SIXTH EDITION

CONTEMPORARY LOGISTICS

JAMES C. JOHNSON

ST. CLOUD STATE UNIVERSITY

DONALD F. WOOD

SAN FRANCISCO STATE UNIVERSITY

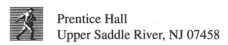

Prentice Hall
Upper Saddle River, NJ 07458

Library of Congress Cataloging-in-Publication Data

Johnson, James C.
    Contemporary logistics / James C. Johnson, Donald F. Wood. -- 6th
ed.
        p.   cm.
    Includes bibliographical references and index.
    ISBN 0-13-398249-1
    1. Physical distribution of goods.   2. Business logistics.
I. Wood, Donald F.   II. Title.
HF5415.6.J6   1996
658.5--dc20   95-40389
                                                                    CIP

Acquisitions Editor: David Borkowsky
Production Supervisor: Publication Services
Project Manager: Lynne Breitfeller
Associate Managing Editor: Carol Burgett
Marketing Manager: John Chillingworth
Cover Design: Jayne Conte
Copy Editor: Joe Vittitow
Production Editor: Larry Adelston
Permissions Editor: Jan Fisher
Manufacturing Buyer: Vincent Scelta
Editorial Assistant: Theresa Festa

©1996 by Prentice-Hall, Inc.
A Simon and Schuster Company
Upper Saddle River, New Jersey 07458

Printed in the United States of America

10 9 8 7 6 5 4 3 2 1

ISBN   0-13-398249-1

Prentice-Hall International (UK) Limited, *London*
Prentice-Hall of Australia Pty. Limited, *Sydney*
Prentice-Hall Canada Inc., *Toronto*
Prentice-Hall Hispanoamericana, S. A., *Mexico*
Prentice-Hall of India Private Limited, *New Delhi*
Prentice-Hall of Japan, Inc., *Tokyo*
Simon & Schuster Asia Pte. Ltd., *Singapore*
Editora Prentice-Hall do Brazil, Ltda., *Rio de Janeiro*

To Cammy and Doreen

CONTENTS

v

LIST OF FIGURES

LIST OF TABLES

PREFACE

The subject of logistics is dynamic and interesting, filled with both problems and opportunities for practicing and future logistics managers. This was true when we wrote the first edition of this text, then titled *Contemporary Physical Distribution,* and continues to be the case today with the publication of the sixth edition, *Contemporary Logistics.* The title of the book was changed in its fourth edition to reflect the broadening responsibilities of those who practice in the field.

This edition has been updated to take into account the many real-world happenings of the 1980s and 1990s. Recent events that will lead logistics and supply-chain thinking into the twenty-first century include the fallout from transportation deregulation, the prodigious use of computers (especially small computers in the workplace), a greater concern for recycling, and the growing popularity of electronic data interchange (EDI). International operations continue to grow in importance.

Several of the case studies that appear at the end of chapters have been revised in a way that requires the use of a computer. Instructors planning to use these cases should make certain that the computers and software are made available to students. The software can be obtained in advance from Prentice Hall Publishing Company. Finally, through the courtesy of Consolidated Freightways, its tariffs are utilized in a number of case studies.

A separate instructor's manual is available.

ACKNOWLEDGMENTS

We are grateful to the following individuals, whose help and support made possible the writing of this and previous editions of *Contemporary Logistics:* Glen Adams of Standard Oil Company; Fred Altstadt of Four-phase System; Scott A. Ames of Logistics Associates; Folger Athearn Jr. of Athearn & Company; Donald W. Baldra of Schering Corporation; Charles L. Ballard of Hudson Valley Community College; Carl Bankard of York College of Pennsylvania; James H. Barnes of the University of Georgia; Warren Blanding of Marketing Publications, Inc.; James F. Briody of Fairchild Camera and Instrument Company; Hank Bulwinkel of Towson State University; W. R. Callister of Del Monte Corporation; Neil D. Chaitin of Challenge Equipment Corporation; W. M. Cheatham of Specialty Brands; Bill Cunningham of Memphis State University; Bob J. Davis of Western Illinois University; Rick Dawe of Southern Pacific; Gary Dicer of the University of Tennessee; John R. Doggett of *Warehousing Review;* W. R. Donham of Cambridge Plan International; A. J. Faria of the University of Windsor; Donald C. Garland of Zellerbach Paper; Stanley Groover of Towson State University; Carl Guelzo of Towson State University; Mark Haight of the University of Wisconsin Center at Barron County; Jay Hamerslag of Hamerslag Equipment Company; Gerald Hampton of San Francisco State University; Lowell Hedrick of Phillips Petroleum Company; Weldon G. Helmus of Hewlett Packard; Lynn Hill of Heublein, Inc.; Stephen G. Hill of Dole Packaged Foods Company; Stanley J. Hille of the University of Missouri at Columbia; Donald Horton of the American Warehousemen's Association; Rufus C. Jefferson; Creed Jenkins of Consolidated Distribution Services; J. M. Johnson of Johnson & Johnson; J. Richard Jones of Memphis State University; Robert E. Jones of F. E. Warren Air Force Base; Henry M. Karel of Shelby State Community College; R. L. Kemmer of GTE Service Corporation; Bob Kingston of Kaiser Permanente Medical Care Program; C. John Langley Jr. of the University of Tennessee; Art LaPlant of Schlage Lock Company; Joseph R. Larsen of CIBA Pharmaceutical Company;

Ron Lennon of Towson State University; Douglas Long; Harry Loomer of the University of Wisconsin Center at Barron County; Irving C. MacDonald; Ernest Y. Maitland of the British Columbia Institute of Technology; Don Marsh of United Air Lines Maintenance Operations; Darwyn Mass of the Rocky Mountain Motor Tariff Bureau; Frank McDonald; Michael McGinnis of the University of South Alabama; Chinnubbie McIntosh of Warren Petroleum Company; Jim Meneley of American Honda Motor Company; Edward J. Meyers of Pacific Gas & Electric Company; Donald D. Mickel of the Sacramento Army Depot; Lowell S. Miller; Joseph F. Moffatt of the University of Southwestern Louisiana; Paul R. Neff of Boeing Company; Donald P. Nelson of the National Distribution Agency; David Norton of Nabisco; Thomas Paczkowski of Cayuga Community College; Donald Pefaur of Trammell Crow Distribution Corporation; Ray Perin of Perin Company; Andru M. Peters of Andros, Inc.; Robert R. Piper; Lee Plummer of North Carolina State University; Richard L. Rickenbacher of Safeway Stores; Frank R. Scheer of the University of Tennessee; Karl Schober; Skip Sherwood of California State University at Fresno; Charles S. Shuken of Metropolitan Warehouse Company; Melvin Silvester; David A. Smith of the State University of New York at Buffalo; Jerome V. Smith of Consolidated Freightways; F. J. Spellman; Jack M. Starling of North Texas State University; Joseph J. Stefanic of Agrico Chemical Company; Wendell M. Stewart of Kearney Management Consultants; Stephen Stover; T. M. Tipton of USCO Services, Inc.; Teddy N. Toklas of the Oakland Naval Supply Center; Lee Totten of Western New England College; Frances Tucker of Syracuse University; Roy Dale Voorhees of Iowa State University; Peter F. Walstad; Bill Walton of Pacific American Warehousing & Trucking Company; Daniel Wardlow; Boyd L. Warnick of Utah Technical College; Mary Margaret Weber of Missouri Western State College; Terry C. Whiteside of the Montana State Department of Agriculture; Lynn Williams of Logisticon; Kenneth C. Williamson of James Madison University; Warren Winstead of George Washington University; Suzan C. Woods of Logisticon; Jean Woodruff of Western New England College; Ronald S. Yaros; James Ziola of Consolidated Freightways; and Howard Zysman of Morada Distribution, Inc.

We also want to thank Frank Burinsky, Carolyn Coggins, Joseph Garfall, David Kupferman, Christopher Low, Michael McGinnis, Ira Pollack, Doreen Wood, and Mark Zborowski for providing useful material for several of the case studies. For pretesting some of the cases in class, we are indebted to Rory K. Miller of the California Maritime Academy. At Prentice Hall we wish to extend our thanks to our editor, David Borkowsky, our production manager, Lynn Breitfeller, and our cover designer, Jayne Conte.

James C. Johnson
St. Cloud, Minnesota

Donald F. Wood
San Francisco, California

Part One

Overview of Logistics

Part 1 sets the stage for the text by introducing the many dimensions of the complex and dynamic subject of logistics. The first three chapters of *Contemporary Logistics* are designed to serve as the structural foundation on which the remainder of the text is built.

Chapter 1 discusses logistics concepts and examines the reasons for their recent growth in importance in business firms. It also introduces terms such as *materials management, inbound logistics,* and *strategic logistics.*

Chapter 2 looks at the supply-chain management concept, which links together one's suppliers' suppliers and one's customers' customers. Several of the marketing channels are also discussed: the ownership channel, the negotiations channel, the promotions channel, the financing channel, and the logistics channel.

Chapter 3 examines the relationships within the firm and between the firm and its suppliers. It covers topics such as purchasing, just-in-time deliveries, recycling, and the relationship of logistics to marketing's four *P*s.

Logistics Systems: Their Development and Growth

This steam locomotive, the *Reno*, was originally built in 1872 for use by the Virginia and Truckee Railroad, which served in the silver-mining area of Nevada. The engine survived and was shipped to the Southwest, where it appeared in many movies (including *Union Pacific* and *Annie Get Your Gun*) and television shows (such as *Gunsmoke* and *Little House on the Prairie*). In 1988 it was loaned to the Swiss Transport Museum, and here we see it being loaded aboard a container ship, the MV *Star Eagle*, at the Port of Houston. It is on a flatbed container platform, which will be loaded into a container-holding slot. A second container will be used for the locomotive's tender. (Credit: Ray Soto, Port of Houston Authority.)

[To] create demand for recycled corrugated, McDonald's ordered its suppliers—the companies that sell everything from meat to coffee cups to McDonald's—to use boxes with a minimum of 35 percent recycled content.

Rolling Stone
August 22, 1991

Logistics have become central to product strategy because, it is increasingly clear, products are not just things-with-features. They are things-with-features bundled with services.

Joseph Fuller, James O'Conor, and Richard Rawlinson
Harvard Business Review
May–June 1993

Because of the competitive advantage provided by the logistics system, many organizations are attempting to determine if their system is world class. But what does it mean to be world class in logistics? I would include the following ten dimensions in defining world-class performance: Customer service, quality, the supply chain, transportation, warehousing, materials handling, purchasing, information systems, environmental impact, and financial performance.

John A. White
Modern Materials Handling
August 1994

Key Terms

- Cost trade-off
- Inbound logistics
- Integrated logistics
- Leading-edge logistics
- Logistics
- Materials management
- Physical distribution
- Stock-keeping unit (SKU)
- Strategic logistics
- Systems approach

Learning Objectives

- To differentiate among physical distribution, materials management, and logistics
- To examine briefly the history of physical distribution and logistics
- To understand why logistics has become more important in recent years
- To note the importance of computer utilization for logistics management
- To examine a number of logistics systems in action

LOGISTICS: WHAT IT IS AND WHY IT IS IMPORTANT

Whenever there is rapid change in a field, new terms and definitions abound. Logistics is no exception. Business logistics, physical distribution, materials management, distribution engineering, logistics management, and supply-chain management are only some of the terms being used to describe approximately the same subject, logistics.

In this book we use five important key terms: logistics, inbound logistics, materials management, physical distribution, and supply-chain management. **Logistics** describes the entire process of materials and products moving into, through, and out of a firm. **Inbound logistics** covers the movement of materials received from suppliers. **Materials management** describes the movements of materials and components within a firm. **Physical distribution** refers to the movement of goods outward from the end of the assembly line to the customer. Finally, supply-chain management is somewhat larger than logistics, and it links logistics more directly with the user's total communications network and with the firm's engineering staff. Our use of these terms is somewhat arbitrary, though all professionals and academics will recognize them and their application. (See Figure 1-1.)

While on the subject of terminology, let us quote C. John Langley:

> While many authors go to great lengths to provide concise definitions of each of these terms, the fact is that in actual business practice these terms many times are used interchangeably. Each professional in this field has at least a slightly different interpretation of what each of these terms means. For this reason, terminology will not be an issue if it is assumed that there is some common understanding that any or all of these terms refers generally to a comprehensive set of activities relating to the movement and storage of product and information. These activities are all undertaken to achieve two common goals, namely, providing an acceptable level of customer service, and operating a logistics system to provide overall conformity to customer requirements.[1]

In 1991 the Council of Logistics Management (CLM), a prestigious professional organization, defined logistics as "the process of planning, implementing, and controlling the efficient, effective flow and storage of goods, services, and related information from the point of origin to the point of consumption for the purpose of conforming to customer requirements."

Although physical distribution/logistics was neglected in the past, it has been receiving more attention in recent years, and the reasons for this new interest are closely tied to the history of American business. At the beginning of the Industrial Revolution in the early 1800s, the emphasis was on production. A firm stressed its ability to decrease the cost of production of each unit. In the early 1900s production started to catch up with demand, and businesses began

---

[1] C. John Langley Jr., "The Evolution of the Logistics Concept," *Journal of Business Logistics* (September 1986), p. 2.

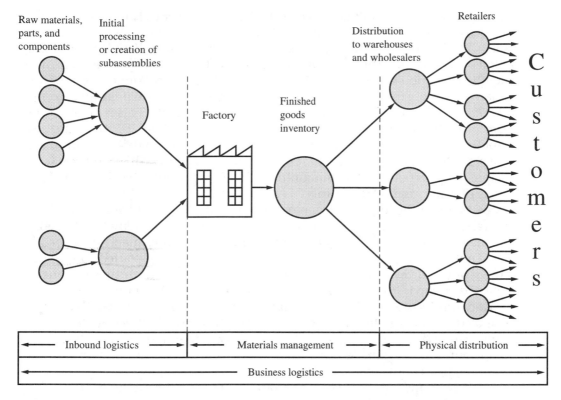

Figure 1-1   Control over the flow of inbound and outbound movements. In this drawing the circles represent buildings where inventories are stored, and the lines with arrows represent movement performed by carriers, a stop-and-start process. Current thought deals more with flows, possibly in different volumes and at different speeds, but without the inventory standing still.

to recognize the importance of sales. But physical distribution/logistics, as we know it today, was still ignored by the business community until much later.[2]

The word *logistics* was first associated with the military. In 1905 Major Chauncey B. Baker wrote, "That branch of the Art of War pertaining to the movement and supply of armies is called logistics."[3] During World War II military forces made effective use of logistics models and forms of systems analysis to ensure that materials were at the proper place when needed. One indication of the increased use of the term *logistics* at that time can be seen in the frustration of Chief of Naval Operations Admiral Ernest H. King, who

[2] Bernard J. LaLonde and Leslie M. Dawson, "Early Development of Physical Distribution Thought," in Donald J. Bowersox, Bernard J. LaLonde, and Edward W. Smykay (eds.), *Readings in Physical Distribution Management* (New York: Macmillan, 1959), pp. 9–18.

[3] Chauncey B. Baker, *Transportation of Troops and Material* (Kansas City, Mo.: Hudson Publishing, 1905), p. 125.

reportedly said, "I don't know what the hell this logistics is that [Army Chief of Staff General George C.] Marshall is always talking about, but I want some of it."[4] The term is still widely used in military and military-type applications. During the Ethiopian famine relief efforts of the 1980s, the term was applied to food-supply activities. World Vision International, one of the many relief organizations at work there, produced a manual entitled *Getting It There—A Logistics Handbook for Relief and Development.*[5] This is an appropriate place to point out that most of the principles in this textbook are also applicable to the workings of governmental and nonprofit undertakings. During the land war in Iraq, for example, a U.S. armored division could consume daily "5,000 tons of ammunition, 555,000 gallons of fuel, 300,000 gallons of water, and 80,000 meals."[6]

Many of the logistical techniques learned during World War II were temporarily ignored during the postwar surge in economic activity. Marketing managers turned their attention to filling the postwar demand for goods. It was not until the recessions of the 1950s that managers started to examine their physical distribution networks. The 1958 recession and profit squeeze created an environment in which business began searching for more effective cost-control systems. Almost simultaneously, many firms realized that physical distribution and logistics were activities whose cost had neither been carefully studied nor coordinated. A number of other trends were becoming apparent, and they made it necessary to focus attention on product distribution. Eight trends can be identified.

First, transportation costs rose rapidly. Traditional methods of distribution had become more expensive, and management became aware of the need to control these costs better. In the 1970s these factors became more critical, with fuel prices soaring and spot shortages occurring. Transportation could no longer be considered a stable factor in the business planner's equations. Higher-level management had to become involved in transportation-related aspects of logistics at both the operating and policy levels because of the many new decisions that had to be made to adapt to the rapid changes in all areas of transport. Starting about 1980, deregulation of common-carrier transportation changed many of the long-established "rules of the game" that had governed shippers' use of transportation. Many new operating- and policy-level decisions had to be made by the users of transport in order to take advantage of the new laws.

[4] U.S. General Accounting Office, *Welcome to the Logistics & Communications Division* (Washington, D.C.: Government Printing Office, 1974).

[5] The manual's chapters cover operations, organization, coordination, procurement, transport by truck, other modes of transport, ocean freight, materials management, maintenance, other logistics functions, and personnel. The manual, published in 1987, is available from the organization at 919 West Huntington Drive, Monrovia, CA 91016.

[6] *Transport Topics,* March 4, 1991, p. 7.

Second, production efficiency was reaching a peak. It was becoming very difficult to generate significant additional cost savings because the "fat" had been taken out of production. Physical distribution and logistics, however, were relatively untouched.

Third, there was a fundamental change in inventory philosophy. At one time retailers held approximately half of the finished product inventory, and wholesalers and manufacturers held the other half. During the 1950s more sophisticated inventory-control techniques, especially in the grocery business, reduced total amounts of inventory and changed the proportions to only 10 percent held by retailers and 90 percent by distributors and manufacturers.

Fourth, product lines proliferated, a direct result of the marketing concept of giving each customer the exact product he or she desires. For example, until the mid-1950s products such as light bulbs, appliances, and facial tissue were largely functional in nature. More recently, differences in the products are no longer limited to real structural dissimilarities. **Stock-keeping units (SKUs),** or line-items of inventory (each different type or package size of a good is a different SKU) increase exponentially. "Toilet SKUs grew from approximately 300 in 1970 to 900 in 1991" and the "number of models in Apple Computer's Macintosh line has grown from one in 1984 to more than twenty."[7]

The fifth trend was computer technology. Management of the logistics approach involved a tremendous amount of detail and data. The following are examples of the information that must be available: (1) location of each customer; (2) size of each order; (3) location of production facilities, warehouses, and distribution centers; (4) transportation costs from each warehouse or plant to each customer; (5) available carriers and the service levels they offer; (6) location of suppliers; and (7) inventory levels currently available in each warehouse and distribution center. The sheer magnitude of these data rendered manual analysis virtually impossible. Fortunately, just as the physical distribution concepts were being developed, along came the computer, which allowed the concepts to be put into practice. Without the development and use of the computer at this time, logistics and physical distribution concepts would have remained interesting theories with few real applications.

The sixth factor is related to the increased use of computers because even if a specific firm does not use computers, its suppliers (vendors) and customers do. It became possible for firms to study systematically the quality of service they received from their suppliers. Based on this kind of analysis, many firms were able to pinpoint suppliers who consistently offered substandard levels of service. Many firms were rudely awakened and made to realize the need to upgrade their distribution systems. And as manufacturing firms shifted to

---

[7] Michael H. Sargent and Keith P. Creehan, "Managing the Complexities of Product Proliferation," *Mercer Management Journal*, 1993, unpaged.

just-in-time (JIT) systems, their materials delivery requirements placed very exacting demands upon their parts suppliers and the delivering carriers.

The seventh factor is the increased public concern for the recycling of products, which is likely to become even more important in the twenty-first century. This has many interfaces with logistics, namely, packaging and developing return channels for the recycled materials. Consumers are demanding that firms be actively engaged in recycling activities.

The eighth factor has been the growth of several new, large retail chains, or mass merchandisers, with large demands and very sophisticated logistics service. They frequently bypass traditional channels of distribution, and they turn their inventories so quickly that they have often sold the product and collected payment for it before their payment to the supplier for the product is due. They have demanded, and received, very special attention from their suppliers.

In discussing the development of physical distribution and logistics, Donald Bowersox notes that early physical distribution operations involved coordination of transport, warehousing, inventory policy, and order processing to achieve timely, cost-effective customer service. "The movement toward coordinated physical distribution resulted in the identification of the cost elements and improved the overall accuracy in the measurement of customer service."[8] Bowersox continues that the next plateau was firms' decisions to regroup staff so as to manage physical distribution and materials management activities more efficiently. "The term logistics gained popularity as a label for the comprehensive management responsibility for the strategic deployment of inventory from point of raw material acquisition to final customer destination." Bowersox notes that during the 1980s the concept of **integrated logistics** evolved and that an integrated logistics system moves inventory through a constant and consecutive chain of value-added steps, with it arriving when needed in the proper quantity and form. Value added means that each party involved acts to enhance the value of the product or service for those who will be receiving it. Another writer states, "Logistics may integrate distribution, production, and supply in order to synchronize rhythms and flows; this system, known as integrated logistics, is often found within the leading consumer goods manufacturers."[9]

Bowersox believes that the 1990s will continue to focus on **strategic logistics,** which is a step beyond logistics:

> Management focus is moving beyond the walls of existing business structure to encompass suppliers and customers. Strategic logistics is defined as using logistical competency and channel-wide partnership alliances to gain competitive advantage. The development and maintenance of interorganizational logistical alliances that span organizational boundaries is not easy to achieve. A firm with

[8] Donald J. Bowersox, "Logistics Strategic Planning for the 1990s," *Council of Logistics Management Fall 1987 Annual Conference Proceedings,* vol. 1 (Oak Brook, IL: CLM, 1987), p. 233.

[9] J. Colin, *The Role of Shippers and Transport Operators in the Logistics Chain* (Paris: European Conference of Ministers of Transport, 1987), p. 13.

true strategic capability is willing to commit performance capabilities to customers in advance and then perform as expected under microscopic scrutiny. Effective strategic logistics requires the leveraging of combined assets of a company with key suppliers of material and services.

The net result of a strategic orientation is that logistic managers are beginning to spend less time in internal company operations and more time interfacing with suppliers and customers.[10]

Here is an example of the close interfacing between a carrier and a shipper. The carrier is Conrail, and the shipper is American Honda's Marysville, Ohio, plant, where approximately 1,500 new Hondas are shipped out every day.

Conrail Trainmasters Gary Homan and Wayne Malz, both of whom are based right at the Honda facility, play key roles in managing the flow of rail cars in and out of the plant. "We work closely with the contractor that handles the loading of the autos onto the rail cars," explained Homan. Both trainmasters are in constant touch with Conrail's Columbus, Ohio–based train dispatchers and with Conrail's busy Buckeye Yard, also in Columbus. The trainmasters, working with other local operating people, help ensure that the day's orders make the right connections with Conrail trains departing the area for those cities so that they can meet Honda's delivery standards.[11]

More recently, Bowersox et al. adopted the term **leading-edge logistics** in the following context:

A small number of leading-edge North American firms enjoy a superior level of logistical competency. These companies use logistics as a competitive weapon to secure and maintain customer loyalty. They are more responsive and flexible, are more committed to their customers, are more aware of their results, work more closely with their suppliers, are more likely to embrace technology, and are more involved with their firm's strategic direction.

The leading-edge firms do many things differently. First, leading-edge organizations seek to use logistical competency to gain and maintain competitive superiority. Secondly, excellent companies seek to add value to the products and services they market, supporting this goal by operating a cost-effective logistics system. And lastly, leading-edge firms leverage their assets by forming strategic alliances with service suppliers. These alliances help the firms achieve preferred-supplier status with key customers.[12]

THE TOTAL-COST APPROACH TO LOGISTICS

Logistics is a classic example of the systems approach to business problems. From a company's point of view the systems approach indicates that the company's objectives can be realized by recognizing the mutual interdependence

---

[10] Bowersox, "Logistics," pp. 234–235.

[11] "Competitiveness in a World Market," *Conrail Update*, Fall 1988, p. 5.

[12] Donald J. Bowersox, Patricia J. Daugherty, Cornelia L. Droge, Dale S. Rogers, and Daniel L. Wardlow, *Leading-Edge Logistics: Competitive Positioning for the 1990s* (East Lansing: Michigan State University, 1989), pp. i, vi.

of the basic functional areas of the firm (marketing, production, and finance). The same reasoning can be applied to the areas of logistics. The logistics manager must balance each functional area and see that none is stressed to the point where it becomes detrimental to others. One definition of **systems approach** is as follows: "The systems approach to a problem involves not only a recognition of the individual importance of the various elements of which it is composed but also an acknowledgment of their interrelationship. Whereas field specialists concentrate restrictively on their own particular bailiwick, the more versatile systems people, in their capacity as generalists, seek the optimum blend of many of these individual operations in order to fulfill a broader objective."[13]

As noted at the start of the chapter, three important terms used in this book are *logistics, physical distribution,* and *materials management.* The objective of a physical distribution system is to minimize, with a specified level of service provided to customers, the costs involved in physically moving and storing the product from its production point to the point where it is delivered. The objective of materials management, which is concerned with the inbound flows of materials, is to meet the firm's need for those materials in an orderly, efficient, and low-cost manner.

The objectives of logistics encompass efforts to coordinate physical distribution and materials management in order to save money or improve service. (Figure 1-2 is an advertisement for the Cargill Salt Company. Note that because salt is basically a homogenous product, Cargill differentiates its product by stressing a dependable logistical system to serve its food-processing customers.) Examples of such coordination are the use of the same truck both to make deliveries and to pick up supplies, and the use of a computer program that monitors orders being processed and determines how filling the orders will deplete stocks of goods on hand, require new production runs, and consume raw materials in the new production runs. To achieve these objectives, the logistics manager uses the total-cost approach. This approach is built on the premise that all relevant functions in moving and sorting materials and products should be considered as a whole, not individually. The following functions are included in the total-cost approach to logistics because they often fall under a firm's logistics umbrella:

1. Customer service
2. Demand forecasting
3. Documentation flow
4. Interplant movements
5. Inventory management

---

[13] Colin Barrett, "The Machine and Its Parts," *Transportation and Distribution Management,* April 1971, p. 3.

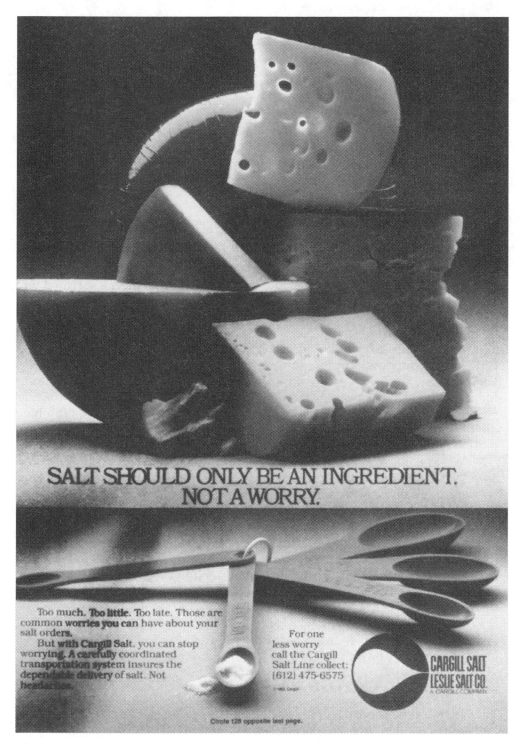

Figure 1-2 The utilization of logistics service as a major selling point. (Reproduced with permission of Cargill, Incorporated.)

6. Order processing
7. Packaging
8. Parts and service support
9. Plant and warehouse site selection
10. Production scheduling
11. Purchasing
12. Returned products
13. Salvage scrap recycling and disposal
14. Traffic management
15. Warehouse and distribution center management

The list is long, and in many firms responsibility for some of the activities is shared with other departments. The key to the total-cost approach is that all cost items are considered simultaneously in attempting to meet a specified service level. When testing alternative approaches, the costs of some functions will increase, others will decrease, and still others will remain unchanged. Thus the objective is to find the approach with the lowest total cost.

Cost trade-offs are used, acknowledging that changing patterns or functions of distribution cause some costs to increase and others to decrease. For example, high inventory-carrying costs prompt firms to adopt various methods, usually computer-based ones, to control and reduce inventories. As George Gecowets of the Council of Logistics Management explains, "Double-digit inflation in the early 1980s meant logistics managers had to trade information for inventory."[14]

When employed in the logistics decision-making process, the total-cost approach forms what is commonly called the total logistics concept. This concept is unique not because of the function performed, since each function (traffic, warehousing) is the same, but because of the integration of all functions into a unified whole that seeks to minimize distribution costs for a given level of customer and in-firm service. Note that the logistics concept is frequently extended to include suppliers and customers. Supply-chain management, to be covered in the next chapter, focuses on developing a smooth flow all the way from raw material sources to the customer, and it ties logistics to some of the firm's other functional areas.

Logistics is now a widely accepted and adopted function of business. Professional logistics meetings now often deal with the topic of re-engineering logistics, meaning how to improve a system that is already in place.

FIVE LOGISTICS SYSTEMS IN ACTION

This section provides partial descriptions of the logistics systems of five well-known firms, including one that is a provider of logistics service.

[14] *KLM Cargovision*, January–February 1988, p. 10.

Kraft, Inc.

Kraft sells about $10 billion of food and food products each year. It is divided into eight domestic operating divisions and one overseas division. Its major customers are retail food chains and grocery wholesalers. Distribution of its many products is complicated by the fact that some are frozen, some are refrigerated, and many have different shelf lives. Operating out of seven distribution centers, Kraft ships nearly a million cases per day. One of the company's customer service accomplishments is that it ships 98.5 percent of all cases ordered. Each distribution center has a toll-free 800 telephone number that customers may call to advance order dates, add products to current orders, or expedite shipments.

The firm's operations are an example of integrated logistics. "The distribution structure successfully links it to other parts of the material flow chain including purchasing, asset management, production scheduling, inventory control, and transportation."[15] Kraft operates three truck fleets, one to handle interplant shipments, one to make deliveries to customers, and one for administrative and service purposes.

Within the materials management unit at Kraft, decisions are made regarding inventory locations, transportation modes to be used, and sourcing. The main objectives of the materials management group include the following:

- Cost competitiveness in each aspect of procurement, distribution, and transportation.
- Unwavering commitment to quality, including assured quality from suppliers and carriers.
- Effective utilization of computers.
- Development of individualized relationships with providers of materials and services.
- Management development to attract, hire, and develop people in each position with a net outflow to other organizational units of Kraft.[16]

Note the objective of developing "individualized relationships with providers of materials and services." This is an example of strategic logistics, that is, forming alliances with outside firms. One such alliance between Kraft and the carriers that serve it results in additional trailers being provided so truckers do not have to wait for unloading. This benefits both the trucker and the Kraft distribution center, which has more time to unload the trailers.

---

[15] Miles L. Marsh, "Achieving Realistic Leadership," *Transportation and Distribution,* 1988–1989 Presidential Issue, p.16.

[16] Marsh, "Leadership," p. 17.

Bayer AG

Bayer AG is a huge chemical company headquartered in Leverkusen, Germany, with annual sales equivalent to $25 billion. It operates 320 plants in sixty-seven different nations, and it distributes 25,000 different products, ranging from biochemical and pharmaceutical items to herbicides and plastics. The firm's work force totals 173,000, and this includes 2,200 who work in the field of logistics. Bayer's annual logistics budget is about $5 billion; it involves 3,000 different distribution points handling about 740,000 different shipments.[17]

In terms of tonnage shipped, over half of what Bayer ships is considered hazardous, meaning that it requires special handling, packaging, and documentation. These hazardous materials result in two differences in Bayer's distribution patterns, compared with those of most other firms. Some hazardous materials cannot be placed in the same vehicle, so shipment consolidation (the grouping of many small shipments into a single larger one that moves at a lower rate per pound) is more difficult to achieve. Even if only one of the products is hazardous, its presence may slow the handling of the entire shipment. Second, Bayer's customers have been moving to just-in-time inventory systems and want smaller, more frequent shipments to arrive by air. Many hazardous materials do not move by air, so it is more difficult for Bayer to provide just-in-time deliveries.

Bayer's president, Hermann Josef Strenger, notes that not only is taking care of the environment an important social responsibility of the chemical industry but it will also make the industry more acceptable to the public. Bayer is taking a variety of measures to prevent environmental disasters.

> Since transport is, environmentally speaking, the weakest line in the Bayer chain, checking, re-checking, and tightening up safety measures during shipment has become daily work. Should something go wrong, trained specialists are on twenty-four-hour standby at strategic points throughout the world.[18]

Canon, Inc.

Canon, a Japanese-based firm originally known only for its cameras, is now known for its office equipment as well, especially its copy machines. In addition, it produces video equipment, optical products, laser-beam printers, and semiconductors. The firm is on *Fortune's* list of the largest one hundred multinational corporations. In the late 1980s Canon had a "global corporation plan" that included three parts:

> First, by restructuring trade patterns, we promote increased production overseas. A higher level of local procurement and larger imports of quality materials and components will help redress trade imbalances. Our second policy is to explore

---

[17] Hans Kops, "Learning by the Numbers," *KLM Cargovision,* July–August, 1988, p. 8.
[18] Ibid., p. 9.

new business areas and new product concepts. Our third policy is to strengthen worldwide marketing capability.[19]

In Europe, Canon developed plants in Germany, France, and Italy as well as a research facility in England. Its European headquarters is near Amsterdam. At this site is the company's major distribution center, stocking eight thousand different products and eighty thousand components for distribution to four hundred sales outlets in forty different countries in Europe, Africa, and the Middle East. In 1990 that facility received 51,000 tons of materials—5 percent by air, 64 percent by sea, 29 percent by truck, and 2 percent by combined water and air. Outbound shipments from the facility usually move by truck, with 85 percent to 90 percent delivered within three days. At present, the European operation is groping with two challenges: the relaxed trade barriers that are occurring in Western Europe and increased access to markets in Eastern Europe.

Worldwide, Canon is concerned with environmental issues. Its ecology department in the international headquarters in Japan recently began a recycling program for the cartridges used in printers and copiers: "We ask our customers to return all the cartridges to us, and we send them to the Dalian plant in China where they are disassembled and recycled. It is a huge and costly program, but Canon does not want to see its name in the news for polluting the environment."[20] In the United States, where Canon is a well-known firm, buyers of toner cartridges receive a preaddressed UPS label and instructions for returning the empty cartridges to Canon at the company's expense. The cartridges are returned to Brisbane, California, and are then sent by sea to the China plant, where they are disassembled and melted down into raw materials for reuse. In order to encourage customers to return the used cartridges, Canon donates $1 for each returned container in the United States to the National Wildlife Federation and the Nature Conservancy.

Morton Automotive Safety Products

With its headquarters in Ogden, Utah, this firm is one of the world's largest manufacturers of front-seat airbags. (Its parent is Morton International, which also controls the company that produces the well-known Morton Salt.) When shipped, auto airbags are considered to be dangerous or hazardous products because their gas-generating pellets can explode and release gas, as they are intended to when the auto in which they are installed crashes. Morton makes truckload deliveries to its North American customers using reusable packaging. The largest customer of Morton Auto Safety Products is Chrysler.

The firm's markets are growing in both Europe and Asia. In mid-1994 Morton was shipping 70,000 pounds of airfreight weekly to Europe. This included twenty different designs, each intended for installation on a different

[19] *KLM Cargovision,* May–June 1991, p. 8.

[20] Ibid., p. 11. See also *Distribution,* November 1991, pp. 56–58.

style of vehicle. Morton sends two truckloads a week from Ogden to New York's JFK airport. To reach Europe, Morton works with Burlington Air Express in a service partnership that involves "coordinated air cargo movements between the U.S. and Europe: airline ULD (unit load devices) deliveries direct to a central European logistics center, and short-term product storage in that center under Customs bond prior to final delivery to the customer."[21] Special high-quality boxes are used for the product, and they are bar-coded for the entire journey.

Certain styles of airbags can travel as cargo on passenger flights; other styles are restricted to all-cargo flights. The dangerous nature of the cargo also restricts the choice of warehousing and truck delivery routes. Morton feels that it must maintain a certain inventory in Europe to give customers there confidence that they can deliver. At present the European operation turns its inventory twenty-six times per year. At present the firm's European distribution center is in the Netherlands, and it can reach all of Western Europe by truck within two days, except for Spain and Italy, which require three days. The product cannot be carried from the Continent to the United Kingdom via ferry or through the Chunnel.

To reach Asian markets Morton uses ocean freight from West Coast ports. It has a joint-venture arrangement with a Japanese firm, which offers warehousing, JIT deliveries, and sales and marketing support.

Fritz Companies

Best known as an international freight forwarder, this San Francisco–based firm appears to be growing in all directions. Fritz employs over 3,000 people, serves 20,000 clients, has 121 offices worldwide, and has partnership arrangements with 500 firms around the world. It is one of a handful of logistics service providers that is truly global in coverage.

Fritz Air Freight is an international air freight forwarder. (Freight forwarders collect and consolidate small shipments from a number of sources and combine them into larger, single shipments.) Fritz Air Freight can provide real-time information to its clients with regard to the status of their shipments. They can also provide documentation and banking services.

Many of the nation's major companies rely on Fritz. For example, Fritz employees in Memphis handle all the import paperwork for the tens of thousands of parcels that FedEx planes bring in from Europe each evening. In Anchorage Fritz employees process parcels that FedEx brings in from Asia. To help clear these parcels quickly, a three-way electronic data interchange system is used, linking FedEx, Fritz, and U.S. Customs.

Fritz is a long-time ocean freight forwarder. Under its wing is Fritz Transportation International, an NVOCC (non-vessel-operating common carrier).

---

[21] *KLM Cargovision*, November 1994, p. 19. ULDs are large enclosed pallets, and a customs bond is a guarantee to the importing nation's customs that the goods will not be released for sale without moving through customs, at which time duties must be paid.

NVOCCs do not own vessels, but they charter blocs of space, or container slots, on scheduled vessels and then retail these spaces to shippers. Fritz also has a project logistics team, which advises clients that have one-time one-of-a-kind transport needs.

Fritz also offers international warehousing, delivery, and customshouse brokerage services, and it is the largest customshouse broker in the United States. Many major firms have contracted with Fritz to handle all or parts of their international logistics needs.

RESPONSIBILITIES OF LOGISTICS MANAGERS

The logistics manager has a highly complex and challenging position. The major reason is that he or she must be both a technical expert and a generalist. In the first capacity the logistics manager must understand freight rates, warehouse layouts, inventory analysis, production, purchasing, and transportation law. As a generalist, the logistics manager must understand the relationships between all logistics functions. In addition, he or she must relate logistics to other operations of the firm as well as to outside suppliers and customers.

As George A. Gecowets of the Council of Logistics Management observed, "Most people today at the higher levels in distribution are generalists. They are mangers first and distribution professionals second. They could manage any of the corporate functions, not just transportation/distribution."[22]

Logistics is a part of a firm's corporate strategy. Today corporations often have mission statements that define the corporation's purpose. Under the umbrella of the corporate mission statement should be the statements of the various departments within the firm. Professors J.R. Stock and C. Droge surveyed about one hundred logistics departments in major U.S. firms to learn about their mission statements. Most of the statements they received ranged from twenty to forty words in length. The statements were analyzed in terms of the number of times certain words appeared within them. The word *customer,* for example, was most frequently used, appearing in 50 percent of the mission statements. Other words, in descending order of use, were *cost, service, product, distribution, transportation, logistics, system, control, mission, production/manufacturing, management, profit, marketing,* and *effective.*[23]

Logistics managers are responsible for controlling large expenditures. Total logistics expenditures in the United States in 1990 were estimated at $600 billion, including $221 billion in inventory-carrying costs, $356 billion for freight transportation, and $23 billion for administrative costs.[24]

[22] *Traffic Management,* February 1984, p. 35.

[23] James R. Stock and Cornelia Droge, "Logistics Mission Statements," *The Private Carrier,* April 1991, p. 8.

[24] *Distribution,* July 1991, p. 6. Inventory-carrying costs were calculated by applying a 27.2 percent carrying cost to an estimated $800 billion inventory.

LOGISTICS CAREERS

In 1991 the Council of Logistics Management published a booklet for college students entitled *Careers in Logistics*. It profiles people with seven different logistics jobs: inventory control manager, warehousing/operations manager, administrative manager (who supervises three hundred people and is responsible for material, facilities, inventory control, order processing, and the like), administrative analyst/planner, transportation manager, customer service manager, and a consultant. The booklet concludes, "The field of logistics is so large that almost any business organization may be viewed as a potential employer of the logistics manager."[25]

"We created the Materials Management Development Program with the intention of hiring the right people and thoroughly training them to manage our challenging new business," says Keith R. McKennon, president of Dow Chemical USA.[26] The program handles about ten new hires a year and includes a summer internship program.

> We recruit primarily at four universities—Michigan State, Penn State, the University of Tennessee and Arizona State. Recruiting is taken very seriously. We're looking for competent college graduates who possess:
>
> - A bachelor's degree in transportation, logistics, engineering, or a related discipline.
> - Strong human relations and communications skills, since contact with people in a variety of occupations is an integral part of the program.
> - The ability to make decisions quickly and independently.
> - The desire to build a successful career in one of the challenging areas of Dow's materials management.[27]

New employees at Dow Chemical are given hands-on experience, with a typical first assignment being that of an analyst in the distribution function, which enables the individual to become familiar with Dow's products, plant, and distribution operations. Another first assignment is as a planning analyst, who plans the distribution network for a new product. A third new assignment is on the traffic team, working directly with carriers. Jobs are continually changed in this program—approximately every eighteen months. The approach enables cross-training between functions, and movements between departments and divisions is encouraged.

Logistics training is also valuable for individuals who hope to work for carriers because it gives them a better understanding of shippers' needs.

---

[25] The booklet is available from the CLM at 2803 Butterfield Rd., Suite 380, Oak Brook, IL 60521. The quotation is from page 18. The CLM also has a videotape on logistics careers.

[26] Keith R. McKennon, "The Challenge of Attracting Professionals," *Transportation and Distribution,* 1988–1989 Presidential Issue, p. 55.

[27] Ibid.

Each year Professor Bernard LaLonde and his colleagues at Ohio State University survey career patterns in logistics. Their findings, based on information from the highest-ranking distribution executives in major firms, are reported at annual meetings of the Council of Logistics Management. The 1994 survey of logistics managers included over two hundred respondents. About one-third had the title "logistics manager," "logistics director,"or "vice-president-logistics." The median annual compensation for a manager was $75,000; for a director, $95,000; and for a vice president, $146,000. The 1994 survey also asked the respondents to detail how they allocate their time to various logistical activities. Their answers were warehousing, 20 percent; traffic, 19 percent; inventory control, 13 percent; purchasing/procurement, 13 percent; global logistics, 11 percent; order processing, 7 percent; product planning, 7 percent; facility location, 7 percent; order entry, 6 percent; sales forecasting, 5 percent; and packaging, 4 percent; and the remaining time was spent on general management. Nearly all of the respondents had a bachelor's degree, and 41 percent had a graduate degree. Their average age was 45. Only 7 percent of the respondents were women.[28]

LOGISTICS PROFESSIONALISM

Because of the growing importance of logistics, it has achieved a true professional status. A number of professional organizations in logistics are dedicated to advancing the professional knowledge of their members. The rationale for these professional associations is that the state of the art is changing so rapidly that professionals must be constantly educating and reeducating themselves. Some of these organizations offer a certification program, usually requiring the individual to pass one or more examinations.

Council of Logistics Management (CLM)

Formerly known as the National Council of Physical Distribution Management (NCPDM), the Council of Logistics Management (CLM) is the best-known organization for logistics and physical distribution professionals. It is active on the national level and through many local roundtables. Further information can be obtained from Council of Logistics Management, 2803 Butterfield Road, Suite 380, Oak Brook, IL 60521.

Canadian Association of Logistics Management (CALM)

The Canadian Association of Logistics Management (CALM) is for business professionals in Canada interested in improving their logistics and distribution management skills. Contact CALM, 610 Alden Road, Suite 201, Markham, Ontario L3R 9Z1.

[28] Bernard J. LaLonde and James M. Masters, "The 1994 Ohio State University Survey of Career Patterns in Logistics," *CLM Annual Proceedings*, (Oak Brook, IL: CLM, 1994), pp. 89–105.

American Production and Inventory Control Society (APICS)

The American Production and Inventory Control Society (APICS) attempts to develop professional, scientific approaches to methods of inventory control. In 1980 APICS formed a special section to deal with the physical distribution aspects of logistics. They have a certification program consisting of five exams. For additional information write APICS, 500 West Annandale Road, Falls Church, VA 22046.

American Society of Transportation and Logistics (AST&L)

The American Society of Transportation and Logistics (AST&L) was founded to help its members achieve "high standards of education and technical training, requisite to the proper performance of the various functions of traffic, transportation, and physical distribution management." To become a certified member of AST&L, one must pass four comprehensive tests over various aspects of traffic, transportation, and logistics and write an original research paper. For further information write AST&L, 216 East Church St., Lock Haven, PA 17745.

Association of Transportation Practitioners (ATP)

The Association of Transportation Practitioners (ATP) is dedicated "to promote the proper administration of the Interstate Commerce Act and related acts . . . ; to cooperate in fostering increased educational opportunities and maintaining high standards of professional conduct; and to encourage cordial communication among the practitioners." To belong to this organization, one must be an ICC practitioner. This is accomplished by passing a comprehensive test. For further information write Association of Transportation Practitioners, 1725 K Street NW, Suite 301, Washington, DC 20006.

Delta Nu Alpha (DNA)

Delta Nu Alpha (DNA) is a transportation fraternity dedicated to the education of its members. DNA chapters are very active at the local level and foster learning through small educationally oriented discussion groups. For further information write DNA, 530 Church St., Suite 300, Nashville, TN 37219.

Society of Logistics Engineers (SOLE)

The focus of the Society of Logistics Engineers (SOLE) includes commercial and military logistics. The group has a certification program. For more information write Society of Logistics Engineers, 8100 Professional Place, Suite 213, New Carrollton, MD 20785.

Transportation Research Forum (TRF)

The Transportation Research Forum (TRF) is a "joint endeavor of interested persons in academic life, government service, business logistics, and the various modes of transportation. The Forum's purpose is to provide a common meeting ground or forum for the discussion of ideas and research techniques applicable to economic, management, and public policy problems involving transportation." Additional information can be obtained from TRF, 11250-8 Roger Bacon Drive, Suite 8, Reston, VA 22090.

Warehouse and Education Research Council (WERC)

The purpose of the Warehouse and Education Research Council (WERC) is to provide education and conduct research concerning the warehousing process and to refine the art and science of managing warehouses. "The Council will foster professionalism in warehouse management. It will also operate in cooperation with other organizations and institutions." Additional information can be obtained by writing to WERC, 1100 Jorie Blvd., Suite 170, Oak Brook, IL 60521.

SUMMARY

Chapter 1 introduces the topic of logistics, which the Council of Logistics Management defines as "the process of planning, implementing, and controlling the efficient, effective flow and storage of goods, services, and related information from the point of origin to the point of consumption for the purpose of conforming to customer requirements."

The different terminologies in use are discussed, as are the developments that helped shape the field since the end of World War II. Two recent influences are the just-in-time inventory systems and computers.

Portions of logistics systems of several well-known firms are described: Kraft, Inc., Bayer AG (headquartered in West Germany), Cannon (headquartered in Japan), and Morton Automotive Safety Products.

Career opportunities and professional organizations are also discussed.

QUESTIONS FOR DISCUSSION AND REVIEW

1. Comment on the validity of this statement: Traffic management and logistics management are really the same thing! The latter term just sounds more sophisticated, but it is really nothing more than the purchasing of transportation services.
2. What are the technical differences among physical distribution, logistics, and materials management?
3. Discuss the functional areas that combine to form the logistics department.
4. Why has logistics become recognized as an important business function?

5. Why is the phenomenon of product proliferation so difficult from the logistics manager's point of view?

6. Discuss the impact of computer technology on the development of the logistics concept.

7. Deregulation of transportation took place between 1977 and 1980. What has been the impact of this on logistics managers? Why?

8. What is the systems approach to problem solving? Why is this concept applicable to logistics management?

9. Discuss the objectives of physical distribution, materials management, and logistics.

10. Discuss the total-cost approach to logistic management.

11. Give an example of the total-cost approach.

12. Define a cost trade-off. Do you believe this concept is workable? Why?

13. What is integrated logistics?

14. Logistics managers must be both generalists and technicians. Why is this true? Does that fact help to explain why logistics managers are in relatively short supply?

15. Discuss advantages to a career in logistics management.

16. Discuss logistical activities at Kraft.

17. Discuss reasons for environmental concerns at Bayer AG.

18. What is leading-edge logistics?

19. Discuss Canon's involvement with recycling.

20. If you were to join one professional organization, which one would it be? Why?

SUGGESTED READINGS

Bowersox, Donald J., Patricia J. Daugherty, Cornelia L. Droge, Dale S. Rogers, and Daniel L. Wardlow. *Leading Edge Logistics—Competitive Positioning for the 1990s.* Oak Brook, Ill.: Council of Logistics Management, 1989.

Dorsett, Katie G., and Julian M. Benjamin. "Training and Career Opportunities for Minorities and Women." *Annual Proceedings of the Transportation Research Forum.* Arlington, Va.: TRF, 1984, pp. 177–181.

Lynagh, Peter M., and Richard F. Poist. "Women's Perceptions Regarding Careers in Transportation and Distribution." *Annual Proceedings of the Transportation Research Forum.* Arlington, Va.: TRF, 1984, pp. 182–186.

Murphy, Paul R., and Richard F. Poist. "Educational Strategies for Succeeding in Logistics: A Comparative Analysis." *Transportation Journal,* Spring 1994, pp. 36–48.

Stalk, George Jr., and Thomas M. Hout. *Competing against Time.* New York: Free Press, 1990.

Zinszer, Paul H. *A Study of University Programs in Logistics and Industry Demand for Entry Level Logistics Employees.* Oak Brook, Ill.: Council of Logistics Management, 1985, p. 1.

C A S E   1 - 1

SUDSY SOAP, INC.

Frank Johnson was physical distribution manager in charge of outbound movements for Sudsy Soap, Inc. He had held the job for the past five years and had just about every distribution function well under control. His task was made easier because shipping patterns and volumes were unchanging routines. The firm's management boasted that it had a steady share in "a stable market," although a few stockholders grumbled that Sudsy Soap had a declining share in a growing market.

The Sudsy Soap plant was in Akron, Ohio. It routinely produced 100,000 forty-eight-ounce cartons of powdered soap each week. Each carton measured about half a cubic foot, and each working day, fifteen to twenty rail carloads were loaded and shipped to various food chain warehouses and to a few large grocery brokers. Johnson worked with the marketing staff to establish prices, so nearly all soap was purchased in carload lots. Shipments less than a full carload did not occur very often.

Buyers relied on dependable deliveries, and the average length of time it took for a carton of soap to leave the Sudsy production line and reach a retailer's shelf was nineteen days. The best time was six days (mainly to chains distributing in Ohio), and the longest time was forty-three days (to retailers in Hawaii).

Sudsy Soap's president was worried about the stockholders' criticism regarding Sudsy's lack of growth, so he hired a new sales manager, E. Gerard Beever (nicknamed "Eager" since his college days at a Big Ten university). Beever had a one-year contract and knew he must produce. He needed a gimmick.

At his university fraternity reunion he ran into one of his fraternity roommates, who was now sales manager for an imported line of kitchen dishes manufactured in China and distributed by a firm headquartered in Hong Kong. Their quality was good, but competition was intense. It was difficult to get even a "toe-hold" in the kitchen dish market. He and Beever shared a common plight: They were responsible for increasing market shares for products with very little differentiation from competitors' products. They both wished they could help each other, but they could not. The reunion ended and each went home.

The next week Beever was surprised to receive a fax from his old room-mate. It read:

> We propose a tie-in promotion between Sudsy Soap and our dishes. We will sup-ply at no cost to you one hundred thousand each twelve-inch dinner plates, seven-inch pie plates, nine-inch bread and butter plates, coffee cups, and saucers. Each week you must have a different piece in each package starting din-ner plate in week one, pie plates in week two, and so on through end of week five. Recommend this be done weeks of October 3, October 10, October 17, October 24, and October 31 of this year. Timing important because national advertising linked to new television show we are sponsoring. We will give buy-ers of five packages of Sudsy Soap, purchased five weeks in a row, one free place setting of our dishes. Enough of your customers will want to complete table set-tings so they will buy three, five, or seven more place settings from our retailers. Timing is crucial. Advise immediately.

Beever was pleased to receive the offer but realized a lot of questions had to be answered before he could recommend that the offer be accepted. He sent a copy of the fax to Johnson attached to an interoffice memo. The memo said:

> Note attached fax offering tie-in with dishes. Dishes are of good quality. What additional information do we need from dish distributor, and what additional information do you need before we know whether to recommend acceptance? Advise quickly. Thanks.

Questions

1. Assume that you are Frank Johnson's assistant and he asks you to look into various scheduling problems that might occur. List and discuss them.

2. What packaging problems, if any, might there be?

3. Many firms selling consumer goods are concerned with problems of product liability. Does the dish offer present any such problems? If so, what are they? Can they be accommodated?

4. Should the exterior of the Sudsy Soap package be altered to show what dish it contains? If so, who should pay for the extra costs?

5. Assume that you are another one of Johnson's assistants and your prin-cipal responsibility is managing the inventories of all the firm's inputs, finished products, and outbound inventories. What additional work will the dish proposal cause for you?

6. You are Mr. Beever. Your staff has given many objections to the dish tie-in proposal, but you believe that much of the problem is your staff's reluctance to try anything innovative. Draft a letter to the dish com-pany that, although not accepting their proposal, attempts to clarify points that may be subject to misinterpretation and also takes into account some of your staff's legitimate concerns.

C A S E   1 - 2

··

KIDDIELAND AND THE SUPER GYM*

KiddieLand is a retailer of toys located in the Midwest. Corporate headquarters is in Chicago and its seventy stores are located in Minnesota, Wisconsin, Michigan, Illinois, Indiana, Ohio, Iowa, and Kentucky. One distribution center is located in Columbus (for Kentucky, Indiana, Michigan, and Ohio) and one in Chicago (for Illinois, Iowa, Minnesota, and Wisconsin).

KiddieLand markets a full range of toys, electronic games, computers, and playsets. Emphasis is on a full line of brand-name products together with selected items sold under the KiddieLand brand. KiddieLand's primary competitors include various regional discount chains. The keys to KiddieLand's success have been a comprehensive product line, aggressive pricing, and self-service.

Donald Hurst is KiddieLand's distribution manager. He is responsible for managing both distribution centers, for traffic management, and for inventory control. Don's primary mission is "to make sure all stores are in stock at all times without maintaining excessive levels of inventory."

One morning in late January, while Don was reviewing the new year's merchandising plan, he discovered that starting in March, KiddieLand would begin promoting the Super Gym Outdoor Children's Exercise Center. Don was particularly interested that the new set would sell for $715. In addition, the Super Gym is packaged in three boxes weighing a total of 450 pounds. "Holy Cow!" thought Don, "the largest set we have sold to date retails for $159 and weighs only 125 pounds."

"There must be some mistake," thought Don as he walked down the hall to the office of Olga Olsen, KiddieLand's buyer for playsets. Olga was new on her job and was unusually harassed because both of her assistant buyers had just resigned to seek employment on the West Coast.

As soon as Olga saw Don, she exclaimed, "Don, my friend, I have been meaning to talk to you." Don knew right then that his worst fears were confirmed.

The next morning Don and Olga met with Randy Smith, Don's traffic manager; A. J. Toth, general manager for KiddieLand's eight Chicago stores; and Sharon Rabiega, Don's assistant for distribution services. Since the previous year had been unusually profitable, everyone was in a good mood (for once) because this year's bonus was 50 percent larger than last year's.

---

* This is a disguised case prepared by Michael A. McGinnis and Frank Burinsky, Shippensburg University, and reproduced with permission. This case was prepared as a basis for class discussion rather than to illustrate effective or ineffective handling of an administrative issue.

Nevertheless, A. J. got to the point, "You mean to tell me that we expect somebody to stuff a spouse, three kids, a dog, and 450 pounds of Super Gym in their Vega station wagon and not have a conniption?"

Randy chimed in, "Besides, we can't drop ship Super Gyms from the manufacturer to the consumer's address because Super Gym ships only in quantities of ten or more."

Olga was now becoming worried. "We can't back out of the Super Gym now," she moaned, "I have already committed KiddieLand for four hundred sets, and the spring–summer playset promotion went to press last week. Besides," Olga continued, "I am depending on the Super Gym to make my gross margin figures."

By now the scope of the problem had become apparent to everyone at the meeting. At 3 P.M. Don summarized the alternatives discussed. They are summarized here.

1. Purchase a two-wheeled trailer for each store.
2. Find a local trucking company that can haul the Super Gym from the store to the customer.
3. Stock the Super Gym at the two distribution centers and have the truck deliver during the delivery runs to the retail stores.
4. Charge for delivery if the customer cannot get the Super Gym home.
5. Negotiate with the Super Gym manufacturers to ship directly to the customer's address.

When the meeting adjourned, everyone agreed to meet the following Monday to discuss the alternatives. Thursday morning a record-breaking blizzard hit Chicago; everyone went home early. KiddieLand headquarters was closed Friday because of the blizzard. By Wednesday the same group met again, except for A. J. Toth, who was still stranded on a skiing trip in Colorado. However, A. J.'s assistant, Mary Anne Ainsworth, was in attendance.

Don started the meeting. "Okay," Don began, "let's review our options, Sharon. What did you find out about buying trailers for each store?"

"Well," Sharon began, "the best deal I can find is $1,800 per trailer for seventy trailers, plus $250 per store for an adequate selection of bumper hitches, and an additional $50 per year per store for licensing and insurance."

"Oh, no," moaned Olga, "we only expect to sell 5.7 sets per store—that means $368 per Super Gym for delivery," as she punched her calculator, "and $147.00 in lost gross margin!"

Next, Randy Smith summarized the second option. "So far we can get delivery within 25 miles of most of our stores for $38.21 per set. Actually," Randy continued, "$38.21 is for delivery 25 miles from the store. The rate would be a little less for under 25 miles and about $1.50 per mile beyond 25 miles."

Mary Anne chimed in, "According to our marketing research department, 85 percent of our customers drive less than 25 minutes to the store, so a flat fee of $40 for delivery would probably be okay."

Randy continued, "Most delivery companies we talked to will deliver twice weekly, but not daily."

Next, Sharon spoke, "The motor carrier that handles shipments from our distribution centers is a consolidator. He said that squeezing an eighteen-wheeler into some subdivision wouldn't make sense." She continued, "Every time they try, they knock down a couple of mailboxes and leave truck tracks in some homeowner's driveway."

Olga added, "I talked to Super Gym about shipping direct to the customer's address and they said forget it. Whenever they have tried that," Olga continued, "the customer gets two of one box and none of another."

"Well, Olga," Don interrupted, "can we charge the customer for delivery?"

Olga thought a minute. "Well, we have never done that before, but then we have never sold a 450-pound item before. It sounds like," Olga continued, "our choice is to either absorb $40 per set or charge the customer for delivery."

"That means $16,000 for delivery," added Olga.

"One more thing," Don spoke, "if we charge for shipping, we must include that in the copy for the spring–summer brochure."

Olga smiled. "We can make a minor insert in the copy if we decide to charge for delivery. However," she continued, "any changes will have to be made to the page proofs—and page proofs are due back to the printer next Monday."

Questions

1. List and discuss the advantages and disadvantages of purchasing a two-wheeled trailer for each store to use for delivering Super Gyms.

2. List and discuss the advantages and disadvantages of having local trucking companies deliver the Super Gym from the retail stores to the customers.

3. List and discuss the advantages and disadvantages of stocking Super Gyms at the distribution centers, and then having the truck that makes deliveries from the distribution center to the retail stores also make deliveries of Super Gyms to individual customers.

4. List and discuss the advantages and disadvantages of charging customers for home delivery if they are unable to carry the Super Gym home.

5. Which alternative would you prefer? Why?

6. Draft a brief statement (catalog copy) to be inserted in the firm's spring–summer brochure that clearly explains to potential customers the policy you recommended in question 5.

The Supply-Chain Concept

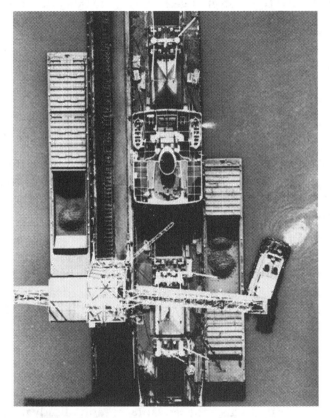

A major concern of logistics is determining transfer points for cargo. This overhead view shows the transfer of coal between an oceangoing ship, in the center, and two barges, one on each side. A small tug is at the right. The picture was taken at New Orleans. During the 1980s the United States both imported and exported coal. Volumes and directions of the coal movements were dependent on the price of oil and the relative value of the U.S. dollar vis-à-vis other world currencies. (Courtesy of Board of Commissioners of the Port of New Orleans.)

Caterpillar Americas Co. has closed a link in its supply chain by teaming its transportation department with its marketing department. It was a step that the Caterpillar Co. subsidiary decided was necessary to get control of customer service between the factory and the dealer.

American Shipper
July 1994

Each function contributing to the "management" of the supply chain has developed processes and systems to meet the individual needs of the the functions; not necessarily in the best interest of the supply chain. Each function strives for excellence, and many achieve it within their functional area of responsibility. But this does not create an optimized supply chain. We suggest that it creates the reverse.

Rod Inger, Alan Braithwaite, and Martin Christopher
Aligning Manufacturing with the Market:
The "How" of Supply Chain Management
1994

Whenever it's a better deal to do it internally, do it. At the end of the day, you're going to be buying a lot from vendors. No company can keep up with an entire product set in a rapidly changing world.

Lars Ljungdahl, of IBM
American Shipper
July 1993

Key Terms

- Channel intermediary
- Facilitator
- Financing channel
- Logistics channel
- Negotiations channel
- Ownership channel
- Partnership
- Promotions channel
- Sorting function
- Strategic alliance
- Supply-chain management
- Third-party logistics
- Value added

Learning Objectives

- To learn about marketing channels and their functions
- To understand how power is used in the channels
- To recognize the importance of the sorting function
- To learn the role of channel intermediaries
- To learn about third-party logistics and logistics partnerships
- To understand the supply chain, how it functions, and how it differs from the marketing channel

INTRODUCTION

The term **supply-chain management** extends the "concept of integration beyond the firm to all firms in the supply chain. Suppliers, customers, and third-party logistics providers share the information and plans necessary to make the channel more efficient and competitive. This sharing is more accurate and detailed than in traditional, more adversarial buyer-seller relationships."[1] All these parties are also part of an arrangement often referred to as *marketing channels,* and a discussion of channels will aid in one's understanding of the supply chain.

MARKETING CHANNELS

Knowledge of marketing channels is useful prior to discussing the supply chain.

> Marketing channels can be viewed as sets of interdependent organizations involved in the process of making a product or service available for use or consumption. From the outset, it should be recognized that not only do marketing channels satisfy demand by supplying goods and services at the right place, quantity, quality and price, but they also stimulate demand through promotional activities of the units (e.g. retailers, manufacturers' representatives, sales offices, and wholesalers) constituting them. Therefore, the channel should be viewed as an orchestrated network that creates value for the consumer through the generation of form, possession, time, and place utilities.[2]

The principal, traditional actors in the marketing channel are the manufacturer, the wholesaler, and the retailer. Each in turn assumes ownership of the inventory of goods. They also assume risks associated with their temporary inventory ownership position. The channel members in this arrangement, carrying out this task, can also be referred to as the **ownership channel.** The same or related parties also get together in other channel arrangements, and these channels are called the **negotiations channel,** the **financing channel,** the **promotions channel,** and the **logistics channel.** The logistics channel handles the physical flow of product, which is the principal topic of this book. All channels and channel activities can be graphed as networks.

Information is also freely carried up and down, back and forth, and between channels. One of the functions of the channel system is to give each

---

[1] Lisa M. Ellram, "Supply Chain Management, Partnerships, and the Shipper–Third Party Relationship," *International Journal of Logistics Management,* vol. 1, no. 1 (1990), p. 1.

[2] Louis W. Stern and Adel I. El-Ansary, *Marketing Channels,* 4th ed. (Englewood Cliffs, N.J.: Prentice Hall, 1992), p. 1.

actor sufficient information so that he or she can make a correct, rational decision. Information availability is important to a channel's functioning: channels will fail if some of the actors feel that necessary information is lacking. Although information flows in both directions, there is some bias in that most channel members are usually more concerned about buyers' needs than sellers' needs. New products, for example, are developed with customers in mind. Selling is carried on more aggressively and is considered more glamorous than purchasing. Of course, one channel member's sale is another channel member's purchase.

In late 1994 an event occurred that is destined to become a textbook example of poor use of information. It had to do with a defective computer chip. Here is but one aspect: An individual in a firm designing computers was encountering many troubles. Eventually an engineer in another company told this individual about a rumored bug in the power management feature of certain Intel 486 chips. This individual then "called Intel for an explanation and was told that in order to learn why one batch [of chips] worked better than the other he and his associates had to sign an agreement not to disclose what they were about to learn."[3] Eventually the defect became widely known, and Intel suffered considerably from bad publicity. The point to make here is that Intel's initial behavior of withholding information about the product's defect was counter to acceptable channel behavior (as well as consumer interests). Both final consumers and parties such as the individual mentioned, who was trying to design a product that would incorporate the Intel chip, were hurt. Firms that used the Intel chip in their final product also suffered because some consumers blamed them for the poor performance of the final product.

It is safe to assume that over 99 percent of the decisions made within channels are for repeat purchases (also called rebuys); hence many of the transactions are not strictly new, but are either exact repeats, or repeats with minor modifications, from whatever was done yesterday or last week. There is also a stock of goodwill included in many transactions. Persons prefer doing business with persons they like. This is especially true today, when we extol "partnership" rather than "adversarial" relationships between buyers and sellers. We prefer thinking about rewarding "good" behavior, rather than penalizing "bad."

Only a few participants are in the action for the first time; they must establish their credibility and learn that channel's rules of the game. Let us look more closely at how the three parties, the manufacturer, the wholesaler, and the retailer, interact in each of the five mentioned channels.

---

[3] *San Francisco Examiner,* January 1, 1995, p. B1.

The ownership channel covers movement of title to the goods. The goods themselves might not be physically present or even exist. If a good is in great demand, one might have to buy it before it is produced, such as a commissioned piece of art or a book yet to be written. Sometimes a product will not be made until there are sufficient financial commitments, which is often the case with new models of airline aircraft. The party owning the good almost always has the right to trade or sell it and bears the risks and costs associated with having it in inventory. Also, while owning the good, one can use it as collateral for a loan, although this may place some restrictions on its use or movement.

The negotiations channel is the one where buy and sell agreements are reached. This could include transactions face to face or by telephone, E-mail, or almost any other form of communication. In many situations there are no actual negotiations; the price for the product is stated and one either buys at that price or does not. In some trades auctions are used, and in others highly structured, organized trading takes place, such as markets for some commodities. One part of the negotiations covers how activities in the other channels are to be handled. For example, each buying party will specify the point and time of delivery and the point and time of payment. Even packaging design may be negotiated. (An old Henry Ford story is that suppliers of some parts were directed to ship in wooden crates built of good lumber and to very exacting specifications. It turned out that the empty crates were then partially disassembled and became floorboards in Ford Model Ts.) Later will be some discussion of channel intermediaries, who fill niches in the supply chain, usually without taking an ownership position. Brokers are intermediaries who play an an important role in the negotiations channel, helping buyers and sellers close a deal.

Each party to the negotiation assigns a cost to each completed transaction. The cost is of the negotiator's time and any associated expenses, say, long distance telephone charges or sales commissions. This is of significance to the logistics channel because the size of an order depends in part on the transaction costs. To the extent that the transaction costs can be spread over an order, it is advantageous to order a larger amount since the transaction costs per unit are then less. The buyer might also negotiate to have the order divided into several segments, with one segment being delivered, say, each week. Options are also employed in which a certain amount of product is purchased and the buyer has the option to repeat the order one or more times within specified limits. In many situations, one combines the transaction costs and the cost of the product. If these combined costs are too high, parties will drop out of the market. They will either seek substitute products or possibly decide to build an item rather than purchase it.

Relevant to the negotiations channel is the issue of power. Parties in the channel possess strengths that vary with their size, their financial assets, or the popularity of the product handled. A never-ending issue in logistics channels is which party should maintain the inventory, and where. A retailer wants to keep a small reserve stock, but also wants the wholesaler to maintain huge reserve stocks and the capability to make almost instantaneous deliveries upon demand. In the past decade mass retailers have been able to make some extraordinary demands on other channel members: A few have decided not to deal with wholesalers at all and insist on dealing directly with the manufacturers.

> Wal-Mart Stores . . . uses a sophisticated point-of-sale information system to monitor sales and automatically replenish goods to its store. Now the company has suggested taking the process a step further by not paying any supplier until its product is sold to the final consumer. Funds would then flow instantaneously to each partner in the supply chain through electronic funds transfer.[4]

A party with power may also develop alternate channels to move some of its product. The most common example is the development of catalog sales, which bypass retail stores and some wholesalers.

The financing channel handles the payment for the goods. More importantly, it handles the issue of credit. The several participants in the channel have different financial strengths, and often one must help another to keep the entire channel alive. For example, a newly opened retail store may have some of its goods placed on consignment, meaning that the wholesaler, not the store, owns them. The retailer will reimburse the wholesaler only for goods sold; the wholesaler bears nearly all the financial risks. Sometimes, in an effort to develop what it believes is a necessary new product line, a wholesaler will assist the manufacturer by putting up cash in advance along with an order. Or the wholesaler will place a large, firm order, and the manufacturer can take that order to a bank and use it as a basis for receiving a loan. The logistics channel is often designed so that a payment must be received in order to trigger the release of the order or part of the order. Credit is important to all parties in the channel; they frequently receive or extend it, and it becomes an integral part of the negotiations. When bills are not paid when due or when credit is over-extended, collection becomes a financing channel function.

The promotions channel is concerned with promoting a new or an existing product. This is probably most closely related to the financing channel because monetary allowances are often part of the promotion effort. However, the promotion channel and the logistics channel are linked in several ways. First, there may be special advertising materials,

---

[4] *Transport Topics,* October 3, 1994, p. 5.

such as coupon books, floor advertising signs, or posters, that must be distributed with the promoted product. Second, some of the cartons or consumer packs may have special labeling, and their placement at retailers must coincide with other promotional efforts. Third, the retailer will be reluctant to take any more of a new product than is necessary, in case the promotion flops. On the other hand, if the promotion is successful, the retailer will demand more product, so it is necessary to keep reserve stocks nearby. Fourth, since logistics personnel handle order processing, they have instantaneous records of actual sales, which indicate the initial success of the promotional efforts. Fifth, since some promotions involve price reductions for large orders, the logistics staff must prepare for making large shipments (and then see shipments drop off). Last, the promotion may involve an entirely different product. For example, some years ago, Kool cigarettes had promotion that required the end of a Kool cigarette carton and some money in order to obtain a sailboat. In this situation, the sailboats moved through an entirely different logistics channel than the cigarettes.

As mentioned before, the logistics channel, its components, and its functioning are the main topics of this book. Logistics covers both the movement and the storage of the product, mainly in the direction of the consumer. Sometimes the reverse move is also of concern. Examples are product recalls and the recycling of products and of packaging.

The most significant contribution that the logistics channel makes to the overall channel process is the **sorting function.** This function involves rearranging the assortment of products as they flow through the channels toward the customer, taking large blocks of single products and rearranging them into quantities, assortments, and varieties that consumers prefer. The sorting function bridges "the discrepancy between the assortment of goods and services generated by the producer and the assortment demanded by the consumer. The discrepancy results from the fact that manufacturers typically produce a large quantity of a limited variety of goods, whereas consumers usually desire only a limited quantity of a wide variety of goods."[5] Nearly a century ago James H. Ritter said that the jobber "assembles various lines of goods, carries a large and assorted stock and by means of travelling salesmen and other agencies, sells these goods to the retailer in small assorted lots, while the retailer supplies the consumer."[6] At one time the word *reshipping* described these procedures.

[5] Stern and El-Ansary, p. 6.

[6] Cited in Mushtaq Luqmani et. al., "Tracing the Development of Wholesaling Practice and Thought," *Journal of Marketing Channels,* vol. 2, no. 1 (1991), p. 85. They cited Ritter's article in the November 1903 issue of the *Annals of the American Academy of Political Science.*

The sorting function has four steps, and these are important to understanding the concept of goods flowing through the logistics channel (and the supply chain).

- *Sorting out* is sorting a heterogeneous supply of products into stocks that are homogeneous.
- *Accumulating* is bringing together similar stocks from different sources.
- *Allocating* is breaking a homogeneous supply into smaller lots.
- *Assorting* is building up assortments of goods for resale, usually to retail customers.

These steps take place between the manufacturer and the consumer. That means that they are performed by the wholesaler, the retailer, or specialist intermediaries. Before moving on, we should briefly mention the handling of hazardous materials. They often move through a logistics channel of their own, utilizing specialized carriers and warehouses and sometimes following different routes.

CHANNEL INTERMEDIARIES

In addition to the major actors, or primary participants in a logistics channel, there are many less well known actors who play minor but very necessary roles. They are called **facilitators,** or **channel intermediaries.**[7] Intermediaries make the entire system function better. They spring up and flourish in areas where communications and other interactions between major parties are not well meshed. For example, in international transactions, translators may be an important intermediary. Intermediaries also function in areas needing orderly routines, such as order processing, and in searching, for example, when customers are looking for products or producers are looking for customers. Intermediaries fill niches, they are very well focused, and they serve as buffers. Usually they do not take an ownership position in the products or goods being handled.

We can look at the five channels discussed above and see where intermediaries function and fit. They are used only when needed, and most channel actors know when to rely on them. For example, wholesaler has its own warehouse but also rents public warehouse space when needed, the public warehouse being the intermediary.

In the ownership channel the most common intermediary is the bank or finance company, which may assume temporary or partial ownership of goods as part of an ongoing transaction. Often this is a condition for the

---

[7] At one time they were called *middlemen*, a word that is no longer politically correct.

extension of credit. Banks routinely loan funds to all parties in the channel, making it possible for goods to be manufactured, marketed, and sold.

In the negotiations channels we often use the term *broker*. A broker is intermediary between a buyer and a seller. Commodities are often traded through brokers. When one contracts with a trucker to carry a truckload of freight, a broker is used. One reason brokers are used in this situation is that the individual trucker feels that his or her time is more profitably spent driving, rather than being on the phone trying to negotiate for the next load. It is easier for the trucker to let the broker find the load and then give the broker 10 to 15 percent off of the top. When one charters ships, two brokers are used, one representing the user, the other, the vessel owner. This is a global market and both brokers have contacts throughout the world.

Intermediaries in the financing field are again often banks, who supply the credit necessary for a deal to be finalized. Sometimes insurance is also a requirement in the agreement, so insurance companies may also serve as intermediaries. Sometimes accountants are called in to verify certain information. For "big ticket" items, such as ships or houses, the buyer almost always borrows money to finance part of the purchase. Providers of finances are intermediaries, as are those who bring together buyers, sellers, and sources of credit.

The promotions channel has intermediaries that aid with promotions. There are firms that design, build, and transport product exhibits for display at trade shows. Others will handle the preparation and media placement of advertising materials. Promotions efforts are coordinated with the firm's overall advertising activities.

The logistics channel has many intermediaries, and many are mentioned in this book. The most common is the freight forwarder, whose function is to assemble small shipments into larger shipments and then tender them in truckload or rail carload quantities to truck lines or to railroads. In international logistics, intermediaries abound; over one hundred different types could be listed. To give an idea of specialization, there are "cargo surveyors" who specialize in coffee, devoting their careers to examining and arbitrating damage claims involving shipments of coffee beans.

WHAT IS THE SUPPLY CHAIN?

Having spent some time discussing channels, let us now move to discussing the supply chain, which is an expansion of the channel concept. In what ways is it different?

Focus.   First, the channel focuses on one product or a set of related products, say, packaged breakfast cereal, and deals with how it moves from the manufacturer to the customer. That is a marketing channel, as is the channel by which the wheat moves from the farm to cereal manufacturer. The supply chain encompasses the entire move from the farm to the consumer buying cereal. Indeed, it might even go back farther and include the farmer's purchases of seed and fertilizer. The logistics manager now looks outward from his or her firm in both directions, toward suppliers and toward their customers, and having done this, visualizes a smooth, continual flow of materials and products starting at the sources and leading to the consumers.

> How long is your supply chain? For many firms, the supply chain extends from their suppliers' suppliers to their customers' customers and beyond. Recognizing the investment levels represented by the supply chain, it is essential that inventories throughout the so-called seamless tube be managed effectively and efficiently. Having accurate information on amounts and locations of suppliers' and customers' inventories allows direct shipments from your suppliers to your customers, bypassing your organization in a strategy some refer to as virtual warehousing.[8]

In the textile and apparel industry, the supply chain might consist of a fiber provider, a yarn manufacturer, a textile manufacturer, an apparel manufacturer, a distributor, and a retailer, as well as any firms supplying transportation, information, or distribution services to those firms that actually manufacture or sell the product.

Figure 2-1 shows the supply-chain travels of materials that eventually become a DuPont toothbrush. From DuPont's standpoint, the movements to the Texas plant consist of inbound raw materials. Responsibility for coordinating these moves is shared by the firm's purchasing and production staffs and its suppliers. These are also marketing channels for the inputs. The moves from the Texas operations to West Virginia and then to Massachusetts involve company-owned material in semiprocessed form. These moves are under the direction of the firm's traffic and production departments and are considered interplant logistics. Finally, the movements of finished product from the DuPont Massachusetts plant are classified as physical distribution and are controlled by DuPont and wholesalers that buy from DuPont. These finished product movements are considered as part of the toothbrush marketing channel. Both the inbound channel and the outbound channel, plus the interplant moves, all make up the supply chain. Hence, the first major difference between a marketing channel and a supply chain is the length.

Reengineering.   The second difference between the supply chain and the marketing channel is that while the channel appears to concentrate

___

[8] John A. White, "In Search of World-Class Logistics," *Modern Materials Management,* August 1994, p. 31.

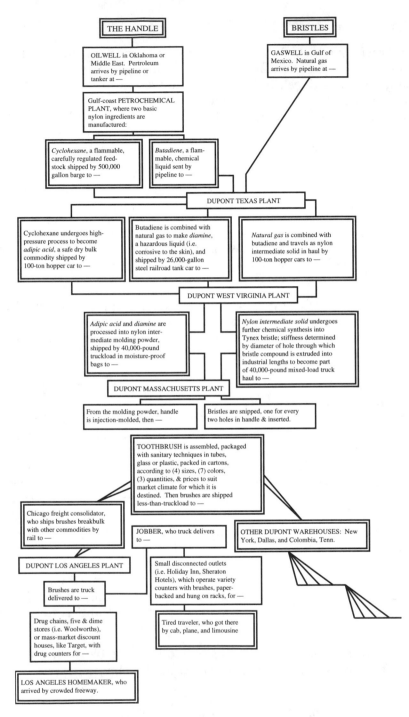

Figure 2-1 From doorstep to doorstep: the travels of a toothbrush. (*Source:* Adapted from Daniel K. Chapman, "Untangling Industry's Toughest Knot: Physical Distribution Systems in the Seventies," paper distributed by Robertson Distribution Systems, Inc., Houston, 1973.)

on existing products, the supply chain appears to include more room for considering the reengineering of products and processes so that the flow through the entire chain is smoother.

> By exploring packing configurations, the company [Caterpillar Americas] has shipped two backhoes in one container rather than shipping them separately. . . . "We're looking deeply into how to configure machines to ship them more cost effectively. That can go all the way down to how to design them to begin with."[9]

With the supply chain concept it is acceptable, even desirable, to negotiate engineering and design changes in products to make them more compatible with the needs of other chain members. The firm and all its supply chain partners are attempting to deliver a quality product through a quality system, and to achieve this, other functions within the firm must be involved. Each firm's core competencies are determined, and the firm should stand ready to relinquish to others in the supply chain responsibilities for tasks that these others can perform more competently. Once a firm has stripped down to its core competencies, it is also in better position to reprioritize sales, enter new markets, develop and serve in new channels and supply chains, and focus on order profitability.

In 1993 IBM examined its logistics competencies and made several decisions regarding the firm's reorientation. "Through the years, IBM has developed proprietary information systems for international trade. Companies have come to IBM and said: 'We want what you've got.'"[10] After considerable study IBM decided that its core competencies dealt with processes, information systems, and international movements, so it made these services available to others on a third-party basis. In terms of domestic distribution, IBM felt that it had no particular core competencies, so it shed those functions, and they are now performed by others who contract with IBM as third-party logistics providers.

Inventory Management.   Third, inventories are better managed, which means smaller. Literature to date discussing the supply chain tends to concentrate on inventory management and on changing the pattern from stop and start to one of continuous flow. Changes in the supply chain are subject to negotiation. An example is supplier lead time, the time necessary for the supplier to replenish some needed stocks. If the supplier's lead time can be reduced, the buyer can maintain smaller inventories. Hence, supplier lead times would be a relevant subject for coverage in the negotiation channel. In the negotiations a clearer understanding of buyer/seller expectations

---

[9] Roger Noonan, regional manager for Caterpillar Americas, quoted in *American Shipper*, June 1994, p. 46.

[10] *American Shipper*, July 1993, p. 38.

must develop. One of the main objectives of supply-chain management is to obtain a smoother and better-controlled flow of inventory with fewer inventory "lumps" along the way.

Pull Strategy.   Fourth, inventories have shifted from "push" to "pull" systems.

> Until recently, large consumer goods manufacturers dominated the retailing channel. Under the "push" strategy, these suppliers used long production runs to gain efficiencies of scale, thus minimizing unit costs and optimizing utilization of their production and distribution assets.
>
>   However, because production is not necessarily aligned with actual retail sales, a surplus of inventory generally exists. This excess product is "pushed out" to the retailers through use of deals and promotions designed to entice the retailers to make large purchases in advance ("forward buying"). Although the "push" strategy can strengthen manufacturers' profits, it also results in excess inventory and inefficient supply-chain management. . . .
>
>   Under the "push" scenario, manufacturers produce what they expect to sell. Under "pull," the system "listens" to the consumer through the retailer, transmits preferences back up the information pipeline and quickly responds with the merchandise demanded. The objective across the supply chain is to reduce the inventory buffer for all trading partners.[11]

R. Inger, A. Braithwaite, and M. Christopher use the phrase "lean logistics" and say that the way to achieve it is through the following:

- [use] shorter planning cycles.
- reduce lead times.
- tightly couple adjacent inventories with frequent replenishments of what has been consumed in the immediately past period.
- introduce single points of decoupling—that is—where the supply chain moves from forecast-push of material, to demand-pull. . . .
- reduce batch sizes in manufacture and distribution.
- defer product explosion to fit several markets by having the greatest stocks in generic product, or even better, in materials and sub-assemblies.[12]

The Inger, Braithwaite, and Christopher list includes factors we have listed as points 3 and 4. Irrespective of whether power shifts are an issue, inventories are reduced and are better managed. In a sense, use of the word *chain* in *supply chain* is a poor choice, since a better analogy would be to cable. If

---

[11] *The Mass Merchant Distribution Channel: Challenge and Opportunities* (Oak Brook, Ill.: Warehousing Education and Research Council, 1994), pp. 7–8.

[12] Rod Inger, Alan Braithwaite, and Martin Christopher, *Aligning Manufacturing with the Market: The "How" of Supply Chain Management* (London: Logistics Consulting Partners, 1994), p. 10.

anything, the channel can be graphed as chain, with links joined together, while the supply chain is better diagrammed as a cable or as a tube through which products flow.

Communication.   Fifth, communications is better integrated with the management of the operation and the flow of the product. Channels and the supply chain depend on huge quantities of real-time information. The use of just-in-time and electronic data interchange (EDI) systems has forced closer relationships. J. Hammond writes, "In order to efficiently achieve quick-response capabilities, companies must choose and/or develop channel partners that have the necessary capabilities and establish coordinating mechanisms that ensure the rapid flow of both product and information through the channel."[13] It is not unusual to have point-of-sale information transmitted directly to suppliers and translated into orders for replenishment stocks. Data bases are shared, and members of the supply chain have some access to the data bases of their partners. A vendor may allow a customer to query the vendor's inventory records to determine what the vendor has in stock before placing an order. This enables the customer to make more accurate plans for the goods it plans on receiving, such as where to stock them or how to use them in a promotion. Bar-code labels follow many items through the entire supply chain. Figure 2-2 is an ad from a logistics service provider; note that the services it offers include "state-of-the-art scanning and sorting" and that it is "EDI compatible."

Coordination.   Sixth, management is different. In earlier systems each manager was concerned with his or her individual function: order processing, inventory control, traffic management, and the like. Consultants describing this would refer to and illustrate each of these functions as being in a bureaucratic silo (with the added inference that some silo dwellers wanted their silos to be wider and higher than the others). As logistics developed within the firm, the activities within silos were coordinated with each other. Supply-chain managers do not think in terms of a separate silo for each function. Instead, they think of a long, continuous flow designed mainly to please the customer. Some firms have customer councils, which are made up of representative customers who meet from time to time to suggest improvements they would like to see. (This is a way of learning how a distributor's competitors are doing, since customers are likely to make comparisons with other distributors.)

Long-Term Agreements.   Seventh, the supply chain is held together by long-term agreements between and among parties. A marketing channel

[13] Janice Hammond, "Coordination in Textile and Apparel Channels: A Case for 'Virtual' Integration," in *Papers: The 1991 OSU Transportation and Logistics Research Fund Proceedings* (Columbus: Ohio State University, 1991), p. 114.

Figure 2-2 Ad from a logistics services provider. (Courtesy Eastern America Transport and Warehousing, Inc.)

can function with daily or hourly buy/sell transactions between parties and no long-term commitments. A firm graduates from the marketing channel to the supply-chain concept by entering into contractual arrangements, or other forms of agreement, with sources, customers, and intermediaries. As more and more of these arrangements develop, the firm is increasingly bound in both directions, as are the firms with which it contracts.

Barriers to Supply-Chain Management

Several barriers to the supply-chain management approaches are

> tradition, organizational, legal, and nonintegrated management systems. Traditionally, supply chains of necessity have been managed and controlled functionally. The management objectives and measures for each of these functions are in fundamental conflict. Inventories, for example, are "owned" and managed separately.[14]

There are concerns other than efficiency; the firm, for example, may not want to be completely dependent on one source of supply. In 1953 GM's transmission plant in Livonia, Michigan, was completely destroyed by fire. At that time it was GM's only source of the Hydra-Matic transmissions used in Pontiacs, Oldsmobiles, and Cadillacs.[15]

Numerous studies and surveys conducted in the early 1990s showed rather limited acceptance of many of the integrating tools mentioned here. Some partners are reluctant to share proprietary data. Point-of-sale information, gathered at retail checkout counters is, in many instances, too voluminous to manage. Bar coding, while used by larger firms, is not used by others, and as these others adopt bar-code-reading equipment, they will find that the industry leaders have abandoned the zebra code for a small, more complex two-dimensional symbol containing considerably more information in the same space. EDI, while used for many transactions, is still limited in coverage, with firms reporting, say, that they receive only 10 to 20 percent of their orders via EDI, although these orders may account for over half their sales. In a 1994 survey only 26 percent of the nation's grocery manufacturers had EDI links to customers, and only 15 percent had EDI links to warehouses.[16] Many war stories exist concerning the inadequacies or mismatches

---

[14] Thomas C. Jones and Daniel W. Riley, "Using Inventory for Competitive Advantage through Supply-Chain Management," *International Journal of Physical Distribution and Materials Management,* vol. 17, no. 3 (1987), p. 104.

[15] "The Great Livonia Fire," *Fortune,* November 1953, pp. 132–135, 171–178. It took about four months to resume full production of Hydra-Matic transmissions. In the interim, Chevrolet's Power-glide transmissions were placed in Pontiacs, and Buick's Dynaflow transmissions were placed in Oldsmobiles and Cadillacs.

[16] *Transport Topics,* October 9, 1994, p.12.

of computer systems. One apparent casualty has been the vendor-managed inventory. Many vendors have been unable to meet their customers' expectations in this area of logistics performance.

Several decades ago many of the supply-chain arrangements in use today would have been considered illegal under certain antitrust statutes. Long-term commitments do stifle competition to the extent that they make it more difficult for others to enter the market. It is still wise to have some legal advice before entering into some of these arrangements today.

SUPPLY-CHAIN MANAGEMENT AND INTEGRATION

Usually a firm is involved in many supply chains, and it is difficult to know whether to bundle or disassemble them. A manufacturer of food products sells to grocery chains, institutional buyers, specialty firms (which may, say, use products in gift boxes), and industrial users (who use the product as an ingredient in another product that they manufacture). Last would be export sales, with sales to each different country following a unique chain (or channel). Buyers in each chain have their own expectations. Sales expertise is also divided; special knowledge of the product would be needed when making sales to other producers, and knowledge of export/import regulations would be necessary when selling to customers overseas.

The individual firm may choose how much of each chain it wishes to own as well as the degree of control (usually through contract) it seeks to exercise over other segments or members of the chain. At one extreme is the vertically integrated firm; for example, the Ford Motor Company of the 1920s owned forests and steel mills and exercised tight control over its dealers. At the other extreme, for instance, is an individual who deals in postage stamps for collectors and who buys, sells, receives, and delivers the stamps through the mail. Most firms fall somewhere in between the two extremes, owning some logistical functions and relying on vendors or customers to perform the others.

During the late 1970s, when unionized Teamsters' wages were very high, some firms gave up their private fleets and used common or contract carriers instead, which may have increased their transportation costs. However, when negotiating with other operating unions within their own plants, management no longer had to explain why it was paying its unionized Teamsters so much.

The discussion to this point has treated the manufacturer, wholesaler, and retailer as being independent firms. That is not always so. Some firms own all three functions, with the most common examples being some lines of paint and of tires. Lumber companies often own their sources of raw materials. Chains are also integrated through wholesalers that are cooperatively owned by retailers. Some of these exist in the hardware and grocery fields. Another common form of integration is through franchises, which attempt to combine the benefits of tight integration of some functions along with the ability to be very flexible while performing other functions. Note that all the arrangements listed in this paragraph are more formalized and probably longer lasting than those in the traditional channel consisting of three independents. They may also make less use of intermediaries, since one of their rationales for organizing more formally would be the cost savings resulting from eliminating some intermediaries.

We do see vertically integrated marketing systems evolving from supply chains.

THIRD-PARTY LOGISTICS RELATIONSHIPS

Today some companies are farming out some of their logistics functions to outside firms, such as FedEx, which offers such services as just-in-time agents.

> By using its sophisticated tracking system, Federal is managing inventories of high-priced goods for customers at its sorting hubs in Memphis, Oakland, and Newark. Federal began warehousing parts for IBM work stations. By using Federal's airplanes and couriers, delivery costs were cut, and IBM could begin closing 120 parts depots.[17]

These farming-out arrangements are known as **partnerships, strategic alliances,** and **third-party logistics** or contract logistics.

B.J. LaLonde and M.C. Cooper define four different logistics relationships, including partnerships, in this way:

1. A partnership is "a relationship between two entities in the logistics channel that entails a sharing of benefits and burden over some agreed-upon time horizon."
2. A strategic alliance is "a contractual relationship between two independent entities in the logistics channel to achieve specific objectives and benefits."
3. A third-party arrangement involves "an agent in the logistics channel who enters into a temporary or longer-term relationship with some other entity in the logistics channel."
4. Contract logistics is "a process whereby the shipper and the third party(ies) enter into an agreement for specific services at specific costs over some identifiable time horizon."[18]

[17] *Business Week,* November 9, 1987, p. 62, 66.

[18] Bernard J. LaLonde and Martha C. Cooper, *Partnerships in Providing Customer Service: A Third-Party Perspective* (Oak Brook, Ill.: Council of Logistics Management, 1989), p. 6.

These precise definitions are not used by all writers, but they are useful in distinguishing the different types of arrangements. D.L. Anderson defines contract logistics as "the use of outside distribution companies (carriers, warehouses, or third parties) to perform all or part of a company's product distribution functions (including transportation, storage, inventory control, customer service, and logistical information networks.)"[19] These third-party firms do not take an ownership position in the inventories they manage for others. Most providers of contract logistics services are affiliates of large carriers.

However, some non-carrier-related firms also offer contract logistics advisory and management services. They argue that they can be more objective than a carrier-related firm, since shippers are uneasy about giving all of their freight to a company that has a heavy investment in transportation facilities. The best-known of these have spun off from two large manufacturers, Caterpillar Tractor and Kaiser Technologies. "Caterpillar Logistics Services, a $25 million subsidiary of Caterpillar, Inc., provides worldwide industrial products distribution for companies such as Navistar, Chrysler, and Land Rover."[20] In a study of the newly developing industry, Professor D.L. Wardlow traces three other sources of firms offering logistics integrated services: warehouse chains, providers of information technology, and a labor contractor.[21]

Contract logistics operations are common in many industries. Many well-known fast-food chains are supplied by contract firms. In the auto industry, Customized Transportation, Inc. (CTI) picks up "from as many as 360 vendors of 33 loop runs, from 25 to 1,800 miles away," for the auto plant, where it makes deliveries in "two-hour time windows."[22] Ad agencies use contract firms because the agencies often have one-time needs to distribute large quantities of materials quickly. In the international field, Sears contracts with Fritz Companies to handle Sears's international traffic and logistics management. Fritz now maintains one or two full-time persons in each of Sears's overseas offices. "Fritz personnel supplanted Sears traffic and logistics people overseas, and Sears's international services division has trimmed its Chicago staff somewhat."[23]

[19] David L. Anderson, "Third-Party Logistics," *American Shipper,* February 1988, p. 44.

[20] *American Shipper,* January 1991, p. 48.

[21] Daniel L. Wardlow, "Strategic Dimensions of Integrated Services Providers," Ph.D. dissertation, Michigan State University, 1991, pp. 6–8.

[22] *Distribution,* January 1988, p. 29. A *delivery window* is the span of time within which a scheduled delivery must be made.

[23] *American Shipper,* February 1991, p. 51. "Also working in Fritz Companies' favor, according to one source close to the situation, is that the firm does not have the kinds of high-cost fixed assets that ocean carriers do."

Figure 2-3   Ad for logistics partnerships. (Courtesy of the Dornbush Group.)

These long-term relationships between a firm and its suppliers and customers have developed in the past decade. Agreements are drawn up in a way
that rewards all partners when cooperative ventures are successful. They also
provide incentives for all parties to work toward success. Often they require
both parties to make some specific investments that are necessary for fulfilling the relationship. They also share risks (see Figure 2-3). The service expectations of shippers and carriers are becoming more congruent.

These relationships exist throughout the supply chain and are not
restricted to logistics operations. According to Gary Kowalski, at New United
Motors:

> Suppliers [are selected] by using the fundamental criteria of quality and cost;
> however, supplier attitude and commitment have also been important factors in
> our selection process. Our intent is to develop close, long-term, and stable rela-
> tionships with qualified suppliers. As a result, we will all share the risks and the
> responsibilities of producing a quality product, at a reasonable cost.[24]

It is crucial to consider the entire network of channels in which a firm
operates before deciding on the most appropriate form of supply-chain organization.

CUSTOMER POWER

Supply chains recognize the power of customers and view customers as
assets. In the past decade there has been a clear shift of power away from the
manufacturer to the customer. Many changes are justified as being customer-
driven. When setting up a channel or a supply chain, the most common
alignment is with the best (usually, largest) customers.

Chains such as Wal-Mart, Kmart, and Target are called mass retailers or
mass merchants. Some of the demands they are placing on suppliers are 98+
percent order fill rates, no backorders, on-time deliveries with delivery windows assigned, Universal Product Code markings on all cases and cartons,
customer-specific case packs, and advance shipment notification. They also
attempt to shift to the vendors responsibilities for managing their (the mass
retailers') inventories.[25]

QUALITY AND VALUE ADDED

Quality and *value added* are current buzzwords in logistics circles. In the engineering and design of supply chains, both concepts are extremely important.

---

[24] Gary Kowalski of New United Motors, comments made at the national meeting of the
Warehousing Education and Research Council, San Francisco, May 25, 1988.

[25] *The Mass Merchant Distribution Channel: Challenge and Opportunities*, p. 5.

Over the years vendors have noticed that buyers' tolerance for errors is getting smaller. Ten years ago a buyer might have accepted 1 percent errors in components purchased, five years ago it might have 0.5 percent, and today it might be 0.1 percent. Logistics managers everywhere are running tighter ships. Quality is important to supply-chain thinking because, literally, the supply chain is no better than its weakest link. Whichever link in the supply chain is responsible for questionable quality will be the first eliminated. Another supplier will be found or a connected partner will take over the function.

Value added is important to all participants in the supply chain. They must convincingly demonstrate that their contribution adds value to the entire process and that this value exceeds whatever their contribution costs. An example of a value-added service offered by carriers that is not traditionally part of the common carrier obligation is the "early warning of a late shipment, which permits contingency plans to be executed to keep production lines running and customers supplied down the channel."[26]

FINANCIAL PERFORMANCE

Good financial performance is always a business goal. All the efforts at configuring or reengineering a supply chain must have the bottom line in mind. A firm must think of its own bottom line, as well as the bottom lines of all other participants. Some concern must be shown for the partners' bottom lines since they are unlikely to move forward with new ideas unless they can be persuaded that their profitability will improve. One advantage of partnerships is the leveraging of each partner's assets. Properly combined, the assets will earn more than the sum of what each would earn independently.

John A. White writes "A world-class logistics system will deliver bottom line benefits. By providing superior service to customers, market share will increase. As many top firms have discovered, having world-class logistics will permit a company to charge premium prices for the services it provided."[27]

ENVIRONMENTAL IMPACT

Today's business world is concerned with the impacts that it is making on the environment. Even if a specific profit-minded businessperson does not care, he or she may find that consumer groups boycott a product because the firm is apparently guilty of some transgression against the environment. Hence,

[26] LaLonde and Cooper, p. 31.
[27] White, loc. cit.

one must be certain that all partners in the supply chain are following environmentally correct practices.

INTRAFIRM LOGISTICS

Before closing, we must acknowledge that the most elementary segments in a supply chain are the operations within each firm in the chain. A firm must handle its internal movements successfully if it is to be a useful member of a supply chain. Sometimes the phrase *materials management* applies to intrafirm movements. Every firm has both inbound and outbound movements of freight. An extreme example is a firm the size of General Motors, which has 120 parts plants, which feed into about thirty GM auto and truck assembly plants. General Motors also depends upon 2,500 suppliers. These numbers count inbound movements only; the completed autos leave the GM assembly plants for dealers throughout the United States and in other countries.

For some firms, one type of movement may be more important; for other firms, inbound and outbound movements may share equal importance. The importance of movement type often depends on the industry as well as on whether competition is felt in the buying or selling sector. Another factor is the geographic range over which products are sold or raw materials are purchased.

The logistics staff is responsible for all movements of materials between a firm's various plants and warehouses. Note that the production plant sees two types of inbound transportation: (1) the inbound movements of materials purchased from various outside suppliers and (2) the interplant movement of materials and components between plants owned by the same firm. The firm's logistics managers work with others to schedule the firm's overall production in whatever manner top management believes is most desirable.

SUMMARY

Marketing channels consist of sets of manufacturers, wholesalers, and retailers that are linked together in order to make the product available to consumers. Within the marketing channel are several interrelated channels dealing with ownership, financing, negotiation, promotions, and logistics. The power of channel members varies and sometimes changes. Channel intermediaries fill niches and help the entire channel function more effectively.

One of the channel's functions is sorting, which means rearranging goods received from suppliers into mixes that are desired by those in the next stage of the channel.

Partnerships, alliances, and third-party logistics are all arrangements for improving channel design and performance.

The supply chain is more than a marketing channel, and it is designed to ensure a smooth continuous flow from one's suppliers' suppliers to one's customers' customers. Firms in a supply chain specialize in performing their core competencies, and all parties are amenable to redesigning their product if it smooths the flow through the entire channel.

Issues in supply-chain management include links and their strengths, customer power, financial performance, and environmental impacts.

QUESTIONS FOR DISCUSSION AND REVIEW

1. What is a marketing channel? Is it a single or a multiple channel?
2. What is the ownership channel? What functions does it perform?
3. What is the financing channel? What functions does it perform?
4. What is the negotiations channel? What functions does it perform?
5. What is the promotions channel? What functions does it perform?
6. What is the logistics channel? What functions does it perform?
7. How are the five channels, mentioned in questions 2 through 6, related? Discuss.
8. What is the sorting function? What is its significance to logistics?
9. Who, or what, are channel intermediaries? What are their functions? Are they necessary?
10. What are brokers? What functions are they likely to perform in the logistics field?
11. Are all parties in a marketing chain completely independent from each other? Discuss.
12. What is third-party logistics? In what situations is it used? Is it the same as contract logistics?
13. What are logistics partnerships? When would they be used?
14. What is a strategic alliance in logistics? When might one be used?
15. What is the supply chain?
16. In what ways does a supply chain differ from a marketing channel?
17. What are push and pull inventories? When is each likely to be used?
18. What are apparent barriers to further use of the supply-chain concept?
19. What is intrafirm logistics?
20. What factors link a supply chain?

SUGGESTED READINGS

Anscombe, Jonathan. "The Fourth Wave of Logistics Improvement: Maximizing Value in the Supply-Chain." *Logistics Focus,* (1994), p. 36–40.

Cavinato, Joseph L. "A Total Cost/Value Model for Supply Chain Competitiveness." *Journal of Business Logistics,* vol. 13, no. 2 (1992), pp. 285–301.

Erdem, S. Altan. "An Investigation of the Concept of Power and Power Taxonomy in Channels of Distribution: A Transaction Cost Analysis Perspective." *Journal Of Marketing Theory and Practice,* vol. 2, no. 1 (Fall 1993), pp. 62–79.

Flanagan, David J. et al. "From Logistics Management to Integrated Supply Chain Management." In James Masters (ed.), *Logistics at the Crossroads of Commerce,* (Columbus: Ohio State University Transportation and Logistics Research Fund, 1994), pp. 163–181.

Fuller, Joseph B., James O'Conner, and Richard Rawlinson. "Tailored Logistics: The Next Advantage." *Harvard Business Review,* vol. 71, no. 3 (May–June 1993), pp. 53–57.

Luqmani, Mushtaq, Donna Goehle, Zahir A. Quraeshi, and Ugur Yavis. "Tracing the Development of Wholesaling Practice and Thought." *Journal of Marketing Channels,* vol. 2, no. 1 (1991), pp. 75–99.

Maltz, Arnold B. "The Outsourcing Decision: What the Data Say." In James Masters (ed.), *Logistics at the Crossroads of Commerce.* Columbus: Ohio State University Transportation and Logistics Research Fund, 1994, pp. 123–138.

Powers, Thomas L., and David J. Closs. "An Examination of the Effects of Trade Incentives on Logistics Performance in a Consumer Products Distribution Channel." *Journal of Business Logistics,* September 1987, pp. 1–28.

C A S E   2 - 1

JOHNSON TOY COMPANY

Located in Biloxi, Mississippi, the Johnson Toy Company is celebrating its seventy-fifth year of business. Amy Johnson, who is president, and Lori Johnson, who is vice president, are sisters and are of the third generation of their family to be involved in the toy business. The firm manufactures and sells toys throughout the United States. The toy business is very seasonal, with the majority of sales occurring before Christmas. A smaller peak occurs in the late spring–early summer period, when sales of outdoor items are good.

The firm relies on several basic designs of toys—which have low profit margins but are steady sellers—and on new designs of unconventional toys whose introduction is always risky but promises high profits if the item becomes popular. The firm advertises regularly on Saturday morning television shows for children.

Late last year, just before Christmas, the Johnson Toy Company introduced the Jungle Jim the Jogger doll, modeled after a popular television show. Sales skyrocketed, and every retailer's stock of Jungle Jim the Jogger dolls was sold out in mid-December; the Johnson Company could have sold several million more units if they had been available before Christmas. Based on the sales success of this doll, Amy and Lori made commitments to manufacture ten million Jungle Jim the Jogger dolls this year and to introduce a wide line of accessory items which they hoped every doll owner would also want to have. Production was well under way, and many retailers were happy to accept dolls in January and February because they were still a fast-selling item, even though the toy business itself was sluggish during these months.

Unfortunately, in the aftermath of a Valentine's Day party in Hollywood, the television actor who portrayed Jungle Jim the Jogger became involved in a widely publicized sexual misadventure, the details of which shocked and disgusted many readers and TV viewers, and we would be embarrassed to describe them. Ratings of the television series plummeted, and within a month it had been dropped from the air. On March 1, the Johnson Company had canceled further production of the Jungle Jim the Jogger dolls, although it had to pay penalties to some of its suppliers because of the cancellation. The company had little choice because it was obvious that sales had stopped.

On April 1 a gloomy group assembled in the Johnson Company conference room. Besides Amy and Lori, those present included Carolyn Coggins, the firm's sales manager; Cheryl Guridi, the logistics manager; Greg Sullivan, the controller; and Kevin Vidal, the plant engineer. Coggins had just reported that she believed that there were between 1.5 million and 2 million Jungle Jim the Jogger dolls in retailer stores, and Sullivan had indicated that there were 2,567,112 complete units in various public warehouses in Biloxi. Vidal said that he was still trying to count all of the unassembled component parts, adding that one problem was that they were still being received from suppliers, despite the cancellation.

Amy said, "Let's wait a few weeks to get a complete count of all the dolls and all of the unassembled component parts. Lori, I'm naming you to work with Carolyn and Kevin to develop recommendations as to how we can recycle the Jungle Jim item into something we can sell. Given the numbers involved, I'm willing to turn out some innocuous doll and sell it for a little more than the cost of recycling because we can't take a complete loss on all these damned Jungle Jim dolls! Greg says we have nearly 2.6 million of them to play with, so let's think of something."

"Your 2.6 million figure may be low," said Coggins. "Don't forget that there may be nearly 2 million in the hands of the dealers and they will return them."

"Return them?" questioned Amy. "They're not defective. That's the only reason we accept returns. The retailers made a poor choice. It's the same as if they ordered sleds and then had a winter with no snow. We are no more responsible for Jungle Jim's sex life than they are!"

Cheryl Guridi spoke up: "You may be underestimating the problem, Amy. One of our policies is to accept the dealer's word as to what is defective and right now there are a lot of dealers out there claiming defects in the Jungle Jim dolls. One reason that Kevin can't get an accurate count is that returned dolls are showing up on our receiving dock and getting mixed up with our in-stock inventory."

"How can that happen?" asked Amy, angrily. "We're not paying the freight, also, are we?"

"So far, no," responded Guridi. "The retailers are paying the freight just to get rid of them."

"We've received several bills in which the retailer has deducted the costs of the Jungle Jim dolls and of the freight for shipping them back from what he owes us," said Sullivan. "That was one item I wanted to raise while we were together."

"We can't allow that!" exclaimed Amy.

"Don't be so sure," responded Sullivan. "The account in question has paid every bill he's owed us on time for forty years. Do you want *me* to tell him we won't reimburse him?"

"This is worse than I imagined," said Amy. "Just what are our return policies, Lori?"

"Well, until today, I thought we had only two," said Lori. "One for our small accounts involves having our salespeople inspect the merchandise when they make a sales call. They can pick it up and give the retailer credit off of the next order."

"Sometimes they pick up more than defective merchandise," added Coggins. "Often they'll take the slow movers out of the retailer's hands. We have to do that as a sales tool."

"That's not quite right," interjected Vidal. "Sometimes the returned items are just plain shopworn—scratched, dented, and damaged. That makes it hard for us because we have to inspect every item and decide whether it can be put back into stock. When we think a particular sales-person is accepting too many shopworn items, we tell Carolyn, although it's not clear to me that the message reaches the salespeople out in the field."

"I wish I had an easy solution," said Coggins. "We used to let our sales-people give credit for defects and then destroy everything out in the field. Unfortunately, some abused the system and resold the toys to discount stores. At least now we can see everything we're buying back. I agree we are stuck with some shopworn items, but our salespeople are out there to sell, and nothing would ruin a big sale quicker than for our salespeople to start arguing with the retailer, on an item-by-item basis, as to whether something being returned happens to be shopworn."

"Is there a limit to what a salesperson is permitted to allow a retailer to return?" asked Amy.

"Well, not until now," responded Coggins. "But with this Jungle Jogger snafu we can expect the issue to occur. In fact, I have several phone queries on my desk concerning this. I thought I'd wait until after this meeting to return them."

"Well, I think we'd better establish limits—right now," said Amy.

"Be careful," said Lori. "When I was out with the salespeople last year, I gathered the impression that some were able to write bigger orders by implying that we'd take the unsold merchandise back, if need be. If we assume that risk, the retailer is willing to take more of our merchandise."

"Are there no limits to this policy?" asked Amy.

"Informal ones," was Coggins's response. "It depends on the salesperson and the account. I don't think there is much abuse, although there is some."

"How do the goods get back to us under these circumstances?" asked Amy.

"The salespeople either keep them and shuffle them about to other customers, or—if it's a real loser—they ask us what to do," replied Coggins.

"Greg," said Amy, "do our records reflect these returns and transfers?"

"Oh, fairly well," was his response. "We lose track of individual items and quantities, but if the salesperson is honest—and I think ours are—we can follow the dollar amount of the return to the salesperson's inventory, to another retailer, or back here to us. We do not have good controls on the actual items that are allowed for returns. Kevin and I have difficulty in reconciling the value of returned items that wind up back here. Carolyn's records say they're okay for resale, and Kevin says they're too badly damaged."

"I insist on the reconciliation before we allow the goods back into our working inventory," said Guridi. "That way I know exactly what I have here, ready to ship."

"You know, I'm finding out more information about inventories and returns than I thought existed," said Amy.

"Too many trips to Paris, dearest," said Lori, and the others all suppressed smiles.

Amy decided to ignore Lori's remark, and she looked at Guridi and asked, "Are you satisfied with your control over inventories, Cheryl?"

"I have no problem with the ones here in Biloxi," was Guridi's response, "but I have an awful time with the inventories of return items that salespeople carry about with them, waiting to place them with another retailer. I'm not always certain they're getting us top dollar, and each salesperson knows only his or her own territory. When Carolyn and I are trying to monitor the sales of some new item, we never know whether it's bombing in some areas and riding around in salespeople's cars as they try to sell it again."

"Have you now described our returns policy, such as it is?" asked Amy, looking at everybody in the room.

"No," was the response murmured by all. Sullivan spoke: "For large accounts we deduct a straight 2 percent off wholesale selling price to cover defectives, and then we never want to hear about the defectives from these accounts at all."

"That sounds like a better policy," said Amy. "How well is it working?"

"Up until Jungle Jim jogged where he shouldn't it worked fine. Now a number of large accounts are pleading 'special circumstances' or threatening to sue if we don't take back the dolls."

"They have no grounds for suit," declared Amy.

"You're right," said Coggins, "but several of their buyers are refusing to see our sales staff until the matter is resolved. I just heard about this yesterday and meant to bring it up in today's meeting. I consider this very serious."

"Dammit!" shouted Amy, pounding the table with her fist. "I hope that damned jogger dies of jungle rot! We're going to lose money this year, and now you're all telling me how the return policy works, or doesn't work, as the case may be! Why can't we just have a policy of all sales being final and telling retailers that if there is an honest defect they should send the goods back here to us in good old Biloxi?"

"Most of the small accounts know nothing about shipping," responded Vidal. "They don't know how to pack, they don't know how to prepare shipping documents, and they can't choose the right carriers. You ought to see the hodgepodge of shipments we receive from them. In more cases than not, they pay more in shipping charges than the products are worth to us. I'd rather see them destroyed in the field."

Sullivan spoke up. "I'd object to that. We would need some pretty tight controls to make certain the goods were actually destroyed. What if they are truly defective, but improperly disposed of, then fall into the hands of children who play with them and the defect causes an injury? Our name may still be on the product, and the child's parents will no doubt claim the item was purchased from one of our retailers. Will we be liable? Why can't we have everything come back here? We have enough volume of some returned items that we could think in terms of recycling parts."

Vidal responded: "Recycling is a theoretical solution to such a problem, but only in rare instances will it pay. In most instances the volume is too small and the cost of taking toys apart is usually very high. The Jogger Jim product involves such a large volume that it is reasonable to think up another product that utilizes many of the parts. It would even pay to modify some machines for disassembling the Jogger Jim doll."

"As I listen to this discussion," said Lori, "one fact becomes obvious. We will never have very good knowledge about volume or patterns of returns until it's too late. That's their very nature."

Guridi asked, "Could we have field representatives who do nothing but deal with this problem? The retailers would be told to hang onto the defectives until our claims reps arrive."

Coggins answered, "This would be expensive, because most retailers have little storage space for anything and would expect our claims rep to be there p.d.q. Besides, it might undermine our selling efforts if retailers could no longer use returns to deal with as they talked about new orders."

"That may be," interjected Amy, "but we cannot continue having each salesperson tailoring a return policy for each retailer. That's why we're in such a mess with the jogger doll. We have to get our return policy established, made more uniform, and enforced. We cannot go through another fiasco like Jungle Jim the Jogger for a long time. We're going to lose money this year, no matter what, and I have already told Kevin that there will be virtually no money available for retooling for next year's new products."

Questions

1. From the standpoint of an individual concerned with accounting controls, discuss and evaluate Johnson Toy Company's present policies for handling returned items.

2. Answer question 1, but from the standpoint of an individual interested in marketing.

3. Propose a policy for handling returns that should be adopted by the Johnson Toy Company. Be certain to list circumstances under which exceptions would be allowed. Should it apply to the Jungle Jim dolls?

4. Should this policy, if adopted, be printed and distributed to all of the retailers who handle Johnson Toy Company products? Why or why not? If it should not be distributed to them, who should receive copies?

5. Assume that it is decided to prepare a statement on returns to be distributed to all retailers and that it should be less than a single page of double-spaced type. Prepare such a statement.

6. On the basis of the policy in your answer to question 3 develop instructions for the Johnson Toy Company distribution and accounting departments with respect to their roles and procedures in the handling of returns.

7. Assume that you are Cheryl Guridi, the firm's logistics manager. Do you think that the returns policy favored by the logistics manager would differ from what would be best for the firm? Why or why not?

8. Until the policy you recommend in your answer to question 3 takes effect, how would you handle the immediate problem of retailers wanting to return unsold Jungle Jim the Jogger dolls?

C A S E   2 - 2

WYOMO GROCERY BUYERS' COOPERATIVE

Located in Billings, Montana, the Wyomo Grocery Buyers' Cooperative served the dry grocery and produce needs of about 150 food stores in the area from Great Falls to Butte in the northwest and from Casper to Cheyenne in the southeast. All dry groceries were shipped out of a 20,000-square-foot warehouse in Billings, built by the co-op in 1968. Produce was handled out of the Billings warehouse and small rented warehouses in Cheyenne and Great Falls. At these warehouses the co-op bagged some bulk products, such as potatoes, onions, and oranges, into five, ten, and twenty-pound bags carrying the co-op label. The warehouses also stocked items used by the stores, such as butcher paper, cash-register tape, plastic produce bags, and various sizes of brown bags.

The co-op had its own fleet of fifteen tractors and nineteen trailers which operated out of Billings, and six straight trucks with refrigerated bodies, with two each working out of Billings, Cheyenne, and Great Falls. Dry grocery deliveries were made once or twice a week, and produce deliveries were handled separately and were made two or three times a week, depending on each store's volume. Both dry grocery and produce trucks traveled approximately the same routes each week, and goods for both large and small stores were carried aboard the same truck. Stores were responsible for placing orders with the co-op, although a co-op representative would call on a weekly basis, and one of her or his functions was to help some store operators complete their order forms.

The co-op was owned by member grocery stores and run by a board of directors elected by the member stores. The directors hired the general manager, Peter Bright. Directors were elected with member stores having at least one vote. Stores with larger sales volumes got more votes, although their additional votes were not proportional to their additional sales. (This was because several years ago smaller stores realized that they could lose their power, so they capped the additional votes a larger store could be given.)

Goods were currently sold to members on the basis of cost to the co-op plus 23 percent to cover warehousing and transportation from the warehouses to the members' retail stores. Each year the co-op's revenues exceeded costs by a small margin; 20 percent of this excess was returned to the members in direct proportion to their purchases from the co-op, and the remainder was considered capital and reinvested in the co-op. The co-op's level of business was not growing. Its members were losing sales to chain food stores and chain discount department stores, which were moving into the region.

A continual problem facing the board of directors was the political split between small and large stores belonging to the co-op. Small grocery stores stocked only 1,000 to 2,000 different items or lines of merchandise (SKUs) carried by the co-op, whereas larger members needed to carry 6,000 to 8,000 SKUs to compete with the chains. The latter group of co-op members consisted of the more aggressive merchants, most of whom felt that the co-op should forget about its small members and instead help them battle the chains. From time to time they threatened to form their own co-op.

The "tissue issue" was a long-standing controversy that was debated at every quarterly meeting of the co-op's directors. Indeed, it had been a problem since the 1950s, when tissue manufacturers started manufacturing toilet paper and facial tissues in colors in addition to white. Later they introduced floral patterns for facial tissue and, more recently, started packaging in a variety of designer dispenser boxes. The tissue manufacturers did this to capture more shelf space in retailers' stores. For example, if only white tissue were sold, it could be displayed on a shelf and occupy only twelve inches of shelf space (measured along the front). If white, pink, yellow, blue, and green tissue were all to be displayed, each would require its own twelve inches of shelf space, so a total of sixty inches of shelf space would be needed. The same held for toilet paper (and many other products).

From the co-op's standpoint, five colors of tissue multiplied the warehouse workload since each color of tissue was handled as a separate product, or SKU. Each required a line on order forms, each required its own slot in the warehouse, and each had to be picked separately. However, total volume of tissue handled remained the same. The volume that was once white was now merely spread over five colors. From the co-op's warehousing standpoint, the only result had been to raise handling costs as a percentage of sales volume.

The co-op's small store members, which continued to carry only white tissue and toilet paper, thought that it was unfair for the co-op to raise its handling charges because some of its larger members now wanted to carry five colors of tissue. Larger members retorted that they had to carry this variety if they were to compete successfully with the chains.

The main warehouse, built in 1968, had now reached its capacity. Actually, it was over capacity. It was built and engineered to carry 7,000 to 7,500 SKUs, but it was now carrying just over 8,000. Some items were doubled up in slots or left in aisles or at one of the docks, but these practices were causing operational difficulties and driving up costs.

At the directors' quarterly meeting, there was a proposal for raising the co-op's charges to its members from 23 percent to 27 percent in order to generate more funds for capital investment. Money was needed for a new 32,000-square-foot warehouse in Billings that could handle up to 10,500 SKUs.

At the meeting, Seth Hardy, a long-time director who operated a small store at Absarokee, Montana, and who generally spoke for the small store members said, "Our warehouse now handles over 8,000 different items. We're told that we need a new one, costing God-knows-what so we can handle 10,000 to 11,000 different items. It's the tissue issue all over again. The manufacturers want to make the same thing in ten colors and want ten times the shelf space and ten separate bins in our warehouse!"

"Big stores see things differently," said Peter Bright, the co-op's general manager. "Manufacturers are so anxious to get shelf space for new products that they'll even bribe the store owner to give them space on a shelf. They call it a 'stocking allowance.'"

"That hasn't happened to me," retorted Hardy. "Is it because my store is too small or that I look too honest?"

"Probably both," was Bright's reply.

"How's the bribe paid?" asked Chris Jones, a director who owned a large store.

"I'm not sure that I should know the answer to that," said Bright, "but I've been told that if they're dealing with the store owner they offer several free cases of other items in their product line that the store is already carrying. If they're dealing with a salaried manager, they may slip him or her some cash, or so I've been told."

"Maybe we can get them to bribe us to stock their goods in our warehouse," commented Jones.

Hardy gave Jones an angry look, and then snapped: "We're straying from the topic. Our business as a co-op is not increasing. Therefore, I make the following motion: Resolved, that to keep the number of different items our warehouse handles limited to 8,000, all Wyomo buyers be limited to a certain number of SKUs, with the total assigned to all buyers totaling 8,000. If a buyer wants to add an SKU, he or she will have to drop another."

Questions

1. Co-op members presently pay for goods "on the basis of cost to the co-op plus 23 percent to cover warehousing and transportation from the warehouses to the members' retail stores." Is this a fair way to cover warehousing costs? Can you think of a better way? If so, describe it.

2. Answer the problem posed in question 1 with respect to transportation costs.

3. Toward the end of the case, Bright describes how some manufacturers pay bribes in order to get shelf space in retail stores. Should retailers accept such bribes? Why or why not?

4. The case says, "Stores were responsible for placing orders with the co-op, although a co-op representative would call on a weekly basis, and one of her or his functions was to help some store operators complete their order forms." Is this a function that the co-op should be performing? Why or why not?

5. The case mentions that some of the larger stores that belonged to the co-op sometimes threatened to form their own co-op. Assume that you are hired by some of them to study the feasibility of such a move. List the various topics that you would include in your study.

6. How would you vote on Hardy's motion? Why?

7. Would it make a difference whether you represented a large or small store? Why?

8. Are there other strategies that the co-op might pursue to overcome this problem? If so, describe.

Logistics Interfaces with Suppliers and within the Firm

This young lad, who peddled milk in Cascade, Idaho, in 1920, combined inbound and outbound logistics. On the saddle are two rows for holding bottles. The upper one, covered by a canvas flap, is for full bottles; the bottom one is for empties. (Source: Forest Service, U.S. Department of Agriculture.)

[The 1992 Mercury Marquis] has enough foreign parts in it to avoid being classified as a domestic car. The reason is the arcane politics of something called the corporate average fuel economy (CAFE), the federal requirement that an auto maker's new car fleet average 27.5 miles per gallon. The kicker is that an American car company cannot include its foreign-sourced little cars to raise its average. Likewise, the government cannot use the company's foreign-sourced big cars to lower its CAFE standing. The upshot is that Ford Motor Company is using enough parts from Mexico, Germany, and several other countries to make the Marquis LS "foreign."

San Francisco Chronicle
May 30, 1991

A recent survey of 1,700 companies found that only 33% in North America had begun to integrate the supply chain with distributors and suppliers, 7% had internally integrated operations, and 24% had integrated with customers.

Transport Topics
October 3, 1994

Quick Response inevitably depends upon information technology that has advanced rapidly in recent years. QR would be impossible without an alphabet soup of anagrams describing such innovative tools as electronic data interchange (EDI), point-of-sale (POS), electronic scanners, automatic replenishment systems, Universal Product Code (UPC) bar coding, Shipping Container Marking (SCM), and Advance Shipment Notification (ASN).

William C. Copacino, Kenneth R. Ernst, and Bruce S. Richard
Logistics Perspectives
Fall 1994

Key Terms

- Delivered-pricing system
- Efficient consumer response (ECR)
- Freight absorption
- ISO 9000
- Just-in-time (JIT)
- Manufacturing resource planning (MRP II)
- Materials requirements planning (MRP I)
- Phantom freight
- Recycling
- Reverse logistics
- Uniform delivered price

Learning Objectives

- To note the interaction between purchasing and logistics
- To identify the concepts of MRP I and MRP II
- To learn about return movements
- To understand some of the relationships between logistics and other functional activities of the firm
- To examine the relationship of pricing activities to logistics

LOGISTICS INTERFACES WITH SUPPLIERS AND WITHIN THE FIRM

Logistics has gained increased importance and recognition in corporate planning. It is considered to be as important as the work of producing and selling products. Logistics is now at the center of most of any firm's strategic planning decisions. Supply-chain management includes the involvement of other departments in the firm that until now have not usually been directly associated with logistics. As a result, the logistics department interacts with all other major functional players within a firm. One advantage of a career in logistics is the high level of personal exposure that is gained through contact with other areas of a firm.

The movement of materials can be inbound, outbound, or interplant. The relative importance of each type varies among firms and may also depend upon the point from which they are viewed. In this and the following chapters, the specific functions of inbound, outbound, and interplant movements are broken down for analysis to make them easier to understand. However, it should be noted that all logistics operations within a firm need to be integrated so they can work together most effectively; they must also be integrated with others within the supply chain.

Chapter 3 examines the logistical relationships between a firm and its suppliers; reverse logistics, which covers recycling; and the logistical and administrative relationships among the various other major functional areas within a firm. Most of the remaining chapters are oriented toward outward movements, that is, the logistical relationships between a firm and its customers. This present chapter differs in that it is written about the relationship with one's suppliers and with others in one's own firm. All relationships should be considered as a part of one or more supply chains.

INBOUND MOVEMENTS

For purposes of discussion, the inbound goods will be broken into three categories. The first comprises inputs or components to be used in the manufacture of another product. The second category includes products purchased for resale, such as products purchased by a wholesaler or a retail chain or store. The third category includes products or packaging materials that are being returned as part of a recycling effort.

Purchasing is the organized acquisition of inputs or of materials for resale. Purchasing is an important corporate function. Professors J. Pooley and S. C. Dunn analyzed a thirty-year sample of purchasing job ads in *The Wall Street Journal* to determine how the desired skills had changed. Over the period, there was an increase in mention of materials management, computer, international, and communications skills.[1]

---

[1] John Pooley and Steven C. Dunn, "A Longitudinal Study of Purchasing Positions: 1960–1989," *Journal of Business Logistics,* vol. 15, no. 1 (1994), pp. 193–214.

In almost all purchasing situations the items purchased must be physically moved to where the buyer needs them. Assuming that one wishes to gain better control of the logistics associated with a firm's inbound movements, a number of steps should be followed. One should:

1. Analyze current inbound freight costs, which is done by looking at paid freight bills. For products purchased on a delivered basis one would need to calculate approximate costs to the buyer if it were to pay the freight charges directly.

2. Convert buyers (the purchasing staff) to the logistics concept. This would include an appreciation of the costs of maintaining inventory and the advantages of on-time deliveries. Also, buyers should insist that vendors separate transportation costs from other costs.

3. Determine the most favorable terms of purchase, taking into account risks and the time value of money. Some large firms have blanket insurance coverage and could assume risks of ownership on inbound movements.

4. Review freight allowances offered by vendors. (A freight allowance is what the vendor allows the buyer if the buyer provides its own transportation.)

5. Set up rules for inbound routing, and penalize vendors that do not follow them. For example, establish delivery windows or specify a carrier.

6. Create alliances with vendors, working on matters of mutual benefit, such as bar coding for an item that can be used through the entire supply chain. Figure 3-1 shows how bar codes are used as an integrating tool within a single production facility.

7. Work with carriers and determine whether there would be advantages to designating one or a small number of them to handle one's inbound movements. The possible advantages would be lower rates, advance notice of delivery (often via EDI), or single-time delivery of all shipments.

8. Develop an inbound monitoring system, which usually would be part of one's computerized ordering system. If the monitoring system is especially accurate—such as through use of earth satellites to locate trucks—it has the benefit of making the inbound goods considered as part of your inventory. (This is a subtle, but important point. Goods that are merely on order are less likely to be considered as part of your stock than goods that, say, have already covered 990 miles of the 1,000-mile journey toward you.)[2]

---

[2] This is loosely based on a presentation by Bill Porter at the CLM national meeting in Cincinnati, October 18, 1994.

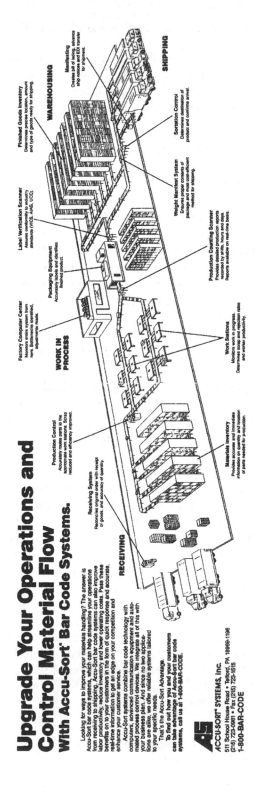

Figure 3-1 Use of bar codes throughout a manufacturing process. (Courtesy Accu-Sort® Systems, Inc.)

Purchase for Use in Manufacture

Inbound logistics for a manufacturer works to improve vendor relations and sourcing quality, cut incoming transportation time and costs, enhance materials management, and meet new production goals of quality products at competitive prices. All of this is part of supply-chain management. Vendors play a pivotal role in cost management programs. Both parties must carefully work together in developing sound alternatives for cost control. These include (1) improved make-or-buy analysis; (2) redefined terms of payment; (3) realization of quantity discounts; (4) employing scientific value analysis; (5) material, part, or supply substitution; (6) changes in production, fabrication, or processing methods; (7) salvage or scrap reduction; (8) modification in tolerances or specifications; (9) mandating reasonable vendor programs related to cost reduction and control; and (10) consolidating orders.[3]

Beginning about twenty years ago, inbound logistics has increasingly received attention for several reasons. First, increased fuel prices made it necessary for shippers to apply more controls to transportation costs. One way to control those costs was to increase the utilization of equipment. Firms thus began to balance inbound and outbound shipments. Second, when transportation regulatory barriers were relaxed in 1980, it was possible for more firms to use otherwise empty carrying capacity in their private fleets. Third, management science has led to increased interest in inbound movements. Terms such as *materials requirements planning, manufacturing resource planning,* and *JIT* (just-in-time), or *kanban,* became popular as firms turned their attention to better management of the stocks and inventories of materials destined for use on the assembly line. Fourth, these movements were fueled by the very high interest rates of the 1980s, which increased the costs of carrying production and other inventories.

An important focal point is the production-purchasing interface. Within a firm, production scheduling is carried on at a fairly high level. Sales forecasts determine what should be manufactured. A master production schedule (MPS) is developed, and a bill of materials (BOM) listing all of the necessary inputs is drawn up. The bill of materials also indicates when the inputs are needed. In addition, there is a sequential relationship. Some inputs are not needed until others arrive and are installed. Paint for a finished product is one example. Purchase orders are then placed with vendors indicating the quantities desired and the dates by which or on which the materials must be delivered.

Materials requirements planning (MRP, or MRP I) is a computer-assisted method of managing production inventory. It takes into account the firm's master production schedule, sales forecasts, open orders, inventories,

---

[3] William B. Wagner, "The Role and Relevance of Improved Purchasing for Logistics," *Journal of Business Logistics,* March 1987, p. 62.

and bills of material. Materials requirements planning recognizes that the demand for all components depends on demand for the final product and, while the demand for the final product may be uncertain, "there is no need to treat the demand for parts and subassemblies as being uncertain."[4] Traditionally, firms maintained large inventories of components along the assembly line because supervisors did not want the lines shut down because of a part shortage on their part of the line. This practice was expensive in terms of inventory holding or carrying costs. Materials requirements planning directly challenges this concept: It maintains that very limited production inputs are required to have an efficient system that can respond to most production situations. First, the firm establishes its MPS. This is based on a sales forecast or may be generated from orders that have already been received. From the MPS a BOM can be ascertained, which is a list of the specific inputs required to produce the products called for in the MPS. When producing a number of products simultaneously, there is a strong likelihood that the same component will be utilized in a number of different products. Therefore, a computer is typically necessary to keep track of the exact number of parts required for all products to be produced during a particular time period, usually one week. The computer thus lists, or *explodes,* the production inputs needed for each product and then *aggregates* each part needed for all products to be produced during each MRP cycle. This MRP planning cycle takes place a number of weeks prior to the actual production. At this point the firm places orders with its vendors for production inputs, and delivery is scheduled for arrival just before the inputs are required in the production process. If the firm manufactures its own inputs, they are scheduled to be produced so that they are available shortly before the final assembly of the finished product.

Manufacturing resource planning (MRP II) has evolved from taking into account materials requirements planning (MRP I) and adding to it the functions of marketing, finance, and purchasing.[5]

A firm's logistics staff fits into the production scheduling and MRP processes in at least four ways. First, order processing often gives the firm its most accurate data regarding actual sales. This information can be read by skilled market analysts in a manner similar to that of a physician listening to a pulse or heartbeat. For example, a firm receives orders from its branches via EDI. The information on the order forms is processed so that goods will be shipped, and, of interest here, the data on the order are fed into the firm's

[4] Alan J. Stenger and Joseph L. Cavinato, "Adapting MRP to the Outbound Side—Distribution Requirements Planning," *Production and Inventory Management,* Fourth Quarter 1979, p. 1.

[5] Norman E. Hutchinson, *An Integrated Approach to Logistics Management* (Englewood Cliffs, N.J.: Prentice Hall, 1987), p. 114. See also "Inventory and Capacity Planning Augment MRP II," *Manufacturing Systems,* July 1993.

forecast equations and then into its master production scheduling process. This then triggers raw materials purchase orders for materials needed to manufacture the precise items that the customer has just ordered or to replenish stocks that will be depleted once the customer's order is filled.

Second, the logistics staff is concerned with scheduling and managing inbound products that have unique handling or storage characteristics. The logistics staff might also have contingency plans for finding and moving critical parts in cases where the initial source of supply proves to be inadequate or unsatisfactory.

Third, the logistics staff is responsible for all movements of materials between a firm's various plants and warehouses. Note that the production plant sees two types of inbound transportation: the inbound movements of materials purchased from various outside suppliers and the interplant movements of materials and components between plants owned by the same firm.

Fourth, a logistics staff works with carriers to implement the firm's goal of better management of production inventories. "Purchasing agents are restructuring buying decisions and, in so doing, influencing the work and performance of logistics managers."[6] A 1987 survey of purchasing managers found that 20 percent had made changes in their patterns of buying inbound transport. Some "moved from rail to truck or from truck to air—in many cases to meet the speedier delivery needs of Just-in-Time inventory. And others say they have done one or more of the following: (1) shifted from multiple- to single-carrier sources, (2) put more emphasis on discount LTL (less-than-truckload) carriers, or (3) started the process of liquidating in-house trucking operations because of high insurance costs."[7] Deliveries of parts and components must be highly disciplined. Arrival "sometime next week, or the following Monday for sure" is not just-in-time thinking. Instead, truckers might be assigned a sixty-minute window on a specific day to make their deliveries. If they miss, they have to pay some financial penalties; if they miss very often, they lose the contract. Just as the quality of product inputs must improve in a JIT system, so must the quality of the carriers delivering them. Also, just as the JIT system means that the manufacturer works with fewer suppliers of components, it also works with a smaller number of carriers, because it expects more service from them than could be expected if a carrier is used for but one shipment.

Just-in-Time Systems

Already mentioned is a production inventory system that has received attention in recent years, known as **just-in-time** (JIT), or by its Japanese name, kanban. This concept has been effectively utilized by Japanese manufacturers,

---

[6] William B. Wagner, "The Role and Relevance of Improved Purchasing for Logistics," *Journal of Business Logistics,* March 1987, p. 63.

[7] *Purchasing World,* March 1987, p. 49.

and now it is being widely implemented in the United States. Customers place orders with their suppliers on basically set schedules that frequently involve daily or hourly delivery by suppliers to their customers. Ordering costs are assumed to be negligible; hence, firms order frequently in order to minimize inventory holding costs. "Although any manufacturer is concerned with material lead times and delivery reliability, the JIT manager must seek to minimize lead times and maximize delivery reliability."[8]

The JIT system is widely used in manufacturing products needed to fill orders. It is used less often in retailing because of the unpredictability of buyers' demands. In addition, it is not as widely used in industries with seasonal production patterns. Canned peaches, for example, must be processed and canned during a period of a few weeks in late summer and then sold on a fairly even level over the next fifty-two weeks.

Although JIT is often thought of as a new inventory system, the concept actually started in the United States with Henry Ford's integrated production and assembly plants in Detroit in the 1920s. Iron ore would arrive by Great Lakes vessel, and within one day it would be turned into steel in one of Ford's steel plants and then stamped or molded into auto parts, which were assembled within days of the ore's arrival from Minnesota. In 1926 Ford stated, "Waste is that stock of materials and goods in excess of requirements that turns up in high prices and low wages."[9] American businesspeople lost track of Ford's JIT system in the affluence that followed World War II. Professor Bernard J. LaLonde explains why this took place:

> For thirty-five years, most businesspeople in the United States solved most problems by throwing inventory at the problem. And if they throw enough inventory at the problem, everybody in the organization is happy; salespeople don't complain, vendors don't complain, customers don't complain, and so on.[10]

The traditional inventory purchasing systems worked well until two things happened: Interest rates started to increase greatly, causing the cost of holding inventory to skyrocket, and foreign products actively started to enter the U.S. market.

In the 1950s U.S. firms were not very concerned about inventory costs, but Japanese manufacturers were trying to rebuild their industrial capacity. Because their war damage had been so great, they effectively started from

---

[8] Bruce Ferrin, "Planning Just-in-Time Supply Operations: A Multiple-Case Analysis," *Journal of Business Logistics,* vol. 15, no. 1 (1994), p. 53.

[9] Brian C. Kullman and Robert W. Haessler, "Kanban, American Style," *Annual Proceedings of the NCPDM* (Chicago: NCPDM, 1984), p. 101. See also Arthur J. Kuhn, *GM Passes Ford, 1918–1938—Designing the General Motors Performance-Control System* (University Park: Pennsylvania State University Press, 1986).

[10] R. Scott Whiting, "Public Warehousing and the 'Just-in-Time' Production System," *Warehousing Review,* Distribution Executive Issue, 1982, p. 3.

scratch. They invited Professors W. Edwards Deming and Joseph Juran from the United states to instruct them on quality-control techniques and on how to minimize production costs. (Appropriately, Japan's most coveted industrial honor is the Deming award for quality.) The firm that most vigorously adopted kanban in the 1950s was the Toyota Motor Company.[11] As initially used in Japan, kanban was not a computerized inventory system. *Kanban* literally means *card,* and the system involves two basic types of cards, or placards. The first is the *move* card, which is utilized by assembly workers to indicate that they are getting low on an input. This card is given to workers, who bring inventory stored in the plant to the assembly line so employees can easily reach the parts necessary to assemble the final product. When the move card requires a container of inputs to be brought to the assembly line, the *production* card is taken from the container. The production card is initially placed in the container by the manufacturer of the input. This production card is then sent back to the manufacturer so the input can be replaced before another move card calls for more parts at the assembly line. (In some cases the firm manufactures its own inputs, so the production card is sent to the section of the plant that produces the input so that it can be manufactured.)

Today the terms *kanban* and *JIT* are used interchangeably, although, as we have seen, kanban is a specific type of JIT system. Let us look at how Toyota uses kanban and contrast its production system with the traditional methods used in the United States. Toyota looks at inventory as waste.[12] In the United States inventory has traditionally been considered insurance.

The key to reducing inventory, the Japanese believe, is to look at suppliers as partners in the production process. In the United States suppliers were often viewed as each other's adversaries, so the buyer constantly played one against another to get lower prices. Multiple suppliers (vendors) were frequently utilized in the United States to encourage price competition; it is considered safer because if one vendor is shut down, for example, by a labor dispute or a fire, the other vendor can supply the firm's requirements. In Japan one supplier for each production input is the rule. Thus, at one time, Toyota had 250 vendors and General Motors had 4,000.[13] Toyota uses the following method, which is typical of kanban. Vendors are included when the firm establishes its ninety-day production schedule. Each vendor receives an informal order for inputs required during this time period—but only the first thirty days is an actual order from Toyota. The production schedule tells exactly what will be needed each day for the next thirty days. Then, at the first of each month, another ninety-day schedule is given to each vendor, with the first thirty days again a

[11] George C. Jackson, "Just-in-Time Production: Implications for Logistics Managers," *Journal of Business Logistics,* vol. 4 (1983), pp. 1–2.

[12] Walter E. Goddard, "Kanban Versus MRP II—Which Is Best for You?" *Modern Materials Handling,* November 5, 1982, p. 42.

[13] Kullman and Haessler, "Kanban," p. 105.

firm order and the next sixty days Toyota's best estimate of what production will be during this time period. Note that this system enables vendors to plan their production schedules to coincide with Toyota's.

United States firms traditionally use safety stock to protect against defective parts, late deliveries, and incorrect inputs sent to the manufacturer. Because each of these problems can shut down an assembly line, safety stock was looked at as a necessary but expensive requirement. Kanban says that safety stock only covers up problems. The time to key in seriously on problems, identify them, and correct them quickly is when assembly lines stop.

Kanban works best in two situations, both of which are found at Toyota. First, the product should have relatively few variations, so that the ninety-day production schedule is accurate. This is why Toyota offers so many luxury items on their cars as standard features. It is actually cheaper to produce cars that are all about the same and then brag about the impressive list of typically extra-cost options that are standard on Japanese cars.

The second condition is that vendors be physically located close to their customers. In Japan almost all auto production parts and the cars themselves are assembled in three city clusters: Tokyo, Nagoya, and Hiroshima.[14] All of Toyota's vendors ship their products, often many times per day, less than sixty miles to the assembly plants. Many vendors are located in the same industrial parks as the Toyota assembly plants.

Two primary advantages accrue when the JIT inventory system is used. The first is that the level of production inputs on hand at any given time is less than without JIT. With inventory holding costs high, reduced levels of inputs can be a major cost-reduction program, because less money is tied up in inventory, less storage space is required, and less physical deterioration occurs. Another effect is more inventory turns, indicating that less inventory sits around waiting to be assembled. Assume, for example, that a firm needs 9,000 units of a given input in a year. If the firm has three inventory turns, then, assuming steady production and no safety stock, the firm has an average inventory of 1,500 units. (That is, 9,000 divided by 3; half of this is 1,500. We take half because, when the 3,000 units are received, we start to use them immediately, and on the average we have half the order on hand.) However, if a firm can achieve an inventory turn of ten, the average level of inventory in stock is then reduced to 450 units. (Ten deliveries of 900 units divided in half.) An example is Bendix Corporation's establishment of kanban/JIT at a production facility in Japan that supplied Toyota. Within two years after the new inventory method was established, inventory turns increased from ten to thirty times annually.[15] Another illustration is Harley-Davidson, a U.S. motorcycle manufacturer. In order to compete with Japanese manufacturers, it started to use JIT. Inventory turns increased on an

---

[14] Whiting, "Public Warehousing," p. 4.

[15] Jackson, "Just-in-Time," pp. 8–9.

annual basis from three to sixteen, decreasing the firm's costs so much that its prices could be reduced, and its market share increased.[16]

The second advantage of kanban/JIT is quality control. It is explained by James Harbour, a management consultant to the auto industry:

> Use your own logic. If you're a supplier and you ship me junk and I have no inventory, guess what happens? The [production] line shuts down. Guess what happens next? Everybody is aware of the quality problem and it gets fixed then and there. If you ever ship junk again, you're done. We get a new supplier.[17]

Like it or not, suppliers must live with the JIT systems adopted by their customers. This has meant that they must turn out a much higher quality product and deliver it in a more disciplined way. The benefits are longer relationships with customers and less dependence upon being able to continually submit the low bid. Professor J. H. Perry has noted that "the involvement of suppliers in many phases of the firm's decision making is increasing, and supplier development has been a central operating concept for most JIT firms."[18] As noted earlier, current logistics thought advocates the development of long-term, mutually beneficial relationships with outside firms that are part of the supply chain.

> To be fully effective, JIT requires complete integration of all functions between supplier and customer. The process begins by capturing information on product movement in real-time at the actual point of sale. From there, the sales information is accumulated at convenient intervals, item by item, and can be used to reorder, forecast sales (by store, distributor, or market segment), set production schedules, route shipments, analyze the effectiveness of sales and marketing efforts, and map out future distribution requirements.
>
> In other words, the manufacturer and supplier now can operate to meet exact daily requirements. Together they can maintain ongoing sales/inventory/resupply management by customer delivery point. Shipping operations and daily routing/dispatch can be planned in a timely, cost-effective manner and in accordance with customer needs. Internal operations, including inventories, also can be planned to meet optimal needs, using all of the computer-integrated procedures that manufacturing and JIT permit.[19]

ISO 9000 Certification

Today many vendors are expected to have "quality" programs. Obviously, many have worked for years to achieve such a reputation. One way for newer entrants to convince potential buyers that they, too, are capable of quality

---

[16] James Cook, "Kanban, American Style," *Forbes,* October 8, 1984, p. 66.

[17] Whiting, "Public Warehousing," p. 3.

[18] James H. Perry, "Firm Behavior and Operating Performance in Just-in-Time Logistics Channels," *Journal of Business Logistics,* February 1988, p. 25.

[19] Harvey N. Shycon, "Operating Effective Pipelines," *Transportation and Distribution,* 1988–1989 Presidential Issue, p. 47.

performance is through a program known as **ISO 9000** certification. (ISO stands for International Standards Organization.) Firms demonstrating a commitment to quality through training, reviews, and audits can receive an ISO 9000 certification. ISO 9000 is a set of generic standards used to document, implement, and demonstrate quality management and assurance systems. Applicable to manufacturing and service industries, these standards are intended to help companies build quality into every core process in each department.[20] These programs are not limited to manufacturers; a number of carriers are also engaged in ISO 9000 programs.

By late 1994 each of the major U.S. auto builders had its own quality assurance program in place that it developed for its specific suppliers. At that time, these three automakers plus truck manufacturers Freightliner, Mack, Navistar International, Paccar (which builds Kenworth and Peterbilt) and Volvo-GM mailed a new quality assurance document to the industry's 13,000 suppliers. The document included "word-for-word the requirements contained in ISO 9001 (one of the documents in the ISO 9000 family) plus all of the additional requirements on which the eight [auto and truck] OEM [original equipment manufacturers] could harmonize."[21] The auto and truck builders are also requiring the 13,000 suppliers to hold *their* suppliers to the document's quality requirements. (This is the supply chain concept at work.)

JIT II

An enhancement of JIT systems, associated with the BOSE Corporation, a manufacturer of sound systems located in Framingham, Massachusetts, has been called *JIT II*. It involves close integration of the buyer and seller and is used in industrial purchasing. "In practice, a vendor employee sits in the purchasing office of the customer, replacing the buyer and the salesman. He is empowered to utilize the customer purchase orders and places orders on himself in effect. The vendor in-plant person is also empowered to practice 'concurrent engineering' from the in-plant location, attending any and all design engineering meetings involving his company product area."[22]

If it functions properly, JIT II should eliminate the inventory surpluses that occur on both the buying and selling sides of the transaction. In addition, the buyer and the seller can both make longer-range plans more effectively. This relation is a form of partnership.

Purchase for Resale

Retail chains deal with many vendors. Some averages calculated in 1992 showed that the average department store dealt with 4,526 vendors; mass merchandiser, 1,468; specialty apparel store, 670; home center, 838; and

[20] *World Trade*, April 1994, p. 46.

[21] *TENews*, September 1994, p. 1.

[22] Handout distributed by the Council of Logistics Management (Oak Brook, Ill.), September 12, 1992.

supermarket and drugstore, 1,029. On the average, each vendor provided twenty-two **stock-keeping units** (SKUs)—distinct items in a stock-keeping or record-keeping sense.[23]

For an example of a large retailer's inbound system, one can look at one segment of J.C. Penney Co.'s import system, which supplies 1,300 retail department stores, six catalog distribution centers, and 470 Thrift drugstores. The system described here is for apparel. Planning begins twelve to fifteen months in front of sale with computer images of fashion designs transmitted between the Dallas home office, stores, and overseas sources. In the ten months before the selling season, sales forecasts are prepared. Seven to eight months before, foreign suppliers are identified and initial production and costs are negotiated. Six months out, buyers conclude their plans and advertising is planned. "The buyer works with the distribution department to figure out how suppliers can pack shipments so that stores can get the variety of sizes and colors they need while ordering by the case. . . . This 'pre-packing' is important because it reduces the need for warehousing once the shipment reaches the United States."[24]

Five to six months out, buyers present their merchandising plans to stores, including the packing assortments that are available. Stores place orders, and Penney makes the orders firm with suppliers. The goods are manufactured, and Penney must then calculate transit time. Using the example of a shipment from Korea to Columbus, Ohio, by sea:

3 days at consolidator

13 days port to port by ship

3 days at U.S. customs

1 day at Penney's Buena Park, California, distribution center

8 days in the company's transportation system (a contract trucker)

By air:

1 day at consolidator

2 days airport to airport

3 days at U.S. customs

1 day in Penney's Buena Park, California, distribution center

8 days in the company's transportation system

Penney uses three overseas consolidators; buying terms are that manufacturer must deliver goods to consolidator. The consolidator may take up to

---

[23] *Chain Store Age Executive,* April 1992, p. 14A.

[24] Joseph Bonney, "Penney's System for Imports," *American Shipper,* November 1991, pp. 51–52. Penney's manager of distribution services Byron A. Peterson said Penney figures that warehousing adds about 6.5 percent to the cost of merchandise—3.5 percent for handling and 3 percent for inventory costs. Handling prepack costs 0.5 percent.

five days to load a container with goods from different sources. Penney gives the consolidators routing instructions and criteria for selecting carrier. These imports are purchased FOB supplier.

After the shipment is booked, a copy of documents is sent to Penney's Salt Lake City office and entered into its import reporting system, which monitors goods through Penney's domestic distribution system. A computer directs the printing of carton labels to be applied in Buena Park. Labeled cartons go directly to outbound trucks without passing through a warehouse.

Efficient Consumer Response (ECR)

At the risk of over-simplification, one can consider **efficient consumer response** (ECR) to be the near-equivalent of just-in-time adapted to consumer products. Related to ECR is *quick response* (QR). Quick response involves manufacturers and retailers implementing computerized automatic product identification technologies to perform routine business transactions, with the emphasis on product movement. Efficient consumer response includes QR and focuses on purchasing, distribution, and product promotion.

An industry study of ECR users estimates that ECR practices result in a saving of 10.8 percent of consumer prices. These savings are from four different areas:

1. More efficient store assortments and better use of store space (1.5 percent). Better utilization of retail space because of less space devoted to inventory, and increased inventory turns.
2. More efficient replenishment (4.1 percent). Flow-through logistics (i.e. inventories moved continuously, rather than stopping and starting; automated rather than manual ordering).
3. More efficient promotion (4.3 percent). Less warehousing costs for "forward buy" inventories. Previously "price-cutting deals" would result in large "lumps" moving through the system every so often, followed by a drop-off in activity.
4. More efficient product development (0.9 percent). Fewer unsuccessful product introductions, better value products.[25]

Both ECR and QR are widely used in the grocery industry and by other mass merchandisers. Usually point-of-sale data are used to trigger replenishment. Both ECR and QR represent a change in wholesaling and promotion channel behavior. Previously, price-cutting deals were offered and the retailer would buy a large block of stock at a lower price and then sell the product at a reduced retail price. Sometimes a retailer would delay placing an order or would reorder in very small amounts because it was waiting for the next deal

---

[25] *Modern Materials Handling*, December 1994, p. 13.

to be announced. ECR and QR, instead, are keyed to a more orderly, regular flow of product and to smaller inventories.

Similar replenishment systems exist in the service industries. Here is a partial description of a continuous replenishment planning (CRP) system used by Kendall Healthcare Products Company for supplying hospitals:

> The inventory on hand balances and open customer orders are transmitted . . . for updating into Kendall's item balance record for each location and item. The sales tracings of what Kendall products were sold the day before . . . to the hospital are used for daily forecast consumption and transmitted. Once the CRP order is created by Kendall and sent to the distribution center for picking, purchase order confirmation is sent to create a purchase order receiver plus provide visibility to customer service of what will be delivered on the next truck. The following day after the order has been shipped from the Kendall distribution center the Advance Shipment Notification provides the transportation information. When the order is received a receipt is sent to confirm quantities and to relieve the intransit inventory.[26]

REVERSE LOGISTICS

"Reverse Logistics is a broad term referring to the logistics management skills and activities involved in reducing, managing, and disposing of hazardous or non-hazardous waste from packaging and products. It includes reverse distribution, which causes goods and information to flow in the opposite direction of normal logistics activities."[27] While we tend to think of materials or goods as moving through the supply chain in the direction from raw materials toward consumers, there are certain movements in the reverse direction that must be planned for. One is product recall, which occurs when a product that has already reached consumers is found to be defective to the extent that it must be gathered up and returned. Product recalls are discussed in a later chapter. Other reverse movements will be discussed here. Some are depicted in Figure 3-2.

Inbound for Redistribution

In some trades goods are sent to distributors with the understanding that unsold ones may be returned, subject to certain conditions set by the manufacturer or the distributor. In essence this is an incentive for later members of

[26] Fred R. Ricker and Peter Sturtevant, "Continuous Replenishment Planning (CRP): The Driving Force in the Healthcare Industry," *Annual Conference Proceedings of the Council of Logistics Management,* 1993, p. 529. The phrase "relieve the intransit inventory" means that a separate inventory record exists for goods in transit.

[27] *Reuse and Recycling—Reverse Logistics Opportunities* (Oak Brook, Ill: Council of Logistics Management, 1993), p. 3. Reverse distribution is defined as "the process by which a company collects its used, damaged, or outdated products and/or packaging from end-users."

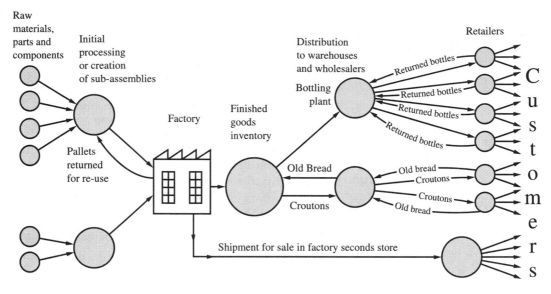

Figure 3-2   Diagram of the flow of inbound, outbound, and recycled movements.

the supply chain to hold more inventory since the risks of unsold inventory are borne by their suppliers.

> For one example, Warner/Elektra/Atlantic Corporation runs a national returns center in Chicago, which handles video and audio cassettes, along with compact discs (CDs) that are distributed by Time-Warner record companies, as well as Warner Home Video. . . . A product becomes a return when a retailer feels overstocked on an item and wants to return the CD, video tape or audio cassette to the manufacturer. On a typical day this center will receive about 150,000 items! After processing, about half go back to one of four regional distribution centers.[28]

All returns have to be preauthorized, and there are tight controls on allowing and issuing credits. All old shrink wrap and price tags are removed, and new shrink wrap applied. The repackaged items are accumulated by title (done by reading their bar codes) and then placed into cartons and returned to distribution centers for redistribution.

Recycling

The growing public interest in the recycling or reuse of materials began as a protest against a throwaway society in which empty beverage containers litter the landscape. During the 1970s, **recycling** obtained more of an eco-

---

[28] *Modern Materials Handling,* June 1994, p. 57.

nomic rationale when it was discovered that the use of recycled materials could reduce significantly the economy's use of energy. For purposes of discussion, a firm's recycling efforts fit into two categories: recycling of product and recycling of packaging.

Some recycling examples are shown in Figure 3-2. The recycling of a retail product is shown: old loaves of bread that have not been sold by the end-of-shelf-life date. The old bread is removed from the shelves and returned through reverse channels to a facility near the finished goods inventory. Here it is further dried, cut up into small cubes, packaged as croutons, and placed again into the firm's outbound new products channels.

A similar example is used motor oil:

> Since last fall, such companies as Exxon Corp. and Kragen Auto Parts have opened their own oil-recycling centers in California and many other states. They see it as a way to bolster sales in the hotly competitive lube oil business. After all, customers who bring in used oil are likely to replace it at their outlets.[29]

Oil has some hazardous characteristics and so requires special handling on its return through the channel. Batteries pose a challenge to both the environment and workers at the recycling yards. Frankly, many are sent to other countries for recycling because of these other nations' lax efforts at enforcing environmental protection and worker safety laws.

Another form of recycling diagrammed in Figure 3-2 shows the results of a decision to market factory seconds through a special store. In this instance the product might be clothes, such as items that did not pass final inspection because of stains or minor defects in the fabric. The factory seconds store bypasses the firm's conventional exchange and transaction channels and, to a limited degree, competes with them.

Firms may also choose to collect products for recycling so that they do not fall into competitors' hands. Used equipment competes with new equipment. This is a concern in the telephone industry, where "once an item has been disconnected, if it's not picked up in a timely fashion, it could be sold or illegally used by a third party."[30]

Figure 3-2 also shows the recycling of glass beverage bottles. In this instance the firm has two sources of bottles: the bottle manufacturer and used bottles returned through the reverse distribution channels (or bottle collection efforts). The reuse of pallets between a plant that creates subassemblies and the main factory is also shown in the figure. Drivers returning to the subassembly plant are expected to bring with them the pallets that were unloaded at the factory. The shipping dock supervisor at the subassembly plant has two pallet sources: the pallet manufacturer and the pallets that

---

[29] *San Francisco Chronicle*, March 9, 1992, p. B1.

[30] *Distribution*, September 1991, p. 64.

drivers bring back to the plant. If the returned pallets are damaged, the super-visor can either buy new pallets or assign a worker to repair the damaged ones.

The rising prices of recycled materials make it increasingly desirable for a firm to manage its flow of recyclables. This process occurs throughout the entire production and distribution network and must become an additional concern of managers at all levels. In a sense, the one-time scrap is collected, sorted, assembled, baled, placed on the firm's shipping dock, sold, and loaded aboard the recycler's trucks in a manner similar to that by which many of the firm's other products are handled.

Ultimately, many systems will have to be redesigned to pay more atten-tion to recycling. BMW, for example, now has a disassembly line, on which old BMWs are taken apart and studied to determine what can be reused and what design changes will give future models more reusable components. "The car of the future will not be measured alone by its motoring comfort, safety, economy, and ease of service. Rather, designers are now also required to build cars which can be recycled as completely and economically as pos-sible."[31]

Firms can expect increased pressure from consumers, consumer groups, and socially responsible investors to increase their recycling efforts. Product and packaging design activities can also help by using less material or recy-cled or recyclable material. Firms (and consumers) can also assist the recy-cling effort by showing preference for buying either recycled products or products that have a certain content of recycled materials. Some government purchase orders already require that certain products contain a specified per-centage of recycled content. "Companies may also restructure their supply chains to address regulatory pressures or capture financial benefits."[32] When laying out a supply chain, one could also show preference for partners that practice recycling.

> In industries where recycled material is beginning to comprise a significant per-centage of inputs, the supply chain may be largely restructured. For example, minimum content laws for newsprint have tipped the balance of newsprint pro-duction from Canadian mills located in remote areas next to large forests to U.S. mills operating near large cities. When states began enacting recycled content mandates for newspapers in the late 1980s, Canadian mills had just one deink-ing plant, while U.S. mills had eight such plants. Newspaper publishers switched to the U.S. suppliers, who also began siting additional facilities near urban areas.
> To prevent massive erosion of their customer base, the Canadian producers have been slowing or eliminating production at virgin mills and building deink-

[31] BMW, *BMW Factbook: Recycling of Plastics* (1991).
[32] Reuse and Recycling—Reverse Logistics Opportunities, p. 100.

ing capacity. For raw material, the Canadian mills are importing old newsprint by rail from the Midwest and Northeast United States.[33]

LOGISTICS RELATIONSHIPS WITHIN THE FIRM

In its discussion of supply chains, the previous chapter appeared to emphasize relationships outside the firm. Relationships within the firm are at least equally important. For the beginner they are even more important, since one must demonstrate an ability to work well with others within the firm before he or she will be allowed to represent the firm to outsiders.

Earlier in this chapter was the statement that manufacturing resource planning (MRP II) has evolved from taking into account materials requirements planning (MRP I) taking into account materials requirements planning (MRP I) and adding to it the functions of marketing, finance, and purchasing. We shall discuss the relationship of logistics to each of these activities.

Marketing Interfaces

Early in this chapter there was discussion of materials planning as it related manufacturing to purchasing. Two new topics deserve mention before we move on: distribution requirements planning and distribution resource planning, both referred to as DRP and both having approximately the same meaning. These terms are somewhat related to the materials requirements planning programs: "Although using proven techniques borrowed from MRP, DRP has evolved as a fundamentally different tool which accounts for the effect of distribution lead time and existing inventory on requirements."[34] Nabisco Foods defines distribution requirements planning as the "coordination between the various activities involved in filling customer orders [in order] to maximize customer service [and] minimiz[e] inventory investment" and DRP as "a way of managing the product flow through the distribution network so that all flows are driven by the expectations of customer demand."[35] Nabisco has $20 million invested in its new DRP system. The process "turned Nabisco's operations upside-down. Or more precisely, backwards. Marketing, in accord with distribution, began producing very sophisticated sales forecasts, upon which DRP is based. In turn, DRP became the

---

[33] Ibid., p. 102.

[34] Jeryl R. Wolfe, "Enterprising Logistics: The Right Tool for the Job," *International Journal of Logistics Management,* vol. 1, no. 20 (1990), p. 44. See also Robert L. Bregman, "Enhanced Distribution Requirements Planning," *Journal of Business Logistics,* vol. 11, no. 1 (1990), pp. 49–68.

[35] *Logistics Systems of the 90s* (a Nabisco newsletter), various issues (Parsippany, N.J.: Nabisco Foods Company, 1989–1991). Note that the definition refers to both maximizing and minimizing at the same time. One could contend that this cannot be done; rather, one can minimize costs for a given level of customer service at a given level of expenditure.

engine which drives production planning."[36] Quoting Nabisco's vice president of distribution: "A lot of people have been skeptical about JIT because it often just pushed the 'bubble of inventory' back to the supplier. Well, we think this system will help eliminate the 'bubble of inventory' altogether."[37] Obviously, outbound logistics, inbound logistics, and interplant logistics are themselves bound together.

Figure 3-3 shows the integral relationship between outbound logistics and the other parts of a firm's marketing staff. Sales is probably the most important single function, although the chart does not detail all the sales activities. Although the figure resembles an organizational chart, it is actually more like a flowchart because the earlier actions are shown on the left. In this particular arrangement we are concerned only with the outward flow of material.

Outbound logistics is a positive sales-generating asset, which explains its popularity among people in marketing. Outbound logistics interfaces with each of the four basic parts of the marketing mix: place, price, product, and promotion (sometimes referred to as the four *P*s). The following discussion will be based on the four *P*s.

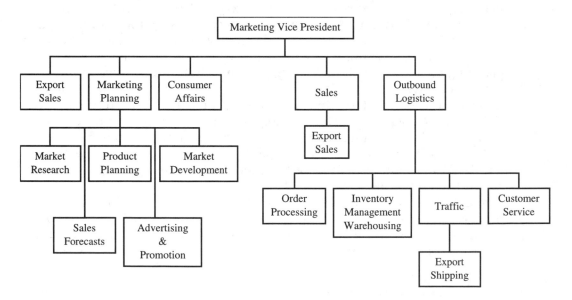

Figure 3-3   Outbound logistics as it fits functionally and organizationally.

[36] *Distribution*, September 1990, p. 34.
[37] Ibid.

Place Decisions

One important marketing concern is place. Decisions regarding place involve two types of networks: logistics and the marketing channel. Logistics decisions concern how most effectively to move and store the product between where it is produced and where it is sold. A later chapter is devoted solely to the subject of site selection.

An effective logistics system can provide positive support by enabling the firm to attract and utilize what it considers to be the most productive channel and supply chain members. Frequently the channel members are in a position to pick and choose which manufacturer's products they wish to merchandise. If a manufacturer is not consistently able to provide a certain product at the right time, in the right quantities, and in an undamaged condition, the channel members may end their relationship with the supplier or cease active promotion of the supplier's product.

Place decisions may also involve new strategies of reaching customers. One rapidly expanding nationwide pizza chain has no restaurants; buyers must have the pizza delivered or pick it up (the latter option offers no competitive advantage over existing pizza purveyors). This chain's use of computer-assisted communications and routing enables it to offer a high level of service (usually with a refund if delivery takes more than thirty minutes from the time the order was placed). Delivery people usually provide their own vehicles, and the chain has an insurance policy that supplements the auto policies carried by the individual drivers.

Another example from the service industries is the automatic teller machine (ATM) provided by banks. There are some logistical considerations: Each machine must be serviced once or twice a day to pick up deposit envelopes and restock the cash and ticket forms. In addition, crews must maintain the machines on a regular basis and answer repair calls.

Price Decisions

It is only good business sense to recognize that a firm cannot be profitable and grow—in fact it can be doomed—if it does not control its logistics costs. Obviously, the price of a product must cover all costs associated with its production, and if a firm has serious waste in its logistics system, it will either have to pass these costs on to its customers—and thus make its price higher than its competitors—or cause the firm to reduce the quality of its product and thus possibly lose customer loyalty.

Transportation cost factors are especially important in determining the method used to quote the firm's selling price. A firm can handle its transportation costs by using one of several pricing methods, the two most common being FOB-origin and **delivered-pricing systems.** An FOB-origin price does not include any transportation costs to the purchaser. With this

type of pricing, the buyer is responsible for the selection of the transport carrier because the buyer assumes the expense of the transportation. This system
of pricing is easy for the seller to administer and always yields the same net
return from each sale.

A drawback of FOB-origin pricing is that it complicates marketing strategies that call for a uniform retail price for the product on a regional or
national basis. Retailers are reluctant to follow the manufacturer's suggested
retail price for a product because their landed price varies depending on the
distance between them and the manufacturer. (Landed price includes the
price of the product at the source plus the transportation costs to wherever it
is delivered.) Because retailers typically have a predetermined margin based
on total landed costs, the result is that each retailer has a different retail
price.

Another, more subtle, problem is probably the most important. Donald
V. Harper observes that FOB-origin "may mislead the manufacturer into
thinking that outbound transportation costs are of no concern [when], in
fact, they are still quite important to the extent that the buyer of a product is
concerned with the total landed cost of the product, rather than just the
price of the product alone."[38] In a **delivered pricing system,** the seller
quotes the purchaser a price that includes both the price of the product and
the transportation cost of the product to the purchaser's receiving dock. The
seller has the prerogative to select the carrier to deliver the product.

An average amount of transportation costs is added to the cost of each
product the firm makes to determine the **uniform delivered price.** The
transportation component of this price reflects the cost of shipping the
goods to a point that is the average distance from the seller's place of business. Buyers located relatively close to the seller's point (closer than the average) pay more than their share of freight charges. (It is said that these buyers
pay **phantom freight.**) The opposite situation occurs when the buyer actually pays less freight than the seller incurs in shipping the product. This
situation is known as **freight absorption** because the seller actually pays
part of the transportation costs involved in the shipment. Freight absorption
and phantom freight are illustrated in Figure 3-4 for shipments originating in
Omaha.

Sellers find delivered pricing advantageous for several reasons. The first
is that it enables a manufacturer to expand the geographic area to which its
product is sold because distant customers in a region do not pay the full costs
of transportation. Second, this system of pricing simplifies the use of suggested retail pricing by the manufacturer. Third, delivered pricing is favored
by the manufacturer's salespeople because they can easily quote the total cost
of the product to the buyer. Finally, product distribution is managed by the

---

[38] Donald V. Harper, *Price Policy and Procedure* (New York: Harcourt, 1965), p. 208.

National Single-Zone Pricing

Every customer in the United States pays $11 per unit.

Multiple-Zone Pricing

There are three zones: The midwestern zone, paying $10.00 per unit, and the East Coast and West Coast zones, paying $11.95 per unit.

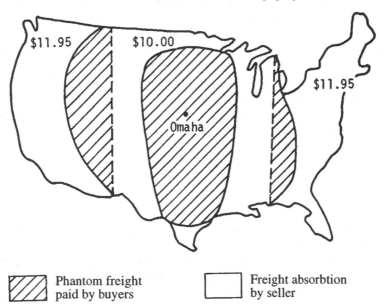

▨ Phantom freight paid by buyers	☐ Freight absorbtion by seller

Figure 3-4   Phantom freight and freight absorption.

seller, who can control the logistics network, making it function in a manner that is most beneficial to the firm's overall objectives.

There are also some negative aspects to delivered-pricing systems. The first is that the firm does not receive the same net for each purchase because an average transportation cost (rather than the actual cost) is added to the purchase price of each product. Second, over time, the locational mix of customers will change. This can be especially troublesome if sales continue to increase in the more distant markets in which the firm is already absorbing a portion of the freight charges. A problem also occurs when astute customers realize that since they are located relatively close to the vendor, they are being forced to pay phantom freight. Some sellers, to avoid alienating these customers, allow customers to order FOB-origin if they so desire. Buyers with their own truck fleets often ask vendors to quote both FOB-origin and FOB-delivered prices and then decide whether to perform the haul themselves.

Logistics managers play an important role in product pricing. They are expected to know the costs of providing various levels of customer service and therefore must be consulted to determine the trade-offs between costs and customer service. Because many distribution costs produce per unit savings when larger volumes are handled, the logistics manager can also help formulate the firm's quantity discount pricing policies.

Related to pricing are terms of sale. Most sellers have several and allow the customer to pick. Buyers often ask for quotations using several different terms and then select the most advantageous one. One concern may be how quickly the buyer must pay for the goods. Buyers that operate their own fleets may want the option of using their own equipment. A seller that sells on a delivered basis provides a freight or backhaul allowance for customers that provide carriage for the goods.

Another concern is ownership of the goods in transit. The party that owns them should be certain that the goods in transit are insured. Another concern is which firm (the buyer or seller) is in a better position to deal with the carrier in case there is a claim for damaged freight. Usually the party that pays the freight bill is in the better position.

Firms wish to control transportation on their inbound traffic for two reasons: to avoid excess freight charges and to funnel their traffic into a single or a small number of inbound carriers. Buyers may negotiate contracts with truckers that have volume incentives, and use the inbound tonnages to qualify for larger discounts. In addition, a trucker that receives shipments from several sources will consolidate them on one truck to make a single delivery each day to the buyer, and this is less disruptive than having several truck lines each deliver a single shipment.

Three FOB-origin terms are

FOB-origin, freight collect: The buyer pays freight charges and owns the goods in transit. This is the most common FOB-origin term.

FOB-origin, freight prepaid: The seller pays the freight charges, but the buyer owns the goods in transit.

FOB-origin, freight prepaid and charged back: The seller pays the freight charges in advance but bills the buyer for them. The buyer owns the goods in transit.

Three delivered terms are

FOB-destination, freight prepaid: The seller pays the freight charges and also owns the goods in transit. (This is what is generally referred to as delivered pricing; the remaining two charge the exact shipping charges to the buyer.)

FOB-destination, freight collect: The buyer pays the freight charges when the goods arrive, and the seller owns the goods while they are in transit.

FOB-destination, freight prepaid and charged back: The seller owns the goods in transit, prepays the freight charges, and bills the buyer for the freight charges.

In all these situations the logistics staff is concerned with freight charges, whether paying them or quoting them to prospective buyers. One must also see what competitors are doing and try not to pay more in transportation costs. International terms of sale and purchase are much more complicated.

Product Decisions

The most important objective of the interface between a firm's production and logistics departments is to ensure that the product itself arrives where and when it is needed in an undamaged state. If this objective is not met, a stockout may occur.

The production and logistics departments must agree on protective packaging and other materials-handling procedures that will result in a minimum of product damage. Design of the product may also be altered. Apple Computer saved $100,000 annually in shipping charges by reducing the dimensions of one of its products by one-quarter inch.[39]

The logistics staff is also involved with product design. It provides information on distribution costs (packaging, warehousing, transportation, and the like) for various new products under consideration. Later chapters will talk about a classification number that carriers assign to freight based on its handling characteristics, with a lower classification resulting in lower freight charges. For example, in the case of metal wastebaskets, the classification number for wastebaskets that can be nested (placed inside each other) is less than the number for wastebaskets that cannot. The logistics staff also advises on the costs of servicing planned products and of providing supplies and repairs.

[39] Warehouse Education and Research Council Tour of Apple Distribution Center of Santa Clara, Cal., March 26, 1989.

Promotional Decisions

Many situations require close coordination between the promotion department and logistics personnel. One important support function concerns the availability of highly advertised products, such as so-called specials. Marketing experts contend that few things are more damaging to a firm's good will than being stocked out of an item that is being heavily promoted in a large sales campaign. Another involves quantities being sold in large lots, such as cases. Some time ago, Peter R. Attwood, a British consultant, related the following situation, which would be amusing if it were not so serious.

> An example to illustrate the need for unified planning concerns an American manufacturer who ran a massive sales promotion campaign a few years ago. Customers were given a large discount for orders requiring twenty-five cases of goods at one time. It had been planned that this discount would be covered by the savings from processing large orders. Unfortunately, the campaign flopped, because distribution costs increased out of proportion. These increases were due to handling in uneconomic batches, because a pallet load of goods comprised twenty-four cases.[40]

Once a decision is made to introduce a new product, the logistics staff assumes responsibility for having the product in place on the day of release. For example, when the novel *Scarlett,* the sequel to *Gone With the Wind,* was released on September 25, 1991, copies had to be in bookstores in the morning of that exact day. Roadway Express was chosen to distribute three hundred thousand copies of the book. Roadway had the books stored in three hundred terminals throughout the country; the books had Day-Glo labels attached to them instructing the terminal managers to deliver on September 25. The terminal managers also received written and telephoned instructions about delivery. There was only one early delivery of *Scarlett,* which Roadway had returned to its terminal, and there were only two deliveries that arrived later than planned on.[41]

The logistics system is not simply a neutral factor in promotion. Outstanding distribution is a positive selling point. This is especially true for such commodities as paper products. The Scott Paper Company, for example, continually monitors the size of shipments being sent to its customers. Whenever it appears that a relatively small increase in an order will substantially lower the freight charge per unit, the sales department is notified. The opposite happens too often. As Professors R. J. Sampson and M. T. Farris point out, sales personnel always prefer to sell large orders but will sell in a smaller quantity if they cannot get a larger order. If the traffic department

---

[40] Peter R. Attwood, *Planning a Distribution System* (London: Gower, 1971), p. 55.

[41] *Distribution,* December 1991, pp. 34–35.

establishes too many esoteric rules about minimum order sizes, consolidated shipments, and the like, the salespeople will simply ignore these rules.[42]

Financial and Accounting Interfaces

The logistics department constantly interfaces with both the financial and the accounting departments. A key reason for this interdependency is that distribution and logistics managers' decisions are only as good as the quality of the cost data with which they are working. The finance staff, which is always predicting future cash flows, is often dependent upon the logistics staff for information concerning the status of finished products that are somewhere between the end of the firm's production line and the purchaser's receiving dock.

The finance staff often is charged with the responsibility of allocating the firm's limited funds to projects desired by the various operating departments. Finance personnel use several methods, such as the return on invested capital method, to determine which projects should be funded. Policies regarding investments in new inventory should also be subject to comparable financial analysis.

Accounting operations also serve to integrate a firm. Figure 3-5 shows a software company's total financial control accounting package for truck body manufacturing firms. Note that the inventory and order entry accounts are tied both to accounts receivable and to the general ledger.

Inventory valuation is a matter of concern when reports are being prepared about the company's worth. In times of inflation, identical items added to the inventory at different times may each have a different cost, and it makes a difference if one uses cost or current value as an indicator of the total inventory's worth. Professor J. Cavinato uses the phrase *inventory float* to refer to the cash flow associated with holding inventory. In general terms, the inventory costs are for the time period from when one pays a vendor until the time one collects from the customer for the same goods. The rate of interest is the opportunity cost, that is, what the firm could have been earning on other investments during this same time span. One's inventory can turn over at a different rate than the cash flow, meaning that the inventory turns over, say, every four weeks but the lag between paying vendors and collecting from customers might be, say, six weeks.[43]

One difference between the accounting staff and the logistics staff is that the accountants count inventory in dollars while the logistics staff count numbers of units. If one has an inventory of, say, grain, its value fluctuates

---

[42]Roy J. Sampson and Martin T. Farris, *Domestic Transportation: Practice, Theory and Policy,* 3d ed. (Boston: Houghton, 1975), p. 294.

[43] Joseph Cavinato, "What Does Your Inventory Really Cost?" *Distribution,* March 1988, pp. 68–72.

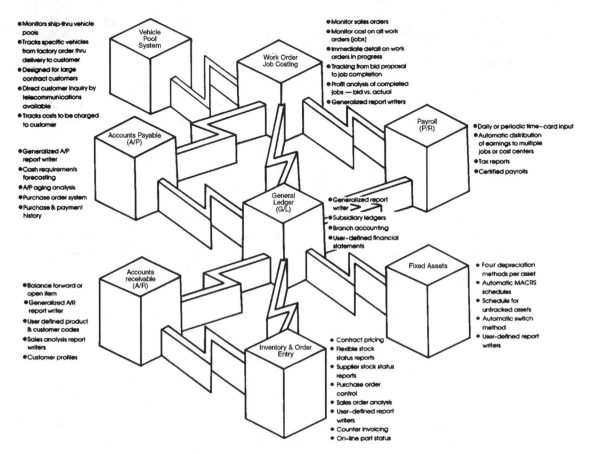

Figure 3-5 An integrated financial accounting system. (Courtesy of Spokane Computer, Inc., Spokane, Washington.)

with the commodity markets even though its quantity remains unchanged. Or the accountants may depreciate an inventory by a certain amount, even though the physical size of the inventory remains unchanged.

Over the years, logistics staffs have attempted to have accounting analysis performed in a way that is more useful to those managing logistics operations. This would include recognition of cost drivers and of the structural determinants of a firm's logistical activities. These cost drivers should then be measured in such a manner that their interactions can be understood, rather than merely tallying costs.[44]

[44] Terrance L. Pohlen and Bernard J. LaLonde, "Implementing Activity-Based Costing (ABC) in Logistics," *Journal of Business Logistics,* vol. 15, no. 2 (1994), pp. 3–4.

Purchasing Interfaces

Purchasing was discussed early in this chapter, as was its relationship to logistics. The logistics staff can make valuable contributions to purchasing and even new product design issues. Individuals concerned with materials handling want items to be designed in a way that facilitates their movement through the entire supply chain.

SUMMARY

Chapter 3 examines the logistical interfaces within a firm (i.e., the relationships with others who have the same employer). These close working relationships sometimes extend outside the firm to long-time suppliers and customers.

Inbound logistics is the movement of raw materials, components, and subassemblies into the manufacturing and processing plants. Two new management concepts are materials requirements planning (MRP I) and manufacturing resource planning (MRP II); the latter is more integrative in nature.

While one thinks of products moving outward, there is always a small return flow. Part of the return movement is caused by an increased interest in recycling of both products and their packaging.

Logistics impacts on marketing's place, price, product, and promotional activities. Many customers value a seller's ability to deliver goods and provide product support. The cost of delivering goods to the customer are very much a cost of doing business. Zone pricing, freight absorption, and phantom freight are discussed.

QUESTIONS FOR DISCUSSION AND REVIEW

1. Logistics necessarily interfaces with all other functional areas of a firm. Which interaction do you believe is most important? Which is least important? Why?
2. What are some of the steps one would take to gain control over a firm's inbound logistics?
3. Why might a firm wish to control inbound transportation?
4. What skills are needed by an individual who wishes to work in purchasing?
5. What is MRP I? Discuss the interface between MRP I, purchasing, and logistics.
6. What is an MRP II system?
7. What is a just-in-time system?
8. What is ISO 9000?
9. What is JIT II?
10. Does logistics interface with the firm's promotional activities? How, if at all?
11. Discuss the basic interfaces between inbound logistics and those responsible for production.

12. Discuss the relationship between recycling and a firm's logistical operation.

13. How can logistics activities provide positive sales-generating situations? Discuss.

14. Discuss briefly each of the four basic aspects of the marketing mix and how each interfaces with the logistics function.

15. What does FOB-origin pricing imply? What are the advantages and disadvantages of using this type of pricing system? Discuss.

16. What is the basic theory or rationale of zone pricing? Why is it done, and what information is necessary to implement such a pricing system?

17. Discuss briefly the concepts of phantom freight and freight absorption.

18. What activity is typically assigned to the finance group that directly affects logistics activities? Discuss.

19. Discuss a number of situations in which the logistics and accounting functions can assist each other in performing more efficiently.

20. Which is more important: inbound or outbound logistics? Why?

SUGGESTED READINGS

Bowersox, Donald J. "The Strategic Benefits of Logistics Alliances," *Harvard Business Review*, July–August 1990, pp. 36–45.

Cooke, James A. "Should You Control Your Inbound?" *Traffic Management,* February 1993, pp. 30–33.

Dobler, Donald W., David Burt, and Lamar Lee Jr. *Purchasing and Materials Management,* 5th ed. New York: McGraw-Hill, 1990.

Dunn, Richard L. *Practical Purchasing Management.* Barrington, Ill.: Purchasing World, 1984.

Ferrin, Bruce. "Planning Just-in-Time Supply Operations: A Multiple-Case Analysis." *Journal of Business Logistics,* vol. 15, no. 1 (1994), pp. 53–69.

Gentry, Julie J., and Martin J. Farris. "The Increasing Importance of Purchasing in Transportation Decision Making." *Transportation Journal,* Fall 1992, pp. 61–72.

Killen, William A. "Partnership in Profit through Inbound Transportation Management." In *Annual Proceedings of the Council of Logistics Management,* vol. 2. Oak Brook, Ill.: CLM, 1987, pp. 315–320.

Larson, Paul D., and Jack D. Kulchitsky. "Logistics Implications of Single Sourcing and Supplier Certification." In James Masters, ed. *Logistics at the Crossroads of Commerce.* Columbus: Ohio State University Transportation and Logistics Research Fund, 1994, pp. 81–95.

Leenders, Michiel R., Harold Fearon, and Wilbur England. *Purchasing and Materials Management,* 9th ed. Homewood, Ill.: Irwin, 1989.

Myers, Charles F., Joseph L. Fanelli, and Dan C. Boger. "Assessing the Impact of Consolidation on Inbound Vendor Traffic." *Journal of the Transportation Research Forum* (1987), pp. 230–236.

Pohlen, Terrance L., and Bernard J. LaLonde. "Implementing Activity-Based Costing (ABC) in Logistics." *Journal of Business Logistics,* vol. 15, no. 2 [1994], pp. 1–23.

Pooley, John, and Steven C. Dunn, "A Longitudinal Study of Purchasing Positions: 1960–1989." *Journal of Business Logistics,* vol. 15, no. 1 (1994), pp. 193–214.

Reuse and Recycling—Reverse Logistics Opportunities (Oak Brook, Ill.: Council of Logistics Management, 1993).

Turner, Greg, Stephen LeMay, and Mark Andrew Mitchell. "Solving the Reverse Logistics Problem: Applying the Symbiotic Logistics Concept." *Journal of Marketing Theory and Practice,* Spring 1994, pp. 15–27.

C A S E   3 - 1

JUST-IN-TIME IN KALAMAZOO

Jim Ballenger was president of a medium-sized firm that manufactured mini motor homes in Kalamazoo, Michigan. The firm had expanded from a local Midwest market to a national one, including southern California and New England. As markets had expanded, so too had sources of supply for the company, with major suppliers located in southern California, the Pacific Northwest, and Michigan. The decision to found the company in Michigan had been made for two reasons: Jim's former associates in the auto industry were there, and the largest single component of the mini—the truck or van chassis upon which the rest of the vehicle is built—was purchased from one of the "Big Three" U.S. automakers.

Like others in the field, Jim's company actually manufactured very few of its components. Virtually the entire product was assembled from components purchased from outside vendors. There was, however, a well-defined order in which the components could most efficiently be installed in the vehicle. Recently it had become clear to Jim that transportation and inventory costs were a relatively large portion of his component parts expenses, and that they might be ripe for a substantial reduction. He had been hearing about "just-in-time" systems. According to some notes he had taken at a professional meeting: The JIT production system was developed by the Toyota Motor Company over thirty-five years ago. It involves an approach to inventory that, in turn, forces a complementary approach to production, quality control, supplier relations, and distributor relationships. The major tenets of JIT can be summarized as follows:

1. Inventory in itself is wasteful and should be minimized.
2. Minimum replenishment quantity is maintained for both manufactured and purchased parts.
3. Minimum inventory should be maintained of semifinished goods—in this case, partially completed motor homes.
4. Deliveries of inputs should be frequent and small.
5. Reduce the time needed to set up production lines to the absolute minimum.
6. Treat suppliers as a part of the production team. This means that the vendor makes every effort to provide outstanding service and quality and that there is usually a much longer lasting relationship with a smaller number of suppliers than is common in the United States.
7. The objective of the production system is zero defects.
8. Deliver the finished product on a very short lead time.

To the American inventory planner, vice president of logistics, or production planner, an operation run on the preceding principles raised a number of disturbing prospects. Jim Ballenger was very aware of the costs that might arise if a JIT production system were to be established. From the materials management standpoint, the idea of deliberately planning many small shipments rather than a few large ones appeared to ensure higher freight bills, especially from more distant suppliers, for which LTL rates would make the most difference.

With regard to competition among suppliers, Jim often had the opportunity, in the volatile mini-motor-home market, to buy out parts and component supplies from manufacturers that were going out of business. Those components could be obtained at a substantial savings, with the requirement that inventory in the particular parts be temporarily increased or purchases from existing vendors be temporarily curtailed. Perhaps the greatest question raised by JIT, however, had to do with the probability of much more erratic production as a result of tight supplies of components. Both with suppliers' products and with his own, Jim operated with the (generally tacit) assumption that there would be some defective components purchased and that there would likely be something wrong with his product when it first came off the assembly line. For this reason, the Kalamazoo minis were extensively tested (their advertising said, "We hope you'll never do what *we* do to your Kalamazoo mini"), as were the components prior to installation. To the extent that only a few of a particular type of component were on hand, the interruption in the production schedule would be that much greater. It might entail expensive rush orders for replacement components, or equally expensive downtime for the entire plant.

Jim was also concerned about his relationship with his suppliers, as compared, say, to a large auto manufacturer. In the mini-motor-home business, generally the manufacturers are small and the component makers are large. In this situation, it was somewhat more difficult to see the idea of the supplier as a part of the production team—in the sense that the supplier would be expected to make a special effort in terms of either quality control or delivery flexibility on behalf of one of its almost miniscule accounts.

Despite these concerns, Jim was painfully aware that he was using a public warehouse near his plant that usually contained between $500,000 to $1,000,000 in inventory, on which he paid over 1.5 percent per month for the borrowed funds used to buy it, as well as expenses relating to the use of the warehouse itself. In addition, his firm was now producing so many different models (one with a bath, one with a shower only) and using so many different appliances (various types of radios, three varieties of refrigerator, and so forth) that the costs of a safety stock for each component were going up every day.

As an aid to making his decision on whether to try a JIT orientation at his plant, Jim's executive assistant, Kathy Williams, drew up a table that summarized the anticipated impacts of a JIT system (see Exhibit 3-A). The figures are based on random samples of inventory items. The major component of any mini motor home—the chassis—would in all events be purchased on a one-at-a-time basis from Ford, Chevrolet, Dodge, or International. With rare exceptions, it was always available on demand. It would be delivered through the local dealer. If the dealer did not have one in stock, one could easily be obtained from another area dealership.

Exhibit 3-A is a representative 10 percent sample of Ballenger's components inventory, and it covers weekly use of each item, the current lot size purchased, and so on. Before figuring out the total costs under the present and JIT systems, several additional facts must be noted. First, Ballenger's inventory carrying costs are assumed to be 20 percent per year on the average investment in inventory on hand (including its acquisition and transportation costs). Second, under the current system, here is how to calculate the number of units of each type of component kept in stock. For those items purchased from vendors more than 500 miles away, a safety stock representing four weeks' use is maintained. For items from vendors between 100 and 500 miles away, a safety stock representing two weeks' use is maintained. For items from closer sources, a safety stock representing one week's use is maintained. In addition to safety stocks, the average inventory of any item is the current lot size purchased, divided by 2.

If you are familiar with Lotus 1-2-3 or other spreadsheet software, you might try applying it here, although it is not necessary.

Questions

1. What is the total annual cost of maintaining the components inventory under the present system?

EXHIBIT 3-A TEN PERCENT RANDOM SAMPLE OF COMPONENT INVENTORY

Item	Distance from vendor (in miles)	Current system				Using JIT		
		Average number of units used each week	Current lot size purchased	Unit cost	Average freight cost per unit	JIT lot size	Unit cost	Average freight cost per unit (surface)
Gas range	1,145	10	200	$100	$20	10	$105	$22
Toilet	606	10	240	80	18	10	100	18
Pump	26	56	125	16	3	7	15	4
Refrigerator (large)	22	6	120	110	20	6	113	25
Refrigerator (small)	22	7	15	95	15	1	85	15
Foam cushion	490	675	1,500	8	2	75	7	3
CB radio (type D)	1,800	9	24	136	11	3	130	26
Dome lights	3	824	1,720	2	none	36	4	none
Awning brackets	48	540	1,200	4	1	60	5	1
Insect screens	159	570	1,240	7	1	50	7	2

Note: The plant operates fifty-two weeks per year and produces ten mini motor homes per week.

2. What would be the total annual cost of maintaining the components inventory under the JIT system (assuming no safety stocks)?

3. Are there other costs or benefits from the JIT system that Ballenger should take into account? If so, what are they?

4. If the JIT system is adopted, are there safety stocks of any item that should be maintained? If so, which ones and how much?

5. If the JIT system was adopted, what changes, if any, should occur in the relationships between Ballenger's firm and his suppliers of components? Discuss.

6. Assume that Ballenger has switched to the JIT system. He receives a surprise phone call from a competitor who is going out of business. The competitor wants to sell Ballenger 7,000 dome lights of the type listed on Exhibit 3-A. Should Ballenger buy them? If so, at what price?

7. Carrying costs are 20 percent. Is there a level of carrying costs at which both Ballenger's present system and a JIT system have similar costs? If so, what is it?

C A S E   3 - 2

OBREGON RESTAURANT
SUPPLY COMPANY

The Obregon Restaurant Supply Company was a partnership owned by two brothers, Juan and José Obregon, and located in Bakersfield, California. It sold nonfood supplies to restaurants. Paper supplies, silverware, and dishes were its three principal lines and accounted for 80 percent of the firm's sales. The other 20 percent was accounted for by a wide range of articles, such as napkin dispensers, toothpick dispensers, kitchen pans, and utensils. The sales territory included the area bounded by Fresno, San Luis Obispo, Santa Barbara, and Barstow, all in California. (See Exhibit 3-B.) The firm did not sell in the Los Angeles area, and there was no market to speak of east of Bakersfield. Juan and José took turns staying in the office and selling on the road. Four other full-time salespeople were also employed.

The firm's market was the relatively unsophisticated restaurants throughout the entire territory. Salespeople drove small vans in which they stocked the new items they were trying to sell and a variety of small replacement items for which there was frequent demand. Most of the restaurants were regular customers. A salesperson would call at a fairly regular time each week and take an order. At the end of the day, the order would be handed in to the

Exhibit 3-B Obregon Restaurant Supply Company's market area

Bakersfield office (or phoned in if the salesperson were staying away overnight). The next day either Juan or José, whoever's turn it was to be in the office, would tally all of the orders and in turn place Obregon's order with about six principal suppliers. These suppliers were located in Bakersfield, Fresno, and the Los Angeles area. All these goods were bought on an FOB plant or warehouse basis, and, late in the afternoon on the day after the Obregons placed the order, the goods would be picked up by an Obregon truck that had finished delivering supplies to restaurants. Obregon trucks would then take them to the small Obregon office/warehouse, where the goods would be unloaded. That night, outgoing orders would be made up and loaded aboard the Obregon trucks.

    The truck routes for delivery were fairly regular, as were the pickups of supplies. During the afternoon, one of the Obregon brothers would write out the delivery documents and pickup instructions for each of tomorrow's drivers. That evening a night crew of two would assemble the next day's outgoing orders, load them—in reverse order of delivery—aboard each truck, and then clean and lock up the premises.

About 90 percent of Obregon's business was handled in the manner described. Some kitchen utensils had to be ordered from firms in the East and would be mailed or sent via parcel service to the Obregon office and then delivered on an Obregon truck. Some of Obregon's outgoing shipments went by motor common carrier. These were usually those destined toward San Luis Obispo, and since there was no backhaul for Obregon trucks from that area, it was cheaper for the Obregons to use common carriers. Common carrier truck service was relatively good despite the small size of the Obregon shipments because Obregon had a regular volume of business. Obregon's salespeople also made a few deliveries each week, mainly to restaurants in isolated locations. In these instances, the salespeople would deliver last week's order while taking the order for delivery next week.

In the past two years, the Obregons had been losing business to a Los Angeles–based competitor who gave next-day delivery, which meant that the supplies would be delivered to the restaurant one day after the salesperson took the order. (The comparable time for an Obregon order was three to four days after the order was given.) The Los Angeles firm's salespeople just called on larger restaurants on the principal north-south highways between Los Angeles and South San Francisco, where their firm also maintained a warehouse. One day a truck's delivery route would be Los Angeles to South San Francisco, and the next day its route would be from South San Francisco to Los Angeles along Interstate 5. Their other truck went on Highway 101.

The Obregons lost some of their best accounts to this new competitor. The restaurants that switched said that the main reason for switching was improved delivery times. If trends continued, the Obregons would be left serving only two categories of restaurants: small ones in isolated areas that nobody else wanted to serve, and those owned by Americans of Mexican descent who preferred to do business with others of similar origin.

The Obregons decided that in order to remain competitive they would have to maintain an inventory of all supplies in Bakersfield. They could also provide next-day delivery along the north-south highways where their competitor was active.

They were somewhat surprised when they calculated that their dollar investment in inventory would not be large. This was because they would be buying in much larger volumes and would enjoy substantial quantity discounts. Some of the suppliers indicated that if the Obregons ordered in rail carload quantities, they could receive goods directly from the factory at even greater savings.

In their investigation the Obregon brothers talked with several public warehousers in Bakersfield. In addition, the warehouse supervisors in their suppliers' warehouses were helpful, especially with suggestions with respect to handling their own types of product. It was agreed by all that the Obregons would need about 10,000 square feet of warehouse space. The question then was whether to use a public warehouse or to buy a private warehouse. In addition to the 10,000 square feet of space, they needed a loading/unloading dock wide enough that three trucks could be handled simultaneously, parking space for six trucks and six autos, 200 square feet of office space, and, perhaps, a location on a rail siding so that they could receive by rail. Their products were of moderate value and could be handled with relatively unsophisticated warehouse equipment. The suggestion was made that about 1,000 square feet of the area be fenced with chicken wire and kept locked most of the time. Inside it would be kept open cases.

José Obregon investigated the public warehousing available in Bakersfield and found three different firms with which he would be willing to do business. José believed that if the decision was made to use public warehouse facilities, he would talk with users of all three to determine which offered the best service. José was sold on public warehouses and told Juan of their advantages. "The main advantage is flexibility," he said. "Our business may be more volatile than we think, and if competition increases, we may have a smaller volume of sales and inventory. Then we'll be stuck with empty space. Also, if we're making the right decision, all three public warehouses have rail sidings so we could start receiving paper products by rail. Our only big cash outlay is for inventory. We'd be stretching our credit rating to borrow for a building. Interest rates are such that we'd be paying 18 to 20 percent."

"What would monthly charges at a public warehouse be?" asked Juan.

"That depends on what we're handling and the amount of labor. For our mix of product, renting the space would be about $1,400 per month. In addition, we'd need about 300 hours of warehouse labor per month, which is figured at $11 per hour."

"That's high," said Juan.

"You're right," said José, "but we use two people for eight hours every night here."

"Yeah, but they cost us only $7 per hour. If we had a private warehouse, one could work the day shift and receive and stock the goods and the other could work at night, loading outgoing trucks."

"What would a private warehouse cost us?" José asked his brother.

Juan answered: "There are two private ones we can rent. One is 12,000 square feet, which we could have for 10 cents a square foot a month on a five-year lease. The second one would be 10,000 feet in a larger structure that a consortium of local investors wants to build. We could get 10,000 square feet at 13 cents a square foot, but we'd have to sign a ten-year lease. That site has rail siding, the first one doesn't."

"I don't like those long leases," said José. "In a public warehouse we could change the amount of space rented every month. We'd also have to buy equipment for a private warehouse, wouldn't we?"

"Yes, but let me finish talking about private warehouses," said Juan. "We could build a 10,000-square-foot structure on a site with plenty of room for expansion for about $85,000, including a lot and building. We'd have to pay 40 percent down, and the rest would be paid over 15 years, in annual payments of $7,000 each (which includes 11 percent of the unpaid balance)."

"What about property taxes?" asked José.

"They'd run $1,500 per year for the land and building. We'd also pay an inventory tax, but in this state it makes no difference whether you're in a public or a private warehouse. As I see it, we'll need only a crew of two for forty hours a week apiece, and our wages are only $7 per hour."

"Yes, but they need equipment," exclaimed José.

"We won't need much more than we use around here to load and unload trucks," responded Juan. "The only immediate need would be a fork-lift so we can stack higher. We'd only be using it an hour or so a day, and I think we could assume, if we bought a used one, that the cost would be about $1,000 a year."

José asked, "Did the sites you consider have rail sidings?"

Juan said that they were alongside rail tracks and that the Obregon firm would have to pay the cost of the siding on their land. If they generated enough traffic the railroad would not charge them for the costs of the siding that was on railroad property.

Questions

1. The Obregons have decided that "in order to remain competitive they would have to maintain an inventory of all supplies in Bakersfield." How will their new inventory carrying costs compare with those under the former system? What are some of the elements that will contribute to the change in costs?

2. How would you go about calculating the value to the Obregon brothers of locating on a railroad siding?

3. Obregon salespeople sometimes phone in their orders. Design a form to be used in the Obregon office when a salesperson calls in with an order. What information is needed, and in what order should it be arranged? (Restrict the size of your form to no more than one 8½ by 11-inch sheet of paper.)

4. Obregon salespeople "drove small vans in which they stocked the new items they were trying to sell and a variety of small replacement items for which there was frequent demand." How would you go about determining which items should be stocked in the vans? Draft a memo for

the Obregons to use indicating which items salespeople can and cannot stock in their vans.

5. Based on the information given so far, which warehousing alternative would you recommend? Why?

6. Before making the decision that the Obregon brothers are going to have to make, what additional information would be useful?

Part Two

Elements of Logistics Systems

Part 2 presents a detailed examination of many elements of logistics systems. It is written with an emphasis on outbound movements.

Chapter 4 looks at the order processing and customer service systems. Order processing deals with incoming orders, and customer service deals with keeping one's existing customers happy. Protective packaging and materials handling are covered in Chapter 5; both are related to the product's physical movement.

Two chapters are devoted to transportation. Chapter 6 covers the domestic transportation system that is available to shippers, and Chapter 7 covers the nitty-gritty aspects of traffic management.

The topic of Chapter 8 is selecting the site for one's factory or distribution center. Often this is to fit within one's entire network. Inventory management, possibly the key to successful logistics management, is handled in Chapter 9. Inventories are kept in warehouses and distribution centers, the subject of Chapter 10.

The last chapter in this section, Chapter 11, deals with international logistics. Actually, certain other aspects of international logistics are touched upon in other chapters as well. International logistics management is a fast-growing field, and in each revision of the book, more space is devoted to it.

Order Processing and Customer Service

Customer service includes paying attention to the unique needs of customers and to a firm's own marketing staff. The photo shows a Lear jet on a barge in New Orleans. The new plane landed at the New Orleans Lakefront Airport and was then carried by derrick barge to a wharf near the New Orleans Convention Center, where it was displayed at a trade show. (Courtesy of Board of Commissioners of the Port of New Orleans.)

Understand and solve a customer's business problem and you've deepened the relationship.

Fortune
September 19, 1994

Of all the modern tools that retailers and manufacturers are using to synchronize their supply chains, few are as potentially powerful as the Advance Shipping Notice.

American Shipper
October 1994

Companies do not create value for customers and sustainable advantages for themselves merely by offering varieties of tangible goods. Rather, they offer goods in distinct ways, presuming that consumers value convenience, reliability, and support.

Joseph Fuller, James O'Conor, and Richard Rawlinson
Harvard Business Review
May–June 1993

General Motors' new approach to repairing its newest engines is not to fix them at all. Instead, it is paying dealers to remove engines with problems and replace them with new ones. GM hopes the program will bolster its image among customers by reducing complaints about engines that are not fixed properly or promptly.

San Francisco Chronicle
November 9, 1991

Key Terms

- Customer service
- Load planning
- Order cycle
- Order delivery
- Order handling
- Order picking and assembly
- Order processing
- Order transmittal
- Packing list

Learning Objectives

- To understand how a firm processes incoming orders
- To understand the importance of customer service to a firm's marketing activities
- To relate the role of logistics in the customer service area
- To examine why customer service standards should be specific and measurable
- To describe how a customer service program is established and maintained

INTRODUCTION

This chapter deals with two closely related logistics activities: order processing and customer service. Order processing is obviously an early step in the logistics channel. The order, possibly transferred from the negotiations channel, must now be handled. In a supply chain today's order may be just one of many repeat orders executed under negotiations completed a long time ago.

Customer service is loosely defined as keeping existing customers happy. With that definition one might think that it belongs at the tail end of the logistics process. That is not quite so because for some products, customer service begins as soon as the sale is made. A simple example might be an order for printing: A customer service representative would be assigned to work with the buyer to make certain that the text, artwork, and layout of the job are satisfactory before the actual printing. Second, in many fields quality customer service results in repeat orders that require very little sales effort. Customer service is the catalyst for reorders along the supply chain. Last, the principles of customer service can be practiced throughout the entire logistics channel described in this and following chapters.

ORDER PROCESSING

Order processing has several definitions, which differ only in the degree of precision with which they are applied. In general terms, the phrase means how a firm handles incoming orders; more specifically, order processing is the activities that take place in the period between the time a firm receives an order and the time a warehouse is notified to ship the goods to fill that order. For purposes of clarity, we shall use the phrase *order handling* when using this second definition.

Order cycle is a related phrase, also with several meanings, depending upon one's perspective. From the seller's standpoint it is the time from when an order is received from a customer to when the goods arrive at the customer's receiving dock. From the buyer's standpoint, the order cycle is from when the order is sent out to when the goods are received. (This is also known as the replenishment cycle for goods needed on a regular basis.) The shorter and more consistent the order cycle is, the less inventory is needed by one's customers.

> Kmart . . . formed cohesive partnerships with its motor carriers and vendors and significantly reduced the time it takes to deliver merchandise to its 2,400 stores.
>
> "In 1988, our delivery turnaround time was 120 hours. In 1990, we pared it down to less than three days," said Tom D'Ambrosio, Kmart's vice president of transportation.
>
> Now, Kmart's 150 lowest volume outlets receive shipments three times a week, its Super Center and 100 high-volume stores enjoy deliveries within 24 hours of placing requests, while all other stores get their orders within 48 hours.[1]

[1] *Journal of Commerce*, November 23, 1994, p. 2B.

Today the word *quality* is frequently used in conjunction with logistics systems and is usually associated with customer service. It is assumed that delivery systems are subject to the same types of quality inspections as those associated with conventional assembly lines. Firms also benchmark their performance against that of other firms.

Many firms analyze their customer service standards in terms of five aspects, or stages, of the order cycle: order planning, order transmittal, order handling, order picking and assembly, and order delivery.

Order Planning

In order to even out workloads, some firms develop plans that space orders more evenly. A major problem area in achieving an efficient order-handling system (either centralized or decentralized) is *bunching*. Bunching results when a high percentage of customers make their orders at approximately the same time. Such an overload on the order-handling system causes delays in handling. The results, of course, are that the entire order cycle time is increased and the firm's customer service is lowered. The key to reducing bunching problems is to control when customers place their orders. If customers' ordering schedules can be influenced, a firm can balance them out and thereby minimize the peaks and valleys in the order-handling workload.

Three techniques are commonly used to control customer ordering patterns. The first is the use of field, or outside, salespeople, who take orders when they call on customers. Many customers prefer the ease of ordering directly from salespeople because of their extensive knowledge of the product lines. Thus, when customers know that a firm's representative arrives the first Monday of every month, they usually hold their orders for that salesperson.

The second procedure involves the use of phone salespeople (or inside salespeople). A firm's representative calls the customer at one or more given times during the month and takes the customer's order. This method is especially attractive because it is easy.

The third technique is to offer a substantial price discount to customers that place their orders on certain dates, such as every fourth Monday. Avon Products, whose representatives make door-to-door sales, uses this method. Each representative has "a specific day to submit the order every two weeks. By selecting the day of the week an order is submitted, we are able to balance the workload in our branches and consolidate orders into truckload quantities for maximum service at a reasonable expense."[2]

Order Transmittal

Order transmittal is the series of events that occur between the time a customer places or sends an order and the time the seller receives the order. In recent years this aspect of the order cycle has received increasing attention

[2] Comments by W. R. Dykes, director of corporate transportation for Avon Products, Inc., at the American Package Express Carriers Meeting, San Francisco, June 7, 1979.

for two reasons. First, firms that calculate the order transmittal time to be between two and five days via the U.S. Postal Service feel that this is unreasonably long. Second, there are unpredictable variations in mail service, making it difficult to provide consistency in fulfilling orders on time. (The buyer assumes that the seller receives the order almost immediately after it is mailed.)

To correct these deficiencies in order transmittal, many companies arrange for their salespeople and customers to order directly by phone or some other electronic method. The use of telephone ordering, especially the use of toll-free 800 telephone numbers, has grown considerably in recent years. Some firms that receive orders have a caller I.D. program keyed to the incoming phone number, which gives the person receiving the order a record of other recent orders from the same phone number. Other recent developments are FAX machines and electronic data interchange (EDI). Sears, for example, offers its "vendors free EDI software, worth an estimated $3,000, in addition to free training and other technical assistance. Sears [plans to] spend $5 million in this effort and expects to recoup the investment within three years."[3] Radio is also used to transmit orders. In some cities Coca-Cola distributors use salespeople to get retailers' orders, which are then radioed in via handheld radio units.

Another method of order transmittal that is becoming more common utilizes scanners and bar codes. McKesson Corporation, a wholesale company supplying drugstores, utilizes this method. The firm provides each of its retail customers with an electronic ordering machine that is only somewhat larger than a handheld calculator. The store employee walks through the store at a regular time and notices which products are low on inventory. He or she then passes a pencil-like scanner, which is attached to the ordering device, across a label affixed to the shelf. The scanner automatically reads the label. After all the products with low inventory have been scanned, the employee places the order by dialing McKesson's phone number and then placing the phone in a device (known as an acoustic coupler) that sends information from the ordering machine. Orders are shipped to the drugstore the following day.[4]

Some of the largest chain stores have their ordering system linked to their point-of-sale registers. For some products, each retail sale sets in motion an order for a replacement. More often, a running total is kept of the sales and when a specified level or number is reached, a reorder is transmitted.

Order Handling

Order handling typically includes such activities as the following: (1) The order information is checked for completeness and accuracy; (2) a credit

---

[3] *WERCsheet*, October 1990, p. 2.

[4] *San Francisco Chronicle*, September 3, 1984, p. 54.

check is made by the credit department;[5] (3) the marketing department credits the salesperson with the sale; (4) the accounting department records the transaction; (5) the inventory department locates the closest warehouse to the customer, advises it to pick the shipment, and updates the firm's master inventory controls; and (6) the traffic department arranges for the shipment's transportation from the warehouse site.

The various activities associated with order handling are shown in Figure 4-1. Along the bottom one could show days or hours. Incoming orders are divided into two categories. Electronic data interchange links with established buyers bypass the routine steps that might be applicable to first-time buyers. The order triage function segments the orders into different customers' specific needs. Some might want only 100 percent complete orders; another might want shipments in truckload quantities only; a third might want custom labeling or bar-coding. There may also be some emergency orders for, say, repair parts.

Working within the supply-chain concept, buyers will specify when they want the goods, often within as narrow an opening as a two-hour delivery window (time span within which an order must arrive). In these situations the seller must look at the right side of the chart first and take into account the time that the goods will be in transit. Adding these two times, the seller would know when to place the order into the queue of orders being handled so that it leaves at the needed time.

> What Kmart wanted was for all its vendors to adhere to a centralized appointment system and a vendor route guide so that transit times are included in production schedules.
>
> Kmart takes a firm stance on compliance.
>
> If shipment is more than one day late for its scheduled delivery, a thorough investigation is conducted which can result in penalties to manufacturers. . . .
>
> Truckers . . . must work within Kmart's guidelines and when appropriate, refuse to pick up a vendor's order because of improper lead times.[6]

As the goods leave, an advance shipping notice (ASN) is sent to some consignees via EDI. Consignees then think of these goods as incoming inventory rather than as goods on order. Figure 4-1 also shows us that the goods are being sold F.O.B.-source since the transportation costs must be determined before the final bill is prepared, so that they may be added to the invoice. At the very end of the process, the invoice is sent via mail or EDI to the customer.

---

[5] For much computerized order processing today, a customer credit unit is built into records; the computer either approves credit for the order or sets it aside it for a person to decide.

[6] *Journal of Commerce*, November 23, 1994, p. 2B.

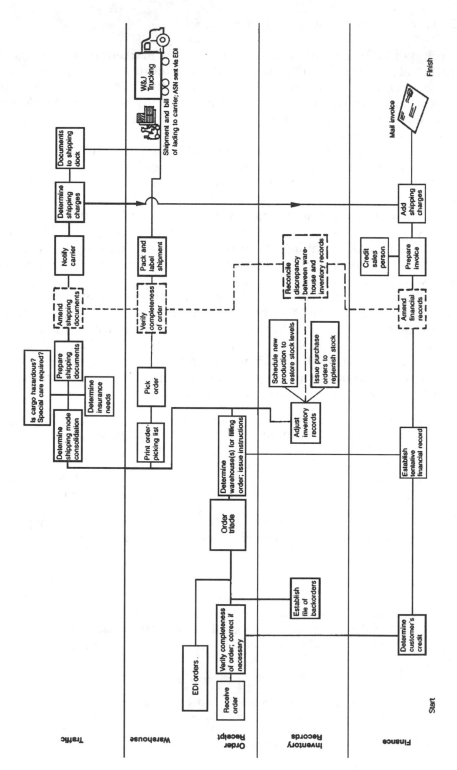

Figure 4-1 Flowchart of order-handling (order-processing) system.

110

Nearly all major firms have computerized certain aspects of their order-handling systems. Order forms, whether printed or in computer format, are designed so that the use of computers by both the customer and the vendor is facilitated. The billing of customers is increasingly done through computerized and electronic networks. For example, "sending invoices electronically from Levi's offices to retailers eliminates paper handling and re-keying by retailers. The invoices may also serve as advance shipping notices."[7]

Mack Trucks, Inc., has a computer network linked with its dealers. Called MACKnet, the system enables distributors to prepare and submit warranty claims to the home office, check on the status of warranty claims, place truck orders, use the Mack truck locator service (a list of all other dealers' unsold inventory), and track the status of a new truck order.[8] The MACKnet system can be enhanced by adding the capability to inventory and order parts.

One additional situation that every firm must contend with is a stock-out. In most cases the best procedure is to notify the customer of the situation as soon as possible. This can be done immediately if the seller's inventory system is computerized and the customer is ordering via EDI or a phone call-in system. If the order has been mailed, the customer should be contacted via phone or mail. In any case the customer should be notified as to when the order will be shipped and given the option of accepting similar products currently in stock.

Figure 4-2 is a simplified chart showing how an export order might be handled. In this case the order arrives in the form of a letter of credit, which is a bank document guaranteeing payment after all conditions are met (usually meaning that the product is delivered to the buyer in good order). If the seller cannot meet the specified conditions, the seller moves to have the letter of credit amended, which must be agreed to by the buyer. An international freight forwarder is retained both to prepare shipping documents and to make arrangements with the ocean carrier. (Note that in this example the forwarder consolidates this exporter's cargo with cargo of other clients.) A number of documents must be assembled, and some are delivered to the port of export. If some are late, they are flown to meet the cargo at the port of import. Once the shipment arrives in good order, the bank is notified and the seller paid.

Order Picking and Assembly

One of the stages of order handling is **order picking and assembly:** producing a document telling a specific warehouse to assemble a given order for a customer. An actual order-picking list, indicating which items are to be

[7] *Marin Independent Journal*, January 24, 1988, p. G6.

[8] "First Phase of Mack Trucks' Distributor Communications System Fully in Place," *Mack Bulldog*, no. 3, 1988, p. 10.

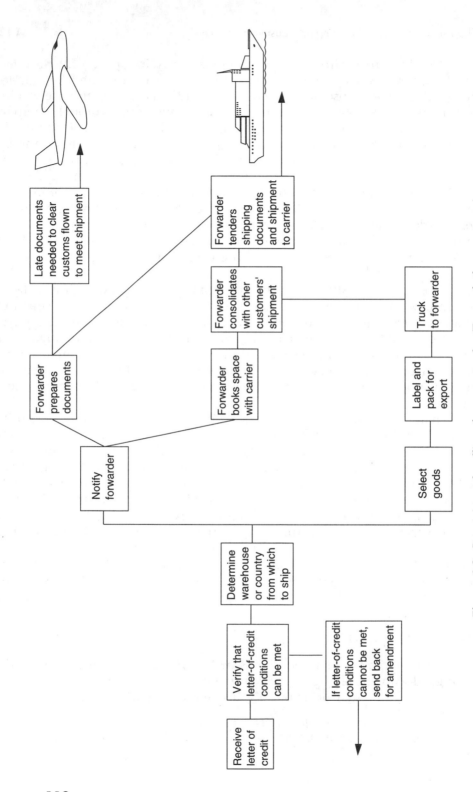

Figure 4-2 Processing or handling of an export order. (Terms of sale are not specified; they would indicate point to which exporter is involved.)

assembled, is given to a warehouse employee. The order-picking and assembly function includes all activities from the time the warehouse receives an order to ship items until goods are loaded aboard an outbound carrier.

The trend is for the order pickers' activities to be scheduled by computer. At the L.L. Bean distribution center in Freeport, Maine, each order picker is given a computer printout that specifies which products to pick, where to find them, and in what sequence the products should be gathered for each order. This system has provided impressive results. During the peak of Bean's shipping season, the firm's sixty order pickers select from 13,000 products in a 50,000-square-foot picking area and can process over 33,000 orders per day.

A further refinement in the use of computers in the order-picking process is reported by the E.J. Brach Company, a large manufacturer of candy. Each order picker carries a handheld computer that functions as an order-picking terminal. It tells the picker what to pick, the quantity to pick, and the location of the product. When each product has been picked, the employee presses the button labeled "task done." The warehouse computer then shows the employee his or her next assignment on the handheld terminal. The phrase *paperless warehouse* is used to describe warehouse operations in which computers have replaced the use of paper documents.

After orders have been picked, the assembled orders are checked to ensure that they were accurately picked. If there is a stockout on a particular item, the information is sent back to the order-handling department so that original documents can be adjusted. A **packing list** is enclosed with each outgoing order, indicating what items were picked and the initials of the individuals who prepared the order for shipment. The consignee is expected to check the packing list on receipt of the order and verify that all items are present.

The final phase of the order cycle is **order delivery,** the time from when a carrier picks up the shipment until it is delivered to the customer's receiving dock. Professors R. W. Haessler and F. B. Talbot suggest that even **load planning** (i.e., the arrangement of goods within the trailer or container) could become a customer service element.[9]

Carriers establish their own service standards, and shippers using them have to incorporate the carrier's estimated delivery times into calculations of the entire length of the order cycle. Later chapters examine the various transportation alternatives available for order delivery. In some situations carriers guarantee a delivery schedule; the carrier will pay a penalty payment to the shipper if the delivery is later than a specified time.

---

[9] Robert W. Haessler and F. Brian Talbot, "Improving Customer Service through Load Planning," *Journal of Business Logistics*, vol. 12, no. 2 (1991), pp. 115–127.

Importance of the Order Cycle

When the five stages of the order cycle—order planning, order transmittal, order handling, order picking, and order delivery—are carefully run and skillfully coordinated, impressive gains in performance can be realized. The firm is then able to use the order cycle as a potent marketing and sales tool.

An efficient order cycle can also be a valuable internal tool. Many of the same steps occur for intrafirm transactions, and some steps, such as credit verification, can be eliminated or modified. Intrafirm movements can also be conducted at very high service levels. As Avon's director of corporate transportation commented:

> Avon's policy is a maximum seven-day order turnaround to the sales representative; that is, an order submitted to Avon on Monday must be delivered no later than the following Monday, but consistently on the same day of the week each time. This system allows two days for order submission, one day for Avon branch handling, and one to four days for delivery of the order to the sales representative's residence, dependent upon the distance to the representative. Our entire marketing program is very service oriented, and the minimum acceptable on-time delivery performance is 99 percent.[10]

CUSTOMER SERVICE

Customer service is the collection of activities performed in filling orders and keeping customers happy, or creating in the customer's mind the perception of an organization that is easy to do business with. It is an excellent competitive weapon. It has a special advantage over price competition. If a firm cuts its selling price, its competitors can initiate a matching price reduction immediately and eliminate the first company's comparative advantage. Customer service improvements take longer to establish, and they are much more difficult for competitors to imitate.

Customer service serves as an integrating activity in two ways. First, several different functional areas in a firm must work together in order to keep the firm's customers happy. Second, developing special supplier-user relationships over a period of time helps integrate relationships within logistics channels. "Customer service is a process for providing significant value-added benefits to the supply chain in a cost-effective way."[11] In this context *value added* means some extra services supplied that make one's product and service stand out as slightly better than those of competitors. One example is to provide bar-code labels on cartons, which make it easier for all parties in the logistics chain to handle and tally the cartons. Another example is to arrange a carton (or a pallet or truck) in the same sequence that the user

[10] W. R. Dykes, loc. cit.

[11] Bernard J. LaLonde, Martha C. Cooper, and Thomas G. Noordewier, *Customer Service: A Management Perspective* (Oak Brook, Ill.: CLM, 1988), p. 5.

wishes to use or unload it. A third example is to have an accessible order status system so that any party in the logistics chain can obtain prompt and accurate information concerning the status of an order.

To give an idea as to where customer service fits within firms, a 1987 survey found that 51 percent of manufacturers had customer service report through sales and marketing, 14 percent through general administration, and 13 percent through distribution/logistics.[12]

Since this chapter deals with reaching the customer, it is necessary to place the costs of customer service activities in focus as a cost of doing business. According to logistics consultant Herbert W. Davis, "warehousing, transportation, order processing/customer service, distribution administration, and inventory are an integral part of selling the product and servicing the customer."[13] Davis has been keeping track of these costs, by industry, for some years. In 1994, for example, the cost elements expressed as percentages of sales were transportation of finished goods, 3.09 percent; warehousing, 2.12 percent; customer service/order processing, 0.47 percent; distribution administration, 0.35 percent; and inventory-carrying cost at 18 percent, 1.93 percent—a total of 7.72 percent.[14] The cost elements expressed in dollars per hundred pounds of product were transportation of finished goods, $15.11; warehousing, $13.64; customer service/order processing, $8.96; distribution administration, $3.31; and inventory-carrying cost at 18 percent, $19.43—a total of $57.59.

The Importance of Customer Service Standards

Elements of customer service occur in three phases. Some occur before the transaction, others are involved as part of the transaction, and still others occur after the transaction has been completed. Professor Paul H. Zinszer once divided all customer service elements into eight major activities.[15] Two activities are in the pretransactional phase: developing a corporate customer service policy and explaining the policy to customers. Activities 3, 4, and 5 are related directly to the sales transaction phase. Activity 3 is provision by the seller of up-to-date status reports of its own inventory, enabling the customer to make a substitute order immediately if a first choice is not in stock. Activity 4 includes all the elements of the order cycle, which was discussed earlier in the chapter. Activity 5 concerns those elements of the transaction

[12] *Distribution*, March 1988, p. 14.

[13] Herbert W. Davis, "Physical Distribution Costs: Performance in Selected Industries, 1987," *Council of Logistics Management, Fall 1987 Annual Conference Proceedings*, vol. 1 (Oak Brook, Ill. CLM, 1987), p. 372.

[14] Herbert W. Davis and William H. Drumm, "Physical Distribution Cost and Service, 1994," *Council of Logistics Management, Annual Conference Proceedings, 1994* (Oak Brook, Ill.: CLM, 1994), p. 120.

[15] Paul H. Zinszer, "Customer Service: The Customers' Perspective," *Applied Distribution Research* (1977), pp. 39–43

that deal with invoicing the buyer, handling returns, and making adjustments in cases of error.

Zinszer groups the last three activities into the posttransactional phase. They cover provision of additional technical services the customer may need, support materials and supplies, and repairs.

Establishing Specific Objectives

Some companies distinguish goals from objectives when establishing customer service standards. Goals tend to be broad, generalized statements regarding the overall results that the firm is attempting to achieve. Objectives, the means by which the goals are achieved, have certain minimum requirements. Usually a company determines a minimum set of requirements needed to meet an objective and then attempts to improve on it. The E.I. Du Pont de Nemours & Company's goals and objectives adopted some time ago illustrated this difference:

> Our Primary Goal is to provide a level of service equal to or better than major competition in select area markets of opportunity, and in other areas, improvements requiring little or no physical system change.
>
> Our Secondary Goal (in support of the primary goal) [is to have]: adequate stock available at all times to satisfy customer requirements promptly; dependable shipments and delivery service of products within the established objectives or the date specified by the customer; and prompt notification to customer upon any deviation from standard terms.[16]

Objectives are more specific than goals. One example of an objective is to reduce the number or rate of errors in shipment from, say, 3 per 1,000 shipments to 2 per 1,000 shipments. Although many measures can be used to achieve specific objectives, the following four areas deserve special attention:

1. The total elapsed time from when the customer places an order until the customer receives the order
2. The percentage of customer orders that can be filled immediately and completely from stock located in the warehouse
3. The total elapsed time from receipt of the order until the shipment is tendered to the transport mode for delivery to the customer
4. The percentage of customer orders that are picked and sent correctly

L.L. Bean, Inc., for example,

> uses several measures to assess customer convenience in dealing with the company via telephone, including: the percentage of customer calls connected with

---

[16] T. R. Elsman, "Export Customer Service," *Annual Proceedings of the NCPDM* (Chicago: NCPDM, 1972), p. 172.

an agent (or recorded message) within 20 seconds and the percentage of abandoned calls. The established objective for the former measure is to respond to between 85 and 90 percent of all calls within 20 seconds. From the customer's point of view, this corresponds to a response in no more than three rings. The target abandoned-call-rate is less than two percent.[17]

Unfortunately, many firms' statements of customer service goals are couched in platitudes lacking specific objectives specifying how the goals are to be achieved. This is a serious problem because if the customer service objectives or standards are not stated in specific terms, they may be ignored or be too vague to provide any real guidance to operating personnel. In addition, the logistics department may become the scapegoat for the marketing department. If a new product flops, the marketing department might argue that the new product introduction failed because customer service standards were too low. Without specific guidelines the customer service staff lacks a base to prove that acceptable levels of customer service were maintained.

The solution to the preceding quandary is obvious. Customer service objectives or standards should be similar to the Du Pont statement: detailed and specific. With detailed objectives it is easier to determine whether the customer service staff did, in fact, "drop the ball." In addition, the customer service department is in a better position to provide good service as well as to refute allegations of not meeting established objectives. In some firms the standards are very specific, such as "97 percent of all orders filled completely and accurately, and shipped within twenty-four hours of receipt," and then management and employee bonuses are tied to achieving such goals.

Since customer service is a competitive tool, one must also determine what one's competitors are doing. Caterpillar, Inc., periodically tests itself and its major competitors (both original equipment manufacturers and firms that build only replacement parts). "The testing method employed by Caterpillar is straightforward. First, it selects specific machine or engine models to be tested. Second, it selects normal repair situations. Third, it selects repair parts for purchase and/or availability checks. Fourth, it selects geographic territories to be checked."[18] It then tests how well it and its competitors perform.

Returned Products

One important posttransactional customer service activity is the handling of returned materials or merchandise. Like recycling, one of the effects of returns is to set up new flows of products. (A specialized type of return movement, the product recall, is discussed in Chapter 13.)

Goods and materials are returned for a variety of reasons. Sometimes the shipper makes an error when filling an order. Sometimes the goods are

---

[17] LaLonde, Cooper, and Noordewier, *Customer Service*, p. 119.

[18] LaLonde, Cooper, and Noordewier, *Customer Service*, p. 101.

damaged in transit and the carrier responsible for the damage wants the shipper to determine the costs of repairs. Sometimes the customer makes an error in ordering, such as writing down the incorrect part number. Or, in this day of sophisticated electronics, some customers just cannot get whatever they bought to work. "Experts say that even in a good year, as many as ten percent of computers sold will be returned to stores by disgruntled customers."[19] These are relatively straightforward reasons for which merchandise might be returned.

The most difficult part of maintaining good relationships within channels is the return of defective goods. Defects discovered by the customer immediately after unpacking a shipment are usually easy to handle, but sometimes defects are not discovered until later, as when a retail customer attempts to return a purchased good, often after heavy use, claiming it is defective. Or a merchant may have overordered an item that is not selling well and then decide to examine the materials again and again until he or she discovers defects and then has a reason for returning the entire lot.

As part of their customer service policy, companies should establish procedures for handling, inspecting, and allowing claims on returned materials. A hypothetical example of such a policy in the sporting goods field follows:

> Returns of merchandise for credit or exchange will not be accepted under any conditions unless a return authorization form obtained from and signed by John Doe Co. is enclosed with the items. A minimum of 10 percent restocking charge will be made on all return merchandise unless it is for reasons caused by the John Doe Co. Any cost for work or repairs necessary to put returned merchandise into new, saleable condition will be made in addition to the 10 percent restocking charge. Include the invoice number and the price of the merchandise returned. Returns must be shipped prepaid and insured. If a return is made because of John Doe Co.'s error, carrier fees will be credited. Returns will always be credited at your wholesale or current wholesale cost, whichever is lower. Claims must be made within four weeks of invoice date.[20]

The policy may seem strict, but the industry is one where over 85 percent of merchandise returned to the manufacturer is claimed to be defective.

Another reason for returned goods is related to spare parts. The customer may know that something is wrong with the clutch, for example, and order a new, complete clutch assembly. After disassembling the defective clutch, the customer discovers that only a small bolt is needed and then wants to return all the other parts for credit.

Logistics personnel dealing with customer service can expect to confront problems arising from claims and must be able to develop procedures for handling them. Retailers making claims against manufacturers are often caught between a customer who has returned the good, claiming it is defective and wanting his or her money back, and the manufacturer claiming that

---

[19] *TIME,* January 5, 1995, p. 61.

[20] "Return Goods Haunt Dealers," *Sporting Goods Dealer,* May 1980, p. 50.

nothing is—or was—wrong with the good in question. It is usually best to settle claims quickly since the customer or retailer will be unhappy while awaiting settlement. Firms keep records of claimants and take into account the number and nature of complaints already filed by the same party.

Returned goods must be examined by the manufacturer to determine whether they can be placed back in the finished goods inventory or require some additional repairs. Other alternatives are to dispose of them as seconds or to disassemble them, saving the usable parts.

In some retail operations it is necessary to haul away the product that the newly sold item replaces. Common examples are mattresses and refrigerators. The traded-in items usually have no positive value, but the practice is necessary to making the sale.

Grocery reclamation centers located in major cities deal with damaged grocery products as well as products not sold prior to their expiration date. Retail stores often use empty banana boxes to accumulate these goods, which are then sent to the reclamation centers. At the reclamation center the conventional checkout scanner is used to record the products received, item by item, and to note both the store from which they came and their manufacturer. The goods can then be

Repackaged for resale

Donated to charities that feed the homeless

Resold to small retailers that handle and resell damaged goods

Sold to pet food industries for use as filler (e.g., some cereals and pasta)

Hauled to a landfill site if they have no value

The discarded packaging and containers can be recycled.

Manufacturers often have their own policies as to how they want their goods handled in the reclamation centers. For example, many do not want the goods resold to retailers that handle damaged goods because of the possibility that they (the manufacturer) are still liable for defective products. The centers are expected to hold products for a certain number of days in case the manufacturer wishes to conduct an audit. Some manufacturers argue that retailers use the system for disposing of merchandise that they overordered. The customer service element of reclamation centers is that the grocery manufacturers support a system that allows retailers to dispose of damaged or overage items and then receive credit for them.

THE ROLE OF LOGISTICS IN ESTABLISHING CUSTOMER SERVICE GOALS AND OBJECTIVES

Because customer service standards can significantly affect a firm's overall sales success, establishing goals and objectives is an important senior management decision. Distribution is closely related to customer service, so the outbound logistics department plays an important role in the establishment of customer service goals and objectives.

Adviser to Marketing

Generally the marketing department is very influential in establishing customer service standards. As a part of marketing, the outbound logistics operation serves a particularly important advisory function. Marketing executives are occasionally guilty of equating *sales maximization* and *profit maximization*. Some marketing practitioners still believe that the most important objective of a firm is to increase sales. The result is that the customer service goals and objectives are set at unreasonably high levels that ignore the costs incurred to achieve them.

The outbound logistics department must then act as marketing's conscience by asking, Are you aware that the goals and objectives you want established are going to cost ———? Relatively small increases in the overall level of customer service objectives can substantially increase the costs of maintaining the increased level of customer service. As management consultant John F. Magee noted back in 1960, "approximately 80 percent more inventory is needed in a typical business to fill 95 percent of the customers' orders from stock than to fill only 80 percent."[21] Figure 4-3 illustrates what Magee's statement can mean to a company. The curve indicates the necessary inventory to meet a customer service goal. Up to 90 percent, it goes up at a rate that increases only slightly. But by the time the line reaches 95 percent, it is going almost straight up. This example shows the need to consistently keep the costs of the firm's customer service goals and objectives in mind. Most firms have delegated this authority to the logistics department. Noted customer service consultant Warren Blanding observes that the physical distribution group must

> help set customer service standards. Note the word help. Physical distribution can outline the alternative means of delivering products to customers and calculate the cost for different levels of customer service: the size of inventories, the number of shipping points, the order-processing requirements, warehousing, and transportation. It can do all this, but it cannot (or at least should not) set actual customer service standards. That is management's job, with sales and marketing helping to determine the levels of customer service that the competitive situation requires—and that pricing policies and profit objectives will permit.[22]

Establishing a Customer Service Program

A central element in the establishment of customer service goals and objectives is determining the customer's viewpoint. This means asking customers what they feel is important about service.

[21] John F. Magee, "The Logistics of Distribution," *Harvard Business Review,* July–August 1960, p. 92.

[22] Warren Blanding, "Yes, There Is Such a Thing as Too Much Customer Service," *Sales Management*, October 14, 1974, pp. 41–42.

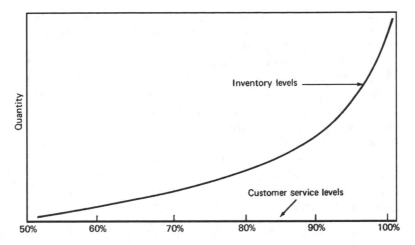

Figure 4-3   The relationship between inventory levels and customer service levels. (Source: Mason and Dixon Lines, Inc., "Needed: Credible Measures of Customer Service Costs and Penalties," *Procurement/Distribution Ideas and Methods,* undated, c. 1975, p. 101. Used with permission.)

The first aspect involves asking questions about additional elements of service. What services would the customer like to receive that are presently not available? For example, could the method of order transmittal be improved? If yes, how? Would it be helpful to have order shipment notification? If yes, why?

The second aspect of customer service involves determining which aspects of service are most important to the customer. Is the present speed of the order or replenishing cycle acceptable? If not, why? A key question for those who indicate that some aspect of the current customer service level is unsatisfactory is, Are you willing to pay more to receive a higher level of service?[23] Actually, many customer variables are involved. When Professors J. U. Sterling and D. M. Lambert surveyed firms in the office systems and furniture field with regard to customer service, they used a list of nearly one hundred different variables.[24] Depending upon definitions, some of these variables might be considered other parts of the marketing mix.

The third aspect, which is very important, is how the customer evaluates the service levels of competing vendors. Some purchasing agents release this information, as it can be helpful in establishing the necessary minimum levels of customer service.

When all of the preceding information has been gathered and analyzed, management can establish the firm's customer service goals and objectives.

[23] See Carl H. Majeczky and Peter A. Smith, "Competitive Customer Service Planning at Sara Lee," *Annual Proceedings of the NCPDM* (Chicago: NCPDM, 1983), pp. 602–607.

[24] Jay U. Sterling and Douglas M. Lambert, "Establishing Customer Service Strategies within the Marketing Mix," *Journal of Business Logistics,* March 1987, pp. 7–25.

Professor James L. Heskett once identified three basic categories of information: (1) economics, (2) the nature of the competitive environment, and (3) the nature of the product.[25]

Economic considerations involve the cost of different levels of customer service. Higher levels of service, of course, are more expensive. Rapid order delivery generally requires premium transportation and its higher rates. If all orders are to be picked in the warehouse within twenty-four hours of receipt, say, it is necessary to maintain a larger workforce to fill such orders. Do customers want this level of service? Do they want it enough it pay for it? Do we have sufficiently detailed and accurate costs for each activity? Eastman Kodak once provided the same level of customer service for all products, but it then realized that its users' needs varied by degrees. Alex Bezney, Kodak's director of customer operations support, noted:

> For example, a photo finisher, if he runs out of paper, he has to send his people home. If a retailer runs out of film for amateur photographers, it's not as crucial. Of course we don't want him running out of film, but it's not as crucial as sending people home.[26]

The nature of the environment relates to industry standards. Information about customer expectations and competitors' customer service standards is invaluable in establishing competitive standards.

The nature of the product also affects the level of the customer service that should be offered. Substitutability is one aspect. It refers to the number of products that a firm's customers can choose from to meet their needs. If a firm has a near monopoly on an important product, a high level of customer service is not required because a customer that needs the product will buy it under any reasonable customer service standard. However, if there are many products that basically perform the same task, then customer service standards become important from a competitive marketing point of view. One should also observe where the product is in its product life cycle. A product just being introduced needs a different kind of service support than one that is in a mature or declining market stage. Professor J. Cavinato comments about the decline stage:

> Purchasing and distribution strategies in the decline stage stress cash management. Inventory control—and the entire materials management—is more crucial than ever. Inventory is viewed as a poor second to cash. Accountants push materials and distribution to evaluate inventories for obsolescence write-offs. Capital expenditures are rarely considered. Cannibalization and substitute uses of warehouse space are more fruitful.[27]

[25] James L. Heskett, "Controlling Customer Logistics Service," *International Journal of Physical Distribution*, June 1971, pp. 140–145.

[26] "Customer Service: How Much Is Enough?" *Distribution*, May 1988, p. 33.

[27] Joseph Cavinato, "Product Life Cycle: Logistics Rides the Roller Coaster," *Distribution*, September 1987, pp. 12–20.

Establishing minimum acceptable order sizes is an increasing problem for physical distribution managers since many of their customers, driven by JIT philosophies, want to order small quantities at more frequent intervals. Professors D. M. Lambert and M. L. Bennion developed an analytical framework that shows the diminishing (and eventually negative) contributions to profits made by orders of decreasing size. In any particular marketing situation, some detailed analysis is needed regarding both why small orders are placed and the possible reactions of existing customers to a new policy that requires either a large minimum order size or a surcharge on small orders to offset losses.[28]

When customer service information has been thoroughly analyzed, it is possible to put customer service goals and objectives in writing. It has been said that talk is cheap and actions dear. In other words, grandiose statements regarding a firm's level of customer service represent little more than rhetoric unless the customer service standards are actually implemented. To accomplish the latter, a systematic program of measurement and control is required.

MEASUREMENT AND CONTROL OF CUSTOMER SERVICE

The ability to measure is the ability to control, and effective control is what management is all about. The value of any corporate objective or goal depends to a large extent on the tools used to measure it. A firm's customer service program must be written and monitored.

A problem encountered when measuring actual customer service standards is determining what factors to measure. Many firms choose those aspects of customer service that are the easiest to measure, rather than those that may be the most important from the customer's point of view. For example, instead of measuring the complete order or replenishment cycle, some firms may only measure order-handling and order-picking times because these elements are readily available to them. The problem, of course, is that measurement of these aspects tells nothing about the quality of other parts of the order cycle, such as order transmittal and delivery, which are more difficult to measure and consequently most susceptible to problems.

How can a firm most effectively measure those aspects of customer service that the customer values? One technique that appears to be gaining popularity is the performance model. It is based on a questionnaire designed to determine the percentage of times the firm accomplishes its customer service goals and objectives. This can be done on a sampling basis. Sometimes it can be accomplished by enclosing a return postcard with each product for the buyer to fill out and mail. This also gives an idea as to how long it took the carrier to deliver the shipment. Figure 4-4 is a form used by a firm located in

---

[28] Douglas M. Lambert and Mark L. Bennion, "Establishing a Minimum Order Policy," *Journal of Business Logistics*, September 1986, pp. 91–108.

CONTROL DEL TIEMPO DE TRANSPORTE

*Estimado cliente: estamos intentando reducir al mínimo el tiempo de transporte de nuestro almacén al suyo. Le agradeceríamos mucho si nos indica el día y la hora aproximada en que recibió este material y **nos pasa este documento por fax***

Albarán n° [   ]

RECIBIDO EL DIA [/   /   ]   **HORA APROXIMADA** [:   ]

COMENTARIOS _____
_____
_____

Nuestro número de FAX es el 98 / 579 32 71

¡ MUCHAS GRACIAS POR SU AYUDA !

DPL/011/00

Figure 4-4   Form used by a Spanish firm to learn time length of transportation.
(Courtesy TEMPER, S.A./Marcelino González.)

Spain for its customers to report when goods were delivered. (Logistics practices and infrastructure in Western Europe and parts of Asia are as advanced as—or even ahead of—those in North America.)

Another way of measuring performance is to audit credit memos: the documents that must be issued to correct errors in shipping and billing. Comparing them with the volume of error-free activity gives a measure of relative activity accuracy in performance. This system is not foolproof, however, since customers who receive more than they are billed for may not call that type of error to the shipper's attention. The same might hold if the goods received are not those requested but are of similar value.

MEETING CUSTOMER DEMANDS

Our discussion thus far has focused on the measurement of customer service goals and objectives: also important is control. Control is the process of taking corrective action when measurements indicate that the goals and objectives of customer service are not being achieved. Measurement by itself is merely wasted time and effort if no action is taken based on the feedback received. The actions taken after the deficiencies have been identified make for a strong and effective customer service program.

Firms are demanding higher levels of customer service for a number of reasons. First, reliable service enables a firm to maintain a lower level of inventory, especially of safety stocks. The lower average level of inventory produces lower inventory holding costs. Second, the increased use of vendor quality control programs necessitates higher levels of customer service. In recent years many firms, especially retailers and wholesalers, have become more inventory-conscious. This emphasis has resulted in computer-assisted analysis to identify vendors who consistently give either good or bad levels of service. In the past, with manual systems, it took repeated and serious customer service errors before a vendor's activities were singled out for corrective action. Today these factors are automatically programmed into the computer, and companies are able to closely monitor the quality of service they receive from each vendor.

Third, in an increasingly automated and computerized world the relationships between customers and vendors often become dehumanized. This situation is both frustrating and often inefficient from the customer's viewpoint. The firm that can offer a high level of customer service, especially on a personal basis, finds it has a powerful sales advantage in the marketplace.

What happens to a supplier that consistently provides less-than-acceptable levels of customer service? This question was asked of a large number of companies, and Figure 4-5 summarizes the answers. The most common response was that the customer reduced the volume of business given to the vendor involved. Almost one-fifth of the respondents stated that they had stopped all purchases with suppliers who provide inadequate levels of customer service.

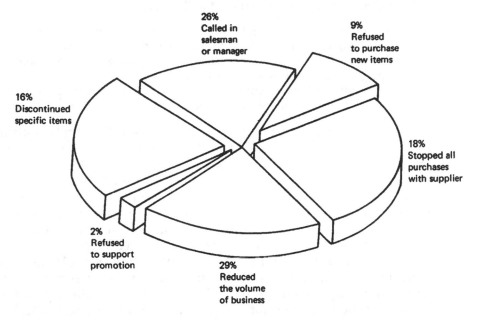

Figure 4-5 Penalties for customer service failures. (Reprinted with permission of *Traffic Management,* September 1982.) (© 1982 by Cahners Publishing Company.)

OVERALL CUSTOMER SERVICE POLICY

There are many elements of customer service, as we have seen in the preceding discussion. Figure 4-6, developed by consultant Warren Blanding, shows a checklist of internal and external customer service policies. A firm that can handle all of the situations described in the checklist is likely to have a fairly complete customer service policy.

Here is an example: In 1991 Campbell Soup Company announced its so-called C 3 program—"Campbell's Customer Care"—in a lavish twelve- by fourteen-inch color brochure filled with many photographs of Campbell memorabilia. The program and booklet, addressed to Campbell's wholesalers and retailers, covered topics mentioned earlier in this chapter as well as others. For example, in its discussion of ordering, the booklet mentioned the company's use of delivery windows, order tracking, EDI links with customers, end-aisle display shippers (product cartons that can be used to display the featured product in a retail store), and order cycle times (averaging eight days for all Campbell shipping points). Another part of the brochure dealt solely with issues involving the use of pallets. Campbell noted that it was switching from a forty-four- by forty-eight-inch pallet to a forty- by forty-eight-inch pallet, the size recommended by the Grocery Manufacturers Association (GMA). In addition, case sizes were reduced to under fifty pounds, with one exception, meeting another GMA goal to reduce the weights that workers must lift. Return of damaged or distressed merchandise was also discussed. Ongoing performance was monitored in this way:

> Each month, Campbell gathers and reviews data from every one of our plants concerning customer service. This includes statistics on warehouse load/unload times, on-time pickup/delivery performance, order and case fill, shipping errors, damage levels, [and] backhaul delivery schedules.
>
> Additional input comes from regularly scheduled focus meetings and operating reviews with our customers.[29]

Also discussed in the brochure were programs that apply statistical quality performance measures to carriers that Campbell uses, consultation services regarding the warehousing of Campbell products, use of scannable bar codes on cases (they were already being used on individual consumer packages and cans), Campbell's toll-free 800 telephone numbers for handling retail customers' complaints, and working with retailers on product promotions.

Note mention of the toll-free phone numbers for customers to call. They are often called "consumer hot lines" and are used by customers to call for a variety of information, and sometimes with complaints. (At the CLM's 1994 annual meeting in Cincinnati, in a discussion following a presentation, the distribution manager of one of the nation's largest firms said that each week the subjects of the consumer hot-line calls to his firm were tallied and classified, and that he frequently used this information to start his weekly staff meeting.)

---

[29] *Campbell's Customer Care* (Camden, N.J.: Campbell Soup Company, 1991), p. 9.

CUSTOMER SERVICE POLICY CHECKLIST

Published as a special supplement to CUSTOMER SERVICE NEWSLETTER by Marketing Publications Inc., National Press Building, Washington, DC 20045

NOTE: This checklist is intended only as a general guide to formulation of customer service policy and makes no attempt to separate elements of external policy from those of internal policy. It also recognizes the overlap between terms of sale and customer service policy. Some elements of customer service policy may be influenced by legal requirements and/or trade customs, and in that respect may be interpreted by individual firms in the light of their own situation.

☐ **CREDIT RULES AFFECTING CUSTOMER SERVICE**
- ☐ Must credit be established prior to acceptance of orders?
- ☐ If open account orders are acceptable, are there limits?
- ☐ Are there credit limits for established accounts?
- ☐ When will orders not be filled for credit reasons?
- ☐ Is a responsible credit person readily accessible to customers?

☐ **CONDITIONS GOVERNING ACCEPTANCE OF ORDERS**
- ☐ Are there any restrictions on method of receiving orders? (These might include requirements for placing orders through salesmen, brokers, etc., or a prohibition of phone orders.)
- ☐ Will the customer be required to order from a specific order-receiving location?
- ☐ What information is required on the order?
- ☐ What authority is required? (Formal purchase order, or restrictions on phone or verbal orders.)
- ☐ Are COD orders accepted?
- ☐ Are there legal limitations? (This would cover restrictions applicable to controlled substances, export-import, licensing or other credentials required by the purchaser.)
- ☐ What is the policy when purchase orders conflict with terms of sale?

☐ **MATERIALS IN SHORT SUPPLY**
- ☐ Is there a suitable allocation policy?
- ☐ Is it legal?
- ☐ Is there a single person in charge who is accessible to customers, customer service personnel and salesmen at all times?

☐ **CUSTOMER SERVICE ORGANIZATION AND PERSONNEL**
- ☐ Has the mission of the customer service organization been fully defined?
- ☐ Do the managers have the tools necessary to accomplish their tasks, including personnel, information systems, communications, etc.?
- ☐ Do they have sufficient authority?
- ☐ Are there formal selection and training policies for personnel?
- ☐ Are customer service reps to be assigned by account, or by product line?
- ☐ Is there a policy whereby customer service managers spend a certain amount of time in the field contacting customers on-location?
- ☐ Are there provisions for monitoring customer service reps' contacts with customers, i.e., by phone or in correspondence?
- ☐ Are managers and personnel compensated in line with comparable positions elsewhere in the firm?

☐ **JURISDICTION OF SALES VS. CUSTOMER SERVICE**
- ☐ Are salesmen permitted to set shipping dates, or does a standard lead time apply?
- ☐ Are salesmen permitted to determine shipping locations, or do standard decision rules apply?
- ☐ Have guidelines been established for the respective participation of salesmen and customer service personnel in each of the following areas?

Prospect inquiries	Carrier claims	Credits
Product inquiries	Reorders	Merchandising service
Product complaints	Order processing	Technical support
Delivery complaints	Order status reporting	Credits
Shipment tracing	Billing problems	Inside selling

(and other jurisdictional areas specific to the individual firm)

☐ **COMPLAINT PROCEDURE AND RIGHT OF APPEAL**
- ☐ Is there a standard procedure for handling complaints?
- ☐ Is there a policy for automatic resolution of complaints involving payments or replacement below a certain dollar level?
- ☐ Is the authority to resolve complaints placed at the lowest level consistent with good business practice?
- ☐ Is there a standard policy of keeping customers informed of the progress of complaints or claims?
- ☐ Is there an established routine for moving complaints to higher levels of authority when they can't be resolved initially to the customer's satisfaction?
- ☐ Are customers made aware of their "right of appeal?"

☐ **MINIMUM ORDER AND STANDARD ORDER QUANTITIES**
- ☐ Is minimum order size set by unit of shipment, or by dollar value?
- ☐ If it is set by unit of shipment, does the unit reflect current distribution economics?
- ☐ If it is set by dollar value, is it a reasonable figure?
- ☐ Is the minimum order size large enough to discourage costly hand-to-mouth buying by customers, but not so large as to discourage them from buying at all?
- ☐ Are there standard order quantities which the customer can translate to palletloads, truckloads, carloads, etc.?
- ☐ Is there provision for overflow truckloads or carloads, i.e., where there is more than enough for one full load but not enough for two?
- ☐ Does the seller retain the option to add or subtract "variance items" to achieve best transport utilization?
- ☐ Are there penalties or extra charges for non-standard orders?
- ☐ Are customer service reps charged with upgrading orders and advising customers of most economic order quantities?

☐ **ORDER CYCLE AND LEAD TIME**
- ☐ Are salesmen and reps given a standard lead time to quote to customers?
- ☐ Is the lead time realistic in terms of materials availability and production capacity?
- ☐ Is it realistic in terms of finished goods inventories?
- ☐ Is it based on maximum transportation economies consistent with competitive requirements?

page 2

Figure 4-6 Customer service policy checklist. (Copyright © Warren Blanding. Reproduced with permission.)

☐ Has a consolidation and pool-shipment program been investigated and implemented if practical?

☐ Have order cutoffs and schedules been established and made known to reps, salesmen and customers?

☐ Has a plan been developed to sell such a program to customers on the basis of increased reliability?

☐ Is it in fact more reliable?

☐ Have standard times been developed for the following:

Inbound transmission of orders   Non-exception order processing
Order assembly and shipping   Invoicing
Transit and delivery

☐ SPECIAL ORDERS AND VARIANCES

☐ Are there extra charges for emergency shipments?

☐ For telephone orders (where phone is nor normally used)?

☐ Have rules been established governing change orders, including cutoff or lead time requirements in terms of originally promised shipping date?

☐ What are the conditions under which the order will be recycled?

☐ Have rules been set forth on changes in order cycle caused by addition of items to order which have a longer cycle than other items already ordered?

☐ Has a schedule of penalties been established for cancellation or reduction in order size?

☐ HANDLING OF STOCKOUTS AND BACKORDERS

☐ In the case of partial or complete stockouts, does the policy indicate whether the seller will:

a) Hold order until all items are available?
b) Make partial shipment, with balance to follow?
c) Make partial shipment and cancel balance?
d) Make substitutions for out-of-stock items?
e) Cancel entire order?

☐ Have subroutines been developed for order processing systems to handle stockouts and other exceptions in terms of individual customers' requirements?

☐ If substitutions are acceptable, have criteria been established in terms of pack, size, color, style, model, value, etc.?

☐ Has provision been made for effective monitoring of stockouts?

☐ Has provision been made for timely notification of customers regarding stockouts?

☐ If substitutions are acceptable, have criteria been established in terms of pack, size, color, style, model, value, etc.?

☐ TIME DELIVERIES (IF APPLICABLE)

☐ Has a clear statement of the company's extent of liability in the case of time deliveries to jobsites and elsewhere been formulated and made known to customers?

☐ Have conditions imposed on customers (e.g., 24-hour phone contact) been made known?

☐ Have rules been established for handling chargebacks imposed by customers for late deliveries?

☐ CLAIMS, RETURNS AND CREDITS (see also COMPLAINTS)

☐ Have clear rules been established for acceptance of returns?

☐ Have similar rules been established for filing of non-carrier claims and/or chargebacks and subsequent issuance of credits?

page 3

☐ Has responsibility for filing of carrier claims been established as between seller and buyer?

☐ Has the seller company established a dollar cutoff below which it will not dispute claims or chargebacks by customers?

☐ Is it established a similar dollar cutoff for carrier claims?

☐ ORDER PICKUP BY CUSTOMERS IN THEIR OWN VEHICLES

☐ Is customer pickup permissible?

☐ Are lead time and advance notification requirements set forth so as to minimize disruption to warehouse operations?

☐ Has a minimum order size been established for pickup?

☐ If a freight allowance is granted, is it legal?

☐ PROVISION FOR PRODUCT RECALL

☐ Is lot identification and control adequate to permit efficient product recall as required by the Consumer Product Safety Act?

☐ Are the full requirements of the Act known to all concerned?

☐ Are buyers made aware of their responsibility under the Act to participate in recall activities?

☐ Are communications and information systems adequate to perform product recall as required?

☐ MADE-TO-ORDER PRODUCTS

☐ Has policy been established for acceptable overruns and underruns?

☐ Have penalties been set forth for cancellations and changes?

☐ INVENTORY POLICY

☐ Has a comprehensive inventory policy been developed, based on desired levels of customer service?

☐ Is it adequate?

☐ Have decision rules been developed covering all likely events?

☐ Have adequate monitoring and feedback systems been developed to adjust production schedules and inventory levels as necessary?

☐ Has the firm committed itself to an effective forecasting system?

☐ Is it decided on acceptable stockout levels? By line item fill? By dollar fill?

☐ Have the inventory investment requirements and profit contribution implications been fully explored and spelled out?

☐ Have alternatives like air freight and centralized warehousing of low-volume, high-value items been considered?

☐ CUSTOMER SERVICE LEVELS AND STANDARDS

☐ Have customer requirements in terms of service levels, shipment mode, etc., been fully researched using accepted market research techniques?

☐ Have customer service levels of competitors been similarly researched?

☐ Have customer service levels and standards been formulated accordingly?

☐ Have investigations been conducted to determine customers' willingness to trade speed of delivery for improved reliability?

☐ Have standards been established for speed of response to order status and other inquiries from customers?

☐ Has provision been made for an ongoing system for monitoring customer service performance according to standards, and communicating the information in timely fashion to the appropriate quarters?

page 4

Figure 4-6 (Continued)

SUMMARY

Order processing deals with the handling of orders. Customer service is defined as the collection of activities that includes order processing and keeping the customer happy. Customer service helps integrate the seller's logistical activities, since they must pull together to help the customer.

This chapter also discusses the order cycle and order processing and order handling. The customer views the order cycle as the period of time from when the order is placed until it is received. The seller has a shorter view: from the time the order is received until the goods are shipped. Today many orders are placed through computerized and electronic networks.

Customer service standards are important yardsticks of performance. Often they are told to customers (who may even collect reimbursement if the standards are not met). Customer service standards are an important competitive tool and take time to develop and maintain.

Policies for returned products are discussed, as is the role of the logistics staff in helping establish customer service goals. Finally, a booklet about Campbell Soup's customer service is examined.

QUESTIONS FOR DISCUSSION AND REVIEW

1. Discuss why customer service is often considered an important aspect of outbound logistics management.
2. Who in the firm should establish the customer service goals and objectives? Which departments should assist in arriving at this decision? Why?
3. Define in general terms customer service goals and customer service objectives. Give a specific example of each.
4. What are the most commonly used specific objectives for customer service programs?
5. Does the consumer buy a product, or does the consumer buy a product that is bundled with accompanying services? Discuss.
6. Define and describe the order cycle. Why is it considered an important aspect of customer service?
7. Discuss fully the basic parts that combine to form the order cycle.
8. Which part of the order cycle do you believe is the most important? Why?
9. Discuss the customer service aspects of returned products. Do you believe returned products will become a more or less serious problem in the late 1990s? Why?
10. The establishment of customer service goals and objectives is a basic corporate responsibility. What information should the various departments in the firm provide for making this important decision? Why?
11. The text indicates that the role of the logistics staff is to act as an adviser to the marketing department regarding customer service standards. Explain the rationale for this statement.

12. Assume that you are asked to establish a firm's customer service goals and objectives. What information should you collect, and how would you gather it?

13. Discuss the importance of measurement and control in achieving an effective customer service program.

14. A potential weakness in the measurement of customer service standards is that the wrong elements may be measured. Discuss why this could happen.

15. It has been argued that customers are demanding higher levels of customer service from their vendors. Why is this happening?

16. Examine the extensive customer service policy checklist compiled by Warren Blanding (Figure 4-6). Which major section do you believe is the most important? Why? Which do you believe is the least important? Why?

17. Discuss the Campbell Soup Company's customer service brochure.

18. What procedures should firms employ to handle returned merchandise?

19. How important is the customer service offered by one's competitors? Why?

20. Have you ever stopped doing business with a firm because of poor customer service? If so, describe the circumstances.

SUGGESTED READINGS

Akaah, Ishmael, and George C. Jackson. "Frequency Distributions of the Weights of Customer Orders in Physical Distribution Systems." *Journal of Business Logistics,* September 1988, pp. 155–164.

Allen, Mary K., Robert L. Cook, M. Bixby Cooper, Omar Keith Helferich, and George D. Wagenheim. "Enhancing the Customer Service Edge with Knowledge Base Transfer." In *Annual Proceedings of the Council of Logistics Management, 1991,* vol. 1. Oak Brook, Ill.: CLM, 1991, pp. 71–98.

Bowersox, Donald J. "Improving the Logistics Marketing/Sales Interface." In *Annual Proceedings of the Council of Logistics Management, 1991,* vol. 1. Oak Brook, Ill.: CLM, 1991, pp. 243–256.

Foster, Jerry R., Sandra Strasser, and Alicia Thompson. "The Effect of Written Customer Service Policies on Customer Service Implementation by Carriers and Shippers." *Transportation Journal,* Spring 1992, pp. 4–10.

Harrington, Thomas C., Douglas Lambert, and Martin Christopher. "A Methodology for Measuring Vendor Performance." *Journal of Business Logistics,* Spring 1991, pp. 83–104.

Innis, Daniel, and Bernard J. LaLonde. "Modeling the Effects of Customer Service Performance on Purchase Intentions in the Channel." *Journal of Marketing Theory and Practice,* Spring 1994, pp. 45–69.

Jackson, George, M. Christine Lewis, David Williams, and Hugh Cannon. "Increasing Sample Reliability in Customer Service Control Systems Using Empirical Bayes Estimation." *Journal of Business Logistics,* Fall 1991, pp. 143–156.

Mathe, Herve (ed.). *Service-Mix Strategies.* Cergy Pontoise Cedex, France: European Center for Research in Operations and Service Management, 1990.

Murphy, Paul R., and Richard F. Poist. "The Logistics-Marketing Interface: Techniques for Enhancing Cooperation." *Transportation Journal,* Winter 1992, pp. 14–23.

O'Neil, Brian F., and Jon L. Iveson. "An Operational Procedure for Prioritizing Customer Service Elements." *Journal of Business Logistics,* Fall 1991, pp. 157–191.

Voorhees, Roy Dale, R. Kenneth Teas, Benjamin J. Allen, and Earl T. Dinkler. "Changes in the Marketing-Logistics Relationship." *Journal of Business Logistics,* February 1988, pp. 34–50.

Xu, Kefeng. "Customer Service, Customer Response and Corporate Performance: A Test of the U.S. Airline Industry." *Proceedings, 35th Meeting of the TRF, 1993,* pp. 265–275.

C A S E   4 - 1

CHEEZY WHEEZY

Starting as a small retail store in New Glarus, Wisconsin, the Cheezy Wheezy firm had slowly grown into a chain of nine retail shops located in southern Wisconsin and northern Illinois. In recent years nearly all of its competitors had begun issuing catalogs, widely distributed in late October, advertising gift packages of cheese, jam, jellies, and other fancy food items. Henry Wilson, son of the firm's founder, had convinced his father that Cheezy Wheezy should also issue a catalog.

It was then March, and the last snows were melting. Henry Wilson had called his third staff meeting in as many weeks to discuss the catalog project. Present were Henry (whose title happened to be vice president); Susan Moore, the sales manager; Jeff Bell, the inventory manager; and Robert Walker, the traffic manager. Also present was Robert Caldwell, from a Milwaukee-based ad agency that was handling many aspects of the catalog project. Moore and Caldwell had just finished describing the catalog's tentative design and the allocation of catalog pages to various product lines. Caldwell then said, "We are up to the point where we must design the order form, which will be stapled inside the center pages. It will be a single 8½- by 11-inch sheet. The customer will remove it from the catalog, complete it, fold it into the envelope shape, lick the gummed lines, and mail it in. The order form will be on only one side of the sheet. On the reverse will be the instructions for folding and Cheezy Wheezy's mailing address in New Glarus; the remainder of the space will be ads for some impulse items. Right now we're thinking of a Santa Claus–shaped figure molded out of cheese."

"Enough of that," said Wilson, "this group isn't here to discuss Santa dolls. We're here to design the order form. We may also have to talk a little about selling terms. Susan?"

Responding to her cue, Moore said, "Our biggest problem is how to handle the transportation and shipping costs. We've studied all of our competitors' catalogs. Some absorb the costs into the product's price, some charge by weight of the order, some charge by money value of order, and some ship COD."

"How important are shipping costs, Susan?" asked Bell.

"Plenty," was her response. "They run $2 to $3 for a one- or two-pound package. If you take a pound of cheese that we sell in our retail stores for $2, here are our costs if it goes by catalog: our cost of goods, $1; order processing, 50 cents; overhead including inventory carrying costs, 50 cents; packaging for shipment, 50 cents; and transportation costs to any point in the United States ranging between $1.75 and $3.20. If, however, we're dealing with bigger shipments, the relative costs vary."

"I'm not following you," said Wilson.

"It's like this," responded Moore: "The wholesale cost of cheese to us is the same per pound, no matter how much is sold. Order-processing costs are approximately the same for each order we'll be receiving by mail. Overhead and inventory carrying costs are always present but may be allocated in a variety of ways. Packaging costs are also about the same per order. They go up only a few cents as we move to larger cartons. Transportation costs are hard to describe because of their tapers. Right now our whole catalog project is bogged down with the problem of transportation cost tapers."

"Tapers?" said Wilson, turning to Walker. "You've never told me about tapers before. It sounds like some kind of animal."

"That's tapir, t-a-p-i-r," said Walker. "We're talking about tapers, t-a-p-e-r-s."

"Oh," said Wilson. "What are they?"

"When one ships small packages of cheese," said Walker, "rates are based on two factors, the weight being shipped and the distance. As weight or distance increases (or both), the rates go up, but not as quickly. This is called the tapering principle. To ship two pounds of cheese from New Glarus to St. Louis costs $2.40; three pounds cost $3.30; five pounds cost $4.60; and so on. A hundred pounds—no, fifty pounds is a better example because some of the parcel services we'll be using won't take one hundred pounds—fifty pounds would cost $21. There's also a distance taper. The two-pound shipment that costs $2.40 to St. Louis is $3.40 to Denver and $4.15 to L.A."

"Can't we use the average transportation costs?" asked Bell. "That's what we do with inventory carrying costs."

"Won't work," said Caldwell. "You'll be overpriced for small, short-distance shipments and will lose sales. For heavy long shipments you'll be underpriced and will make so many sales that you might soon go belly up."

Wilson shuddered and inquired, "Does that mean we charge by weight and by distance?"

Moore answered, "It's not that easy. In the cheese business, people buy by the pound, but shipping weights—which include packaging—are actually more. A customer who orders three pounds of cheese is in fact receiving three pounds of cheese plus six ounces of packaging materials. I wish we could sell a pound of cheese that consisted of fourteen ounces of cheese and two ounces of packing material, but that would be illegal at worst, and of questionable ethics, at best."

"We have the same problems with distance," added Walker. "We're trying to sell in fifty states, but who knows how far they are from New Glarus? We could have tables and maps in the catalog, but they take up valuable selling space. Also, if it looks too complex, we may just cause some potential customers to 'turn off' before completing their order."

"There's another problem some of our clients have," added Caldwell, "and that is split orders. The customer will want ten pounds of cheese, but it will be five two-pound packages sent to five different locations. That has an impact on both packaging and transportation costs."

"So, what do we do?" asked Wilson.

Questions

1. Assume that Cheezy Wheezy goes into the catalog order business. What policy should it adopt for handling stockouts—that is, what should the company do when it receives mail orders that it cannot completely fill because one or more of the desired items are out of stock?

2. Some mail customers will complain that the items Cheezy Wheezy shipped never arrived. What policy should Cheezy Wheezy adopt to deal with this?

3. Should the order form, which will be stapled into the center of the catalog and be addressed to Cheezy Wheezy, be of the postage-paid type, which means that Cheezy Wheezy will pay the first-class postage rate plus a few cents on each envelope delivered to it, or should the customer be expected to add a first-class stamp to the order before he or she mails it? Discuss.

4. Cheezy Wheezy's headquarters are in New Glarus, but the company also operates in southern Wisconsin and northern Illinois. Is New Glarus the best address to use for receiving mail orders for cheese? Might there be advantages, perhaps, in having the mail addressed to a more major city—say, Madison, Milwaukee, or Chicago? Discuss.

5. From the facts that have been presented in the case, how would you handle the matter of charging for the *packaging* costs of each shipment? Why?

6. How would you handle the matter of charging for the *transportation* costs of each shipment? Why?

7. Taking your answers to questions 5 and 6, write out in either text or tabular form the explanation of shipping charges that your catalog customers will read. (Note: As used here, *shipping* includes both packaging and transportation.)

8. On a single 8½- by 11-inch sheet of paper, design a catalog order form for use by Cheezy Wheezy.

C A S E   4 - 2

HANDY ANDY, INC.

Handy Andy, Inc., produced garbage/trash compactors at a factory in St. Louis, Missouri, and sold them throughout the United States. Nearly all sales were in large urban areas where trash-collection costs were high.

The basic unit was about 3 feet high, 2 feet deep, and 1½ feet wide. A deluxe model had the same dimensions but contained more features. Since most of the sales represented units to be placed in existing kitchens, a wide variety of colors and trims were manufactured, providing an exterior that would match almost any kitchen decor. The standard model came in five colors with three different trims for a total of fifteen different combinations. The deluxe model came in eight colors and four different trims for a total of thirty-two different combinations. Retail prices were set by the dealer, with prices for the standard model ranging between $310 and $350 and for the deluxe model between $390 and $450. Sales in an area were usually slow until trash collectors, faced with rising landfill costs, raised their rates per can of refuse picked up.

Because of the sporadic sales patterns and the wide number of colors and trims available, retailers usually stocked only a display unit or two. They had available an expensively printed brochure that had paint chips so buyers could select the color and finish they wanted. When the retailer completed the sale, he or she would take the order and promise delivery and installation within a given number of days. In each major city there was one major Handy Andy dealer, titled the factory distributor. This dealer maintained a complete stock of all styles and trims of the Handy Andy compactors. (Handy Andy, Inc., insisted that these factory distributors stock at least five units each of the forty-seven different styles available.) The general agreement between the factory distributors and Handy Andy was that the factory distributor would deliver and install the compactor within five days after the dealer who had made the sale informed the factory distributor. For the delivery and installation, the factory distributor received 9 percent of the unit's wholesale price, half paid by the dealer who had made the sale and half paid by Handy Andy as a credit against future orders.

Jose Ortega worked in Handy Andy's distribution department in the St. Louis headquarters. He currently was working on a project to determine whether the compactor's warranty should be extended from one year to two years. The units were well built, and there had been almost no warranty work requested in the first year of each model's life. Since Handy Andy would have no records of work performed after the one-year period had expired, Ortega was contacting random buyers, using long-distance phones. Their names and phone numbers came from postcards they had mailed in at time of purchase to register the warranty (see Exhibit 4-A). The phrase at the bottom of the card referring to Handy Andy's records was to keep the buyer from waiting for a problem to occur and then mailing in the card. Whether this statement was necessary was unknown since so few defects had been reported. Ortega was in the process of contacting five hundred purchasers who had owned the compactors for between one year and four years (when they had first been introduced) to determine whether the compactors had required repairs and, if so, the extent and cost of the repairs. In talking to purchasers, Ortega was impressed by the fact that there were remarkably few complaints involving the durability of the compactors.

Another type of complaint did arise, however, one that Ortega had difficulty understanding until he heard many buyers, usually from the same few cities, tell an almost identical story. It appeared that in these cities the factory distributor would contact individuals who had purchased Handy Andy compactors from other, smaller dealers and attempt to have them cancel the original order. The factory distributor told the buyer that the model they had originally requested was out of stock but that they could supply a better model for the same price. The factory distributors also indicated that the buyer would receive better service if they bought from them since they claimed to provide service for all Handy Andy models sold in their area. In addition, the factory distributors in these few cities indicated that they, not Handy Andy, Inc., stood behind the one-year warranty.

Ortega realized that he was uncovering a larger problem than he had been assigned to deal with. He chatted briefly with his supervisor and she told him to revise the format of his interview to include a few more questions concerning the installation. She also told him to begin calling individuals who had owned compactors for less than a year. Ortega did this, and the only new information he uncovered was that the factory distributors in almost all cities did a better job of installing compactors that they had sold than they did those sold by smaller dealers. The delivery was faster (in terms of elapsed time since sale), more time was spent explaining to the customer how the compactor worked, and phone calls were made to the customer

MAIL WITHIN FIVE DAYS OF INSTALLATION!

Serial Number _____
(8-digit number under the switch)
Purchased from:
Dealer's name_____

City_____

Date of purchase_____/_____/199_____
              MONTH   DAY
Your
name_____

Address_____

City_____State_____ZIP_____

This card requires no postage. Just fill out and drop in any mailbox. Your warranty is good for one year from the date of purchase, as determined by our records. Contact your dealer first if you have questions.

HANDY ANDY, INC.
St. Louis, MO 63129

Exhibit 4-A   Return postcard.

three days and ten days after installation to make certain that the customer had no additional questions concerning the compactor's operation. When a compactor that had been sold by a smaller dealer was delivered, it was frequently left in the middle of the kitchen with scarcely a word exchanged between the customer and the installation personnel.

Ortega had another meeting scheduled with his supervisor. As he entered her office, he was surprised to see Handy Andy's vice president of marketing also sitting in the office. Ortega's supervisor asked him to tell the vice president of the results of his interviews.

The marketing vice president asked Ortega, "Do you think this pattern exists in all markets?"

"No," was Ortega's reply. "I'd say it was a problem in Jacksonville, Baltimore, Cleveland, Louisville, Denver, and San Diego. It may be a problem in Dallas and New Orleans. My sample wasn't very well structured in a metropolitan market sense; you will recall that it was a nationwide sample that was trying to look at repairs."

Questions

1. Is this a customer service problem? Why or why not?

2. Marketing channels are the arrangement of intermediaries (wholesalers, retailers, and the like) that the firm uses to achieve its marketing objectives. Is the problem discussed in Handy Andy's marketing channels? Why or why not?

3. Logistics channels handle the physical flow of goods or service. Is the problem discussed in Handy Andy's logistics channel? Why or why not?

4. It appears that the factory distributors are exploiting the smaller dealers. Yet from what we can tell, Handy Andy in St. Louis has heard no complaints from the smaller dealers. Why wouldn't they complain?

5. What should Handy Andy's marketing vice president do? Why?

6. Redesign the warranty postcard, staying within the same dimensions, and include questions or statements that will make it easier for Handy Andy headquarters to detect whether installation practices of the type discussed in the case occur.

7. In the case is the statement, "The factory distributors in these few cities indicated that they, not Handy Andy, Inc., stood behind the one-year warranty." Is this a problem for Handy Andy? Why or why not?

8. (This is a continuation of question 7.) Assume that it is a problem. How should the firm deal with it?

Protective Packaging and Materials Handling

Bagged sugar is loaded into a vessel's hold through the use of two giant rotating spiral loaders. (Courtesy of Port of Antwerp Promotion Association. Photo by F. Coolens.)

The letter was fairly straightforward—all orders shipped to the customer would soon have to be marked with a bar coded label. Failure to comply by a specific date meant no more orders.

Modern Materials Handling
May 1993

Logistical packaging is one of the most "systemic" of all logistical activities. The same shipping container is transported, sorted, and stored throughout a firm's distribution channels by each participant. It must meet each channel member's functional requirements for protection, communication, and efficiency.

Diana Twede
Journal of Business Logistics
1992

3M and Du Pont . . . are realizing substantial savings from reducing hazardous waste material they must pay to have disposed of properly. Secondly, they benefit on the public relations front for their pro-environmental activities.

WERCsheet
March 1994

Products such as steering wheels and seat belts used to arrive in cardboard boxes—which cost Chrysler an average of $30 per vehicle. But durable plastic and wood containers can be used over and over again, saving the automaker up to $90 per ton in disposal fees.

Modern Materials Handling
June 1994

Forgiving is the word we use to describe a material handling system that adjusts easily to errors in input or unexpected changes. Automated material handling systems are not forgiving by nature; they have to be taught how to forgive. The automated baggage handling system at Denver International Airport is learning the hard way: it's being rethought, reworked, and rerouted.

Material Handling Engineering
October 1994

Key Terms

- Building-blocks concept
- Bulk materials
- Ergonomics
- Materials handling
- Package testing
- Pallet
- Recycled content
- Slip sheet
- Unitization
- Unit loads

Learning Objectives

- To know how product features affect packaging and materials handling
- To identify the functions performed by protective packaging
- To analyze the utilization of unit loads in materials handling
- To appreciate how the environmental protection movement has affected packaging and package choice
- To learn materials handling principles

INTRODUCTION

This chapter deals with the physical handling of products. Packaged goods are handled by the package. **Bulk materials** are free-flowing or loose rather than in packaged form and are handled by pumps, shovels, or conveyor devices. Each product has unique physical properties that, along with the accepted volumes or quantities in which it is traded or moved, determine how the product is packaged. The distinction is not absolute, because a good may move in bulk form from the manufacturer to a wholesaler that packages it for retail distribution.

Packaging and materials handling are closely related to several topics currently considered on the cutting edge of logistics thinking and operations. Materials requirements planning (MRP) is concerned with obtaining more efficient management over the flow of all materials and products in a firm's production system. Robotics, although still used mainly in manufacturing, is being introduced in a number of functions related to the physical handling of both packaged and bulk materials. Packaging is also closely tied to choice of transportation mode, and varying packaging costs are one part of the equation as the shipper looks for a solution of low total cost. Last, choice of packaging is related to many recycling issues.

PRODUCT CHARACTERISTICS

Each product has unique physical properties. For example, density of bulk materials varies. The ability to withstand exposure to the elements is another quality. Coal piles can be exposed to the rain; salt piles cannot. Some products can be exposed to freezing weather; others cannot. Nearly all substances exist in three forms—solid, liquid, and gas—and the form that they happen to be in is a function of temperature.

The physical characteristics of some goods change while they are moving in the logistics channel. Fresh fruits and vegetables are the best-known example. Even after they are picked, they continue to give off gases and moisture and to generate heat—a process known as respiration. Fruits and vegetables are harvested before they are ripe so that they will reach the retail stores as they ripen. Ripening processes can be delayed through the use of lower temperatures or application of gases. Products such as fresh produce, meats, fish, and bakers' yeast are referred to as perishables. They require special packaging, loading, storage, and monitoring as they are moved from source to customer. Even a dry product such as pet food or potato chips settles in bags as it moves through the logistics system.

Some years ago an experiment was conducted to determine whether Colorado and California carnations should be picked and shipped as buds rather than as full flowers. The buds had better transport characteristics because they were less voluminous (more could be loaded into a carton) and they weighed less because the stem with the bud contained less water than the stem with the full flower. An advantage at the receiving end of the shipment was that the buds had a longer shelf life because ripening could be delayed by keeping the buds at a low temperature. The disadvantages were at the receiver's end, because ripening the carnations required temperature-controlled space and some labor to trim and place the stems into buckets of ripening solutions.[1]

Producers of fresh fruits were also interested in developing systems to slow ripening. Consider this item from 1994:

> The two ships that called at Wilmington over the last week are the first of six climate-controlled vessels the Chilean company is building in Japan. They represent a major step forward in controlled-atmosphere technology, which has been evolving for about 15 years.
>
> The technology seals a ship's cargo holds and rapidly reduces the oxygen level from a normal of about 20 percent to three percent, halting the ripening process. Precise instruments in the control room constantly monitor oxygen level.
>
> [The owners] expect that the demand for certain crops will increase. Chilean winter blueberries, which now must travel by air and often sell for $3.99 per half-pint can go by ship now—and sell for 59 cents a half-pint.[2]

In addition to physical characteristics, products possess chemical characteristics that affect the manner in which they should be handled. Certain pairs of products are incompatible. For example, "commodities which are sensitive to ethylene such as mangoes, bananas, and broccoli should never be held for more than a few hours in the same area as those products which emit ethylene, such as apples, avocados, and cantaloupes."[3]

The various properties of goods must also be made known to consumers to help them to make the correct buying decision and care for the product properly. Figure 5-1 is a portion of a fabric care label that goes on Levi's jeans sold in Japan.

Hazardous Cargo

Under certain conditions, almost any material can possess hazardous qualities. Flour dust can explode, and grain in elevators can self-ignite and burn. Special care is needed to handle these and many other substances. There are governmental regulations involving the movements of hazardous materials, which are often classified into seven categories: explosives, compressed gases,

[1] *Transport and Handling of Carnations Cut in the Bud Stage—Potential Advantages*, Report no. 899 (Washington, D.C.: U.S. Department of Agriculture, Agricultural Research Service, Market-ing Research, 1971).

[2] *Journal of Commerce*, February 16, 1994, p. 1B.

[3] *A Commitment to Excellence in the Shipment of Perishable Commodities* (Elizabeth, N.J.: Sea-Land Service, Inc., 1980), p. 4.

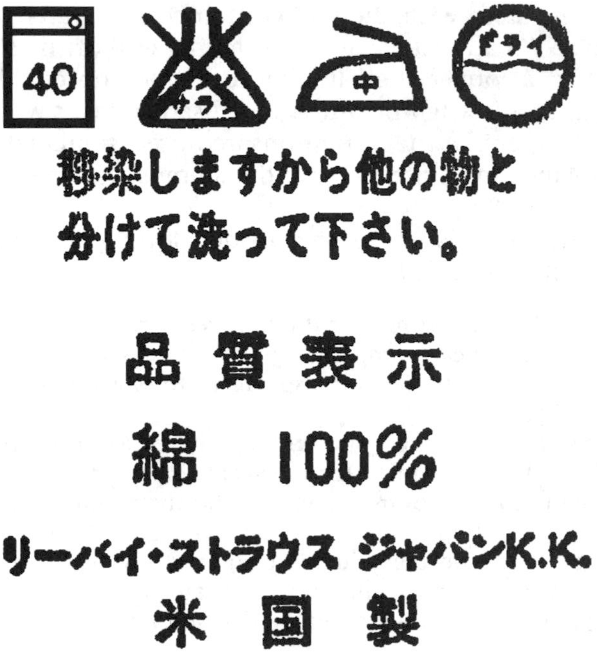

Figure 5-1 Portion of fabric care label for Levi's jeans sold in Japan. From left to right, the pictures say, Wash at 40° centigrade; use no chlorine bleach; iron at the medium temperature setting; the jeans can be dry-cleaned. The text below the label gives the fabric content, the nation of origin, and the name *Levi Strauss*. (Courtesy Levi Strauss, Japan K.K.)

flammable liquids, oxidizers, poisons, radioactive materials, and corrosive materials.

The specific requirements differ for each hazardous commodity, but all of them involve labeling, packaging and repackaging, placing warnings on shipping documents, and notifying carriers in advance. A common requirement on transferring flammable materials is that the vehicle and the receiving or discharging device both be electrically grounded. Care must be taken to properly clean tanks, pumps, hoses, and cleaning apparatus to avoid contamination of the next cargo that is handled.

Numerous regulations are issued by all levels of government, and there are differences between domestic and international moves. Effective on October 1, 1994, the United States adopted for domestic use the global hazardous materials packaging and labeling regulations developed through the United Nations. However, these regulations are not used in all nations. At the local level there are sometimes prohibitions on the use of certain tunnels or bridges during specified hours by trucks carrying explosives or other dangerous cargo. Shipping documents must also indicate whether the cargo is of hazardous nature, and sometimes additional documentation is required.

Packages, containers, trailers, and railcars carrying hazardous materials must carry distinct signs, or placards, identifying the hazard.

Environmental Protection

Public concern for environmental protection has had an impact on packaging and materials handling practices. Many materials used in packaging can be recycled. Use of disposable packing materials is often viewed as wasteful, and it is increasingly expensive as costs increase for dumping in landfill sites. Wooden pallets have tripled in price, creating an incentive for many firms to devise methods for reusing them rather than indiscriminantly disposing of them.

Dust and vapors produced during bulk-cargo transfer operations are also being scrutinized more closely by public agencies. Coal dust can be blown for several miles from a large coal pile. In port areas bulk materials that were once stored outside are now in enclosed structures. For products still left outside, elaborate vacuum systems are used to capture the dust created by handling, and ditches around the facility capture rainwater runoff so that it can be run through filters. Some states require handlers of petroleum products, including retail gasoline stations, to install vapor recovery systems. For liquids with vapor-escape problems, the transfer processes are redesigned so that tanks and other receptacles are loaded from the bottom rather than the top.

The environmental protection movement has had a profound impact upon the packaging industry, and on a worldwide basis. Receiving considerable publicity are the German requirements for recycling. Retail stores are required to accept from customers all packaging of the retail product. (If you bought a new TV, you could take it home in its carton, unpack it, and then take all the packaging materials back to the retailer's shop for the retailer to worry about.) In a similar manner, retailers could return to wholesalers whatever additional packaging had been used for the move from the wholesaler to the retailer. Likewise, the wholesaler could return the transportation-related packaging and packing materials to the manufacturer. (Rumors are that in some areas the law is not working as intended; the scrap material is collected and then sent for disposal in neighboring nations that have yet to enact sufficient restrictions.) Nonetheless, the law is indicative of the direction in which the world is moving. One problem facing those trying to choose packaging materials is that each nation's (and, for that matter, each state's) regulations differ regarding which packaging is acceptable.

One reason that regulations differ is that different areas view environmental problems differently and enact regulations that address the issue of current concern to them. Many regulations in the United States are aimed at reducing the amount of material that ends up in landfills. Landfill is, of course, only part of the problem. One study that attempted to look at a wider range of environmental issues dealt with soft drink containers. Containers studied were four sizes of plastic PET (polyethylene terephthalate) containers, aluminum cans, and four sizes of glass container including one that was refillable. It was assumed that 20 percent of the plastic containers were recycled, 50 percent of the aluminum cans, and 10 percent of the glass containers, except for the refillable bottles, which were used eight times. Environmental impacts measured were energy needed to produce the container and three forms of waste associated with the containers' disposal: air (atmospheric), waterborne, and solid (landfill). The reusable glass bottle required the least energy, the aluminum can contributed the least to solid waste by volume, and the plastic containers scored best in atmospheric wastes and in solid waste by weight.[4] The findings were very dependent upon the assumed rates of recycling of the container types.

Purchasers may also show a preference for products packed in recycled materials, and recycling has an impact upon choice of materials used in packaging. For example, here is a possible requirement for the packaging of a product purchased by a state government given by a Maryland official: "The packaging must consist only of corrugated board, which can be recycled, and not include plastic cushioning, which must be thrown out because it's not readily recyclable now."[5]

Firms can adopt environmentally friendly packaging strategies that follow one of four routes, although portions of the routes may be combined. The first is to reduce the amount of packing materials used. This is easier said than done since carriers that are responsible for the goods while in transit insist that packaging be adequate. Later chapters that describe carriers' rate-making procedures, including classifying freight, will note that the packaging to be used is often specified very precisely.

At this early point the shipper could follow a second strategy by using packaging materials that are more environmentally friendly. Unfortunately there is little consensus as to what those specific materials might be. A consumer with a fireplace or wood-burning stove would view scrap wooden packing material in a different manner than a consumer without one (although fireplace fires are themselves suspected of being environmentally unfriendly). The shipper could use packaging that is made of recycled material, although again there are disagreements as to how packaging with **recycled content** can be labeled.

> Since 17 states and the Federal Trade Commission now have laws and guidelines for environment labeling, logistics managers may want to acquaint themselves with these laws. . . . When making a claim of recycled content in anything, state laws require full disclosure. That is, you must use a full sentence and explain what the percentage of post-consumer content is in the package. For example,

[4] *Comparative Energy and Environmental Impacts for Soft Drink Delivery Systems,* prepared for the National Association for Plastic Container Recovery by Franklin Associates, Prairie Village, Kansas, 1989.

[5] Charles R. Goerth, "Affirmative Procurement: A New Factor in Package Development," in *Performance Packaging and Transportation, Proceedings of the 1988 Annual Meeting of the National Safe Transit Association* (Chicago: NSTA, 1988), p. 92.

you cannot say "recycled" but you can say "This box contains 35 percent post-consumer recycled fibers; 60 percent total recovered fibers." Since there are no agreed-upon definitions of recycled paper, ask your paper supplier how they define "post-consumer" content.[6]

A third strategy is to use reusable containers. Refillable glass beverage bottles are the best example. This cannot be done for all products since problems arise when goods in reused containers are contaminated by traces of whatever product had been carried earlier. It was necessary for the FDA to issue an order restricting the reuse of containers to avoid food contamination. Dressed poultry often carries salmonella organisms (which are killed in cooking), and the organisms survive in the wooden crates and spread to vegetables if they are transported later in the same crate. This strategy works best in closed-loop systems, in which there are carriers in place to haul the empty containers back to their origin. The best example is in the auto industry, where parts suppliers send parts packed in reusable containers and the same trucks delivering parts haul the empty containers back to the suppliers for another load.

The John Deere plant at Horicon, Wisconsin, which manufactures riding lawn mowers, uses returnable containers for approximately 30 percent of its inbound parts volume. Deere relies on Roadway Logistics to track, clean, sequence, and route the containers in both directions. Ten container types are used, and they can hold 80 percent of all tractor components. "The John Deere Horicon Works expects to save over 13 million dollars during the next eight years with an initial two million dollar investment. The number of solid waste loads sent to a landfill has steadily decreased from a high of 1,500 in 1988, to less than 280 in 1992."[7] Because the containers were designed for reuse, they are much easier to pack and unpack and there are fewer lacerations from using utility knives to open cartons.

The fourth strategy is to retain or support services that collect the used package and recycle it. The economies of scale principle works here; if sufficient amounts of similar waste materials are collected it is easier to process them for reuse.

Xerox used contract carriers to install new copy machines. After installation, it is easy for drivers to collect EPS [expanded polystyrene] foam that protected the machine, then return spent packaging material to the carrier's plant location. The closest AFPR [Association of Foam Packaging Recyclers] member coordinates collection of the EPS from the carrier for recycling.[8]

[6] *Transportation and Distribution,* October 1994, p. 50.

[7] Glenn Hildebrandt, "Case Study: Installation of Inbound Returnable Containers at the John Deere Horicon Works," in *CLM Annual Conference Proceedings, 1993* (Oak Brook, Ill.: CLM, 1993), p. 292.

[8] *Material Handling Engineering,* September 1994, p. 24.

There are also package recovery firms that specialize in handling used containers that carry pharmaceutical products. When the container of a product is first shipped to the customer, the container also has a prepaid shipping label addressed to the package recovery firm. At the package recovery firm, the used containers are inspected and either returned to the manufacturer for reuse or sent to a recycler. There are also pallet recovery/recycling firms.

Note that both the third and fourth strategies add a returned packaging loop to the supply chain.

Packaging Scrap Disposal

Firms that receive larger quantities of packaged goods must make provision for reusing or scrapping the waste materials. Several recycling methods were just mentioned that should reduce, if not nearly eliminate, the accumulation of used packaging to be dealt with. It is still sometimes necessary to collect and reduce used packaging so that it can be disposed of. Today that often means reducing it to a state in which it can be "sold" to a recycler for either a positive or a negative price, with a negative price meaning one still pays the recycler to haul the material away. Depending on the prices that the recycler may receive from its buyers, it may either sell the scrap or haul it to a landfill site. From a supply-chain standpoint, ending up in a landfill must represent the end of the line. If the materials are recycled, they are fed back into a loop or into somebody else's supply chain.

Figure 5-2 shows a pallet shredder used to reduce wooden pallets and crating to pieces of wood averaging fifty square inches in plane area. This reduces the cubic volume of the scrap by about 75 percent, making it easier to ship and to process.

Metric System

More and more products are being packaged and sold in metric units. New packages are in metric units, and the nonmetric equivalents are printed in smaller type. Although the entire change may take several decades, many of the steps necessary to implement the adoption of the new system must be taken in the next few years.

One U.S. industry that has converted to metric containers is the wine- and liquor-producing industry, which has introduced new sizes of bottles. The conversion was successful, in spite of the fact that the industry is subjected to more than its share of regulation because its product is heavily taxed and many of the taxes were drawn up to be applicable to containers of other sizes.

United States exporters are coming under increasing pressure to market their products overseas in metric units. Some importing nations levy fines against products that are not sold in metric measurements.

Figure 5-2   A pallet shredder designed to reduce the cubic volume of wooden pallets and crating so that they cost less to transport. (Courtesy Blower Application Company, Inc.)

PACKAGING

Packaging can be thought of in terms of the **building-blocks concept:** The smallest units are the retail, or consumer, packages or cartons on the shelves of stores. These are packed into boxes of one to two cubic feet, which are light enough in weight to be carried by a stock clerk. This discussion of the building-blocks concept emphasizes rectangular containers, though it can be applied to other shapes as well.

The building-blocks hierarchy is important to remember because each of the different building blocks is inside another and their total effect must be to protect the product. They function in a complementary sense. When the consumer-sized package, as one sees on the shelves of stores, is very solid, the larger packaging elements require less-sturdy packaging materials because the smaller packages are themselves sturdy. At the other extreme are light-bulbs, with a retail packing of single-face corrugated fiberboard that may protect them from breakage but contributes nothing to the internal strength of the larger container.

Sales Functions of Boxes

Although boxes are thought primarily to be protective, they may also contain features with a sales orientation. Some products are sold in either a consumer-size pack or a larger box or case. Some merchants build displays using box or case lots of goods to create the impression they have made an extra-large purchase of a certain item—presumably at a lower price per unit that is being passed on to the consumer. In this instance it would be appropriate to display some advertising on the outside of the box. Some boxes are designed so that they do not have to be unpacked by the stock clerk for stocking on shelves. Instead, the stock clerk cuts away the top two-thirds of the box and places the bottom third, with its contents still in place, on the shelf. Figure 5-3 illustrates a display box that has been packed as we see it at the factory. The retailer needs only to remove the front and add the header card at the top.

The advertising and protective functions of packaging sometimes conflict. Although from a retailing standpoint it may be desirable to have an attractive advertising message on the outside of each box, when these boxes are in a warehouse the same message might make it easier for a thief to determine quickly which boxes contain the most valuable items. Using code numbers alone on the outside of the box slows down the thief.

Sometimes the marketing staff wants a package with a large surface so that large advertising artwork can be used. An extreme example is from the music industry, where record jackets for twelve-inch records have much more space for artwork than tape or CD cases. Mass merchandising usually means very little sales help on the floor, so for many products customers can only examine the printing and pictures on closed cartons before making their choices.

Figure 5-4 illustrates another issue involving sales and protective packaging. The razor blade container, shown at the bottom, is quite small. Because razor blades are often displayed next to chain store checkout stands, from a marketing standpoint it is useful to display them on a rack. However, to reduce the problem of shoplifting, it is necessary to mount the blades on a stiff card that is larger than most people's pockets. The net effect of these two steps is to increase the *cube*, or volume, of each razor blade package by over 700 percent. Other small products, such as camera film, batteries, and compact discs, must also be placed in large packages to reduce shoplifting. Airlines want packages that they handle to be at least one cubic foot in size. One reason is that this is large enough to be difficult to conceal on one's person, making theft and pilferage more difficult.

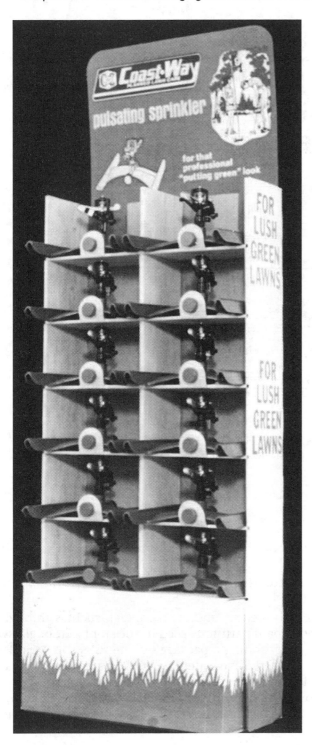

Figure 5-3 Shipping and display carton. (Courtesy of Stone Container Corporation.)

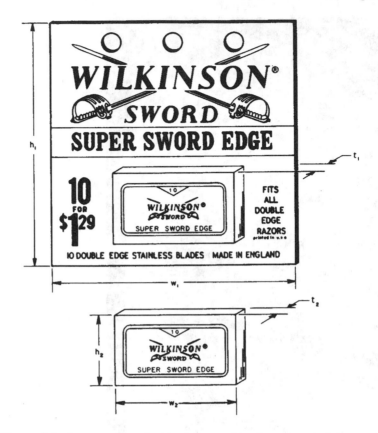

Figure 5-4   Impact on item's cube due to packing it so it can be hung on rack. (Courtesy of E. Ralph Sims, Jr., and Associates.)

Protective Functions of Packaging

A protective package should perform the following functions:

1. Enclose the materials, both to protect them and protect other items from them.
2. Restrain them from undesired movements within the container when the container is in transit.
3. Separate the contents to prevent undesired contact, such as through the use of corrugated fiberboard partitions used in the shipment of glassware. (A unique example of separating a package's contents is shown in Figure 5-5, a package used for expensive water faucets. The plumber pulls at the horizontal tab, which is between the top and bottom of the box. This removes the top, outer half, giving the plumber access to all of the fittings necessary to install the faucets, which is the most time-consuming

Figure 5-5   Package separating plumbing fixture parts into sequence when needed. (Courtesy of Georgia-Pacific Corporation.)

of the plumber's tasks. The bottom part of the package holds the expensive faucets themselves, which are used last in the installation process. Because the plumber will not remove them until they are needed, they are less likely to be lost, scratched, or dirtied.)

4. Cushion the contents from outside vibrations and shocks.

5. Support the weight of identical containers that will be stacked above it as part of the building-blocks concept. This could mean, in some situations, stacks in a warehouse that are up to twenty feet high.

6. Position the contents to provide maximum protection for them. If one were packaging combined sets of wastebaskets and lamp shades, the package would be designed so that the lamp shades were protected by the wastebaskets.

7. Provide for fairly uniform weight distribution within the package, because most equipment for the automatic handling of packages is designed

for packages whose weight is evenly distributed. Also, individuals handling packages manually assume that the weight inside is evenly distributed.

8. Provide enough exterior surface area that identification and shipping labels can be applied along with specific instructions such as "This Side Up" or "Keep Refrigerated." Today this would also mean providing a uniform location for the application of bar codes. Handling symbols, such as a picture of an umbrella, meaning "Keep Dry," might also be used. ("We are finding that more of our distribution personnel don't read or write any English.")[9]

9. Be tamper-proof to the extent that evidence of tampering can be noticed. We think of that mainly at the retail level of packaging for some foods and drugs.

10. Be safe in the sense that the package itself (both in conjunction with the product carried and after it has been unpacked) presents no hazards to consumers or to others.

Figure 5-6 is a checklist prepared by the Fibre Box Association indicating the range of considerations that go into package choice. Firms that sell packaging material are helpful sources of information to potential users. Often they provide technical advice.

Carriers' tariffs and classifications influence (if not control) the type of packaging and packing methods that must be used. In freight classification documents the type of packaging is specified. The commodity is listed, followed by a comma and then by a phrase such as "in machine pressed bales," "in barrels," "in bales compressed in more than 18 lb. per square foot," "folded flat, in packages," "celluloid covered, in boxes," "SU" (set up), or "KD" (knocked down, or disassembled and packed so that it occupies two-thirds or less of the volume it would occupy in its set-up state). The carriers established these different classifications for two main reasons. First, packaging specifications determined by product density encourage shippers to tender loads in densities that make best use of the equipment's weight and volume capabilities. Figure 5-7 shows how a bicycle is broken down so that its carton takes up less cube. Second, specifications that deal with protective packaging reduce the likelihood of damage to products while they are being carried; this, in turn, reduces the amount of loss and damage claims placed against the carrier. Figure 5-8 shows the type of label that motor carriers and railroads require on fiber boxes used for shipping freight. The label is the fiber box manufacturer's assurance to the motor carriers and railroads that

[9] Robert B. Footlik, "Performance, Packaging, and Distribution: Who Are We Performing For?" in *Performance Packaging and Transportation, Proceedings of the 1988 Annual Meeting of the National Safe Transit Association* (Chicago: NSTA, 1988), p. 11.

checklist for box users

The corrugated box contains and protects your product, but it can also serve many functions which aid in packing, storage, distribution, marketing and sales. This checklist is a guide to the information you'll want to supply to your box maker. He can then offer suggestions and recommendations to utilize every value-added advantage that corrugated can offer.

YOUR PRODUCT

	yes	no
1. Have you given your box maker a description of your product and its use, the exact dimensions, weight and physical characteristics?	☐	☐
2. Is the product likely to settle or shift?	☐	☐
3. Is it perishable, fragile, or hazardous in any way?	☐	☐
4. Will it need extra protection against vibration, impact, moisture, air, heat or cold?	☐	☐
5. Will it be shipped fully assembled?	☐	☐
6. Will more than one unit be packed in a box?	☐	☐
7. Will accessories, parts or literature be included with the product?	☐	☐
8. Have you provided your box maker with a complete sample of your product as it will be packed?	☐	☐

YOUR PACKING OPERATION

	yes	no
1. Is your box inventory adequately geared to re-order lead time?	☐	☐
2. Is your box inventory arranged to efficiently feed your packing lines?	☐	☐
3. Is your inventory of boxes properly stored?		
4. Will you be setting up the boxes on automatic equipment? (If so, what type? Size? Method of closure?)	☐	☐
5. Will your product be packed automatically? (If so, with what type of equipment?)	☐	☐
6. If more than one unit or part goes into each box, have you determined the sequence?	☐	☐
7. Will inner packing—shells, liners, pads, partitions—be inserted by hand?	☐	☐
8. Is your closure system—tape, stiches, glue—compatible with the box, packing line speed, customer needs and recycling considerations?	☐	☐
9. Will the box be imprinted or labeled?	☐	☐
10. Will a master pack be used for a multiple of boxes to maintain cleanliness or appearance?	☐	☐
	☐	☐

YOUR STORAGE

	yes	no
1. Have you determined the gross weight of the filled box?	☐	☐
2. Does the product itself help support weight in stacking?	☐	☐
3. Will the bottom box have to support the full weight in warehouse stacking?	☐	☐
4. Will boxes be handled by lift trucks which use clamps, finger lifts or special attachments?	☐	☐
5. Will filled boxes be palletized? (The size of pallet and pallet pattern may justify a change in box design or dimensions, if only to reduce or eliminate overhang.)	☐	☐
6. Would a change in box style or size make more efficient use of warehouse space?	☐	☐
7. Will filled boxes be subject to unusual conditions during storage—high humidity, extreme temperatures, etc.?	☐	☐
8. Is the product likely to be stored outdoors at any time during its distribution?	☐	☐
9. Would color coding simplify identification of various packed products?	☐	☐

YOUR SHIPPING

	yes	no
1. Have you reviewed the appropriate rules of the transportation service you intend to use (rail, truck, air, parcel post, etc.)?	☐	☐
2. Is your container authorized for shipment of your product?	☐	☐
3. If the package is not authorized, have you requested appropriate test shipment authorization from the carrier?	☐	☐
4. Does your product require any special caution or warning label or legend for shipment?	☐	☐
5. Have you determined the actual inside dimensions of the transportation vehicle so that you can establish how your filled boxes will be stacked or braced?	☐	☐

YOUR CUSTOMER

	yes	no
1. Does your customer have any special receiving, storage or handling requirements that will affect box design?	☐	☐
2. Will the box be used as part of a mass display?	☐	☐
3. Is the box intended as a display-shipper?	☐	☐
4. Will it contain a separate product display?	☐	☐
5. Will it be used as a carry-home package, requiring a carrying device?	☐	☐
6. Does it need an easy-opening feature?	☐	☐
7. Can surface design, symbols or colors relate to promotional materials or to other products of the same corporate family?	☐	☐
8. Should instructions or opening precautions be printed on the box?	☐	☐
9. Can the box be made to better sell your product?	☐	☐

Figure 5-6   Checklist for box users. (Courtesy of Fibre Box Association.)

Figure 5-7   A partially disassembled bicycle in front of its carton. The seller's catalog says, "For our custom bicycles, we set up and adjust every component, from the bearings to the brakes to the shifting. Then, we partially disassemble the bike and ship it to you as shown." (Courtesy The Colorado Cyclist, Inc.)

Figure 5-8   Box-maker's guarantee. (Courtesy of Fibre Box Association.)

the boxes will be sturdy enough to meet their handling specifications. Note that a number of measures are used.

Carrier specifications are precise. Here is an excerpt from an item that was considered by the motor carriers' National Classification Committee in early 1992:

> Subject 24: Proposes to amend Package 1254, which is authorized for the shipment of dishwashers as named in item 119540, by adding the following options for the base and the corner posts: the specifications for the base would include the following wording: "Expanded polystyrene foam base pad having a minimum density of 1.6 pcf, providing a thickness at bottom of 5/8-inch and 7/8-inch at sides, with sides extended upward a minimum of 2-7/8 inches"; and the specifications for corner posts would include the following option: "a 3/4-inch clearance must be maintained between article and inside wall of container by mandrel-formed tubular L-shaped solid fibre corner posts."[10]

In today's deregulated environment, it is difficult to know exactly how much carrier tariffs and classifications control shippers' packaging. Responsibility for damage in transit is one issue subject to contract negotiation; if the carrier remains liable, the carrier specifies the level of packaging protection to be used. If the shipper assumes responsibility, the shipper may choose the type of packaging to use. Carrier deregulation allows corrugated packaging "manufacturers and their customers to innovate with performance outside of the [packaging] rules."[11] As specific contract rates are negotiated and drawn up between individual carriers and shippers, packaging requirements may, of course, be one element of negotiation. (However, when a group of West Coast traffic managers participating in a panel at San Francisco State University were asked whether packaging requirements were an element in their negotiations with carriers, they answered no. They said that in the negotiations the carriers desired to limit their own liability for loss and damage claims so much that the shippers were subsequently reluctant to cut back on their packaging because most of the risk for damage in transit had been passed to them.)

Airlines, express delivery companies, and the Postal Service also have packaging requirements, although they are somewhat less detailed than those used by rail and motor common carriers. Export packing is discussed briefly in Chapter 11. The International Air Transport Association regulates packaging of air shipments. There are fewer requirements regarding ocean shipments. However, exporters nearly always buy additional insurance coverage for their export shipments, and the type of packing influences the insurance rates.

[10] *Transport Topics*, February 24, 1992, p. 25.

[11] Bruce Benson, "Corrugated Standard Issues," in *Performance Packaging and Transportation, Proceedings of the 1988 Annual Meeting of the National Safe Transit Association* (Chicago: NSTA, 1988), p. 102.

Package Testing

When new products or new packaging techniques are about to be introduced, it is sometimes advisable to have the packages pretested. Various packaging material manufacturers and trade organizations provide free **package testing.** Independent testing laboratories can also be used. The packages are subject to tests that attempt to duplicate all the expected various shipping hazards: vibration, dropping, horizontal impacts, compression (having too much weight loaded on top), overexposure to extreme temperatures or moisture, and rough handling.

To design a protective package system properly, the engineer requires three important kinds of information:

1. Information on the severity of the distribution environment.
2. Information on the fragility of the product to be protected.
3. Information on the performance characteristics of various cushion materials.[12]

Sometimes specialized tests are devised. The following quotation describes tests conducted on a new type of pallet:

> After bearing a 2,400-pound load for 48 hours and being checked for deformation, the pallet was again loaded with a 2,400-pound load and run through a series of tests.
>
> Twenty times picked up and set back down on the four by fours in a rough and careless manner.
>
> Four times picked up off the supporting beams with one fork under the center of the pallet only and lifted to a height of 4 feet; then rapidly lowered and raised. This attempt was to crack the pallet in the center.
>
> Ten times raised 6 inches by a fork that had a fast fork drop rate, and then very rapidly dropped back on its supporting beams.
>
> We then tried to mutilate the loaded pallet by
>
> 1. Twisting the forks within the pallet-fork openings; that is, backing up at an angle before disengaging the forks from the pallet. We were able to put a slight tear near the corner of one fork opening.
> 2. Roughly, we pushed the pallet to different positions while flat on the floor with one fork. This was done in the attempt to split the outside corners.[13]

Computer software has been devised to test different packaging. One program enables the user to simulate the use of various grades of lumber and different numbers and sizes of nails to be used in constructing wooden pallets. For each combination of lumber and nails the software calculates the average life expectancy of a pallet and the average cost before it needs repair.

---

[12] Herbert H. Schueneman, "Re-examining the Package Drop-Height Environment," in *Performance Packaging and Transportation, Proceedings of the 1988 Annual Meeting of the National Safe Transit Association* (Chicago: NSTA, 1988), p. 72.

[13] Anonymous source.

In addition to the testing of new products or new packages, shippers should keep detailed records on all loss and damage claims. Statistical tests can be applied to the data to determine whether the damage pattern is randomly distributed. If it is not, efforts are made toward providing additional protection for areas in the package that are overly vulnerable. Carriers also have provisions that allow shippers to follow special rules while testing new packaging materials. UPS allows customers to ship sample parcels to various UPS district offices, and UPS employees at those sites then report back with comments about how well the packaging withstood the UPS trip.

Related to package testing is actual monitoring of the environment the package must pass through. This is done by enclosing recording devices within cartons of the product that are shipped. The measuring devices may be very simple, such as hospital-like thermometers that record only temperature extremes and springs that are set to snap only if a specified number of g's (a measure of force) is exceeded. Figure 5-9 shows one such device being inserted in the side of a package. More sophisticated devices record over time a series of variables, such as temperature, humidity, and acceleration force and duration (in several directions). Acceleration force and duration are usually

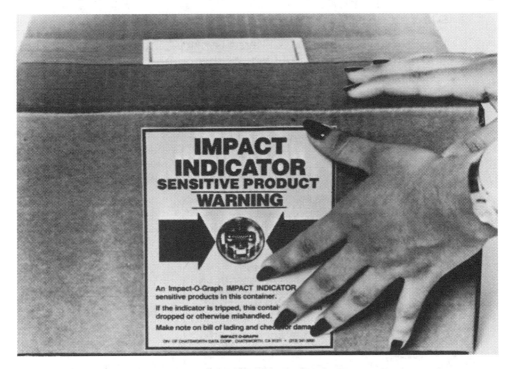

Figure 5-9 An impact indicator. The indicator is implanted in the package's side, and the consignee is instructed to see whether the mechanism was tripped during shipment. If it was, the consignee is supposed to indicate that in the shipping document. (Courtesy of Impact-O-Graph, Chatsworth, California.)

recorded along three different axes, making it possible to calculate the precise direction from which the force originated. Kaiser Aluminum, which was troubled with problems of water-stain damage, devised the small sticker with the happy face shown in Figure 5-10. Above the happy face's smile are two eyes, but one of the eyes is printed in a special ink that dissolves when it comes into contact with moisture. If the receiver of the shipment notices that the eye is distorted, he or she can assume that the shipment has been exposed to moisture and should be inspected for damage.

Sophisticated monitors are expensive, but they may be necessary to solve a problem of recurrent in-transit damage. Less complicated devices are used to record temperatures and may or may not be used as the basis for a damage claim against a carrier. They may be used aboard a shipper's own equipment to ensure quality control. A frozen food distributor wants to be certain that its product had not thawed and been refrozen in transit. Large shipments of apples are accompanied by a mechanical temperature recorder, which provides the receiver with a greater workable knowledge of each load, such as information on temperature variation that may affect the speed at which the receiver should handle and merchandise the apples.

Labeling

Once the material being packaged is placed into the box and the cover is closed, the contents are hidden. At this point it becomes necessary to label the box. Whether words or code numbers are used depends upon the nature of the product and its vulnerability to pilferage. Retroflective labels that can be read by optical scanners may also be applied. Batch numbers are frequently assigned to food and drug products, so that they may be more easily traced in case of a product recall.

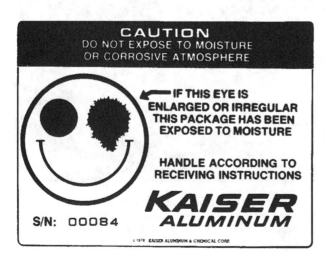

Figure 5-10   Kaiser Aluminum's moisture-alert label. When the product is shipped, both eyes are normal; that is, they look like the eye on the left. The figure shows how the label looks after the product is exposed to moisture. The receiver is to record the conditions of the label in the shipping document.

Many regulations govern the labeling of consumer-size packages, including the labeling of weight, specific contents, and instructions for use. Today many of these must also be placed outside the larger cartons as well, because some retail outlets sell in carton lots and the buyer does not see the consumer package until he or she reaches home.

Packaging is usually done at the end of the assembly line. Package labeling also occurs here, since using this location avoids accumulating an inventory of preprinted packages. This is also a key point for control because this is where there is an exact measure of what comes off the assembly line. As the packaged goods are moved from the end of the assembly line, they become stocks of finished goods and become the responsibility of the firm's outbound logistics system. Near the point where product packaging occurs, it is necessary to maintain complete inventory of all the packages, packing materials, and labels that will be used. Today, with laser printers, it is possible to print labels as needed, for example, twenty-four labels in French. This has lessened the requirement for inventorying printed labels.

The discussion in the last few paragraphs, and for much of this chapter, emphasizes the outward movements of finished goods. For sophisticated materials management systems it is also necessary to label inbound parts and components so that their location can be continually monitored. Bar codes are commonly used, and they are read by scanners, or sensors. (Figure 5-11

Figure 5-11   Two handheld bar-code applicators. (Courtesy SATO PROMO Touch Hand Applicators.)

shows simple hand-held bar-code label applicators, and Figure 5-12 shows a bar-code laser scanner.) Scanners often do more than signal the presence of a container or part. They also give the computer as much information as it needs about that part to maintain accurate production and inventory records and to determine the routing of that part from one workstation to another. Leading firms are moving away from the one-dimensional bar code to a code with two dimensions, which can hold considerably more information in a small space.

Today nearly all logistics operations rely heavily on bar codes and scanners as a means of linking the supply chain. There are some exceptions. Sometimes parties in the supply chain fear that their customers will link up directly with their suppliers, bypassing them. "Orders are typically sent from . . . suppliers, many of which are in Illinois, to a freight forwarder in Chicago and shipped out by ocean freight. To protect its sources from distributors, the forwarder removes identifying labels and lists itself as shipper on all documents."[14]

Figure 5-12 A handheld laser scanner scanning labels on a pallet load of product sitting in a warehouse rack. (Courtesy PSC Inc.)

[14] *Journal of Commerce,* September 24, 1993, p. 4A.

UNIT LOADS IN MATERIALS HANDLING

As mentioned earlier in the chapter, the packaging of materials is based on the building-blocks concept: putting products in containers that will provide efficient yet manageable units. This section discusses **unit loads,** an extension of the building-blocks concept to very large quantities. The basic unit in unit loading is the **pallet** or skid. Unit loading involves the securing of one or more boxes to a pallet or skid so that the boxes can be handled by mechanical means, such as a forklift. The boxes or other containers secured to a pallet are known as a *unit load.* The term **unitization** is used to describe this kind of handling. Figure 5-13 is a computer printout showing twenty-eight different possible ways to arrange twelve- by eight- by six-inch cartons on a forty- by forty-eight-inch pallet.

More often than not, the unit load is placed on a wooden pallet. Although somewhat lowly in status, wooden pallets receive considerable attention both

```
                        PALLET PATTERN CONFIGURATIONS
   PALLET    PATTERN      TOTAL     NO. OF     TOTAL     TOTAL      SPACE
   NUMBER     TYPE      ON COURSE   COURSES  ON PALLET  WEIGHT    UTILIZED
     1      Unitblock      18         9         162       972      90 %
     2      Unitblock      20         9         180      1080     100 %
     3      Multiblock     20         9         180      1080     100 %
     4      Multiblock     18         9         162       972      90 %
     5      Multiblock     18         9         162       972      90 %
     6      Multiblock     19         9         171      1026      95 %
     7      Multiblock     17         9         153       918      85 %
     8      Pinwheel       18         9         162       972      90 %
     9      Pinwheel       18         9         162       972      90 %
    10      Pinwheel       18         9         162       972      90 %
    11      Pinwheel       20         9         180      1080     100 %
    12      Irregular      18         9         162       972      90 %
    13      Irregular      17         9         153       918      85 %
    14      Irregular      19         9         171      1026      95 %
    15      Irregular      19         9         171      1026      95 %
    16      Irregular      20         9         180      1080     100 %
                      12 more patterns to see

 < KEY RETURN=SELECT;SPACE=DOWN;BACKSPACE=UP;B=BACK SCREEN;N=NEXT SCREEN

                        PALLET PATTERN CONFIGURATIONS
   PALLET    PATTERN      TOTAL     NO. OF     TOTAL     TOTAL      SPACE
   NUMBER     TYPE      ON COURSE   COURSES  ON PALLET  WEIGHT    UTILIZED
    17      Irregular      19         9         171      1026      95 %
    18      Irregular      19         9         171      1026      95 %
    19      Irregular      18         9         162       972      90 %
    20      Irregular      19         9         171      1026      95 %
    21      Irregular      20         9         180      1080     100 %
    22      Irregular      19         9         171      1026      95 %
    23      Irregular      19         9         171      1026      95 %
    24      Irregular      17         9         153       918      85 %
    25      Irregular      19         9         171      1026      95 %
    26      Irregular      18         9         162       972      90 %
    27      Irregular      18         9         162       972      90 %
    28      Irregular      17         9         153       918      85 %
               THESE ARE ALL POSSIBLE PALLET SOLUTIONS
```

Figure 5-13   Computer printout showing alternative ways to arrange cartons on pallets. (Courtesy of Professional Micro Systems.)

in trade journals and at trade meetings. The degree of attention is usually correlated with the price of lumber, and pallets are no longer thought of as free. Shippers are requiring consignees to return the same number of pallets or billing them separately for unreturned pallets.

One disadvantage of the conventional pallet is its height (approximately six inches). A pallet may occupy as much space as a layer of cases of canned soft drinks. When goods are loaded aboard pallets into rail cars, trailers, or containers, the space occupied by the pallet is unproductive. The alternative is to place a sheet of flexible heavy plastic or fiberboard material, known as a **slip sheet,** under the unit load in place of the pallet and then strap the unit load to the slip sheet. The disadvantage is that handling time is increased because the forklift operator must use the equipment much more carefully to avoid damaging the product.

Even though the wooden pallet occupies space in a vehicle, its construction and physical properties provide a favorable cushioning effect. However, the quality of individual pallets varies widely. The grocery industry once attempted to establish a pallet interchange pool that was to have minimum standards of quality, but it lost interest because some members believed that slip sheets would replace pallets in unit loading. There is considerable disagreement concerning the relative merits of slip sheets and wooden pallets. However, both involve unit loads and unitization. The disagreement is over the best way to handle them.

In place of the pallet pool, Chep USA, a private firm, performs almost the same function by renting out wooden pallets. Chep USA works mainly in the grocery industry. Most of its deliveries of empty pallets go to food processors and manufacturers. Later it takes back the empty pallets from retail stores. The pallets are inspected, repaired or replaced if necessary, and fed back to manufacturers. From a supply-chain perspective, note that this is a loop that operates alongside the main product chain.

The grocery industry is currently thinking of plastic pallets made from recycled plastic containers. The plastic pallet has no nails that might protrude to injure handlers, damage cargo, or scratch floors in retail stores. The problem is getting a sturdy plastic pallet that will weigh under fifty pounds (reflecting a goal in the industry to have everything that is manually handled under fifty pounds in weight). Plastic pallets are finding markets in closed-loop systems, that is, where the same pallets sent out always come back. Metal pallets are expensive and are used only in closed-loop systems, the largest user being the airfreight industry.

The unit load offers several advantages. It gives some additional protection to the cargo because the cartons are secured to the pallet by straps, shrink-wrapping, or some other bonding device. This provides a sturdier building block. Pilferage is discouraged because it is difficult to remove a single package or its contents. Also, a pallet can be stacked in such a manner that the cartons containing the more valuable or more fragile items are on the inside of the unit load. The major advantage of the unit load is that it enables mechanical devices to be substituted for hand labor. Many machines have been devised that can quickly build up or tear down a pallet load of materials. One example, a depalletizer, is shown in Figure 5-14. A full pallet, waiting to be depalletized, is shown on the far left. On the right is a pallet load, which has been turned a full ninety degrees, with grips pressing in on its sides. One level of cases is being shown as it is being lowered from the pallet load, which is on its side. The entire operation is tilted downward toward us, and the layer of cases will pass toward us on the roller system. Robots are used when much more sophisticated integrated movements are needed for loading or unloading pallets. An example of robot-assisted palletizing and depalletizing exists in the printing industry, where bundles of printed pages must be stacked in a specified order.

The unit load does not have its limitations, however. It represents a larger quantity of an item than a single box—often thirty to fifty times as

Figure 5-14 A depalletizer at work. (Design superceded Columbia Machine, Inc.)

much. Therefore, it is of limited value to shippers or consignees who deal in small quantities. Some shippers recognize this and have a price break at both the pallet-load quantity and the pallet-layer quantity. Thus, a canner ships in pallet loads to a distributor, which sells to retailers that may buy only in pallet layers or loads. All of the distributor's items are in boxes that can be arranged on the conventional forty-eight-inch by forty-inch pallet (although the number of boxes that would cover one layer varies). Nonetheless, the distributor's price break is at the pallet-layer quantity, so the retailer might decide to order one layer (which might be twelve boxes or cases) of canned peaches, two layers (which might be fifteen cases each) of catsup, and so on. The distributor would load each layer separately, yet the goods would leave its warehouse as a full pallet, or unit load. The distributor would have given an even lower price if the retailer had purchased a full pallet load of a single item because in that instance the distributor would have avoided manual handling of the product completely; it would have merely shipped out one of the full pallet loads it had received from the canner.

The military also uses pallet-sized boxes having the forty-inch by forty-eight-inch base:

> Of all the materials handling equipment used by U.S. Forces in the Persian Gulf, a simple wooden box turned out to be one of the most versatile items around.
>
> One version of the box, constructed of 1/4-inch thick plywood and patented hardware and measuring 48 inches long by 40 inches wide by 27.5 inches high, was used to handle and move everything from foodstuffs to ammunition. Designed to be shipped and stored in a knocked-down format (at a 5:1 ratio), the easy-to-assemble box can be assembled with a rubber mallet and a screwdriver in just 10 minutes.[15]

Lift trucks are the common workhorse used around warehouses to move pallets. They come in many designs. Figure 5-15 shows a lift truck used for picking stock in warehouses; note that in this model the operator rides with the load rather than at ground level.

Before moving to the next step in the building-blocks concept, we should make one additional point. Our discussion has emphasized the building of loads from small blocks into large blocks. The reverse is also true; that is, the large units or blocks must be broken down into their smaller component blocks, with the very smallest unit being the single item that the retail customer carries home. This is illustrated in Figure 5-16, which shows a high-rise warehouse four tiers high. At the right, a lift truck places full unit loads into a gravity-flow rack system. As they are used, the pallets move to the left, where order pickers break down the unit loads into single boxes.

[15] *Modern Materials Handling,* July 4, 1991, p. 61.

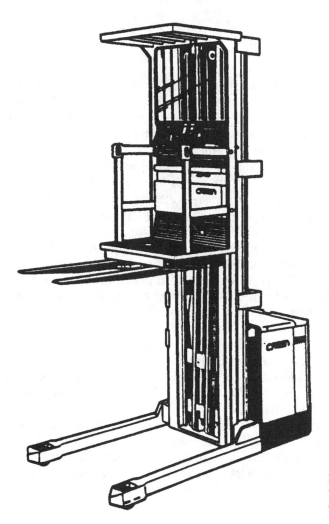

Figure 5-15 A battery-powered lift truck used for stock picking. (Courtesy of Crown.)

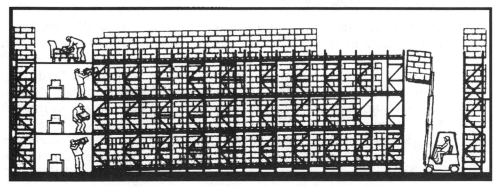

Figure 5-16 A warehouse where unit loads are broken down into boxes. (Courtesy of the Interlake Corporation.)

CONTAINERS

For surface cargo, the next-sized block beyond the unit load is the intermodal container, which is usually 8 feet wide, 8 or more feet high, and 20, 28, 35, 40, or more feet long. Containers are widely used in U.S. foreign trade and domestic trade, although containers used domestically are usually 102 inches wide. Because they are interchangeable among rail, truck, and water carriers, containers can be used in intermodal applications and reap the advantages offered by each of several modes. Both ocean carriers and railroads have developed methods of handling two or more containers at one time, thereby reducing the number of individual lifting and storage moves.

Most containers are dry-cargo boxes. Some are insulated and come with temperature-controlling devices; others contain one large tank; still others are flatbed. There are also specially designed containers for the transport of livestock and automobiles: "With Autostack, as many as six autos are rolled into a rack that a special loader mechanically inserts into a container for transport. The racks are collapsible and can fit six to a container when they are knocked down."[16]

Some airlines use eight- by eight- by twenty-foot containers constructed of lightweight metals, which are interchanged between air and motor carriers. Only the largest jumbo jets carry containers of this size. Most other aircraft containers have somewhat irregular shapes, dictated by the contours of the fuselage into which they must fit.

Manufacturing operations often receive components from their suppliers loaded on custom-made reusable racks, which are then returned to the supplier for reloading. The racks are designed with certain palletlike characteristics because they are handled with mechanized equipment and, ideally, maximize use of the vehicle's cubic carrying capacity.

Equipment Loading

The next step in the building-blocks process is to stow the unit-load pallets into a waiting truck trailer, railcar, or container van. Figure 5-17 shows a computer printout from load-planning software; it suggests how to load a container with different sizes of cartons and tells where the loads for several customers should be loaded. The software recognizes, for example, that some cartons cannot be laid on their sides or cannot have other cartons placed on top of them.

Slight clearances must be maintained between pallets to allow for the loading and unloading processes. Bracing or inflatable dunnage bags are used to fill narrow empty spaces. When inflated, they fill the void space

---

[16] American Shipper, April 1991, p. 59.

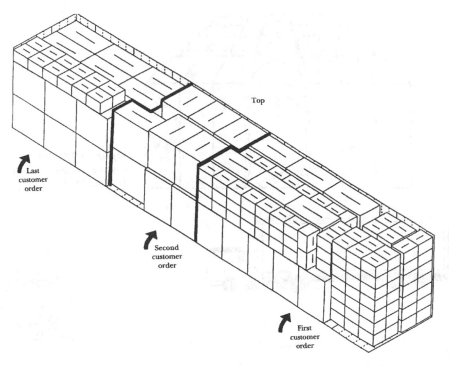

Figure 5-17   Computer-generated load plan. (Courtesy of TOPS Engineering Corp.)

and function as both a cushion and a brace. Figure 5-18 shows inflated dunnage bags. A problem involved with any bracing or cushioning device is that the load is subjected to forces from all directions. Figure 5-19 shows five of the forces to which a surface-sea load may be subjected. Sea loads are subjected to more forces than the ones illustrated in the figure because a vessel in rolling seas can encounter almost any pattern of forces. Even when cargoes are properly braced, the various forces can still cause damage: Continued vibrations may loosen screws on machinery or cause the contents of some bags or packages to settle, changing the type of support they give to the materials packed above them. For products that present this problem, special preloading vibrators are used to cause the load to settle immediately.

Some goods are so heavy that they utilize the railcar's, trailer's, or container's weight capacity without filling its cubic capacity. These loads, such as heavy machinery, must be carefully braced, and the weight must be distributed as evenly as possible. In highway trailers, for example, it is dangerous

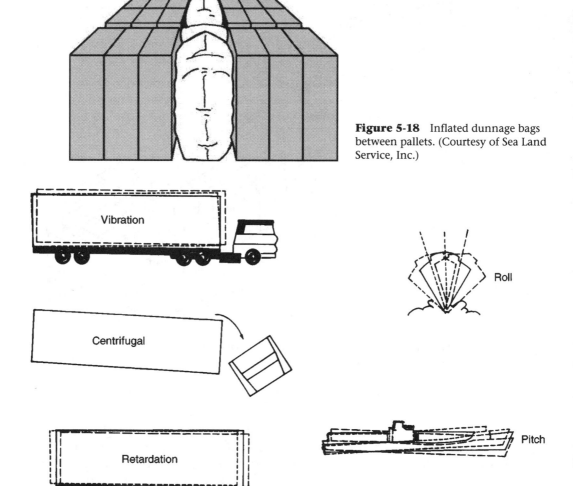

Figure 5-18 Inflated dunnage bags between pallets. (Courtesy of Sea Land Service, Inc.)

Figure 5-19 Various forces to which cargo is subjected. (Courtesy of Sea Land Service, Inc.)

to have one side loaded more heavily than the other. In addition the load should be distributed evenly over the axles. Figure 5-20 shows the bracing and straps used to secure a load inside a railcar.

Do not block at ends of leg-type frame.

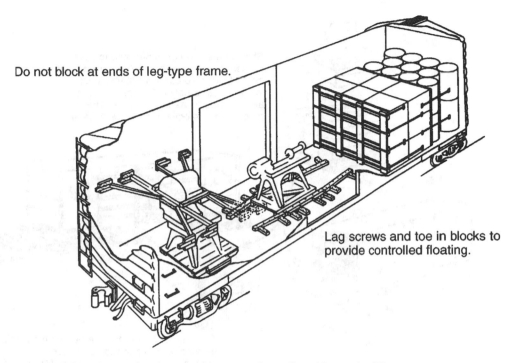

Lag screws and toe in blocks to provide controlled floating.

Figure 5-20   Bracing of heavy machinery inside a railcar. (Courtesy of Damage Prevention & Loading Services, Association of American Railroads.)

Finally, the building-blocks concept includes the container or vehicle load, although carriers offer rate incentives for multiple-container, -trailer, or -railcar shipments. Indeed, most carrier-shipper contracts today involve movements in those quantities. Interestingly, CSX Transportation offers special grain rates in fifteen-car lots, in part because that number of cars is equal to one barge load.[17]

Figure 5-21 summarizes the building-blocks concept insofar as it relates to building up a load. The concept does, of course, also work in reverse, going back down to the consumer-size pack.

[17] CSX Transportation's entry in the *Modern Railroads* Golden Freight Car Competition, 1990, unpublished.

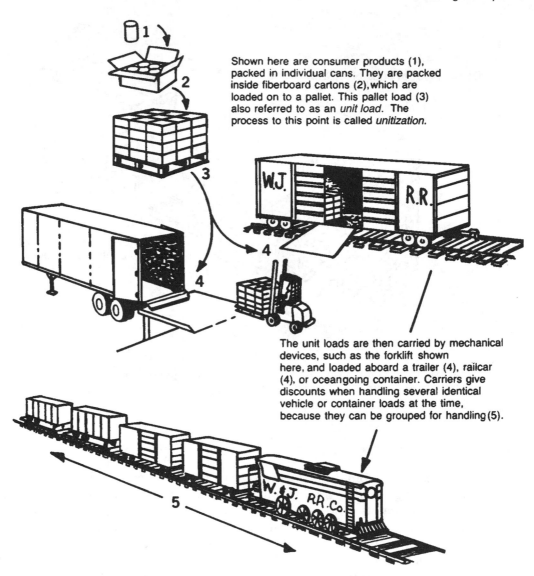

Shown here are consumer products (1), packed in individual cans. They are packed inside fiberboard cartons (2),which are loaded on to a pallet. This pallet load (3) also referred to as an *unit load*. The process to this point is called *unitization*.

The unit loads are then carried by mechanical devices, such as the forklift shown here, and loaded aboard a trailer (4), railcar (4), or oceangoing container. Carriers give discounts when handling several identical vehicle or container loads at the time, because they can be grouped for handling (5).

Figure 5-21   The building-blocks concept of packaging: a summary.

MATERIALS HANDLING

Materials flow through the supply chain. How they are handled physically is the subject of **materials handling.** Mechanical devices are often used for all or parts of movement.

To this point the emphasis has been on the movement of products that are packaged, often in consumer-size boxes, bottles, or cans. Nearly all are handled by the building-block concept of packaging that has already been described. The other way that products, especially large quantities of products, are handled is in bulk. Bulk materials are loose rather than in packaged form and are handled by pumps, shovel devices, conveyor belts (see Figure 5-22), or the mere force of gravity. The decision must be made as to where in the supply chain the bulk materials should be placed into smaller containers for further sale or shipment. Sometimes bagged and bulk quantities of the same material are part of the same shipment. In vessels, bagged rice is placed on top of bulk rice to provide load stability.

Bulk cargoes have various handling characteristics. One is density. The Great Lakes steamer *Richard J. Reiss* uses only two-thirds of its cubic capacity when carrying ore, yet the 15,800 tons of ore lower the vessel to its maximum allowable draft of twenty-four feet, eight inches. When loaded with coal, the vessel cubes out; that is, the cubic capacity is filled and the vessel is lowered to only twenty feet, six inches. Grain loads are even lighter; the *Richard J. Reiss*'s draft with grain is slightly less than twenty feet.[18] Port facilities for handling three different bulk materials—coal, iron ore, and grain—are illustrated in one of the transportation chapters.

A material's angle of repose is the size of angle that would be formed by the side of a conical stack of that material. The greater the angle, the higher the pile of materials that can be placed on a specific land area. Anthracite coal has an angle of repose of approximately twenty-seven degrees, whereas for iron ore the figure is thirty-five degrees. This means more cubic yards of ore can be stockpiled on a given site and the ore can be carried on a slightly steeper, narrower conveyor belt.

Bulk liquids also have unique handling characteristics. Resistance to flow is measured as viscosity, which can be lowered by increasing the temperature of a liquid. Molasses, cooking oils, and many petroleum products are heated before an attempt is made to pump them.

Gases have unique handling properties, although most of them are handled within completely enclosed pipeline systems. An exception is liquefied natural gas, or LNG, which is cooled and compressed into liquid form that is 1/630 of its volume in gaseous state. In its liquefied, highly pressurized state, it is transported by oceangoing vessels in special tanks.

The handling process itself may change the characteristics (or quality) of the product. Rice grains cannot fall far without being broken. This influences the design of loading and unloading facilities so that the grains of rice never drop more than a few feet at any one time. When sugar is handled, a

[18] Correspondence from the Reiss Steamship Company to the authors.

Figure 5-22   Imported raw sugar moving along and up a conveyor belt in Galveston. (Courtesy Port of Galveston.)

dust is formed because of abrasion between sugar crystals. This dust is also sugar but in much finer form and with different sensitivities to moisture. The dust must be separated from the rest of the sugar or the quality of the final bakery product in which the sugar is used will be affected.

An ideal equipment configuration for one bulk cargo may not be able to handle another. Another consideration is the size of particle of the cargo in question; there are costs involved in pulverizing to a uniform size so it can be handled by pneumatic or slurry devices.

Materials Handling Principles

Materials handling is a branch of engineering and deals with the movement of the material between two or more different points. As a supply chain is linked together, one of the concerns of those involved with logistics is the physical transfer of the product from one party to another: How will it be handled? In what type of vehicles will it arrive? In what form will it be? In what quantities? What kind of equipment is needed to handle or to store it? Materials handling processes generally receive little public attention. An exception to this has been the luggage-handling system at the new Denver Airport, which was initially defective to the extent that it delayed the airport's opening by many months.

The College-Industry Council on Materials Handling Education has developed and refined a list of twenty-four materials handling principles. Most materials handling systems are designed and tested through rigorous engineering analysis. The principles are more important when laying out the intended design or when troubleshooting to learn why a system is not performing well. The principles follow:

1. The *orientation principle* requires that one look at the entire system first to learn how and why it operates. One would also look at relationships to other systems and to physical limitations.

2. What is the system expected to do? The *requirements principle* focuses on answering that question.

3. All storage and handling operations must be coordinated, and that is known as the *integrated system principle*.

4. The *standardization principle* means just that. It is important in the selection of packaging to be used. Other things being equal, it is advantageous to standardize on as small a number of packages or wraps as possible.

5. The *just-in-time principle* holds that products are not moved until needed.

6. The *unit-load principle* conflicts with the just-in-time principle in that it emphasizes the importance of handling materials in large blocks, such as the unit loads mentioned earlier in the chapter.

7. Systems should be set up so that loads move for the shortest distances; this is the *minimum travel principle*.

8. The *space utilization principle* requires one to make good use of space. Some materials handling equipment is designed to fit into otherwise underutilized space.

9. **Ergonomics** involves an understanding of how the human body functions as it performs physical tasks. The *ergonomic principle* is used to justify manufacturing and materials handling systems that protect workers from performing difficult and repetitive functions that ultimately result in injuries or disability.

10. The *energy principle* aims at reducing energy consumption by the materials handling activities.

11. The *ecology principle* calls on us to devise systems that are environmentally friendly, with an example being the choice of materials to use in packaging.

12. Using machines, where justified, to replace human effort is called the *mechanization principle.*

13. The *automation principle* involves the development of equipment that is preprogrammed, or self-controlled. Some machines can be programmed to make simple decisions given certain conditions. Some equipment today can respond to radio signals or even voice commands.

14. The *flexibility principle* is important for systems in which there are changes from time to time in the tasks that the system is expected to perform.

15. The *simplification principle* means what it says: Avoid overly complicated systems.

16. The *gravity principle* is easy to understand; one should rely on gravity to move materials wherever possible. Many figures in this book showing materials being handled involve the use of gravity to accomplish part of the task. Note, for example, Figure 5-16.

17. The *safety principle* emphasizes the importance of having equipment that is safe to operate and to be near.

18. The *computerization principle* recognizes the widespread use of computers to operate both individual pieces of equipment and massive supply chains spread across several continents. Computers allow better, faster use of information. Material flows are integrated with information flows.

19. The *systems flow principle* calls for an orderly and logical flow of materials.

20. The *layout principle* requires that the system be laid out in a manner that takes all these listed principles into account.

21. The *cost principle* recognizes that all materials handling alternatives have associated costs and that these costs must be carefully considered as the system is devised. Investment proposals must be presented to top management for approval.

22. Once in operation, a system must be maintained. This is recognized by the *maintenance principle,* which includes taking various maintenance alternatives into account.

23. Many existing systems include equipment that has been in service for some time. The *obsolescence principle* recognizes that this equipment must be phased out, taking into account its usefulness, as well as tax and accounting considerations.

24. The *team solution principle* means that materials handling challenges are sufficiently large and complex that often teams of people are needed to devise the best system.[19]

Figure 5-23 shows a massive piece of railroad equipment designed to handle taconite pellets and limestone. The entire unit consists of a transfer car plus fifteen hopper cars stretching a total of 1,013 feet along railroad tracks, plus the length of the locomotive needed to move it. It is used for winter movements of ore pellets in Cleveland, which have been stockpiled at other Cleveland docks by Great Lakes vessels during the open navigation season. This is a shorthaul movement, but because it occurs during the winter, persons loading the cars must break up large frozen chunks of pellets that would clog the system. A conveyor belt runs the length of the sixteen cars and is controlled and operated hydraulically. A special heater was installed to keep the hydraulic fluid from congealing.[20]

Materials Handling in the Supply Chain

Products are designed so that they can move throughout the entire supply chain. Auto frames, for example, are built so they can be packed together compactly on their journey to the assembly line. They may also come with brackets that are useful on the assembly line but have no particular value once the auto is assembled. Much of this discussion of packaging has dealt with a system that built loads up into truckload quantities. The warehousing chapter will describe how these large loads of individual products are received at a warehouse, broken down, and assembled and shipped out in entire different arrays as desired by the next party along the chain.

A few products are even built with reuse in mind. For example, the odometer on autos is tamperproof; the matter would be of less consequence if we expected autos to have only a single owner. As recycling practices increase, we will see products designed with disassembly in mind; their reusable parts will be segregated and placed back into use.

[19] See "The 24 Principles of Material Handling," prepared by the College-Industry Council on Materials Handling Education and appearing in *Material Handling Engineering Directory Issue, 1993–1994,* pp. A13–A18.

[20] Entry in the *Railway Age* 1993 Golden Freight Car Competition, submitted by the River Terminal Railway Company, of Cleveland, unpublished.

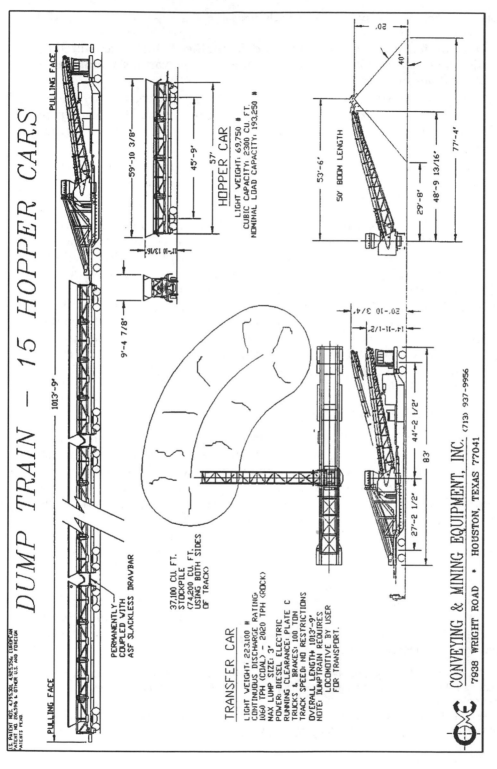

Figure 5-23 A dump train consisting of fifteen hopper cars that feed to a transfer car. The cars are permanently coupled, and a conveyor belt runs the entire length of the train, feeding material from left to right to the transfer car, which has a fifty-foot boom that can be elevated to twenty feet and can reach both sides of the car. This allows it to place materials in stacks twenty feet high on either side of the train. The device can unload 1060 tons of coal per hour and 2020 tons per hour of rock. (Courtesy David C. Curtis, Manager Traffic & Marketing LTV Steel Railroads.)

SUMMARY

As Chapter 5 demonstrates, there are many considerations to take into account as one chooses protective packaging. Much depends upon the physical characteristics of the specific product. Some products are hazardous to either the environment or to persons handling them, and they require special packaging and attention. Common carriers often specify the packaging that must be used. Concerns about recycling and environmental protection also have an impact upon the choice of packaging materials.

Packages have a sales function as well, and a sturdy package contributes to a product's solid image. In recent years retail packages have been provided with protective seals, which make it easier to detect tampering.

Retail packages are placed into cartons, which are loaded onto pallets to form unit loads. Then the unit loads are loaded by forklifts into containers, truck trailers, or railcars. Palletization and unitization both refer to the utilization of pallet loads as a form of building block.

QUESTIONS FOR DISCUSSION AND REVIEW

1. What is the difference between the selling and protective functions of packaging? How are the two functions related? Explain.
2. Describe the function of conventional pallets. What are their advantages? Disadvantages?
3. Discuss the specific protective functions that a protective package must accomplish. Does every package have to accomplish every function? Discuss.
4. What impacts has the recycling movement had upon packaging?
5. What environmentally friendly packaging strategies might a firm adopt?
6. For what reasons might a liquor or camera distributor choose not to print its cartons' contents in plain English?
7. What are the various physical forces to which a package in transit might be subjected? What other hazards might it encounter?
8. What is shrink-wrap packaging?
9. What is unit loading?
10. Why should a load's weight be distributed evenly inside a truck trailer?
11. What information is needed to design a protective package properly?
12. How does supply-chain integration affect packaging? Discuss.
13. What is the building-blocks concept? How is it applied to the handling of packaged goods?
14. Discuss the relationship between the level of protective packaging used relative to the packaging requirement of common carriers. How has carrier deregulation affected shippers' packaging? Discuss.
15. Give some examples of package testing.
16. Describe some of the devices that are used to monitor conditions during the journey that a shipment makes.

17. What are materials handling principles? What function do they serve?

18. Describe a materials handling situation with which you are familiar and point out those materials handling principles that you think are applicable.

19. Is materials handling an issue within a firm, or is it a supply-chain issue? Discuss.

20. Give some examples of package recycling efforts with which you have been involved.

SUGGESTED READINGS

Bookbinder, James H., and Dominique Gervais. "Material-Handling Equipment Selection via an Expert System." *Journal of Business Logistics,* vol. 13, no. 1 (1992), pp. 149–172.

CIGNA. *Ports of the World—A Guide to Cargo Loss Control,* 15th ed. Philadelphia: CIGNA, 1992.

Cox, Ralph M., and Kenneth G. Van Tassel. "The Role of Packaging in Physical Distribution." In *The Distribution Handbook.* New York: Free Press, 1985, pp. 737–773.

Fibre Box Association. *Fibre Box Handbook.* Chicago: Fibre Box Association, 1989.

Haessler, Robert W., and F. Brian Talbot. "Improving Customer Service through Load Planning." In *Annual Conference Proceedings of the Council of Logistics Management,* vol. 2. Oak Brook, Ill.: CLM, 1990, pp. 251–256.

Hildebrandt, Glenn. "Case Study: Installation of Inbound Returnable Containers at the John Deere Horicon Works." In *CLM Annual Conference Proceedings,* 1993. Oak Brook, Ill.: CLM, 1993, pp. 289–292.

Sea-Land. *Shipping Guide for Perishables.* Iselin, N.J.: Sea-Land, 1988.

Twede, Diana. "Logistical Packaging Course Module: A New Logistics Education Initiative." In James Masters (ed.), *Logistics at the Crossroads of Commerce.* Columbus: Ohio State University Transportation and Logistics Research Fund, 1994, pp. 63–80.

Twede, Diana. "The Process of Logistical Packaging Innovation." *Journal of Business Logistics,* vol. 13, no. 1 (1992), pp. 69–94.

C A S E   5 - 1

LET THERE BE LIGHT LAMP SHADE COMPANY

Started in Madison, Wisconsin, after the student unrest of the sixties had died down, the Let There Be Light Lamp Shade Company served an upscale local market for many years. They designed and custom-built both lamp shades and lamp globes. In the mid-1980s some architects who had once studied under Frank Lloyd Wright in nearby Spring Green were commissioned to design several large public buildings in Asia. A total of 5,400 identical lights were to be installed, and Let There Be Light Lamp Shade Company wished to bid on the work. Terms of sale would be delivery to the foreign port where the buyer would take possession.

Transportation costs would be a hurdle. In the initial design the shades were cylinders that were eleven inches high and eleven inches in diameter and were packed into boxes that were twelve by twelve by twelve inches. The packages cost 60 cents each and weighed one pound each. We shall refer to these shades as style A. The shades cost $4 each to manufacture. They weighed nine pounds each and ten pounds packaged.

They would be shipped to the port of Oakland. The land rate to Oakland was $1,000 per forty-foot container, without regard to weight, although the weight of the load could not exceed 44,000 pounds per loaded container because of highway weight restrictions. The interior dimensions of the intermodal container were 8 feet wide by 8.5 feet high by 40 feet long.

Ocean rates from Oakland to the overseas port were $22 per ton (2,000 pounds) except that the ocean conference used a measurement ton that indicated that for bulky loads every forty cubic feet would equal one ton for rate-making purposes. (That is, a shipment weighing, say, 130 pounds and occupying eighty cubic feet would cost as though it weighed 4,000 pounds) Insurance costs were 2 percent of the value of the shipment ready to be loaded aboard ship in Oakland. (This is calculated as all of the company's costs up to this point.)

Because of the large size of the order, Let There Be Light Lamp Shade Company realized that it could "custom" design a shade that, rather than being a cylinder, would be shaped like a cone. The advantage to that was that the shades could be nested. Some padding would be required between the shades, but the nested shades would also help protect each other. However, cutting out material for conical shapes results in waste, so production costs would be higher. Two alternative cone-shaped designs were proposed, and they shall be referred to as style B and style C.

Style B cost $5 per shade to manufacture. They could be shipped nested in packages of six. The package dimensions were twelve by twelve by forty-eight inches, and when holding six shades, a package weighed sixty-two pounds. Each package cost $2, and this included padding between the shades.

Style C cost $6 per shade to make. They could be shipped nested in packages of ten. The package dimensions were twelve by twelve by fifty inches, and when holding ten shades, a package weighted 101 pounds. Each package cost $3, including padding between the individual shades.

Questions

1. How many style A shades can be loaded into an intermodal container?
2. How many style B shades can be loaded into an intermodal container?

3. How many style C shades can be loaded into an intermodal container?
4. What are the total costs of delivering the style A shades to the port of importation?
5. What are the total costs of delivering the style B shades to the port of importation?
6. What are the total costs of delivering the style C shades to the port of importation?
7. Which style would you recommend? Why?

C A S E   5 - 2

JACKSON'S WAREHOUSE

(Note to the instructor: This case should be assigned only if students are familiar with STORM software, although, possibly, other general business analysis software programs might be used. The terminology and approach are not exactly the same as in the text, especially the use of Sigma lead times, which are measured in units and can be explained as measuring the "dipping" into safety stocks.)

Located in Memphis, Tennessee, Jackson's Warehouse stores only twelve different items, which are sold to a select number of customers. Each item is known only by its SKU number. Exhibit 5-A shows each SKU number, the

EXHIBIT 5-A   JACKSON'S WAREHOUSE'S NEEDS

SKU number	Demand (weekly)	Unit cost to Jackson's	Lead time (in weeks)	Standard deviations of demand per week (in units of product)
402	4	$1,500	2	40
940	20	720	1	50
660	12	500	2	60
829	30	65	1	80
301	35	250	1	90
447	48	190	1	100
799	8	200	1	30
597	12	40	2	35
27	4	210	1	50
196	20	35	1	60
258	42	250	1	115
62	180	8	1	700

annual demand for each, the unit cost to Jackson's warehouse, the lead time (the lapse of time between Jackson's ordering from its supplier and receiving the goods), and Sigma lead time (the standard deviation of lead time demand, expressed as the number of units by which safety stocks are drawn down in times of heavy demand).

For SKUs with a unit cost of less than $500, it costs Jackson's $30 to process an order for any number of units of that single SKU; and for SKUs with a unit cost of $500 or above, it costs Jackson's $75 to process an order for any number of units of that single SKU.

Carrying costs are calculated as 30 percent of the average inventory of each SKU. The average inventory is the safety stock plus one-half the size of each order. (It is assumed that goods move outward in a fairly even flow so, at any one time, the amount in stock is halfway between the size of a full order and zero, plus safety stock.)

Assume that the warehouse wants to stock enough of each SKU to fill orders 95 percent of the time.

Questions

1. Perform an ABC analysis. Is it of much use if the firm maintains only twelve SKUs? Why or why not?

2. Find the reorder point for each of the SKUs expressed as the point to which existing inventory must drop to trigger a replenishment order.

3. How large a safety stock should be maintained for each SKU?

4. How much money will Jackson's have as its average investment in inventory?

5. Interest rates drop, and Jackson's now assumes that its carrying costs are 20 percent, rather than 30 percent. How will this change your answers to questions 2, 3, and 4, if at all? Explain.

6. Disregard your answers to questions 4 and 5. Answer question 3, this time assuming that Jackson's wants to keep enough of each SKU to fill orders 90 percent of the time.

The Domestic Transportation System

6

One of the problem areas regarding regulation of U.S. carriers is that of coordinating different modes of transportation. This is especially true if one mode represents domestic moves connected with another mode that is international. These interfaces are also often focal points of technological change. Shown here are some of the advances in truck-to-ship transfers of cargo. The upper picture, taken in 1926, is titled "New Port of St. Petersburg on Florida's West Coast." The bottom photo, taken in 1983 in Seattle, shows one of American President Line's container ships, the *President Lincoln*. In the older picture, the cargo-handling equipment is on the vessel; in the newer picture, it is based on shore. (Credit: Library of Congress and Don Wilson, Port of Seattle.)

Regardless of which party is controlling the transportation of purchased goods, it is crucial that the transportation providers be included in the strategic partnership planning to some extent. The long-term agreement between a buyer and a supplier should not be finalized until the transportation service requirements are thoroughly discussed and evaluated on both cost and quality measures.

Julie J. Gentry
International Journal of Purchasing and Materials Management
Summer 1993

Overall, it is calculated that more than 75 percent of the value of all goods and service produced in the U.S. is carried by truck.

Transportation Statistics, Annual Report 1994

Barge freight rates are based on a percentage of a 1974 tariff, the last one published by the Interstate Commerce Commission before deregulation of the barge industry.

Journal of Commerce
November 3, 1994

The Supreme Court on Monday returned to the trucking undercharge controversy for the fourth time in four years, agreeing to determine whether Interstate Commerce Commission regulations can override retroactive freight claims filed by bankrupt trucking lines.

Journal of Commerce
April 19, 1994

Key Terms

- Broker
- Bulk cargo
- Common carrier
- Consignee
- Dedicated equipment
- Freight classification
- Freight forwarder
- LTL
- Nesting
- Parcel
- Parcel carrier
- Private transportation
- Project cargo
- Routing guide
- Shippers' cooperative
- Slurry system
- Terminal
- Ton-mile
- Unit train

Learning Objectives

- To relate the mode of transport to the user's shipping volume
- To understand the use of routing guides
- To realize the role of freight forwarders and other intermediaries
- To understand the difference between LTL and TL motor carriers
- To understand how slurry pipelines function
- To appreciate the use of terminals as transfer points for bulk materials
- To appreciate trade-offs when using vehicles with self-loading/unloading equipment
- To learn about project cargo
- To learn the basics of freight rate determination

INTRODUCTION

Transportation is the movement of goods between two points. While many other logistics activities are site specific, transportation is not. At one time logistics systems were thought of as inventory storage points (nodes) connected to others by transport carriers (links). Goods in transit between two modes were almost in a state of limbo. Their removal from the shipping point would be recorded by subtracting them from that facility's records. When they arrived at their destination, they would be unloaded and added to that facility's inventories. Today, much closer tabs are kept on inventories in motion, and carriers are so well disciplined that goods in transit can always be counted upon to arrive when needed. (Well, almost always.)

This chapter looks at the nation's domestic transportation system, starting with service available to the shipper of small amounts and moving up to shippers that think in terms of trainloads or barge loads. It assumes that readers have some knowledge of parcels and smaller freight shipments, and it spends more time on carriers that handle large movements of bulk materials. Chapter 11 will cover international transport.

Transportation is pivotal to the successful operation of any logistics system:

1. Transportation costs are directly affected by the location of the firm's plants, warehouses, vendors, and customers.
2. Inventory requirements are influenced by the mode of transport used. High-speed, high-priced transportation systems require smaller amounts of inventories near customer locations.
3. The transport mode selected determines the packaging required, and carrier classification rules often dictate package choice.
4. The type of carrier used dictates a manufacturing plant's materials handling equipment, such as loading and unloading equipment and the design of the receiving and shipping docks.
5. An order-processing methodology that encourages maximum consolidation of shipments between common points enables a company to give larger shipments to its carriers and take advantage of volume discounts.
6. Customer service goals influence the type of carrier selected by the seller.

In our own heads we generally know when to use mail, fax, phone, or E-mail. Much is based on trial and error. If we know that we will be making certain shipments in the future, we may call around to determine prices and services available or the other party to our transaction may advise or instruct us. **Routing guides** (sometimes called *shipping guides*), used by almost all shippers, contain instructions for choice of mode and carrier to handle each shipment. In the shipping room of many firms, the routing guide was often a three-ring binder, and if one had a forty-two-pound shipment that had to reach Atlanta in four days, the guide would tell the lowest-cost method to use.

Today many of these guides are computerized, and the decision of how to ship is determined at the time of order processing, the appropriate shipping documents and labels being produced by a computer. One of the authors recently toured a computer-manufacturing plant in California's Silicon Valley. At the shipping dock three trailers were being loaded as packaged computers and accessories came off the end of the packing line. Above each trailer was a banner (supplied by the carrier) saying, "FedEX," "UPS," or "Consolidated Freightways." Each of the three carriers offered a different class of service, and the manufacturer's own computerized system was programmed to make the carrier selection. Routing guides are also sometimes supplied to vendors with specific instructions as to how incoming goods must be routed.

Brief mention was made above of nodes, which are points to and from which shipments are made. They are an integral part of the transportation and logistics system. They represent points where one achieves access to or exit from a transport system, and where cargoes are exchanged between modes or carriers or vehicles. Figure 6-1

Figure 6-1   Switching milk cans from a farmer's buggy to a truck on a rural road in North Carolina, 1929. (Photo courtesy of U.S. Department of Agriculture.)

shows a simple node, circa 1930. Many nodes are known as **terminals.** Here the word *terminal* has two meanings: a transfer point or the end of a move. Often inventories are kept at terminals to provide a cushion to accommodate the different patterns of inbound and outbound flow. The bulk terminals described later in this chapter, and the warehouses described in a later chapter, all hold inventories.

SMALL-VOLUME SHIPPERS

The smallest of businesses are probably operated out of one's home. Mail and parcel post can reach any address in the United States and virtually any address elsewhere in the world (with varying degrees of reliability). At the very beginning level one can purchase supplies on a delivered basis, and the seller has to arrange for transportation. One can also sell F.O.B. (free on board) source, in which case customers will have to come to pick up their purchases. One's own auto or light truck can be used for local carriage of goods. In some cities taxis can be used to deliver packages; there are also local delivery services that will pick up and deliver packages within a certain geographic area. For purposes of discussion, we will assume that we are dealing with packages weighing up to 100 or 150 pounds. These are often referred to as **parcels,** and firms that specialize in their carriage are called **parcel carriers.**

In recent years a franchise of shipping/packaging outlets has located in shopping centers, office buildings, office parks, and industrial parks. Operating out of storefronts, walk-in customers bring materials to be packaged and sent via mail, UPS, or other forms of transport. They often have fax machines, photocopiers, and mailboxes and sell packaging materials and some office supplies. They give the occasional shipper access to all forms of carriage, and they relieve the shipper of the need to inventory packaging supplies. They charge the carriers' rate plus an additional percentage, and they arrange for insurance. These franchises offer an entry into all services that the occasional shipper of small packages needs. They will also represent their customers in case some problem with the carrier occurs at some later stage. They have access to the on-line computer services that carriers offer to enable the shipper to trace a shipment or query as to its status.

As one's volume of shipments increases, one studies the various services available for handling small movements of product. Parcel post is a service of the U. S. Postal Service. There are definite size and weight limitations (approximately seventy pounds). Charges are based on weight and distance and are relatively low. In most cases the parcel must be carried to the post office, but it will be delivered to the receiver. The Postal Service also offers various levels of mail and parcel service and some parcel pickup.

Probably the best-known parcel carrier is UPS, which now operates in nearly 200 countries, and financially dwarfs any other trucking company in the United States. This company has experienced growth because it has earned a reputation for very reliable service. UPS rates include both pickup and delivery. It offers a range of service relying on several modes of transport; users of its air service can purchase next-day, second-day, or third-day deliveries. UPS also provides computer software to assist with documentation and to allow the customer access, via a modem, to those segments of the UPS computer system that the customer needs to learn of the status of his or her shipment. UPS has several imitators.

Federal Express runs on a similar concept, relying on a huge fleet of planes to carry parcels to and from several major hubs each night. Its specialty is overnight delivery. It also has imitators. In most major markets there are at least half a dozen companies offering overnight delivery of small packages. Both UPS and Federal Express offer service to many foreign countries, and as a part of this service, also handle the many documentation needs associated with export/import transactions.

Passenger carriers also carry small packages, which usually have to be delivered to and picked up from the carrier's terminal. Bus package service is offered by intercity bus companies. The maximum weight per package is from 100 to 150 pounds. The packages travel in special compartments on the intercity buses. The service is fast and reliable, and packages delivered thirty minutes before a bus's departure will be aboard that bus. There is no pickup or delivery service. Amtrak has similar service on its trains. Some airlines offer next-flight-out service and accept parcels at the passenger ticketing and check-in gates at the airport's terminal.

LTL SHIPPERS

As one starts dealing with larger shipments, the next step in the progression is referred to as **less-than-truckload,** or **LTL,** traffic. Shipments in this category range from about 150 to, say, 5,000 or 10,000 pounds. They are often too big to be handled manually, yet they do not fill a truck. Trucks that carry LTL freight have space for and plan to carry shipments of other customers at the same time.

The LTL category has the majority of the nation's large trucking firms. Since deregulation, a handful have developed high-quality, nationwide service for less-than-truckload amounts. Leaders are Yellow Freight, CF Motor Freight, Roadway Express, Overnite Transportation, and ABF Freight System. All operate in virtually the same manner. They have numerous terminals spread throughout the nation. From each terminal, small *bobtail* trucks go out to customers delivering and picking up shipments. These shipments are then taken to the terminal, where they are loaded aboard line-haul trucks, which are driven to a terminal near the freight's destination (sometimes this line-haul move occurs with a container or trailer riding on a railcar). The goods are unloaded from the line-haul carrier, move through the terminal, and are loaded aboard a bobtail truck for local delivery.

Consignees are receivers of freight. Some consignees consolidate their inbound freight by specifying that all shipments made to them be routed via a specific LTL or parcel carrier. In that carrier's local terminal, all shipments to be delivered to the specified consignee are loaded on one truck. There is therefore only one delivery each day of several packages, rather than numerous deliveries, each by a different carrier with a single package.

Shipments of this size also move by air. They can be tendered directly to the airline at an airport, or they can be given to a **freight forwarder** for consolidation. Most air freight is carried on passenger airline aircraft, and only about 10 percent of passenger airlines' revenue comes from air freight. A small number of airlines carry freight exclusively. The following product groups represent the largest users of air freight: wearing apparel; electronic or electrical equipment and parts; printed matter; machinery and parts; cut flowers and nursery stock; auto parts and accessories; tapes, televisions, radios, and recorders; fruits and vegetables; metal products; and photographic equipment, parts, and film. As this list illustrates, products that are air freighted tend to be high in value and are often of a perishable nature or otherwise require urgent delivery.

Air freight moves in air cargo containers. Air cargo containers have varying shapes, designed to take into account the plane's interior contours. Each airline uses only containers that fit into its own aircraft. Some air cargo containers are interchangeable between different models of aircraft. For example, in its booklet describing containers that can be used aboard its aircraft, KLM, the Royal Dutch Airlines, lists about twenty different sizes of containers and pallets.[1] The largest container is eight by eight by twenty feet, which looks like the rail/truck/water container. However, its tare (empty) weight is much less, and it is engineered to higher standards because it is designed to be an integral part of the loaded aircraft. That container is used on the main deck of wide-bodied aircraft. The next smaller KLM container is half that size, eight by eight by ten feet, also designed for the main deck on wide-body planes. There are igloo-shaped containers for main-deck placement on smaller all-cargo jets, and lower-deck containers having one bottom corner tapered to fit inside the plane.

Freight Forwarders and Other Consolidators

Freight forwarders are not modes, but from the shipper's viewpoint they are analogous to other carriers. The two types of domestic freight forwarders—surface and air—can best be thought of as consolidators of freight.

Freight forwarders operate as agents. Both surface and air carriers give volume discounts to customers shipping large quantities of freight at one

[1] *Unit Load Devices—Your Way to Greater Profits* (KLM, ca. 1986).

time. For example, the motor carrier rate from City A to City B might be $5 per 100 pounds for shipments of less than 20,000 pounds. This is called an LTL rate. The TL (truckload) rate might be $2 per 100 pounds when shipments of 20,000 pounds or more are tendered. The freight forwarder exists by offering a service to shippers that must use LTL rates because they do not generate enough volume to use TL rates. Without the freight forwarder, the small shipper has to use the $5 LTL rate. The freight forwarder, however, offers the same transportation service for a rate between the LTL and TL rate, say, $4. This is possible because the freight forwarder consolidates all the small shipments it has and gives them to the carrier (a trucker in this case) and hence qualifies for the $2 TL rate. The freight forwarder typically offers pickup and delivery service but does not perform the line-haul service. This is done by the motor carrier or railroad involved. Forwarders also function as traffic departments for small firms, performing other traffic-management functions.

Some forwarders specialize in certain cargoes. A common example is in the garment industry, in which many small garment firms send large numbers of a few garments each to retail shops in most large cities. The garment forwarders use special containers in which the garments can hang from hangers and be ready for display on arrival. Another specialized forwarder has been described this way:

> Air Animal, of Tampa, Florida, moves everything from tropical fishes to horses, but most of the company's business involves providing national and international transportation for dogs and cats.[2]

The firm handles health inspection prior to shipment, arranges for cages and quarantines (if required), books flights, and handles all documentation. The majority of their business is household pets. Rock-it Cargo, in Los Angeles, specializes in carrying cargo for rock groups:

> In one of its most ambitious tasks, Rock-it Cargo is helping the Rolling Stones send their equipment to concert sites. . . . Each of the six stages being moved around the world for the group's "Voodoo Lounge" tour fills 16 40-foot cargo containers. In addition, the Rolling Stones travel with 500,000 pounds of musical, video and lighting equipment.[3]

The air forwarding industry works with the air carriers. The forwarders consolidate shipments and tender them in containers that are ready for aircraft loading. This results in significant ground-handling time savings for the airlines. Therefore, airlines encourage forwarder traffic since it results in an agreeable division of labor: The forwarders provide the retailing function and deal with each individual shipper and consignee, and the airline concentrates

---

[2] *Journal of Commerce*, December 19, 1994, p. 3.
[3] Ibid.

on wholesaling—moving the forwarders' loaded containers between major cities. The following excerpt from a routing guide differentiates nicely as to when to use an air freight forwarder and when to deal directly with an airline:

> Harcourt Brace & Company utilizes air freight forwarders whose responsibilities (from door to door) [are] generally a requirement of our business, whereas an airline's primary concern is to move freight between airports with secondary emphasis on pickup and delivery. Both offer immediate tracing service.
>
> For the most part, our air freight shipments can run anywhere from five pounds to three hundred pounds. Depending upon destination plus service requirements, it would be well to utilize the airline itself for the movement of shipments in excess of three hundred pounds in order to effect cost savings and accomplish our intent.[4]

Shippers' cooperatives perform basically the same function as surface and air freight forwarders, except they do not operate as profit-making organizations. All profits achieved through their consolidation program are returned to members. This type of consolidation program has been well received by shippers. An example of a shippers' co-op is the Washington-Oregon Shippers Cooperative Association, which has 1,200 members, a staff of forty-three, and annual billings of about $25 million. The co-op has terminals in Seattle, Portland, Anchorage, Charlotte, Atlanta, Memphis, and Los Angeles.[5]

The term **broker** is used frequently in transportation. A broker is a facilitator that brings together a buyer and seller. Some brokers handle LTL shipments. They consolidate shipments and then turn them over to truckers, forwarders, or shippers' associations.

To this point we have covered parcels and less-than-truckload shipments. This is the type of transportation the vast majority of U. S. firms use. The ubiquitous brown UPS truck and other delivery trucks are familiar to all readers. Trucks (including truckload carriers, yet to be discussed) receive over three-quarters of all money spent on domestic freight transportation. It is for parcels and LTL shipments that carriers use published rates, similar in format to those described toward the end of this chapter. These rates are based on three factors, the size of the shipment, the distance traveled, and the product's handling characteristics.

TRUCKLOAD AND CARLOAD SHIPPERS

Once one's individual (or consolidated) shipments reach weights of, say, 20,000 to 30,000 pounds, one can start thinking of truckload (TL) or surface containerload shipments. The exact weight depends upon the product, and it

---

[4] *Harcourt Brace & Company Logistics Services Procedures Manual* (Orlando, Fla.: Harcourt Brace, 1994), pp. 16–17.

[5] *American Shipper,* June 1988, p. 80.

is close to the amount that would physically fill a truck trailer. For glassware this might be 18,000 pounds; for canned goods it might be 40,000 pounds. If one's shipments are larger, railcars are viable, although carload (CL)[6] weights tend to be heavier. The shipper can also use intermodal surface containers. These containers used in domestic trades are usually 102 inches wide, 8½ feet high, and 40 feet long.[7] The shipper probably handles these shipments like a truck shipment; the trucker, however, will turn the container over to a railroad for a portion of the move.

Truckload shipments cost less per pound than LTL shipments. This is for three reasons:

- The shipper loads and the consignee unloads the trailer.
- The load goes directly from shipper to consignee without passing through terminals.
- Paperwork, billing, and control costs are no more for a truckload than they would be for a ten-pound LTL shipment.

The same logic explains why containerloads and rail carloads cost less per pound than LTL shipments. We have also reached the size of shipment at which the rate for each haul may be negotiable. The price is a function of supply and demand for transportation. For example, when the demand is high for trucks to carry fresh agricultural product eastward from California, the rate per truckload is often six times as high as it is for trucks heading from the Midwest to California.

Not all truck- or other vehicle-load contracts are on a one-shot, or trip, basis. They may be negotiated to cover a span of time, say, two truckloads a week for one year. There are also additional services that might be negotiated as part of the contract, such as a split delivery, in which the truck carries a full load but delivers portions of that full load to several addresses.

Truckload freight haulers specialize in truckload lots, using either their own equipment or contracting with owner-operators. The largest firm in this category is Schneider National Van Carriers, and nearly the same size is J.B. Hunt Transport. Other firms are smaller. Firms in this industry tend to be less well known because they advertise less often and do not need to maintain a nationwide presence. Truck firms in this category do make use of owner-operators to perform much of their hauling. Many have long-term relationships profitable to both.

---

[6] CL can be applied to either rail carloads or surface containerloads. Rail carloads tend to be heavier than truckloads because of the railcars' greater carrying capacity. Containerloads are often similar to truckloads since containers often move on the highway.

[7] Intermodal containers used for international moves are ninety-six inches wide and range in length from twenty to fifty-five feet.

It is also for these larger quantities that the user can think of specialized trucks or railcars to handle the movement. Sometimes the shipper provides them; sometimes the carrier does. When the shipper provides and operates its own equipment, it is known as **private transportation. Dedicated equipment** is carrier-owned but assigned to serve specific customers for an indefinite period. To give an example of the variety of specialized truck bodies, here is a list: A-frame glass-carrying, acid tank, air compressor, armored car, asphalt tank, bakery, beer, beverage, bookmobile, bottler, brick-loading/unloading, bulk cement, cable splicer, canopy, cargo van, cattle rack, cement mixer, cleaner and dyer, coal, concessionaire, concrete, contractor, dairy, delivery, department store, dry freight, dump, farm, feed, fertilizer spreading, florist, food product, frozen food, fuel oil, furniture, garbage, gas cylinder, gas line construction, gasoline transport, grain, grocers', high-lift, horse van, ice-control spreader, ice cream, insulated, laundry, limestone spreader, livestock, logging, lumber, meat packer, milk delivery, oil field equipment, open-top, pallet-loading, parcel delivery, pickup, pie distributors', platform, produce, public utility service, radio unit, refrigerator, road-building, self-unloading, stake, telephone installation, tree trimmer, and wrecker.[8] Some of these are used for more purposes than transporting goods, but the list demonstrates that in some trades, one uses a truck, and often owns that truck, to carry products and sometimes workers. There are also specialized railcars and specialized barges, although the lists would not be as long.

Shippers utilizing conventional railroad service need to have a railroad siding on their property, and must also make certain that the consignee is able to receive shipments by rail. Railroads specialize in transporting raw materials and unprocessed products in carload quantities. At one time almost all businesses of any size had rail sidings, but today that is no longer true. At one time railroads typically shipped general merchandise in boxcars, and because this portion of their business is in a long-term decline, the industry finds itself with excess general-purpose boxcars. It has been speculated that the rail industry will never again purchase this type of car and will specialize in container and piggyback-trailer handling equipment instead.

Chartered Cargo Aircraft

It is also possible to charter (or rent) an entire aircraft to handle specific shipments. Sometimes small aircraft are chartered to deliver repair parts to combines that are stranded in grain fields. The largest of planes, the Boeing 747, can carry about 100 tons (see Figure 6-2). Chartered aircraft are expensive, compared with other modes of transport. Livestock are often moved on chartered aircraft because extended durations of travel are hard on livestock.

[8] Donald F. Wood, *Commercial Trucks* (Osceola, Wis.: Motorbooks International, 1993), pp. 205–206.

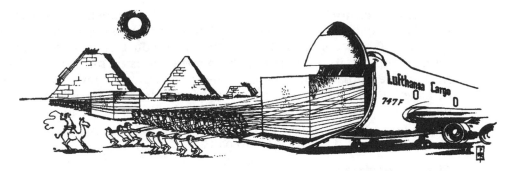

Figure 6-2   Air freight capabilities. (Courtesy of Lufthansa Cargo.)

LARGE BULK SHIPPERS

Bulk materials are loose rather than in packaged form and are handled by pumps, scoops, conveyor belts, or the force of gravity. The decision must be made as to where in the distribution system the bulk materials should be placed into smaller containers for sale or shipment to the next party in the supply chain.

Bulk cargoes have various handling characteristics. An ideal equipment configuration for one bulk cargo may not be able to handle another. Another consideration is the size of particle of the cargo in question; there are costs involved in pulverizing to a uniform size so it can be handled by pneumatic or slurry devices.

Materials shipped in bulk move in truckload, rail carload, or vessel-size lots or via pipeline. Lot sizes differ. A truckload may be 20 to 30 tons, a railcar load runs from 40 to 80 tons, a barge holds about 1,000 tons, a Great Lakes vessel holds 25,000 to 50,000 tons, and the largest of ocean vessels can carry 500,000 tons.

Truckload Hauls

Trucking of bulk materials involves either for-hire or private trucks, with specialized bodies if necessary. For-hire trucks are retained for a specific haul or for a span of time or for a task (say, to move tomatoes from fields to a cannery). Brokers are often used by shippers to find and contract with independent truckers; the broker takes a certain percentage off the top of the rate.

Railroads

Rail rates and contracts encourage multiple-car shipments since the railroad can switch and haul a number of cars as easily as one. The largest of rail hauls are handled on **unit trains.** This is a train of permanently connected cars that carries only one product nonstop from origin to destination. It can be thought of as a conveyor belt. Once the product is delivered, the train returns empty to its origin and makes another nonstop run. Unit trains benefit both the railroads and their customers: The trains achieve a very high percentage of car utilization and usually provide less expensive and more dependable service. Currently over 90 percent of all coal movement is by unit trains. General Motors uses a unit train from Chicago to Los Angeles for carrying assembled autos and auto parts.

Water Carriers

There are domestic movements of freight by water on the Great Lakes and on our inland waterways—or barge—system. There is also waterborne commerce via oceangoing vessels between the mainland ("lower forty-eight") states and Alaska, Hawaii, and Puerto Rico. One of the largest domestic movements is oil from Alaska, which moves on large tankers from Valdez to Panama. The tankers are nearly 1,000 feet long, carry 1.5 million barrels, and are too large to transit the canal. At Panama the oil is unloaded at a tank farm and pumped via pipeline across the isthmus to a tank farm on the Atlantic. There it is reloaded aboard smaller tankers and taken to U.S. Gulf and East Coast ports.

The inland waterway system, not counting the coastal routes, the Great Lakes, or the St. Lawrence Seaway system, is made up of about 16,000 miles that are dredged to a depth of nine feet, which is the minimum required for most barges. Most of this system is concentrated in the southeastern region of the United States along the Mississippi River and its tributaries.

Domestic water carriers have specialized in transporting bulk products at very low prices at slow average speeds (six miles per hour). Petroleum and related products account for 36 percent of total barge commerce. Coal is second, with 28 percent. Other products that move extensively in the inland waterway system are grain and grain products, industrial chemicals, iron and steel products, forestry products, cement, sulphur, fertilizers, paper products, sand and gravel, and limestone. In most cases these products are tendered to the carriers of barge-load lots. There are also barge-oriented freight forwarders offering services on the inland waterways system. Their main sales tool is to offer a smaller minimum tender requirement to shippers. One forwarder bases its rates on shipments as small as 100 tons, whereas common carrier barges serving the same area require minimum shipments of 800 tons.

A problem faced by inland waterway carriers operating in the northern states and on the Great Lakes is the fact that ice closes their systems and prevents year-round operation. This means their customers must stockpile inventories in the fall to last through the winter months. Studies are under way to determine the feasibility of extending the open navigation system into the winter months. This stockpiling of large inventories runs counter to most current logistical thinking.

Pipelines

There are two types of oil pipelines: crude oil and product. Crude oil lines transport petroleum from wells to refineries. There are approximately 150,000 miles of crude oil pipelines in the United States. There are two types of crude oil lines. Somewhat more than half of the crude oil line mileage is in the form of gathering lines, which are six inches or smaller in diameter and are frequently laid on the ground. These lines start at each well and carry the product to concentration points. Trunk lines are larger-diameter pipelines that carry crude oil from gathering line concentration points to the oil refineries. Their diameter varies from three to forty-eight inches; eight- to ten-inch pipe is the most common size. A large pipeline's capacity is also impressive. The forty-eight-inch Trans-Alaska pipeline, which is 789 miles long, has a discharge capacity of two million barrels (forty-two gallons each) per day.

The other type of petroleum pipeline is called a product pipeline and carries products such as gasoline or aviation fuel to tank farms located nearer to customers. The products are stored at the tank farms and then delivered to customers by truck or by rail.

Slurry systems involve grinding the solid material to a certain particle size, mixing it with water to form a fluid, muddy substance, pumping that substance through a pipeline, and then decanting the water and removing it, leaving the solid material. Railcars can also carry slurry. For example, kaolin (a clay used in paper making) is mined and separated from the accompanying sand by a water process. The sand-free clay is then subjected to a number of mechanical processes that reduce its moisture content to about 35 percent. The result is a substance that has the viscosity of heavy cream, which is about the consistency desired by the paper-making plants, so it is shipped in this form, despite the fact that, by weight, a substantial percentage of what is shipped is water. In this instance, the economics are such that it is less costly to transport the water than it is to remove it near the quarry and add it after shipment at the paper mill.

A large coal slurry line in operation today is the Black Mesa pipeline, which transports pulverized coal in an eighteen-inch pipe 273 miles from strip mines in northern Arizona to an electric-generating station on the Colorado River near Davis Dam, Nevada. The slurry line was constructed because unit-train operation was not feasible over the terrain involved. The 50 percent water, 50 percent coal mixture moves at four miles per hour and makes the trip in three days. The speed of the movement must be carefully maintained because excessive speed makes the coal powder act like sandpaper on the inside of the pipe, and insufficient speed causes the coal powder to fall out of suspension and build up on the bottom of the pipe. When the slurry solution reaches destination, centrifuges spin the water out. The coal is then fed into the furnaces.

Dry Bulk Handling Systems

Systems for handling dry bulk materials are often large and custom engineered to fit specific needs. Three examples of terminals are illustrated here to give an idea of the scale at which these facilities are designed and constructed and to give an indication of the equipment used to load and unload vehicles. Figure 6-3 is a cross-sectional view of a coal car–unloading facility. The cars carrying coal are joined in a unit train, whose cars are permanently

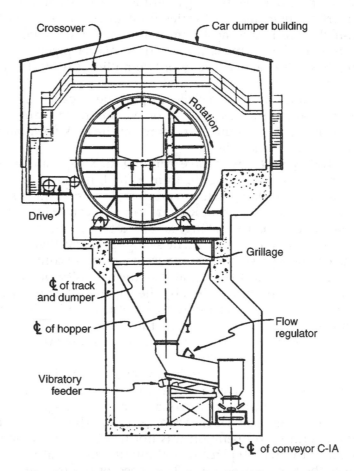

Figure 6-3   Cross-section of a coal car–dumping building in St. Louis, Missouri. [Courtesy of McNally Wellman (a Svedala Group Company).]

coupled. However, this coupling is unique because it allows each car to swivel and be turned upside down while still remaining coupled. The train comes to a stop with the first coal car in exact position within the rotating drum. Grips extend from the drum to secure the car, and it is rolled over, nearly 180 degrees, dumping the coal. It is rolled back and released, and the train moves ahead until the next car is in position. It takes 90 seconds to unload each car, which can hold 100 tons of coal. The unit train consists of 110 cars.

A taconite loading facility is shown in Figure 6-4. It is located at Two Harbors, Minnesota, on the western end of Lake Superior. Taconite is partially processed iron ore in pellet form. The site in question can store two million tons of taconite (about 20,000 rail carloads). The ore is received by unit train at the unloading station shown at the top of the figure (which is similar to the facility shown in Figure 6-3). The ore pellets are then moved out to the storage piles, where they are held until loaded aboard a vessel via conveyor belts. One reason such a large storage area is needed is the difference in receiving and shipping seasons. Taconite is received year-round but is shipped only during an eight-month season because most of the Great Lakes are closed to navigation during the winter.

Figure 6-5 illustrates another bulk cargo handling facility: a large grain elevator located at the Port of Seattle. The facility receives grain both by rail and by truck. In the figure, note the references to dust collection and dust

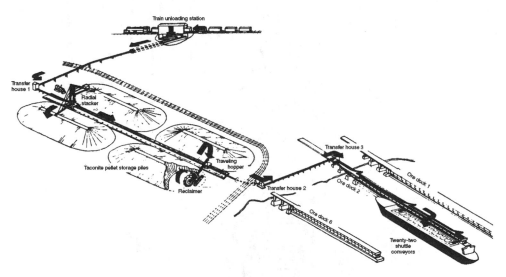

Figure 6-4   Taconite storage and loading facility at Two Harbors, Minnesota. (Source: Duluth, Missabe, and Iron Range Railway Company.)

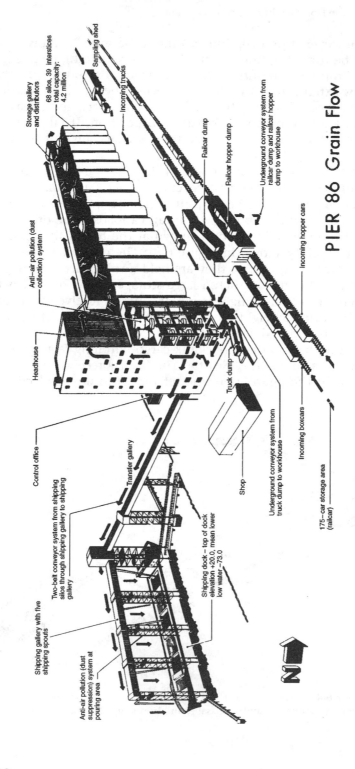

Storage gallery and distributors

68 silos, 39 interstices total capacity: 4.2 million

Sampling shed

Incoming trucks

Railcar dump

Railcar hopper dump

Underground conveyor system from railcar dump and railcar hopper dump to workhouse

Incoming hopper cars

PIER 86 Grain Flow

Anti–air pollution (dust collection) system

Headhouse

Truck dump

Control office

Transfer gallery

Shop

Incoming boxcars

Underground conveyor system from truck dump to workhouse

175–car storage area (railcar)

Two–belt conveyor system from shipping silos through shipping gallery to shipping gallery

Shipping gallery with five shipping spouts

Shipping dock – top of dock elevation +20.0, mean lower low water –73.0

Anti–air pollution (dust suppression) system at pouring area

N

Figure 6-5 Export grain elevator at the Port of Seattle. (Courtesy of Port of Seattle.)

198

suppression systems. Also note that incoming trucks have their grain sampled. The grain is graded to determine its price. (Shipments received by rail have already been graded at the initial inland elevator where they were handled, whereas most truck shipments received here are direct from the farm.)

Vehicle and Vessel Equipment Choice

Bulk cargo movements are unique in that they almost always utilize a vehicle's entire capacity. A bulk cargo shipper thinks in terms of truckloads, barge loads, railcar loads, or ship loads. Various types of equipment are used to transport and transfer bulk materials. One must think of the entire segment of the supply chain through which the cargo will pass. One equipment innovation that has replaced carriage and handling of bagged dry cargo is the use of pneumatic systems for the rapid loading and unloading of dry-cargo truck trailers, railcars, and barges. Approximately one hundred flowable commodities, such as cement, chemicals, and grains, are now carried in this type of equipment.

Many handbooks and newsletters are published to serve those attempting to match up cargoes, origins, destinations, and means of carriage. Figure 6-6 shows a page from one such handbook, *Greenwood's Guide to Great Lakes Shipping.* The page deals with self-unloading vessels. The vessel's exterior measurements are important because in many Great Lakes ports there are physical restrictions, such as narrow bridge openings, that limit the size of vessel that can reach certain docks. The vessels have several compartments (holds) that are important in shipping different grades of coal. The boom length and degrees of swing indicate how far inland the vessel can discharge. The farther inland the boom reaches, the more material can be stockpiled. Note that the vessel's allowable safe draft changes by season; this is significant if a dense cargo, such as iron ore, is being handled. *Greenwood's Guide* has similar data for shoreside facilities, indicating how large a vessel can be accommodated and the loading/unloading equipment available.

Choice of equipment is also influenced by the investment the shipper and consignee want to make. Great Lakes coal docks using self-unloaders do not have to invest in vessel unloading facilities—the vessel owner has made the investment in the conveyor and discharge system. Great Lakes vessel rates for carrying coal on self-unloaders are about 10 percent higher than for vessels that the consignee must unload. The consignee can pay that higher rate or invest in its own shore-based unloading equipment.

Another consideration with respect to bulk cargo handling deals with equipment ownership. The several handling facilities discussed in this chapter involve massive investments in fixed facilities and specialized vehicles. From a logistics management standpoint, bulk cargoes require unique, often

FIRST LINE: Fleet No. — Vessel

SECOND LINE: Cubic feet per Compartment with coal capacity shown in Net Tons

NOTE: Coal stowage factor 42 C.F. per Net Ton similar to slack coal

Fleet No. / Vessel	Size	Gross Reg. Tons	Net Reg. Tons	Keel	B.P.	O.A.	Beam	Depth	Compartments	Mid-Summer Draft	Summer Draft / Degrees Boom Can Swing Right/Left	Intermediate Draft / Type of Self-Unloader	Winter Draft / Chutes	Capacity at M.S. / Boom Length
6 Hutchinson, John T. B 16-½-24	38x11	9,775	6,964	595'0"	605'0"	620'0"	60'0"	35'0"	4	24'6"	23'11" / 120	23'0" / Conveyor	21'11" / None	14,650 / 250'
2 Jodrey, Roy A. (Can.) 18–24	#1 P & S 12 x 11; #2 2–18; 49 x 11	Can. 16,154 U.S. 13,974	11,133	603'3"	619'7"	640'6"	72'0"	40'0"	4	28'6"	27'10"	26'10" At 26'0" –Seaway—	25'7" –Seaway—	23,500 20,500
6 Kling, John A. 30–12	38x9	6,829	5,413	538'0"	546'6"	561'3"	56'3"	30'3"	7	21'1"	20'9" / 100	19'11" / Conveyor	19'0" / None	10,850 / 205'
6 Kyes, Roger M. 20-24	49'6" x 11 5-5-5-5			664'6"	664'6"	680'0"	78'0"	42'0"	4	27'6"	27'6" / 96	27'6" / Conveyor	27'6" / 30'	25,650 / 260'
35 Lakewood B 4–uneven	1–23x12 2–23x64 3–23x84 4–23x14	3,751	2,708	370'0"	377'6"	390'0"	48'0"	28'0"	4	19'5-½"	19'5-½" / 100	19'1-½" / Conveyor	18'7-½" / None	3,950 / 142'
60 Leadale (Can.) 27–12	36x9	7,073	4,701	504'0"	512'0"	524'0"	56'0"	30'0"	6	20'2"	19'9" / 120	19'2" / Conveyor	18'5" / 30'	8,950 / 200'

Second-line (cubic feet per Compartment with coal capacity in Net Tons):

- **Hutchinson, John T.:** 1) 94,070 C.F. – 2,320; 2) 171,170 C.F. – 3,870; 3) 168,390 C.F. – 3,820; 4) 135,095 C.F. – 3,070 Total: 13,080 N.T.
- **Jodrey, Roy A.:** B 1) 229,230 C.F. – 5,470; 2) 179,495 C.F. – 4,275; 3) 179,495 C.F. – 4,275; 4) 234,885 C.F. – 5,580 Total: 19,600 N.T.
- **Kling, John A.:** B 1) 58,850 C.F. – 1,400; 2) 26,950 C.F. – 670; 3) 52,800 C.F. – 1,250; 4) 64,050 C.F. – 1,500; 5) 47,200 C.F. – 1,130; 6) 58,850 C.F. – 1,400; 7) 65,500 C.F. 1,540 Total: 8,900 N.T.
- **Kyes, Roger M.:** B 1) 234,545 C.F. –5,600; 2) 227,980 C.F. –5,425; 3) 227,980 C.F. –5,425; 4) 213,930 C.F. –5,100 Total: 21,500 N.T.
- **Lakewood:** 1) 12,700 C.F. – 200; 2) 47,000 C.F. – 1,450; 3) 64,000 C.F. – 1,900, 4) 15,600 C.F. – 400 Total: 3,950 G.T. Sand or Stone
- **Leadale (Can.):** 1) 63,500 C.F. – 1,600; 2) 50,100 C.F. – 1,350; 3) 49,600 C.F. – 1,400; 4) 87,000 C.F. – 2,300; 5) 49,900 C.F. – 1,300; 6) 53,000 C.F. – 1,200 Total: 9,150 N.T.

Figure 6-6 A page from *Greenwood's Guide to Great Lakes Shipping*. (Reproduced by permission from *Greenwood's Guide to Great Lakes Shipping*, Freshwater Press, Inc., 1975.)

custom-built handling facilities, and there is always uncertainty as to who should provide them—the buyer, the seller, or a third party.

A marketing problem may be that a specialized unloading device will pay for itself only if a specified number of customers install a new type of receiving equipment. What kinds of financial incentives should the seller offer so that customers will install the new receiving equipment? What types of long-term commitments must each party make to the other to ensure a necessary return from the required investment? An example of this situation comes from the food industry, where liquid egg distributors supply the contents of shelled eggs or egg-base concentrates to food processors, commercial bakeries, and institutional food service industries. Because eggs in the shell have unfavorable transportation characteristics, a truck carrying the eggs' contents after they are shelled can carry about twice as much weight in the same space as a truck carrying eggs in conventional cartons. The supplier must invest in an egg-breaking machine located near the egg farms, as well as in trucks with refrigerated tank trailers that can pump out their own contents. Sanitation is important and must be maintained. The customers' investments are in one or more tanks to receive the yolks, the egg whites, or a mixture of both. Even without knowing the quantities or the costs involved, it is clear that quite a few calculations would have to be made and numerous alternatives considered.

Some liquid cargoes are heated so that they will flow more easily. Sometimes the heating equipment is at the shipping point, and sometimes the heavily insulated truck, railcar, or barge also carries its own heating system to maintain a high temperature. A common example is trucks that haul liquid asphalt at over 400 degrees Fahrenheit directly to construction sites. Careful calculations must be made of the time distance of the haul and the outdoor temperatures to determine the temperature to which the cargo should be heated.

PROJECT CARGO

Recurring shipments usually lend themselves to logistics analysis that results in either lower-cost shipments or a more efficient method of handling the shipment or both. In some industries, however, each movement is so unique and so difficult that a specialized engineering-logistics study is needed to determine how the move should be accomplished. Examples are the delivery of generators to dam sites and of oilfield and pipeline materials to Prudhoe Bay in northern Alaska. The phrase **project cargo** describes these one-of-a-kind movements.

One of the most spectacular project moves occurred during the late 1970s, when two specially designed Japanese barges were used to tow two halves of a woodpulp-processing plant, built in Japan, to a site in Brazil's Amazon River basin. Two barges were built in the Japanese yard, and then the pulp plant and the accompanying power plant were built on top of each. Very careful attention was paid to determining how the weight of the pulp and power plants would be distributed on their respective barges. The plants were then towed by tugs the entire way to a site on the Jari River in Brazil that had been partially enclosed by a dike. At the places inside the diked area where the plants were destined to be placed, wooden pilings had been driven into the bottom. When the two barges with the plants arrived, they were towed inside the diked area and moored next to the pilings. The dike was then extended to enclose the area completely, and water was pumped in to raise the barges. The barges were floated directly above the piles and the water was drained, so the barges holding the two plants were then resting on top of the piles. Windows were cut in the sides of the barges, and the barges became the lower floors of the pulp and power plants. It was estimated that construction costs were reduced by 20 percent and that two years were saved by having the plant built in Japan and towed to Brazil rather than having it constructed at the Brazilian site.[9]

Another example of a project cargo occurred in 1991, when a U.S. engineering firm, the Bechtel Group, organized and orchestrated the movement of 200,000 tons of cargo to fight the oilwell fires in Kuwait after the Persian Gulf War:

> From April through [the] fall [of 1991], Bechtel collected about 8,000 pieces of construction equipment, including bulldozers, cranes, computers, and ambulances. It also dispatched everything from terrycloth towels for mopping up the sticky crude to fire-resistant underwear for the crews who were fighting the 2,000-degree blaze.[10]

OVERSIZED MOVES

Sometimes a product, such as a machine, is assembled at the factory to make sure that it functions, and then is disassembled for shipment because it is too large for any one type of carrier to deliver. Therefore it is delivered in pieces and reassembled at the site. Clearly there can be savings if the amount of disassembly and reassembly involved can be reduced. Therefore, studies have to be made of shipping routes and procedures that will accommodate shipments with unusual dimensions.

---

[9] "Shipbuilder in Japan Delivers Completed Pulp Plant to Brazil," *Surveyor,* May 1978, pp. 14–18.

[10] *San Francisco Chronicle,* November 4, 1991, p. B1.

High-weight trucks are sometimes used. Heavy dollies, which are additional axles, are placed under the load so that less weight is exerted on each axle. When passing over a bridge of limited capacity, the dollies must be spaced sufficiently far apart that no more than the allowable weight is on the bridge at any one time. Once the bridge is crossed, the load is stopped, and the dollies are placed closer together again to make it easier to negotiate curves. Special permits and escort vehicles are required, and police might keep other traffic off the road. Highway engineers along the route determine the maximum allowable load. If bituminous pavement is involved, the move may be restricted to cooler times of the year or day since the cooler pavement is less likely to be permanently marked by the tires of the dollies. Equipment such as this can carry loads of 500 or more tons, if enough dollies are used.

Weight is only one limitation of special moves. There also may be height restrictions, such as electric wires (which can be moved) or tunnels (which cannot). Modular housing (prebuilt structures that are transported to home sites) is not especially heavy, but it tends to be large. A study regarding industrial sites for manufacturing the modules noted that

> because the housing modules themselves are high and wide, access from the plant to the market areas both by over-the-road and rail becomes a critical portion of the investigation. Access to the Interstate System is of absolute necessity. And siding needs for outbound shipment from the plants are vastly different than for ordinary industrial sites. When going by rail, the modules will travel on long cars and in trainload lots. Minimum curvatures of about 400 feet and accessible siding lengths of about 250 feet are required.[11]

Curvature of the road or steepness of grade imposes still other limitations. The move must be carefully analyzed by individuals who are familiar with both the transportation complexities and the equipment being moved. Allowable highway widths have been increased from 96 to 102 inches, making it possible for truck trailers and buses to be built wider. Other products shipped on highways can also now be built wider, an example being trailered boats. Some railroad tunnels are being raised, mainly to accommodate double-stack container trains. Other high cargo will also benefit.

Figure 6-7 is an information sheet issued by one railroad to indicate the weight of loaded railcars that can be handled on various tracks within its system. The same carrier also issues sheets that indicate height limitations throughout its entire system.

[11] Carl J. Liba, "The Transportation Market Potential in Modular Housing," in *Proceedings of the Sixty-second Annual Meeting of the American Railway Development Association* (ARDA, 1971), pp. 27–32.

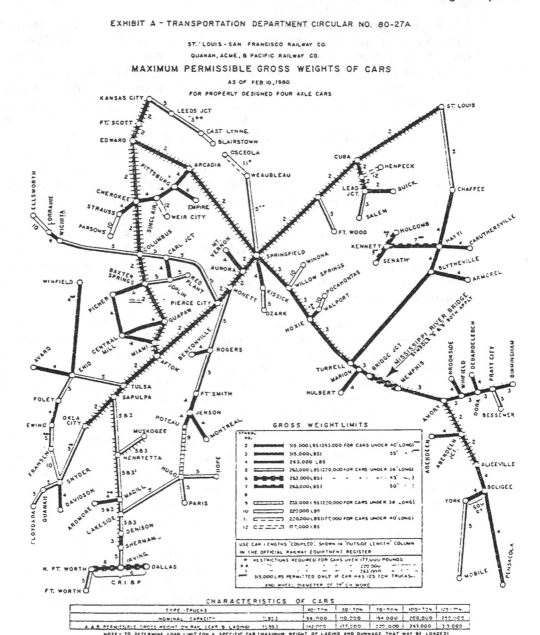

Figure 6-7 Railroad weight limits. (Courtesy of Burlington Northern Railroad.)

HAZARDOUS MATERIALS

Hazardous materials have the potential of endangering the carrier's equipment, other products, people, and the environment. While they can go on any mode of transport, they are subject to many restrictions. They usually move in very special dedicated or shipper-owned equipment. Railroads seem to haul more than their share of hazardous materials. This is because of their equipment, their routes, and their relatively low incidence of accidents.

Both state and federal regulations cover the movement of hazardous materials. For example, in late 1994 the National Park Service banned commercial vehicles carrying hazardous materials from using the twenty-two miles of U.S. Highway 191 that passes through Yellowstone National Park.[12] Employee training programs, special packaging, and marking is often required. Readers have seen the diamond placards on the sides of trucks.

COMPARISON OF MODES

We have surveyed the essential operating characteristics of each transportation alternative available to the user. Every logistics manager must decide which transportation mix will best meet the company's objectives. Earlier editions of this book compared modes in terms of speed, dependability, rates, fuel efficiency, and so on, and also reported the results of surveys as to which service features appealed most to traffic managers making the choice of modes. Such comparisons are less relevant today. This is for three reasons.

The first is intermodalism, which has already been discussed. An intermodal carrier can combine the various service and cost aspects of several modes in order to offer the mix desired by the shipper.

Second, negotiated contracts between carriers and shippers are now widely used. Through negotiations the shipper can express exactly what it does or does not want and can expect to see this reflected in the final bottom-line price it must pay.

Third, carriers are no longer constrained with respect to the variety of services they may offer. Professor J. R. Stock notes:

> Before deregulation, the purchase of transportation was a fairly straightforward corporate decision because of regulated pricing and service controls. After deregulation some carriers not wishing to become a part of an undifferentiated market with only price as a competitive variable, developed strategies to distinguish themselves from others.[13]

Stock goes on to describe how some carrier firms provide services allowing shippers access to the carrier's computers to track freight, give shippers

[12] *Transport Topics,* September 26, 1994, p. 22.

[13] James R. Stock, "The Maturing of Transportation: An Expanded Role for Freight Carriers," *Journal of Business Logistics,* September 1988, pp. 15–16.

monthly analyses of their flows of freight, manage shippers' inventories, and provide warehousing. These additional services help the carrier form strategic alliances with its customers.

Having said this, we will make some broad comparisons to emphasize that there are still some differences. Using current national transportation data, one can compare, in rough terms, the intercity revenues and ton-miles carried by each mode to get an idea as to the relative costs per ton-mile. (A **ton-mile** is one ton of freight carried one mile.) Pipeline costs are about 1.3 cents per ton-mile, with water being a close second, at 1.7 cents per ton-mile. Rail costs are about twice as high, 2.9 cents per ton-mile. Truck costs are over ten times higher, or 36 cents per ton-mile, while air freight is 89 cents per ton-mile.

Differences in speed are obvious, with air being the fastest, and water or pipeline being the slowest. One reason that water transport is slow is that many navigation routes are circuitous. For short hauls, truck is faster than rail. For longer hauls, truck and rail are more evenly matched, although the truck must have more than one driver. A railroad that wants the speed advantage in a certain market can obtain it by assigning high priority to that specific train.

On-time delivery is often used as a criterion. The air express services and some truckers probably have the best records. Weather does affect all modes except pipelines. Water transportation in the north shuts down completely during winter months. A bad snowstorm can bring air, truck, and rail traffic to a halt. Flooding is another disaster that can interfere with transport operations. During the floods on the Mississippi River in 1993, impacts were significant. Portions of the Mississippi, Missouri, and Illinois Rivers, totaling 1,600 miles, were closed to barge navigation for lengths of time ranging from ten to forty-five days. At least one lock on the Mississippi was closed for a duration of fifty-two days, thereby blocking use of the entire river. Grain exports from New Orleans declined during this period because of the drop in barge deliveries. About 3,800 miles of rail line were shut down, and over 1,000 trains were rerouted, with delays of up to five days for some freight cars. There were many highway closures, especially in Missouri, and long detours became common. Finally, thirty-four small airports were closed.[14] In this disaster, barges were interrupted the most, then rail, and then truck.

In a benchmarking study of several modes performed for the Council of Logistics Management by Anderson Consulting, shippers were asked to rate the carriers by several criteria using a scale of 4 (outstanding) to 1 (below average). Here is a portion of the findings, using criteria that have not been discussed to this point:

[14] *Transportation Statistics, Annual Report 1994* (Washington, D. C.: U.S. Department of Transportation, 1994), pp. 90–98.

- Level of communication: LTL, 2.63; truckload, 2.57; intermodal, 2.25; rail, 2.08; and parcel, 2.20
- Ability to handle volume peaks: LTL, 2.99; truckload, 2.88; parcel, 2.62; intermodal, 2.61; and rail, 2.32
- Geographic coverage: parcel, 3.21; LTL, 3.10; truckload, 3.07; intermodal, 2.37; and rail, 2.34
- Availability of carrier executives: LTL, 2.82; truckload, 2.49; rail, 2.37; intermodal, 2.14; parcel, 1.73
- Responsiveness of operations: truckload, 2.93; LTL, 2.71; intermodal, 2.45; railroads, 2.11, and parcel carriers, 1.87 [15]

TRANSPORTATION REGULATION AND DEREGULATION

For many years most of the nation's transportation service was subject to economic regulation, meaning that the services offered and rates charged were subject to approval by a government agency. This applied to both interstate and intrastate movements. Carriers were allowed to operate as monopolists or oligopolists and in return assumed the **common carrier** obligation. The common carrier has four specific obligations: to serve, to deliver, to charge reasonable rates, and to avoid discrimination. These obligations date to English common law.

Beginning in the late 1970s, various sectors of the transportation industry were deregulated. This move has continued into the 1990s. As of January 1, 1995, the federal government eliminated state economic regulation of motor carriers; this ban removed regulations that about forty states were still enforcing. Some carriers are still subject to economic regulation. They include

- railroad service to captive shippers, i.e., those that have no viable alternative means of transport (the most common example being mines and coal-burning electricity-generating plants)
- household goods movers
- many petroleum pipelines
- many natural gas pipelines
- some inland waterway traffic
- some water transport and some joint motor-water transport between the mainland and Hawaii, Puerto Rico, and Alaska

Today's traffic manager must be able to operate in both the deregulated and regulated transportation environments. There are also numerous regulations

---

[15] *Purchasing*, January 16, 1992, p. 111.

by all levels of governments regarding vehicle operations, dimensions, and the safety of operators and the general public.

The existing structure of the nation's transportation industry was heavily influenced by regulation and by deregulation. Many of its problems are also blamed on either regulation, deregulation, or both. A troubling series of court cases in the early and middle 1990s undermined some of the steps that had been taken toward deregulation. In what is referred to as the Maislin case, a trucking firm had gone bankrupt; its trustees in bankruptcy then filed claims against former shippers with whom the carrier had contracted to carry goods, because the rates agreed to in the contracts were less than those on file with the Interstate Commerce Commission (ICC). The issue went to the Supreme Court, which decided in favor of the bankruptcy trustees; that is, the rates on file with the ICC were the ones to be used. The ruling left many shippers vulnerable. Attempts at legislative relief were blocked by Teamster opposition, since many of the bankrupt trucking firms owed money to the Teamsters' pension fund, and the Teamsters wanted to see the shippers pay so that some of this money would go into their pensions. A law providing relief was enacted, but the matter still remains in the courts. Tens of thousands of shippers remain potentially liable.[16]

TRANSPORTATION RATES

Transportation rates are complex, and the structures employed date to the time of regulation, when rate bureaus (committees of carriers) would establish rates subject to the approval of some state or federal regulatory agency. The rate structure deals with three different factors:

- Relationships between different products, in terms of their handling characteristics, for example, the difference between carrying 2,000 pounds of ballpoint pens and 2,000 pounds of live chickens
- Relationships between shipments of different weights, for example, shipments of 1 pound each, 100 pounds each, or 100,000 pounds each
- Relationships between different distances the products are carried, for example, from Boston to Albany or from Atlanta to Spokane

Ratemaking has to define all three relations in numeric form, and then has to devise methods of typing those numbers into a rate of so many cents per hundredweight (CWT) for a specific haul. The three relationships mentioned above are of continual importance to the logistics manager because if they can be altered, the total transportation charges will be lowered. With respect

---

[16] The campus bookstore at the school of one of the authors paid $6,000 to settle a claim by trustees of a bankrupt carrier.

to handling characteristics, density is especially important. Waste baskets that are perfect cylinders will cost more to ship than wastebaskets that have a tapered shape and can be packed with one partially inside the other (known as **nesting**). Freight consolidation means assembling many small shipments so that one large shipment can be tendered to the carrier. Distances are also significant: It almost always costs more to ship a product for a longer distance.

While many rates today are negotiated between carriers and shippers, the rate structures and the common carrier obligation are both referred to in the negotiation process. Often they are points of departure from which negotiations begin. An understanding of traditional freight rate determination is still necessary. The reason is that carriers, as they compete, often quote prices in terms of percentage discounts from existing, or published, rates.

What follows is a discussion of traditional railroad class rate determination. Class rates are standard rates that can be found for almost all products or commodities shipped. These rates are found with the help of a classification tariff. This tariff gives each shipment a rating, or class, ranging from 400 to 13 in the widely used *Uniform Freight Classification (UFC)*. It contains thirty-one separate ratings, or classes, and is used extensively by the railroads and many truckers and water carriers. The other widely used classification tariff is the *National Motor Freight Classification (NMFC)*, which has ratings, or classes, from 500 to 35, with twenty-three separate ratings. The higher the rating, the greater the relative charge for transporting the commodity. A multitude of factors are involved in determining a product's specific class or rating. However, the ICC in recent years has stated that the following four factors should be primary inputs to determine a **freight classification:** (1) density of the product (how heavy it is in relationship to its size), (2) stowability (how easy it is to pack into a load), (3) ease or difficulty of handling, and (4) liability to damage and theft. The last factor is also related to the value of the product; in 1990 motor freight Class 50 had a maximum average value per pound of $0.71; Class 100, $17.82; Class 200, $35.65; and Class 400, $71.29.[17] Motor carrier classification numbers are established by the National Motor Freight Traffic Association, a group representing trucking firms. Classification numbers are very important since they are code words that describe cargo in a manner that carriers and shippers understand.

Once the commodity rating, or class, is determined, it is necessary to establish the rate bases number from the applicable tariff. This number is the approximate distance between the cities of origin and destination. With the

[17] Ray Bohman, quoted in *Traffic Management,* April 1991, p. 25. Of the four factors influencing classification, Bohman considers density to be the most important.

commodity rating and the rate bases number, the specific rate per hundred pounds can be located in another tariff. Finally, to establish the specific cost of moving commodity A between City B and City C, one must use the following formula:

Weight (in hundred-pound units) × rate (per hundred pounds) = charge

An example will help to clarify this. Assume that a professor of archaeology is retiring and moving from Sioux Falls, South Dakota, to Hannibal, Missouri. He has collected 30,000 pounds of bones during his long career. He wants to use railroads since his shipment is in no particular hurry. To establish the rating (class), it is necessary for him first to find the commodity in the *UFC* index. Figure 6-8 contains the page from the index that contains human bones. Note that the letters *noibn* follow human bones. This stands for "not otherwise indexed by name." We are referred to item number 13350. Figure 6-9 is the page in the *UFC* that contains item number 13350. This tariff also specifies how the human bones are to be packaged for presentation to the carrier. (This is important for all products: The classification *dictates* how products must be packaged.) On the right-hand edge of Figure 6-9 are the appropriate ratings, or classes. The first rating of 200 is the less than carload (LCL) rating. Then it states that if 20,000 or more pounds are tendered to the carrier, the carload (CL) rating is 100. Because this shipment involves 30,000 pounds, the CL rating of 100 will be used. The next requirement is to determine the rate bases number. Figure 6-10 illustrates a typical tariff page containing this information. The appropriate rate bases number between Sioux Falls, South Dakota, and Hannibal, Missouri, is 448. Finally, it is necessary to establish the specific rate per hundred pounds. Figure 6-11 contains a tariff page that uses the rating (class) and rate bases number to determine the rate, which is $3.07 in this example. The total charge can now be determined using this formula:

Rate (per hundred pounds) × weight (in hundred-pound units) = charge

or

$$\$3.07 \times 300 = \$921$$

Computerization of Freight Rates and Tariffs

One of the most dismal problems of the U.S. transportation system since World War II was the enormousness and complexity of its rate structure. So complex (and frequently illogical) is the system that it was once believed impossible to computerize. This meant that a shipper's traffic department was the last bastion in the firm to resist the time-saving advances that computers were providing to all other aspects of business enterprise.

UNIFORM FREIGHT CLASSIFICATION 7

INDEX TO ARTICLES

STCC No.	Article	Item	STCC No.	Article	Item
	Hulls₋Concluded:			Huskers₋Concluded:	
20 914 45	Cottonseed,mixed with meal	37130	35 225 23	Corn,and fodder shredders, combined,ot hand, SU	3370,†4050
20 914 25	Cottonseed,not ground	31250,†31270	34 236 79	Corn,hand (husking gloves)	36260
20 939 46	Fleaseed (psyllium)	33800,80090	35 225 60	Corn,noibn,ot hand, KD	3360,†4050
34 412 15	Launch,steel	11690	35 225 59	Corn,noibn,ot hand,SU, on wheels	3360,†4050
37 329 12	Launch,wooden,in the white, KD	11490	35 227 30	Green corn	62530
37 329 13	Launch,wooden,in the white, SU	11490	34 236 79	Husking gloves,corn (corn huskers)	36260
20 939 55	Nut,noibn	86140	34 236 80	Husking pins	36500
20 418 30	Oat	47110	01 199 30	Husks,corn (shucks)	37350
20 999 25	Peanut,crushed or ground	37530	33 219 16	Hydrants,or sections	29520
20 939 20	Peanut,not crushed nor ground	37540	28 311 51	Hydrastis canadensis (golden seal) roots,ground or powdered	33590,33800
20 939 46	Psyllium seed (fleaseed)	33800,80090	01 915 13	Hydrastis canadensis (golden seal) roots, not ground nor powdered	33620,33800
20 449 15	Rice,ground and rice bran, feed	37580	35 329 10	Hydraulic accumulators,mining, ore milling or smelting	63480
20 449 20	Rice,ground,feed	37590	32 411 15	Hydraulic cement	21680,†77130
20 449 25	Rice,unground (rice chaff), feed	37600	35 999 16	Hydraulic cylinders,ot rotary,steel	60780
09 131 55	Shrimp	δ	35 691 45	Hydraulic rams	†61240,64890
20 923 16	Soybean,ground	37640	35 329 10	Hydraulic rotary swivels,oil, water or gas well	72070
20 923 17	Soybean,not ground	37640	29 912 10	Hydraulic system fluid,ot, petroleum	14690
20 939 56	Sunflower seed	83440		Hydraulic wheel presses	†66800
20 939 27	Tung nut	52790	34 434 38	Hydro-pneumatic tanks,copper, cylindrical closed at both ends	89040
20 939 64	Velvet bean,ground	95550	34 434 40	Hydro-pneumatic tanks,silicon bronze,cylindrical,closed at both ends	89050
20 939 66	Velvet bean,not ground	95560			
28 311 21	Human blood,liquid,frozen or chilled	11355	34 434 42	Hydro-pneumatic tanks,steel,14 gauge or thicker,cylindrical, closed at both ends	89060
39 998 21	Human bones,noibn	13350	38 213 15	Hydrobarometers	32990
39 994 10	Human hair	48320	28 139 92	Hydrocarbon gas,noibn	45630
39 994 20	Human hair goods,noibn	48390	35 599 78	Hydrocarbon recovery systems	δ
39 994 15	Human hair samples,mounted on cardboard	48360	28 194 50	Hydrochloric (muraitic) acid	2340,33800
40 291 47	Human hair waste,not stumps nor combed hair	95490	28 194 34	Hydrocyanic acid	2260
	Humidifiers:		28 194 42	Hydrofluoric and sulphuric acid, mixed	2280,33800
41 111 10	Air and blowers or fans combined, mounted on freight automobile	73400	28 194 38	Hydrofluoric acid	2270,33800
35 857 20	Air and blowers or fans combined, noibn	†30450,58510	40 251 65	Hydrofluoric acid waste, aqueous	δ
35 857 45	Air bakers',cast iron	†58610,†58720	28 194 46	Hydrofluosilicic acid	2290,33800
37 142 12	Coolers and filters,air, automobile,non-electric	8125	28 139 20	Hydrogen bromide,anhydrous, liquefied	45410
34 336 49	Hot air house heating furnace,automatic	12700	28 139 22	Hydrogen chloride,anhydrous, liquefied	45420
34 299 30	Humidors,ot display	52800	28 199 31	Hydrogen dioxide	24020,33800
14 917 15	Humus	27320	28 134 60	Hydrogen gas	45640
33 992 50	Hungarian nails,noibn,brass, bronze or copper	†49771,50810	28 199 31	Hydrogen peroxide	24020,33800
33 152 25	Hungarian nails,noibn,steel,with ot steel or zinc heads	†49781,50820	28 139 46	Hydrogen sulphide	45650
33 152 30	Hungarian nails,noibn,steel, with steel heads	†49781,50830	20 469 10	Hydrol (corn,sorghum grain or wheat sugar final molasses)	37360
33 152 35	Hungarian nails,noibn,steel, with zinc heads	†49781,50840	38 219 14	Hydrometers	33000
	Hurdles,track,steel with wooden cross bars, noibn	7580	28 186 20	Hydroxy acetic acid	2300,33800
	Hurdles,track steel with wooden cross bars,uprights folded to base,or SU nstd, in nests of five or more	7580	40 251 62	Hydroxy aldehydes,waste, containing not less than 40% water	96090
22 995 73	Hurds,hemp or ramie	52810	28 612 20	Hypernic extracts,dry	35860
35 225 29	Huskers and pickers combined, corn	3390,†4050	28 612 21	Hypernic extracts,liquid or paste	35870
35 225 61	Huskers and shellers,combined, corn,ot hand	3380,†4050	40 291 57	Hypo-mud,photo silver	95720
	Huskers:				
35 225 24	Corn and fodder shredders, combined,ot hand,KD	3370,†4050			

Figure 6-8 Index page from freight classification. (Reproduced by permission of tariff publisher.)

Fortunately, things have changed. Considerable progress has been made to render carrier and rate bureau tariffs into a form that computers can accommodate. In general terms, the industry is revising its description of commodity items, its listing of routes and junctions, and its listing of

Item	ARTICLES	Less Carload Ratings	Carload Minimum (Pounds)	Carload Ratings
	BOILERS, FURNACES, RADIATORS, STOVES, RELATED ARTICLES OR PARTS NAMED (Subject to Item 11960)—Concluded:			
	Group No. 1			
13250	Coal hods (scuttles) or vases, steel; cookers or steamers, stock feed, noibn; furnaces, house heating, hot air, with or without equipment of air conditioning apparatus or thermostats; griddles, kettles, pots, skillets or spiders, sheet steel; holloware, cast iron, as described in Item 49880; house heating furnace casing parts; sugar or syrup evaporator kettles, iron; stove or range cabinets, closets or high shelves, steel; stove or range ovens; stove or range parts, iron or steel, other than castings, noibn; stove pipe drums or drum ovens; stove pipe or elbows, sheet iron, steel or tin plate, side seams closed; stove pipe thimbles, plate or sheet iron or steel or tin plate, side seams closed; stove or range reservoirs or reservoir attachments; tee joints and draft regulators combined, stove pipe.			
	Group No. 2			
13260	Air registers, noibn, including air louvres, iron or steel; andirons, iron; ash scrapers; heating furnace pipe or elbows, sheet iron, steel or tin plate; house heating furnace castings, iron; burners, gas, for coal, oil or wood stoves, see Note 58, Item 13271; oil burning outfits for brooders or coal or wood stoves; pans, baking, dripping or frying, sheet steel; fire pokers, iron; sad irons, with or without stands, other than self-heating; stove boards, iron or metal clad wood or fibreboard; stove cover lifters, iron; stove or range castings, iron; stove pipe, sheet iron, steel or tin plate, side seams not closed, nested; dampers, noibn, iron; stove pipe thimbles, cast iron or plate or sheet iron or tin plate, side seams not closed, nested; stove shovels, sheet steel; water heaters, noibn			
13261	Note 52.—Weight of articles in Group 2, Item 13260, must not exceed 50% of weight upon which charges are assessed.			
13265	Mixed CL of two or more of the following articles, viz.: Stoves or ranges, iron or steel; dampers, noibn, iron; electric logs, see Note 54, Item 13266; fireplace grates or grate baskets, with or without heating units; fireplace grate parts, noibn; gas logs; heaters, gas, with or without clay radiants; andirons (fire dogs); fenders or fireplace guards or screens, brass, see Note 54, Item 13266; fenders or fireplace guards or screens, iron or steel, plain or brass coated or plated, or with brass trimming; fireplace sets (shovels and tongs), with or without hearth brushes, holders or pokers, brass or brass and iron combined, see Note 54, Item 13266; fireplace sets (shovels and tongs), with or without hearth brushes, holders or pokers, iron; lighters, fire, brass or iron, see Note 54, Item 13266; or wood holders or racks, fireplace, see Note 54, Item 13266.	....	24,000R	45
13266	Note 54.—Aggregate weight of articles subject to this note must not exceed 50% of weight upon which charges are assessed.			
13267	Note 55.—Section 2 of Rule 34 is not applicable.			
13270	Superheaters, other than locomotive:			
	SU, loose or in packages	70	24,000R	40
	KD, or superheater parts, KD, loose or in packages	65	24,000R	40
13271	Note 58.—Ratings apply only on burners for converting coal, oil or wood stoves into gas stoves.			
13272	Note 60.—Weight of articles subject to this note shall not exceed 10% of weight upon which charges are assessed.			
13280	Tanks, oil stove, sheet steel, 26 gauge or thicker, capacity not exceeding 5 gallons, in boxes or crates	110	16,000R	60
13281	Note 66.—Ratings also apply on stoves or ranges designed for separate permanent installation of oven and surface cooking units.			
13282	Note 68.—CL ratings will include iron or steel garbage or offal incinerators, not exceeding 25% of the weight upon which freight charges are assessed.			
13295	Bolster rolls for beds, couches or lounges, fibreboard with plywood ends and reinforcing ribs, upholstered, in Package 9F	150	10,000R	100
12300	Bolster rolls for beds, couches or lounges, noibn, in boxes or crates	200	10,000R	100
13310	Bone, charred filtering (animal charcoal), other than spent, in bags or barrels	70	36,000	35
13320	Bone, charred filtering (animal charcoal), spent, in bags	50	40,000	20
13330	Bone, charred filtering, synthetic, in bags or barrels	70	36,000	35
13340	Bone ash, in bags, barrels or boxes	55	36,000	30
13350	Bones, human, noibn, prepaid, in barrels or boxes	200	20,000R	100
13360	Bones, noibn, ground or not ground, LCL, in bags or barrels, or in barrels with cloth tops; CL, loose or in packages	50	40,000	22½
13370	Book ends, moulded wood or plaster, in boxes	85	24,000R	55
13380	Book stacks, library, consisting of iron brackets, floor framing, stairs, railings, standards, and shelves, in packages; also CL, loose	70	36,000	40
13390	Boot or shoe arch supports or arch support insoles, in boxes	100	20,000R	70
13400	Boot or shoe forms or trees, in barrels or boxes	85	20,000R	55
13410	BOOTS, SHOES, OR BOOT OR SHOE FINDINGS:			
13420	Boot or shoe findings, noibn, in bales, barrels or boxes, or in barrels with cloth tops	100	16,000R	70
13430	Boots or shoes, noibn, see Note 1, item 13431, in boxes; in trunks in crates; in salesmen's sample trunks, locked; in Packages 277 or 1197; also in straight CL in Package 1126	100	24,000R	70
13431	Note 1.—Ratings also apply on Huaraches (Mexican leather sandals) in bamboo baskets or hampers, tops securely closed.			
13440	Boots or shoes, old, used, leather, having value other than for reclamation of raw materials, prepaid, see Note 2, Item 13441, in packages; also CL, loose	85	36,000	50
13441	Note 2.—Old used shoes rebuilt or repaired, will be rated as shoes, noibn.			
13450	Boots or shoes, plastic, rubber or rubber and canvas, felt or wool combined, in bales or boxes	100	15,000R	70
13460	Boots or shoes, wooden or leather with wooden soles, in packages	92½	24,000R	65
13470	Box toe boards, in packages; also CL, loose	70	36,000	35

Figure 6-9   Page showing classification of articles. (Reproduced by permission of tariff publisher.)

Freight Tariff No. W-1000

APPLICATION OF RATE BASES

BETWEEN (See Item 100)

AND (See Item 100)

RATE BASES APPLICABLE

BETWEEN / AND		Greeley Centre, Neb.	Green Bay, Wis.	Greenbush, Minn.	Granville, S.D.	Grinnell, Iowa	Grover, Colo.	Hallock, Minn.	Hannaford, N.D.	Hannibal, Mo.	Harvard, Ill.	Harwarden, Iowa	Hartun, Colo.	Hays, Kan.	Hasen, N.D.	Herington, Kan.	Hermansville, Mich.	Hermosa, S.D.	Herreid, S.D.	Hettinger, N.D.	Hibbing, Minn.
Rugby	N.D.	716	716	233	340	680	944	202	128	855	768	465	914	939	306	825	687	609	714	461	372
Rulo	Neb.	240	619	712	627	237	846	718	621	251	477	244	438	318	699	179	715	619	347	669	636
Russell	Kan.	335	844	919	834	479	474	925	828	457	606	451	482	27	906	121	941	695	506	875	868
St. Cloud	Minn.	489	350	262	223	317	828	287	241	495	401	250	737	712	433	596	367	558	487	461	193
St. Francis	Kan.	309	918	935	850	568	502	941	844	620	809	467	363	363	922	332	985	646	487	892	884
St. Ignace	Mich.	937	256	681	735	619	1277	713	722	659	392	713	1186	1098	914	959	166	1064	935	966	477
St. James	Minn.	358	380	430	345	220	697	436	363	408	388	133	607	581	488	465	414	498	356	457	314
St. Joseph	Mo.	281	579	737	652	213	587	743	646	207	437	269	479	293	724	154	676	657	383	694	614
St. Louis	Mo.	583	458	854	812	303	890	880	833	⊕	⊕	545	783	561	983	414	553	940	668	952	719
Sabetha	Kan.	223	640	740	655	273	524	747	649	267	498	272	414	277	727	155	736	604	349	697	666
Sabula	Iowa	492	246	639	597	146	832	665	618	⊕	⊕	364	741	625	792	486	343	756	572	762	504
Sac City	Iowa	250	464	545	460	143	589	552	472	317	362	115	499	462	561	347	540	510	302	530	442
Salem	S.D.	330	539	456	359	313	670	442	304	488	512	76	579	553	383	438	572	340	328	352	437
Salina	Kan.	258	767	842	757	402	526	848	751	380	619	374	405	104	829	44	864	618	429	798	791
Salisbury	Mo.	412	515	778	734	201	720	804	757	91	362	383	612	393	838	253	611	771	497	808	649
Sanborn	Minn.	376	407	396	311	238	715	402	329	427	415	151	625	599	454	483	430	470	374	423	325
Sanish	N.D.	793	817	368	428	768	962	336	247	942	871	543	933	1016	227	901	815	628	791	447	506
Sargent	Neb.	102	750	766	681	408	475	773	675	530	641	298	389	406	754	308	816	538	314	723	716
Sauk Centre	Minn.	517	392	234	181	359	857	254	199	537	443	279	766	740	391	625	409	546	515	419	228
Sault Ste Marie	Mich.	955	273	685	739	664	1294	717	726	708	452	730	1203	1144	767	1161	184	1082	953	984	481
Sawyer	Kan.	405	872	987	903	522	656	994	897	480	719	520	552	210	975	158	968	765	576	944	923
Schley	Minn.	648	427	146	276	476	988	178	258	654	518	409	897	871	450	756	399	670	646	522	82
Scott City	Kan.	461	959	1044	959	594	437	1051	953	572	811	576	486	244	1032	228	1055	726	632	1001	993
Scottsbluff	Neb.	365	980	897	804	638	175	883	746	729	871	529	145	565	765	467	1046	222	544	735	946
Sedalia	Colo.	490	1105	1095	1001	762	130	1081	943	832	996	554	180	361	963	505	1171	420	669	932	1071
Sedalia	Mo.	413	568	831	787	254	709	857	792	144	415	415	603	371	870	224	664	794	529	840	702
Seney	Mich.	891	210	605	660	601	1231	637	646	644	388	667	1140	1080	838	941	120	1012	889	906	401
Severy	Kan.	375	757	920	835	410	643	926	829	364	605	452	522	231	907	141	854	735	521	877	811
Sharon Springs	Kan.	355	965	082	897	608	317	988	891	623	851	514	366	140	969	287	1031	606	534	938	931
Shawano	Wis.	690	38	553	544	403	1030	585	570	447	190	498	939	882	956	743	107	860	721	763	351
Shawnee	Wyo.	479	1023	864	771	231	165	850	677	843	948	539	259	612	732	581	1056	190	575	702	940
Sheboygan	Wis.	700	63	613	604	356	1040	645	631	397	129	522	949	835	817	696	159	905	745	822	411
Sheldon	Ill.	653	275	802	760	304	986	828	781	⊕	⊕	533	881	717	962	578	372	925	738	931	601
Sheldon	Iowa	267	471	464	379	216	607	471	392	395	415	43	516	490	480	375	505	429	265	449	404
Shenandoah	Iowa	218	531	657	572	189	547	663	566	268	429	189	441	383	644	243	556	577	303	614	562
Sheridan Lake	Colo.	536	1034	1120	1035	669	361	1126	1029	647	886	652	411	319	1107	303	1131	651	707	1077	1069
Sidney	Neb.	328	943	906	813	601	102	894	757	691	834	492	73	504	776	429	1009	233	507	746	909
Simpson (Johnson Co.)	Ill.	733	522	995	953	446	1040	1021	974	⊕	⊕	686	933	711	1123	564	649	1081	818	1093	835
Sioux City	Iowa	211	527	512	427	236	550	518	421	398	453	44	459	434	499	318	561	444	209	468	461
Sioux Falls	S.D.	299	499	437	340	273	639	444	337	448	473	46	548	522	422	407	533	380	297	392	397
Bisseton	S.D.	537	503	318	193	439	831	304	230	627	552	284	786	760	385	645	521	496	535	354	370
Smithboro	Ill.	625	432	858	816	309	932	884	837	⊕	⊕	549	825	604	987	464	528	944	705	956	711
South Beloit	Ill.	588	150	634	592	242	928	660	613	⊕	⊕	433	837	721	805	581	247	819	653	802	434
Sparta	Ill.	637	490	908	866	359	944	934	887	⊕	⊕	599	837	607	1036	460	587	994	732	1006	769
Spencer	Iowa	303	443	500	415	180	643	507	428	359	379	79	552	527	516	411	486	465	302	486	386
Spooner	Wis.	570	253	353	379	473	909	385	394	510	328	345	818	786	586	659	247	697	568	599	149
Springfield	Ill.	580	369	794	752	261	894	820	773	⊕	⊕	501	786	584	938	445	466	895	665	908	642
Stafford	Kan.	360	841	942	858	479	568	949	852	449	688	475	507	165	930	113	937	720	531	899	880
Stanley	N.D.	795	804	348	419	759	1023	317	214	934	856	544	993	1018	315	903	799	668	793	535	486
Stapleton	Neb.	212	827	843	759	485	423	850	753	575	718	376	365	411	831	313	893	519	391	800	973
Sterling	Colo.	343	958	948	855	616	106	934	796	707	849	507	33	460	816	443	1024	273	522	785	924
Stiles Jct.	Wis.	722	28	576	575	419	1061	607	602	463	207	530	971	899	788	759	75	892	753	794	371
Stockton	Kan.	271	838	867	782	481	539	874	776	477	707	399	418	217	854	157	914	630	442	824	817
Strasburg	Colo.	477	1086	1003	1015	730	144	1094	957	779	973	635	194	299	977	443	1153	434	546	946	1053
Stratton	Neb.	256	866	883	798	516	275	889	792	586	757	415	202	329	870	298	932	442	435	839	832
Streator	Ill.	583	297	732	690	231	916	758	711	⊕	⊕	460	811	648	888	508	370	852	668	858	556
Streeter	N.D.	582	630	304	241	547	810	290	134	721	687	332	780	805	257	690	648	475	580	327	411
Studley	Kan.	330	923	956	871	558	388	963	865	536	775	488	398	157	944	200	1006	677	409	913	908
Sturgeon Bay	Wis.	762	58	630	621	449	1102	662	648	492	236	570	1011	928	834	788	154	994	793	839	428
Sublette	Kan.	479	971	1062	977	606	473	1069	971	580	819	594	523	261	1049	240	1067	763	650	1019	1007

⊕ For rates refer to I. F. A. Tariff No. I-1002. I. C. C. No. 757, R. G. Raasch, Agent.

Figure 6-10 Tariff page showing point-to-point rate bases. (Reproduced by permission of tariff publisher.)

Tariff W-1000

CLASS RATES IN CENTS PER 100 POUNDS

RATE BASIS NUMBERS	400	300	250	200	175	150	125	110	100	97½	95	92½	90	87½	85	82½	80	77½	75	73½	72½	70	67½	65
5	328	246	205	164	144	123	103	90	82	80	78	76	74	72	70	68	66	64	62	60	59	57	55	54
10	356	267	223	178	156	134	111	98	89	87	85	82	80	78	76	73	71	69	67	65	65	62	60	59
15	384	288	240	192	168	144	120	106	96	94	91	89	86	84	82	79	77	74	72	71	70	67	65	63
20	408	306	255	204	179	153	128	112	102	99	97	94	92	89	87	84	82	79	77	75	74	71	69	67
25	420	315	263	210	184	158	131	116	105	102	100	97	95	92	89	87	84	81	79	77	76	74	71	69
30	448	336	280	224	196	168	140	123	112	109	106	104	101	98	95	92	90	87	84	82	81	78	76	74
35	460	345	288	230	201	173	144	127	115	112	109	106	104	101	98	95	92	89	86	85	83	81	78	76
40	480	360	300	240	210	180	150	132	120	117	114	111	108	105	102	99	96	93	90	88	87	84	81	79
45	492	369	308	246	215	185	154	135	123	120	117	114	111	108	105	101	98	95	92	90	89	86	83	81
50	504	378	315	252	221	189	158	139	126	123	120	117	113	110	107	104	101	98	95	93	91	88	85	83
55	524	393	328	262	229	197	164	144	131	128	124	121	118	115	111	108	105	102	98	96	95	92	88	86
60	536	402	335	268	235	201	168	147	134	131	127	124	121	117	114	111	107	104	101	98	97	94	90	88
65	556	417	348	278	243	209	174	153	139	136	132	129	125	122	118	115	111	108	104	102	101	97	94	92
70	564	423	353	282	247	212	176	155	141	137	134	130	127	123	120	116	113	109	106	104	102	99	95	93
75	572	429	358	286	250	215	179	157	143	139	136	132	129	125	122	118	114	111	107	105	104	100	97	94
80	588	441	368	294	257	221	184	162	147	143	140	136	132	129	125	121	118	114	110	108	107	103	99	97
85	600	450	375	300	263	225	188	165	150	146	143	139	135	131	128	124	120	116	113	110	109	105	101	99
90	616	462	385	308	270	231	193	169	154	150	146	142	139	135	131	127	123	119	116	113	112	108	104	102
95	624	468	390	312	273	234	195	172	156	152	148	144	140	137	133	129	125	121	117	115	113	109	105	103
100	636	477	398	318	278	239	199	175	159	155	151	147	143	139	135	131	127	123	119	117	115	111	107	105
110	656	492	410	328	287	246	205	180	164	160	156	152	148	144	139	135	131	127	123	121	119	115	111	108
120	676	507	423	338	296	254	211	186	169	165	161	156	152	148	144	139	135	131	127	124	123	118	114	112
130	700	525	438	350	306	263	219	193	175	171	166	162	158	153	149	144	140	136	131	129	127	123	118	116
140	720	540	450	360	315	270	225	198	180	176	171	167	162	158	153	149	144	140	135	132	131	126	122	119
150	740	555	463	370	324	278	231	204	185	180	176	171	167	162	157	153	149	144	139	136	134	130	125	122
160	756	567	473	378	331	284	236	208	189	184	180	175	170	165	161	156	151	146	142	139	137	132	128	125
170	784	588	490	392	343	294	245	216	196	191	186	181	176	172	167	162	157	152	147	144	142	137	132	129
180	796	597	498	398	348	299	249	219	199	194	189	184	179	174	169	164	159	154	149	146	144	139	134	131
190	812	609	508	406	355	305	254	223	203	198	193	188	183	178	173	167	162	157	152	149	147	142	137	134
200	828	621	518	414	362	311	259	228	207	202	197	191	186	181	176	171	166	160	155	152	150	145	140	137
210	852	639	533	426	373	320	266	234	213	208	202	197	192	186	181	176	170	165	160	157	154	149	144	141
220	868	651	543	434	380	326	271	239	217	212	206	201	195	190	184	179	174	168	163	159	157	152	146	143
230	884	663	553	442	387	332	276	243	221	215	210	204	199	193	188	182	177	171	166	162	160	155	149	146
240	900	675	563	450	394	338	281	248	225	219	214	208	203	197	191	186	180	174	169	165	163	158	152	149
250	940	705	588	470	411	353	294	259	235	229	223	217	212	206	200	194	188	182	176	173	170	165	159	155
280	964	723	603	482	422	362	301	265	241	235	229	223	217	211	205	199	193	187	181	177	175	169	163	159
300	996	747	623	498	436	374	311	274	249	243	237	230	224	218	212	205	199	193	187	181	181	174	168	164
320	1032	774	645	516	452	387	323	284	258	252	245	239	232	226	219	213	206	200	194	190	187	181	174	170
340	1060	795	663	530	464	398	331	292	265	258	252	245	239	232	225	219	212	205	198	192	189	186	179	175
360	1092	819	683	546	478	410	341	300	273	266	259	253	246	239	232	225	218	212	205	201	198	191	184	180
380	1116	837	698	558	488	419	349	307	279	272	265	258	251	244	237	230	223	216	209	205	202	195	188	184
400	1148	861	718	574	502	431	359	316	287	280	273	265	258	251	244	237	230	222	215	211	208	201	194	189
420	1180	885	738	590	516	443	369	325	295	288	280	273	266	258	251	243	236	229	221	217	214	207	199	195
440	1204	903	753	602	527	452	376	331	301	293	286	278	271	263	256	248	241	233	226	221	218	211	203	199
460	1228	921	768	614	537	461	384	338	307	299	292	284	276	269	261	253	246	238	230	226	223	215	207	203
480	1260	945	788	630	551	473	394	347	315	307	299	291	284	276	268	260	252	244	236	232	228	221	213	208
500	1288	966	805	644	564	483	403	354	322	314	306	298	290	282	274	266	258	250	242	237	233	225	217	213
520	1308	981	818	654	572	491	409	360	327	319	311	302	294	286	278	270	262	253	245	240	237	229	221	216
540	1344	1008	840	672	588	504	420	370	336	328	319	311	302	294	286	277	269	260	252	247	244	235	227	222
560	1368	1026	855	684	599	513	428	376	342	333	325	316	308	299	291	282	274	265	257	251	248	239	231	226
580	1396	1047	873	698	611	524	436	384	349	340	332	323	314	305	297	288	279	270	262	257	253	244	236	230
600	1420	1065	888	710	621	533	444	391	355	346	337	328	320	311	302	293	284	275	266	261	257	249	240	234
620	1448	1086	905	724	634	543	453	398	362	353	344	335	326	317	308	299	290	281	272	266	262	253	244	239
640	1476	1107	923	738	646	553	461	404	369	360	351	341	332	323	314	304	295	286	277	271	268	258	249	244
660	1508	1131	943	754	660	566	471	415	377	368	358	349	339	330	320	311	302	292	283	277	273	264	254	249
680	1532	1149	958	766	670	576	479	421	383	373	364	354	345	335	326	316	306	297	287	282	278	268	259	253
700	1560	1170	975	780	683	585	488	429	390	380	371	361	351	341	332	322	312	302	293	287	283	273	263	257
720	1592	1194	995	796	697	597	498	438	398	388	378	368	358	348	338	328	318	308	302	292	289	279	269	263
740	1616	1212	1010	808	707	606	505	444	404	394	384	374	364	354	343	333	323	313	303	297	293	283	273	267
760	1640	1230	1025	820	718	615	513	451	410	400	390	379	369	359	349	338	328	318	308	301	297	287	277	271
780	1672	1254	1045	836	732	627	523	460	418	408	397	387	376	366	355	345	334	324	314	308	303	293	282	276
800	1700	1275	1063	850	744	638	531	468	425	414	404	393	383	372	361	351	340	329	319	312	308	298	287	281
825	1724	1293	1078	862	754	647	539	474	431	420	409	399	388	377	366	356	345	334	323	317	312	302	291	284
850	1756	1317	1098	878	768	659	549	483	439	428	417	406	395	384	373	362	351	340	329	323	318	307	296	290
875	1784	1338	1115	892	781	669	558	491	446	435	424	413	401	390	379	367	356	346	335	329	323	312	301	294
900	1812	1359	1133	906	793	680	566	498	453	442	430	419	408	396	385	374	362	351	340	333	328	317	306	299
925	1840	1380	1150	920	805	690	575	506	460	449	437	426	414	403	391	380	368	357	345	338	334	322	311	304

Figure 6-11 Tariff page showing application of rate bases to charges. In this table, interpolation is not used. Instead, if you cannot find the exact number in the left-hand column, use the next-highest printed value. (Reproduced by permission of tariff publisher.)

geographic points, so that they are amenable to computer processing. Precise steps include the following:

- The removal of minor differences in the place and commodity descriptions used by different modes
- The removal of peculiarities in working tariffs and tariff rules that are difficult to convert to computerized format—one example being overuse of the word *except*
- The requirement that new tariff and tariff rule submissions to the ICC for approval be in a specific computer-oriented format

Much of the credit for creating the framework that makes computerized freight rates possible goes to the Electronic Data Interchange Association (EDIA), formerly known as the Transportation Data Coordinating Committee (TDCC). The TDCC was started in 1968 as a nonprofit corporation designed to develop, foster, and maintain a program to coordinate transportation data and information systems by standardizing descriptions, codes, tariff formats, systems, and procedures for transportation and distribution. Today, EDIA's membership is composed of both shippers and carriers, and its goals are endorsed by federal agencies.

The initial thrust of the EDIA was to encourage further development of standardized code categories—to serve as the building blocks of the Tariff Modernization Program. The objectives of this program were to simplify and further computerize transportation documentation and rate determination. The codes developed dealt with describing commodities, carriers, patrons (shippers and consignees), and geographic points.

By now most shippers and carriers have computerized many aspects of their freight-moving activities. Buyers, sellers, and carriers regularly exchange data via electronic means, including EDI.

Assume that a traffic department decides to computerize the carrier rate determination function. A basic issue becomes, Should the computerization be performed internally or externally? An internal system implies that the firm will own or lease its own computer facilities and that the entire rate retrieval operation will be performed by employees of the company. The use of an outside contracting company is the key aspect of the external system. Here the computer itself and its rate-retrieval or other programs are operated and continually updated by the contracting company. Its business is to provide accurate and expeditious rate determination for its traffic manager customers.

One reason some firms choose to use an external computerized rate service is that it is less expensive to start up and can be operational in less time (a few months) than an internal service. Firms that choose to have an internal rate automation system can purchase software packages. These are detailed programs that have been fully checked for bugs—errors—and can therefore be utilized almost immediately.

An increasingly common tariff for less-than-truckload shipments transported via common carrier trucker is the computerized rate system that can be run on most shippers' personal computers. These rate systems are being used by the following trucking companies: American Freight Systems, Arkansas Best Freight, ANR Freight Systems, Carolina Freight Systems, Consolidated Freightways, Overnite Transportation, and Yellow Freight System.[18] These are all for less-than-truckload shipments. Most work about the same way: Usually one enters in the origin and destination ZIP codes, the weight and classification of each shipment, any supplemental services needed, and whatever discount the carrier has awarded the shipper. (In practice, most rates calculated by the diskettes are high, but shippers negotiate for discounts in the 20–30 percent range, with a few discounts being as high as 60 percent.)

Figures 6-12 through 6-17 are generated from the Yellow Freight System's ZIP Disk, a two-disk system. Figure 6-12 is similar to a title page on a printed tariff. Figure 6-13 is the primary menu. Figure 6-14 lists the different accessorial charges, and the *MM*s indicate two that we have highlighted for inclusion. The specific amounts of the accessorial charges are shown on Figure 6-15. Note that there are some minimum and maximum charges. In Figure 6-16 we see the total charges for a shipment of items in three different classifications. We have added two accessorial charges and took a 15 percent

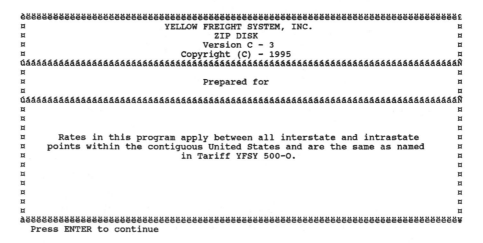

Figure 6-12   Title page for Yellow Freight's ZIP Disk. (Courtesy of Yellow Freight System.)

[18] "Disk Rating Systems," *Distribution*, November 1987, pp. 46–60.

```
                        YELLOW FREIGHT SYSTEM, INC.
                                ZIP DISK
                        Rates Effective January 1, 1995
                                Primary Menu
       Date: 6-29-95                                    Time: 09:22:39


                   1     Freight Bill Rating

                   2     Rate Inquiry / Print Zip Sheets

                   3     Freight Bill Rating With Data File Creation

                   4     Rate Inquiry With Data File Creation

                   5     Enter Discounts

                   6     Use Programmed Discounts  On  Off

                   X     Exit Program

     Enter Selection Number
```

Figure 6-13   Yellow Freight ZIP Disk menu. (Courtesy of Yellow Freight System.)

```
              COD Fee
              Change COD
              Inside delivery
              Marking or tagging
              Notify before delivery
              Redelivery
              Residential delivery
              Sorting and segregating
              Storage
              Miscellaneous Charge




           Repeat function on/off, press "R".
 Select/deselect accessorial by positioning arrow then press space bar.
   F1  Explanation of Accessorial Charges                   F10  Finished
```

Figure 6-14   List of accessorial charges. (Courtesy of Yellow Freight System.)

discount. The ZIP Disk system also enables us to perform some analysis. In Figure 6-17 we see rates for Class 70 shipments between ZIP code area 01100 and six other areas. The numbers are rates per hundred pounds for the sizes of shipments shown across the top. Note that two of the ZIP code areas are within the same state, so the program prints out that those are interstate rates for reconsignments.[19]

[19] Intrastate movements were deregulated on January 1, 1995. This tariff was issued before then, so it probably did not cover intrastate movements.

Explanation of Accessorial Charges

```
COD Fees:   COD <=700    40.00        Change COD: 23.00
            COD <=800    46.00        Notify before delivery: 22.00
            COD <=900    51.50        Residential delivery: 33.00
            COD <=1000   57.50
            COD > 1000   COD * 0.05750
            Maximum :    1000.00      Storage: 1.10 per CWT * days
                                        Daily Minimum: 6.00
Marking:    Pieces * 1.00               Shipment Minimum: 31.00
            Minimum: 17.00
                                      Single Shipment (Weight < 500):
Sorting and segregating:                17.40 or 10.50 depending on zip
        Pieces * 0.35 or
        0.60 per CWT                  Redelivery:   3.30 per CWT
                                        Minimum:  25.00
                                        Maximum: 435.00


                                      Inside delivery:   4.00 per CWT
                                        Minimum:  50.00
                                        Maximum: 500.00


Press ENTER to continue
```

Figure 6-15 Amounts charged for accessorial services on Yellow Freight's ZIP Disk system. (Courtesy of Yellow Freight System.)

```
YFSY 500-O    From zip code 16201(PA) to zip code 44401(OH)   YFSY 500-O
Shipment : Direct

    CLASS                WEIGHT              RATE              EXTENSION

     100                  478                2261               108.08
      70                 4598                1641               754.53
     200                  544                4610               250.78

Subtotal                                                       1113.39
Discount                                    25.0%               278.35
Residential delivery                                            33.00

Total                   5620                                    868.04
```

Figure 6-16 Freight bill calculated with Yellow Freight's ZIP Disk program. (Courtesy of Yellow Freight System.)

Outbound from zip code 01101(MA)   Class 70

to zip zone	MIN	L5C	M5C	M1M	M2M	M5M	M10M	M20M	M30M	M40M
022 (MA)	8701	3219	2496	1819	1652	1189	1063	641	469	439
033 (NH)	8730	3410	2672	1977	1801	1334	1189	737	553	496
044 (ME)	8730	3897	3060	2291	2145	1663	1485	975	720	686
066 (CT)	8303	2854	2214	1600	1471	1030	924	548	398	367
077A(NJ)	8688	3571	2671	2009	1690	1361	1213	774	593	560
077B(NJ)	8671	3549	2652	1994	1676	1353	1206	769	589	556

Figure 6-17 Use of ZIP Disk program for rate analysis. (Courtesy of Yellow Freight System.)

Intrastate trucking deregulation took place on January 1, 1995. In late 1994 several large LTL carriers began introducing single-page, intrastate rate sheets for each shipper. Geographic zones were used, and for each individual shipper a classification number was determined based on the shipment weights and the product's handling characteristics.[20] Current discounts would be built into the net rates shown on the price sheets. Classifications are also now the subject of negotiation between individual shippers and carriers, and usually the classification number must be agreed to before a rate sheet will be prepared.

By mid-1995 it appeared that some of the new intrastate rates had been cut too much. Several long-time motor carriers that had served only intrastate markets dropped out of business.

Some carriers have their rates on a mainframe computer and allow access via the Internet system, feeling that potential shippers can access rates via that route. For some carriers, rates are not fixed, in the sense that they are trying to fill space every day. Hence, if considerable uncommitted space exists on tomorrow's plane, railcar, or barge, the rate for tomorrow may be reduced in an attempt to fill the space. So some shippers may have to "surf" the Internet to find the best rates.

Note that this rate determination takes the mystique out of the function. A class rate determination that previously took six or more steps can now be accomplished in a matter of seconds by keying a few numbers into one's personal computer. It is also possible to use the same computer software to generate the various shipping documents that are needed by the carrier. In addition, other documents useful to the traffic manager and to the logistics manager can be generated at the same time.

SUMMARY

Transportation is the links portion of the links and nodes that make up the logistics operation. Transportation is pivotal to the success of any logistics operation. The shippers of small quantities rely on the Post Office or parcel carriers such as UPS or Federal Express. The next step is to ship by an LTL motor carrier, which picks up goods and takes them to a local terminal, where they are loaded aboard a linehaul truck to a terminal near the consignee. A small truck then makes deliveries from the terminal. In terms of numbers of shippers, the vast majority use only parcel or LTL services.

The next step, in terms of shipment size, is to ship in truckload, railcar load, or barge load volumes or to use a pipeline. The rates are negotiable, and service considerations become part of the negotiations. Carriers encourage multiple truckloads, multiple railcar loads, and so on. Specialized equipment

---

[20] *Transport Topics*, December 5, 1994, p. 23.

is also used with these volumes of traffic. Specialized terminals are also custom designed for handling each different type of bulk commodity.

Parcel and LTL shippers pay rates established in carrier tariffs. To prepare a tariff, the carriers need three different types of information before they know the exact rate for a specific shipment. The information needed is length of haul, size of shipment, and the cargo's handling characteristics. Cargo handling characteristics are usually incorporated into a product's classification number. This number is heavily influenced by the product's density. This, in turn, is taken into account when the product is designed and when packaging is selected.

Today, many tariffs are computerized on PC software, and this had made the entire process of rate determination much easier.

QUESTIONS FOR DISCUSSION AND REVIEW

1. What are terminals? What functions do they serve?
2. Why is transportation important to a firm's logistical operations?
3. What are routing guides? How are they used?
4. With some guidance from your instructor, contact your local post office and offices of UPS, FedEx, some motor carriers, airlines, and so on to learn of the services they offer and the rates they charge for typical domestic shipments.
5. What is LTL traffic? How is it handled by the LTL carriers?
6. List some products that frequently move by air freight. Why do you think that air freight was selected as the mode to use?
7. What are freight forwarders? How do they function? What services do they perform?
8. What is a shippers' cooperative?
9. How do truck TL operations differ from truck LTL operations?
10. What is bulk cargo?
11. What is a unit train? How does it function?
12. What types of product move by barge? In what ways would they differ from typical products carried by air?
13. What are slurry systems? How do they function?
14. Why are self-unloading vessels employed? What are their advantages and their disadvantages?
15. What is project cargo, and what is oversized cargo? What are the differences between them?
16. Compare the five modes of transport—air, motor, pipeline, rail, and water—by at least three different criteria that you think are important.
17. What impacts did the Mississippi River flooding of 1993 have on the various transport modes?
18. What is product classification as used by carriers?

19. Why was it difficult to computerize freight rates?

20. How does one use an LTL motor carrier's computerized tariff?

SUGGESTED READINGS

Ashar, Asaf, Anatoly Hochstein, and Kevin Horn. "Projects for River/Ocean Short-Sea General Cargo Shipping in the United States." *Journal of the Transportation Research Forum* (1988), pp. 94–100.

Babcock, Michael W., and H. Wade German. "Transportation Policy in the 1990s and the Railroad/Motor Carrier Market Shares." *Journal of the Transportation Research Forum,* vol. 31, no. 1 (1991), pp. 63–74.

Bahn, Henry M., Kenneth L. Casavant, Gene Griffin, and Daniel Zink. "Use of Rail Rate Contracting on Varying Transportation Competitive Environments and Its Impact on the Competitive Structure of Grain Merchandising." *Journal of the Transportation Research Forum* (1987), pp. 168–176.

Baker, J. A. "Emergent Pricing Structures in LTL Transportation." *Journal of Business Logistics,* Spring 1991, pp. 191–202.

Bookbinder, James H., and Wendy W. Qu. "Comparing the Performance of Major American Railroads." *Journal of the Transportation Research Forum,* vol. 39, no. 1 (1993), pp. 70–85.

Bradley, Michael D., and Alan Robinson. "Determining the Marginal Cost of Purchased Transportation." *Journal of the Transportation Research Forum* (1988), pp. 169–176.

Brown, Terence A. "Freight Brokers and General Commodity Trucking." *Transportation Journal,* Winter 1984, pp. 4–14.

Burdg, Henry, B., and James M. Daley. "Shallow-Draft Water Transportation: Marketing Implications of User and Carrier Attribute Perceptions." *Transportation Journal,* Spring 1985, pp. 55–67.

Corsi, Thomas, and Philip Fanara. "Deregulation, New Entrants, and the Safety Learning Curve." *Journal of the Transportation Research Forum* (1988), pp. 3–8.

Coyle, John J., Edward J. Bardi, and Robert A. Novack. *Transportation,* 4th ed. St. Paul: West Publishing, 1993.

Dempsey, Paul Stephen, and William Thoms. *Law and Economic Regulation in Transportation.* New York: Quorum Books, 1986.

Gooley, Toby B. "All-Cargo Airlines: Airfreight's Best-Kept Secret." *Traffic Management,* August 1993, pp. 45–48.

Harper, Donald V., and Philip T. Evers. "Competitive Issues in Intermodal Railroad-Truck Service." *Transportation Journal,* vol. 32, no. 3, Spring 1993, pp. 31–45.

Kindred, Hugh M. "Slow but Sure: Responsibility for Delay in the Delivery of Multimodal Cargoes." *Journal of the Transportation Research Forum,* vol. 30, no. 2 (1991), pp. 418–424.

Larson, Paul D. "Transportation Deregulation and Logistics Costs." *Transportation Quarterly,* January 1992, pp. 19–35.

Morlok, Edward K., and Lazar N. Spasovic. "Redesigning Rail-Truck Intermodal Drayage Operations for Enhanced Service and Cost Performance." *Journal of the Transportation Research Forum* (1994), pp. 16–31.

Muller, Gerhardt. *Intermodal Freight Transportation,* 3rd ed. Westport, Conn.: Eno Foundation, 1995.

National Transportation Statistics, Annual Report, September 1993. Washington, D.C.: Bureau of Transportation Statistics, U.S. DOT, 1994.

Ozment, John, William A. Cunningham, and Grant M. Davis. "Motor Carrier Fuel Efficiency and Equipment Utilization: Effects of Deregulation." *Journal of the Transportation Research Forum,* vol. 30, no. 2 (1990), pp. 431–441.

Sonstegaard, Miles. "Separate Freight Rates for Weight and Cube." *Journal of the Transportation Research Forum* (1987), pp. 342–345.

Tolliver, Denver D., Frank J. Dooley, and Daniel Zink. "Short Line Operation of Light Density Rail Networks: Economics and Public Policy." *Journal of the Transportation Research Forum* (1987), pp. 277–282.

Winston, Clifford. "Conceptual Developments in the Economics of Transportation: An Interpretive Survey." *Journal of Economic Literature,* March 1985, pp. 57–94.

Wood, Donald F., and James C. Johnson. *Contemporary Transportation,* 5th ed. Englewood Cliffs, N.J.: Prentice Hall, 1996.

C A S E   6 - 1

BOONE SHOE COMPANY

"Red" Boone founded the Boone Shoe Company in St. Joseph, Missouri, during the 1930s. Unable to find work as a sheet metal worker, Red started to make moccasins for friends who had always admired the ones he had made for himself. Over time, the reputation of Boone's shoes spread, and Red expanded his product line and hired additional employees. The real growth of the company took place during World War II. In 1942, almost as a joke, Red submitted a bid to the War Department to produce 100,000 pairs of combat boots. Much to his surprise, the contract was accepted, probably because Red noted in the bid that a sufficient noncombat labor force (females and retirees) existed in the area to produce boots.

The main production input, leather, was easily obtained at the nearby Kansas City stockyards. After the war, the Boone company expanded its production of civilian shoes and related products and also continued to supply the military services with all types of leather footwear. Red Boone's son, Barry, was in charge of all marketing and distribution activities.

Larry Gitman functioned as the firm's warehouse, purchasing, and traffic manager. After two years' experience as a management trainee with a large motor common carrier, Larry had accepted the position at Boone Shoe Company. Because of the firm's steady annual growth rate of 15 percent, Barry Boone had authorized Larry to hire an assistant.

Steve Knapp, just out of high school, was working part-time from 1:00 to 6:00 P.M. and also attending the local community college. Steve had progressed so rapidly that Larry felt comfortable taking a three-week vacation, his first extended vacation in some years.

During Larry's vacation, Steve assumed Larry's responsibilities. As Steve sat in his office, the intercom buzzed and Barry asked Steve to pick up line 3 and take part in the conversation. The call was from Tom Cook, Boone's salesman for Minnesota and Wisconsin. Tom stated, "I'm calling from the buying office of Lawson Department Stores in Green Bay. Although they're currently overstocked in shoes, they are interested in buying a sizable quantity of our 'Light Stride' arch-support insoles. They plan on giving them away with their shoes in order to stimulate shoe sales. They want to buy FOB destination. I need to know in the next few minutes the cost of sending 17,000 pounds of the arch supports from St. Joseph to Green Bay."

Steve asked, "Will they accept a rail shipment? It's less expensive, and we usually receive fairly good rail service on our northbound shipments."

Tom replied, "The buyer said he expected the shipment to come via rail."

Barry came on the line and asked, "Steve, can you look up this info for Tom?"

Steve said, "No problem. I'll call you back with the answer in fifteen minutes or less."

Questions

1. Assume there are no commodity or exception rates in effect for this shipment. Using Figures 6-9, 6-10, and 6-11, calculate the applicable charge.

2. Steve remembered that he had heard Larry speak of shipping "wind." This involved paying the CL minimum weight in order to receive the CL rate, even if the shipment actually weighed less than the carload minimum weight. Should this technique be used for the shipment? Why or why not?

3. The buyer will pay upon receipt of the shipment, which is valued at $21,000 plus any transportation charges. Boone Shoe Company borrows money from the bank regularly on an open line credit and is currently paying interest on its debt at the rate of 15 percent per year. If rail LCL service is used, delivery time to Green Bay will be about ten days. If rail CL service is used, delivery time will be six days. What is the additional advantage to Boone Shoe Company if it chooses to use CL service?

4. (This is a continuation of question 3.) Boone Shoe Company also owns several large trucks, although Steve is uncertain whether they are avail-

able for immediate use. He knows that they could make the delivery to Green Bay in two days. He checks the highway distance from St. Joseph to Green Bay and finds that it is 588 miles. Larry had once told Steve that it cost the company 85 cents per mile to operate its highway trucks. Do you think that a truck should be used if it is available? Why?

5. (This is a continuation of questions 2 and 3.) Another alternative is to make the shipment by rail from Boone's St. Louis warehouse. Rail delivery time will be four days. What price should Tom Cook be told to quote to Lawson's?

6. Boone Shoe Company often sells large quantities—from 10,000 up to 30,000 pounds—of arch-support insoles on an FOB-delivered basis. After referring to Figure 6-9, do you think there is a minimum weight (in this 10,000 to 30,000 pound range) that customers should be encouraged to order? If so, what is it?

C A S E   6 - 2

FINDING THE RATE

(*Note:* To use this case, you will need two 5¼-inch floppy computer disks that have been supplied by Prentice Hall to your instructor. The disks may be copied. They are labeled CF OMNIRATE DISK 1 and CF OMNIRATE DISK 2, and they were provided through the courtesy of Consolidated Freightways and the Rocky Mountain Motor Tariff Bureau, Inc. These same disks are also needed for Cases 8-1 and 12-2.)

You will also need an IBM-compatible PC with a single-disk drive and 256K of built-in memory. After booting your computer with your DOS, insert OMNIRATE DISK 1 into drive A, type "CF," and press the ENTER key. The screen will prompt you to remove OMNIRATE DISK 1 and place OMNIRATE DISK 2 into A drive. A MENU screen will arrive, giving you three options. For this case, use the RATING option, except for question 6, for which you should use the RATE SHEET option.

Questions

1. Freight rates are discussed in this chapter. One needs to know the size of a shipment, its origin and destination, and its classification in order to determine the charges for the shipment. How are these three factors handled on this computerized tariff? Discuss.

2. Who issued this tariff? Is it on file with any regulatory bodies? If so, which ones?

3. In this chapter an example is given concerning an archaeologist's shipment of bones. Assume that the same classifications are used by motor carriers as were used in the example. The ZIP code for Sioux Falls, South Dakota, is 57069, and for Hannibal, Missouri, is 63401. What are the charges?

4. Assume further that the archaeologist was going to sell the bones for $10,000 plus the cost of shipping and wanted to have the carrier collect the COD charges. What would the total delivered cost be to the buyer?

5. Assume all the conditions in question 4, but assume that the buyer may want the shipment redelivered to another address (still inside the Hannibal commercial zone). What would this redelivery cost?

6. (For this question, you may use the RATE SHEET capability of the program.) Assume that your product's origin is in Des Moines, Iowa (ZIP code 50302) and that you will be supplying a salesperson whose territory is five major cities in Idaho: Coeur D'Alene (ZIP code 83811), Lewiston (ZIP code 83522), Boise (ZIP code 83645), Twin Falls (ZIP code 83333), and Pocatello (ZIP code 83255). Your product's classification is 70, and it is sold in 1,100-pound lots. Each is a single shipment, and there are no discounts or accessorial charges involved. Your salesperson wants a rate sheet showing what it would cost to ship 1,100, 2,200, 3,300, 4,400, and 5,500 pounds to each of the five cities. Prepare such a sheet, using a five-by-five table.

The Traffic Management Function

The equipment available for shipping products has changed. The top photograph shows a tank car from 1865, built by placing two wooden tubs on a flat car. The bottom photograph shows a tank car as it is used today. The sign in the center of the car includes a toll-free telephone number for product emergencies. (Photos courtesy of Union Tank Car Company.)

Matson Navigation, Inc., one of two principal ocean carriers in the U.S.-Hawaii trade, said it will increase its rates across the board by nearly 4% early next year. The Federal Maritime Commission and Interstate Commerce Commission will review the increases and decide by early next year whether to allow them.

Journal of Commerce
November 22, 1994

Union Pacific to hike fees for late return of cars.

Journal of Commerce
April 28, 1992

Colgate-Palmolive goes outside for freight bill auditing.

Transportation & Distribution
March 1994

Key Terms

- Bill of lading
- Break-bulk
- Demurrage/detention
- Diversion
- Expediting
- Hazardous materials
- Loss and damage
- Make-bulk
- Private transportation
- Reparations
- Rate determination
- Rate and service negotiation
- Reconsignment
- Shipment consolidation
- Tracing
- Transit privilege

Learning Objectives

- To examine the background of the traffic management function
- To discuss the functions of traffic management
- To identify the role negotiations play in the traffic management function
- To examine the new options available for private carriage
- To understand the purpose of freight consolidation

TRAFFIC MANAGEMENT: BACKGROUND AND SCOPE

Today senior management is concerned about traffic management more than ever before because transportation represents a major expense item. In general terms, freight transportation accounts for 6 percent of gross national product. Today, riding on the crest of enthusiasm for the logistics concept, the traffic manager is considered an important member of the management team. Restructuring of carriers since deregulation has also sparked top management's interest in transportation issues.

It is difficult to generalize about how deregulation has changed the traffic manager's responsibilities. Many of the preregulation rules remain in effect; what we read or hear about are negotiations concerning departures from these established rules. A simple example is claims for loss and damage; the carrier was and still is responsible unless, in the course of negotiations, the shipper relieves the carrier of part or all of its obligation.

In conjunction with the American Society of Transportation and Logistics, Professor B. J. LaLonde et al. studied the changing status of the corporate transportation function. They found that

> the 1980s were a period of change for the corporate transportation function. The change was pervasive. It extended all the way from the chief transportation executive of the firm to the rate clerk. In most firms, it required a redefinition of the relationship between shipper and carrier as well as a redefinition of the expectations from this continuing relationship both in a domestic and global context. It required the option of new technology, not for purposes of getting ahead, but just to stay even. All these factors converged as a result of deregulation during the 1980s. The traffic function which emerged at the end of the decade was far different from the traffic function at the beginning of the decade.[1]

The traffic department was among the last operations in a firm to computerize, usually because of the complexity of rates. Today large carriers have either placed their rates on mainframe computers to which shippers have access, or they distribute their rates on PC disks (see Chapter 6). Hundreds of specialized software programs are available for traffic managers to use. Or they may adopt workhorse programs, such as Lotus 1-2-3, to their own uses. One trade journal article describes how Ray-O-Vac used Lotus for thirteen different applications, including the following:

1. Allowances (determines the allowance to give to the customer that picks up freight)
2. Claims files
3. Export/import (monitors shipments)
4. Pallets (lists use and location)

[1] Bernard J. LaLonde, James M. Masters, Arnold B. Maltz, and Lisa R. Williams, *The Evolution, Status, and Future of the Corporate Transportation Function* (Columbus: Ohio State University, 1991), pp. 3–4.

5. Fuel consumption analysis (monitors private fleet)
6. LTL rates (stores applicable rates, by ZIP code)
7. Volume rates (stores applicable volume rates)

Other uses enable the tracking of loads among plants, distribution centers, and customers. Last, there are some uses in conjunction with a word-processing program that generates original letters to vendors showing Ray-O-Vac's preferred routings.[2]

The study of LaLonde et al. found that traffic managers divide their time in this way: rate negotiation, 23 percent; carrier selection, 14 percent; managing private fleets, 14 percent; billing and auditing, 10 percent; routing, 9 percent; carrier assignment, 9 percent; tracing and expediting, 7 percent; and claims, 6 percent.[3]

The following sections of this chapter discuss the primary duties of today's traffic department. First, though, it should be pointed out that traffic managers are also involved with many other operations of the firm. They assist marketing by quoting freight rates for salespeople, suggesting quantity discounts that can be based on transportation savings, and selecting carriers and routes for reliable delivery of products. Traffic managers help manufacturing by advising on packaging and materials handling and making certain that an adequate supply of transportation is available when it is needed. Figure 7-1

Figure 7-1   Shipper-owned switch engine spotting a tank car at a large soybean oil refinery. (Courtesy Union Tank Car Company.)

[2] *Distribution,* February 1988, p. 44.

[3] LaLonde et al., *Evolution,* pp. 106–107. The sum of the figures given here is less than 100 percent.

shows a small, shipper-owned switch engine used to move cars around a major industrial complex. Traffic managers aid the outbound shipping process by providing simplified shipping or routing guides, drawing up transportation documents, and encouraging shipment consolidations. Finally, they help purchasing by advising about methods to control the costs and quality of inbound deliveries and by tracing and expediting lost or delayed shipments of important inputs.[4]

RATE DETERMINATION AND NEGOTIATION ACTIVITIES

Chapter 6 dealt with published carrier rates. From the traffic department's standpoint, we can divide rate-associated duties into four categories. The categories are interrelated because they may all involve rates for the same shipment, and whichever category results in the lowest rate is the one utilized. The categories are (1) published rate determination, (2) working with carrier classification bureaus to publish new, usually lower classifications (available to all shippers with identical products), (3) negotiating with a specific carrier for a contract rate to carry most of the shipper's business, and (4) appearing before a regulatory board in those few instances in which they still have jurisdiction.

Rate Determination

Rate determination is very important to every traffic manager. Although the carrier has a legal obligation to determine the correct rate, this is an extremely complex process that is usually open to a broad range of interpretations.

In most situations many applicable rates can be found in tariffs. If the carrier representative is left to determine the correct rate, he or she has no incentive to search the tariffs for the lowest applicable rate. Instead, the carrier representative typically uses the rate that is easiest to find. A long-time industry rule of thumb was that the "correct" freight charge quoted by the carrier averages about 10 percent higher than the lowest applicable legal rate. Figure 7-2 is a page from a Port of Houston tariff that has loading/unloading charges plus wharfage charges (assessed for using the port). Note that the specific page is in its sixtieth revision. The traffic manager must search many tariffs to find the lowest rate. Some tariffs are printed; some are in computer form.

Freight Classification

Recall from Chapter 6 that the freight classification values relate to the handling characteristics of freight and are one of the factors determining freight charges. Such classifications are taken as given in contract negotiations between shippers and carriers. Rate classification bureaus are made up

---

[4] Leon W. Morse, *Practical Handbook of Industrial Traffic Management,* 7th ed. (Washington, D.C.: Traffic Service Corp., 1987), pp. 415–416.

PORT OF HOUSTON
TARIFF NO. 8

SECTION FIVE: Sixtieth Revised Page No. 87

ITEM NO. 65   LOADING, UNLOADING AND WHARFAGE CHARGES
(CONT'D.)   ALL HANDLING charges are in cents per 100 pounds and apply
                     to all shipments at actual weight, except as otherwise noted.
                     ALL WHARFAGE charges are in cents per ton of 2,000 pounds and
                     apply to all shipments at actual weight, except as otherwise noted.

COMMODITY	Loading or Unloading Except as Noted	WHARFAGE Export/Import, Intercoastal, Coastwise, and Intracoastal	ARTICLE NUMBER
Vehicles, Machinery (Self Propelled) Automobiles, Trucks, Trailers, Utility Vehicles, Military Ordinance Vehicles, Agricultural Machinery, (Tractors, Combines, etc.)			
Driven On/Off Land Carrier Equipment......	51	(I) 429	867A
Lift on or Lift Off Carrier Equipment.....	122	(I) 429	867B
Knock Down, Parts........................	99	(I) 310	867C
Exception 1 (Driven On/Off Carrier Equipment) Minimun Charge: $ 37.80 Maximum Charge: $162.00			
Exception (Wharfage Only) 1: Agricultural Machinery		(I) 220	867D
Exception (Wharfage Only) 2: Used Grading or Road Making Machinery being returned to the United States		(I) 220	867E
Note: Outfits consisting of vehicles modified or equipped with attachments, apparatus, or implements will be rated as above.			
A service charge of $35.00 each applies to vehicles, imported or to be exported, when necessary to drain or add fuel or water or disconnect or connect battery cables.			

Issued: November 24, 1993   Effective: January 1, 1994

Figure 7-2 Page from a Port of Houston tariff showing some loading, unloading, and wharfage charges. (Courtesy Port of Houston Authority.)

231

of carrier representatives and enjoy immunity from antitrust prosecution. Traffic managers appear before the bureaus in attempts to have the classification of specific commodities or movements lowered. Shippers must also combat the carriers' attempts to increase classification numbers. An issue in early 1994 was the classification of flashlights:

> Flashlights in boxes, without batteries are designated less-than-truckload class 100 or truckload class 55 with a minimum weight of 20,000 lbs. Flashlights with their normal complement of batteries are considered LTL class 70 or truckload class 45 with a minimum weight of 24,000 lbs.[5]

Because the classification committee felt that flashlights without batteries were too light in the sense that a truck filled with them would cube out, that is, be full but still have unused weight capacity, they proposed classifications of 150 LTL and 100 TL, increases of 50 and 82 percent, respectively. The classification committee conducted surveys showing that the density of the flashlights shipped without batteries was 6.9 pounds per cubic foot. Shippers countered with their surveys showing densities ranging from 10.5 to 11.3 pounds per cubic foot.

Figure 7-3 shows an excerpt from the National Motor Freight Classification Committee's hearing docket concerning a proposal to adopt new classifications for spark plugs. The present classification is described first in the figure, and then the proposal is shown. Note that changing density appears to be an important factor. Figure 7-4 shows an applicant's completed worksheet for submission to the Classification Committee.

Rate and Service Negotiations

When contract carrier **rate and service negotiations** are being dealt with, both rates and service are brought to the table for negotiation. In 1978 the ICC allowed railroads to enter into contracts with shippers, a move that helped make railroads more competitive with contract motor carriage. However, because of legal challenges, rail contracts were of questionable legality until 1980, when they were authorized by the Staggers Rail Act. Since then thousands of rail contracts have been filed with the ICC, and the number still grows. Following are summaries of some of the contract elements of the agreements negotiated between railroads and individual shippers:

> In an agreement between the Chicago and Northwestern and General Foods Corporation involving the carriage of grocery products from Northlake, Illinois, to eight consignees in the St. Louis area, the shipper agreed to pay the railroad an additional amount (ranging from $117 to $159 per car) when the car was delivered on a precise, previously scheduled, day.

> In an agreement between Ford Motor Company and the Missouri Pacific Railroad involving the movements of new autos and auto parts between several

[5] *Journal of Commerce*, February 3, 1994, p. 2B.

PROPOSED

PRESENT CLASSIFICATION: (Show specific NMFC item number and description under which commodity is now being classified.)

ITEM NO.	DESCRIPTION	LTL	TL	MW

PRESENT

177080	Spark Plugs, NOI, in boxes:			
Sub 1	Card mounted, blister packed or skin packed	100	55	24
Sub 2	Other than card mounted, blister packed or skin packed	85	45	30

PROPOSED AMENDMENTS: (Show description. classes and MW exactly as you propose them to be established in the Classification.)

ITEM NO.	DESCRIPTION	LTL	TL	MW

PROPOSED

177080	Spark Plugs, NOI, in boxes:			
Sub 1	Card mounted, blister packed or skin packed	100	55	24
Sub 2	Other than card mounted, blister packed or skin packed :			
>Sub 3	Density less than 30 pounds per cubic foot; or actual value exceeding $6.00 per pound; or where no density or value is shown at time of shipment	85	45	30
>Sub 4	Density in pounds per cubic foot of 30 or greater, and actual value not exceeding $6.00 per pound, see Note, item NEW	70	37.5	36
NEW	NOTE -- Shipper must certify on shipping orders and bills of lading at time of shipment that density is 30 pounds or greater per cubic foot and that the actual value per pound does not exceed $6.00.			

JUSTIFICATION: Due to the density, value per pound and ease of handling of the involved commodities, the proposed changes are warranted.

If you have any questions regarding the proper execution of these forms or require technical assistance please contact our staff at (703) 838-1869.

Figure 7-3 Motor carrier classification docket proposal for changing the classification of spark plugs. (Permission to reproduce this material has been granted by American Trucking Associations, Inc.)

specified points, the railroad agreed to give the shipper an allowance if thirty or more cars were tendered at one time or if the cars arrived at their destinations late. In return Ford agreed to ship 95 percent of this business via Missouri Pacific.

In an agreement between the Santa Fe Railroad and General Foods Corporation for shipments of grocery products moving in trailers aboard flatcars from Houston to Chicago, the shipper agreed to ship a minimum of six million pounds per year. The shipper further agreed to pay an additional $75 per trailer when 90 percent or more of the trailers completed the rail movement within 96 hours. The railroad agreed to furnish sufficient trailers to meet the six million pounds per year volume requirement.

TRANSPORTATION CHARACTERISTICS

I. **DENSITY:** (Please base your calculations on the exterior dimensions and the shipping weight of the commodity as packaged for shipment.)

Model	Description of Package	Length	Width	Height	Weight	Density*
Spark	packaged individually,	38"	38"	42"	1280 #	36.5
plugs	then packaged into cartons					
(boxed)	of 10, then packaged into					
	cartons of 100. Shipped					
	in master cartons on skids.					

*To determine the density (pounds per cubic foot), multiply the three dimensions of the article as packed for shipment. If the result is in cubic inches, divide by 1728 to convert to cubic feet. Then divide the weight by the cubic feet. To determine the cubic feet of space occupied by a drum, pail, or other cylindrical container, square the greatest diameter and multiply that result by the height or length. If the package is of irregular shape, use the greatest dimensions, including all projections.

II. **LIABILITY**

1) Claim value per package (Please match the models with those reported under **DENSITY**)

Model	Description of Package	Weight	Dollar Amount	Value Per Pound
Spark	packaged individually,	1280 #	$7200	$5.63
plugs	then packaged into cartons			
(boxed)	of 10, then packaged into			
	cartons of 100. Shipped			
	in master cartons on skids.			

2) Does the commodity require temperature control?   NO

3) Is the commodity subject to U.S. Department of Transportation Regulations governing hazardous materials? Yes ___ No XX If yes, what HMT commodity description and label are required?

4) Does commodity have protruding edges?   NO

5) Is commodity liquid NO dry NO paste NO

Figure 7-4 Worksheet for motor carrier classification docket proposal for changing the classification of spark plugs. (Permission to reproduce this material has been granted by American Trucking Associations, Inc.)

II.   **LIABILITY - continued**

    6) Claims Experience (Motor Common Carrier Shipments):

        a) Number of claims (one year period) __NONE_____

        b) Dollar amount of claims _____   Amount Paid _____

        c) Total number of shipments made (one year period) _____

        d) Total amount of freight paid (one year period) _____

        e) Claims filed by shipper _____ receiver (consignee) _____

        f) If the information is available, please indicate the percentage of claims for:

           loss _____   damage _____

III.   **HANDLING:**

    1) Is freight palletized? Yes XX   No ____   If yes, are pallets unitized? Yes XX   No ____

    2) Does the commodity require more than one person to load or unload? Yes ____   No XX

    3) Does the product as packaged for shipment require the use of mechanical handling equipment?
Yes XX____   No _____   If yes, what type? pallet jack or forklift

    4) Does the commodity require special handling in loading or unloading? Yes ____   No XX
If yes, please explain what care and attention is necessary.

        _____

    5) Are there other instructions or precautionary markings on the shipping packages or shipping documents?
Yes ____   No XX   If yes, please state what they are:

        _____

IV.   **STOWABILITY**

    1) Form of shipment: SU XX KD ____ KD Flat ____ Folded ____ Folded Flat ____
Nested _____   Nested Solid _____ (See Definitions Below)

    2) Is commodity capable of being tiered for shipment? Yes XX No ____
If yes, how high? ____two_____

    3) If the shipping package is other than square, rectangular or cylindrical, please attach a diagram or photo

    4) Does commodity have any projections or extensions which are not enclosed by the package?
          NO
        _____

    5) If commodity is wheeled, does the article rest on its wheels during shipment? Yes ___   No XX

DEFINITIONS OF SHIPPING FORMS

These definitions are derived from Item (Rule) 110, Sections 12 and 13, of the National Motor Freight Classification and are the applicable ones for classification purposes:

"Set Up (SU)" means the article is in its assembled condition or is disassembled, folded or telescoped but not meeting the definitions of "Knocked Down," "Knocked Down Flat," "Folded " or "Folded Flat."

"Knocked Down (KD)" means that the article is taken apart, folded or telescoped in such a manner as to reduce its bulk at least 33 1/3 percent from its normal shipping cubage when set up or assembled.

"Knocked Down Flat (KD Flat)" means that the article is taken apart, folded or telescoped in such a manner as to reduce its bulk at least 66 2/3 percent from its normal shipping cubage when set up or assembled.

"Folded" means that the article is folded in such a manner as to reduce its bulk at least 33 1/3 percent from its normal shipping cubage when not folded.

"Folded Flat" means that the article is folded in such a manner as to reduce its bulk at least 66 2/3 percent from its normal shipping cubage when not folded.

"Nested" means that three or more different sizes of the article are placed each smaller within the next larger or that three or more of the same article are placed one within the other so that each upper article does not project above the next lower article by more than one-third of its height.

"Nested Solid" means that three or more of the same article are placed one within or upon the other so that the outer side surfaces of the one above are in contact with the inner surfaces of the one below and so that each upper article does not project above the next lower article by more than 1/4 inch.

Figure 7-4   *(Continued)*

These contract provisions illustrate the various aspects of service that are important to the shipper and that may be subject to negotiation. They also indicate that shippers are willing to pay for improved quality of railroad service. Once a contract is entered into, the burden of meeting the shipper's obligations and monitoring the carrier's performance rests on the shipper's traffic manager.

Contracts with other modes of transport can follow some of the objectives indicated in the rail examples just given. Another form of service is for the carrier to assign one or more vehicles to the exclusive use of the shipper for a specified amount of time. A retail store may contract with one or more truckers to help with holiday deliveries.

> "Futures" markets also exist for barge service and for blocs of railroad cars. The Burlington Northern Railroad allows shippers to bid up to 6 months in advance for blocs of cars in fourteen corridors (point-to-point markets). Bidding is done by telephone or fax. The successful bidder must then pay 50 percent immediately and the remainder when the shipment is made. The railroad guarantees to make the cars available and the successful bidder may sell its "rights" to others.[6]

An example of contracting for air freight is provided by Nabisco Brands. The firm spends huge sums on surface transportation for its products. Its use of air freight, often for carrying promotional products, was difficult to tally. After some investigation Nabisco determined that it was spending between $2 million and $4 million per year on air freight. It then decided to contract with two air carriers—one for correspondence, another for freight—to handle this entire business. After consultation with regional offices, the following specifications for air freight carriers were drawn up:

1. Service available twenty-four hours per day, 365 days per year
2. Carrier service and service representatives at cities where Nabisco had offices
3. Deferred service option (i.e., lower rates for less urgent shipments—second-, third-, and fourth-morning delivery)
4. Door-to-door rates
5. Nondimensional rates (some of Nabisco's advertising was oversized)
6. Loss and damage liability of $9.07 per pound
7. Temperature-controlled cargo space
8. Tracing services
9. Proof-of-delivery service
10. Computer-reporting process

[6] Burlington Northern Railroad's entry in the *Modern Railroads* 1989 Golden Freight Car Award Competition, unpublished.

11. Electronic data interchange capability
12. End-of-month reports concerning Nabisco's traffic patterns

The requirements were mailed out along with a volume history of Nabisco's air shipments, a questionnaire intended to determine the carrier's strength and weakness, and a request for rate proposals. After receiving responses, Nabisco invited seven carriers to make presentations, and two—an air-express company and a forwarder—were selected. "The final issues were service first and price second."[7]

Since carrier deregulation, many articles and checklists have been prepared to help both sides in the shipper-carrier negotiation process. One such list in a shipper-carrier contract included the following items of importance: contract duration, contract termination, renegotiation and reopening of contract, transportation service level, carrier insurance, lead times, waiver of terms, detention time, articles and commodities covered, how loss and damage claims are handled, schedule of rates and charges, estimated traffic volume, billing procedures, carrier equipment and drivers, carrier notification requirements, confidential contract, arbitration, audit rights, pallet loading, proof of delivery, adjustments to rates, and basis for charges.[8]

As noted in the earlier chapters, one important change in logistics thinking has been to encourage long-term relationships with suppliers and customers. Contracting with carriers is one way of doing this, although the contracts may be for more than the carriage of products. An example is the five-year agreement between Norfolk Southern Railroad and the Ford Motor Company for an auto distribution facility at Meridian, Mississippi. Norfolk Southern assumed the responsibility of distributing Ford, Lincoln, and Mercury products from assembly plants directly to dealers in Mississippi, Florida, Alabama, and Louisiana. Norfolk Southern built the facility, which sits on a seventeen-acre site. The railroad also contracted with Motor Convoy, an auto-haulaway trucking firm, to handle movements from Meridian to the dealers; however, Ford deals only with the railroad. Two computer programs are used in the operation. One monitors damage to new autos and links it to the haulaway driver. The other program gives the haulaway carrier shipment information early so the truck movements to dealers can be planned. Norfolk Southern also has a contractor that unloads the railcars and pre-stages the autos in position for each truck trailer. "The unloading contractor has a Ford originated printout before the vehicles arrive at Meridian. He knows immediately where to place the vehicle upon arrival."[9]

---

[7] June S. Bischof, comments made at the National Forum of Air Cargo, Inc., Oakland, Ca., July 30, 1987. Bischof is a senior transportation analyst for Nabisco Brands.

[8] Jack Barry, "Negotiation-Application," *Council of Logistics Management Fall 1987 Annual Conference Proceedings,* vol. 2 (Oak Brook, Ill.: CLM, 1987), p. 20.

[9] Norfolk Southern's entry to the *Modern Railroads* 1988 Golden Freight Car award contest, unpublished.

Under deregulation carriers lost much of their immunity from antitrust laws. As a result there are some antitrust considerations that negotiators should take into account before negotiations begin.

Another agreement with carriers that the traffic department also must negotiate and administer is an average weight agreement. This involves agreements as to weights of various items shipped repetitively, so that each individual shipment does not have to be weighed.

Rate Regulatory Bodies

In a few instances transportation rates are still subject to the approval of a regulatory body. In that situation the traffic manager follows the quasijudicial hearings and participates to represent his or her company's interests. For example, in instances in which rail users are dependent upon a single railroad for service, they are referred to as being captive shippers and are still subject to protection by the ICC. By some rulings, their rates are limited to 180 percent of the railroad's out-of-pocket costs. One attorney complained that this

> gives any railroad in the transportation chain a free hand to exact higher freight rates—as long as the arbitrary standard of 180 percent of cost on the through rate isn't exceeded.
>
>   Would you accept this situation if your through rates are, say, at 175 percent of the railroad's costs, while your competitors' rates are 25 to 30 points lower? Assuming, of course, that you can find out how much lower your competitors' rates are in these days of exempt and contract traffic.[10]

In a similar type of case settled in 1994, the ICC adopted the "stand-alone cost constraint" in which the ICC "estimates the cost of an efficiently designed and operated hypothetical stand-alone railroad"[11] with which to compare the rates charged to the captive coal customer.

In the cases just described, the issues may seem esoteric, but that was often the nature of rate regulation. The point to realize here is that in these situations the traffic manager is expected to proceed in a lawyer-like manner.

CARRIER SELECTION

Selecting the mode and then the specific carrier within that mode are other fundamental activities of the traffic department. However, the decision regarding which transport mode or modes to use may not be exclusively determined by the traffic manager. In many corporations the decision to use more expensive forms of transportation (such as air freight) is made by senior

---

[10] Edward D. Greenberg, "The Troubling Effects of the Midtec Decision," *Inbound Logistics*, November 1988, p. 18.

[11] *Journal of Commerce,* October 25, 1994, p. 3B.

management. Indeed, initial decisions to locate facilities may have been based on modal choice: the traditional site for a warehouse was often the point where it was most cost-effective to have shipments go in by rail and out by truck.

Carrier selection is a topic for which an abundance of studies have been carried out. John Grabner of the Ohio State University and Richard Brand of Goodyear Aerospace were involved in two studies conducted ten years apart, in 1975 and 1985. They found relatively little change in the factors, with two exceptions: First, shippers made more use of modal and multimodal alternatives. Second, there was an increased use of bids and negotiated rates. (The process for selecting carriers changed more than the criteria used for selecting them.) Regarding changing carriers, "there wasn't much difference between the 1985 and 1975 findings. In both cases, poor service was the most important reason for considering a carrier change."[12]

Professors G. Chow and R. F. Poist studied how the quality of service influenced the carrier selection process. They found that twenty-two different factors were used. The ten most important, in descending order, were door-to-door rates or costs, freight loss and damage experience, claims-processing experience, transit time reliability, experience with carrier in negotiating rate changes, shipment tracing, door-to-door transit time, quality of pickup and delivery service, availability of single-line service, and equipment availability.[13] Several other service factors (discussed later in the chapter) were shipment expediting (ranked eleventh), in-transit privileges (ranked sixteenth), and diversion/reconsignment (ranked seventeenth). More recently, Professor M. A. McGinnis analyzed a number of studies concerning the freight transportation choice and found that service is more important than cost.[14]

A 1990 study of small manufacturing firms found that shipment pickup is the most important criterion for selecting a motor carrier.[15] This perhaps reflects the indifferent and inconsistent performance of some motor carriers when they serve very small accounts.

Buyers of freight transportation may have their own weights that they give to carrier service factors. Michael L. Johnston, transportation manager of GM's Delco Remy Division, suggests these factor weightings:

[12] John Grabner and Richard Brand, "The Carrier Selection Process Has Changed," *Transport Topics,* April 14, 1986, pp. 13, 17.

[13] Garland Chow and Richard F. Poist, "The Measurement of Quality of Service and the Transportation Purchase Decision," *Logistics and Transportation Review,* vol. 20, no. 1 (1984), 29.

[14] Michael A. McGinnis, "The Relative Importance of Cost and Service in Freight Transportation Choice: Before and after Deregulation," *Transportation Journal,* Fall 1990, pp. 12–19. See also the same author's "A Comparative Evaluation of Freight Transportation Choice Models," *Transportation Journal,* Winter 1989, pp. 36–46.

[15] Kenneth R. Evans, Howard D. Feldman, and Jerry Foster, "Purchasing Motor Carrier Service: An Investigation of the Criteria Used by Small Manufacturing Firms," *Journal of Small Business Management,* January 1990, pp. 39–47.

1. Carrier's area of geographic coverage, 0.5
2. Carrier's marketing efforts, 0.4
3. Carrier's transit performance, 1.8
4. Equipment availability and cleanliness, 1.1
5. Customer service (shipper-carrier computer interface available, shipment status reports, and so on), 1.4
6. Pricing, 1.4
7. Billing accuracy and timeliness, 1.2
8. Loss and damage claims handling, 1.2
9. Carrier financial stability, 1.0

Each factor can be scored from 0 to 10. Johnston believes that employees having direct contact with the carrier's efforts should do the scoring and that the completed scoresheets should be given to the carrier.[16]

PRIVATE TRANSPORTATION

In the field of domestic logistics, the term **private transportation** is used when firms own and operate their own trucks, railcars, barges, ships, and airplanes. Weyerhauser Corporation has a subsidiary that runs seven ships. These ships carry mainly Weyerhauser cargo but also carry other cargo during slow periods. Figure 7-5 shows an equipment availability roster of a service that allows private shippers (that own railroad tank cars) to lease or sublease them back and forth as their needs for this specialized type of equipment fluctuate.

Traffic managers who are frustrated with inconsistent service on some shipments are sometimes forced into private trucking. Most firms also run a few small trucks and vans for use around plants or for trips to and from the post office and airport (usually the traffic manager's responsibility).

The growth of private trucking is related to a number of factors. The most important single factor is the improved level of customer service that private trucking makes feasible. Another advantage of private trucking is the advertising of products by way of the billboards that appear on the trucks. This factor can be especially important when the vehicles are attractively designed and have courteous drivers, creating a positive impression on the thousands of potential customers who see the vehicles each day. When the traffic manager uses both private carriage and contract carriage, he or she has a good working knowledge of the costs of running trucks and is in a better position to evaluate

[16] Michael L. Johnston, "Do Your Carriers Measure Up?" *Handling & Management,* June 1986, p. 64. The 1-to-10 score is multiplied by the weighting factor, with the top score being 100.

UTIL-I-FAX® SHEET

A LISTING OF RAILCARS AVAILABLE FOR SUBLEASING

PUBLISHED BY UNION TANK CAR COMPANY • A MEMBER OF THE MARMON GROUP OF COMPANIES

EASTERN	CENTRAL	SOUTHEAST	MIDWEST	SOUTHWEST	WEST COAST
71 Arch Street	205 Manor Oak One	5775 Peachtree-Dunwoody Rd.	111 W. Jackson Blvd.	16225 Park Ten Place	2815 Mitchell Drive
Greenwich, CT 06830	Pittsburgh, PA 15220	Atlanta, GA 30342	Chicago, IL 60604	Houston, TX 77084	Walnut Creek, CA 94598
(203) 661-8000	(412) 341-8003	(404) 255-8859	(312) 431-5000	(713) 578-8859	(415) 932-2075

FEBRUARY 1, 1991

SPECIALTY CARS NEEDED TO SUBLEASE.
NOTE OUR 'UTIL-I-FAX NEEDS' SECTION.

No. Cars	New	DOT Class	Capacity	Last Contents	Truck	Unloading	Lining	Remarks
INSULATED, EXTERIOR COILED TANK CARS								
3		111A100W3	4,000	PROPYLENE GLYCOL	40FR	T & BOP	NO	LONG TERM ONLY
1		111A60W1	8,000	CRUDE VEG OIL	50	BTM	NO	AVAIL TIL 11-92.
1		111A100W3	10,000	PULP MILL LIQUID	50	BTM	NO	FOR NON-REG LOADING
1		111A60W1	10,000	RESIN SOLUTION	50	T + BOP	NO	AVAIL LONG TERM.
3		111A100W6	10,000	ROSIN	50	T + BOP	NO	STAINLESS TANK
5		111A60W3	10,000	STOCK OIL	70FR	T + BOP	NO	AVAIL THRU 1-93
20		104W	10,000	LUBE	70FR	BOP	NO	AVAIL LONG TERM
25		111A60W1	10,000	FUEL OIL	50	BOP	NO	AVAIL LONG TERM
5		111A60W3	10,500	SYNTHETIC RESINS	50	T + BOP	NO	AVAIL LONG TERM
1		111A100W3	16,000	NEW COATING	100	T + B	P 2310	AVAIL LONG TERM. S/VEN
3		111A60W1	16,000	POTASSIUM HYDROXIDE	100	T & B	YES	AVAIL LONG TERM
35		111A100W3	16,000	CAUSTIC	100	T & BOP	P-2310	NEW LININGS-LONG TERM
60		111A100W3	16,000	SODIUM ALUMINATE	100	T & B	YES	AVAIL LONG TERM

* IDENTIFIES NEW LISTINGS QUICKLY.
CALL YOUR LOCAL CUSTOMER SERVICE REPRESENTATIVE
OR UTIL-I-FAX REPRESENTATIVE WILLIAM R. HANSEN AT (312) 431-5050 / FAX: (312) 347-5707.

UTIL-I-FACT: THE FIRST RECORDED USE OF A "REFRIGERATOR" CAR IN THE USA
WAS ON JULY 1ST, 1851. IT CARRIED EIGHT TONS OF BUTTER.

UTIL-I-FAX — SINCE 1970 — 21 YEARS OF SERVICE TO OUR CUSTOMERS.

Figure 7-5 Excerpt from a listing of rail tank cars available for leasing and subleasing. (Courtesy of Union Tank Car Company.)

the merits of carrier rate proposals. Petroleum companies like to have deliveries to filling stations made in tank trucks carrying their brand name, rather than having the station's tanks filled from an unmarked truck.

For many companies private trucking also offers the advantage of being less expensive than motor common carriers. This is typically the case when the private trucking operation is able to achieve full loads in both directions. Figure 7-6 shows a trailer designed to carry new autos in one direction and general freight in the other. Many private fleet managers use the services of a broker to ensure a backhaul load of agricultural products.

In 1978 the ICC, for the first time since the 1940s, allowed a private carrier to operate also as a for-hire carrier. The company involved was known as the Toto Purchasing and Supply Company. Today, when a private carrier applies to the ICC to become a common or contract carrier, it is known as applying for Toto operating rights. Another new option for private fleets is known as compensated intercorporate hauling. Until the 1980 Motor Carrier Act it was illegal for one division of the same company to use the private fleet of another division or subsidiary. This restriction has been removed.

Also available to private fleet managers is the option of establishing an in-house brokerage service. Anyone can become a broker by applying to the ICC and paying an application fee. A firm typically also applies to the ICC under Toto authority to become a contract or common carrier. The private fleet manager can now, acting as a broker, solicit additional business for the firm's for-hire trucking service. The firm can also generate business for other for-hire carriers and be paid by them, usually between 5 percent and 10 percent of the transportation charges.

With the development of third-party logistics, private fleets are being formed in conjunction with warehousing and distribution services. Quality Express of Arlington, Texas, was formed by a Missouri trucking firm and a Texas warehousing and logistics company to distribute Whirlpool appliances. The trucks carry the Whirlpool logo and the new firm's drivers "not only take the goods to the retailer [but also] call ahead. The trucking company put cellular phones in the cabs and ramps or liftgates on the vehicle."[17]

The decision to enter into a private trucking operation should be carefully researched and analyzed well in advance. One factor commonly ignored in the cost calculations of private trucking is the requirement that the operation be managed by a professional. All too often traffic managers assume that, along with their many other responsibilities, they will also supervise the private trucking operation. Later, when it is discovered that all but the smallest fleets each require a full-time manager (to supervise vehicle scheduling, maintenance, labor relations, and so on), the firm is faced with a large, unanticipated expense.

Private fleets are also subject to safety regulations. In 1991 the federal DOT's Office of Motor Carrier Safety closed down the fleet operated by the transportation division of a New Jersey food distributor for flagrant safety

---

[17] *Transport Topics*, February 10, 1992, p. 11.

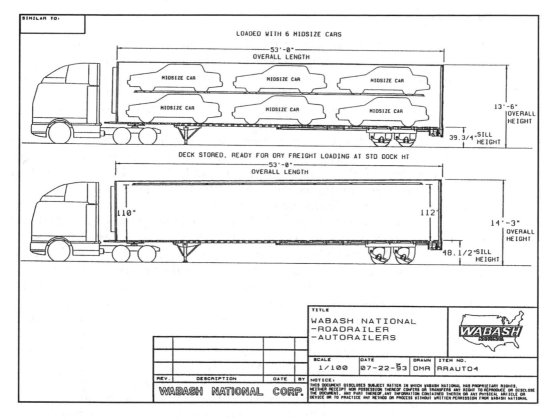

Figure 7-6   RoadRailer trailer designed to carry autos in one direction and general freight in return. Note rail wheels on rear; rig can operate on highways or on rails. (Courtesy RoadRailer Division, Wabash National Corp.)

violations. "According to the OMC, the carrier failed to conduct annual vehicle inspections, test its drivers for drugs, keep hours-of-service records and daily vehicle inspection reports, and maintain minimum insurance."[18]

Private trucking fleets are often very large. Giant Foods, for example, has a fleet that serves 153 supermarkets in the Washington-Baltimore area. In late 1991 the company's roster of equipment included 270 truck tractors, 537 refrigerated trailers, 115 freezer trailers, 835 dry van trailers, and 330 other vehicles (such as vans, light trucks, straight trucks, and support vehicles). "About 150 of the older dry vans are detailed to Giant's construction division, which builds its stores, mostly for on-site storage and for transporting materials."[19]

[18] *Transport Topics,* April 15, 1991, p. 27.

[19] *Transport Topics,* September 30, 1991, p. 12.

DOCUMENTATION

The traffic department is responsible for completing all of the documents needed to transport the firm's products. Today many carriers provide software that enables the shipper to use computers to generate all of the commonly used documents. Shippers also have their own order-processing software, which also is capable of generating transportation documents.

The most important single transportation document is the **bill of lading,** which is the basic operating paper in the industry. The bill of lading functions as a delivery receipt when products are tendered to carriers. Upon receipt of the freight, the carrier signs the bill of lading and gives the original of it to the shipper. The signed original of the bill of lading is the shipper's legal proof that the carrier received the freight.

The bill of lading contains a binding contract specifying the duties and obligations of both carrier and shipper. The bill of lading contract for surface carriers is basically standardized by law and greatly simplifies the traffic manager's job because it specifies exactly the duties of the shipper and carrier.

There are two types of bills of lading: the straight and the order. On a straight bill of lading, which is printed on white paper, the name of the consignee is stated in the appropriate place and the carrier is under a strict legal obligation to deliver the freight to the named consignee and to no one else. Ownership of the goods is neither stated nor implied. On the order bill of lading, which is printed on yellow paper, the name of the consignee is not specified. For example, assume that a lumber company in Seattle has loaded a boxcar of plywood that it has not yet sold. It would use an order bill and tender the shipment to the Burlington Northern Railroad, which would start the car moving toward Chicago. Once a buyer for the plywood is found, the shipper would send via mail the original copy of the order bill to a bank near the buyer and would also tell the buyer which bank had possession of the order bill. The buyer would take it to the bank and pay for the plywood, and the bank would give the original copy to the buyer. The buyer would take it to the railroad, and the railroad would deliver the carload of plywood. (Order bills are used in one other situation—that involving slow payers—because they guarantee that the customer must pay for the products prior to receipt.)

An additional classification of bills is the specific form: long, short, and preprinted. The long-form bill of lading, which may be either an order or straight bill, contains the standard information on the face of the bill (see Figure 7-7), and on the reverse side it contains the entire contract between carrier and shipper. The reverse side is printed in extremely small print. Because of the difficulty of reading the long-form contract and the printing costs of including the contract on all bills, in 1949 the railroads and motor carriers adopted the short-form bill of lading. The short form has the following statement on its face: "Every service to be performed hereunder shall be subject to all the terms and conditions of the Uniform Domestic Straight Bill of Lading."

UNIFORM FREIGHT CLASSIFICATION 7

(Uniform Domestic Straight Bill of Lading, adopted by Carriers in Official and Western Classification
territories, March 15, 1922, as amended August 1, 1930, and June 15, 1941.)

UNIFORM STRAIGHT BILL OF LADING

Original—Not Negotiable

Shipper's No..........

(To be Printed on "White" Paper)

Agent's No.............

Company

RECEIVED, subject to the classifications and tariffs in effect on the date of the issue of this Bill of Lading,

at.., 19...

from...

the property described below, in apparent good order, except as noted (contents and condition of contents of packages unknown), marked, consigned, and destined as indicated below, which said company (the word company being understood throughout this contract as meaning any person or corporation in possession of the property under the contract) agrees to carry to its usual place of delivery at said destination, if on its own road or its own water line, otherwise to deliver to another carrier on the route to said destination. It is mutually agreed, as to each carrier of all or any of said property over all or any portion of said route to destination, and as to each party at any time interested in all or any of said property, that every service to be performed hereunder shall be subject to all the conditions not prohibited by law, whether printed or written, herein contained, including the conditions on back hereof, which are hereby agreed to by the shipper and accepted for himself and his assigns.

(Mail or street address of consignee—For purpose of notification only.)

Consigned to..

Destination...State of.........................County of.....................

Route...

Delivering Carrier.....................................Car Initial........................Car No.....................

No. Pack-ages	Description of Articles, Special Marks, and Exceptions	*Weight (Subject to Correction)	Class or Rate	Check Column	Subject to Section 7 of conditions, if this shipment is to be delivered to the consignee without recourse on the consignor, the consignor shall sign the following statement:
					The carrier shall not make delivery of this shipment without payment of freight and all other lawful charges.
					.... (Signature of consignor.)
					If charges are to be prepaid, write or stamp here, "To be Prepaid."
					....
					Received $................ to apply in prepayment of the charges on the property described hereon.
					Agent or Cashier.
					Per................ (The signature here acknowledges only the amount prepaid.)

"If the shipment moves between two ports by a carrier by water, the law requires that the bill of lading shall state whether it is "carrier's or shipper's weight."

Note.—Where the rate is dependent on value, shippers are required to state specifically in writing the agreed or declared value of the property.

The agreed or declared value of the property is hereby specifically stated by the shipper to be not exceeding

Charges advanced:

....per........

$....................

....Shipper.   ....Agent.

Per..   Per........................

Permanent postoffice address of shipper..

Figure 7-7   A long-form bill of lading. (Reproduced by permission of tariff publisher.)

Another type of bill of lading, which may be a long, short, order, or straight, is preprinted. In theory, the bill of lading is prepared and issued by the carrier. In fact, however, most shippers buy their bills and then have them preprinted with a list of the products they regularly ship. Figure 7-8 illustrates a preprinted short-form bill of lading. Shippers go to the expense of buying and printing their own bills because, in practice, they frequently prepare them prior to calling the carrier. The preparation is part of their computerized order-processing procedures. The preprinted bill can be prepared

Figure 7-8 A preprinted short-form bill of lading.

more rapidly and with less chance of error. The shipper can insert the correct classification rather than letting the carrier determine it.

Another basic document that the traffic manager must be familiar with is the freight bill. It is an invoice, submitted by the carrier, requesting to be paid. Often the traffic manager must approve each freight bill before it is paid. An issue involving freight bills that received considerable attention in 1994 was referred to as off-bill discounting. In this situation, the carrier would send the freight bill to the shipper, who would add the charges on the bill to the costs of goods on the invoice sent to the buyer. Unknown to the buyer of the goods, the shipper would receive a rebate for a portion of the transportation charges shown on the freight bill.

FREIGHT PAYMENT AND AUDIT SERVICES

The ICC requires that carriers be paid within specific numbers of working days. Shipper-carrier contracts also specify how quickly bills must be paid. In an attempt to meet these time limits conveniently, many traffic managers participate in bill-paying services. These services were originally known as bank payment plans, since banks were the first to offer the service. Now a variety of other firms, in addition to banks, offer these automated freight bill-paying services. Once the traffic manager initiates the program with the payment service, the carriers submit their freight bills directly to the service. The payment service treats the freight bills as checks drawn on the shipper's freight account and then pays the carriers.

These payment plans are growing because shippers appreciate the convenience of the payment service handling the paperwork involved in paying freight bills. Carriers support the concept because of the speed with which they are compensated for their transportation services. The payment service provides summaries of traffic activity that are useful to shippers when planning future freight consolidation. Computerized programs are also used to detect duplicate billings. Payment services also offer bill auditing service; that is, they ensure that the proper rate was charged. Some prepayment services have the tariffs their clients use loaded into their computer database and preaudit the bill prior to paying it.

Some shippers also audit their own freight bills. If this work is conducted by employees of the company, it is known as an internal audit. The external audit is performed by an independent third party; some freight-bill auditors also offer freight payment services. Both types of audit are designed to detect current errors that result in overcharges and to correct these errors in the future. Figure 7-9 is an example of a form letter used by a freight-bill auditor to request that a common carrier reimburse the auditor (on behalf of the auditor's client) for the carrier's overcharges.

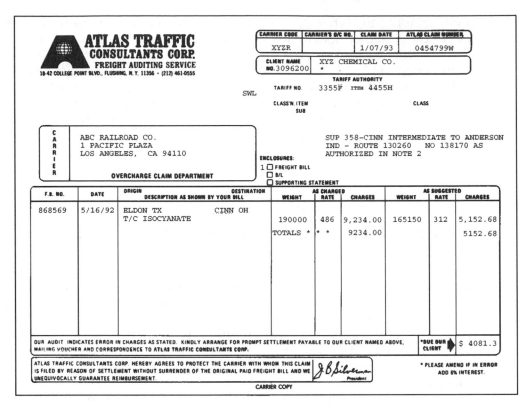

Figure 7-9   An overcharge claim form. (Courtesy of Atlas Traffic Consultants Corporation, Flushing, N.Y.)

A trade journal article in 1994 indicated that external audit companies were finding that their clients were being overcharged on an average of between 4 and 5 percent.[20] The usual arrangement is to split 50-50 the amount recovered between the audit service and its client.

ROUTING

The top sections of Figures 7-7 and 7-8 show a line entitled *route*. Shippers have the right to select the carriers along the route to their shipment's destination. For domestic shipments today, this is almost a nonissue since LTL motor carriers have nationwide authority and rail mergers have resulted in many geographic areas being served by a single railroad.

[20] *Transportation and Distribution,* March 1994, p. 53.

In addition to the traditional routing contract considerations, there are other routing concerns. With respect to hazardous material movements, local restrictions on highway movements and warehouse storage of certain hazardous materials often place severe limitations upon routes the hazardous goods can move. Even some cargoes are incompatible or at least disliked by carriers; see Figure 7-10. Urban traffic congestion is costly to trucks; in addition, truck movements and parking are sometimes restricted to permit more auto traffic to be handled. Sometimes firms with excess inventory deliberately choose slow routing, using the carrier as a temporary warehouse.

"IT'S CARRYING A LOAD OF FERTILIZER."

Figure 7-10   Undesirable cargo. (Reproduced by permission of *Jet Cargo News.*)

Computers are widely used for routing today. Figure 7-11 shows some computer-generated truck routes for the St. Louis area.

Firms sometimes issue routing guides as part of their purchase orders and expect vendors to follow instructions. If they do not, the vendors become liable for penalties. K-mart received about $2 million from vendors in 1986 as charge-back fees because the vendors did not follow the instructions in K-mart's routing manual. "To reinforce the importance of its routing guide, K-mart charges back the entire cost of the move if the vendor uses the wrong carrier."[21]

[21] *Inbound Logistics,* September–October 1987, p. 33.

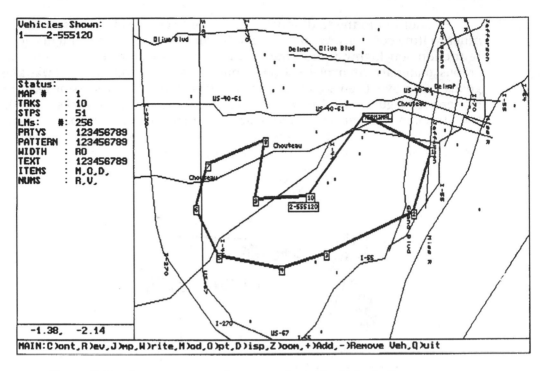

Figure 7-11 Computer-generated route map for trucks, St. Louis. (Source: Microanalytics Inc., of Arlington, Va.)

The traffic manager must also plan for contingencies and have alternative routes and, sometimes, carriers. In the early 1990s, when water levels in the Mississippi River system were low, grain shippers had to switch from barge to rail for many of their downbound shipments. In 1993 the Mississippi was high, and grain shippers sent exports out on the Great Lakes–St. Lawrence River route. In early 1994 there was a Teamsters' strike, and shippers needed to use alternate carriers. As a long-term strategy, the traffic manager sometimes gives a small amount of regular business to different modes or carriers for insurance purposes, such as would be needed in the situations just mentioned.

One allowable exception to the carrier's service obligation is an embargo. This usually happens when excessive congestion is found at a destination or when delivery is impeded because of storm-related damage to the carrier's right-of-way or terminals. After the initial Mount St. Helen's eruption, both the Burlington Northern and the Union Pacific railroads had to place embargoes on traffic destined to several ports because ash and mud from the volcano had blocked the navigation channels between the ports and the ocean and had snarled all transportation facilities.

DIVERSION AND RECONSIGNMENT

Diversion occurs when the shipper notifies the carrier, prior to the shipment's arrival in the destination city, of a change in destination. **Reconsignment** is similar, but it occurs after the car has arrived in the destination city. These services are commonly used in conjunction with order bills of lading. They are also used by shippers of perishables that start their loads in direction of the market and sell it while it is en route.

The tariff of Matson Navigation covering westbound container freight from the mainland to Hawaii devotes an entire page to "Reconsignment, Diversion, or Redelivery." Matson charges $7.85 for amending the bill of lading, and then its charges vary according to (1) whether the destination port in Hawaii was changed, (2) whether it was necessary to rehandle the container, and (3) whether the shipment had already left the port.[22]

TRACING AND EXPEDITING

Tracing is the attempt to locate lost or late shipments. When the traffic department determines that a shipment has not arrived at destination on time, it may contact the carrier to whom it tendered the shipment and ask the carrier to trace the shipment. This is a no-cost service offered by common carriers. Tracing should be requested only when a shipment is unreasonably late. Many airlines and large trucking companies, as well as almost all railroads, have computer systems that monitor the progress of freight movements throughout their systems. This enables almost instantaneous tracing by the carrier.

As carriers become more computerized, they can better keep track of equipment and shipments. Many computer programs allow shippers to access portions of their systems. Figure 7-12 is from American President Lines. It lists a toll-free 800 telephone number and then shows a card that fits on a touch-tone phone, indicating which number the shipper should push to make an inquiry. Shippers are given a password that limits their computer inquiries to their own shipments. Drivers for some parcel delivery companies carry the equipment that enables them to record and report the instant each parcel is delivered.

Expediting is another no-cost service of common carriers. It involves notifying the carrier as far in advance as possible of the need to expedite or rapidly move a shipment through the carrier's system. The carrier makes every effort to ensure that the shipment is delivered to destination with maximum speed. The carrier must have sufficient lead time to alert its employees regarding the shipment to be expedited. For the railroads this involves alerting the

---

[22] *Westbound Container Tariff No. 14F, effective January 14, 1994* (San Francisco: Matson Navigation Company, 1994), p. 46.

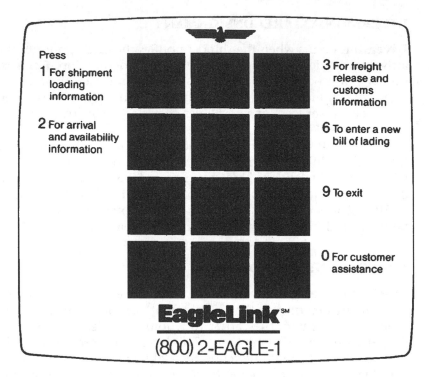

Figure 7-12   EagleLink numbers to be placed on the shipper's telephone. (Courtesy of American President Lines, Ltd.)

yardmaster at each relevant classification yard so that the expedited car can be singled out when it arrives and immediately switched to the proper outbound train. Motor carriers generally notify the operations manager of each freight terminal that the product will be flowing through; in this way, the operations manager can ensure that the product will be quickly placed on the next outbound vehicle. (A specific responsibility sometimes assigned to a shift supervisor in a motor carrier terminal is to see that each piece of expedited freight is removed from the inbound truck and placed on the next outgoing truck.)

LOSS AND DAMAGE

Cargo **loss and damage** has been the bane of the transportation industry since day one. Common carriers traditionally were slow in handling loss and damage claims. Therefore, in 1972 the ICC issued a regulation—the law of loss and damage—that placed three requirements on all surface common carriers. First, common carriers must acknowledge receipt of each loss and damage claim within thirty days. Second, carriers are charged with the responsibility of promptly investigating all new claims. Third, all claims must be resolved within 120 days of their receipt or else the claimant must be given a written explanation as to why the carrier has neither paid the claim nor officially rejected it. Filing claims against carriers is a routine matter; Figure 7-13 shows a loss and damage claim form used by Zellerbach Paper Company.

If a carrier and shipper are not able to resolve a dispute over a loss and damage claim, the dispute is handled by the court system, not the ICC. There are time limitations within which the claim must be filed. Note that there are administrative costs in handling freight claims that are absorbed by the shipper or consignee.

One of the most difficult and challenging aspects of claim work is the determination of the exact dollar amount of the damage. The law states that the common carrier is responsible for the full actual loss sustained by the shipper or consignee. How can this figure be determined? A common rule of thumb is the following:

> The basic thought underlying the federal statutes which define the liability and prescribe the measure of damages in cases of this kind is that the owner shall be made whole by receiving the proper money equivalent for what has actually [been] lost; or, in other words to restore [the owner] to the position he [or she] would have occupied, had the carrier performed its contract.[23]

A key factor in determining the value of the full actual loss is the word *earned*. Assume that a retailer owned the products shipped via a common carrier and that they were damaged beyond repair. The question arises, Should the retailer recover the wholesale price or the retail price? If the products destroyed were going into a general inventory replacement stock, the retailer would recover the wholesale price plus freight costs (if they had been paid) because the retail price has not been earned. Assume, instead, that a product is ordered especially for a customer. When the product arrives, it is damaged and the retailer's customer states that he or she will wait no longer and cancels the order. In this situation the retailer is entitled to the retail price because the profit would have been earned if the carrier had properly performed its service.

Another difficult area for shippers and carriers alike involves concealed loss or damage. If a shipment arrives in damaged condition and the damage is detected before the consignee accepts the goods, the issue is not whether the carrier is liable but the dollar amount of the claim that the carrier must pay. However, concealed loss and damage cases are more difficult to handle because the exterior package does not appear to be damaged or tampered with.

---

[23] *Atlantic Coast Line Ry. Co. vs. Roe*, 118 So. 155.

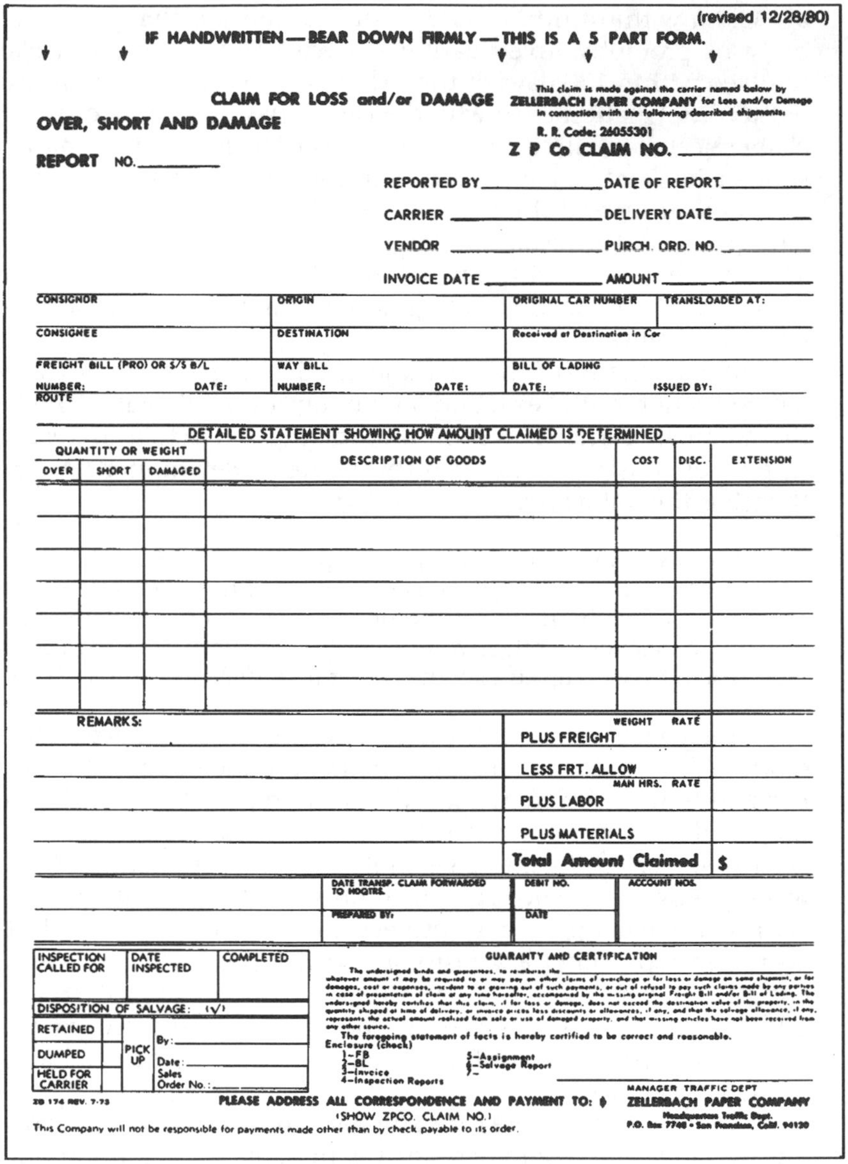

(revised 12/28/80)

IF HANDWRITTEN—BEAR DOWN FIRMLY—THIS IS A 5 PART FORM.

CLAIM FOR LOSS and/or DAMAGE

OVER, SHORT AND DAMAGE

REPORT NO.______

This claim is made against the carrier named below by ZELLERBACH PAPER COMPANY for Loss and/or Damage in connection with the following described shipments:

R. R. Code: 26055301

Z P Co CLAIM NO. ______

REPORTED BY______ DATE OF REPORT______

CARRIER ______ DELIVERY DATE______

VENDOR ______ PURCH. ORD. NO. ______

INVOICE DATE ______ AMOUNT ______

CONSIGNOR	ORIGIN	ORIGINAL CAR NUMBER	TRANSLOADED AT:
CONSIGNEE	DESTINATION	Received at Destination in Car	
FREIGHT BILL (PRO) OR S/S B/L NUMBER: DATE:	WAY BILL NUMBER: DATE:	BILL OF LADING DATE: ISSUED BY:	

ROUTE

DETAILED STATEMENT SHOWING HOW AMOUNT CLAIMED IS DETERMINED

QUANTITY OR WEIGHT			DESCRIPTION OF GOODS	COST	DISC.	EXTENSION
OVER	SHORT	DAMAGED				

REMARKS:	PLUS FREIGHT (WEIGHT RATE)	
	LESS FRT. ALLOW	
	PLUS LABOR (MAN HRS. RATE)	
	PLUS MATERIALS	
	Total Amount Claimed	$

DATE TRANSP. CLAIM FORWARDED TO HDQTRS.	DEBIT NO.	ACCOUNT NOS.
PREPARED BY:	DATE	

INSPECTION CALLED FOR	DATE INSPECTED	COMPLETED

DISPOSITION OF SALVAGE: (√)

RETAINED		PICK UP	By:
DUMPED			Date:
HELD FOR CARRIER			Sales Order No.:

GUARANTY AND CERTIFICATION

The undersigned binds and guarantees, to reimburse the ______ whatever amount it may be required to or may pay on other claims of overcharge or for loss or damage on same shipment, or for damages, cost or expenses, incident to or growing out of such payments, or out of refusal to pay such claims made by any parties in case of presentation of claim at any time hereafter, accompanied by the missing original Freight Bill and/or Bill of Lading. The undersigned hereby certifies that this claim, if for loss or damage, does not exceed the destination value of the property, in the quantity shipped at time of delivery, or invoice prices less discounts or allowances, if any, and that the salvage allowance, if any, represents the actual amount realized from sale or use of damaged property, and that missing articles have not been received from any other source.

The foregoing statement of facts is hereby certified to be correct and reasonable.

Enclosure (check)

1–FB
2–BL
3–Invoice
4–Inspection Reports
5–Assignment
6–Salvage Report
7–

______
MANAGER TRAFFIC DEPT

ZB 174 REV. 7-73

PLEASE ADDRESS ALL CORRESPONDENCE AND PAYMENT TO: ZELLERBACH PAPER COMPANY
Headquarters Traffic Dept.
P.O. Box 7748 • San Francisco, Calif. 94120

(SHOW ZPCO. CLAIM NO.)

This Company will not be responsible for payments made other than by check payable to its order.

Figure 7-13 Loss and damage claim form used by shippers. (Courtesy of the Zellerbach Paper Company, San Francisco.)

At a later date, the consignee opens the package and finds that the product is damaged or missing. As can be appreciated, carriers are reluctant to pay concealed loss and damage claims for two reasons. If the package came through the shipment with no exterior damage, then there is a strong possibility that the product was improperly protected on the inside. If this is the case, the carrier is exempted from liability, since improper packaging is a fault of the shipper. Second, the possibility exists that the consignee's employees broke or stole the products. One writer notes that "carriers do not have a monopoly on damaging freight or on employing 'light-fingered' employees."[24]

Since deregulation, the volume of claims activity has dropped because, during the negotiation process, the shipper may agree to hold the carrier less liable for claims in return for lower transportation charges. In addition, the transportation deregulation acts have reduced carrier liability. The Staggers Act permits railroads to establish *released value* rates (wherein the shipper agrees that a commodity is worth no more than $—— per hundred pounds in case a claim is filed in return for a lower rate) without prior ICC approval. Related to this is the ability of railroads to have *deductibles* in damage claims (wherein the shipper assumes responsibility for the first $—— of a claim in return for a lower rate). Last, the "Staggers Act expressly permits rail carriers to negotiate contracts that specify all terms of the shipping transportation, including those related to liability."[25] The 1980 Motor Carrier Act made changes in motor carrier liability requirements; however, by no means were the requirements eliminated.[26]

Traffic managers and carriers also work together to reduce freight claims, since any reduction benefits them both. Figure 7-14 shows a map produced by CSX Transportation through use of earth satellites. The CSX railcar carried a solar-powered radio that was activated when the rail ride became unusually rough so that its location could be recorded. At the bottom we can see that the events occurred at three different times on April 11, 1993, and that the shock measurement is shown along three dimensions.

In 1979 several shipper and carrier organizations formed the Transportation Arbitration Board (TAB). Shippers and carriers may use this as a means of settling claim disputes. When a claimant and shipper (or consignee) agree to submit their case to TAB, they both pay a fee. The claimant prepares the claim file, including a written statement why it is felt the claim should be paid. This is sent to the carrier, which adds its file and contentions to the file. It is then returned to the claimant, which has a final opportunity to offer a rebuttal brief, with a copy of the rebuttal to go to the carrier. The claimant then sends the entire file to TAB, where a decision is reached.

A policy issue that the shipper must address with respect to claims deals with salvage rights to the damaged goods. Ordinarily, the carrier, or the carrier's insurer, takes possession of the damaged goods after paying the freight claim.

[24] Richard R. Sigmon, *Miller's Law of Freight Loss and Damage Claims,* 3d ed. (Dubuque: Brown, 1967), p. 141. See also William J. Augello, *Freight Claims in Plain English,* 2d ed. (Huntington, N.Y.: Shippers National Freight Claim Council, 1982); and the same author's "The Great Claims Debate," *Distribution,* May 1985, pp. 39–46.

[25] Paul Stephen Dempsey and William Thoms, *Law and Economic Regulation in Transportation* (New York: Quorum Books, 1986), p. 263.

[26] Ibid., pp. 264–266.

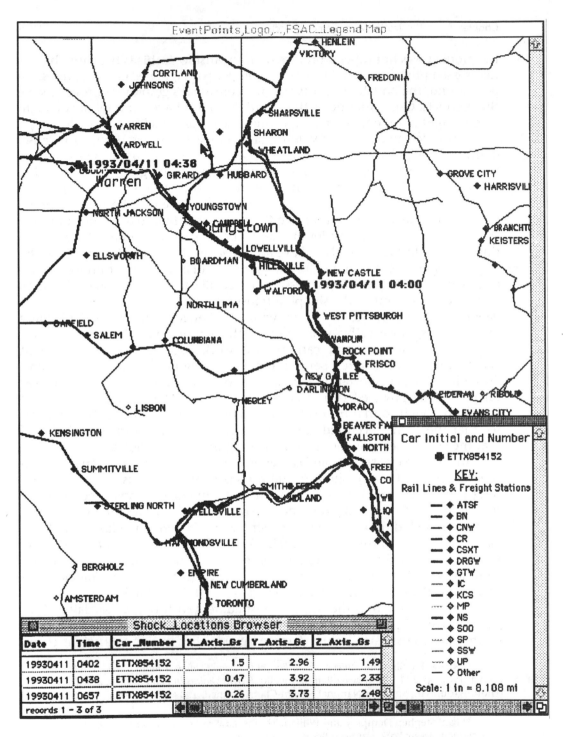

Figure 7-14 Map showing incidence of rough rail rides. (Courtesy CSX Transportation, Inc., Jacksonville, Fla.)

However, there are some disadvantages to the shipper. First, to the extent that the damaged goods are salvaged to the point they can be sold, they will compete in the marketplace with the shipper's own product. Second, if a consumer buys a salvaged product that turns out for some reason or another to be defective, the consumer will go after the original manufacturer of the product.[27]

TRANSIT PRIVILEGES

Transit privileges allow cargo to be stopped en route between its initial origin and final destination and to be unloaded, stored, or processed and then reloaded for shipment to its final destination. Although the products move from A to B and, later, from B to C, the total charges are only for A to C. Because of tapering rates, one long shipment is less costly to the carrier than two shorter trips equal in distance to the long trip.[28]

In an attempt to disperse storage and other activities—often onto land they owned because of the federal land grant program—railroads initiated transit privilege. It allows products or raw materials to be shipped to an intermediate location, where they can be stored, compressed, blended, mixed, milled, inspected, refined, reconditioned, fabricated, assembled, and so on. The regular freight rate is the rate from origin to the intermediate location. Then, generally up to one year later, the products can be shipped from this intermediate location to destination, and only the remainder of the long-haul through rate will be charged.

In-transit operations often imply that the goods are stored for a while. This is a common practice in seasonal situations (that is, for products harvested once a year but consumed over a twelve-month period, or vice versa). However, for products produced and consumed in more even patterns, modern logistical thinking scrutinizes carefully any strategy that encourages storage of inventories. Since the rail industry has moved to contract rate-making, many transit privileges have been eliminated.

REPARATIONS

Reparations can occur only in the few remaining regulated segments of the transportation industry. **Reparations** are payments made to a shipper by a carrier that has charged illegally high rates in the past. The traffic manager must be assertive to protect the interests of his or her company even if it involves alienating carriers. Hence, if a regulatory body finds that past rates

---

[27] James V. Baker Jr., "No, the Carrier Doesn't Have the Right to Salvage Your Damaged Goods," *Inbound Logistics,* February 1988, p. 16.

[28] Tapering transportation costs, or rates, expressed in terms of cents per mile, increase as distance increases, but at a slower rate. That is because the carrier's terminal costs are spread over a larger number of miles.

were illegal, the shipper must then attempt to collect the difference between what was charged and what the regulatory body determined should have been charged.

A late 1988 example of reparations can be found in an ICC decision concerning rates from various points to a salvage yard in Texas. The salvage yard was served by one railroad and was hence a captive customer. In such situations, the Staggers Act limited rail rates to 180 percent of variable cost. The ICC decided that the rate charged in this instance exceeded that limit and ordered the railroad to refund the difference plus interest.[29]

DEMURRAGE AND DETENTION

Demurrage is a penalty payment made by the shipper or consignee to a railroad for keeping a rail car beyond the time when it should be released back to the carrier. Demurrage is also collected by inland water carriers if their barges are kept by the shipper or consignee for a longer period than allowed. Pipelines are involved with demurrage if oil stored in tanks at destination is not removed within specified time limits. **Detention** is basically the same concept as demurrage except that it usually refers to the trucking industry. Users of containers owned by the airlines are subject to similar charges. The carriers' concern is that their equipment will be used as temporary warehouses by either shippers or consignees.

For many traffic managers, handling demurrage and detention are important responsibilities. The rail demurrage tariffs typically state that demurrage payments will start after the expiration of the applicable *free time*. For example, the tariff of South Orient Railroad, which operates in Texas and connects with the Mexican railroad system, says, "Free time for each car will be 36 hours," and the charge is "$50.00 per car day or fraction thereof."[30]

Many traffic managers who are large users of railcars find it advantageous to enter into averaging agreements with the railroads. In an averaging agreement, an accounting system of debits and credits is established. A credit is received every time the shipper or consignee releases a railcar one day early, and a debit is recorded each time a car is surrendered to a carrier one day late.

Since deregulation carriers are able to modify some of their detention and demurrage policies. In late 1988 the Southern Pacific announced a "+3" plan for its intermodal trailers. Customers are allowed three days of free time to either unload or load a trailer, with credits given for early return and debits charged for delayed returns. Debits and credits are reconciled at the end of each month, and if credits outweigh debits, shippers receive $5 for each surplus credit.

Students familiar with commodity markets know that commodities are traded for both immediate and future trades. There are futures markets for rail grain cars. Traffic managers order grain cars for future use, but under a Burlington

---

[29] *On Track,* December 1988, p. 4.

[30] Tariff issued in 1994. The railroad's entire demurrage rules were one full page.

Northern plan, they must use the cars or, if they do not use the cars, pay a $50 cancellation fee or sell their right to use the cars to another shipper.[31]

TRANSPORTATION OF HAZARDOUS MATERIALS

A **hazardous material** is defined in the Hazardous Materials Transportation Act of 1974 as "a substance or material in a quantity and form which may pose an unreasonable risk to health and safety or property when transported in commerce." Hazardous materials are very common and include some everyday household items.

The potential danger involved in the transportation of hazardous materials has been recognized for some time—the federal government began regulating their transport in 1838. The amount of hazardous materials being produced in the United States has increased rapidly, especially in recent years. The 1838 law, called the Act to Provide for the Better Security of the Lives of Passengers on Board Vessels Propelled in Whole or in Part by Steam, specified proper packaging, marking, and stowing requirements for such products as camphene, naphtha, benzene, coal oil, petroleum, oil of vitriol, and nitric acid. In 1866 Congress passed a law stating that the newly discovered superexplosive nitroglycerin could not be transported in the same vehicle or boat that was carrying passengers.

Since 1866 there have been hundreds of changes in federal statutes dealing with the transportation of hazardous materials. Federal regulations deal with the movement, storage, and packaging of hazardous materials. Today one is required to know, track, and record the location of all hazardous materials that one owns or controls or that are being generated. Originating shippers' documents must include a phone number that will be answered twenty-four hours a day. The traffic manager as well as many other managers in a firm's logistics operation are concerned with hazardous materials. In addition, U.S. regulations are being modified to resemble more closely those issued by the United Nations regarding international movements of dangerous goods.

States have their own hazardous materials transportation regulations. Several assess special fees or taxes on shippers of hazardous matter and use the funds to help support local hazardous spill response teams.

Traffic managers working for firms that handle hazardous materials have several important responsibilities. While the hazardous materials are under the manager's control, he or she must see that the materials are moved safely. There are also federal requirements pertaining to the training of personnel to handle the materials, the packaging of the product, the marking and labeling of the packages, the placarding of the vehicles that transport the materials, and the information required on shipping documents. Sometimes only certain routes may be used to move the cargo. The color, symbols, and numbers of the diamond-shaped placards seen on truck trailers, containers,

---

[31] *On Track,* November 1–15, 1988, p. 4.

and railcars identify the hazardous properties of the products being carried. Fire and rescue personnel arriving at the scene of an accident involving a hazardous-materials carrier can take information from the placard and call (via an 800 phone number) Chemtrec, the Washington-based office of the Chemical Manufacturers Association, for immediate advice.

Hazardous wastes are a related topic, for they are a subset of hazardous materials.

> An example of the confusion that can arise [between hazardous waste and hazardous materials] was related by the manager of a trucking terminal.
>
> A gallon container of a liquid material considered hazardous was accidentally punctured by the fork of a lift truck. His employees were trained in handling this sort of incident and reacted quickly, using sawdust to absorb the mildly hazardous common household liquid. The sawdust absorbent was placed into a plastic container along with the damaged gallon pail. When it came time to dispose of the sawdust, they discovered that from what had been only hazardous material, they had created hazardous waste. Disposal problems took a quantum leap from that point.[32]

CONSOLIDATING SMALL SHIPMENTS

The small shipments problem represents one of the most bewildering situations faced by the traffic manager. Small shipments are usually defined as those that weigh more than 100 or 150 pounds and less than 500 pounds. Shipments under those weights can be handled relatively expeditiously and inexpensively by either the Postal System or UPS.

The nature of transportation costs is that it costs less on a per-pound basis to ship a larger quantity. This is because certain costs (fixed, administrative, or terminal) are the same per shipment. When the shipment is larger, such costs can be allocated over a larger weight. The traffic manager is therefore always trying to consolidate large numbers of small shipments into small numbers of large shipments. Some **shipment consolidation** activities are shown in Figure 7-15.

> Virtually all forms of shipment consolidation involve the aggregation of customer orders across time or place or both. Aggregation across time occurs when the shipper holds orders or delays purchases to consolidate shipments. Rather than ship each order immediately, the shipping plan might schedule the release of shipments every second, third, or fourth day. Aggregation across place involves the consolidation of shipments to different destinations within the same general area.[33]

[32] *Material Handling Engineering,* February 1992, pp. 55–56.

[33] John E. Tyworth, Joseph L. Cavinato, and C. John Langley Jr., *Traffic Management: Planning, Operations, and Control* (Reading, Mass.: Addison-Wesley, 1987), p. 265. See also Randolph W. Hall, "Consolidation Strategy: Inventory, Vehicles, and Terminals," *Journal of Business Logistics,* September 1987, pp. 57–73.

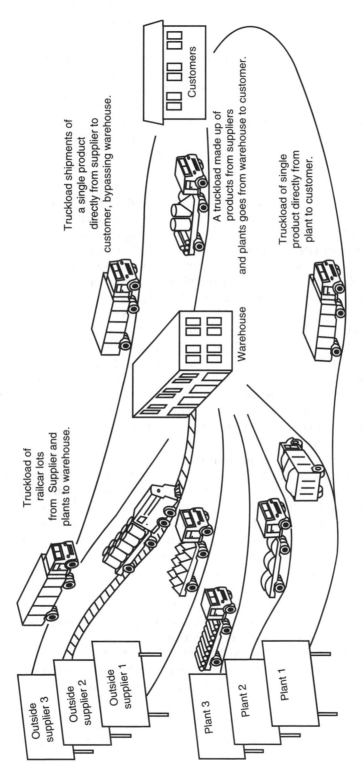

Figure 7-15   The traffic manager consolidates shipments whenever he or she can.

Truckload shipments of a single product directly from supplier to customer, bypassing warehouse.

A truckload made up of products from suppliers and plants goes from warehouse to customer.

Truckload of single product directly from plant to customer.

Truckload of railcar lots from Supplier and plants to warehouse.

Customers

Warehouse

Outside supplier 3

Outside supplier 2

Outside supplier 1

Plant 3

Plant 2

Plant 1

Related to consolidation analysis is an understanding of the postponement principle, which is the deliberate delay in shipping, labeling, or otherwise committing inventory. One of the reasons for this is to be able to consolidate shipments. Also, once inventory is committed, it no longer is available for filling other orders, even though its carrying costs continue. Professors W. Zinn and D. J. Bowersox have analyzed the use of the postponement principle. They believe there are five types of postponement. Four of these deal with form: labeling, packaging, assembly, and manufacturing. The fifth one is time itself.[34]

Smaller shipments are problems for shippers for two reasons. First, truckers are reluctant to accept certain small shipments because of their physical characteristics. These products are often light in weight and called balloon traffic. Typical products in this category are toys, stuffed animals, and furniture. Second, motor common carriers are reluctant to accept small shipments based on the low volume of shipments tendered by the shipper, since carriers often feel that they lose money on "low volume" customers.

The traffic manager must be innovative to compensate for the high cost and poor service given to small shipments. While there are numerous solutions, several approaches appear to be most readily used. One involves the use of interfirm consolidation, or shipper cooperatives. A second type of solution involves intrafirm consolidation. In this case the traffic manager seeks ways to consolidate shipments within his or her own firm. This typically involves a systematic study of the firm's past shipments in order to locate consolidation possibilities. The result of this analysis is the use of either **make-bulk** or **break-bulk** distribution centers. Products move rapidly through these facilities.

A consolidation, or make-bulk, center is illustrated in Figure 7-16. Here a U.S. chain store importing consumer goods from various Asian countries establishes a consolidation point in Hong Kong. All the Asian vendors are instructed to ship their products to the Hong Kong consolidator, which loads them into containers and ships the full containers to the United States.

Figure 7-17 illustrates a break-bulk operation. It shows a three-compartment recycling container of the type we see frequently. It is used as an early step in the recycling process. Each of us is asked to take the metal, plastic, and glass containers from our trash and place them into the recycling container's three compartments. We do the original sorting, and the containers are emptied into trucks that also have three compartments to keep the glass, plastic, and metal separate. In this situation we individuals who separate the containers in our trash perform a break-bulk function. The trucks that unload the recycling container into their own larger compartments are performing a make-bulk function as they add the segregated contents of more and more recycling containers.

---

[34] Walter Zinn and Donald J. Bowersox, "Planning Physical Distribution with the Principle of Postponement," *Journal of Business Logistics,* September 1988, pp. 117–135.

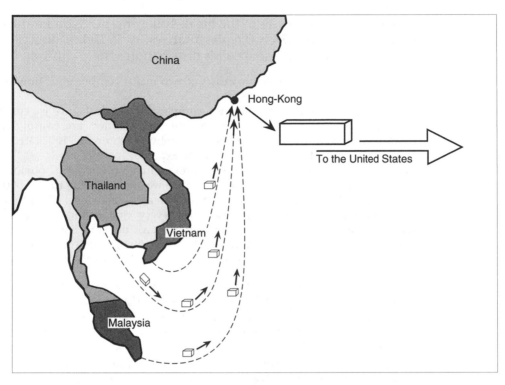

Figure 7-16   Using a consolidation point in Hong Kong for goods bound for the United States. United States chain stores buying in southeast Asia have goods shipped to a consolidator in Hong Kong, who sends full containers to the United States.

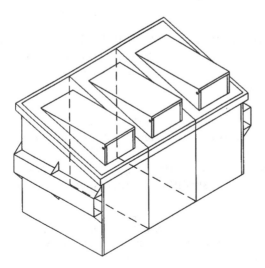

Figure 7-17   A three-compartment recycling container. (Courtesy Consolidated Fabricators Corp., Vernon, Cal.)

Some years ago, one user of the break-bulk concept, Avon Products, distributed cosmetics to its 375,000 representatives. W. R. Dykes, director of corporate traffic for the firm, described his distribution system this way:

> The Avon distribution system consists of two major components: line haul and delivery.
>
> *Line haul* service to the delivery company is practical since we control the shipping date for each order. A geographic area's orders are consolidated for truckload service to the city where the delivery company is located, which ensures high-speed service at a reasonable expense.
>
> *Delivery company* service to the representative's residence is, obviously, the major factor in our distribution system since we are delivering to 375,000 representatives every two weeks. . . . The minimum acceptable level of on-time delivery performance is 99 percent. We serve every city in the United States of 60,000+ population via an independent package delivery company. In doing this, we use the services of 185 delivery companies. The delivery companies are identified as local, extended or contract. Let me briefly explain the differences:
>
> - Local delivery companies serve the commercial zone of the city in which they are located. Their delivery market is urban/suburban.
> - Extended delivery companies, as the name implies, extend their service beyond the commercial zone. They serve the urban/suburban market plus other towns, rural routes, etc.
> - Contract delivery companies are generally dedicated to serving Avon exclusively. They operate five days each week for us and serve the largest metropolitan areas. Their delivery market includes urban, suburban, other town and rural routes.
>
> *UPS* is used in those markets which cannot practically be served by a delivery company, and *Parcel Post* or *Bus* service is used for a very small percentage of our deliveries where delivery company service or UPS is not available.[35]

Shippers study the rate structures of UPS and other parcel delivery firms to determine at which point it is least expensive to tender the shipments to the parcel carrier. L. L. Bean uses UPS to make deliveries, but often it finds it cheaper to send a trailer or container load to the West Coast and there tender it to UPS for local deliveries.

Computer programs that make consolidations easier to achieve are now available. Figure 7-18 shows a route and schedule computer printout for grocery deliveries. The printout shows only the results of the consolidation analysis. According to the software firm, the routing logic considers store time commitments, order sizes, equipment constraints, and road speeds and distances. There

[35] Comments of W. R. Dykes, director of corporate transportation for Avon Products, Inc., at the American Package Express Carriers Meeting, San Francisco, June 7, 1979. Commercial zones are established by the ICC in metropolitan regions to include all areas that should be considered the same as the central city for rate-making purposes.

CAPITAL FOOD COMPANY
ROUTE DATA SUMMARY
ROUTE GROUP:MONDAY

ROUTE:002   CLASS:1   TYPE:L   DRIVER 1:BENNER   DRIVER 2:   TRACTOR:*007   TRAILER:*42R

SN	IDENTIFIER	ARRIVE	DEPART	TZ	DRIVE	OD	WAIT	SVC	DIST	WEIGHT	VOL	PCS	PAL
DI	CAPITAL FOOD COMPANY	10/10/88 03:47	04:02	E				:15		23128	1427	197	197
01	CHAMBERTAIN PIZZA	10/10/88 05:00	05:18	E	:58			:18	11.7	512	55	9	
02	VALUE MARKET	10/10/88 05:21	05:45	E	:03			:24	0.7	248	125	15	
03	CADYVILLE BAKERY	10/10/88 05:56	06:12	E	:11			:16	3.1	1146	67	7	
04	SINCLAIR'S DELI	10/10/88 06:30	06:48	E	:18			:18	3.3	713	65	9	
05	LANDMARK GRILL	10/10/88 07:01	07:23	E	:13			:22	3.8	2235	82	13	
06	FLAME RESTAURANT	10/10/88 07:34	07:50	E	:11			:16	2.0	912	57	7	
07	PIKE PASTA	10/10/88 08:08	08:38	E	:18			:30	3.5	2835	167	22	
08	CHICKEN SHACK	10/10/88 08:41	09:10	E	:03			:29	0.4	2925	117	20	
09	BRADDOCK ROAD ONE STOP	10/10/88 09:25	09:41	E	:15			:16	2.9	1053	39	7	
10	MURPHY'S	10/10/88 09:56	10:28	E	:15			:32	8.4	3699	177	24	
11	MCLEAN DINER	10/10/88 10:42	11:00	E	:14			:18	5.4	1128	93	9	
12	GREENWOOD INN	10/10/88 11:11	11:32	E	:11			:21	3.5	1560	104	17	
13	GARDEN CITY PUB	10/10/88 11:35	11:56	E	:03			:21	0.6	1774	74	12	
14	RODNEY'S	10/10/88 12:02	12:36	E	:06			:34	1.9	2388	205	26	
RE	CAPITAL FOOD SUMMARY	10/10/88 13:26	13:41	E	:50			:15	11.5				
					4:09			5:45	62.7	23128	1427	197	197

*** END OF REPORT ***

Figure 7-18 Computer printout showing route and schedule for grocery deliveries. (Reprinted with the permission of STSC, Inc., 2115 E. Jefferson St., Rockville, MD 20852.)

is also an order-splitting and consolidation feature that can be set to deal with greater-than-truckload splits, making it easier to prevent overflows and less-than-truckload splits and thus achieve better equipment utilization.

ACHIEVING TRANSPORTATION QUALITY

In both this and the previous chapter considerable mention has been made of efforts of carriers and shippers to improve the quality of service in the transport sector. Transportation performance can be measured and usually improved upon. By almost all measures of quality, carriers are doing better now than five to ten years ago. The customers are insisting upon it and are monitoring their performance using hourly—rather than daily—measures.

SUMMARY

Chapter 7 covers traffic management: the purchasing or use of transportation services. Since carrier deregulation, a firm's traffic manager has had to become more agile in dealing with carriers.

The traffic manager has many specific duties. One duty is determining the correct lowest published rate or negotiating with carriers for an even lower rate. In negotiating for a contract, the shipper must also recognize the carrier's needs, some of which are monetary. Other carrier needs are to fill empty backhauls or otherwise improve equipment utilization.

The traffic manager is responsible for correctly preparing many of the documents associated with the shipment, including the bill of lading. He or she may also determine the precise routing that carriers must use. Computers assist in these and many other traffic management operations.

Other traffic management responsibilities include handling loss and damage claims, attempting to receive reparations in situations of carrier over-charges, minimizing demurrage and detention charges from failure to return carrier equipment promptly, and tracing lost or delayed shipments. The shipment of hazardous materials requires additional care. An ongoing responsibility of the traffic manager is to consolidate traffic because carrier rates per pound are always less for larger shipments.

Some firms operate their own private fleets of trucks or other vehicles; these are also a part of the traffic manager's responsibilities.

QUESTIONS FOR DISCUSSION AND REVIEW

1. Discuss briefly the major differences between the responsibilities of the traffic manager and those of the director or vice president of logistics.
2. In recent years senior corporate management has stressed the importance of the traffic management function. Discuss briefly the factors responsible for this trend.

3. Why should a traffic manager be concerned with freight rate determination if the carrier is willing to tell her or him the correct rate? Discuss fully.

4. Why are freight classifications important?

5. When a shipper wishes carriers to prepare contract bids for carrying its cargo, what information must the shipper provide?

6. In your opinion, why have rail contract rates become so commonly utilized in recent years? What are some common factors that are typically addressed in rail contracts?

7. What types of government regulations may have an impact upon a traffic manager's duties?

8. What are average weight agreements? Why are they used?

9. Assume you are the traffic manager of a large furniture manufacturer. What information would you want to know before making your carrier selection decision?

10. What factors influence a shipper's choice of carrier?

11. The bill of lading is the most important single document in transportation. Discuss the three basic functions it performs.

12. Discuss briefly the purpose of the transit privilege.

13. What is the basic rule of thumb regarding the determination of the full actual loss sustained by the shipper or consignee in a loss or damage claim situation?

14. Discuss the basic issues, conflicts, and problems involved in concealed loss and damage claims.

15. What procedure is necessary in order to collect reparations from a carrier?

16. Discuss the basic idea of demurrage and detention and how averaging agreements can be helpful in this area.

17. Discuss the basic types of freight bill auditing. Why is this procedure necessary in the first place?

18. Discuss the involvement of the federal government in the interstate transportation of hazardous materials.

19. Private transportation has been experiencing growth during recent years. Discuss the factors responsible for this growth.

20. What is freight consolidation? Why is it performed?

SUGGESTED READINGS

Abshire, Roger D., and Shane R. Premeaux. "Motor Carriers' and Shippers' Perceptions of the Carrier Choice Decision." *Logistics & Transportation Review,* vol. 27, no. 4 (December 1991), pp. 351–358.

Barrett, Colin. "How to File a Claim." *Distribution,* August 1987, p. 88.

Casavant, Ken L., and Jonathon Newkirk. "Moving Pacific Northwest Fruits and Vegetables: What Costs Are Important?" *Journal of the Transportation Research Forum,* vol. 32, no. 1 (1991), pp. 33–40.

Chow, Garland, and Richard F. Poist. "The Measurement of Quality of Service and the Transportation Purchase Decision." *Logistics and Transportation Review,* vol. 20, no. 1 (1984), pp. 25–43.

Courtney J. L. "Technological Change and Multimodal Freight Competition." *Annual Proceedings of the Transportation Research Forum.* Arlington, Va.: TRF, 1984, pp. 116–121.

Crum, Michael R., and Benjamin J. Allen. "Three Logistics Strategies." *The Private Carrier,* February 1991, pp. 24–31.

Forsythe, Kenneth H., James C. Johnson, and Kenneth C. Schneider. "Traffic Managers: Do They Get Any Respect?" *Journal of Business Logistics,* vol. 11, no. 2 (1990), pp. 87–100.

Foster, Jerry R., and Sandra Strasser. "Carrier/Modal Selection Factors: The Shipper/Carrier Paradox." *Journal of the Transportation Research Forum,* vol. 31, no. 1 (1991), pp. 206–212.

Gibson, Brian J., Harry L. Sink, and Ray A. Mundy. "Shipper-Carrier Relationships and Carrier Selection Criteria," *Logistics & Transportation Review,* vol. 29, no. 4 (December 1993), pp. 371–382.

LaLonde, Bernard, James M. Masters, Arnold B. Maltz, and Lisa R. Williams. *The Evolution, Status, and Future of the Corporate Transportation Function.* Columbus: Ohio State University, 1991.

Lambert, Douglas M., Christine M. Lewis, and James R. Stock. "Customer-Focused Strategies for Motor Carriers." *Transportation Journal,* vol. 32, no. 4 (Summer 1993), pp. 21–28.

MacDonald, James M. "Transactions Costs and the Governance of Coal Supply and Transportation Agreements." *Proceedings, 35th Meeting of the TRF, 1993,* pp. 277–291.

Morse, Leon W. *Practical Handbook of Industrial Traffic Management,* 7th ed. Washington, D.C.: Traffic Service Corp., 1987.

Mundy, Ray A. "Evolution of the Small Shipment Problem." *Annual Conference Proceedings of the Council of Logistics Management,* vol. 1. Oak Brook, Ill.: CLM, 1990, pp. 285–294.

Murphy, David J., and Martin T. Farris. "Time-Based Strategy and Carrier Selection." *Journal of Business Logistics,* vol. 14, no. 2 (1993), pp. 25–40.

Pilarski, Kim, and M. Ted Nelson. "Impacts of the 1990 Clean Air Act Amendments on Coal Transportation in the U.S.: An Initial Inquiry." *Waterways and Transportation Review,* vol. 2, no. 1 (1994), pp. 35–47.

Piper, Robert R. "Trucking Productivity As Viewed from the Loading Dock." *Proceedings, 35th Meeting of the TRF, 1993,* pp. 227–238.

Pisharodi, Ram. "Modeling the Motor Carrier Selection Decision: A Preliminary Report." *Papers, CLM 1988 Annual Meeting,* vol. 1. Oak Brook, Ill.: 1988, pp. 237–242.

Rao, Kant, William Grenoble, and Richard Young. "Traffic Congestion and JIT." *Journal of Business Logistics* (Spring 1991), pp. 105–121.

Rao, Kant, and Alan J. Stenger. "A Logistics Cost Model for Purchasing Transportation to Replenish High Demand Items." *Journal of the Transportation Research Forum,* vol. 32, no. 1 (1991), pp. 146–157.

Sharp, Jeffery M., Robert A. Novack, James M. Masters, Arnold B. Maltz, and Lisa R. Williams. "Purchasing Hazardous Waste Transportation Service: Federal Legal Considerations." *Transportation Journal,* vol. 31, no. 2 (Winter 1991), pp. 4–14.

Smith, David G. "Transportation Pricing and Profitability Planning: An Application of Pen-Based Computing." *Journal of Marketing Theory and Practice,* Winter 1993, pp. 12–21.

Tyworth, John E., Joseph L. Cavinato, and C. John Langley Jr. *Traffic Management: Planning, Operations, and Control.* Reading, Mass.: Addison-Wesley, 1987. Reissued by Waveland Press, Prospect Heights, Ill.

Tyworth, John E., and Haw-Jan Wu. "Conformance-to-Standard for On-Time LTL Transportation: How Much Is It Worth?" *Journal of the Transportation Research Forum,* vol. 39, no. 1 (1993), pp. 109–127.

Walter, Clyde Kenneth. "Longer Combination Vehicles: Issues and User Attributes." *Proceedings, 35th Meeting of the TRF, 1993,* pp. 215–226.

Walter, Clyde, Benjamin J. Allen, and Al Rouviere. "Inbound Freight Transportation Management by State Governments: Extent and Experience." *Journal of Business Logistics,* Fall 1991, pp. 95–113.

C A S E   7 - 1

MOM'S TACOS

Mom's Tacos was a fast-growing food franchise chain. Its motto was "Mom's secret is the sauce," which applied to the sauce served with the tacos. There was no "Mom" as such. The firm was the creation of a group of college dropouts, living in Lubbock, Texas, who had been engaged in communal living and, as a commercial venture, had tried making large batches of tie-dyed shirts. The tie-dye shirt craze passed, and that market collapsed. However, some of the organic dye ingredients were left over, and the group used them in experimental cooking. They managed to produce an excellent-tasting taco sauce and sold the sauce to various restaurants near college campuses. The group then purchased a rundown coffee house, changed its name to "Mom's Tacos," and a legend was born. Within nine years the group, now incorporated, of course, had over three hundred franchised restaurants along the West Coast, in the Southwest, and in the Midwest. It was now considering expansion into the South.

Jenny Wong, logistics manager for the group, was also responsible for purchasing. Others supervised the construction and operation of the franchised restaurants. Restaurant operators were governed by very strict rules regarding cleanliness, personnel, amounts of food in each serving, and the like. The restaurant operators were allowed to purchase all foods they needed locally, provided that specifications, set forth by Mom's Tacos, were met. The only ingredient the restaurant operators had to purchase from Mom's was the taco sauce itself. It allegedly was a combination of secret ingredients known only to "Mom." The sauce was manufactured at Mom's plant in Del Rio, Texas, where it was shipped by the rail carload to Mom's distribution points in Los Angeles (for the West Coast) and Chicago (for the Midwest). There was also a distribution point in Del Rio. After careful market analysis prepared by the well-known marketing consultant Edsel, Tucker, and Frazer (ET&F), Mom's was ready to move into the South. ET&F had recommended Savannah, Georgia, as the location for Mom's southern distribution point. Franchise agreements had already been signed for operations in Savannah, Atlanta, and Augusta, Georgia; Tallahassee and Jacksonville, Florida; and Columbia, South Carolina.

The phrase "Mom's secret is the sauce" was not true, at least in its reference to Mom. The rest of the phrase was true, however. The various herbal ingredients were kept secret, and some of them were still chemically active. They were added at the last moment, and under carefully monitored and guarded conditions, before the sauce left the distribution point bound for the various restaurants. Once mixed, the sauce had a useful life of only ten days, after which the restaurant operations were under the strictest instructions to destroy it. Hence the shipping pattern of the sauce was in the form of a small, steady move from the distribution point to each restaurant.

The shipping container was a plastic bottle inside a fiberboard box. The cost of the containers to Mom's was $46 per hundred for the five-gallon size and $81 per hundred for the twenty-gallon size. When shipped, the five-gallon size of sauce weighed 47 pounds, and the twenty-gallon size weighed 183 pounds. The five-gallon container was an eighteen-inch cube. The twenty-gallon container was twenty-four inches square at the base and forty-eight inches high. The main reason for using the five-gallon container was that in some states an employee could not be required to lift more than fifty pounds. The twenty-gallon container required additional mechanical handling equipment in the restaurant. However, Mom's priced the taco sauce so that the restaurants had a strong incentive to use the twenty-gallon container. At first, all of them would use the five-gallon container, but within a year of starting operations, over half the restaurants moved to the twenty-gallon container.

A small or beginning restaurant would use a five-gallon container every day or day and a half. The largest, and most successful, Mom's Taco Restaurant (in Lubbock, and referred to as the "Mother Mom's") was now using six twenty-gallon containers per day.

Because of its interest in maintaining quality and its realization that restaurants would order fewer shipments of larger quantities of sauce, in order to benefit from lower per-pound shipping rates, Mom's Tacos paid the freight charges on shipments of taco sauce from distribution points to restaurants. Shipments were made to each restaurant twice a week. At any one time, a restaurant would have a three- to six-day supply on hand. In the weekly report to Mom's Tacos' home office, the restaurant operator would indicate the serial or batch number on each unused can in stock as well as the amount to be shipped the following week.

The price of the taco sauce, as charged to each restaurant, consisted of three elements: (1) a charge for the sauce, (2) a discount for ordering in twenty-gallon containers, and (3) a transportation charge based on zone, each zone being a certain distance away from the distribution point. The ordinary zone map looked like a bull's-eye target with the distribution point in the center.

Restaurants that used over forty gallons of sauce per week had the option of ordering in twenty-gallon containers. The price in twenty-gallon containers was somewhat lower and was to reflect the lower cost (on a per-gallon basis) of the container and (on a weight or gallon basis) of shipping. It was Wong's assignment to work on a pricing zone system for distribution from the new Savannah facility. She was to include the price of the sauce at $7 per gallon. In addition to this, she was to add charges for the container (taking into account that larger containers cost less per gallon) and for transportation, using the concentric rings, or zone, approach. The profits were already in the charge for the sauce, so the charges for the containers and transportation were to (1) cover costs and (2) reflect the cost differences in reaching each restaurant as accurately as possible. While the initial zone system would apply only to Savannah, Atlanta, Augusta, Tallahassee, Jacksonville, and Columbia, it would be in effect for any other new restaurants that were opened in the area. In fact, Mom's Tacos' representatives would use Wong's cost chart when talking with potential restaurant operators in other southern cities.

Wong recalled that she had a file folder labeled "price zone construction" that she had put together after working out the price zones in the Southwest from the Del Rio distribution center. In it she found three notes she had written to herself.

The first note said, "Use fifty-mile rings" and was dated April 3, 1986. She remembered that after long discussions with both Mom's Tacos' management and with some restaurant operators, it seemed most reasonable to draw circles around the distribution center with radii of 50 miles, 100 miles, 150 miles, and so on and then set the same price for deliveries inside each ring.

The second note, "Remember the Alamo," was dated March 31, 1988. Wong remembered that on that date Alamo Junior College in Brownsville, Texas, had won the state basketball tournament. The Mom's Taco Restaurant operator in Brownsville had promised free tacos to everyone in case Alamo Junior College won the tournament. That wild night he needed 700 gallons of Mom's taco sauce (his usual weekly use was 75 to 80 gallons), and Mom's Tacos had to pay an air freight bill of over $1,000. The note was in Wong's file to warn her the next time zone prices were set up, some sort of rule would have to be set up so that the home office could avoid the excess freight charges in instances such as "the Alamo."

The third note said, "Newer operations cost more to reach" and was dated February 22, 1989. This was after a year-end audit had disclosed that Mom's Tacos was losing money on reaching most of its new restaurants being served out of Del Rio. The reason was that initial franchises were located in large cities, to which transport rates from Del Rio were relatively low. However, newer restaurants were in smaller cities, and while still within 50, 100, or 150 miles of Del Rio, the costs of reaching them were somewhat higher, mainly because they were in areas with poorer transportation service, less carrier competition, and higher rates. The auditor has suggested to Wong that the next time rates are established, she calculate average rates to a number of points inside each ring, rather than just to points where restaurants were in operation.

Wong then took a map of Georgia and the adjoining areas and, using a compass, drew circles with 50-mile, 100-mile, and longer radii, from Savannah. (See Exhibit 7-A.) She then got on the telephone and started tracking down the various types of motor carriers that would handle the deliveries from the Savannah distribution point. Some carriers were excluded from consideration because they did not provide both pickup and delivery service. Delivery service

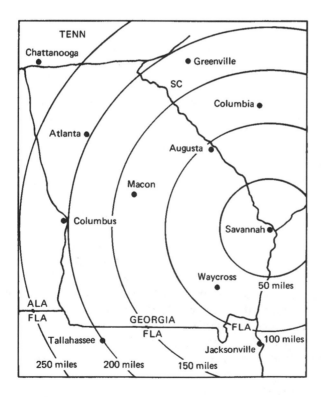

Exhibit 7-A　Mom's Tacos market area.

to restaurants was considered especially important because few restaurant operators had trucks of their own.

Within Savannah, there were several local drayage services that could operate anywhere within the city limits. Their rates were $5.30 per cwt for shipments up to 100 pounds, $4.30 per cwt for shipments between 100 and 499 pounds, and $3.30 per cwt for shipments between 500 and 999 pounds. The minimum charge for any shipment was $5, and they would not handle any shipment over 1,000 pounds.

Acme Parcel Service also served most cities in the South. Its rate would be $10 per week (irrespective of volume, but it would guarantee that a truck of theirs would stop twice a day at Mom's Tacos' Savannah distribution point to pick up any outgoing orders). Mom's Tacos used Acme Parcel Service for other shipments and thus already paid the weekly fee. Their rates would be for deliveries within Savannah, $4 per cwt; for deliveries outside Savannah but within fifty miles, $4.50 per cwt; for deliveries between 50 and 100 miles, $5.75 per cwt; for deliveries between 100 and 150 miles, $6.50 per cwt; for deliveries between 150 and 200 miles, $7.50 per cwt; and for deliveries between 200 and 250 miles, $8 per cwt. It would not handle any single parcel weighing over 50 pounds, which meant that, say, a 150-pound shipment would have to be made in three separate parcels, each one weighing 50 pounds.

Motor common carrier rates for deliveries within Savannah were $5 per cwt for shipments under 200 pounds, $4 per cwt for shipments between 200 and 999 pounds, and $3.50 per cwt for shipments over 1,000 pounds. The minimum charge on any delivery within Savannah was $6.00. Exhibit 7-B shows their rates for shipments outside Savannah. The chart was based on the applicable motor carrier tariffs in effect.

EXHIBIT 7-B   MOTOR COMMON CARRIER RATES, IN CENTS PER HUNDRED POUNDS, FOR SHIPMENTS OUTSIDE SAVANNAH*

Rates are in Cents per Hundred Pounds

Distance from Savannah in miles	If shipment is between			
	0–99 lbs	100–399 lbs	400–999 lbs	Over 1,000 lbs
Up to 50	650	600	500	400
50–100	750	700	500	450
100–150	850	800	600	500
150–200	950	850	650	550
200–250	1,000	900	700	600
250–399	1,100	1,000	750	650

*The minimum charge for any shipment is $6.00.

Questions

1. Ignoring the three notes Wong wrote to herself, construct a price chart for varying amounts of sauce delivered to different locations in Exhibit 7-A using the lowest-cost transportation.

2. Modify the chart (which can be done by adding a note at its bottom) that will protect Mom's Tacos in case another "Remember the Alamo" situation occurs.

3. How, if at all, would you modify the chart to take into account the fact listed on Wong's third note ("newer operations cost more to reach")?

4. The text of the case says, "Mom's priced the taco sauce so that the restaurants had a strong incentive to use the twenty-gallon container." Assume that another Mom's employee, looking at the price chart constructed in answer to question 1, feels that there is not enough incentive in those prices to encourage use of the twenty-gallon containers. What would you do to modify the chart—or Mom's other practices—to take into account this criticism?

5. Assume that Wong wants to have only certain carriers haul the sauce. Does the product have unique requirements that call for high-quality truck service? Outline what you think Wong should tell carriers about what carrier service Mom's Tacos wants.

6. What if some franchise holders want to carry the sauce on their own vehicles? Should Mom's allow this? If so, what price should be charged for taco sauce sold FOB Mom's plant?

7. Should Mom's charge its franchise holders the exact amount of the transportation charges paid to the carriers, or should it mark up the charges and earn some additional revenue? Discuss.

C A S E   7 - 2

RAKOWSKI INDUSTRIAL VACUUM COMPANY

Headquarted in Chattanooga, Tennessee, Rakowski Industrial Vacuum Company made a high-quality industrial vacuum that was marketed throughout the United States. All sales were FOB plant (Chattanooga), so the only transportation of immediate concern was that of inbound materials and movements between plants. Rakowski had another plant in Birmingham, Alabama, and a close relationship with a supplier in Atlanta, Georgia. So many of Rakowski's shipments moved between Chattanooga, Birmingham, and Atlanta that after interstate motor carriage was deregulated in 1980, Rakowski decided to attempt to negotiate a contract with a single trucking firm to handle all of Rakowski's business among three points. Exhibit 7-C shows the weekly pattern of the movements Rakowski wants covered in the contract. Product type A is high priority and must be delivered the day after it is picked up. Product type B is material scheduled for recycling; it must be picked up at least once a week (to empty the storage bins) and be delivered within seven working days.

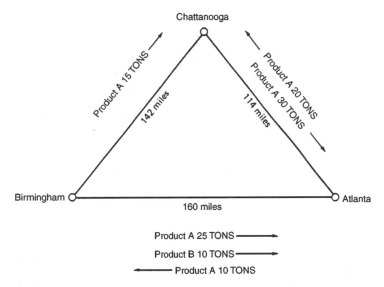

Exhibit 7-C   Weekly interplant tonnages. Last year's tonnage divided by 52. Each week's activity is within 10 percent of figures shown above.

After a preliminary screening of about twenty carriers, Rakowski narrowed the field down to two large nationwide carriers with which it had already done business. Both were reputable firms, unionized, and in fairly good financial condition. One was Sherwood Trucking, headquartered in California, and the other was Voorhees Express, headquartered in Iowa. Rakowski intended to negotiate a tentative contract with each carrier and then select the one trucker whose contract was most favorable to Rakowski.

As it turned out, there were many items to be negotiated. Rakowski and the two trucking companies knew of all the information presented in the case. (Although the two competing truck firms do not exchange information directly, they have been involved in enough competitive bidding situations to know something about each other's costs and strategies.) The various contract items to be negotiated are listed in Exhibit 7-D along with some data concerning the position of Rakowski Industrial Vacuum, Sherwood Trucking, and Voorhees Express.

EXHIBIT 7-D POSITIONS OF PARTIES BEFORE NEGOTIATIONS

	Issue	Rakowski's position	Sherwood's position	Voorhees's position
I.	Loss and damage to product	Product A is valued at $3 to $4 per pound. It is subject to pilferage and to damage in handling. Last year, when dealing with common carrier truckers, Rakowski filed loss and damage claims of $17,000. Product B is worth 25 cents per pound and is not subject to damage or theft. Rakowski wants claims paid promptly.	Willing to assume that annual loss and damage will be $17,000. Will build this into cost of carriage. Will pay claims "promptly."	Wholesale value of product A is less than $2 per pound. Freight claims Rakowski refers to were settled for only $11,000. Prefers that Rakowski assume risk up to a certain amount; this will eliminate petty paperwork.
II.	Outside insurance	Rakowski wants truckers to carry insurance protection with an outside firm to cover loss of cargo as a result of a truck accident, fire, and so on.	Agreeable. Already has coverage.	Agreeable. Already has coverage.
III.	Scheduling of payments to truckers	Rakowski prefers to delay payments because working capital costs 1.5 percent per month interest.	Prefers prompt payment, with penalties for late payments.	Prefers prompt payment with an incentive, or discount, for early payment.
IV.	Packaging	The product is currently packaged according to rules of the Motor Carriers Freight Classification. Rakowski wants the contract to allow it to use less costly packaging.	No experience with other types of packaging for this product. Worried about additional claims for damaged freight.	Concerned about damage claims. Also, Voorhees's terminals are set up to handle palletized freight much more easily than nonpalletized items.
V.	Next-morning delivery	For product A, Rakowski wants freight picked up one day to be delivered the next, with penalties if it is not. These penalties should be large because production would be upset.	Agrees, except for when cause of delay is beyond control of trucker.	Same as Sherwood's position.

VI.	Appointments, or windows, for pickup and delivery of freight	Wants to establish one-hour openings within which the trucks will show up. This is needed to help schedule the plant's work. Wants to assess penalties for trucks showing up before or after the sixty-minute window.	Will agree reluctantly. Prefers to be penalized only after missing by an excessive number of minutes. Wants exemption when cause is beyond control of trucker.	Will agree very reluctantly. Prefers to be penalized after missing a certain number of windows per month. Wants exemption for causes beyond trucker's control.
VII.	Charges for picking up and carrying freight	The tonnage to be carried is shown in Exhibit 7-C. Products are loaded on pallets; the trucker is responsible for loading and unloading. Note: All this freight is handled on an LTL basis, which means it moves to the trucker's terminal in the city, where it is picked up, carried on a line-haul truck to a terminal in the city of destination, and then transferred to a small truck for local delivery. Product A must be delivered on a next-day basis. It should be picked up once a day. Shipments of Product A tend to be heavier later in the week. Product B must be picked up at least once a week. Each loaded pallet carries one ton.	Pickup charges (including carriage to local terminal) are $20 per stop, including the first five minutes; then $2 per minute. It takes one minute to load or unload a pallet. Line-haul costs (from city to city) are 10 cents per ton-mile. Delivery costs and times are the same as pickup costs. All costs include normal profits.	Pickup costs (including carriage to the local terminal) are $20 per stop, plus $1 per minute for each minute spent at the stop. It takes one minute to load each pallet. Line-haul costs are 11 cents per ton-mile for the first 100 miles covered; 10 cents per ton-mile for miles over 100, up to 149; and 9 cents per ton-mile for miles over 149, up to 299. (A ton, moving a distance of 113 miles, would cost $100 \times 11¢ + 13 \times 10¢ = \$12.30$.) All costs include normal profits.

(Continued)

EXHIBIT 7-D *(Continued)*

Issue	Rakowski's position	Sherwood's position	Voorhees's position
VII-A. Charges for picking up and carrying freight. (Note: This is an optional item, which complicates the negotiations. *The course instructor should decide in advance whether it should be included. If it is, all conditions and statements made for VII hold as well.*)	Although shipments of Product A are heavier toward the end of the week, Rakowski is willing to agree to ship approximately the same amount each day of the week (Monday through Friday). If truckers want even more of Product A to move early in the week, Rakowski will have to manufacture it the week before. The cost of manufacture is $2 per pound, and the rate of interest on borrowed working capital is 1.5 percent per month.	The average line-haul costs given in issue VII hold. However, in the Atlanta-Chattanooga-Birmingham area, Sherwood's line-haul trucks are only 40 percent full on Monday nights and carry freight that pays only 5 cents per ton-mile. On Tuesdays and Wednesdays trucks are half full and carry freight paying 10 to 15 cents per ton-mile. On Thursdays they are nearly full and carry cargo paying about 15 cents per ton-mile. On Fridays they are full and carry freight paying 25 cents or more per ton-mile.	The average line-haul costs given in issue VII hold. Voorhees has a policy of analyzing all its traffic in lanes between points and asking more in the direction of predominant flow, in an attempt to achieve balance. From Atlanta to Birmingham, Voorhees wants to charge about twice as much per ton-mile as for the reverse direction. From Atlanta to Chattanooga, it wants to charge at least 1.5 times as much for the reverse direction. In the lane between Birmingham and Chattanooga there is no imbalance.
VIII. Special pickups of freight	Sometimes Rakowski will want the carrier to make an additional pickup of freight—in addition to the pickups already agreed to and scheduled.	Will allow a certain number of "freebies" a month; beyond this it will assess a charge.	Will charge for additional unscheduled pickups unless the shipment is above a certain weight.
IX. Annual volume of freight	Wants the contract to cover volume of freight shown in Exhibit 7-C, plus or minus 10 percent.	Wants the contract to cover the amount of freight shown in Exhibit 7-C, with penalties if it drops below that volume. Penalties should be justified in terms of additional costs to the carrier.	Wants the contract to cover the amount of freight shown in Exhibit 7-C, with incentives if greater volumes are shipped. Incentives should be justified in terms of the savings to the carrier.
X. Subsequent adjustments to take into account: increase in costs of living (or inflation)	Recognizes that the contract is written in dollars. Inflation may drive carrier costs up, and it would be reasonable for them to be paid more dollars (of deflated currency).	In the middle to late 1970s, fuel and labor costs climbed faster than the general cost of living. This was less of a problem in the 1980s.	Holds the same position as Sherwood. Believes that labor costs will have more of an influence on pickup and delivery costs; fuel costs will impact more on line-haul costs.

(At this point, the instructor should divide the class into three negotiating teams: one representing Rakowski Industrial Vacuum Company, one representing Sherwood Trucking, and one representing Voorhees Express. Negotiations between the Rakowski and Sherwood teams must be conducted separately from negotiations between the Rakowski and Voorhees teams. It will be considered unethical for the Rakowski team to use a concession negotiated from one trucking company as leverage to obtain a greater concession from the other trucking company. The object of the exercise is to draw up tentative contracts with the Sherwood and Voorhees firms. Then the instructor with the assistance of the Rakowski team will select the contract that is the more favorable to Rakowski Industrial Vacuum. Note, however, that Rakowski Industrial Vacuum is very ethical and is concerned about positive long-term relationships with its suppliers. Therefore it will not knowingly enter into a contract that is obviously so disadvantageous to a trucker that the trucker is likely to lose money in performing the agreement.)

The items or issues to be negotiated are listed in Exhibit 7-D, along with the viewpoints of Rakowski and the two truckers. Each should be negotiated separately and, to the extent possible, independently of the other issues. After the Rakowski team and a trucker's team agree on how to handle an issue, the agreement must be written or typed, as though it were to be one paragraph in a multiparagraphed agreement.

Distribution Center, Warehouse, and Plant Location

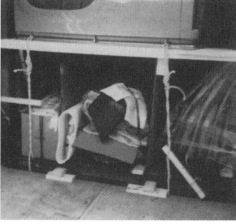

Foreign trade zones are land areas near international ports and airports under control of U.S. Customs. Products in the zones have not yet entered the United States. Eventually, they might enter, or they could be shipped to a third nation. These pictures show a truck disassembly process taking place at a foreign trade zone in Jacksonville. The 168 Mitsubishi trucks were assembled in Japan and shipped to the Jacksonville foreign trade zone. Their ultimate destination is Brazil. Brazilian tariffs on imported vehicles are 100 percent, and on import vehicle parts they are 25 percent, so each truck was disassembled into 157 parts. The picture on the left shows the chassis being attached to a large wooden pallet. In the picture on the right we see parts that have been wrapped and stowed. (Pictures courtesy of GATX Logistics, Inc.)

Under federal law, a polluting company that seeks to move to or expand in a dirty [air] area must first obtain emissions reductions or "offsets" from existing plants in the same locale. Some regions, including the [San Francisco] Bay Area, allow firms to cut their emissions and then "bank" pollution credits for later sale to those who need them.

San Francisco Chronicle
March 21, 1994

Components for Chrysler's assembly plants now are shipped an average of 357 miles. The automaker figures that it can save about $450,000 for every mile that average is reduced.

American Shipper
February 1994

In May, 1993, 188 workers died and nearly 500 more were injured in the fire at the Kader Industrial Co.'s toy factory on the outskirts of Bangkok.

Harsh working conditions and poor safety standards—narrow stairwells and hallways also used for storage, unsafe exits and improper building design—were blamed at the time for the heavy loss of life.

"Given the intensely competitive market for toys, there is a danger that progress in improving working conditions in one country will be undermined by a flight of production to others where workers' basic rights at the workplace are abused," the International Confederation of Free Unions said.

Journal of Commerce
December 19, 1994

Key Terms

- Center-of-gravity approach
- Commodity flow
- Dovetailing
- Enterprise zone
- Facility relocation
- Foreign trade zone
- Grid system
- Maquiladora
- Right-to-work law
- Tax-free bond
- Weight-losing product

Learning Objectives

- To examine the screening or focusing concept of plant/warehouse location
- To describe the major factors that influence location decisions
- To explain the general process of determining the optimum number of facilities
- To explain systems to determine the location that minimizes transportation costs
- To examine a site's specialized location characteristics
- To learn about foreign trade zones

INTRODUCTION

In Chapter 8 we turn to facility location. In particular, the chapter discusses locating warehouses and distribution centers in ways that accommodate the movement of inventories to customers. It also discusses locational issues regarding production facilities. In retailing, it's often said that the three factors necessary for success are: "location, location, and location." Location of distribution centers to serve these retail outlets is also important in terms of cost savings and the ability to efficiently manage the production and flow of materials as they move along the supply chain.

The major factors influencing locational decisions are markets and resource availability. Most facilities are located near one or the other. Also important are labor, taxes, and the availability of transport services. Labor is of special analytical significance because it can be considered both a necessary resource (in human form) as well as a market (for final products).

The transportation system examined earlier moves goods and materials from their initial origin to the ultimate consumer. Chapter 8 deals with locating the facilities along the transport routes where goods are processed, manufactured, and stored. The transportation system makes the other factors mobile and allows the firm to combine factors of production that originate great distances apart.

The chapter also deals with the major influences on facility location, describes briefly some of the elementary techniques used for choosing general locations, and discusses site selection and facility relocation.

Communications improvements have had considerable influence on locational decisions. For example, it is now possible to diagnose electronic equipment malfunctions from a distance and even to have recovery programs transmitted to the ailing equipment. Telemarketing, personal computer, and telephone-linked marketing have changed the needs of retail outlets. Lower-priced clerical labor can be employed at some distance from large cities to perform data-entry functions. Airline passenger and freight reservation systems are often located in small communities serving the nation through long-distance phone lines.

Another factor influencing facility location is mergers between firms with related product lines. One potential cost saving comes from being able to consolidate two separate systems of distribution centers. Although this chapter follows the traditional approach to facility location, it should be pointed out that the approach is challenged by critics such as Stalk and Hout:

> The traditional pattern for a firm has been to provide the most value for the least cost. The expanded pattern is to provide the most value for the least cost in the least elapsed amount of time. These new-generation competitors use flexible factories and operations to respond to their customers' needs rapidly by expanding variety and increasing the rate of innovation. A company that builds its strategy on this cycle is a more powerful competitor than one with a traditional strategy based on low wages, scale, or focus. These older, cost-driven strategies require managers to do whatever is necessary to drive down costs: move production to, or source from, a low-wage country; build

new facilities or consolidate old plants to gain economies of scale. Such tactics reduce costs but at the expense of responsiveness to customer needs—a dangerous exposure.[1]

The locational decision process involves several levels of screening or focusing, with each step becoming a more detailed analysis of smaller areas or sites. A Mercedes-Benz official, describing the company's 1993 decision to locate a facility in Alabama, said: "a six month, worldwide site search eventually came down to 150 locations in the United States; then six, in Alabama, Georgia, Nebraska, North Carolina, South Carolina, and Tennessee; and finally three, in Alabama and North and South Carolina."[2]

The initial focus is on the region, which for a multinational company might mean selecting a nation in which to locate a facility. For a nationwide operation it might mean choosing a state or group of states. The next focus is more precise; it usually involves selection of the metropolitan area or community in which the facility will be located. This is illustrated in Figure 8-1,

Figure 8-1 Advertisement showing a site's location as an advantage in reaching British and continental European markets. (Source: Warrington and Runcorn Development Corporation, England.)

---

[1] George Stalk, Jr., and Thomas M. Hout, *Competing against Time* (New York: Free Press, 1990), p. 60.

[2] *Journal of Commerce,* March 30, 1994, p. 7A.

from a brochure describing a site in the Manchester-Liverpool area of England.

Final analysis involves a detailed inspection of various sites of land. Figure 8-2 shows a map of a specific site along the Little Calumet River, between Chicago and Hammond. The site has a barge dock, access to three railroads, and numerous existing buildings.

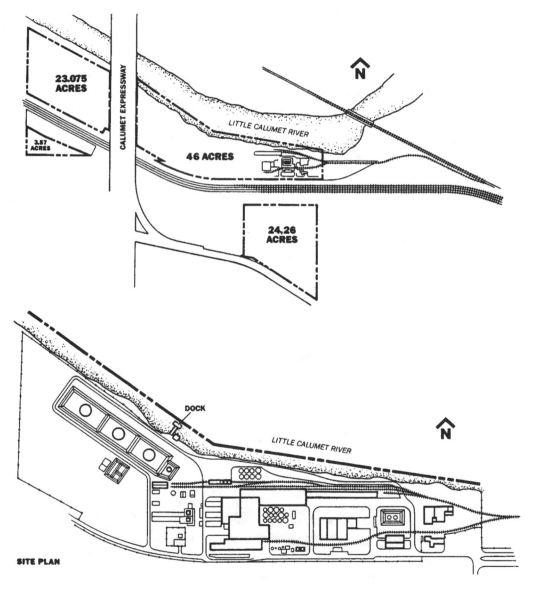

Figure 8-2 Location map and site plan for an available industrial site on the Little Calumet River. (Courtesy of Donald F. Schroud of Hiffman Shaffer Anderson, Inc.)

DETERMINING THE NUMBER OF FACILITIES

A separate, though related, decision involves determining the total number of facilities that a firm should operate. After this is known, the firm proceeds to the site-location analysis.

Few firms start business on one day and need a nationwide distribution system the next day. Distribution and production facilities are usually added one at a time. Marginal analysis is employed to test whether one more (or fewer) distribution facility is required. The drawback of marginal analysis is that one may miss the overall picture. Painstaking analysis may be applied to the question, Do we need a thirty-seventh distribution facility, and if so, where should it be located? when the question should have been, Do we need approximately thirty-five to forty distribution facilities, or is there some other total number that would serve us better?

The number of retail stores served by a distribution center varies by type of business.

> Overall, each distribution center serves an average of 55 stores. Department stores have the lowest store to distribution center ratio, with an average of just 24 stores served by each distribution center. This ratio is nearly one-half that for mass merchandisers who, on average, serve 40 stores with each distribution center. Specialty apparel retailers are at the other extreme with each distribution center serving 78 stores.[3]

Most analytical procedures for determining the number of distribution centers are computerized because of the vast number of alternatives that must be considered. Through simulation techniques, varying hypothetical demands are forecast, and the ability of each facility and the supply chain as a whole to avoid stockouts and provide a specified minimum of service is tested. Testing an entire system is difficult because the neighboring distribution centers are each designed to serve a specified number of locations as well as to serve as backup for each other. For example, a firm testing a system for upstate New York, with one of the points being considered in Syracuse, must also measure the ability of Syracuse to back up facilities at Rochester, Binghamton, and Schenectady, and vice versa. Given these four points, Syracuse would probably be the best backup point because it is located between the other three. However, determining its value as a backup facility is more difficult because Rochester could also draw on Buffalo and Binghamton could rely on a facility at Scranton, Pennsylvania; thus this backup value must be shared with other locations as well. One can see that the complementary relationship between adjoining distribution facilities makes manual analysis of distribution system design difficult. If, in addition,

---

[3] *Chain Store Age Executive,* April 1992, p. 11A. Supermarkets and drugstores had a ratio of sixty-two stores per distribution center; and home centers had fifty-six stores per distribution center.

varying levels of service are being tested, one might find that for each level of service an entirely different series of distribution sites would prove to be ideal. Clearly, these are network problems that are handled on mainframe computers with software developed by consultants. One such example dealt with the firm Franchise Services, Inc., a distribution subsidiary of Pepsico that handles the logistics for the Pizza Hut chain. The Pizza Hut chain's 4,500 restaurants were supplied by Franchise Services' fourteen regional distribution centers. Franchise Services was involved in an ongoing strategic five-year plan that

> included an effort to optimize the size and location of Franchise Services' distribution centers. A goal of the five-year plan was to judge whether these facilities were strategically located for the future in light of the projected growth of the chain. More fundamentally, Franchise Services asked itself whether fourteen was the right number of warehouse locations to begin with.[4]

The software selected

> minimized warehousing and distribution costs. To accomplish this, the system require[d] several types of data: transportation costs, geographic coordinates of delivery locations, various sizes and weights, customer densities, etc.
>
>   Franchise Services used demographic and sales data to ask its two questions: How many distribution centers would it take to serve the restaurant chain most efficiently and where should these facilities be located. The software could have determined the most profitable network for any number of facilities or could relocate existing facilities.[5]

There is a situation in which those planning the introduction of a new product have many options: when an existing firm is adding a new item to its product line. The persons planning for the new product have the option of determining how many and which distribution centers should carry inventory, who should be trained to provide customer service, and so on.

FACTORS INFLUENCING FACILITY LOCATION

Most products are the result of combining raw materials and labor and are made for sale in specific markets. Thus these factors—raw materials, labor, and markets—all influence the decision of where to locate a manufacturing or processing facility. Distribution warehouses exist to facilitate the distribution of products. They are located between, and influenced by, the locations of plants whose products they handle and the markets they serve. The discussion that follows covers the location of manufacturing, processing, and distribution facilities along the supply chain. The relative importance of each factor varies with the type of facility, the product being handled, its volume,

---

[4] Quoted in *Chilton's Distribution,* June 1986.
[5] Ibid.

and the geographic locations being considered. Although much of the discussion deals with single facilities, the decision process often involves a combination of facilities, in which case one must take into account the relationships among them.

Natural Resources

The materials used to make a product must be extracted directly from the earth or sea (as in the case of mining or fishing) or indirectly (as in the case of farm products). In some instances, these resources are located great distances from the point where the materials or their products will be consumed. If the materials must be processed at some point between where they are gathered and where they are needed, their **weight-losing** characteristics become important. For materials that lose no weight in processing, the processing point can be anywhere between the raw material source and the market. If the materials lose considerable weight in processing, then the processing point will be near the point where they are mined or harvested. Or if they gain weight, the processing point will be close to the market (e.g., bottled soft drinks).

In addition to its use for bottling, water, in one form or another, is a requirement for the location of many facilities. For many industrial processes, water is used for cooling. In some climates, it is possible to use naturally flowing water for air conditioning during warm months. Many processing operations require water both for cleaning purposes and as a medium for carrying away waste. Water is also necessary for fire protection; the fire insurance premiums charged are dependent upon the availability of a municipal—or other—water supply.

Originally, when writing about natural resources and facility location, one thought of raw materials on their way to consumers. Today one must also look at natural resources in terms of the environment and be concerned with controls on environmental pollution. Two examples from California show the possible influence of environmental controls upon facility location. In the San Francisco Bay Area, New United Motor Manufacturing Inc. (NUMMI, a joint venture of GM and Toyota) filed an 84-page application with the Bay Area Air Quality Management District

> seeking to obtain a pollution permit so it can build up to 180,000 trucks a year at its Fremont plant. NUMMI already emits 4.01 tons of organic compounds each day, that makes the plant the Bay Area's sixth-worst source of emissions.[6]

In southern California, a railroad filed a protest with the California Coastal Commission over the Port of Long Beach's issuance of a permit for expansion of a truck-based container operation. The railroad charged that the additional trucks would add more air pollution in "an air basin that's a

---

[6] *San Francisco Chronicle*, November 8, 1988, pp. C1–C4.

non-attainment area"—a tactful way of describing an area that does not meet federal standards for air quality.[7]

Population Characteristics

Population can be viewed as both a market for goods and a potential source of labor. Distribution planners for consumer products follow shifts in population carefully. Not only are changes in population size of interest to planners, but so are changes in the characteristics of the population—especially when those characteristics can be translated into buying power. In the United States, a comprehensive census is conducted each decade by the U.S. Bureau of the Census. Between decades, one must rely on data such as estimates made by moving companies of the number of households whose goods are moved from state to state. Figure 8-3 is based on one moving company's records. State and regional planning bodies possess additional information concerning populations within their areas of jurisdiction.

U.S. census data are scrutinized to determine where populations are growing and at what rates. Between 1980 and 1990, the U.S. population increased by about 9.7 percent. The states with the highest growth rates were Nevada (51 percent), Alaska (35 percent), Arizona (33 percent), Florida (32 percent), and California (27 percent). Some states actually lost population during the decade, including (in alphabetical order) Illinois, Iowa, Kentucky, Louisiana, North Dakota, West Virginia, and Wyoming. In late 1993 the Census Bureau released estimates of population changes since 1990. States with growth rates of 2 percent or greater were Arizona, Colorado, Georgia, Idaho, Montana, Nevada, New Mexico, Oregon, Texas, Utah, and Washington. Absolute losses were estimated for Connecticut, the District of Columbia, and Rhode Island.[8]

The racial mix of population may also be a consideration. Many firms, especially those with a national or international presence, have a workforce made up of many races. They may be hesitant to establish a facility in a community that is not racially diverse, since it would be difficult to transfer some workers from other areas to that site. One Maryland firm was offered several incentives to relocate in a midwestern state. "It would flee the nerve-rattling East Coast and settle here in America's heartland—fresh air, quiet streets, smiling faces. But after a closer look . . . , the company noticed that almost all those faces, smiling or not, were white. The offer was ultimately rejected."[9]

Labor

Labor availability is of prime concern in selecting a site for manufacturing, assembling, and even warehousing. Businesses are concerned with the size of the available workforce, its skills, the prevailing wage rates, and the extent to

---

[7] *Pacific Maritime Magazine,* November 1988, p. 14.

[8] *San Francisco Chronicle,* December 29, 1993, p. A9.

[9] *San Francisco Chronicle,* May 1, 1994, p. 4.

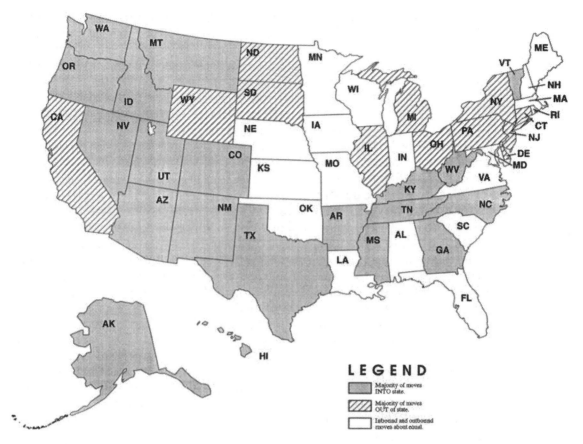

Figure 8-3 United States migration patterns in 1994, based on a moving company's records. (Source: 1994 traffic statistics of Allied Van Lines, Inc.)

which the workforce is or will be unionized. Firms looking for sites often prefer areas where unions are not strong. Some states and communities pride themselves on the fact that unions in their area are not well developed. These states often have **right-to-work laws,** which means that an individual cannot be compelled to join a union. At the same time, some unions are expanding their jurisdiction nationwide and making it more difficult for firms with union contracts to open nonunion operations elsewhere. Industrywide bargaining agreements result in fairly uniform wages and work standards, although there is often less uniformity nationwide than commonly believed because so-called nationwide settlements have to be ratified locally, at which point both labor and management may bargain for additional terms. State labor laws must also be examined because often they are applicable. Such laws deal with issues including minimum wages and management-labor disputes, and may differ from federal statutes, although they do cover firms engaged in intrastate commerce. Trade magazines often show labor data, by state, to give an idea of differences. For example, in 1988 hourly wages paid to manufacturing employees ranged from $7.59 in Mississippi and $7.83 in North Carolina to $11.73 in Ohio and $12.97 in Michigan. The percentage of the workforce belonging to unions ranged from 3.10 percent in South Dakota and 3.59 percent in South Carolina to 50.27 percent in New York and 51.94 percent in Michigan.[10] One location-advising consultant maintains county-by-county records dating back 25 years, listing the results of all National Labor Relations Board–conducted elections.[11]

Local economic conditions also can influence negotiated agreements. In the late 1970s and the 1980s some unionized workers at plants about to be closed softened their demands in hopes of keeping the plants open.

In the United States the skills of individuals seeking employment are fairly well catalogued. Therefore, someone who is comparing different communities in which to locate should work with representatives of the state employment office. An employer needing additional workers possessing certain skills could have state or federal agencies conduct job-training courses to provide the necessary skills. In some areas, unions agree to supply the necessary labor force. In areas with chronic unemployment, job retraining programs are available. Vocational-technical schools and community colleges frequently train persons to work in distribution or manufacturing functions, and these educational institutions can be relied upon to train additional personnel. Not all personnel at a new operation will be new employees of the firm. A small number of supervisory staff are frequently transferred from one location to another.

In expanding operations into foreign countries, there are sometimes limits to the number of supervisory personnel that can be brought in. The foreign government may insist that its own nationals be trained for and employed in most supervisory posts. Once one considers locations outside the United States, wage rate differentials become much larger. The U.S. Department of Labor estimated that hourly labor costs (including fringe benefits) for manufacturing labor in the United States in 1992 averaged $16.17. Figures for Belgium, Denmark, Netherlands, Norway, Sweden, and Switzerland were all between $20.00 and $25.00, and for Germany the figure was $25.92. For Mexico the figure was $2.35, for Hong Kong $3.89, and for Taiwan $5.19.[12]

---

[10] "Distribution's 1988 Site Location Index," *Distribution,* September 1988, p. 42.

[11] The source wishes to remain anonymous. The National Labor Relations Board conducts elections at sites where workers wish to decide whether to unionize, to select (certify) a union to act as bargaining agent, to decertify a union, and so on.

[12] *World Trade,* June 1993, p. 122.

Just south of the United States–Mexican border assembly plants known as **maquiladoras** are flourishing. They pay low wages to the Mexican workers, and the relative value of these wages dropped even more in early 1995 as the peso suddenly dipped in value. In Tijuana,

> more than 40,000 people work in this city's maquiladoras—border assembly factories that operate under Mexican laws permitting 100 percent foreign ownership as long as all the goods they produce are exported.
>
> One maquiladora operator, who asked not to be identified, said his firm has helped companies chased out of Southern California by environmental inspectors to locate in Tijuana. Mexican officials found no problem with a furniture maker's discharges of sawdust into the air or varnish into the sewers that Los Angeles inspectors complained about.[13]

Taxes and Subsidies

While labor availability and practices are an important consideration in any location decision, taxes are frequently more important, at least insofar as distribution facilities are concerned. The reason is that distribution facilities, and the inventories they contain, are often viewed as "milk cows" by local tax collectors. From the community's standpoint, warehouses are desirable operations to attract because they add to the tax base without requiring much in the way of municipal services.

Tax burdens differ by location, and it is necessary to ask tax consultants to determine the actual tax burden associated with each site. Even when areas have what appear to be identical taxes, there are frequently significant differences in the manner in which assessments are made or in which collections are enforced. Some localities are so anxious to attract new industries that they either formally or informally agree to "go easy" on the new operation for its first several years.

> A sign of the times is the importance attached to the [corrugated cardboard and wastepaper recycling] mill's environmental contribution, which gained tax-exempt financing. The recycling of some 300,000 tons of waste cardboard and paper not only qualified Cedar River Paper Co. for tax-exempt solid waste reduction bond financing, but gave [the state of] Iowa a big boost toward fulfilling its solid waste reduction plan.[14]

The term **enterprise zone,** or *free enterprise zone,* is sometimes used to describe areas, often in declining regions or portions of cities, where special tax inducements are offered to industry.

[13] *San Francisco Chronicle,* March 1, 1988, pp. A1, A8. A current problem facing maquiladoras is that shipments headed into the United States are delayed because of searches for smuggled drugs or aliens.

[14] *Journal of Commerce,* March 30, 1994, p. 6A. The article continued: "Site selection . . . became a one-stop shopping deal: Iowa Electric System, which owned the 120-acre site, will also supply steam and electricity, and its short-line railroad, the Crandac Railroad, serves the property. It is adjacent to U.S. 30, near Interstate 380."

Some localities even subsidize new industry by issuing **tax-free bonds** to prepare plant sites and construct buildings. Municipalities can borrow money for less than private firms can; hence it is to the firm's financial advantage to locate in such a subsidized setting and reimburse the local unit of government for its interest and debt retirement costs for preparing the site and building. While commendable insofar as attracting new industries, this arrangement frequently places a burden on existing taxpayers.

While no list of taxes is complete, a partial list includes sales taxes, real estate taxes, corporation franchise taxes, taxes associated with the exchange of real estate, business income taxes, motor fuel taxes, unemployment compensation taxes, and severance taxes (for the removal of natural resources). Of particular interest to logistics managers is the inventory tax, analogous to the personal property tax paid by individuals. In states with inventory taxes, the assessment date is usually in the spring (chosen by rurally dominated legislatures as the date for assessing all personal property and the date that would find farmers' holdings at a minimum). When only one date is used, it is to the advantage of logistics managers to have their inventories as low as possible at that time.

Most states have inventory taxes, although frequently they exempt items of political importance. Wisconsin exempts natural cheese in storage for aging, Virginia exempts tobacco still in possession of its producer, Georgia exempts all farm products, and Maryland exempts imported olive oil and coffee beans. Several states exempt property used for pollution abatement. Other exemptions deal more precisely with distribution functions. Some states exempt goods in public warehouses; one exempts goods brought into the state by water transport so long as they are still stored in the county of the entry port; and other states exempt goods passing through the state on a storage-in-transit bill of lading. Many states exempt goods moving on carriers passing through the state and covered by an active bill of lading.

As if taxes are not difficult enough to understand, they are but one side of the coin in determining the costs that must be paid to government entities. The other is to know the value of services received from these same government entities. If water supply is inadequate or fire protection is poor, the result will be higher fire insurance rates. If a plant cannot discharge its waste into a municipal sewage collection and treatment system, it may be forced to install facilities of its own. It may be difficult to attract workers to a community with a poor school system because they are concerned about their children's education. A poor school system ultimately places a greater training burden on employers, so the saving in taxes may not be as great as initially thought.

To complicate matters further, governments often subsidize new industries or firms as an inducement for them to locate. Use of a state or municipality's ability to issue tax-exempt bonds has already been mentioned. Other subsidies common in the United States are massive site improvements, including installation of roads and sewers. In late 1993 Mercedes-Benz announced that they would build and open a new assembly plant near Tuscaloosa, Alabama. The firm will invest $300 million in the plant, which is expected to open in 1997 and to employ 1,500. Vendors to Mercedes will invest an additional $19 million and employ 500 people near the Mercedes site. "The state is rolling out a green carpet of capital incentives worth $253 million, and an annual operating incentive of $9.27 million."[15] The incentives include providing offices and temporary living quarters for key Mercedes personnel. The Tuscaloosa city and county governments spent $30 million to purchase and improve the site, which shall be sold to Mercedes for $100. The state passed a law that gave Mercedes property, corporate, and income tax abatements.

The West Virginia Economic Development Authority "provides low-interest loans from a revolving fund for land acquisition, building construction, and equipment purchases. The loan programs are geared toward manufacturing firms with an emphasis on new job creation."[16] West Virginia also has a "small" business tax credit applying to firms with payrolls of no more than $1.5 million annually and a median salary of at least $11,000 per year. The small business must create at least ten new jobs to qualify for the tax credit.

On the international level, nations subsidize or otherwise promote or protect many types of commerce. The term *national competitive strategy* is employed in reference to a nation's attempts to adopt policies that will strengthen its economic position vis-à-vis the rest of the world.

Transportation Services

When considering a new location, the individual performing the analysis must calculate the transportation costs from sources of supply to each proposed site and to markets that must be served from the site. Costs are calculated in terms of both money paid to carriers (or for one's own vehicles) and the investment in products while they are being carried. Figure 8-4 reflects this concern and shows distances for truck shipments leaving Oklahoma. It also shows major highways and a waterway route.

Competition among carriers is often important. Some electric utilities located in Great Lakes ports adjacent to deep-draft navigation channels have not installed equipment to unload coal from vessels. However, their waterfront site allows them to obtain a lower rate from the railroad because they may threaten to install vessel-handling equipment and switch to water

---

[15] *Journal of Commerce*, March 30, 1994, p. 7A.

[16] Brochure issued by Governor's Office of Community and Industrial Development, Charleston, W.V., 1988.

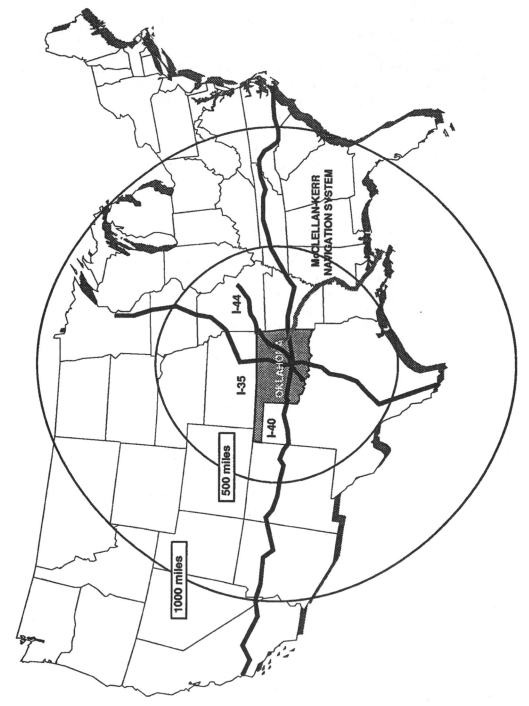

Figure 8-4 Truck distances from Oklahoma. (Source: Oklahoma Department of Commerce.)

transport. Service by several modes also means that a plant is less threatened by strikes in any one mode.

Finding and Satisfying Customers

In addition to resources, labor, taxes, and transportation factors, customers are of great importance. Most distribution facilities are oriented more toward customers than toward other factors. Finding and satisfying customers is discussed in basic marketing texts. For consumer products, a firm usually seeks a population with buying power and designs its distribution system to carry out the firm's marketing objectives. Figure 8-5 shows a computer-generated map produced by a program that relates distribution site locations to markets.

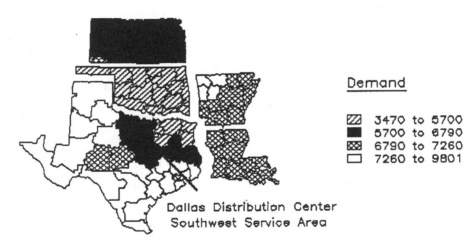

Figure 8-5   Computer image showing a distribution center location. (Source: Microanalytics, Inc., of Arlington, Va.)

Sellers of industrial products also locate near their buyers. A study of plant location decisions made by firms that located in Greensboro, North Carolina, described a specific type of customer orientation referred to as **dovetailing:**

> Dovetailing is the process whereby a supplier locates [a] plant in close proximity to a large customer. The most obvious examples of dovetailing in the United States are the several tin can plants abutting food or beverage packers.

For this particular dovetailing situation the tin can conveyor belt is actually extended through a common wall so the finished cans are never touched before they are filled with product. Nonelectrical machinery dominates the dovetailing orientation in Greensboro. These machinery factories were constructed to build machinery for use by the local textile and furniture industry. The other four plants dovetail as follows: The textile plant manufactures woven elastic for the apparel industry; the apparel plant does contract sewing for a large garment manufacturer; the chemical plant manufactures textile chemicals; and the furniture plant does contract upholstering for furniture assemblies.[17]

More recently, Volvo GM ran an ad with text reading: "Volvo GM Heavy Truck Corporation built an 80,000 square foot parts distribution center at the airport in Memphis. Which happens to be the headquarters of Federal Express. That means we get parts faster to you than anyone. Because when you're serious about parts delivery, you don't just *use* Federal Express. You move next door."[18]

Energy Sources

All distribution and manufacturing facilities use electricity, and some manufacturing processes are dependent on other forms of energy. Questions should be asked about energy costs and the likelihood of shortages. Electric utilities rely on a number of sources of energy to generate electric power, and some of these sources are more likely to be subjected to price increases than others.

This is another area where local subsidies to new industries are given. A study of factors influencing plant location in small Texas communities stated that it is important to determine "whether the utility company is owned by the city, a public organization, or a private concern. The importance is that often cities may offer utility rebates to induce industries to locate there."[19]

Commodity Flows

Firms producing consumer goods follow changes in population in order to better orient their distribution systems. There are also shifts in markets for industrial goods. General sources of data regarding **commodity flows** are

---

[17] Charles R. Hayes and Norman W. Schul, "Why Do Manufacturers Locate in the Southern Piedmont?" *Land Economics,* February 1968, pp. 177–121.

[18] Ad appearing in *Private Carrier,* February 1995.

[19] Ronald Linehan, C. Michael Walton, and Richard Dodge, "Variables in Rural Plant Location: A Case Study of Sealy, Texas," Memo 21 (Austin: University of Texas Council for Advanced Transportation Studies, 1975), p. 21.

studied, much like population figures, to determine changes occurring in the movements of raw materials and semiprocessed goods. Government data in these areas are generally complete, but the degree of coverage varies. There may be excellent reports concerning the supply and demand for a specific agricultural commodity, but almost no data concerning other, more significant products. Some trade organizations report data concerning their members' activities.

Although population shifts are especially important to marketing decisions, commodity flow data are usually related to production. Two vital pieces of information are (1) how much is being produced and (2) where it is being shipped. If a firm is concerned with a distribution system for its industrial product, this information would tell how the market is functioning and, in many instances, how to identify both the manufacturers and their major customers. At this point the researcher would understand the existing situation and would try to find a lower-cost production-distribution arrangement. Should the firm join the existing patterns of trade (which is easier to do in an expanding market), or should it produce at a point where no manufacturers of similar products are located?

FINDING THE LOWEST-COST LOCATION

Many products are a combination of several material inputs and labor. Traditional site location theory can be used to show that one or several locations will minimize total transportation costs. Figure 8-6 shows a laboratorylike piece of equipment that could be used to find the lowest-cost location for assembling a product consisting of inputs from two sources and a market in a third area. This equipment, as shown, can only be used to minimize transportation costs. Most solutions to locational problems are reached through the use of computerized analysis. Frequently, large geographic areas are under consideration, and initially all possible sites are considered eligible. But ultimately, the firm must decide where to locate specifically. A firm exporting into Europe may decide that it must locate a manufacturing operation inside one of the Common Market countries so it can avoid the higher tariff barriers facing exports from outside. A U.S. firm located in Pennsylvania may decide that the time has come to locate an additional distribution facility west of the Mississippi River. This section illustrates a method for finding the low-cost location and discusses the various sources of geographic coding data, available in the United States, that might be needed for any computerized analysis of a locational problem. It assumes that the decision has been made to open only one additional facility and that the problem has been reduced to finding the best location for that facility.

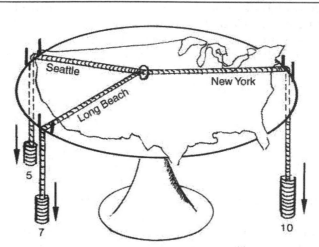

This is a simplified demonstration showing the various "pulls" which exist to determine the industrial location which minimizes the total ton miles of transportation used to transport both inputs and output. This method can be used for situations where there are "pulls" in three directions—either two sources of supply and one market, or one source of supply and two separate markets.

Assume we have two inputs, one produced in Long Beach and one produced in Seattle. The two inputs are combined to make a product which is sold in New York City. Assume further that to produce ten tons of the product consumed in New York, we must combine seven tons of the product which comes from Long Beach with five tons of the product which comes from Seattle. Assume finally that a transportation system is available anywhere and that the transport costs per ton mile are the same for either input or for the final product.

We take a circular table, placing a map of the U.S. on it and pairs of pegs on the table edge in the vicinity of Long Beach, Seattle, and New York as they are on the tabletop map. The pairs of pegs are so that a piece of string can pass between them.

We knot together three pieces of string, with all of them ending in one knot. To one of the pieces of string, which we pass through the pegs near Seattle on our map, we attach five identical metal washers (each one representing one ton). We attach seven washers to a second piece of string and pass it through the pegs in the vicinity of Long Beach on our tabletop map. To the third piece of string we attach ten washers and place it through the pegs in the vicinity of New York.

Then we take the knot and gently lift it to a point above the center of the table, with the washers on all three strings pulling down. We then drop the knot and it comes to rest at the spot on the map which represents the point in the U.S. where the manufacturing operation (for combining these two inputs into the single product) should locate. No other point will require less transportation effort—measured in ton-miles of freight moved.

(If transportation costs, or rates, differ on a per ton mile for each of the commodities or products involved, this can be taken into account by having the number of washers "weighted" to take into account the varying rates as well as the differences in weight being shippped. If for example in the situation described above carriers charged twice as much per ton mile to carry the finished product as they charged for carrying inputs, one would attach 20 washers (2 × 10) on the string reaching toward New York.)

Adapted from: Alfred Weber, *Theory of the Location of Industries*, translated by Carl J. Friedrich (Chicago: Univ. of Chicago Press, 1929).

Figure 8-6   Example of transportation forces dictating plant location.

The Center-of-Gravity Approach

The **center-of-gravity** approach is frequently used for locating a single facility so that the distance to existing facilities is minimized. Figure 8-7 shows a **grid system** placed over a map of five existing retail stores. Assuming that each store receives the same tonnage and that straight-line (or "as the crow flies") distances are used throughout, the best location for a warehouse to serve the five retail stores is determined by taking the average north-south coordinates and the average east-west coordinates of the retail stores. In Figure 8-7 the grid system has its lower left (southwest) corner labeled point zero, zero. The vertical (north-south) axis shows distances north of point zero, zero, and the horizontal (east-west) axis shows distances to the east. In the example, the average distance north is 3 + 1 + 3 + 2 + 3 divided by the number of stores, 5, so the answer is 12/5, or 2.4 miles. The average distance east is 1 + 2 + 3 + 4 + 6 divided by 5, or 3.2 miles. The best warehouse location is one with coordinates 2.4 miles north and 3.2 miles east of point zero. (The term *best* is used, but the method described here only approximates the optimum solution.)

Approaches such as this one provide approximate locations of centralized facilities, at least in a transportation sense. However, adjustments have to be made to take into account taxes, wage rates, volume discounts, the cost and quality of transport services, and the fact that transport rates taper.

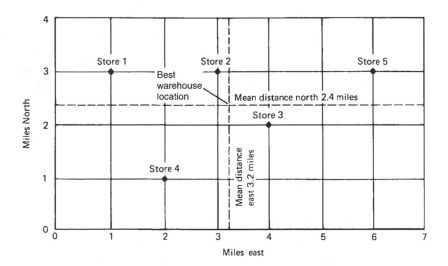

Figure 8-7 Center-of-gravity location for a warehouse serving five retail stores.

Other Grid Systems

Grid systems are checkerboard patterns placed on a map (as in Figure 8-7). Squares are numbered in two directions: horizontal and vertical. Recall from geometry that the length of the hypotenuse of a right triangle is the square root of the sum of the squared values of the right triangle's two legs. It is easy for a computer to calculate the distance between any two points whose grid coordinates are known. Grid systems are placed so they coincide with north-south and east-west lines on a map (although minor distortion is caused by the fact that east-west lines are parallel while north-south lines converge at both poles—a factor that sophisticated computer programs can take into account). Grid systems are important to locational analysis because they allow one to analyze spatial relationships with relatively simple mathematical tools. One may also group and regroup various areas for purposes of analysis.

At least one firm has placed varying types of geographic data on one record. Figure 8-8 shows a layout that uses 126 digits to record twenty-three types of information. Some of the types of information require additional explanation. Item 3, unit type, indicates whether the place is a city or a country or some other governmental unit. Item 4 refers to the airport code developed by the International Air Transport Association (IATA). Items 6 through 8 refer to a numeric code established by Dun and Bradstreet. Items 10 and 11 refer to a Standard Point Location Code developed jointly by the National Motor Freight Tariff Association and the Association of American Railroads for the purpose of providing a scheme for identifying locations in computerized transportation tariffs and in other transportation and logistics systems. Items 15 and 18 are the mean latitudes and longitudes of the counties. Items 19 and 20 refer to a geographic coding system devised by IBM, and items 21, 22, and 23 refer to FIPS—or Federal Information Processing Standards—a system maintained by the National Bureau of Standards. The firm whose form is pictured lists over 132,000 places in the United States.

The discussion thus far has emphasized transportation data. However, marketing data are equally important. In a geographical analysis a locational researcher might include statistics concerning the population and buying power of areas for which distribution centers are being considered. This information is available from the Census Bureau as well as private services.

Specialized Location Characteristics

As discussed earlier in the chapter, there are many general considerations in the selection of a site for manufacturing, distributing, or assembling. Mathematical techniques may indicate that if a facility is located in a certain spot, transportation costs will be minimized. More sophisticated models take other

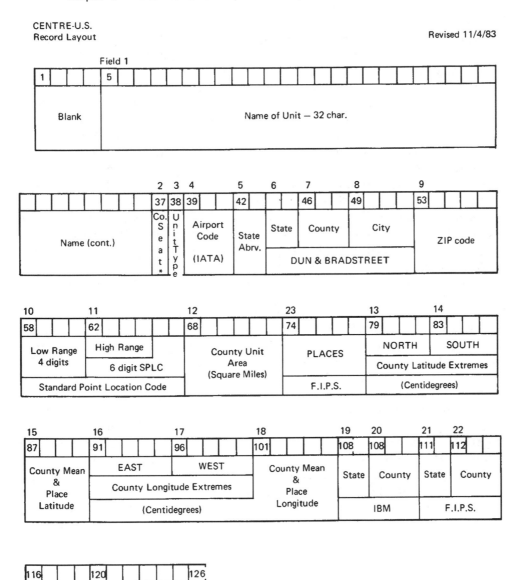

Figure 8-8   An example of the U.S. Geographic Code layout. (Copyright © 1984 by Distribution Sciences, Inc., Des Plaines, Illinois. Reproduced by permission.)

factors into account and indicate an ideal site. This section deals with some specialized considerations that must be recognized in deciding upon a specific area or site. Most of these considerations are "invisible" boundaries that are frequently of great significance.

Within municipalities most lands are zoned, which means that there are limits on the types of uses to which they may be put. For example, a warehouse might be allowed only in areas set aside for wholesale or other specified commercial operations. Restrictions on sites for manufacturing are even more severe, especially if the operation in question is not considered to be a desirable neighbor because of the fumes, smoke, dust, and noise it creates. Distribution centers are believed to be more desirable, the only complaint against them being the volume of truck traffic they cause on neighboring streets. Zoning classifications can be changed, especially if the community in question is attempting to attract industry. Vacant land should be considered only after any possible land use restrictions have been checked out.

Union locals have areas of jurisdiction. A firm's labor relations manager may have preferences as to which locals he or she will be dealing with; the labor relations manager should thus be consulted before any decisions are made. The firm's existing contracts may have some provisions regarding union jurisdiction over new sites. Sometimes unions battle for jurisdiction. In every coastal maritime cargo-handling terminal, for example, there is an invisible line between the jurisdictions of longshoremen and teamsters.

Other invisible lines influencing site locations include boundaries of motor carrier commercial zones and railroad switching districts. Commercial zones are drawn up by the Interstate Commerce Commission around large cities, and the interstate rates between a point in another state and anywhere in a specific commercial zone are the same. Commercial zones along the Mexican border are frequently in the news because they are the limits to how far inside the United States Mexican truckers can drive. Large trucks are sometimes allowed to operate only within certain distances of freeway interchanges. Rail switching districts are established around big cities, and railcars can be transferred within a district at relatively low rates.

Foreign Trade Zones

A highly specialized site in which to locate is a **foreign trade zone,** also known as a free trade zone. There are about 170 in the United States (including subzones). A typical foreign trade zone is an enclosed facility, under customs security supervision, situated in or near an international port. Foreign merchandise may be stored, exhibited, processed, or used in zone manufacturing operations without being subjected to duties and quotas until the goods or their products enter the customs territory of the zone country. The most common advantage of a foreign trade zone is that the payment of duties can be delayed until the goods are ready to be delivered to retailers or customers. For example, liquor purchased in large quantities is stored in a foreign trade zone until needed. Then import duties are paid and federal and state liquor tax stamps are purchased and placed on the bottles. Another distribution function performed in foreign trade zones is to relabel canned and bottled foods with labels that may be required before they can be sold in U.S. markets.

Foreign trade zones are also utilized for inspecting products, prior to paying duties. In some situations this involves considerable savings, since the importer accepts—and pays duty on—only those goods that can be resold at full price. Insurance costs for goods in foreign trade zones are often less, for two reasons. First, the goods' value does not include the import duty; second, the goods are held under more secure conditions.

A foreign trade zone need not be adjacent to a port or airport. It can be inland near the point of manufacture, although customs supervision is required. The advantage for large manufacturers utilizing foreign built components is that they have their stocks on hand but need pay duty only when they actually need the materials on the assembly line.

Other Site Requirements

Once a precise site is under consideration, many other issues must be dealt with before location can proceed. The title must be searched by attorneys to make certain that the seller can, in fact, sell the parcel and that there are no liens against it. Engineers must examine the site to ensure that it will properly drain and to ascertain the load-bearing characteristics of the soil. Architects may indicate what types of buildings can fit on the site and what types of alterations must be accomplished before a building can be started. Today one also investigates who previously owned the site and how it was used. There is considerable concern that without careful investigation, one may end up buying somebody else's abandoned toxic-waste dump site.

Knowledge of the weather is important as well because weather will have some influence on the type of facility that is constructed. One large spice manufacturer-distributor located its facility in Salinas, California, because the area is dry and neither heating nor cooling apparatus is required. Abbott Laboratories, in its choice of a U.S. port at which to consolidate its export shipments, restricted its choices to ports where there is no freezing weather because some of its hospital and infant nutritional products are subject to freezing.[20]

Weather also has an impact upon transportation operations. Air express companies, looking for sites for transfer hubs, check records to see how often airports are closed due to weather. Many warehouses are located in the Reno area to serve markets in northern California. Highway routes from Reno to northern California are closed several times each winter due to snow or mudslides.

FACILITY RELOCATION

A specialized but frequent case of location choice—**facility relocation**—occurs when a firm decides it cannot continue operations in its present facility and must locate elsewhere. Sometimes the problem is merely lack of room for expansion. A common phenomenon in the United States since World War II is the relocation of industrial plants and warehouses from the aging and crowded central cities to spacious sites in the suburbs. In these instances the old site cannot be expanded, and workers, who once rode mass transit to and from work, now demand private parking facilities for their autos. Trucking firms handling pickups and deliveries claim they can provide better service to suburban sites because there is less traffic congestion.

When relocation is being considered, all of the calculations with respect to selecting a new site must be made. In addition, one must compare all proposed alternatives with continuing operations at the existing site. Many existing sites of operation are in satisfactory, if not ideal, locations, and one must choose between expansion at a site that is not ideally located or closing down that site and starting a completely new operation at the ideal location.

Special considerations apply to relocation to distant communities. The first deals with labor. Employees must be kept informed of any planned relocations that might affect them. If not, rumors will destroy morale and workers at the old site will seek other employment. Their departure will affect the output capability of the old operation at a time when it is nearly impossible to hire replacements. Policies must be decided and announced with respect to which employees will be asked to relocate to the new facility and have their relocation expenses paid. Others may not have their relocation expenses paid but will have the right to assume comparable positions at the new facility. Older employees may be granted earlier retirement benefits. Employees who are not going to relocate but will agree to

[20] It selected New Orleans (New Orleans *Port Record,* July 1984, pp. 16–17).

stay at the old operation until it closes will be given additional severance benefits.

Difficult decisions must be made regarding equipment. What should be taken to the new site? What should be left behind? This is compounded by the need to maintain production in the old facility as long as possible. Inventories of manufactured products must be expanded at this time to offset the loss in production between the time the old plant or warehouse closes and the time the new one shifts into operation. There are delays at both sites. At the old site, fewer experienced workers remain, and those who do are not happy. At the new site, "bugs" have yet to be discovered. The physical move of equipment must be timed to minimize total "down" time. When General Foods Corporation relocated some of its facilities, it calculated the trade-off between two costs necessary to maintain an adequate inventory of Jell-O's product lines. The first cost was accumulating a larger inventory produced at the older plants by use of overtime. Included in this were the higher (overtime) costs of labor, additional money invested in inventory, and payments for use of public warehouses. The alternative was to pay overtime to the workforce installing the new and transferred equipment at the new site. The faster that work was completed, the less would be the down time when operations were halted at both the old and new plants. In this instance, the use of additional shifts for installing equipment at the new plant was found to be the better alternative.[21]

Another type of problem occurs when it becomes apparent that a firm has overexpanded and must plan an orderly withdrawal from certain markets. The analytical techniques are the same as for location or relocation, except that the new alternatives involve service to a smaller area. While this is not the best situation to be in, it frequently occurs, especially during periods of economic downturns. In industries with very volatile markets, all locational decisions are made on a less permanent basis. Many examples can be found in today's electronics and computer industries.

A political issue during 1988 involved giving advance notice to employees of a plant's closure. A new law, which became effective in early 1989, requires that employees be given written notices at least 60 days in advance of a facility's closure if it affects at least fifty jobs. Some firms relocate to points outside the United States; Figure 8-9 shows an ad placed by a firm that assists other firms in relocating to Mexico.

---

[21] Edmund S. Whitman and W. James Schmidt, *Plant Relocation: A Case History of a Move* (New York: American Management Association, 1966), p. 79. The study dealt with General Foods' construction of a new plant at Dover, Delaware, that replaced four older plants in the northeastern United States.

Figure 8-9 Ad run by a firm offering services to U.S. firms interested in relocating to Mexico. (Courtesy North American Plant Relocation.)

SUMMARY

This chapter covers the decision process for locating an industrial plant or a warehouse along the supply chain. An early decision has to be made with respect to the number of facilities with which one is concerned. Once that number is known, one can think in terms of ideal sites for a specific facility. This is an area where mainframe computers are frequently employed, since the volume of data that must be analyzed is immense.

Many factors influence the locational decision. To begin with, most sites are somewhere between the raw material sources and the marketplace.

Goods that lose weight in processing are usually processed near the sources; goods that add weight—such as soft drinks—are usually processed near markets. Population is another variable; it represents a market for consumer products as well as a source of labor.

Other concerns include environmental pollution controls, local and state taxes, the labor climate, possible subsidies from local governments, transportation services, and costs of energy.

Some specialized boundaries and sites are also discussed. Examples are foreign trade zones, ICC-designated commercial zones, and maquiladoras. The chapter concludes with a discussion of facility relocation.

QUESTIONS FOR DISCUSSION AND REVIEW

1. What are the important factors influencing the decision to locate a distribution warehouse or manufacturing plant?

2. What factors influence the number of facilities that a firm chooses to operate?

3. What types of questions should be asked regarding transportation services to and from sites under consideration?

4. When an operating facility is moved from one location to another, what special considerations must be given to the labor force?

5. How do population shifts influence decisions to locate distribution or manufacturing facilities?

6. How might the factors considered important for locating a manufacturing facility differ from the factors considered important for locating a distribution warehouse?

7. What is a foreign trade zone (or free trade zone)? What functions might be performed by it?

8. Discuss the use of tax-free industrial revenue bonds. From a public policy point of view, do you believe they are a good idea? Discuss.

9. "Energy costs and availability are becoming fundamental aspects in production plant locational analysis." Comment on the validity of this statement.

10. How do the recent environmental protection programs influence site selection?

11. Figure 8-6 shows a physical model used to find the lowest-cost location for assembling a product. Discuss the strengths and weaknesses of this concept.

12. What does the term *dovetailing* mean when used in reference to industrial location? Give some examples.

13. Under what circumstances might a firm decide to reduce the number of facilities it operates?

14. Discuss the use of grid systems.

15. What are right-to-work laws? Do they influence locational decisions? How?

16. Why do some states tax inventories? Do you think inventories should be taxed? Why or why not?

17. What mode of transport do you think is the most important to firms evaluating new sites? Why?

18. Discuss the aspects that should be considered in examining the labor environment of a particular geographical region.

19. Discuss the importance and types of taxes involved in a locational decision.

20. How might climate affect the choice of a site for manufacturing or a warehouse? Discuss.

SUGGESTED READINGS

Allen, Kathleen. "The Role of Logistics in the Overseas Plant Selection Decision Process of United States-Based Multinational Corporations." *Journal of Business Logistics,* Fall 1991, pp. 59–72.

Ballou, Ronald, H., and James M. Masters. "Commercial Software for Locating Warehouses and Other Facilities." *Journal of Business Logistics,* vol. 14, no. 2 (1993), pp. 71–107.

Cooper, Martha C. "Freight Consolidation and Warehouse Location Strategies in Physical Distribution Systems." *Journal of Business Logistics,* vol. 4, no. 2 (1983), pp. 53–74.

Crew, James, and Kevin Horn. "Port Competition for Imported Automobiles: National and Regional Analysis." *Journal of the Transportation Research Forum,* vol. 31, no. 2 (1991), pp. 239–252.

Ellison, Julian. "Celestial Mechanics and the Location Theory of William H. Dean, Jr., 1930–1952." *American Economic Review,* May 1991, pp. 315–317.

Foggin, James H. "Location Analysis With Computer Graphic Enhancements." In *Distribution Research and Education: Today and Tomorrow* (Columbus: Ohio State University Transportation and Logistics Fund, 1985), pp. 97–117.

Hansen, P. H., Hjortkjaer B. Hegedahl, and Borge S. Obel. "A Heuristic Solution to the Warehouse Location-Routing Problem." *European Journal of Operational Research,* vol. 76, no. 1 (July 6, 1994), pp. 111–127.

Perl, Jossef, and Mark S. Daskin. "A Unified Warehouse Location-Routing Methodology." *Journal of Business Logistics,* vol. 5, no. 1 (1984), pp. 92–111.

Rosenfield, Donald B. "The Retailer Facility Site Location Problem: A Case Study." *Journal of Business Logistics* (September 1987), pp. 95–114.

CASE 8-1
FINDING THE SITE

This case requires the use of the same computer disks as those used for Case 6-2. Refer to the introductory comments for that case.

Questions

1. Your firm is located in Milwaukee, Wisconsin (ZIP code 53201), and manufactures a product used to polish capitol domes. Your only customers are in state capitol cities: Columbus, Ohio (43225); Springfield, Illinois (62708); the twin cities in Minnesota (55455); Des Moines, Iowa (50303); and Lansing, Michigan (48824). Once a month you ship 3,500 pounds of the product to each customer. The carrier gives you a 15 percent discount off the published rates. The product's classification is 100. Each is a single shipment, and there are no accessorial charges involved. What are your present transportation costs?

   You have a chance to relocate your plant to a site in Indianapolis, Indiana (46227). How would this change your transportation costs?

2. You have retail outlets in Tallahassee, Florida (32303); Charleston, South Carolina (29406); Mobile, Alabama (36608); Atlanta, Georgia (30303); and Jackson, Mississippi (39210). Each outlet is open seven days a week and sells a thousand widgets per day. Assume the widgets are class 55. Each widget weighs 1 pound, costs 50 cents to produce, and sells for $1. Since your lease for a factory site is about to expire, you have decided to move the manufacturing operation to the back of one of your five retail outlets. Which outlet should you choose? Note that your motor carrier makes pickups and deliveries only 5 days per week. Where should you relocate your manufacturing operations? Why?

3. (This is a continuation of the situation described in question 2.) Would it be cheaper to make only one shipment per week? Should you still use the same site for manufacturing?

4. (This is continuation of the situation described in questions 2 and 3.) Your partner argues that if 7,000 widgets are shipped at the same time, each of the five outlets would have to spend $100 per week for additional storage space to hold the inventory until it is sold. How does this change your answer to question 3, if at all?

5. You sell appliances. You are thinking of adding to your firm's catalog a COD option for customers who receive deliveries by this type of truck line. How would you explain and specify the charges?

6. Your firm is in Chicago (ZIP code 60639). The firm prints and sells forms used by import brokers at coastal ports in Baltimore (21201), Savannah (31411), Miami (33054), New Orleans (70148), Los Angeles (90840), Portland (97207), and Seattle (98195). You ship 500 pounds per week to customers in each of these cities. The product's classification is 200, each is a single shipment, and there are no discounts or accessorial charges involved. Your Portland customer has excess storage space and suggests that you ship the goods in 12,000-pound lots; some the customer will use, and the rest will be trucked to Seattle and Los Angeles in 500-pound lots. Assume that 12,000-pound lots will be shipped from

Chicago to Portland every eight weeks and that 500-pound lots will be trucked from Portland to Seattle and from Portland to Los Angeles each week. What are the transportation savings, if any? What other costs might be involved?

C A S E   8 - 2

ALBERTA HIGHWAY DEPARTMENT, REGION VI

Region VI of the Alberta Highway Department is responsible for highway maintenance in Alberta in an area west of Lethbridge, Calgary, and Red Deer. One of its most important responsibilities, in the public's mind, is to keep open Canadian Route 1, which travels across all of Canada. At the very west of Region VI are the Rocky Mountains, and in a six-mile stretch between Lake Louise and the British Columbia border, the highway climbs from 3,000 to 6,000 feet. The climb in this stretch is uniform, the road's elevation increasing 500 feet each mile as it moves to the west (see Exhibit 8-A).

A highway maintenance station is near Lake Louise, one mile to the east of the six-mile section. At this station are based several heavy-duty dump trucks that in the winter are mounted with snow plows in the front and sand-spreading devices in the rear.

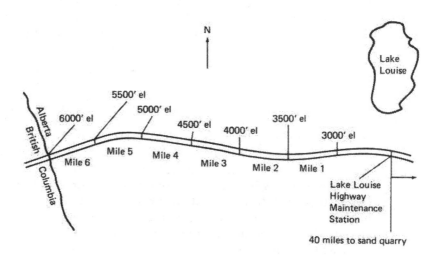

Exhibit 8-A Canadian Route 1.

Sanding is used after frost or freezing rains and in the spring when melting snows refreeze at night. The higher elevations require more sanding because they are subject to more freezing temperatures. For more than ten years, since the highway was opened, records have been kept for the amount of maintenance required by each mile of highway. In terms of sanding, the average number of days per year that each mile requires sanding is as follows:

Mile 1	3000'–3500' elevation	40 days
Mile 2	3500'–4000' elevation	48 days
Mile 3	4000'–4500' elevation	53 days
Mile 4	4500'–5000' elevation	58 days
Mile 5	5000'–5500' elevation	65 days
Mile 6	5500'–6000' elevation	70 days

The dump trucks can carry 10 tons of sand, which is enough to spread over one mile of highway in both the eastbound and westbound lanes. Spreading sand is a slow process because, under slippery conditions, highway traffic moves slowly. Several trucks are needed because when sanding is needed, it is needed quickly.

At the Lake Louise maintenance station are large silos for holding the salt-treated sand. At present, the silos can hold nearly 6,000 tons of sand, some of which is used for lower stretches of highway. During the summer months, the silos are filled by special trailer dump trucks that carry the sand up from a quarry near Bow Valley, 40 miles to the east of the Lake Louise maintenance station. The silo is of such a design that it can be split into two. Split segments of the silo can hold different capacities or equal capacities of sand. However, their total capacity is 6,000 tons.

Through a departmental program for encouraging employee suggestions, a proposal had been received from a sander truck driver that a portion of the Lake Louise sand silos be moved west toward the higher elevation, where more frequent sandings are needed.

The highway was constructed so that at one-mile distances (in this case, at elevations of 3,000, 3,500, 4,000, 5,000, 5,500, and 6,000 feet) it is possible for maintenance trucks to turn around. The shoulders are also wide enough at these points so that the silos can be placed alongside. The silo relocation can be performed during summer months using regular maintenance crews and equipment, with no additional costs.

The principal reason for splitting and relocating a portion of the silos is to place sand closer to where it is needed and to reduce the travel time of maintenance trucks to and from the silos. The work crews are paid a constant rate for a fixed number of hours, and if they are not sanding, they are performing other tasks. Hence, the only relevant costs are those of truck operation.

The facts and assumptions to be used in the analysis follow:

1. Costs of trucking sand from the quarry to the Lake Louise silos or to the relocated silos are 3 cents per ton-mile for the length of the full haul in one direction. (Empty backhaul costs are taken into account by these calculations.)

2. Some sand silo capacity must be kept at the Lake Louise maintenance station.

3. Spreader dump trucks are more costly to operate for carrying sand between silos and to where it is needed. The cost is 10 cents per ton-mile (which also takes empty backhauls into account).

4. There are no costs assigned for spreader trucks to reach silos initially. The reason for this is that they are randomly located on the highway at the time the decision is made to spread sand. Truck crews are then dispatched by radio.

5. If a new silo is located, it must be at one of the turnaround sites between each of the miles.

6. If a new silo is located an even number of miles from the Lake Louise station, a midpoint will be established halfway between the two silos and sanders will load at the silo nearest the mile of road needing sand.

7. If a new silo is located an odd number of miles from the Lake Louise maintenance station, a determination must be made as to which silo will provide sand for the middle one. (This is because maintenance trucks cannot turn at the middle of mile sections.)

8. No costs are assigned to operating the spreaders within a mile on either side of the silo. This is because they start spreading sand immediately upon leaving the silo. However, for sanding a stretch that is, say, between two and three miles from the silo, the cost of reaching the area would be $2 (10 tons × 10 cents × 2 miles).

Questions

1. Should one portion of sand silos at the Lake Louise maintenance station be relocated to a point to the west, at a higher elevation? If yes, where should it be relocated, how much capacity should it have, and what are the projected annual savings in truck operating costs? Show your work.

2. Assume that it is discovered that it would be impossible to split the silo into sections. However, it would be feasible to move the entire silo to another site, farther up the slope. The section of highway from the Lake Louise maintenance station stretching west one mile to where it reaches the 3,000-foot elevation point must be sanded for thirty days per year. All points east of the Lake Louise maintenance station can be serviced from other points. Should the entire silo be moved to another point? If so, to where? What will the savings be? Show your work.

3. Ignore all statements made in question 2 and assume, instead, that the silo can be divided into three sections: one remaining at Lake Louise and the other two located somewhere along the six-mile stretch. If two sections are to be located within the six-mile section, where should they be placed? What will the savings be over the present system? Show your work.

4. This case was written some time ago, when fuel costs were very low. Assume now that the spreader dump truck costs 35 cents per ton-mile to operate (compared to 10 cents) and that the trailer dump truck used to move sand from the quarry costs 20 cents per ton-mile to operate (up from 3 cents). Answer question 1 again, but this time take into account the new truck operating costs.

5. Answer question 2 again but using the new trucking costs outlined in question 4.

6. Answer question 3 again, taking into account the new trucking costs outlined in question 4.

7. Is the situation in this case an example of *partial* systems analysis or of *total* systems analysis? Why?

Inventory Management

9

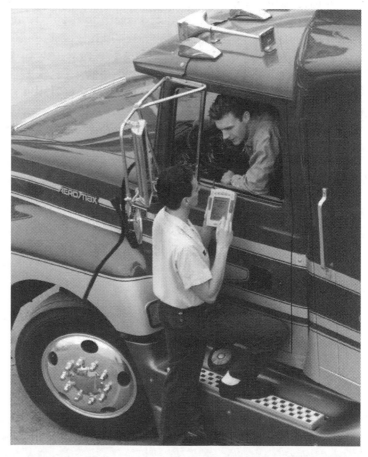

New portable computers, such as the one pictured here, are being used by mobile workers in practically every area of business and industry to collect, process, and communicate real-time inventory information from the source to the management information network. The units contain built-in radio-frequency technology for data communications over local or wide area networks. (Courtesy of the Telxon Corporation.)

All the early Ford V8 engines were built at the Rouge Complex in Dearborn and shipped to other factories for installation. Although each plant had engine storage areas, Ford's largest storage facility was actually the railroad cars filled with engines enroute to the various assembly plants.

Old Car News & Marketplace
June 2, 1994

Rather than relying on safety stock, consider cutting lead times. Big lot sizes and queues on the factory floor or the receiving dock add cost and lengthen the response time.

Modern Materials Handling
May 1994

Nestlé Distribution Company has begun putting its own personnel in customer warehouses to manage inventories.

American Shipper
May 1994

A New York entrepreneur who was awarded the souvenir concession for the New York visit of Pope John Paul II—called off because of the pontiff's health—is the proud possessor of 40,000 T-shirts, 10,000 hats, 15,000 sweatshirts, 10,000 golf shirts, 15,000 rosaries and 10,000 medallions. New York magazine says that he's slashed prices by 50 percent in order to unload the stuff.

San Francisco Chronicle
November 25, 1994

Key Terms

- ABC analysis
- Carload sale
- Distribution resource planning (DRP)
- Economic order quantity (EOQ)
- Fixed-order-interval system
- Inventory carrying cost
- Inventory flow
- Inventory shrinkage
- Obsolescence
- Opportunity cost
- Push or pull inventory system
- Safety stock
- Stockout
- Storage costs

Learning Objectives

- To determine the costs of holding inventory
- To identify the costs associated with a stockout
- To understand the concept of EOQ
- To differentiate the various inventory flow patterns
- To appreciate the role of bar-code scanners in inventory control

INTRODUCTION

Inventories are stocks of goods and materials that are maintained for many purposes, such as resale to others, use in a further manufacturing or assembling process, investment, or for the operation or maintenance of existing equipment. Retailers like large inventories; they attract customers. We've all seen auto dealers' ads on TV proclaiming: "hundreds of new cars in stock!" Professors Larson and DeMaris use the term *psychic stock* to refer to "retail display inventory [that is] carried to stimulate demand."[1] It is necessary to carry this type of stock in order to attract customers who prefer a wide selection of merchandise (for example, men's neckties).

In production and selling processes, inventories serve as cushions to accommodate the fact that items arrive in one pattern and are used in another pattern. If we eat one egg a day and buy them by the dozen, every twelve days we buy a new container of eggs, and the inventory of eggs remaining in our refrigerator declines at the rate of one egg per day.

However, the most prominent ongoing concern about inventories is cost. Inventories are carried as assets on a company's balance sheet. However, an increase in inventories cannot be automatically interpreted as desirable. A firm may manufacture much more than it can sell. Carrying costs for the inventories are significant, and the return on investment to the firm for its funds tied up in inventory should be as high as the return it can obtain from other, equally risky uses of the same funds. Excess inventories are often considered as "waste."

If this was all there were to the "problem," there would be no problem. Firms would keep inventory costs down by keeping inventories extremely low. However, being understocked and having repeated stockouts also can be expensive. (**Stockouts** occur when one is both out of stock and has a willing buyer for the item.) One certain way to lose customers is to be an unreliable source of supply. The solution, then, is to determine the proper balance of inventory and maintain it—our focus in this chapter.

BEARING OR SHARING THE BURDEN OF INVENTORY MANAGEMENT?

Inventory policy integrates all aspects of supply-chain management because the manager must determine the quantity and location of each item to be stored. Buyers prefer situations where they can reduce their inventory levels because they are assured of rapid, on-time replenishment as a result of the supplier's and carrier's dependability.

[1] Paul D. Larson and Robert A. DeMaris, "Psychic Stock: An Independent Variable Category of Inventory," *International Journal of Physical Distribution and Logistics Management,* vol. 20, no. 7 (1990), p. 30.

Because of the high costs associated with maintaining inventories, it is usually desirable to have somebody else do it. In a situation where one distributor supplies several dealers, the distributor tries to force the dealers to carry larger inventories so it can carry a smaller inventory, while the dealers prefer the reverse policy. Some time ago the distribution manager of a pharmaceutical company made the following observation, which could be echoed by many firms: "Inventory management becomes a difficult thing when your customers take the position that they're not going to operate with any more inventory than they possibly have to. Then they push it back to us. We in turn try the same technique with our suppliers."[2] In the automobile industry, the auto companies have such great leverage over some suppliers of components that they buy the components on a consignmentlike basis—meaning they do not pay for them until they are actually installed in cars as they move down the assembly line. The supplier has the financial burden of holding the inventory even though it is committed to the buyer.

Related to the issue of burdens is the issue of terms of sale that deal with how quickly bills must be paid. Within the supply chain, the ideal situation is to have one's suppliers give very generous selling terms with regard to waiting for payment, while one's customers are subject to strict terms, such as having to pay cash for the products on delivery, or possibly even in advance. In this situation the party in the middle always has a "float" of cash.

An inventory order system may be classified as being either a **pull** or **push** type. In a pull situation, the channel members (retailers or wholesalers) request or order products as they are needed from the manufacturer. A current example of a pull system is the market for videotapes of recent movies. At the time they are released, they are heavily advertised, and many consumers then demand to either purchase or rent them from videotape rental stores. Push systems occur when manufacturers force products upon their channel members in an effort to reduce their own inventories. Military operations have push-type systems, with supplies sent forward to troops at the front until an order is received to change the amounts. Local water and electricity systems are push systems; we must turn them off if we don't want them.

This phenomenon occurs even within a single firm. A plant's production manager incurs costs every time he or she changes the type, size, or model of product that a production line is making. The manager would prefer to wait until night or the weekend to make the changes on the line necessary to accommodate the next type of product. Until the change is made, the line continues to manufacture the former product, possibly far in excess of the marketing manager's desires or needs.

This can become even more complex. In the auto industry, as the model year end approaches, the manufacturer has in stock many accessory components

[2] "Inventories: Which Way Now?" *Transportation and Distribution Management* (May–June 1975), p. 27.

for the current year's model that have proven to be unpopular with buyers. Assume that 20,000 autos are still to be built and the following, slow-moving optional items are in inventory: 17,000 vinyl tops, 14,500 rear-seat vanity mirrors, 6,000 AM radios with rear-seat speakers, and 3,000 tinted windshields. In this case the last 20,000 autos will contain one or more of these slow-moving optional items. The result is that none of the optional items are left when the 20,000th, and last, car rolls off the assembly line. The production manager's problem has been solved, but the marketing manager's problem has become more acute because dealers are reluctant to take autos containing an odd assortment of accessories for which buyers have already shown disdain.

In addition to goods for sale and components used in assembly operations, over a dozen other classifications of inventories have been listed by Professor Cavinato: raw materials and components, work-in-process goods, finished goods, resale goods (those purchased from other suppliers and modified slightly for resale, such as a light bulb for an overhead projector or a case for a camera), company supplies, labels and packaging materials, spare parts for sale, promotional materials, traded-in goods, returned goods to be reworked, returned goods that will not be reworked, idle capital goods awaiting installation, scrap and waste, and products that have been recalled.[3] Today, with recycling of products and product packaging, some firms would have even more categories of inventory.

DETERMINING INVENTORY LEVELS

Inventory size determination deals with the amounts, or levels, of inventories a firm attempts to maintain. There are costs of maintaining inventories and costs of being out of stock. The logistics manager must maintain an inventory level that minimizes the total cost of both.

The discussion in this chapter assumes that a firm has already decided on storage sites for its inventories. However, a firm determines the number and location of sites after it determines the desired level of customer service to offer at a specific cost. Decisions about inventory levels are, in a sense, like a closed loop. The approaches discussed here are relatively unsophisticated. In the real world, this is another area where computerized and management science applications abound.

Inventory Carrying Costs

Inventory carrying costs fall into several categories. **Storage costs** are those of occupying space in a storeroom or warehouse. Many inventories must be insured against fire, flood, theft, and other perils, and this is part of the

---

[3] Joseph Cavinato, "Managing Different Types of Inventory," *Distribution*, March 1990, pp. 88–92.

expense of storing goods. Some products lose volume or size over time. **Inventory shrinkage** recognizes the fact that more items are recorded entering warehouses than leaving. In addition, an inventory of tropical fish will shrink as some die. **Obsolescence** recognizes that items in an inventory gradually become out of date. This can be a serious problem with some consumer products such as cosmetics. Related to obsolescence is depreciation, which is a form of deterioration that is a function of time, not usage. For example, upholstery may begin to fade in new automobiles that are stored outside. Interest charges for the money invested in inventories must be added to take into account the money that is required to maintain the investment in inventory.

Inventories are taxed, usually on the basis of the inventory on hand on a certain date, and considerable effort is made to have that day's inventory be as low as possible. The inventory tax and most of the costs associated with avoiding or evading the inventory tax are all part of the inventory carrying costs.

Fresh fish and many types of fresh produce deteriorate (or depreciate) completely in only a few days. Hence, the depreciation portion of a produce company's carrying costs might be 25 percent to 50 percent per day. Dairy products, drugs, bread, some soft drinks, and camera film are examples of items with a form of expiration date before which they should be sold or used. Their rate of depreciation can easily be calculated because, at the expiration date, the unsold items must be removed from the shelf.

Some inventory items have other types of carrying costs because of their specialized nature. Pets or livestock must be watered and fed. Tropical fish must be fed and have oxygen added to the water in which they are kept. Precious items require additional security measures.

Added together, these costs are known as inventory carrying charges. They are usually expressed as a percent of the inventory's value and sometimes are surprisingly high. One old but still widely cited estimate is that carrying costs approximate 25 percent per year of a product's value. Table 9-1 summarizes the component breakdown of the 25 percent figure.

Another cost that should be mentioned, although it is not included in most carrying costs calculations, is **opportunity cost**—the cost of taking a position in the wrong materials. This is more of an issue to those who speculate in holding various types of inventory.

Stockout Costs

If avoiding an oversupply were the only problem associated with inventories, the solution would be simple: store fewer items. But not having enough is as bad as having too many. A **stockout** occurs when the supply of an item is exhausted and a customer wants to buy the out-of-stock item. Stockout costs are difficult to determine and inexact but nevertheless real.

TABLE 9-1 INVENTORY HOLDING COSTS (IN PERCENTAGES)

Insurance	0.25%
Storage facilities	0.25
Taxes	0.50
Transportation	0.50
Handling costs	2.50
Depreciation	5.00
Interest	6.00
Obsolescence	10.00
Total	25.00%

Source: Adapted from L. P. Alford and John R. Bangs (eds.),
Production Handbook (New York: Ronald, 1955), pp. 396–397.

Estimating the costs or penalty for a stockout involves an understanding of customer reactions to a seller being out of stock at the time the customer wants to buy an item. "Without making the effort to quantify the profit consequences of shortages, the logistics manager is flying in the dark when it comes to choosing the most profitable aggregate service level."[4]

Consider the following customer responses to the stockout situation. How should they be evaluated?

A. The customer says, "I'll be back," and this proves to be so.
B. The customer says, "Call me when it's in."
C. The customer buys a substitute product, which yields a higher profit for the seller.
D. The customer buys a less expensive substitute, which yields a lower profit.
E. The customer places an order for the item that is out of stock (known as a back order) and asks to have the item delivered when it arrives.
F. The customer goes to a competitor.

The loss in situation A is negligible; the sale is only slightly delayed. In situation B the information on which to make a judgment is incomplete; it is not known whether the customer will in fact return. In situation C the seller is actually better off than if the item the customer initially desired were in stock; the opposite situation occurs in situation D. Of interest would be the quality of the product the same customer requests the next time he or she comes in. Situation F is most difficult to evaluate because it is unknown

[4] David P. Herron, "Integrated Inventory Management," *Journal of Business Logistics,* March 1987, p. 113.

whether the customer is lost temporarily or permanently. The competitor may also be out of stock. If the customer is lost for good, then it is necessary to know the cost of developing a new customer to replace the lost customer.

For the sake of simplicity, assume the responses can be placed into three categories: sale delayed, sale lost, and customer lost. The third is the most critical. Assume further that, over time, 300 customers who experienced a stockout were queried. It was found that the first alternative occurred 10 percent of the time, the second 65 percent of the time, and the third 25 percent of the time. These percentages (or probabilities of each event taking place) can be used to determine the average cost of a stockout. Table 9-2 illustrates the procedure. Each cost is multiplied by the likelihood that it will occur, and the results are added. A delayed sale has no cost because the customer is brand-loyal and purchases the product when it is again available. The lost sale alternative results in loss of the profit that would have been made on the customer's purchase. The lost customer situation is the worst. The customer tries the competitor's product and prefers it to the product originally requested. The customer is lost, and the cost involved is that of developing a new brand-loyal customer.

TABLE 9-2 DETERMINATION OF THE AVERAGE COST OF A STOCKOUT

Alternative	Loss[a]	Probability[a]	Average cost[a]
1. Brand-loyal customer	$ 0.00	.10	$ 0.00
2. Switches and comes back	37.00	.65	24.05
3. Lost customer	1,200.00	.25	300.00
Average cost of a stockout.		1.00	$324.05

[a]These are hypothetical figures.

Safety Stocks

Firms usually maintain **safety stocks**, or "buffer" stocks, to prevent an excessive number of stockouts. Marginal analysis is generally used to determine the optimum level of safety stocks (see Table 9-3). Assume goods must be ordered from a wholesaler in multiples of ten. The carrying cost of an additional or marginal ten units is $1,200. However, by stocking an additional ten units of safety stock and maintaining it throughout the year, the firm is able to prevent twenty stockouts. Because the average cost of a stockout has already been determined to be $324.05, preventing twenty stockouts saves the firm $6,481.00 ($324.05 × 20). Savings far outweigh costs, and the next alternative is to maintain a safety stock throughout the year of twenty units. This adds $1,200 to the costs but prevents sixteen additional stockouts from occurring, thereby saving $5,184.80.

TABLE 9-3 DETERMINATION OF SAFETY STOCK LEVEL

Number of units of safety stock	Total value of safety stock ($480 per unit)	25% annual carrying cost	Carrying cost of incremental safety stock	Number of additional orders filled	Additional stockout costs avoided
10	$ 4,800	$1,200	$1,200	20	$6,481.00
20	9,600	2,400	1,200	16	5,184.80
30	14,400	3,600	1,200	12	3,888.60
40	19,200	4,800	1,200	8	2,592.40
50	24,000	6,000	1,200	6	1,944.30
60	28,800	7,200	1,200	4	1,296.20
70	33,600	8,400	1,200	3	972.15

The optimum quantity of safety stock is sixty units. With this quantity, the carrying cost of ten additional units is $1,200, but $1,296.20 is saved. If the safety stocks are increased from sixty to seventy units, the additional carrying cost is again $1,200, while the savings are only $972.15. Therefore, the firm would be better off by permitting three stockouts to occur each year. Note that these concerns determine a level of customer service.

Safety stocks also mean that the firm will attempt to replace the item. Not all stores maintain safety stocks. Some mass merchandisers do not, and buyers cannot count on items being replaced. In these situations, customers outfitting a bathroom, for example, should buy all the fixtures at one time; the merchant feels no obligation to replace those specific items or styles once they are out of stock.

ECONOMIC ORDER QUANTITY

As noted in the previous section, the safety stock level is the minimum inventory a firm tries to keep on hand. However, what determines how this level is maintained? How often should stocks be replenished? How much should be ordered each time? The correct amount to order is called the **economic order quantity (EOQ).**

The typical inventory order size problem deals with calculating the proper order size based on minimizing the total of two costs: (1) the costs of carrying the inventory, which are in direct proportion to the size of the order that will arrive; and (2) the costs of ordering, which mainly involve the paperwork associated with handling each order, irrespective of its size. Were there no inventory carrying costs, customers would hold an immense inventory and thus avoid the details of reordering. If there were no costs associated with ordering, one would place orders continually and maintain no inventory at all, aside from safety stocks.

Figure 9-1 shows the two costs on a graph and indicates the point at which they are minimized. Mathematically, the economic order quantity is determined using this formula:

$$EOQ = \sqrt{\frac{2AB}{I}}$$

where

EOQ = the most economic order size, in dollars
A = annual usage, in dollars
B = administrative costs per order of placing the order

and

I = carrying costs of the inventory (expressed as an annual percentage of the inventory's dollar value)

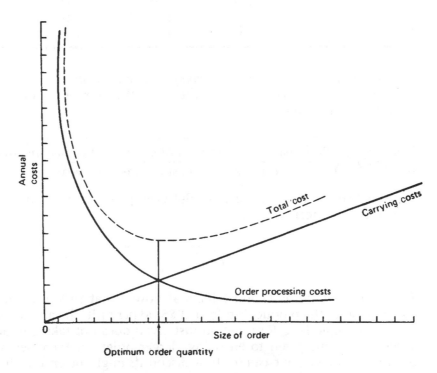

Figure 9-1 Determining EOQ by use of a graph.

If $1,000 of an item is used each year, if the order costs are $25 per order submitted, and if carrying costs are 20 percent, what is the EOQ?

$$EOQ = \sqrt{\frac{2 \times 1,000 \times 25}{0.20}} = \sqrt{250,000} = \$500 \text{ order size}$$

Because of the assumption of even outward flow of goods, inventory carrying costs are applied to one-half the order size that would be the average inventory on hand. (See Table 9-4.) *EOQs, once calculated, may not be the same as the*

TABLE 9-4 EOQ CALCULATIONS

Number of orders per year	Order size	Ordering cost	Carrying cost of average inventory in stock	Total cost
1	$1,000	$ 25	$100	$125
2	500	50	50	100
3	333	75	33	108
4	250	100	25	125
5	200	125	20	145

lot sizes in which the product is commonly sold and bought.

EOQs can also be calculated in terms of the number of units that should be ordered. The formula is

$$EOQ = \sqrt{\frac{2(\text{annual use, in number of units})(\text{cost of placing an order})}{\text{annual carrying cost per item per year}}}$$

Assume that the item in the Table 9-4 example costs $5. Substituting numbers in the new formula yields

$$EOQ = \sqrt{\frac{2\,(200)(25)}{5 \times 0.20}} = \sqrt{\frac{10,000}{1}} = 100 \text{ units}$$

The earlier EOQ formula and Table 9-4 showed that $500 was the best order size, and since the product is priced at $5.00 per unit, the answer is the same.

The simple EOQ formulation just given does not take into account the special discounts given to encourage larger orders or increased volumes of business. However, one can see how discounts might be entered into some of the columns in Table 9-4, which would have an impact on total costs as the figures were added horizontally.

Inventory Flows

At this point the figures from the EOQ and the safety stock calculations can be used to develop an **inventory flow** diagram. Assume that the EOQ in this instance has been determined to be 120 units, that the safety stock level is 60 units, that average demand is 30 units per day, and that the replenishment or order cycle is two days. On day 1 (see Figure 9-2) an EOQ of 120 units arrives. Total inventory (point A) is 180 units (one EOQ plus 60 units of safety stock). Demand is steady at 30 units per day. On day 3, total inventory has declined to 120 units (point B), which is the reorder point, because it takes two days to receive an order and during this time 60 units would be sold. Because safety stock is *not* to be used under normal circumstances, reordering at 120 units means that 60 units (safety stock) will be on hand two days later when the EOQ arrives. The EOQ of 120 units arrives at point C, and then total inventory increases to 180 units at point D.

If the rate of sales doubles to 60 units per day, the reorder point is hit at 120 units (point E), and an additional EOQ is ordered. However, it will not arrive for two days. A day after the reordering, the regular inventory is exhausted, and at point F the safety stock is starting to be used. At point G the EOQ arrives just as the safety stock is about to be exhausted. If the EOQ arrived later than day 8, a stockout would have occurred. The new EOQ boosts the inventory to 120 units, which is also the reorder point. Therefore, at point H another EOQ is ordered. Starting on day 8, the demand settles back to the old average of 30 units per day.

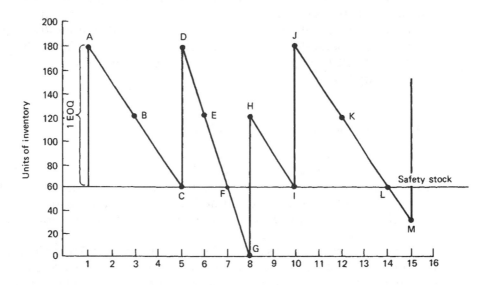

Figure 9-2   Inventory flow diagram.

If it appeared that the demand rate of 60 units per day was going to become the average demand rate, the firm would have to redetermine its EOQ. Recall that a basic input into the EOQ formula is annual sales of the product. If this figure changes, then the EOQ must be recalculated.

Starting at point H, demand is again 30 units per day. The next EOQ arrives on schedule at point I, and total inventory increases to 180 units at point J. The reorder point is at 120 units, and an EOQ is ordered on day 12. Demand stays constant, but the transportation mode delivering the EOQ is delayed one day. Instead of arriving on day 14, it arrives on day 15. Safety stock is entered at point L on day 14. A stockout is again prevented because the EOQ arrives at point M. Note that safety stock protects against two problem areas—increased rate of demand and an increased replenishment cycle.

When an EOQ system is used, as illustrated in Figure 9-2, *the time between orders varies.* The normal time between orders was four days, but when sales doubled the time between orders was only two days. One requirement for the utilization of an EOQ system is that the level of inventory in the system must be monitored constantly. Then, when the reorder point is hit, an EOQ is ordered. With the advent of computerization, many firms have the capability to constantly monitor their inventory and hence have the option of using an EOQ system. A reorder point for each item can be established in the computer's memory so it can indicate when the stock has been depleted to a point where a new order should be placed. Sophisticated computer systems even transmit the purchase order to the vendor electronically.

A variation of the EOQ method is the *fixed-order quantity* method, used in repetitive purchases of the same commodity. An example would be a lumber–construction materials retailer located along the Mississippi River that buys gravel by the barge load (approximately 1,000 tons per load). The retailer would wait until its gravel stockpile was nearly exhausted before ordering another barge load.

FIXED-ORDER-INTERVAL SYSTEM

An alternative inventory concept that is also commonly used is known as the **fixed-order-interval system.** In this system EOQs are not used; instead, orders are placed at fixed intervals, such as every three days or twice a month. In the EOQ system, the time interval fluctuates, with the order size remaining the same. In fixed-interval systems, the opposite holds, and order sizes may vary.

Fixed-interval systems are used in three situations. The first is when the firm does not maintain automatically updated stock levels. Such firms typically have a clerk manually check the levels of all items and determine which stocks are running low. This task is assigned on a regular basis. A second situation is when vendors offer the firm significant discounts if it will place its orders at certain fixed time intervals. Because the discounts are greater than the advantages of using the EOQ system, the fixed-interval ordering system is utilized. Finally, in the third situation, the firm buys FOB origin and tries to utilize its private trucking fleet whenever possible. If one of the firm's trucks deadheads from a point near a supply source back to the firm's plant on a regular basis, the firm may decide to buy FOB origin and carry the supplies in its own truck.

The fixed-order-interval system also is used in conjunction with a safety stock. It usually requires more safety stock than the EOQ system because the latter system constantly monitors inventory levels. In an EOQ system, if sales start to increase, the reorder point will be hit earlier and a new order for an EOQ will be placed automatically. Stockouts can still take place, but only during the replenishment cycle after the new order has been placed. With the fixed-order-interval system, since the inventory levels are not monitored, a stockout can occur during both the order cycle and the time before order placement.

Most fixed-order-interval systems do borrow one element from EOQ systems. Next to each bin or slot in the warehouse is a card indicating the minimum quantity for that product. When the order pickers note that the stocks have been reduced to this level, they notify their supervisor, who decides whether the reorder should occur immediately or on the next scheduled date.

Cyclical buying is a very specialized form of fixed-interval ordering. This practice occurs in the women's fashion industry, where retailers place their orders directly with the manufacturer for each season's fashions, and there is almost no possibility of reorder. Another example is a grocery retailer's purchase of Halloween pumpkins or Christmas trees.

Just-in-Time (JIT) Inventory Systems

An inventory system that has received widespread attention is the just-in-time (JIT) system. The concept is related to the fixed-order-interval system, and customers place orders with their suppliers on set schedules that frequently involve daily or hourly deliveries. With regard to the EOQ system, the concept is based on the assumption that ordering costs are negligible; hence, firms order frequently in order to minimize inventory holding costs. In JIT systems, stocks are small and almost continuously moving.

JIT II systems are a refinement in which the vendor's representatives are stationed at the customer's place of business.

> The original just-in-time practices can stir up hostility by putting pressure on suppliers; JIT II is designed to create harmony and efficiencies for both sides.

Based on sharing of previously guarded data, such as up-to-the-minute sales forecasts, JIT II relies heavily on trust since the companies could face serious conflicts of interest.[5]

INVENTORY REORDERING PROCEDURES

In addition to the JIT inventory system, there are several other, more traditional systems for replenishing inventory stocks. Nearly all inventory systems require some formal stock-level monitoring capability. This section discusses the more common reorder processes.

A separate listing of what the inventory levels should be is usually maintained, and then the actual stock levels are checked against it. A common problem with beginning stock clerks is that when they see that the level of some item is low, they reorder; however, if the stock is exhausted, the clerk forgets completely about the item, especially if adjoining stocks overflow into the empty space. Hence a separate list must be kept, and usually each bin must be labeled. (However, reserving empty space for an out-of-stock item consumes considerable warehouse or shelf space.)

Users' Systems

In chain stores one frequently sees a code number on the shelf next to the price listing for an item. Each day an employee walks up and down each aisle with a bar-code scanner, checking the stocks of items the store is supposed to be carrying. The employee pushes what looks like a grocery cart with a desktop calculator. Attached to the device is a small box with a wire and wand connected to it. The wand is used to scan, or read, the bar code for each product on the shelf front. After scanning the code, depending on how the system is programmed, the employee punches in either the number of items in stock or the number of items to reorder. The record produced by the scanner can be read by a device attached to a telephone; it is used to transmit the order to the firm's warehouse, where the new order is then prepared for shipment to the store.

A more complex variation of the bar-code scanning order system is used for automobile parts. Manufacturers of some popular auto makes establish and enforce rigid repair parts inventory requirements, specifying the minimum number of each item that dealers must keep in stock. On a specified day each month (which varies by dealer so that orders reaching the distributor's warehouse are spread out), the dealer must report inventory to the distributor; the distributor then determines what parts the dealer needs to bring stock up to the minimum levels. This is one type of dealer order.

[5] *The Wall Street Journal,* January 13, 1995, p. 1.

A second type of order is for accessories, sales of which depend on the efforts of new car salespeople. Because these demands are less predictable, the dealer places a supplemental order once a month for accessory items. Parts can be placed on this order, which must be submitted two weeks before or after the next monthly parts order. Note that the dealer has this one chance, midway between its other parts order dates, to request parts that are being used quickly. This distributor pays freight charges on both types of orders just mentioned.

Two other order systems are available, but for these the dealer must pay the freight charges. Emergency orders reach the dealer two or three days after being placed (compared with the usual time of two weeks). A car-down parts order is handled with even higher priority, and the fastest mode of transportation is used for delivery. Frequently, the dealer phones in the order and goes and picks it up. For all types of orders except the car-down order, the distributor handles the paperwork and billing at the time of processing the order. For a car-down order, paperwork is handled after delivery of the part.

Suppliers' Systems

In some industries, especially retailing, the supplier provides the order system. The supplier employs an "order taker," who surveys the stocks on the shelves, in the storeroom, and in the warehouse and then writes out a suggested order for the retailer to sign. When the retailer has a favorable relationship with the order taker, he or she usually signs the order without questioning it. Sometimes the order taker makes a sales pitch for one of the supplier's items and tries to get the retailer to order more of that particular item. Rack salespeople operate in a similar manner. A rack jobber (or driver-salesperson) may maintain the hardware rack in a grocery store and reaches an agreement with the retailer as to the rack's initial inventory. The rack salesperson comes back every other week, replenishes the items that have been removed from the rack, lists the items being replenished on a form, calculates the wholesale prices, and presents the completed form to the retailer as a bill.

Today many suppliers' data base systems are constructed to query the customer around the time that a new order should be placed. Reorder systems can also be viewed as elements of selling; one uses them to make additional sales. In stocks of many products a reorder reminder or form can be found toward the bottom, in place to be used at about the time it's needed. Electronic data interchange (EDI) systems are links throughout the supply chain and are used as combined user-supplier reorder/replenishment systems. EDI is used between buyers and sellers with an established relationship; each shipment is typically covered under the larger umbrella of a sales contract.

Vendor-Managed Inventory

In recent years some buyer-seller relationships have been cemented to the point where

> the manufacturer controls the flow of inventory into the retailer's distribution network, based on daily EDI inputs of the retailer's inventory, demand, and in-transits. The manufacturer determines the orders needed to satisfy the retailer's inventory targets and uses time-phased replenishment plans of the retailer's distribution center needs to help determine its own manufacturing plans.[6]

This is referred to as vendor-managed inventory.

One example of the practice comes from Nestlé and Lucky Stores, which carries about 200 different Nestlé food items. Nestlé has its own personnel in Lucky warehouses, managing Lucky's inventory of Nestlé products. Early results show that the turnover of Nestlé-brand inventory shot up from 18 to between 55 and 60 times annually. Order lead times shrunk from a week to three days.[7]

KEEPING TRACK OF INVENTORIES

Only in a few instances can an individual look around and see the entire inventory with which he or she must be concerned. A logistics manager of a large firm may be responsible for an inventory list of 10,000 to 100,000 different items located at 50 or 100 locations all over the globe. Much of the "inventory" may not be at a fixed location; it may be aboard a moving ship, truck, or railcar. In order to manage an inventory effectively, the manager must maintain records that indicate the current inventory and tell where it is located. These tallies must be adjusted continually to take into account purchases, sales, deliveries, and shortages.

The simplest record for duplicating an inventory—known as the "scratch-in, scratch-out" method—lists all of the different items in the left-hand margin of a sheet of paper, usually attached to a clipboard. A hatch mark is added every time a case is received, and a mark is erased or crossed out every time a case is removed. The number of hatch marks on the sheet is the same as the number of cases in the storeroom. On occasion, it is necessary to take the tally sheet into the storeroom and reconcile the number of hatch marks with the number of cases.

Accounting records are of varying use since they deal with values rather than items. Also, after some items—such as unused parts—are fully depreciated or written off, they disappear from the accountant's records even though they may still be kept in stock. "Taking inventory" is a term familiar to anyone who has worked in retailing, and it represents an annual or more

---

[6] *APICS—The Performance Advantage,* July 1994.

[7] *American Shipper,* May 1994, p. 9.

frequent exercise in which all products are physically counted and compared with recorded inventory. Adjustments are then made both to reconcile records with actual stocks and to make sure that the firm's accounting records reflect lost or damaged stocks. The accountants are mainly interested in the dollar value of the inventory; however, for auditing purposes they will also "spot check" the accuracy of the firm's inventory records. Note that at some level in the firm, inventory is viewed as a dollar amount; at another level, it is seen as the number of items of stock.

Figure 9-3 shows a computerized inventory control worksheet. A few of the worksheet headings need explanation. "PAL-PATTERN" describes the arrangement of cartons loaded on pallets. "QTY DUEIN" refers to stock that is expected with some degree of certainty; it is considered available for commitment. "PEND ORDERS" means that the product is tentatively committed, whereas "HOLD DAMG" refers to products that are being held for some reason such as damage and that cannot be committed without further inspection. "REORD POINT" and "MINQTY REORDER" deal with, respectively, the point or level of inventory at which a reorder is necessary and the minimum size of order that can be made (both values are derived using a computer program).

Tracking Procedures

Multiple Locations.   More sophisticated systems keep track of inventories that are scattered in many locations. For example, United Airlines stocks various aircraft repair parts at its maintenance stations throughout the

PRTREORD   A C C U P L U S   LDS, INC
           INVENTORY CONTROL WORKSHEET   PAGE:

DATE: 12/31/99   FOR: XYZ COMPANY   ABC WAREHOUSE
           CUST#:   0001   BLDG#: 1

PRODUCT CODE	SIZE PACK DESCRIPTION	UNIT WGT	PAL-PATTERN UT/ TP/ UP	ONHAND QTY	QTY DUEIN	AVAIL QTY	PEND ORDERS	HOLD DAMG	NET AVAIL	REORD POINT	CASES NEED	MINQTY REORDER	ORDER QTY	ORDER WGT	PAL ORD
1010	2 15/OZ COOKIE MIX	.1	10/ 10/100												
111	2 16/OZ BROWNIE MIX	3.0	10/ 10/100	90	100	190	10		180						
1111	10 8/OZ MUFFIN MIX	1.0	10/ 10/100												
1212	10 8/OZ CAKE MIX	1.0	10/ 10/100												
222	5 6/OZ PUDDING MIX	3.0	10/ 10/100	100		100	100								
333	5 1/LB ICE CREAM CO	3.0	10/ 10/100	80		80			80						
DSTG1	5 1/LB ICE CREAM BA	5.0	5/ 5/25	60		60			60						
XYZ0000	5 1/LB HOMEMADE C	5.0	5/ 5/25												
XYZ1	3/1LB CLEANING LIQU	3.5	10/ 3/30	310		310	90		220	30		270			
XYZ2	6/1.5 LB CHOCOLATE	9.5	5/ 5/25	200		200			200	25		100			
XYZ3	1/15 LB COFFEE	1.5	4/ 12/ 48							10	10	90	90	135	2
XYZ4	5 1/LB HOMEMADE C	6.0	5/ 5/25							25	25	75	75	450	3
	*** Customer Totals ***			840	100	940	200		740		35		165	585	5

Figure 9-3 Computerized inventory control worksheet. (Courtesy of Accuplus Logistics Management System, by LDS, Inc.)

United States. Because it has numerous commercial flights scheduled between these points every day, it can easily carry a part from one airport location to another. A maintenance mechanic in Chicago who needs to replace a
coffee warmer in the food galley of an aircraft goes to the stock clerk, who in
turn goes to a computer at the maintenance station and finds out where the
item is located in United's repair parts inventory. Even if the part is in
Chicago—possibly just on the other side of the wall from where the clerk is
standing—it is quicker for the clerk to check the computer for the location
of the part than it is to go wandering through the parts room. The computer, in only a few seconds, tells the clerk where the part is stocked. If the
part is not in Chicago, the clerk notes where it is located. If the only ones
are in Detroit and San Francisco, the clerk can ask the computer when the
next United flight from each city will leave for and arrive at Chicago and
then arrange to have the item placed aboard the flight scheduled to reach
Chicago first.

Sometimes a businessperson owns merely two or three outlets and, to a
certain extent, pools the inventory to serve the needs of all the outlets. The
closer together the outlets, the easier this is to accomplish. An example is a
bicycle retailer who owns shops in San Francisco, Berkeley, and Sacramento
and uses a van with racks for carrying twelve assembled bicycles. While most
of the hauls are for bicycles from the San Francisco store, where they are all
received, it is possible for the truck to carry specific bicycles between other
stores if they are needed to fill an order. Videotape rental chains in large
cities "back up" each other. Trucks that carry new tapes also carry tapes from
store to store to replace inventory that is rented out.

Some items such as office equipment, automobiles, cameras, and
firearms are easier to keep track of because they contain identification or
serial numbers. In the case of autos and firearms, government agencies also
keep close control over transfers of the items. Frequently, a government
agency has what amounts to a record of each inventory.

Pharmaceutical drugs and some food items must have batch numbers
on each carton and individual container. In case of product recall, the recall
is by batch or lot number, and all such items must be removed from warehouse stocks and retailers' shelves.

Scanners.   A recent development is the use of printed bar codes that
can be read by electronic scanners. The scanners record inventory data and
may be directly attached to a computer that uses the data to adjust inventory
records and track product movement. Every pair of Levi Strauss jeans is
tagged with a twelve-digit bar code that identifies it by size, style, and color.
Scanners pick up the information when the jeans are sold. Computers accumulate the data and then transmit it to Levi Strauss headquarters. Within
hours a computerized program named LeviLink generates a purchase order to

replace the jeans just sold and can generate a computer model detailing inventory flows. New merchandise arrives in bar-coded cartons, with bar-coded price tags already in place, allowing retailers to log new inventory and display it for sale within hours rather than days.

The most common scanner system is the one associated with the Universal Product Code (UPC). The UPC was initially designed to increase the overall efficiency of grocery stores at the retail level. Computer firms are manufacturing computer checkout systems at grocery stores. The ubiquitous black-and-white vertical-stripe label is now found on almost all grocery products.

The bar-code scanning system involves passing the UPC label on each product over an optical scanner at the checkout counter. The UPC is read and recorded in a computer, which supplies such information as the product's price, tax, if food stamps can be used, and whether it can be legally sold on Sundays. The specific price of each product and its description is then flashed on a monitor screen positioned near the counter. When all the products have been recorded, the customer receives a tape that lists the products purchased, the price of each article, and the total bill. The system is also intended to monitor stock levels, trigger reorder procedures, and the like, but many grocery stores have not adapted the UPC scanner system to a storewide inventory management system, in part because of the great volume of data generated. However, the UPC scanner system is used by some chain stores for complete product tracking and as an inventory management system.

Bar-code scanners are currently the most popular automatic identification system in use. They work to integrate suppliers and customers along the supply chain because all parties read the same labels; in addition, the transfer of the goods between parties can be recorded by simple electronic means. Other automatic identification technologies include optical character recognition (the device reads letters, words, and numbers), machine vision (which can scan, inspect, and interpret what it views), voice data entry (which can record and interpret a human voice), radio-frequency identification (used where there is no line of sight between scanner and label), and magnetic stripes.

Figure 9-4 shows a radio-based warehouse identification system. Its value is that the scanners are linked directly to the firm's mainframe computer. One example of the system's usefulness is when a shipment of a product urgently needed by a customer arrives at the dock. Using the radio-linked scanner, the shipment is recorded as it is received; the mainframe computer then instructs that it be shipped out again immediately to the customer rather than moving through the warehouse.[8]

---

[8] This warehousing practice is known as *cross-docking*.

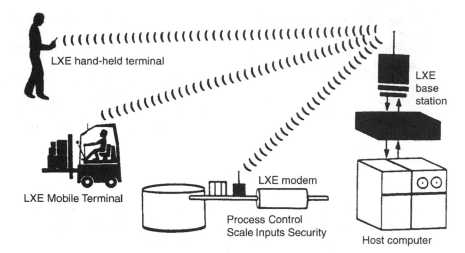

LXE wireless plant communications system including base station, hand-held and mobile terminals and modem.

Figure 9-4   Radio-frequency inventory identification system. (Courtesy of LXE, Inc.)

Inventories in Motion

The person who needs the inventory usually assumes that his or her inventory consists of what is in stock plus what is on order. He or she assigns varying probabilities to goods on order showing up in time to avoid stockouts. The narrowest permissible margin occurs when a salesperson, with a customer out front, discovers the bin empty, but before returning empty-handed to the customer, notices the stock clerk coming down the aisle from the receiving dock with goods to replenish the empty bin. In fact, inventory includes all completed but unsold products as well as those that are on their way from the point of manufacture to the point of sale. On a typical day in the late 1980s, General Motors had 237,000 autos "in transit," that is, moving from its assembly plants to its dealers in North America.[9]

Products moving in railcars, truck trailers, or vessels are considered inventory in motion. For example, railcar diversion and reconsignment privileges are used in the marketing of fresh produce. California lettuce is loaded into railcars and headed east. As the lettuce moves eastward, the owner sells it by long-distance telephone or fax. Once the lettuce is sold, the owner notifies the railroad to deliver it to the buyer.

According to Exxon Corporation, in the 1980s the free world's oil inventory—between the point of production and the point of consumption—was

[9] L. Thomas Gaines, from comments at Burlington Northern's conference "New Links in Transportation," Dallas, November 3–4, 1988.

about 10 billion barrels, which equals about six months' consumption.[10] So large is this inventory that one aspect of its management is to alter the speed at which it flows through pipelines and in tankers at sea. In mid-1981 this tanker fleet, at any one time, was carrying 750 million barrels of oil. If its average speed were increased by one knot, there would be a decrease of approximately 100 million barrels in the amount of oil aboard the free world's tanker fleet at any one time.[11]

The "inventories in motion" concept is also illustrated by the experience of a southern meat packer who closed several warehouses and substituted truck containers that were continually in motion. The refrigerated containers were fifteen feet long and equipped with self-contained legs. A larger truck would carry three containers and make individual stops, where it would meet smaller trucks capable of carrying only one container. (Both the large and small trucks had the capability of lifting into place or discharging a container.) At the meeting point between the large and small trucks, the small truck unloaded an empty container and took on a full container. This operation was repeated at two other sites with two other small trucks; the small trucks then made deliveries from the full containers while the large truck headed back with empty containers to the packing plant. The process was repeated each day. Actually, it was not necessary for the large and small trucks to meet because it was possible to leave the containers in a stationary position.

The phrase *in the pipeline* is used today to describe products on the move. Logistical thinking with regard to product movement is undergoing important changes. Traditional logistical thought showed components or products in one of two situations: (1) in a stationary position in a warehouse, stockpile, or other storage area; or (2) in transit aboard a carrier. Today, however, logistics is turning to continuous flows, and component or product movements are depicted as continually moving through a system of tubes of varying diameters and with changes in velocity to accommodate fluctuations.

Supply pipelines must be flexible, in the sense that they do not always extend between the same two points. During the pre-Christmas season in 1994, Neiman Marcus, the status retailer, used an upscale passenger train, the American Oriental Express, to serve as a rolling retail store for ten days. Five cars were used to display goods, and additional cars provided sleeping and dining accommodations for Neiman Marcus sales personnel. For reasons of aesthetics, the decision was made not to add freight cars to the train in order to stock additional inventory. Instead, trucks were utilized. "Using cellular phones, the train's sales managers notify Neiman Marcus' main distribution center in Dallas about items that need to be resupplied. A 48-foot trailer is

---

[10] *World Oil Inventories* (New York: Exxon, 1981), pp. 3–8.

[11] Ibid., pp. 8–10. Fewer tankers would be needed to move the same amount of oil.

loaded with goods that night and rushed to meet the train at the next scheduled stop."[12]

Improved communications can also speed up delivery processes. An example relates to workstation monitors that come from Asia. Formerly they were imported, and all were moved to assembly sites, many of which were in the midwestern or eastern United States. There they would be combined with a central processing unit and packaged. For those complete units sold on the West Coast, the monitors would travel across the continent again. Under the new system, which relies on electronic data interchange, the companies

> keep half or more of their monitors in inventory on the West Coast. When a West Coast customer places an order, the carrier dispatches an East Coast truck to pick up the central processing unit and a West Coast truck to pick up the monitor. The trucks rendezvous at a predetermined terminal, the workstation is consolidated into one shipment and then delivered to the customer.[13]

At higher levels of management one may think of inventories as always moving, with input materials going in and finished products being delivered to retailers. As a lower level, the person unloading the truck still sees a stationary stock of product that is motionless, waiting to be moved. By way of analogy, the head of a university may think in terms of students flowing into the system as freshmen and leaving as graduates, while the individual instructor sees a roomful of friendly, inquiring faces parked in a classroom for an entire semester.

INVENTORY MANAGEMENT: SPECIAL CONCERNS

Generalizations concerning inventory management are often hard to make. Each commodity has its own handling characteristics. In addition, the framework through which each product is marketed, and all the other supply-chain relationships, vary. What follows, then, is a discussion of factors that affect the management of some inventories.

The inventory manager must divide all materials into *stock-keeping units* (*SKUs*). The phrase *line item* is analogous to *SKU*. It means that a separate horizontal line on inventory record forms is devoted to that product type. Each SKU represents a type of individual item or product for which separate records are maintained. A coal yard carrying five different grades of coal has five SKUs. A large grocery store has between 10,000 and 15,000 SKUs. In addition to designating each product and product variation or size as an SKU, the inventory manager must designate the quantity—or minimum lot

---

[12] *Journal of Commerce,* December 19, 1994, p. 8A.

[13] *Journal of Commerce,* January 24, 1995, p. 3B.

size—with which the inventory records will deal. The retail grocer thinks, or keeps records, in terms of individual items or case lots (a case holds twelve, twenty-four, or some other number of individual items). The warehouse serving that retail store may deal only with case lots or pallet loads (a pallet load contains twenty-five to fifty cases, depending on the product). If the smallest SKU quantity the warehouse wishes to deal in is cases, it accepts orders for one or more cases only. If the distributor selling to the warehouses wants to deal only in pallet loads, it accepts orders for one or more pallet loads only, and so on. Thus, a retailer taking inventory would consider the following as an SKU:

> Lori's tomato paste, 10-oz. can, number of cans

The warehouse person stocking the same product would list the following as an SKU:

> Lori's tomato paste, 10-oz. can, number of 24-can cases

The distributor of the product, which sells to wholesale warehouses, would consider the following an SKU listing:

> Lori's tomato paste, 10-oz. cans, in 24-can cases, number of pallets of 42 cases

Many firms stock hundreds or thousands of items, and to them the problem is one of determining the relative importance of each item. A rule of thumb that can be applied to most inventories is that 20 percent of the items account for 80 percent of the sales. The other 80 percent of the items are much less active. This is known as the 20/80 rule.

The term **ABC analysis** is frequently applied when large inventories are analyzed. An application of ABC analysis might place the top, or fastest-selling, 10 percent of inventory items in category A, the second fastest-moving group in category B, and the slowest in category C. Each of the three groups would be handled separately, and the system designed would take into account their differing inventory-related characteristics. In a repair parts inventory, an additional consideration would be how "critical" a part might be to customers. Hence, category A might include fast-moving repair parts plus a few slow-moving—but still extremely important—repair parts. The reason for including both in category A is that their stock levels require closer surveillance. A stock clerk might be expected to check category A items daily, B items weekly, and C items every three weeks, for example.

ABC analysis can be applied using different measures, with other examples being dollar volume, profitability, or number of items picked. Another criterion might be importance to other partners in the supply chain. A firm supplying medicine to hospitals might need to stock certain items because they are critically important.

Dead Inventory

Some inventory managers use *ABCD analysis,* with *D* standing for inventory items that are dead by one or more criteria. The manager might try to move them out by deals, that is, bunching them with more attractive merchandise. Special care must be taken to make certain they are not reordered. Usually, the order-processing system is informed that orders received for these D products should be handled on a special-order basis only, transmitted to the vendor for the exact amount that the customer requested so that there will be no unsold stock left over. Items can also be dead in an accounting sense, once they have been fully depreciated.

Some dead items can be donated to charities, usually resulting in a partial tax write-off. Figure 9-5 is an ad from a service that helps firms find recipients for inventory donations.

Turn your
excess inventory
into a substantial tax break
and help send needy
kids to college.

Call for your
free guide
to learn how donating your
slow moving inventory
can mean a generous
tax write off
for your company.

Call (708) 690-0010
Peter Roskam
Executive Director

P.O. Box 3021, Glen Ellyn, IL 60138
FAX (708) 690-0565

*Excess inventory today...
student opportunity tomorrow*

"Something's got to go. Fenton. You, me or this inventory—and it's not going to be me."

Figure 9-5   Advertisement from a service that helps firms donate excess inventories to charitable causes. (Courtesy Educational Assistance, Ltd., Glen Ellyn, IL 60137.)

Deals

Deals were just mentioned in the discussion of dead inventory. Sometimes a manufacturer or wholesaler has an unbalanced inventory with too many slow-moving items. To clear the warehouses, the manufacturer or wholesaler may offer retailers a deal, that is, a specific lot of merchandise combining desirable and less desirable items. The price is set so that the retailer is likely to buy in spite of the fact that some of the items will be hard to resell except at a low price. This is offset by the fact that the lot also includes some fast-moving items and that its total price is relatively low. When this lot arrives at the retailer's storage facility, it tends to run counter to inventory management objectives because it contains some unpopular, slow-moving items that may be the same as unpopular, slow-moving items already in stock. An example of a deal occurred after the introduction of color television, which proved to be more popular than expected. Manufacturers had many unsold black-and-white sets and could get dealers to take them only if they were part of a specially priced deal including color sets.

In retailing, the term **carload sale** was often used to mean that the retailer had purchased an entire rail carload of a product and wished to pass the savings in both quantity and discounts from the manufacturer and rail transportation costs on to the retail customer. (Figure 9-6 shows the delivery of a carload of tires to a Miami retailer in the early 1920s.) Moving larger-than-usual quantities through the system may have many advantages from a retailing standpoint, but it may not be related to the goals of good inventory management. Current thought, if anything, is in the opposite direction,

Figure 9-6   Gearing up for a carload tire sale. This photo was taken in Miami in 1921. Note that the trucks in the center and on the left of the photo have solid rubber tires. (Courtesy of the Florida Photographic Collection, Florida State Archives.)

more concerned with orderly on-time replenishment. Today, under the partnership arrangements, deals occur less frequently. The seller and buyer enter into a longer-term agreement whereby the seller agrees to replenish the buyer's stocks and maintain an agreed-upon level.

Another "deal" situation occurs when a competitor goes out of business and offers its entire inventory for sale in a single block. The purchaser must look at this purchase as an investment.

Complementary Inventory Items

An example of inventory items with a complementary relationship pertains to items that are subject to demand in different seasons. Skis are sold for winter use; scuba equipment is sold during the summer. When goods complement each other in this way, their carrying costs are lower since the costs of storage assigned to them are for only a fraction of the year.

Items that are complementary from the retail customer's viewpoint may only intensify the pressures on the retailer or wholesaler concerned with stock maintenance. In the summer, picnic items such as catsup and mustard or wieners and buns sell together. Almost any time an item requiring subsequent purchase of a refill is sold, the refills must be marketed alongside the initial item to demonstrate to buyers that they will not be impossible to find later. Also, customers want to know the price they will have to pay for refills. An example is bags for vacuum cleaners. A store carrying an inventory of vacuums will also carry bags. An initial analysis of inventory procedures might lead the logistics manager to recommend dropping the line of bags because of the high costs involved. Marketing people would then point out that the sale and display of bags is necessary to the sale of new vacuums.

Sometimes it is necessary to stock items that have no market value but must be used as customer service tools, such as the sales literature a wholesaler supplies to retail outlets, spare copies of instruction manuals, or extra copies of book jackets to replace soiled and torn originals. These are justified on the basis of customer service.

The most common complementary relationship between goods in an inventory occurs when incoming goods come from one supplier or outgoing goods go to one receiver or consignee. In these situations the controlling factor may be the dollar, weight, or cubic volume of the entire order. The individual items in the inventories may be of secondary consideration, except for their contribution to totals. A chain food store may schedule a truck to go to a specific retail store on Tuesdays and Fridays. The order to go on Tuesday's truck is small, leaving both volume and weight capacity of the truck underutilized. The warehouse will add to the store's order (without consulting the store) and fill the truck, usually with steady-moving, nonperishable items such as paper towels. In this instance the chain owns the inventory, retail outlet, and warehouse, so its costs of maintaining the inventory remain the same. However, by using the truck's unused carrying capacity, the chain manages to reduce its transport costs by better utilizing its equipment.

In the use of for-hire carriers there are weight breaks—points in tariffs where the charges per hundred pounds drop as the size of shipment increases. If an inventory manager's order were just under one of these points, he or she might save money by ordering more to get the freight savings. Or if the seller pays the freight, a quantity discount may be offered to entice the buyer to purchase a quantity above the weight break involved.

Substitute Items

A more complicated relationship between goods in an inventory occurs when goods are substitutes for each other. Because of this, many food stores are relatively unconcerned about temporary stockouts of food items. They realize that the shopper will not hesitate to substitute a 75-watt light bulb for a 60-watt bulb or one cut of meat for another. Sometimes these substitutions could occur in either direction, but in other cases a one-way relationship exists. For example, a bolt $7/16$ inch in diameter could be used in place of a bolt that was $1/2$ inch in diameter, but the reverse may not hold.

The relationships between goods discussed in this section have implications with respect to determining stockout costs and the sizes of safety stocks to be maintained. If the consumer has no hesitation in making substitutions, it would appear, initially, that there are no penalties for a stockout. However, a point will be reached where customers become sufficiently annoyed at having to make substitutions that they decide to take their business elsewhere. Because of the many possibilities for substituting products, many chain grocery stores aim to have only 95 percent of various products or SKUs in stock. They feel that enough substitutes exist that the customer will look for a substitute item in their store, and not switch to a competing store.

Informal Arrangements outside the Distribution Channel

Competing dealers of the same manufacturer may, in some instances, group their respective inventories for certain purposes. All dealers of a certain make of auto in a city circulate among themselves a list of their inventories of new cars. If one dealer has a ready buyer for a specific model and color of auto that it does not have in stock, the dealer will check the list of other dealers' inventory to see whether they have the model. If one of them does, the dealer will arrange a trade with the other dealer; then the dealer will have the auto in stock that the buyer wants. Dealers also have computer access to each other's parts inventory listings. Franchised fast-food restaurants also sometimes borrow from each other.

In industries with spirited competition between dealers, there is usually little or no competition when it comes to dealers supplying each other with needed repair parts. Informal channels of distribution benefit all parties concerned, including the consumer. They indicate some of the hazards in applying formal inventory analyses to certain situations and overlooking the informal relationship between dealers.

Major U.S. airlines and many foreign airlines that fly U.S.-built aircraft belong to an organization that lists spare parts it has for sale:

> The listing merges the separate data of participating airlines so that items bearing the same manufacturer's part number are grouped together. As an example from a printout, Pratt & Whitney's part no. 484637, an engine strainer, is noted as being offered for sale by five airlines. Also listed are the quantities each seller has available (ranging in this case from 72 to 3,967). Buyers negotiate directly with the sellers.[14]

The procedure does, of course, compete directly with parts sold by the manufacturer, although manufacturers refer to this listing for two purposes. First, they find it cheaper to buy back some parts they originally sold rather than reopen their production line. Second, by noting the quantities available of surplus parts on the airlines' listing, manufacturers can make more accurate predictions of needed production of more units.

Repair Parts

Repair part inventories cause many problems. A truck manufacturer with a nationwide market in mind may advertise that there are a thousand dealers who offer specialized parts and service. This will assure truck buyers that, no matter where in the United States their trucks operate, they are likely to be near parts and service. The individual truck dealer sees things differently. Profits to the dealership come from the sale of new trucks locally, and the dealer feels that the only customers that must be kept satisfied are those local firms that buy new trucks from it. The dealer is less concerned about stocking parts for models of trucks it does not sell. If a cross-country trucker has a breakdown and must wait several days for the repair part to reach the dealer in question, this makes little difference to the dealer. Thus, the manufacturer may require the dealer to maintain a certain basic inventory, which often includes items the dealer would not choose to carry. This relieves the manufacturer of a portion of the burden of maintaining inventories. In situations where the manufacturer requires dealers to maintain a parts inventory, special incentives are frequently offered. The manufacturer may agree to buy back inventory items at cost in situations where obsolescence or depreciation of the items occurs. The manufacturer may absorb shipping charges on items needed to maintain the dealer's required levels of stock.

Note the problem cited here started out as one of marketing: the truck manufacturer wanted to advertise a nationwide network of service and parts.

---

[14] "Worldwide Supermarket of Aircraft Parts," *Exxon Air World*, 1979, p. 28.

Nearly all inventory policies have a relationship to marketing and customer service. Few, if any, decisions are made without speculating about customer reaction. (During the famine relief efforts in Ethiopia during the 1980s, relief organizations preferred using Mercedes trucks in their fleets because there was a Mercedes truck dealership network in Ethiopia that could supply parts.)

FedEx, an airline specializing in rapid delivery of parcels throughout the United States, maintains a warehouse for use by its customers near the airline's Memphis hub. Customers maintain inventories of repair parts at this warehouse and then instruct FedEx to carry or ship them to where they are needed. Several other companies also offer "parts bank" services. An ad for one is shown in Figure 9-7.

Tax Vulnerability

In many jurisdictions, inventories are subject to property taxes. The law usually defines the date on which property will be assessed. Inventory managers attempt to have as little inventory as possible in that jurisdiction on that date. All orders are shipped out while incoming orders are delayed, if not refused. Consider this item from *Journal of Commerce:*

> Houston—Gulf Coast refiners that are trimming crude oil inventories to minimize taxes assessed on their year-end stocks run the risk of potential supply shortfalls if another year-end phenomenon—heavy fog—disrupts the flow of crude oil arriving by tanker. . . .
>
> The inventory trimming has emerged as a prominent market feature in recent days, causing prices of some crude grades to sag as sellers outnumber buyers. . . .
>
> Meanwhile, the refiners may not have to actually dispose of their inventories to achieve reduced tax assessments, according to one trader who suggested the very act of offering it into an amply supplied market may itself depress prices briefly. . . . The taxes are usually based on the January 1 market value of the crude.[15]

Return Items and Recycled Materials

Inventory systems are designed so that goods can flow from the manufacturer to the ultimate consumer. However, in some instances provisions must be made for accommodating a flow, albeit a lesser flow, in the opposite direction. If a customer is unhappy with a defective item and returns it to the store where it was purchased, should the store return it to the wholesaler? Who is authorized to make repairs and then place the item back into stock? If it is not worth returning items, what controls are necessary to avoid fraudulent claims?

Wholesalers wanting retailers to increase their inventories can offer to buy back unsold items at a later date. A distinction has to be made between

---

[15] *Journal of Commerce,* November 24, 1993, p. 11B.

Figure 9-7 Advertisement from a parts bank service. (Courtesy Associated Distribution Logistics.)

returned goods that can be placed back into the wholesaler's stocks and those that are no longer saleable. Some products are repackaged or recycled.

In industries where return items are a major consideration, rack jobbers or driver-salespeople are sometimes employed. They are paid on a salary-plus-commission basis and perform more services than the typical delivery personnel. Some of these services are to check display cases for dated merchandise, remove soiled items, and collect returnable items (such as bottles). Chain food stores frequently rely on driver-salespeople employed by other suppliers to continue to handle items that involve returns. This means that the chain's distribution system need not be concerned with the return flow.

In the parts order system there are also return flows. Some automobile parts are considered rebuildable, and the customer who buys the rebuilt part must be assured that it meets the manufacturer's factory specifications. The foreign manufacturer rebuilds motors in its own country but allows parts such as speedometers to be rebuilt by specific firms in the United States. When a mechanic at the dealer goes to the parts room and asks for a speedometer, the parts clerk may notice that the bin containing speedometers has a special-colored tag that tells him or her to ask the mechanic for the old speedometer. If there is no old speedometer to be traded (as might occur because of an auto accident), the parts clerk charges a higher price to the customer for the new (or rebuilt) speedometer just handed to the mechanic. The used speedometers are sent to the distributor, which sends them to the plant, where they are rebuilt. When finished, they are returned to the distributor and become part of the regular inventory. In this instance the distributor has two sources of supply for speedometers: the factory and the rebuilder.

Distribution Resource Planning (DRP)

Distribution resource planning (DRP) is an inventory method helpful in determining inventory requirements at branch warehouses. Whereas materials requirements planning (MRP-1) deals with production inputs, DRP involves finished products. The key to DRP is centralized order processing by a manufacturer. Many firms receive orders at their regional warehouses, but this can result in an unbalanced inventory of finished products throughout the firm's regional warehouses. With DRP all orders are processed at one location, and then finished products are sent to the appropriate warehouse to replenish inventory that was just sent to the customer who placed the order. The effect is that inventory is balanced throughout the warehouse system. The central inventory planner can also ensure that, if shortages do occur, they can be evenly spread among warehouses, so that no customer must accept complete stockouts while others are receiving almost all of their requested shipments.[16]

[16] See Andre J. Martin, *Distribution Resource Planning* (Essex Junction, VT: Oliver Wight, 1983).

DRP developed as an attempt to apply materials requirements planning principles to outbound distribution. At present, there is some debate as to whether this can be done successfully. According to one critic, "DRP proceeds from a single, flawed premise: that distribution of finished goods can be planned and organized in advance, much the same way that the manufacturing cycle can be scheduled."[17] Professor Masters and others have concluded that "DRP is not viewed as an effective tool to deal with complicated market channel structures."[18] However, we can expect to see its use increase as supply-chain relationships are improved.

SUMMARY

Chapter 9 addresses inventories and inventory management. Since there are many costs associated with holding inventories, a common strategy is to attempt to shift this burden to others.

When deciding what level of inventories to maintain, one tries to minimize the costs associated with both too much and too little inventory. If one maintains too much inventory, the inventory carrying costs (interest, depreciation, insurance, and so on) are too high. If too small an inventory is kept, one risks a stockout (i.e., having a willing buyer but no goods). The worst outcome of a stockout is to lose both the sale and the customer.

EOQ determines an order size that minimizes order-processing and inventory maintenance costs. One managing inventories must also determine reorder points for each item. These are remaining stock levels at which a new order should be placed. Just-in-time inventory systems are widely used in manufacturing operations. They require close monitoring because almost no reserves are kept to offset either late deliveries or flawed parts.

The chapter also discusses reorder procedures, multiple-point inventory locations, complementary inventory items, substitute items, "informal" inventories, and repair parts inventories.

QUESTIONS FOR DISCUSSION AND REVIEW

1. In the section entitled "Bearing or Sharing the Burden of Inventory Management?" what are the important issues discussed?
2. Discuss the costs for holding inventory.
3. Discuss the concept of stockout costs. How can a stockout cost be calculated?
4. What is safety stock? How can its desired level be calculated?

[17] The critic is Robert L. VanDeMark, quoted in *Transportation and Distribution,* May 1988, p. 34.
[18] James M. Masters et al., "On the Adoption of DRP," *Journal of Business Logistics,* Spring 1992, p. 64.

5. What is the logic of the EOQ model?

6. Study Figure 9-2. Present a brief explanation of the inventory flow in this diagram. Be sure to mention the role of the reorder point.

7. "Only unsophisticated inventory managers would prefer a fixed-order-interval system to the EOQ system." Do you agree? Discuss.

8. In 1994 a well-known soft drink company advertised that each one of its cans was "freshness-dated," which meant that a date was stamped on the can and, presumably, the product was best consumed before that time. What problems, if any, would such a program cause persons responsible for managing that beverage company's inventories? Discuss.

9. How do changes in interest rates impact inventory management decisions?

10. In what ways do inventories serve as "buffers"?

11. Who should be responsible for maintaining inventory levels? Why?

12. Should inventories be considered investments?

13. Professor Cavinato listed about a dozen different categories of inventory. Give an example of each.

14. What is vendor-managed inventory?

15. Discuss the utilization of bar-code scanners in inventory control.

16. In the section called "Inventories in Motion," what main issues are discussed?

17. Discuss the concept of complementary inventory items.

18. What are psychic stocks?

19. Do you believe that the area of inventory management will become more or less important relative to the other areas of logistics in the future? Why?

20. Suppose that you operate a cigar stand. Your customers must request the brand of cigars they want, and you usually sell cigars on a one-at-a-time basis. You sell El Smokos for 15 cents each; they cost you only 10 cents apiece. You are out of El Smokos, and on a tally sheet you record the responses of 100 customers who ask for an El Smoko and are told that you are out of stock.

(a) Thirty walk away without making a purchase.

(b) Twenty buy an El Supremo cigar, which sells for 25 cents (and costs you 18 cents).

(c) Forty buy an El Cheapo, at 10 cents (and which costs you 8 cents).

(d) Ten say they can wait and will check with you later in the day to see whether the El Smokos have arrived.

What has it cost you to be out of stock of the 100 El Smoko cigars you could have sold? What is your best estimate? What other information, if any, do you still need?

SUGGESTED READINGS

Axsater, Sven, and Kaj Rosling. "Multi-Level Production-Inventory Control: Material Requirements Planning or Reorder Point Policies?" *European Journal of Operational Research,* vol. 75, no. 2 (June 9, 1994), pp. 405–412.

Billesbach, Thomas J., and Roger Hayen. "Long-Term Impact of Just-in-Time on Inventory Performance Measures." *Production & Inventory Management Journal,* vol. 35, no. 1 (1994), pp. 62–67.

Boylan, John E., and F. R. Johnston. "Relationships between Service Level Measures for Inventory Systems." *Journal of the Operational Research Society,* vol. 45, no. 7 (July 1994), pp. 838–844.

Closs, David J., and Craig K. Thompson. "Logistics Physical Resource Management." *Journal of Business Logistics,* vol. 13, no. 2 (1992), pp. 269–283.

Emmelhainz, Larry, Margaret Emmelhainz, and James R. Stock. "Logistics Implications of Retail Stockouts." *Journal of Business Logistics,* Fall 1991, pp. 129–242.

Groebner, David, and C. Mike Merz. "Solving the Inventory Problem for the Sale of Seasonal Merchandise." *Journal of Small Business Management,* July 1990, pp. 19–26.

Hobbs, O. Kermit, Jr. "Application of JIT Techniques in a Discrete Batch Job Shop." *Production & Inventory Management Journal,* vol. 35, no. 1 (1994), pp. 43–47.

Krupp, James. "Simplified Flow Control Using Kanban Signals." *Production & Inventory Management Journal,* vol. 35, no. 2 (1994), pp. 72–75.

Loar, Tim. "Patterns of Inventory Management and Policy: A Study of Four Industries." *Journal of Business Logistics,* vol. 13, no. 2 (1992), pp. 69–96.

Mahmoud, Mohamed M. "Optimal Inventory Consolidation Schemes: A Portfolio Effect Analysis." *Journal of Business Logistics,* vol. 13, no. 1 (1992), pp. 193–214.

Mentzer, John T., and R. Krishnan. "The Effect of the Assumption of Normality on Inventory Control/Customer Service." *Journal of Business Logistics*, March 1985, pp. 101–120.

Oliver, Nick. "JIT: Issues and Items for the Research Agenda." *International Journal of Physical Distribution and Logistics Management,* vol. 20, no. 7 (1990), pp. 3–10.

Perry, James H. "Firm Behavior and Operating Performance in Just-in-Time Logistics Channels." *Journal of Business Logistics,* February 1988, pp. 19–33.

Scanlon, Patrick C. "Controlling Your Inventory Dollars." *Production & Inventory Management Journal,* vol. 34, no. 4 (1993), pp. 33–35.

Tallon, William J. "The Impact of Inventory Centralization on Aggregate Safety Stock: The Variable Supply Lead Time Case." *Journal of Business Logistics,* vol. 14, no. 1 (1993), pp. 185–203.

Tersine, Richard J., and Michele G. Tersine. "Inventory Reduction: Preventative and Corrective Strategies." *International Journal of Logistics Management,* vol. 1, no. 2 (1990), pp. 17–24.

Young, Jan B. *Modern Inventory Operations.* New York: Van Nostrand Reinhold, 1991.

Zinszer, Paul H. "An Examination of the Cost of Capital and Inventory Stocking Policy." In *Annual Proceedings of the NCPDM* (Chicago: NCPDM, 1984), pp. 603–606.

Zipkin, Paul H. "Does Manufacturing Need a JIT Revolution?" *Harvard Business Review,* January–February 1991, pp. 40–50.

C A S E   9 - 1

LOW NAIL COMPANY

After making some wise short-term investments at a race track, Chris Low had some additional cash to invest in a business. The most promising opportunity at the time was in building supplies, so Low bought a business that specialized in sales of one size of nail. The annual volume of nails was 2,000 kegs, and they were sold to retail customers in an even flow. Low was uncertain how many nails to order at any time. Initially, only two costs concerned him: order-processing costs, which were $60 per order, without regard to size; and warehousing costs, which were $1 per year per keg space. This meant that Low had to rent a constant amount of warehouse space for the year, and it had to be large enough to accommodate an entire order when it arrived. Low was not worried about maintaining safety stocks, mainly because the outward flow of goods was so even. Low bought his nails on a delivered basis.

Questions

1. Using the EOQ methods outlined in Chapter 9, how many kegs of nails should Low order at one time?

2. (This is a continuation of the situation in question 1.) Assume all conditions in question 1 hold, except that Low's supplier now offers a quantity discount in the form of absorbing all or part of Low's order-processing costs. For orders of 750 or more kegs of nails, the supplier will absorb all of the order-processing costs; for orders between 249 and 749 kegs, the supplier will absorb half. What is Low's new EOQ? (If you are assigned this or later questions, it might be easiest to lay out all costs in tabular form.)

3. (This is a continuation of the situation in question 1; temporarily ignore your work on question 2.) Instead of the conditions mentioned in question 2, assume that Low's warehouse offers to rent Low space on the basis of the *average* number of kegs Low will have in stock, rather than on the maximum number of kegs Low would need room for whenever a new shipment arrived. The storage charge per keg remains the same. Does this change the answer to question 1? If so, what is the new answer?

4. (This is a continuation of the situations outlined in questions 1, 2, and 3.) Take into account the answer to question 1 *and* the supplier's new policy outlined in question 2 *and* the warehouse's new policy in question 3. Then determine Low's new EOQ.

5. (This is a continuation of the situation in question 1; temporarily ignore your work on questions 2, 3, and 4.) Low's luck at the race track is over; he now must borrow money to finance his inventory of nails. Looking

at the situation outlined in question 1, assume that the wholesale cost of nails is $40 per keg and that Low must pay interest at the rate of 1.5 percent per month on unsold inventory. What is his new EOQ?

6. (This is a continuation of the situation in questions 2, 3, and 5.) Taking into account all the factors listed in questions 1, 2, 3, and 5, calculate Low's EOQ for kegs of nails.

C A S E   9 - 2

MOM'S TACOS II

(This is a continuation of Mom's Tacos I, Case 7-1. It is necessary to read the text of Mom's Tacos I before beginning this case, although it is not necessary to answer the questions at the end of Mom's Tacos I.)

Sitting in her Lubbock, Texas, office of Mom's Tacos, Jenny Wong—now vice president of logistics—frowned as she looked at the front page of the *Atlanta Constitution* that had been sent to her. A large picture showed a batch of empty Mom's Tacos twenty-gallon sauce containers that had been dropped at the edge of a road in rural Georgia. The article dealt with trash and litter and the need for recycling, and included the statement "Greedy manufacturers avoid doing their share toward cleaning up the environment." While the article did not name Mom's, the words "Mom's Tacos" on the containers were very clear in the picture.

Jenny buzzed her secretary and asked him to make fourteen copies of the newspaper article and send it to the Mom's management, with "F.Y.I.—J. Wong" written at the top. She thought they might want to discuss the topic at their weekly meeting. The firm had never received this type of unfavorable publicity before, and Jenny was uncertain how she, and the firm, should react.

At the weekly meeting, the *Atlanta Constitution* article was barely discussed, although the old joke that "there is no such thing as bad publicity" fell flat. There was consensus that public attitudes toward environmental protection and recycling differed throughout the country. There was also agreement that many individuals who advocated protecting the environment were not willing to pay anything extra to achieve that objective. Jenny was told to look into the costs of using recyclable containers for Mom's sauce, and it was agreed that the information developed for distributing sauce out of the Savannah distribution point would be sufficient for this study. She was also instructed to concern herself only with twenty-gallon containers since—within a year—Mom's would be telling its restaurants that only twenty-gallon containers would be used and that Mom's would provide whatever equipment the restaurants that had been using five-gallon containers required to switch to the larger ones.

At present, Mom's distributed sauce in five-gallon and twenty-gallon containers, consisting of a plastic bottle inside a fiberboard box. The cost of twenty-gallon containers was $81 per hundred. Shipping weight for a twenty-gallon container was 183 pounds (with the sauce weighing 172 pounds and the container weighing 11 pounds).

During the next few months, Jenny was busy with her study. She talked with container suppliers, carriers, restaurant franchise owners, and with those responsible for packaging the sauce after it was created. Mom's also retained an outside consultant on health and cleanliness issues. When the firm had started, cleanliness had not been very important, and in its early days use of unclean vats had—on occasion—given the sauce certain hallucinogenic qualities. That was in the past. Today quality control, cleanliness, and sanitation were of top priority throughout Mom's entire operation, including the franchised restaurants.

After considering over ten alternatives, Jenny narrowed the possibilities to two, which shall be referred to here as A-style and B-style. A-style was close to the present system, using a plastic bottle inside a fiberboard box. B-style was a collapsible plastic container, similar to water containers carried by backpackers, which reduce in size as the water inside is consumed.

For A-style, the cost of twenty-gallon containers was $381 per hundred. Shipping weight for a twenty-gallon container was 189 pounds (with the sauce weighing 172 pounds and the container weighing 17 pounds). Each container could be used about ten times for Mom's products. Each time Mom's inspected and cleaned this A container prior to its reuse, the cost would be 17 cents.

The A-style container could be used even longer for nonfood products, but the more often the containers were cleaned, the more difficult it was to maintain the necessary cleanliness.

For the B-style container the cost was $247 per hundred. Shipping weight for a twenty-gallon container was 180 pounds (with the sauce weighing 172 pounds and the container weighing 8 pounds). The containers could be used about eight times for Mom's products. After that point they had no further use and would have to be disposed of. Each time Mom's inspected and cleaned a B-style container prior to its reuse, the cost would be 11 cents.

Costs of handling either type of container in the processing area within Mom's distribution centers would be the same as present costs. Outbound transportation costs from the distribution center to restaurants were based on motor common carrier rates for single containers from the Savannah distribution point. Twenty percent of Mom's shipments were delivered within Savannah. The rate within Savannah was $5 per cwt (hundredweight) for shipment up to 500 pounds, with a minimum charge of $6. (A 10-pound shipment would cost $6 even though the calculated charges per cwt would total only 0.10 times $5, or $0.50.)

Ms. Wong decided to use the average distance that the sauce traveled outside Savannah, which was between 150 to 200 miles. For shipments between 100 and 399 pounds, it was 8.50 per cwt. (For shipments under 99 pounds, the rate was $9.50 per cwt, and again the minimum charge was $6.)

The same rate structure held for return shipments, except that the only weight being shipped was that of the empty container. In reality, the minimum charge of $6 would apply to most shipments of empty containers.

Ms. Wong had ended up dealing with motor common carriers because they had an obligation to carry all cargo tendered to them. Other classes of carriers indicated that they did not want to handle the returned containers. This was for two reasons. The minor reason was one of cleanliness; the carriers were uncertain how much effort restaurants would put into cleaning a container that they knew would be thoroughly recleaned once it reached Mom's. The second reason was the bulk of the empty containers. These carriers argued that a truckload of returned A-style twenty-gallon containers might consist of 160 empty containers weighing a total of 1,760 pounds, with revenues to the carrier being around $100 for a haul of 100 or 200 miles.

Ms. Wong talked with the motor common carrier who handled most of Mom's business, and they were not enthusiastic about handling the returned containers. They would lose money at either the $6 minimum charge or on any other quantity. They also thought that picking up the empty containers at restaurants would be time-consuming since shipping documents would have to be prepared and most restaurants had no loading docks for handling outbound freight. The carrier's rate manager said that if a volume of empty taco sauce containers developed, the motor common carrier industry would probably ask for a higher rate classification for empty food containers (a higher rate per pound) to reduce their losses in handling the traffic. The reason given was that "it's not fair to use profits from other traffic to subsidize our losses here, even though recycling is socially desirable."

The carrier's rate manager suggested to Ms. Wong that she explore the use of the B-style containers to determine whether they could be collapsed and bundled into a denser, more compact shipment. He even contacted a person who worked with the classification committee of the Southern Motor Carriers' Rate Bureau to help Ms. Wong understand what a desirable density would be. After considerable experimentation, it was determined that the B-style containers could be collapsed and placed inside almost any shipping carton. When the carton was full of empty, collapsed containers, it could be returned to Mom's. Ms. Wong calculated that twelve empty twenty-gallon sauce containers would fit inside a carton. The carton of twelve would weigh about 205 to 210 pounds (depending on the weight of the shipping carton and how clean the B-style containers were). Ms. Wong's contacts with the motor common carriers indicated that if returned containers were returned in this manner—and with this density—the same charges per pound as used for the outbound sauce shipments could be used.

Finally, Ms. Wong talked with a number of restaurants that were already using the twenty-gallon containers. She got a mixed response about recycling the containers. Some restaurants did not want used A-style containers on their premises because of the space they would occupy. Some objected to storing any used containers for fear that, unless they were perfectly clean, they would attract bugs and rodents.

At present, the restaurants were disposing of the containers in a number of ways. One actually sold them to a nearby manufacturer of insect repellant, who used them for product storage. Most restaurants had to pay to have their trash and garbage removed each day, and the containers were just part of the load. Some acknowledged that their garbage-handling charges might be reduced slightly since they were based on volume. None of the restaurants wanted the responsibility for cleaning and bundling the used containers, preparing shipping documentation, or contacting carriers. None wanted to pay any more for the delivered sauce, and only a few thought that being able to advertise that Mom's used recycled sauce containers would be of any value to their franchise.

Questions

1. Given the limited information in the case, compare the outbound transportation costs of the present twenty-gallon containers for styles A and B.

2. Given the limited information in the case, compare the inbound transportation costs of empty twenty-gallon style A and B containers.

3. The carrier's rate manager said that if a volume of empty taco sauce containers developed, the motor common carrier industry would probably ask for a higher rate classification for empty food containers (a higher rate per pound) to reduce their losses in handling the traffic. The reason given was that "it's not fair to use profits from other traffic to subsidize our losses here, even though recycling is socially desirable." Do you agree? Discuss.

4. Based on the limited information in the case, what will use of the new recycled twenty-gallon containers cost, compared with the present system of twenty-gallon containers?

5. The case indicated that the A-style "container could be used even longer for nonfood products" while the B-style container "had no further use and would have to be disposed of." Is this difference between the two styles important? Discuss.

6. Assume that Mom's decides to use recycled containers of the type described in the case. Should all restaurants that use the sauce be forced to recycle their containers? Discuss.

7. What should Ms. Wong recommend? Why?

8. Assume that Mom's decides to go ahead with the idea of using recycled sauce containers. Draft a letter to be sent to all restaurant franchise holders explaining the action and indicating what will be expected from them.

10

Warehousing and Distribution Centers

Warehouse lift trucks and tractors have evolved during this century. The top photo is from some 1920 advertising. The lower left photo shows some equipment currently used for reaching high-rise storage. Robots are also being introduced into warehouse operations, but they tend to look less human than the one pictured in the lower right photo. It is actually an imitation robot, constructed for display in a warehouse equipment trade film. (Top and lower left photos courtesy of Yale Materials Handling Corporation; lower right photo courtesy of Clark Industrial Truck Division.)

In the 1970s, Hershey had 27 full-time stock-keeping locations, 25 public and two private. By 1989 we were down to 17; 15 public, one contract, and one private. In 1994 we are down to eight locations, six of which are public, one private, and one contract. Having a mix of all three allows us to evaluate cost and service effectiveness.

Michael H. Wilson
Manager, Western Distribution
Hershey Chocolate U.S.A.
April 27, 1994

Physically, cross docking is the direct flow of material from the trucks at the receiving dock to the shipping dock without buffering or storage in-between. Delivery trucks and trailers assemble at the shipping dock.

Material Handling Engineering
November 1994

The new 247,000-square-foot facility provides six times the space Delta previously allotted to international cargo in Atlanta and incorporates what the airline claims is the most extensive use of robotic technology in any cargo facility in the world.

Journal of Commerce
March 9, 1992

While electronic surveillance and perimeter fencing are vital to security, they will do little good if transferring inventory is as easy as turning on the computer. Find out how many employees have access to different security levels, and be especially attentive to the experience and background of those individuals who can not only view the inventory information but also delete, add, or alter the information.

Security Management
May 1992

Key Terms

- Bonded storage
- Cross-docking
- Distribution center
- Dunnage
- Field warehouse
- Occupational Safety and Health Act (OSHA)
- Paperless warehouse
- Private warehouse
- Public warehouse
- Sorting function

Learning Objectives

- To understand the role of warehouses and distribution centers in a logistics system
- To identify the various types and functions of warehouses
- To distinguish the various alternatives available in warehouse design
- To examine the different types of handling equipment available
- To analyze the issue of employee safety in warehousing

INTRODUCTION

Warehouses are used to store goods, for varying amounts of time, during their journeys between points of production and to wholesale or retail outlets. This chapter discusses warehouses and their operations.

Inventory analysis can help individual retailers determine whether they should stock all the items in question. Analysis may also show that, if the items in question are stocked only at the factories where they are manufactured, customer service levels may be inadequate because it might take too long to supply customers. Therefore, distribution warehouses represent a compromise. They are justified on the basis of cost analysis that determines that a specified level of customer service can be achieved at minimum cost by locating inventories at certain intermediate locations.

The term **distribution center** is virtually synonymous with *warehouse* since most goods in a warehouse are in somebody's distribution system. In distribution channels, warehouses are intermediate storage points between the manufacturer and the retailers. A distribution center is a warehouse that emphasizes the rapid movement of goods.

Warehouses in the supply chain perform the **sorting function,** meaning that they are the point where goods are concentrated, and from this concentration a new and different assortment of goods is selected and moves forward to be dispersed to the next level. Storage and sorting features are unique to the warehouse. Storage is a somewhat passive function. The sorting function is more dynamic and gets to the basics of logistics and supply-chain thinking. In how many places and at what locations should goods be concentrated so that new and different selections can be assembled and shipped to the next receiver?

The sorting function has four steps, and these are important to understanding the concept of goods flow through the supply chain. The functions involve taking a heterogeneous supply of products and sorting them into stocks that are homogeneous, then bringing together similar stocks from different sources, then breaking a homogeneous supply into smaller lots, and finally, building up assortments of small lots for reshipment, usually to retailers.

Warehouses are also needed because production and consumption do not coincide; canned fruits and vegetables are examples at one extreme, where production occurs during a short period while sales are spread throughout the year. An example at the other extreme is Cleo Wrap, a large manufacturer of Christmas wrapping paper, which sells 90 percent of its output during the last two months of each year.[1] In both instances warehouses serve to match different rates of flow. Sometimes larger quantities of goods

---

[1] *Handling and Shipping Management,* Presidential Issue 1978–79, p. 35.

are purchased than can be immediately consumed. This may occur to prevent anticipated scarcity or to benefit from a seller's advantageously priced deal. Warehousing space is needed to store the surplus supplies.

Warehouses discussed in a distribution textbook would be thought of as primarily *market* oriented. However, some warehouses are production or raw material oriented. Manufacturers that stockpile some of the items they need consider their warehouse selection decision as being *production* oriented.

Implicit in many warehouse functions are assembling or light manufacturing processes. Goods are uncrated and tested. Some goods are repackaged prior to distribution to retail outlets. State tax stamps may be affixed. Minor damage to incoming goods may be repaired (and the carrier or party responsible for the damage billed).

In an era of logistics partnerships, new long-term alliances are being formed between shippers and warehouses. Leveraging is involved in that firms join to use all partners' asset base; the whole is greater than the sum of the parts. For example, customer service representatives of both the distribution center and the supplier make separate calls on the customer; the value-added part is that the distribution center representative also smooths the way for the supplier's product.

> As the relationship builds, additional services may be shifted to the warehouser, such as order receipt and processing, assembly, light repair, pretesting electrical equipment before shipment, and the like. These services can add incremental revenue to the warehouser's operations.[2]

Partnerships are also developing between carriers and warehouses. Starting in 1988, the Santa Fe Railway developed a Quality Distribution Centers (QDC) program that involves about thirty independent warehouses throughout its territory. A single bill of lading covers the movement on rail into and out of the warehouse and delivery to the consignee by truck. The Santa Fe assumes liability for the entire movement.[3]

PUBLIC AND PRIVATE WAREHOUSES

A common distinction between warehouses is whether they are public or private. Distribution centers can be either, although they emphasize distributing rather than storing goods.

---

[2] Bernard J. LaLonde and Martha C. Cooper. *Partnerships in Providing Customer Service: A Third-Party Perspective* (Oak Brook, Ill.: Council of Logistics Management, 1989), p. 75.

[3] Santa Fe Railway's entry in the *Modern Railroads* Golden Freight Car Competition, 1991, unpublished. Railroad boxcars were used, and the target market was shipments that were too small for intermodal containers. In 1990 the Santa Fe handled 9,300 boxcars in this program.

Public Warehouses

Public warehouses are similar to common carriers in that they serve all legitimate users and have certain responsibilities to their users. The Uniform Commercial Code provides the following:

> A warehouse[r] is liable for damages for loss of or injury to the goods caused by [its] failure to exercise such care in regard to them as a reasonably careful [warehouser] would exercise under like circumstances but unless otherwise agreed [it] is not liable for damages which could not have been avoided by the exercise of such care.[4]

Public warehouses are used by firms that either cannot justify the costs of having their own facilities or prefer not making a commitment to owning and operating their own facilities. In most analyses of a firm's warehousing needs, public warehouses are considered as the initial alternative. They offer more flexibility in both space and location than can be offered by any system of company-owned facilities. They require no capital investment, and space is rented as needed.

Some public warehouses are specialized. They may handle only refrigerated goods, steel, or household goods or even be grain elevators.

The following is a list of services that public warehouses provide (and for which they bill customers):

1. *Bonded storage.* There are several types of **bonded storage.** U.S. Customs–bonded warehouses hold goods until import duties are collected. Internal Revenue Service (IRS)–bonded warehouses hold goods until other federal taxes and fees are collected. (In addition, certain federal laws related to storing agricultural products and some state laws require warehouses to be bonded in the sense they must carry insurance to protect their customers.)

2. *Office and display space.* Firms that have large and complex inventory holdings in a warehouse may permanently station one or more of their own staff in the warehouse to perform some of the functions that otherwise would be provided by the warehouser. Display space is used by the selling staff in instances when they want to show products to prospective buyers.

3. *Integrated data-processing equipment.* Integrating data-processing equipment with user's equipment allows the user to communicate with public warehouses in the same manner as with his or her own. Often, the user merely has one of his or her computer terminals placed in the warehouse office, where it can issue queries or instructions to warehouse personnel.

[4] See "Liability of the Warehouseman," *Warehousing Review,* Summer 1979, pp. 2–4; and Kenneth B. Ackerman, "Warehousing Responsibility," *Distribution Worldwide,* February 1978, pp. 42–46.

4. *Inventory-level maintenance.* Users who specify the inventories they want stocked receive inventory-level maintenance, meaning that the warehouse places reorders.

5. *Local delivery or tendering outgoing movements to carriers.* The authority of warehousers to perform delivery services is regulated and varies according to the state in which they are located. In any event, they can handle and prepay the outgoing shipment of goods.

6. *Unpacking, testing, assembling, repacking, stenciling, and price marking.* These are additional commonly performed services, as are break-bulk and assembling functions.

7. *Securing collateral goods for loans.* This can be done either on or off the warehouser's premises. A **field warehouse** is a warehouse temporarily established at the site of an inventory of goods, often the premises of the good's owner. The warehouser assumes custody of the goods and issues a receipt for them, which can then be used as collateral for a loan. Using one's inventory of goods as loan collateral is helpful, although the goods are temporarily frozen in the distribution channel.

Many examples can be cited of a public warehouser's functioning as an integral link in the product's logistics channel. In a city with ten dealers for one make of electrical appliance, none of the dealers might stock an inventory. The only models they possess are on their showroom floors. Once they make a sale, they notify the public warehouse, which delivers a unit directly to the buyer's residence from the warehouse stock. The warehouse notifies the factory of the sale, and the factory replenishes the warehouse's stock. In this instance, the stock in the warehouse inventory belongs to the manufacturer, a factory distributor, or an areawide dealer. The warehouse performs functions that would otherwise have to be performed by the owner of the inventory; the principal advantage is that dealers do not have to maintain large inventories.

In today's logistics thinking, reference is sometimes made to the value-added concept throughout the supply chain. This means that every individual handling the item must do something to enhance its value rather than, say, merely moving it around a warehouse. Examples of such value-added services performed by public warehouses include relabeling goods for export with foreign labels, assembling bicycles, repackaging larger shipments into retail-size quantities and then shrink-wrapping them, price-marking, loading route salespeople's trucks in order of deliveries, and assisting in product recalls.

One manufacturer of batteries ships unmarked products to a warehouse. The warehouse is equipped with decals containing the various brand names under which the battery is sold. If one hundred batteries are sold to a private-label customer, that firm's label is attached to the battery, and the battery is shipped in a box containing the customer's brand name. A single inventory of batteries can thus be used to fill the needs of an infinite number of private-label customers, where before each might have required a separate inventory.[5]

Public warehouses also serve as integral links for other supply-chain functions. For instance, they are used by the auto industry to feed components to the assembly plants on a daily and, sometimes, an hourly basis. With the growing interest in JIT inventory and production systems, there has been some concern as to what role, if any, the public warehouse might play. To a certain extent the manufacturer may reduce inventories of inbound materials on hand by accepting smaller, more frequent deliveries from stocks the vendor maintains—often in nearby public warehouses. This shift in responsibility for holding the inventory results in little net savings unless the vendor is able to do a better job of managing the inventory in warehouses than the user can do in the factory. However, the responsibility for inventory has been pushed back one step in the production-supply process. The more this can happen, the better, because each step back toward the original source represents a delay in the final user's having to pay certain costs.

It is difficult to tell whether public warehouses in the United States are benefitting. One public warehousing leader notes:

> It is revealing to note that it is in the Japanese makeup to consider inventory as inherently "evil." Carrying that train of thought further, one runs headlong into a perceptual problem: What is a warehouse then, but a place to keep inventory, and therefore a place that is inherently "evil"? It is precisely this type of logic that the public warehouse[r] is likely to encounter as [it] begins to market [its] services to an industry that has been preached to unremittingly about the "Japanese Miracle."[6]

The answer may be that better communications are needed. As Marianne Warner of Leaseway Transportation Corporation argues:

> The whole object of just-in-time systems is to reduce the amount of inventory needed to support a manufacturing and distribution process. And just how does a manufacturer or retailer accomplish this, if not simply by moving [its] suppliers closer? One important way is through more sophisticated information systems which, in essence, substitute timely information for inventory. These systems can then be linked to the larger logistics system to achieve greater inventory velocity.[7]

[5] Kenneth Ackerman, cited in James R. Stock., *Strategic Warehousing: Bringing the "Storage Game" to Life* (Oak Brook, Ill.: Warehousing Education and Research Council, 1988), p. 3.

[6] R. Scott Whiting, "Public Warehousing and the 'Just-in-Time' Production System," *Warehousing Review,* Distribution Executive Issue 1983, p. 10.

[7] "Making Standards Pay Off in the Warehouse," *Modern Materials Handling,* August 6, 1984, p. 64. For a discussion of applying JIT systems to a private warehouse, see Robin G. Stegner and Robert E. Murray, *Using Warehousing Operations to Support a Just-in-Time Manufacturing Program* (Oak Brook, Ill.: Warehousing Education and Research Council, 1987).

Private Warehouses

Private warehouses are owned or occupied on a long-term lease by the firm using them. They are used by firms whose warehouse needs are stable enough to make long-term commitments to fixed facilities. (Private warehouse operation also requires commitment to a warehouse labor force.) The largest users of private warehouses are retail chain stores. They handle large volumes of merchandise on a regular basis, and one of their resulting economies of scale comes from integrating the warehousing function with purchasing and distribution to retail outlets.

Manufacturing firms also maintain their own warehouses. Figure 10-1 shows a distribution center built by a toy manufacturer. For a firm manufacturing related products at different locations, each plant ships its items to the firm's regional distribution warehouses so that each of them can stock a complete line of products. There are also products with unique handling characteristics, such as steel beams and gasoline, that, in some areas, public warehousers prefer not to handle. In these instances the manufacturer is forced to develop its own facilities.

Figure 10-1 LEGO Systems, Inc., built this 225,000-square-foot distribution center about one-quarter mile from its factory in Enfield, Connecticut. There was actually an area next to the factory, but if this facility had been built on that site, natural wetlands would have been destroyed. This facility is designed to handle 66,000 cases per day. Note that its design makes the building look like it had been built with giant Legos. (Permission granted by LEGO Systems, Inc.)

Contract Warehouses

Contract warehousing is a form of public warehousing covered by a longer contract between the two parties. Professor Thomas Speh defines the practice as "a long-term mutually beneficial arrangement which provides unique and specially-tailored warehousing and logistics services exclusively to one client, where vendor and client share the risks associated with the operation."[8] This type of arrangement is similar to many partnerships that are evolving along the supply chain.

Plant Warehouses

Associated with most manufacturing operations is the plant warehouse, usually located somewhere near the end of the assembly line. Its principal function is to accommodate the differences in production line output and product demand in the distribution network.

The plant warehouse may also be the single location where every line item in the firm's inventory is stocked. This is especially true for repair parts. Dealers may be required to stock certain items, and regional parts depots may be expected to stock nearly all items. Another centrally located site could perform this function, but it is performed in the plant warehouse because part of the stock of repair parts is merely left-over components from the assembly process.

Distribution Centers

The term *distribution center* is applied somewhat loosely; some public warehouses refer to themselves as distribution centers, which means they emphasize the distribution aspects of warehousing instead of the storage operations. The emphasis is on fast turnover of goods. Service to retailers is required to be of such quality that the distribution center is relied upon to maintain the needed levels of inventory, rather than the individual retailers. The distribution center may also house other customer-oriented services, such as sales, traffic, and credit.

In some trades, distribution centers serve as the staging area for one-shot distribution to retail stores. The Esprit clothing operation is one such example. Their buyers coordinate the buying of outfits for example, coordinated skirts, blouses, belts, sweaters, and jackets. A certain number of each, in different sizes, is programmed to go to each retail outlet. The Esprit distribution center stores, or stages, the pieces from these coordinated offerings until all have been received from vendors. Then they are *all* shipped to retail stores. The distribution center holds no excess stock from which retail outlets can reorder. Instead, the distribution center's efforts are devoted to staging the next offering of a new collection of coordinated outfits.

[8] Cited in *Logistics Today,* no. 2, 1993, p. 2.

WAREHOUSE DESIGN

Public warehouses are usually designed to handle a variety of items, whereas private warehouses are more specialized. Prior to designing a warehouse, the quantity and character of goods to be handled must be known.

Warehouse and Distribution Center Layout

The relative emphasis placed on the storage and distribution functions affects space layout. A storage facility having low rates of turnover is laid out in a manner that maximizes utilization of the cubic capacity of the warehouse devoted to storage. A distribution-oriented facility attempts to maximize throughput rather than storage. (*Throughput* is a term frequently associated with warehouse productivity. It is a measure of how much material passes through a facility within a given period of time.)

Trade-offs.   Trade-offs must be made among space, labor, and mechanization. Spaciousness may not always be advantageous since the distances that an individual or machine must travel in the storing and retrieving functions are increased. But cramped conditions also lead to inefficiencies. Before layout plans are made, each item that will be handled is studied in terms of its specific physical handling properties, the volume and regularity of movement, the frequency it is picked, and whether, compared to related items, it is fast or slow moving.

Many trade-offs are involved in designing both the structure and the arrangement of the equipment inside. Several are listed here. However, the trade-offs are often more complex than they appear in the following list, since all factors in the list affect one another.

1. *Fixed versus variable slot locations for merchandise.* Should one slot always be assigned to each product, resulting in a logical layout but also in low space utilization because many goods have seasonal characteristics? The alternative, which results in higher space utilization, is to assign empty slots to incoming products in an almost random manner.

2. *Horizontal versus high-rise layout.* The cubic capacity of a warehouse is a function of horizontal area times height. A later section in this chapter discusses high-rise storage. The relevant trade-off in utilizing a high-rise operation is between *building costs,* which decline on a cubic-foot basis as one builds higher, and *warehouse equipment costs,* which increase. Figure 10-2 shows what *might* happen to labor.

3. *Order-picking versus stock-replenishing functions.* Should workers who are picking outgoing orders and those who are restocking the warehouse work at the same time? Should they use the same aisles? How much space should be devoted to active or live stocks—stocks the order pickers pick from to fill orders? How much space is devoted to reserve stocks—

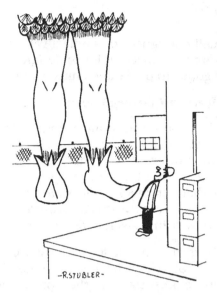

—R.STUBLER—

Sorry to let you go, but we've automated our
high-rise order picking.

Figure 10-2   An example of labor
displaced by machinery. (Reproduced
through the courtesy of *Handling and
Shipping Management* magazine and of
Richard Stubler, the artist.)

those awaiting assignment to the active stock area? If too much space is
devoted to active stocks, the bins are larger and the order picker's travel
time from bin to bin is increased. If the bins are smaller, the active stocks
must be replenished from the reserve stock more frequently.

4. *Two-dock versus single-dock layout.* Conventional warehouses have the
receiving dock on one end and the shipping dock on the other end, and
goods move between them. An alternative uses one dock that receives
in the morning and ships in the afternoon. Viewed from the top, the
goods move in a U-shaped rather than a straight configuration. This
reduces the space devoted to loading docks, but it requires carriers to
pick up and deliver at more specific times.

5. *Space devoted to aisles versus space devoted to racks.* As aisle space increases,
storage capacity decreases. Wider aisles make it easier to operate mechanical equipment but they increase travel distances within the facility. The
typical order picker spends 60 percent of his or her time in a warehouse
moving from location to location.[9]

6. *Labor-intensive versus highly mechanized.* As labor costs increase, many
warehouses place increasing reliance on equipment to perform tasks previously performed manually. Union Carbide built a 12-million-cubic-foot

[9] *Modern Materials Handling,* October 1990, p. 63.

warehouse in West Virginia that could hold 64,000 drums of chemicals. Two persons (one of whom is a computer programmer) handled the entire warehouse.[10]

7. *Picker-to-part or part-to-picker system.* Some sophisticated systems for handling small parts are designed so that the trays with specific, wanted parts can be programmed to appear in front of the individual picking the order. This differs from the older system of having the picker seek out the part at the location where it is stored:

> In part-to-picker systems, the pick location travels to the picker, and the travel time component of total order-picking time is shifted from the picker to the device for bringing locations to the picker. Also, the search time component of total order-picking time is significantly reduced since the correct pick location is automatically presented to the order picker.[11]

8. *Private ownership versus use of space in public warehousing.* This choice influences design because of the tax considerations involved and because of the commitments that must be made to a public warehouser if it is expected to invest in some very specialized handling equipment.

9. *Cross-docking, rather than passing through the warehouse's storage area.* **Cross-docking** involves accepting the product at the receiving dock, where it is "conveyed directly to the shipping dock. There's no need to hold goods in a reserve stock area, or install equipment to store them. Outbound trailers serve as extensions of the distribution center because storage takes place only while trailers are being filled."[12] Food chains often handle beverages in this manner during hot summer months. Computerized control also helps since one can divert goods needed immediately away from the conventional storage and order-picking areas. A facility designed for cross-docking would devote more space to dock operations and less space to product storage.

Examples of Layout.   Distribution centers have varying layout objectives, as the following five examples illustrate:

1. A men's jeans manufacturer/distributor has only a few products. The main difference is in size of jeans. In laying out this facility, jeans could be arranged by size moving from smallest waist and pants length through all lengths with that waist, to the next waist size, through all the lengths with that waist size, and so on. This is the way they are displayed in retail stores. Instead, in order to minimize the time of order

---

[10] "Automated Storage," *Distribution Worldwide*, February 1976, pp. 21–27.

[11] Edward H. Frazelle, *Small Parts Order Picking: Equipment and Strategy* (Oak Brook, Ill. Warehousing Education and Research Council, 1988), p. 4.

[12] *Rapistan Conveyer System Concepts* (brochure), Fall 1991.

pickers, the jeans are arranged so that the most popular sizes are in the locations that are the easiest (i.e., least time-consuming) for the order pickers to reach. The less popular sizes are placed on less accessible shelves.

2. A different approach is taken by an auto accessories chain for its distribution center. First it insists that all of its retail outlets have the same physical arrangement of merchandise. Goods in the warehouse are arranged in the same order. Inventory and reorder forms for use at the retail level are laid out in the same order, which is retained when they are converted to the order picker's form to be used in the warehouse. The warehouse order pickers use metal carts upon which metal baskets can be stacked. The order is picked in the same sequence as it appears in retail shelves, and the baskets are delivered to the retail stores. This enables the retail clerk to rapidly place the items from the basket onto the shelves.

3. A large food chain continually encourages its retail outlets to order the optimum lot size for a specific item. The chain may require or encourage the store to order ant poison by the tube, tomato puree by the forty-eight-can case, and paper towels by the pallet load. Forms supplied to the retail store allow for orders in only these quantities or multiples thereof. The warehouse is split into three sections: for the individual items, for the items handled in case lots, and for the items handled in pallet lots. When assembling an order for a retail store, a computer separates the three types of orders, and assignments are made to order pickers who have different equipment, depending upon the section of warehouse in which they are working. During the course of the year, some items move from one category of minimum lot size to another, and the computer is programmed to make the adjustment readily.

4. Pic 'n Pay's distribution center near Charlotte, North Carolina, operates on such a just-in-time pace that 70 percent of the incoming goods are placed directly for assignment to be loaded onto outgoing trucks.[13] The remaining 30 percent are placed into storage and handled in the conventional warehouse manner. This is an example of cross-docking since 70 percent of the goods do not rest in the warehouse but move continuously through it. Also, there is sufficient confidence that they will arrive on time so that, before they arrive, they are scheduled to be loaded on outgoing deliveries.

5. Del Monte has a new facility in the Port of Savannah, Georgia, for handling imported bananas and pineapples. The warehouse is refrigerated and designed to handle cargo in boxes on pallets, a change in the handling of bananas, which previously moved in bunches on conveyers.

[13] *Modern Materials Handling*, August 1989, p. 46.

Under the old system, the bananas were handled ten times; under the new system, they are handled only four times. (Nine new ships in Del Monte's fleet of thirty-four are designed to handle palletized loads.) Once on land, the pallets of fruit are either loaded directly onto customers' waiting trucks or placed in one of the refrigerated areas. The facility has 25,200 square feet of refrigerated space, a dry-storage warehouse of 25,300 feet, and areas for offices, quality control, and USDA inspections. There are truck and rail docks and electrical outlets in the outside areas for refrigerated containers and truck trailers.[14]

Three Working Systems.   Figure 10-3 shows the top and end views of a distribution center. In this example the replenishment and order-picking functions are completely separated. Order pickers work in the center aisle. Stock replenishers work in the outer aisles, moving goods from reserve to live or active storage. As order pickers empty cartons, they place them and other wrapping materials on the trash conveyer. The trash is carried to another room, where it is probably separated into different types of materials, and each type is baled and then sold to a paper-products recycling plant.

Figure 10-4 illustrates a much more complex, high-rise distribution center that receives pallet loads, breaks them down into carton lots, and then reassembles the carton lots into new, outgoing pallet loads. In that figure, pallet loads are received at point 2, where a computer-controlled stacker takes each pallet and stores it in one of 17,200 openings in the ten-aisle, sixty-five-foot high storage area (point 1). As goods are needed to replenish stocks on the lane loaders (point 4—to be discussed shortly), they are retrieved from area 1 and taken by the pallet carrier to one of several depalletizing stations (point 3). At point 3 the pallets are manually unloaded and the cartons placed aboard a conveyor system, which takes them to the lane loaders (point 4). At the lane loaders at least one lane is assigned to each product and cartons are loaded into the top of each lane. The bottom of the lane feeds onto a moving conveyor belt, which is at right angle to the lanes. The lanes slope downward toward the belt, and at the bottom of each lane (near the conveyor belt) an electrically triggered escapement device releases one case at a time onto the conveyor belt. The lane is of sufficient slope that gravity forces the case out onto the conveyor belt. As orders are assembled on the conveyor belt, they move toward point 5, where they are routed to one of four loading stations and are placed aboard pallets for outgoing shipments. This is also done manually. Hence loading and unloading pallets are the only two manual operations; the other operations are by machine. All operations are computer-controlled.

A highly sophisticated auto-manufacturing parts warehouse is described in Figure 10-5.

[14] *Distribution*, March 1991, pp. 58–60.

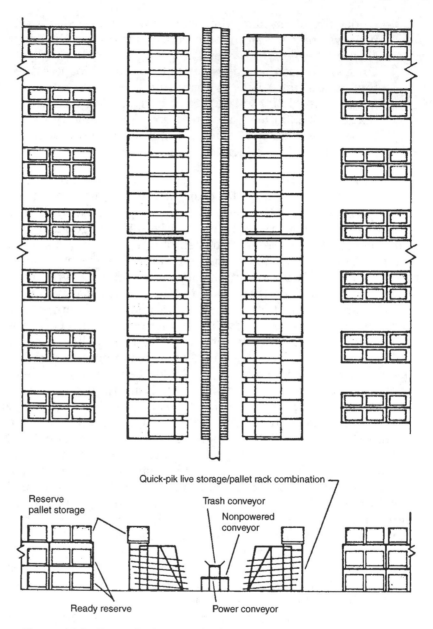

Figure 10-3 Top and side views of a distribution warehouse. The live storage racks slope downward toward the center so that gravity forces cartons to move toward the center. (Courtesy of North American Equipment Corporation.)

Figure 10-4 Large automated distribution center. (Courtesy of SI Handling Systems, Inc.)

WAREHOUSING

AUTOCON: JIT AT ZERO MILES PER HOUR

Making just-in-time (JIT) manufacturing work for a giant auto maker like General Motors takes more than fast trucks and good timing. GM has a network of more than 30 plants in North America and dozens of major suppliers, all of which makes timely, direct shipping for many of its parts movements too complex, too slow, too costly and too undependable.

In the early 1980s, GM decided it needed consolidation points where parts from suppliers could be received, blended with parts from other suppliers and immediately shipped out to assembly plants to meet exacting production schedules. Rather than perform this function in-house, GM looked to outside vendors. A technology-oriented public warehouseman named Russell Gilmore III established a new company, AutoCon, to take on the challenge. Gilmore knew that conventional warehousing techniques and data processing would be too slow and too cumbersome to handle the estimated 500 JIT truck movements per day.

AutoCon certainly does not operate like a traditional storage warehouse. Gilmore has developed a unique system based on bar code software developed by GM. The AutoCon system is a totally electronic data collection and communications system for tracking every part entering, moving in or leaving the AutoCon facility. The computer system receives from suppliers and from Symbol Technology bar code scanners located throughout the facility and on Clark lift trucks. The computer uses this data to transmit instructions to LXE lift-truck mounted radio frequency terminals.

All parts are shipped to AutoCon in steel containers with bar code labels. The suppliers scan the containers as they are loaded on trucks or rail cars and electronically transmit a manifest to AutoCon. While the parts are in transit, the computer determines when the parts will be needed and whether they will be staged for immediate reshipment or put in temporary storage.

When the truck enters the AutoCon yard, the guard enters the trailer number, which brings up the supplier manifest information. As the containers come off the trailer they are scanned to make sure they match up. The central computer transmits to terminals on the lift trucks telling the operator what to do with the container.

More than 60 percent of the inbound parts containers will be reshipped in a matter of minutes or hours and are staged rather than stored. Two-thirds of the 330,000 square foot warehouse is devoted to the staging area. The parts that are needed for shipment that day are scanned and then loaded onto Raymond automatic guided vehicles (AGVs), which take the containers to a storage area determined by the computer. In the storage area, other forklift operators again scan the containers and read on the terminals the exact storage location for the container; once it arrives at its "home," it is again scanned so the computer knows where to get the parts when needed.

Usually, the parts containers are loaded onto outbound trucks almost as fast as they come in the door. The computer tells the lift truck drivers and loaders which parts container goes to which trailer. The computer also tells the warehouse people how to load the truck for maximum efficiency and safety.

After the parts are shipped, the AutoCon system transmits the truck and rail manifests to the destination GM assembly plant. AutoCon takes responsibility for shipments until the final destination is reached, even though its liability technically ends at the loading dock.

The AutoCon system has produced savings in the area of $8 million for GM and its suppliers by increasing the velocity of parts and components from the supplier to the assembly plants, reducing the need for excess inventory, and practically eliminating errors. These savings are produced by the following benefits to GM and its suppliers:

1. On-line, real-time data processing: The AutoCon system links the suppliers, the warehouse and the GM assembly plants with access to real-time data. Instructions, tracing, order status and other information is available instantaneously throughout the logistics network.

2. Minimized handling of product: The majority of product is handled in the staging area only once, reducing handling costs.

3. No paper: The totally electronic system produces no paper, which eliminates clerical costs, data entry, delays and errors.

4. Total Inventory Control: The exact location of every part is known to AutoCon and GM as soon as it comes into the building. Orders can be filled and shipped faster and more accurately. If a supplier sends the wrong part or quantity, this error is detected immediately and communicated to GM. If any parts are found to be defective between the time they leave the supplier and arrive at the assembly plants, they can be pulled from inventory immediately. Physical inventories take less than four hours.

6. Absolute accuracy: The system checks all scanning input for possible error. For example, the system will not allow scanning of the wrong part, incorrect storage locations or incomplete shipments.

8. Greatly increased information access: Response time for accessing any information throughout the warehouse is two seconds, with the latest AutoCon system greatly improving worker productivity and shipment throughput.

9. Throughput leverage: The volume of parts going through the system can be increased greatly with little or no addition to the work force of 54 people.

10. Tight security: Drivers must supply the security guard with the correct trailer number, destination, and bill of lading number before they pick up their trailer. Upon leaving, they show their driver's license and give the guard their full name.

The original AutoCon facility in Dayton has been so successful that Gilmore has added another even more modern facility for GM and its suppliers in Atlanta. Other facilities also in the works will handle customers in addition to GM and the automotive industry. According to Gilmore, his operation team can select a site, perform initial planning, and have the facility ready for full operation within 60 days.

Gilmore also has started another spin-off operation called Scanner Solutions, which is a vendor of the bar code technology AutoCon uses in its facilities.

—Thomas A. Foster

Figure 10-5 Description of an auto manufacturer's warehouse. [Reprinted with the permission of *Distribution Magazine* (December 1987).]

Other Space Needs

In addition to space for the throughput of merchandise, areas must be set aside for other warehouse activities. They require some detailed analysis in terms of space requirements and layout. The following are examples:

1. Areas for vehicles waiting to be unloaded or loaded and employee parking.
2. Receiving and loading facilities for each mode of transport serving the facility.
3. Staging, or temporary storage areas, for both incoming and outgoing merchandise.
4. Office space, including an area for whatever computer facilities may be involved.
5. Employee washrooms, lunchrooms, and the like.
6. Pallet storage and repair facilities. (A large distribution facility that receives unpalletized materials but ships on pallets may require a pallet-assembly operation.)
7. An area to store damaged merchandise that is awaiting inspection by the carrier's claim representative.
8. An area to salvage or repair damaged merchandise.
9. An area for repacking, labeling, price marking, and so on.
10. A room for accumulating and baling waste and scrap.
11. An area for equipment storage and maintenance. For example, battery-powered lift trucks must be plugged into battery chargers overnight.
12. Specialized storage areas for hazardous items, high-value items, warehouse supplies, or items needing other specialized handling (such as freezer or refrigerated space).
13. A returned or recycled goods processing area.

Retail Storerooms

Distribution center design is not an end in itself; it is but one link in the distribution process. The next link is the retail store itself. Some retail stores no longer have storerooms, which means that the goods go from the distribution center directly to the retailer's display shelves. A retail chain often owns two or three times as many trailers as it does tractors. Each time a tractor makes a delivery to a retail store, it leaves a trailer for the store to unload within twenty-four hours. It also picks up the trailer that it left the previous day to be unloaded. Hence, the parked trailer serves as a storeroom and reduces the truck-to-storeroom and storeroom-to-shelves movements to only one because the goods go directly from the parked trailer to the shelves.

This practice does not hold for all industries, however. One furniture retail chain utilizes existing warehouses in urban areas. Part of the warehouse is converted to display space, and if the customer selects the item, an identical one is given the customer from the adjacent storage space.

WAREHOUSE EQUIPMENT

This section discusses computers, scanners, and handling equipment used in warehouses. Much of the equipment discussed in this section is more likely to be found in large warehouses or in specialized distribution centers.

Computers

Warehousing is one field in which the use of computers has exploded in the last decade. At the public warehousing level, the American Warehouse Association (AWA) has developed for its members considerable software for personal computers. One program can develop and analyze the costs of handling a client's potential public warehousing needs. The cost analysis is built on data inputs from nine separate warehousing functions: inbound truck, inbound rail, stocking, order filling, checking, outbound truck, outbound rail, elevator use, and repacking. Standard times are applied to each function, and a 15 percent allowance is added to cover unexpected delays.

Private warehouses tend to have more sophisticated computer systems because they handle more standardized products and are only one segment in the firm's overall computerized system of materials management. Because they handle more standardized products than public warehouses, private warehouses are also more likely to possess sophisticated storage and handling equipment (discussed in the next section). Much of this equipment is controlled, one way or another, by computers or by programmable controllers. For example, some software attempts to minimize the time spent by automatic stacking-retrieving equipment by storing fast-moving SKUs close to the infeed and outfeed addresses, and slow-moving SKUs at the periphery of the warehouse. The system can rely on its own records of warehouse activity to determine how fast-moving an item is, but this must be adjusted manually for products with seasonal variations.

Figure 10-6 shows an example of computerized order picking. The worker is picking an order for a single customer from the racks on the left and placing the items into the box on the right, which moves slowly along the conveyer. On the left, just above the worker's hand, is a small device mounted on the rack under each separate SKU; the device is called a readout unit. When the readout unit is lit, it shows the number of items at that slot that must be picked. After the worker places that number into the large box, he or she punches the clear button on the read-out unit. The worker moves along until he or she reaches the next lit readout unit. The order picker must clear all of

Figure 10-6   An example of computer-assisted order picking. (Courtesy of Rapistan Division, Lear Siegler, Inc.)

the readout units before he or she can move the large box out of the warehouse zone in which he or she is working.

A new development is the use of computer-generated labels for order picking. The order picker is given a sheet of gummed labels, one for each case she or he must pick. As she or he assembles the order, the proper label is attached to each case. Unused labels are returned as evidence of a stockout. This system eliminates the picker's having to read the pick list, mark the list, and continually count the number of cases picked. This saves three to five seconds per case picked, and the "increase in productivity is more than 10 percent."[15]

Both buyers and vendors are likely to have computerized inventory control and warehousing systems. A computerized purchase order might include an item code and a slot number that tells where in the buyer's warehouse the goods should be placed. Some goods even have batch numbers or serial numbers that can be entered into the computerized records. One frozen-food processor cannot release a product until it has been frozen a given number of hours. Computers are programmed to indicate that an item is in stock but not available for delivery until a specified number of hours have passed.

[15]Myron Nerzig, presentation before the San Francisco chapter of the Warehouse Education and Research Council, January 28, 1988.

Scanners are linked to computers for warehouse record keeping, and scanners adjacent to conveyor belts recognize and tally each carton as it passes by. The scanner is tied into a system that sorts each carton with respect to where it should be stored. Once the goods are in storage, inventories can be checked by passing a pen-sized scanner near each label. Some firms link their scanners by radio so that there is no lag in record-keeping information.

The term **paperless warehouse** describes a warehouse that generates and uses few or no paper documents. The order pickers have monitors and scanning wands on their carts. The monitor displays the instructions as to what to pick, and as each item is picked and placed on the cart, the worker scans it with the wand, indicating that the task has been accomplished. Sometimes there are radio communications between the workers on the floor and the warehouse office. The worker's radio is a headset or is hand-held or cart-mounted. Possibly the order was received by EDI and communications and billing will be handled in a similar manner. The only paper used is the bar-code labels and, possibly, shipping labels for the parcels once they leave the warehouse. Software for paperless warehouses also handles receiving and storage of goods and has the ability to inventory products or measure worker productivity.

Storage and Handling Equipment

Conventional single-story warehouses and distribution centers accommodate material at heights up to approximately twenty feet. Although it is possible to store most materials stacked on top of each other, this is inconsistent with the distribution center concept of fast throughput. The oldest pallet would always be on the bottom, and the pallet loads above it would have to be removed in order to get at the older pallet load. Hence, steel shelving or pallet racks are used, and each pallet sets on an individual shelf and can be stacked or removed without disturbing other pallet loads. City building codes regulate rack installation. California building codes discourage high storage racks in an effort to minimize earthquake hazards.

Within the warehouse the goods are moved by a variety of manual and mechanical devices. In small warehouses the lifting device might be on a wheeled cart and have to be pushed along the floor. More sophisticated devices are powered for moving along the floor, and they may or may not contain accommodations for the user to ride in it. The forklift is the standard workhorse in many warehouses.

At one time warehouses had tow lines set in the floor that pulled carts equipped with gripping devices. Today automatic guided vehicles (AGVs) are used. They look like the bumper cars one sees at a carnival, although they operate in a more disciplined manner. In a Delta Air Lines freight facility, the "vehicles are guided by an electronic system in the floor that's linked to a computer providing real-time visual monitoring for Delta employees in the control room."[16]

Most high-rise warehousing equipment moves up and down narrow aisles and services materials on both sides of the aisle. Aisle widths are narrower than in the case of conventional warehouses. Because equipment can move both horizontally and vertically at the same time, the most efficient layout of goods along any one aisle may be a path of upward and downward undulations. This would consume less time than a path that took the equipment along a horizontal path and stopped, then moved up or down and stopped, then continued along the horizontal path and stopped, and so on.

In addition to high-rise systems involving human order pickers, there are completely automated warehouses. They have automated order picking devices that move along an aisle, stop in front of a bin, and, with a lateral handling device, either store or remove a container.

WAREHOUSE OPERATIONS

There are many facets to operating a warehouse. Figure 10-7 is a cost-estimating sheet used by one public warehouse. It demonstrates the wide range of activities that take place within a warehouse operation.

Warehouse management is an exacting task. Work-force motivation is difficult because of the repetitiveness of the operation. The work is strenuous. Only five aspects of operation are touched upon here: worker safety, hazardous materials, facility cleanliness, inventory controls, and handling of stockouts.

Employee Safety

Warehouses are dangerous places to work because of the functions they perform. Goods and workers are in constant motion. A warehouse may receive a pallet that was improperly loaded, and this will not become apparent until a warehouse worker attempts to handle it.

Even with the best of practices, a small percentage of all goods a warehouse receives, stores, and ships is damaged. Special procedures must be established for handling any broken or damaged item just from the standpoint of employee safety (in addition to assuming or assigning responsibility for the breakage). A broken bottle of household ammonia, for example, results in three hazards: noxious fumes, broken glass, and a slippery floor. Aerosol cans pose a hazard that is compounded by the product in the cans. Aerosol cans with shaving cream cause little problem in fires because if they explode, the shaving cream serves to extinguish the fire. That is not the case with aerosol cans with paints or lacquers. Aerosol cans are often kept in cages because in a fire some of them would become burning projectiles.

[16] *Journal of Commerce*, March 9, 1992.

SERVICE SPECIFICATIONS

FOR CUSTOMER USE IN CONTACTING ALLIED MEMBER COMPANIES REGARDING WAREHOUSING SERVICES.

ALLIED DISTRIBUTION INC

5145 N. MILWAUKEE, CHICAGO, ILL. 60646

312/792-0433

FULL AND EXACT NAME OF YOUR COMPANY   DATE

COMPLETE ADDRESS - NUMBER, STREET, STATE, ZIP CODE   AREA CODE - TELEPHONE NUMBER

NAME OF PERSON MAKING INQUIRY   TITLE   ADDRESS, IF OTHER THAN ABOVE

COMMODITY, PACK, TYPE OF CONTAINER	OVERALL DIMENSIONS IN INCHES			GROSS SHIPPING WEIGHT IN LBS.	VALUE OF PACKAGE AND CONTENTS
	LENGTH	WIDTH	HEIGHT		

Estimated Average Stock: _____   Estimated Through-put _____
INBOUND: Rail _____ % Truck _____ % Loose _____ % Palletized _____ % Who Unloads Trucks? _____
    CL _____ % LCL _____ % TL _____ % LTL _____ % Pallet Size: L _____ W _____ H _____ (including pallet)
OUTBOUND CL _____ % LCL _____ % TL _____ % LTL _____ % Who Loads Trucks? _____
    Loose _____ % Palletized _____ % Cartage Needed? _____
Estimated Number of Outbound Orders: _____   Per _____
Outbound Order: Minimum _____ Lbs.   Average _____ Lbs.
No. of Different Items or Separations in Account: _____
B/L Used: Warehouse _____   Customer's _____

Check among the following accessorial services those to be required from the warehouseman in addition to the "Handling" and "Storage" services:

_____ Handling for immediate distribution.
_____ Reporting marked weights, numbers, etc., on receipt and/or delivery.
_____ Making out-of-town shipments.
_____ Prepaying freight charges
_____ Filling orders from a credit list
_____ Invoicing customers for storer.

_____ C.O.D. collection on behalf of storer.
_____ Furnishing reports in addition to usual notification as to receipts and deliveries.
_____ Kind and frequency (attach samples)
_____ Weighing on receipt and/or delivery
_____ Storage-in-transit

Indicate other services required, and give information regarding any special storage characteristics of commodities: (Stacking Limitations, Hazardous, Breaking Cartons, Controlled Temperature, Pick by Package or Serial Number, Odorous or Susceptible to Odors, etc.)

Figure 10-7 Warehouse cost-estimating form. (Courtesy of Allied Distribution, Inc.)

Figure 10-8 is an emergency protective equipment supply room in a container that can be carried on a forklift. It is for use inside a warehouse and would be carried to the site of a hazardous waste spill. It contains equipment needed to rescue workers and contain the contamination.

Warehouse work practices must also attempt to reduce or eliminate worker injuries associated with lifting, carrying too heavy a load, failing to observe proper hand clearances, and the like. The word *ergonomics* means engineering tasks with the goal of not wearing down the worker's body.

Very recently great interest has been shown in back injuries and how to prevent them. To give an idea of how much time a warehouse worker spends lifting, consider this 1993 survey of grocery warehouses, which showed how workers' time was spent: order picking, 37 percent; stock rotation, 17 percent; receiving/unloading, 15 percent; checking/loading, 9 percent; shipping/assembly, 6 percent; sanitation and maintenance, 9 percent; handling returns, 3 percent; and other, 4 percent.[17] Industry practices are moving toward the

Figure 10-8 This emergency protective equipment supply room is used in warehouses and can be carried by a forklift. (Courtesy of Inland Star Distribution Centers, Inc., Fresno, Cal., U.S.A.)

[17] *Modern Materials Handling,* January 1994, p. 7.

belief that fifty pounds be considered the maximum weight that a worker be expected to routinely lift without the aid of mechanical devices. Back support belts are coming into widespread use, but they are of value only if the workers also receive adequate safe lift training.

Warehouses generate large volumes of waste materials, such as empty cartons, steel strapping, broken pallets, and wood and nails used for crating and dunnage. (**Dunnage** is material used to block and brace products inside carrier equipment in order to prevent the shipment from shifting in transit and becoming damaged.) This must be properly handled because it poses a threat to employee safety and may be a fire hazard. One of the purposes of the warehouse trash conveyor belt diagrammed earlier in Figure 10-3 is to remove trash promptly from areas where people are working.

OSHA.   In 1970 the federal **Occupational Safety and Health Act (OSHA)** became law. It resulted in increased federal and state supervision of industrial safety practices. Standards have been set for equipment and operations, and inspectors frequently make inspections. They can issue citations, and monetary fines may be levied. During the 1970s OSHA was among the most controversial issues in the warehousing industry. However, during the Reagan and Bush administrations, enforcement became less rigorous. Nonetheless, OSHA standards are complex and lengthy, and their fines for violations are becoming more costly.

In May 1988 a new set of OSHA regulations, called the *Hazard Communication Standard,* went into effect. It applies to both manufacturing and nonmanufacturing employers whose workers are exposed to hazardous materials. Employers must use warning labels on containers of hazardous materials, make detailed information available to employees concerning the hazardous nature of the materials being handled, and implement employee training programs dealing with hazardous materials. The rules apply also to firms that handle the materials in sealed containers, such as carriers and warehouses.

Employee safety is a matter of continual concern. It involves training, motivation, and never-ending supervision. In the aftermath of the severe blizzards that struck Chicago in early 1979, many warehouses had to send workers up on their roofs to shovel away the accumulated snow.

> One had to be careful to prevent any congregating of men in groups on the roof. If you have a crew of twenty men working on your roof and the foreman calls them all together to give them instructions, you could precipitate a serious collapse by the sheer weight of people clearing snow off the roof. . . . Several warehousemen said that they made it a point to provide all instructions before ascending to the roof and the supervisor ordered that no more than two people could get together to prevent straining the roof.[18]

18 *Warehousing Review,* Summer 1979, p. 18.

Hazardous Materials

Hazardous materials must receive extra attention because of the injuries and property damage they can cause. (See Figure 10-9.) Department of Transportation regulations require that shipping documents indicate the hazardous nature of materials being transported. Warehousers must note these warnings when they receive materials and must be certain that they are included on the outbound shipping documents when the materials leave the warehouse. Warehouse design includes provisions for having the areas where hazardous materials are stored drain into holding tanks and having a dike built around the building so that if the sprinkler system is activated, the combined mixture of water and hazardous matter will be contained.

Yes, sir, I know freezing will not hurt your product, but what will it do to my floor when it thaws?

Figure 10-9   Materials stored in a warehouse can damage other materials or the warehouse structure. (*Warehousing Review,* vol. 6, nos. 2–7 (1977). Drawn by Art Stenholm; courtesy of American Warehouse Association.)

In 1988 the warehousing industry was reacting to a new set of federal regulations referred to as *SARA* (from the law titled *Superfund Amendments and Reauthorization Act*). The law requires warehouses to notify their local communities as to the nature and quantities of hazardous materials they are storing. (This is referred to as the community's right to know, and there is concern that some communities will issue such stringent restrictions on certain materials that they just won't move.) Releases of hazardous materials into the environment must also be reported.

Fires are a constant threat at warehouses. Most materials used for packaging are highly flammable. Plastics, once ignited, can be very difficult to extinguish. High-rise warehouses are more vulnerable to fires, since the vertical spaces between stored materials serve as chimney flues and help the fires burn. Grain dust is also hazardous; two major grain elevators in Gulf ports were destroyed by fires and explosions in the late 1970s.

On July 11, 1988, a Safeway grocery distribution center in Richmond, California, burned almost to the ground. Over five hundred warehouse employees were put out of work.

> The fire originated, according to a Safeway employee, at or near the top of highly combustible pasteboard boxes of paper towels stacked three pallets high near the center of the building. . . . The only known source of heat near the point of fire origin was a newly installed sodium vapor light fixture. This fixture was observed by a Safeway employee to be only a few inches above a burning box, and its light was out.[19]

As an example of partnershipping, manufacturers of chemicals now work more closely with warehouse firms that store their products with regard to safety measures. Examples are training employees for the initial response to a spill and having eyewash stations installed.

Sanitation

Warehouse cleanliness is another ongoing concern. The small amount of space devoted to it here does not do justice to its importance. Sanitation is related to employee safety and morale and to the quality of the products handled.

The U.S. Food and Drug Administration is concerned with the sanitation of food and drugs moving in interstate commerce. Its efforts were strengthened beginning in mid-1975, when the Supreme Court upheld the criminal conviction of the president of a large food chain (nearly nine hundred retail outlets) because of unsanitary conditions in one of the firm's warehouses.[20] This demonstrated that sanitation is a top management responsibility.

Stock Controls

A principal and continuing problem is keeping an accurate count of merchandise moving through the warehouse. If the count is off—either too high or too low—sophisticated handling procedures will be undermined. The initial error occurs when the worker at the receiving dock assumes that all the goods listed on the delivering carrier's bill of lading are, in fact, there. A second type of error occurs when the receiving clerk assumes responsibility for on-the-spot adjustments of overages and shortages. He or she may note that there is one carton too many of brown shoe polish and one too few of black shoe polish. Because the price is the same, the clerk may accept the shipment

---

[19] Report of the Richmond Fire Department, July 27, 1988, unpublished. Press accounts after the fire suggest that an elevated forklift hit the light in question.

[20] *Warehousing Review,* July–August 1975, pp. 2–9.

without noting the discrepancy. The receiving clerk's single error becomes multiplied, because counts for both colors of polish will be off.

Sometimes, as warehouses hold goods, the title of the goods passes from one owner to another. This is especially true of commodities that are traded. Some dental supply firms allow dentists to buy large amounts annually at discounts and then deliver the materials to the dentists' offices as needed. The reason for this is that office rents paid by dentists are relatively high, and so they cannot afford to use them for storing large quantities of materials.

Accurate counts of merchandise leaving the warehouse–distribution center are important, although there is a partial control in that whoever receives the goods next will, if he or she is doing their job properly, report discrepancies. Shortages will be reported. Most methods of control involve the setting up of systems in which any one person's count must be verified— perhaps on a sampling basis—by another individual. Or manual counts may be compared with computerized records. If perishable products are handled, stock controls are needed to move out older stocks (see Figure 10-10).

Stockouts

Stockouts were discussed in detail in Chapter 9, and methods were shown for reducing or eliminating them. Nevertheless they occur. Warehouse–distribution centers must have policies to answer such questions as the following:

1. Will the customer permit substitutions, and if so, what types of substitutes are acceptable?
2. If, because of a partial outage, it is impossible to ship a large enough load to meet minimum load quantities, what should be done?
3. Will the customer accept partial delivery? Will the customer accept back orders? If freight charges are higher because of these split shipments, how shall they be assessed?
4. If shipping dates cannot be met, what actions should be taken?

Highly computerized distribution centers have answers to most of these questions programmed into their system, and the answers can be determined quickly. Unfortunately, not all exceptions can be thought of in advance. It is therefore necessary to know to whom the situation should be reported so that a decision can be made.

These examples relate to the customer service element of logistics. Usually a separate report is made to the salesperson handling the account whose service is being delayed or altered. It may be preferable to have him or her contact the customer waiting for the shipment. If there are some alternative solutions to the problem from which the customer can choose, it may be wise to give the customer the choice. In this case the distribution center's exception policy would be to have the salesperson contact the customer.

Figure 10-10 Stock controls are necessary. If papayas (a tropical fruit) are kept too long, they attract insects. This cartoon accompanied the text of an advertisement for a computerized warehouse-inventory control system. (Courtesy of Logisticon, Inc., Material Management Systems, Santa Clara, Cal.)

SUMMARY

Chapter 10 deals with both warehousing and distribution centers—the sites where inventories are stored for varying periods of time. Warehouses perform what is known as the adjustment function (that is, the goods come in certain collections or assortments and leave in different collections or assortments). Warehouses also serve as consolidation points.

There are both public and private warehouses. Public warehouses have a number of established duties regarding the care of goods placed in them. They can provide bonded storage for goods upon which taxes have not yet been paid. Field warehousing involves holding goods as collateral for securing loans.

Private warehouses are owned by their users, who have large, steady demands. Chain stores are probably the best example. A distribution center is a warehouse located, designed, and operated to support retailing. The emphasis is on quick throughput of goods.

The design of warehouses and distribution centers is discussed. There are many trades-offs, such as between expanding floor dimensions and building higher, and using fixed versus variable slot locations. (In the variable slot location system, goods are placed in any empty slot and their location recorded. In theory, this nearly doubles the warehouse's capacity.) Several examples are given of warehouse layout. This is another logistics area where computers are very important.

QUESTIONS FOR DISCUSSION AND REVIEW

1. Distinguish between a warehouse and a distribution center.
2. List the various functions performed by warehouses and distribution centers.
3. Discuss the liability that public warehouses have for the products stored in the warehouse.
4. What is a bonded warehouse?
5. What is OSHA? How does it affect warehousing?
6. What are the functions of a plant warehouse?
7. Why is the safety of warehouse employees a continuing issue?
8. What is high-rise storage? What limitations, if any, are there on height?
9. Why must accurate counts be kept of merchandise (a) entering, (b) inside, and (c) leaving a warehouse or distribution center?
10. What are the advantages of public warehouses? When would private warehouses be used?
11. What is warehouse *cross-docking?*
12. How are consolidation points selected?
13. Why do warehouses offer incentives for goods loaded on pallets?

14. In a distribution center, which is the more important function—order picking or stock replenishment? Why?

15. Discuss the advantages of fixed and variable slot locations in distribution centers.

16. Discuss the use of computers in warehousing.

17. How are optical scanners used in warehousing operations?

18. What does the term *value added* mean when applied to warehousing or distribution?

19. Why must distribution centers have developed procedures for handling stockouts?

20. What special precautions must be taken when handling hazardous materials in a warehouse? Why?

SUGGESTED READINGS

Before the Fire: Fire Prevention Strategies for Storage Occupancies. Quincy, Mass.: National Fire Protection Association, 1988.

Dadzie, Kofi Q., and Wesley J. Johnston. "Innovative Automation Technology in Corporate Warehousing Logistics." *Journal of Business Logistics*, Spring 1991, pp. 63–82.

Derewecki, Donald J. "Warehouse Planning: Computer-Aided Design." In *Papers, CLM 1988 Annual Meeting*, vol. 1. Oak Brook, Ill. CLM, 1988, pp. 427–458.

Frazelle, Edward H. "The Principles of Order Picking." In *Annual Conference Proceedings of the Council of Logistics Management*, vol. 1. Oak Brook, Ill. CLM, 1990, pp. 129–159.

Jenkins, Michael. "Gaining a Financial Foothold through Public Warehousing." *Journal of Business Strategy*, vol. 13, no. 3 (May–June 1992), pp. 53–57.

Kiernan, Patricia A. "WINS—User Perspective and Update." In *Papers, CLM 1987 Annual Meeting*, vol. 1. Oak Brook, Ill. CLM, 1987, pp. 281–287.

McBride, Jim. *The Public Warehouse Selection Process*. Oak Brook, Ill.: Warehousing Education and Research Council, 1983.

McGinnis, Michael A. *Basic Economic Analysis for Warehouse Decisions*. Oak Brook, Ill.: Warehousing Education and Research Council, 1989.

McGinnis, Michael A., and Lisa A. Forry. *Changing Missions in Warehousing*. Oak Brook, Ill.: Warehousing Education and Research Council, 1986.

McGinnis, Michael A., and Jonathon Kohn. "Warehousing, Competitive Advantage, and Competitive Strategy." *Journal of Business Logistics*, September 1988, pp. 32–54.

Phohl, Hans-Christian, Werner A. Zollner, and Norbert Weber. "Economies of Scale in Customer Warehouses: Theoretical and Empirical Analysis." *Journal of Business Logistics*, vol. 13, no. 1 (1992), pp. 95–124.

Sheehan, William G. "Contract Warehousing: The Evolution of an Industry." *Journal of Business Logistics*, April 1989, pp. 31–49.

Speh, Thomas W., and James A. Blomquist. *The Financial Evaluation of Warehousing Options: An Examination and Appraisal of Contemporary Practices.* Miami, Ohio: Warehousing Research Center, Miami University, 1988.

Speh, Thomas W., Cara Murray, and Christine McCallum. *Warehousing Safety Program Guidelines.* Oak Brook, Ill.: Warehousing Education and Research Council, 1990.

Traveling the Roud of Logistics: The Evolution of Warehousing and Distribution. Chicago: The American Warehousemen's Association, 1991.

Van Oudheusden, Dirk L., and Peter Boey. "Design of an Automated Warehouse for Air Cargo: The Case of the Thai Air Cargo Terminal." *Journal of Business Logistics,* vol. 15, no. 1 (1994), pp. 261–285.

C A S E   1 0 - 1

SANDY'S CANDY

Sandy Nykerk was an operations analyst for Mannix Model Markets, a food store chain headquartered in Omaha, Nebraska, with fifty-five food stores in an area that extended east to Des Moines, Iowa, north to Sioux Falls, South Dakota, west to North Platte, Nebraska, and south to Emporia, Kansas. All the stores were served by daily deliveries five days a week from a large complex of Mannix warehouses in Omaha. There were two exceptions. First, each store's produce department could buy some produce locally, which it usually did during the summer and autumn months. Second, some goods were delivered to the stores by vendors, usually operating through driver/salespeople who would stock the goods on the shelves. Examples of these goods were dairy products, soft drinks, bakery items, name-brand snacks, beer, panty hose, candy, and yogurt. Vendors delivered ice cream directly to the stores west of Grand Island, Nebraska, in part because Mannix was short of trucks with freezer capacity, especially during the summer months.

Mannix Markets was a member of a buying cooperative. The buying cooperative had forced many name-brand manufacturers to make their goods available to it, in which case they would be delivered first to each chain's warehouse and then via chain trucks to individual retail chain stores, where store personnel placed them on the shelves and treated them as any other product. The only good that could not be purchased through the cooperative was beer, because some states had stricter regulations regarding the wholesaling of beer (and other alcoholic beverages), initially to ensure that they received all of their beverage tax receipts (although beer wholesalers opposed legislation to relax these regulations).

Sandy knew that most of the vendor-delivered goods were ones that Mannix Markets did not want to handle through its own distribution system. Milk, for example, would be very expensive to handle because it was costly to ship and had a short shelf life. Bakery products had similar characteristics, although Mannix Markets did buy some bread from a private bakery and sold it in Omaha stores under the Mannix label. Snack foods were also best handled by driver/salespeople working for vendors because they were handled roughly in the Mannix distribution system, and by the time pretzels or potato chips reached the shelves, they were mostly broken and filled only the bottom third of the bag.

The buying cooperative had recently entered into an agreement with Schoenecker's Candies, a well-known regional firm that produced eight different types of candies and caramels sold in cellophane bags. The experience of Mannix Markets was that Schoenecker's candies sold much better than any competing brand, almost irrespective of price, so Schoenecker's was the only brand that Mannix Markets would carry. Sandy had received a note from her supervisor saying that Schoenecker's candies could now be purchased directly through the buyers' cooperative and handled through Mannix Markets' regular distribution system. The supervisor wanted Sandy to calculate whether Mannix Markets should stop having Schoenecker's candies delivered by driver/salespeople and instead purchase the candy through the buying cooperative.

If the cost comparisons were fairly close, Mannix Markets would prefer using its own system for several reasons. The reasons included generalities regarding driver/salespeople and not specifically referring to the Schoenecker driver/salespeople. The three objections to deliveries by driver/salespeople were as follows:

1. Their deliveries could not be scheduled, and sometimes their trucks would tie up an unloading dock, which could delay a Mannix truck waiting to discharge ten or twenty tons of groceries.

2. Some driver/salespeople needed space in the stock room, and this meant that more unknown people were wandering an area where pilferage was sometimes a problem.

3. When a driver/salesperson appeared, this interrupted the store manager or assistant manager, who routinely would have to approve the next order and also have to check in the new merchandise and agree on the amount of returned merchandise the driver/salesperson was removing from the store.

Store clerks disliked some driver/salespeople, claiming that they took shelf-stocking work away from store personnel. Store management discounted this argument because they thought that many store clerks did not like to see how quickly the driver/salespeople worked. (The driver/salespeople were mostly nonunion and worked on a commission basis.) Also, the shelves stocked by driver/salespeople were always neater than those stocked by ordinary store personnel. On occasion, when store clerks disliked a special driver/salesperson, they would sabotage him or her by rearranging the shelves after he or she had left, hiding all the products behind those of a competitor.

Sandy started working on her assignment and found that she was comparing the efficiency of Mannix Markets' distribution system, which handled 10,000 line items, with that of the Schoenecker Candy Company, which handled only eight types of candy in several different-sized packages. Soon Sandy's project became known as the "Sandy Candy Puzzle" among her fellow workers. Finally, to organize her thoughts and provide a basis for comparison, Sandy took a sheet of paper, drew a line down the middle, and listed as many comparisons as possible. Her analysis is shown in Exhibits 10-A and 10-B.

Sandy completed her tally sheets and wondered why sales per store should be higher when driver/salespeople serviced the merchandise. She was told that this was because they did a better job of arranging the goods on the shelves, they kept abreast of changes in demand, and they sometimes placed posters and other small displays on the candy shelves.

Questions

1. Using those items of comparison for which costs can be calculated, determine the cost difference between the two delivery systems.

2. List and compare those factors to which it is difficult to assign precise costs.

3. Given the data that Sandy Nykerk has, do you believe that Mannix Markets should get its Schoenecker Candy through the buying cooperative or continue to rely on direct deliveries by Schoenecker's driver/salespeople? Give your reasons.

4. If you were Nykerk, what additional information would you like to have before being asked to make such a recommendation?

5. Candy sales increase during holiday seasons. Which of the two candy distribution systems do you think would do a better job of anticipating and supplying these seasonal increases? Why?

6. Assume you are in charge of labor relations for Mannix Model Markets. Would you like to see continued reliance on driver/salespeople to supply the markets' candy needs? Why or why not?

Present System	Alternate System
Schoenecker Candy Co. has driver/ salespeople deliver and stock shelves.	Purchase Schoenecker's Candies through buying cooperative and distribute to stores through Mannix Markets' own distribution system.

Buying Terms

Every Friday, the d/s tallies sales for past seven days and store manager approves. Then three days later a bill comes from Schoenecker with 2% discount if paid within ten days (i.e. 13 days after the d/s makes the tally). The entire amount is due within 30 days (or 33 days of d/s tally).	Schoenecker must be paid within seven days after candy is received at Mannix warehouse. No discounts.

Wholesale and Retail Prices of Candy

Package Size	Wholesale Price Paid to Schoenecker	Retail Price	Package Size	Wholesale Price Paid to Schoenecker	Retail Price
3½ oz.	13¢	19¢	4 oz.	10¢	19¢
8 oz.	28¢	39¢	9 oz.	20¢	39¢
12 oz.	42¢	57¢	13 oz.	30¢	57¢

Average Time in Inventory

Goods are on consignment, meaning that Schoenecker owns them and only collects for those that are sold.	Candy would be in the Mannix warehouse for an average of two weeks and on a retail store shelf for an average of one week.

Average Sales per Store per Week

110 3½-oz. pkgs., 70 8-oz. pkgs., and 40 12-oz. pkgs.	100 4-oz. pkgs., 60 9-oz. pkgs., and 30 13-oz. pkgs. (Sales were somewhat lower because store personnel do not take as good care of merchandise on shelves.)

Shrinkage on Store Shelf

(Unaccounted-for loss: 2 percent per week, paid for by Mannix Markets.	2 percent per week, paid for by Mannix Markets.

Exhibit 10-A   Sandy's worksheet.

Present System	Alternate System
Spoilage	
(Package torn open on shelf which cannot be sold): 1 percent a week, absorbed by Schoenecker Candy	Same rate, paid for by Mannix Markets
Ordering Costs	
Absorbed by Schoenecker Candy Co. However, store manager or assistant must approve order, twice a week, taking a total of 10 minutes time. Assistant manager makes $16,000 per year plus 15% fringe.	1½¢ per day, 4 days a week, for each of 24 items (8 types of candy in three sizes of package).
Shelf Stocking	
Absorbed by Schoenecker Candy Co.	20 minutes of clerk's time per week. (Clerk's hourly rate is $3.75 plus 10% fringe.) For every 10 stock clerks there is one supervisor paid $13,000 per year plus 15% fringe.
Warehousing Costs	
Absorbed by Schoenecker Candy Co.	The Mannix warehouse costs $10,000 per day to operate. Its through-put is 750 tons per day, five days a week.
Delivery to Store Costs	
Absorbed by Schoenecker Candy Co.	Only available cost figure is 3¢ per ton-mile, and the average distance from Mannix warehouse to a retail store is 50 miles.
Checking in Goods at Store	
Takes 10 minutes per ____ of manager's or assistant manager's time.	No check-in necessary; controls are at warehouse, and truck is sealed in between warehouse and store.
Billing and Bill-Paying Costs	
Mannix Markets pays $1.00 per week to process and pay the Schoenecker Candy Co. invoice.	Believed to be less since, rather than spot-checking forms from each store, only the Mannix warehouse receipt form need be checked.

Exhibit 10-B Sandy's worksheet.

C A S E   1 0 - 2

MINNETONKA WAREHOUSE

Wayne Schuller managed a warehouse in Minnetonka, Minnesota. His major concern was the number of workers to assign to work at his single unloading dock. After he began contracting with motor carriers for deliveries, he found that they were assessing him stiff penalties if their trucks had to wait to be unloaded. Schuller started adding larger crews at the unloading dock, but often they seemed idle because there were no trucks to unload. Schuller recalled from college that queueing theory might be applicable to such a problem.

The theory of queueing is an analysis of the probabilities associated with waiting in line, assuming that orders, customers, and so on arrive in some pattern (often a random pattern) to stand in line. A common situation is that on the average a facility may have excess capacity, but often there are times when it is more than full, with a backlog of work to be done. Often this backlog has costs associated with it, including penalties to be paid or customers who walk away rather than wait. If a firm expands its capacity to reduce waiting times, then its costs go up and must be paid even when the facility is idle. So queueing theory is used to find the best level of capacity, the one that minimizes the costs of providing a service and the costs of those waiting to use the service.

After some further research specific to his firm, Schuller developed the following facts:

1. Trucks arrive randomly at the average rate of four per hour, with a deviation of plus or minus one.
2. A team of two warehouse workers can unload trucks at the rate of five per hour, or one every 12 minutes.
3. A team of three warehouse workers can unload trucks at the rate of eight per hour, or one every 7.5 minutes.
4. A team of four warehouse workers can unload trucks at the rate of ten per hour, or one every 6 minutes.
5. A team of five warehouse workers can unload trucks at the rate of eleven per hour, or one every 4.45 minutes.
6. The unloading times given in the preceding items (1–5) are average figures.
7. Each warehouse worker receives $14 per hour, must be paid for an entire shift, and because of union work rules, cannot be assigned to other tasks within the warehouse.

8. Because of its contract with the carriers, Schuller's warehouse must pay the motor carriers that own idle trucks at the rate of $60 per hour while the trucks stand idle, waiting to be unloaded.

Use STORM 2.0 or other software that enables you to perform queueing operations. Note that the variable defined as number of servers—# servers— denotes number of teams of workers and accompanying equipment working as a complete server. In the situation given here, the number of teams or servers is always "1," although the number varies in terms of costs and output.

Questions

1. For each of the four work team sizes just mentioned, calculate the expected number of trucks in the queue waiting to be unloaded.
2. For each of the four work team sizes, calculate the expected time in the queue; that is, the expected time a truck has to wait in line to be unloaded.
3. For each of the four work team sizes, what is the probability that a truck cannot be unloaded immediately?
4. Which of the four work team sizes has the lowest cost to Schuller?
5. Schuller is also considering rental of a forklift to use in truck unloading. A team of only two would be needed, but the hourly cost would be $38 per hour ($28 for the workers and $10 for the forklift). They could unload a truck in five minutes. Should Schuller rent the forklift?
6. Disregard your answer to question 5. Labor negotiations are coming up, and Schuller thinks he can get the union to give way on the work rule that prohibits warehouse workers on the unloading dock from being given other assignments when they are not unloading trucks. How much would Schuller save in unloading dock costs if he could reassign warehouse workers to other tasks when they are not unloading trucks, assuming that Schuller has picked a good team of workers and each worker works eight hours a day?

11

International Logistics

A Martinair DC-10 leaving Seattle for Schiphol, flying over several ships in port. Courtesy of Martinair Holland Cargo.

What makes lenders and insurers wary about funding transport and distribution ventures in the former Soviet Union is the tendency of shipments to disappear, sometimes in part, sometimes altogether, sometimes temporarily, sometimes forever.

American Shipper
June 1994

There are now approximately 68 all-cargo B747s and 125 [747] combis flying the world's scheduled routes. The all-cargo B747 has up to 250,000 pounds of cargo capacity, and the combi 125,000 pounds. In addition, dozens and dozens of widebodied passenger aircraft with up to 100,000 pounds cargo capacity in their bellies crisscross the oceans.

CNS Focus
September 1994

United Parcel Service will stop trucking packages to Mexico, effective July 31, but will continue its air delivery south of the border. Treatment by Mexican customs at border crossings and "protectionist regulatory practices" of the Mexican government forced the decision to discontinue ground service, UPS said in a letter to its customers.

Transport Topics
July 17, 1995

About three years ago Sea-Land Service set up a "Global Services Group" as a unit to deal specifically with its largest customers. The group was to appeal to the big shippers who want to deal with Sea-Land as a global service provider, rather than as a company that sells ocean transportation on one or more discrete trade lanes.

American Shipper
December 1994

Key Terms

- Customs house broker
- Documentation channel
- Export management company
- Export packer
- Export trading company
- Import quota
- Incoterms
- International Air Transport Association
- International freight forwarder
- International sourcing
- Irrevocable letter of credit
- Land bridge
- Nontariff barrier
- Nonvessel-operating common carrier (NVOCC)
- Shippers association
- Shipping conference

Learning Objectives

- To examine the importance of international trade to the United States
- To explain the concept of international sourcing
- To identify the reasons for governmental intervention in the area of international trade
- To distinguish among the unique activities of international trade specialists
- To examine issues involved in international air transportation
- To relate activities involved in international ocean transportation

INTRODUCTION

Some aspects of international logistics have been touched upon in earlier chapters. It is difficult to keep separate the practices of domestic and international logistics. International logistics—the movement of goods across national boundaries—occurs in the following situations:

1. A firm exports a portion of a product made or grown, for example, paper-making machinery to Sweden, wheat to Russia, or coal to Japan.
2. A firm imports raw materials (such as pulpwood from Canada) or manufactured products (such as motorcycles from Italy or Japan).
3. Goods are partially assembled in one country and then shipped to another, where they are further assembled or processed. For example, a firm stamps electronic components in the United States, it ships them to a free trade zone in the Far East, where low-cost labor assembles them, and then the assembled components are returned to the United States to become part of the finished product. Currently, there is great interest in Vietnam as a site for performing labor-intensive tasks, since wage rates there are relatively low.
4. Products are assembled in a foreign country for distribution in that and other foreign countries and in the firm's home country. Some autos sold in the United States are assembled in Canada. (Because of a special Canadian-U.S. trade agreement, the U.S. auto manufacturer that relies on Canadian plants to supply a part of its U.S. markets can export to Canada, with few or no tariff restrictions, an equal volume of other models assembled in the United States.)
5. Because of geography, a nation's domestic commerce crosses foreign borders, often in bond (this occurs only rarely). Goods moving by truck between Detroit and Buffalo or between the lower forty-eight states and Alaska, through Canada, travel in bond, which means that the carrier handling them has a special legal obligation to keep them sealed and to make certain that they are not released for sale or use within the country they are traveling through. Products shipped in bond are not subject to normal duties of the country through which they are passing.

Until World War II, concepts of international trade were simple. Industrialized powers maintained political and economic colonies that were sources of raw materials and markets for manufactured products. When dealing with colonies, manufacturers in the main country bought low and sold high. World War II brought an end to the colonial system; since then emerging nations have attempted to develop their own political and economic systems with varying degrees of success. As emerging nations attempt to flex their political and economic muscles, they cause changes in the traditional ways of conducting international business.

Developing nations insist that an increasing proportion of assembling and manufacturing be conducted within their own borders. Because the role of these governments in their own economies is substantial, they are able to exert considerable influence over outside firms desiring to do business within their borders. Local labor must be used whenever possible. Demands are also made that supervisory and managerial talent be recruited from native sources and trained to replace the managers from outside countries.

Developing nations are also becoming more insistent that much of their foreign trade be carried on vessels or planes owned by companies headquartered within their boundaries. In addition they want their local firms to have at least their "fair" share of revenues from the sale of freight-forwarding services, marine insurance, and other transportation and distribution functions.

Traditionally the United States has been a major exporter of manufactured goods and agricultural products. Because of its wealth, the United States has also imported many consumer goods. However, in the last decade, several major changes have upset these traditional patterns. A new equilibrium has yet to be reached. The United States has been running trade deficits annually because of its large purchases of imported oil. In addition many major U.S. industries, once the backbone of the country's industrial might, have found themselves uncompetitive in overseas and even in U.S. markets.

The fluctuating value of the U.S. dollar has an impact on the flow of both exports and imports. When the dollar is weak, it is more costly to import, but foreign customers buy U.S.-built products because to them the prices seem low. When the dollar is strong, the reverse holds true.

In the 1990s several events changed the traditional patterns of how the United States conducts business overseas. The end of Soviet rule in Eastern Europe opened up the opportunity of engaging in much more trade with that major area of the world. As this book is being written one reads of the disintegration of law and order outside of major Russian cities. Insurance firms will not cover shipments to many rural areas in the former Soviet Union. They will cover movements only to major ports and airports, and the buyer must arrange to take delivery at those points. In 1992 Western Europe achieved fuller economic integration, though there remained many barriers to the free movement of goods among all nations. In addition, environmentalists in Europe were attempting to maintain restrictions on truck traffic so that more freight is forced to use rail and waterways. Also in the mid-1990s, the North American Free Trade Agreement (NAFTA) came into being, and steps are under way to achieve closer economic integration among Canada, the United States, and Mexico.

Although this text is written from the standpoint of a U.S.-based firm involved in international trade, another type of firm has recently developed, one that can locate almost anywhere in the world and conduct commerce between any and all nations. The term *global logistics* is more applicable to the logistical challenges of this type of firm.

INTERNATIONAL MARKETING

Marketing overseas is often different from marketing in the United States. Therefore, generalizations are difficult to make since each country of the world possesses unique characteristics when viewed as a market. Conventional marketing analysis is applied, although it must take into account a wider range of differences. Figure 11-1 is an ad placed by a New Jersey public utility offering to assist its customers find trade leads.

In many countries the size or scale of firms used in the distribution operation is much smaller than would be the case in the United States. Street vendors, merchants operating out of "holes-in-the-wall," and small shopkeepers may be the rule. In these countries customers shop on a daily basis and buy small amounts, and retailers are more likely to pull the requested good from a shelf behind the counter so there is less need for the type of packaging used in U.S. self-service markets. (Of course, many countries have retail stores similar to those in the United States.)

Firms selling products under their own brand names are concerned about maintaining a reputation for quality in all markets. This can pose problems with respect to customer service. For example, how many parts depots should be located throughout the world? What kinds of guarantees can a U.S. firm make to foreign buyers? How enforceable are they? What changes must be made in a product to adapt it to export? Because of time differences, one cannot talk with all other parts of the world during one's normal business hours. In tropical nations a siesta is observed, with offices closing from about noon until 4 P.M. In addition, each nation celebrates its own series of holidays.

LEGO's children's construction toys are made by a firm headquartered in Denmark. The product, which was sold worldwide, was uniformly packaged in an elegant see-through carton. In the United States during the late 1980s, however, LEGO lost market share to competitors that packaged a similar product in plastic buckets. Parents who purchased the toys found that the bucket was more functional and helped to encourage children to return the blocks to the bucket for storage.

> LEGO's alarmed U.S. management sought permission from Denmark to package LEGO toys in buckets. The head office flatly refused the request [because] buckets would be a radical deviation from the company's policy of standardized marketing everywhere. Two years later, however, headquarters reversed itself. The impetus was a massive loss of U.S. market share to competitive goods sold in buckets.[1]

In international distribution, push inventory systems are rare because the international credit system is not as well developed as the credit system within the United States or other similarly developed economic areas. In international business, if the buyer is unwilling or unable to pay, collection of the debt can prove difficult or even impossible. Furthermore, even though the buyer or borrower may be willing and able to pay, it may not be permitted to do so because of foreign exchange restrictions, expropriation, or political upheaval.

If the supplier is uncertain about receiving its payments, the supplier is unlikely to push unwanted goods onto its overseas distributors. One of the

---

[1] Kamran Kashani, "Beware the Pitfalls of Global Marketing," *Harvard Business Review*, September–October 1989, pp. 96–97.

Figure 11-1 Ad placed by a New Jersey utility offering to help customers develop export sales leads, agents, and distributors. (Courtesy TradeLink New Jersey, a program from Public Service Electric & Gas.)

ways a supplier can be assured of payment is to insist on payment in advance or else to operate through an **irrevocable letter of credit,** in which a bank guarantees payment provided that the supplier meets certain conditions. (See Figure 11-2 for a sample copy. Note the terms.)

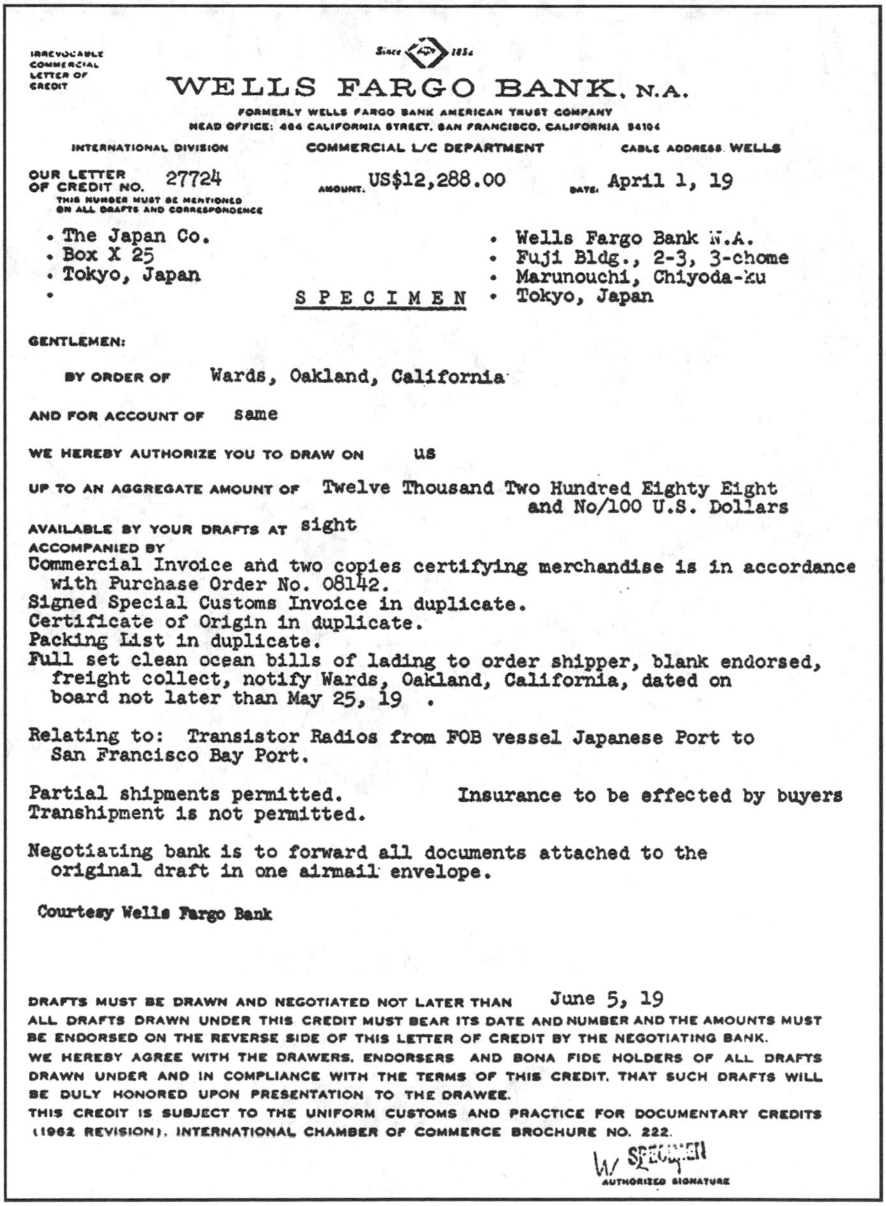

IRREVOCABLE COMMERCIAL LETTER OF CREDIT

Since 1852

WELLS FARGO BANK, N.A.

FORMERLY WELLS FARGO BANK AMERICAN TRUST COMPANY
HEAD OFFICE: 464 CALIFORNIA STREET, SAN FRANCISCO, CALIFORNIA 94104

INTERNATIONAL DIVISION — COMMERCIAL L/C DEPARTMENT — CABLE ADDRESS WELLS

OUR LETTER OF CREDIT NO. 27724 — AMOUNT. US$12,288.00 — DATE. April 1, 19

THIS NUMBER MUST BE MENTIONED ON ALL DRAFTS AND CORRESPONDENCE

- The Japan Co.
- Box X 25
- Tokyo, Japan

SPECIMEN

- Wells Fargo Bank N.A.
- Fuji Bldg., 2-3, 3-chome
- Marunouchi, Chiyoda-ku
- Tokyo, Japan

GENTLEMEN:

BY ORDER OF Wards, Oakland, California

AND FOR ACCOUNT OF same

WE HEREBY AUTHORIZE YOU TO DRAW ON us

UP TO AN AGGREGATE AMOUNT OF Twelve Thousand Two Hundred Eighty Eight and No/100 U.S. Dollars

AVAILABLE BY YOUR DRAFTS AT sight

ACCOMPANIED BY

Commercial Invoice and two copies certifying merchandise is in accordance with Purchase Order No. 08142.
Signed Special Customs Invoice in duplicate.
Certificate of Origin in duplicate.
Packing List in duplicate.
Full set clean ocean bills of lading to order shipper, blank endorsed, freight collect, notify Wards, Oakland, California, dated on board not later than May 25, 19 .

Relating to: Transistor Radios from FOB vessel Japanese Port to San Francisco Bay Port.

Partial shipments permitted. Insurance to be effected by buyers
Transhipment is not permitted.

Negotiating bank is to forward all documents attached to the original draft in one airmail envelope.

Courtesy Wells Fargo Bank

DRAFTS MUST BE DRAWN AND NEGOTIATED NOT LATER THAN June 5, 19

ALL DRAFTS DRAWN UNDER THIS CREDIT MUST BEAR ITS DATE AND NUMBER AND THE AMOUNTS MUST BE ENDORSED ON THE REVERSE SIDE OF THIS LETTER OF CREDIT BY THE NEGOTIATING BANK.

WE HEREBY AGREE WITH THE DRAWERS, ENDORSERS AND BONA FIDE HOLDERS OF ALL DRAFTS DRAWN UNDER AND IN COMPLIANCE WITH THE TERMS OF THIS CREDIT, THAT SUCH DRAFTS WILL BE DULY HONORED UPON PRESENTATION TO THE DRAWEE.

THIS CREDIT IS SUBJECT TO THE UNIFORM CUSTOMS AND PRACTICE FOR DOCUMENTARY CREDITS (1962 REVISION), INTERNATIONAL CHAMBER OF COMMERCE BROCHURE NO. 222.

W/ SPECIMEN
AUTHORIZED SIGNATURE

Figure 11-2 Irrevocable letter of credit. (Courtesy of Wells Fargo Bank.)

From a logistics manager's standpoint, the letter of credit controls the shipment's movement: It names vessels, specifies departure and arrival dates, dictates labeling, and so on. If changes are to be made, both the buyer and seller must agree and the letter of credit must be amended accordingly. The risk is that the value of the product may change after the date of the original agreement, in which case one party to the agreement will seek to renegotiate the price.

INTERNATIONAL SOURCING

The term **international sourcing** applies to buying components and inputs anywhere in the world. It means that the manufacturer, rather than relying solely on its local Yellow Pages, casts out a much wider net in search of sources. Lynn Hutchings of IBM said, "True supply chain services include where you source your product," and "Factors in sourcing decisions include duty rates, politics and trade policies."[2]

Some firms are truly international in stature and try to develop products that can be manufactured and sold in many parts of the world. As one travels in various nations, one sees autos with the Ford emblem that look like first cousins to Fords sold and distributed in the United States. A few decades ago, U.S. manufacturers of autos and appliances would, at the end of a model run, send the various molds, stamping dies, and so on to a factory in a less developed nation, thereby getting a few more years of production out of the original production equipment. That is less likely to occur now because so much of the world has "caught up" with the United States. United States firms also look to develop operations overseas in an attempt to avoid the restrictions that developing countries place on outside firms.

> The term rationalized exchange is used to describe a strategy for holding ground in LDC [less-developed country] markets by locating manufacturing arms in those nations in which the finished products are sold. An interlocking world-wide production scheme of this type enables multinationals to ward off the devastating effects of protectionism in the form of domestic content requirements, tariff barriers, import quotas, taxes, and local ownership laws.[3]

As international sourcing has become more prevalent, firms have incorporated into their new supply chains the most recent inventory-control methodologies. Outboard Marine Corporation (OMC), an engine manufacturer based in Waukegan, Illinois, has tried to adopt the JIT system of managing inbound inventories from new foreign sources, as well as from existing foreign and domestic sources. OMC reduced the number of carriers it used and settled on two ocean carriers to serve each of its three consignment centers.

---

[2] *American Shipper*, July 1993, p. 38.

[3] "Global Sourcing Makes Big Shippers Even Bigger," *American Shipper*, June 1983, pp. 3–4.

"You can solve problems or work with them in a way you can't do with ten or twelve carriers,"[4] claimed Matthew J. Gallagher, OMC's manager of corporate transportation. OMC also had the carriers serving it reduce the number of different applicable rates.

> In the area of customs, always one of the key variables, OMC has managed to eliminate many delays that have been tolerated for years. The company has reduced the number of brokers it works with to just one and has stressed to him the importance of regular, on-time service. Cargo from Hong Kong, for instance, arrives on the West Coast weekly and is transferred to dedicated trains for shipment to Chicago. It arrives bonded in Chicago late Thursday night.
>
> Under the old system, [OMC] did not actually receive the shipment in Waukegan until the following Friday. Although it arrived late the previous Thursday, Gallagher says the company was not notified that the container had arrived until the following Tuesday, at which point arrangements were made for it to be cleared and delivered.
>
> Now [OMC has its] customs broker file with Customs on the Friday it arrives. It is then transferred to the container yard by Monday, inspected if necessary, and received the next day in Waukegan. The net savings is three days.[5]

Michael Sklar of the Temple, Barker, & Sloan consulting firm used the term *worldwide componentry* to refer to the recent developments that demonstrate a need for better worldwide communication, quality control, and ability to trace shipments. Sklar notes that as U.S. firms find themselves exporting fewer goods, they should switch to exporting services, including managerial and entrepreneurial talents.[6]

INTERNATIONAL MARKETING CHANNELS

In the discussion of marketing channels in Chapter 2, which covered the supply-chain concept, there were various arrangements of buyers and sellers in interdependent channels depending upon their function at the time. The five channels were the ownership channel, the negotiations channels, the financing channel, the promotions channel, and the logistics channel. For international transactions, we will add a sixth channel, and call it the **documentation channel**.

Documentation accompanying international shipments is excessive. One shipment to Santiago, Chile, reportedly "required 150 separate documents."[7]

[4] Mark Magneir, "Kanban," *American Shipper*, October 1984, p. 52.

[5] Ibid., p. 54.

[6] Comments made at Port of Oakland's International Transportation Conference, Oakland, Cal., October 23, 1984.

[7] *Davis Database*, October 1983, p. 1.

Preparing these documents, assembling them, and ensuring that they arrive where and when they are needed is no minor logistical operation in itself. For small items such as repair parts, the envelope with the documents will be larger than the packaged part, and the costs of documentation will be greater than the part's value. G. J. Davies claims that the international logistics involves "a system in which documentation flows are as much a part of the main logistical flow as the flow of product."[8]

Terms of Sale

Choosing the terms of sale involves parties working within the negotiations channel, looking at the possible logistics channels, and determining when and where to transfer the following between buyer and seller:

1. The physical goods (the logistics channel)
2. Payment for the goods, freight charges, and insurance for the in-transit goods (the financing channel)
3. Legal title to the goods (the ownership channel)
4. Required documentation (documentation channel)
5. Responsibility for controlling or caring for the goods in transit, say, in the case of livestock (the logistics channel)

Transfer of these five can be specified in terms of calendar time, geographic location, or completion of some actions or tasks. One must think in terms of both time and location.

Here is a list, from the seller's viewpoint, of the different locations, or stages, for quoting a price to an overseas buyer:

1. At the seller's dock: This is known as *ex works.*
2. Free carrier (at a named point): The shipper delivers the goods to a carrier at a specified point. (The term is often used for intermodal movements by container.)
3. Free on rail: This usually means that the goods are loaded aboard rail cars next to the shipper's dock.
4. FOB (free on board) airport: Delivery is made to the airport of export.
5. FAS (free alongside ship) at port of export: The buyer must clear the goods for export and have them loaded aboard the vessel.
6. FOB (free on board) a vessel: The seller is responsible for obtaining export clearance and for loading the ship.
7. C&F: The seller pays costs and freight to a specified destination.

[8] G. J. Davies, "The International Logistics Concept," *International Journal of Physical Distribution and Materials Management,* vol. 17, no. 2 (1987), p. 20.

8. CIF: This is similar to C&F except that the seller is also responsible for insurance.

9. Freight or carriage paid to a specified point: This places risks on the buyer at the point where the goods are tendered to the first carrier.

10. Freight or carriage and insurance paid to a specified point: This is similar to item 9 except that the seller also insures the goods during shipment.

11. Ex ship: The seller makes the goods available to the buyer aboard the ship at the port of import.

12. Ex quay: The seller makes the goods available to the buyer alongside the ship at the port of import.

13. Delivered at frontier: The seller gets the goods to but not through the importer's national customs.

14. Delivered, with duty paid: The seller delivers the goods to the importer's door.

This is a simplified list, and the various terms are often collectively referred to as **incoterms**. Figure 11-3 illustrates the geographic locations of some of them. There are even more variations that might be agreed on, especially if one

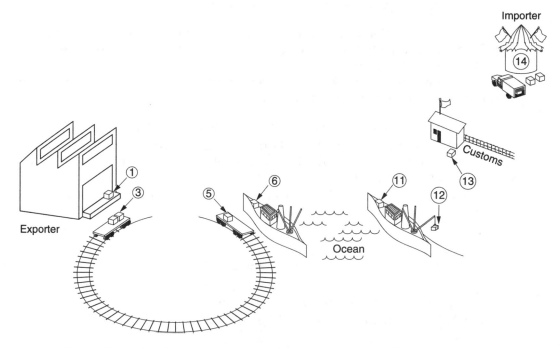

Figure 11-3   Location of some of the various points in an export/import transaction where payment, ownership, and responsibility for freight charges and insurance may be transferred between buyer and seller.

takes into account the many special services and charges associated with moving certain types of goods through some ports or airports.

Choice of currency in which payment is to be made can also be an issue, especially if the payment is to be made in the future. Barter may also be used, rather than sale for cash. This may provide additional duties for the logistics manager because the goods received in payment have to be moved.

GOVERNMENT INFLUENCES ON FOREIGN TRADE

The buying and selling parties are not always free to contract the terms to suit their needs. Often a government pressures firms to insist on terms that will result in that nation's firms performing more of the services associated with moving products. The main goal is to conserve the nation's own currency and improve its balance of payments position. For example, "British exporters have been encouraged by government agencies to sell on a delivered price basis for two reasons. The customer, it is said, wants a price he [or she] can compare locally and the British exporter selling delivered is more likely to nominate a British forwarder or carrier."[9] A nation needing to earn Western currencies, such as China, often buys and takes title at the source; it sells on a delivered basis, using its own national shipping and marine insurance for both imports and exports.

Businesses involved in foreign trade find that the government's role is more significant than in domestic transactions. In part this is because most firms are first developed in domestic markets and take all existing governmental controls as a given factor. As a firm expands into foreign markets, it finds requirements that differ for each nation with which the firm wishes to trade. The U.S. government also places restrictions and paperwork requirements on U.S. firms that buy or sell abroad.

Government Controls on the Flow of International Trade

National governments play a more significant role in international transactions than in domestic transactions for several reasons. The main reason is that governments tax the importation of many items. The taxes are called customs or duties. Goods, including baggage accompanying travelers, are inspected as they cross borders. If any customs are due, they must be paid before the goods can be transported farther.

Customs or duty rates are set high on many goods to "protect" local manufacturers, producers, or growers. Initially, local interests argue that theirs are infant industries and need protection for only a few years in order to prevent foreign-based competitors from dumping goods in the country at prices that are below cost. But once tariff barriers are built, they are not easily

---

[9] Ibid., p. 23.

torn down. Rather than the infant outgrowing the crib, the walls of the crib are built high. The results are that local consumers pay more for goods than if local industries were not protected. In addition, national resources may be allocated in a wasteful manner because they are being used for processes that are inefficient when viewed from a worldwide perspective. Sometimes the tariff the importing nation charges differs according to the nation from which the good is coming. From an international sourcing standpoint, this influences the choice of production site.

Related to tariffs are **import quotas**, which are physical limits on the amount that may be imported from any one country during a period of time. When the quota is reached, the flow of goods stops. Quotas are used for commodities for which no tariffs exist, and they serve to protect local producers in years when local prices are high but foreign prices are low.

Many nations are concerned with stopping the spread of plant and animal diseases and so inspect various commodities or products to make certain that they do not contain these problems. If material is found to be infested, it cannot enter the country until it is cleaned.

Entry of other products may be prohibited because they do not meet safety standards. For example, electrical appliances have different voltage requirements throughout the world. Products that do not meet a country's voltage specifications will not be imported by that country. Another example is the Japanese restriction on imported foods containing the two preservatives benzoic acid and sorbic acid. "The reason for this is that these two preservatives, if permitted for open use in Japan, would be used extensively on all types of fish. Because fish forms a more important part of the Japanese diet than the diets of other nations, there is a clear danger of overconsumption of these two preservatives."[10] Because of the danger of earthquakes in Japan, upright refrigerators must be built so that they will remain upright even when tilted as much as ten degrees.

Products can be modified so that they meet each nation's requirement. Conversion costs per unit are high if only small numbers of units are involved. From an inventory control standpoint, slight variations in acceptable standards mean that products become less homogeneous. Parts are less likely to be interchangeable, and stocks in one country may not be substitutes for stocks of similar products in an adjoining country.

Some nations restrict the outflow of currency. This is because a nation's economy will suffer if it imports more than it exports over a long term. These regulations are not concerned with specific commodities; rather, they are concerned with restricting the outflow of currency. All imports require advance approval, and goods that arrive without prior approval are not allowed to enter. Mexico enacted such restrictions in late 1982, and "only imports approved by the government and for which payment has been authorized by

---

[10] *Japan's Import and Export Regulations* (Tokyo: External Trade Organization, 1974), p. 10.

Mexico's nationalized banks" were permitted to enter.[11] When American Jeeps were first built in China, the Chinese government controlled the process by not allowing funds to be transferred outside China to bring in dies from the United States that would be needed to make a model similar to that made in the United States. This was because the Chinese government wanted Jeep to build a model more similar to an army truck already being made in China.

Firms with operations in several nations are subject to the taxes of each, and any intracompany move between two nations involves a sale for the one subsidiary and a purchase by the other. The transaction, therefore, determines the income, tax, and profit of both subsidiaries.[12] Tax auditors from both countries can also be expected to ask how the price was established for this intrafirm movement and whether one of the results of the price selected was a minimization of tax liability to the country in question.

Figure 11-4 is from a guidebook prepared by an international airline that outlines, in general terms, the various restrictions that apply when shipping to two African nations. From the example of the two nations listed, it is easy to see that exporting involves complications. Note that their embassy locations in the United States are listed. Consular offices are current sources of information regarding their nation's import and currency exchange regulations. Most nations maintain consular offices in major U.S. port cities, and these offices, for a fee, prepare a *consular invoice*, a document that contains approximately the same information as a commercial invoice. The importing nation uses it as the basis for levying applicable import duties.

Political Restrictions on Trade

For political or military reasons, nations ban certain types of shipments. The United States does not ship military equipment or certain strategic materials to certain nations. Political events often lead countries to break off economic relations. For example, United States trade with Cuba is restricted.

Israel and a few Arab nations do not trade with each other, and these Arab nations do not even allow vessels or planes from other nations to sail or fly directly between Israel and themselves. These few Arab nations also refuse, in varying degrees, to do business with firms that also do business with Israel. To complicate matters further, the United States has laws that discourage U.S. firms from complying with the Arab boycott.

Nontariff Barriers

All the actions of various governments described to this point tend to impede the flow of international commerce. Sometimes a government is bound by treaty to grant another nation certain preferential (or lower) tariff charges on

---

[11] *Pacific Traffic*, November 1982, p. 34.

[12] See David Ronen and Michael R. Czinkota, "Order Sourcing and Transfer Pricing in the Multinational Corporation," *Journal of Business Logistics*, March 1983, pp. 65–76.

Part 2   Elements of Logistics Systems

SENEGAL

GOVERNMENT REPRESENTATION

The Republic of Senegal is represented in the United States by an Embassy at 2112 Wyoming Ave., N.W., Washington, D.C. and a United Nations Mission at 51 East 42nd St., New York. Both also act for Canadian affairs.

GENERAL INFORMATION

Customs Airports: Dakar, Saint Louis and Ziguinchor.
Collect Service acceptable to Dakar and Saint Louis only.
COD Service not acceptable.
Free House Delivery not acceptable.

DOCUMENTATION

Commercial consignments—2 commercial invoices containing the following declaration: "Nous certifions que les marchandises denommees dans cette facture sont de fabrication et d'origine (country of origin) et que les prix indiques ci-dessus s'accordent avec les prix courants sur le marche d'exportation."
Sample consignments—Without commercial value: No documents. With commercial value: same as for commercial consignments.
Gift consignments—no documentary requirements.

RESTRICTIONS

Live animals: Health certificate.
Dogs and other domestic animals: Health certificates issued not later than 3 days before shipment and stating that the animals originate from an area free from contagious diseases of the species for the preceding 6 weeks, and in case of cats and dogs, that no rabies has been detected for the same period.
PROHIBITED: Hares and rabbits.
Live plants and plant material: Health certificate.
Arms and ammunition: Special import permit.

PROHIBITIONS

All goods of Portuguese or South African origin; skins of hares and rabbits; beetroot sugar; blankets; cloth of textile fibers; cotton cloth; fibres; flower pots, stoneware, pottery, clay products, matches, ornamental bricks and other clay products for building purposes; outwear, shirts, except shirts over CFA 1700. value; shoes, except fashionable shoes over CFA 400. value; trousers under CFA 1900. value; sisal carpets and rugs; sugar cane, yarn and thread; cotton, apéritifs of alcohol or wine basis; digestives.

IMPORT AND EXCHANGE REGULATIONS

Liberalized items may be imported without quantitative restrictions on the basis of an import certificate, which is made out by the importer, endorsed by the Customs on clearance of the merchandise and delivered to an authorized bank for visa by the Exchange Control Office.
Non-liberalized goods require an import license, issued by the Director General for Economic Services and visaed by the Exchange Control Office. Validity of certificate and license is 6 months.
The currency exchange is obtained through the authorized banks on strength of import certificate or import license. No tolerance in value or quantity shown on import certificate or import license is permitted.
The importation of goods competitive with locally produced items may be prohibited from time to time.
Rate of exchange: 247 C.F.A. Francs = $1.00

SIERRA LEONE

GOVERNMENT REPRESENTATION

Sierra Leone is represented in the United States by an Embassy at 1701 19th Street, N.W., Washington, D.C. and a United Nations Mission at 30 East 42nd St., New York. Both also act for Canadian affairs.

GENERAL INFORMATION

Customs Airport: Freetown.
Collect Service acceptable.
COD Service not acceptable.
Free House Delivery not acceptable.

DOCUMENTATION

Commercial consignments—4 combined certificates of value and origin in English bearing the supplier's letterhead and his seal or stamp against his signature or that of his representative. In case of occasional shipment, when overprinting of the letterhead is prohibitive, the combined certificate must be accompanied with the supplier's own invoice duly signed against his seal or stamp, and containing the certification: "We hereby declare that this commercial invoice is in support of the attached certificate invoice No. . . . and that the particulars shown on the certified invoice are true and correct in every detail."

RESTRICTIONS

Live animals: Import authorization from Veterinary Dept.
Dogs: Additional health and rabies vaccination certificate in English.
Live plants and plant material: Import authorization from Agricultural Department.
PROHIBITED: Aniseed and Indian hemp.
Medicines and narcotics: Import license from Director of Medical services.

PROHIBITIONS

Arms and ammunition from Liberia, obscene photographs, shaving brushes from Japan, traps for night hunting.

IMPORT AND EXCHANGE REGULATIONS

Most goods may be freely imported under "Open General License." Specific import license required for a short list of specified items only . . . issued by the Import Licensing Authority of the Ministry of Commerce and Industry; the validity is generally 12 months.
Exporters should avoid overshipment of goods covered by specific import licenses. No tolerances are permitted.
The currency exchange is obtained through authorized banks. No exchange permit is required. An import license, whether specific or open, automatically entitles the importer to buy the relative foreign exchange.
Rate of exchange: 1 Leone = $1.20

Figure 11-4 Examples of restrictions of exporting to other nations. (Courtesy of Sabena Belgian World Airlines.)

imports. Later, the nation wishes it had not set such low rates but feels bound by treaty to honor the specified rates. An action it then might take is to establish what is known as a **nontariff barrier**, a rule that has the effect of reducing the flow of imports. A widely publicized example in late 1982 was the French decision that all video recorders being imported into France move through the small Customs post at Poitiers, in central France. The move, just before Christmas, caused bottlenecks and delays and prevented many Japanese imports from reaching retailers' shelves before Christmas.[13]

Sometimes the barriers are created by other government agencies, whose primary interests are in matters other than trade. The Canadian province of Quebec requires that the French language be used on all product labels, instructions, and brochures.

Governments' Role in International Transport

As in other aspects of international business, governments are more involved in international transportation than they are in domestic transportation. One reason for this is that ocean vessels and international airline aircraft operate as extensions of a nation's economy, and most of the revenue they receive flows into that nation's economy. To that nation, international carriage functions as an export with favorable effects on the nation's balance of payments. However, to the nation on the other end of the shipment, the effect is opposite since it must import the transport service, and this has an adverse impact on its balance of payments position. Some nations with very weak balance of payments positions issue an *import license*, or permit, on the condition that the goods move on a vessel or plane flying that nation's flag,[14] which means it is importing only the goods, not the transportation service required to carry them. Situations such as this dictate carrier choice.

In order to develop international fleets and airlines, most nations provide subsidies. Many nations train their own merchant marine officers, absorb portions of the costs of building commercial vessels, and engage in other activities to promote their own merchant fleets. Some own ocean carriers in total or in part. Most international airlines are government-owned, although some are moving toward the private sector, a process called *privatization*. International air and vessel rates are frequently established by carrier cartels. Nations rely on carriers that they subsidize to represent national interests as they vote on international rate and service issues.

Less developed nations also desire to carry more of their own waterborne traffic but seem unable to penetrate the existing shipping market, which is dominated by vessel lines from developed countries. In 1983, through the

---

[13] *San Francisco Chronicle*, December 2, 1982, p. 29.

[14] As used here, *flying a nation's flag* is synonymous with being owned by private or public entities in that nation. Flags of convenience are issued by nations with relatively lax maritime safety and work standards to investors of other nations that want to avoid their home nation's control and taxes.

United Nations Conference on Trade and Development, an international agreement was adopted that (in theory) allocates ocean liner traffic between nations on a 40/40/20 split. The exporting and importing nations each have 40 percent of the business, and cross-traders[15] are restricted to 20 percent. If interpreted literally, the 20 percent limitation on cross-traders is severe because in many markets it represents insufficient cargo to keep them in business. To date, the rule has not been effective.

INTERNATIONAL TRADE SPECIALISTS

Few companies involved in international logistics rely solely on in-house personnel to manage all shipping operations. Specialist firms have developed and are known as international freight forwarders (who generally handle exports) and customs house or import brokers. Sometimes the same firm provides both services and has offices in many countries. Most companies involved in international trade eventually use one or more services that these specialists provide. All the specialists are also intermediaries in the marketing channels and in the supply chain.

International Freight Forwarders

International freight forwarders specialize in handling either vessel shipments or air shipments, yet their functions are generally the same.

Advise on Acceptance of Letters of Credit.   When a client receives a letter of credit, the document contains many conditions that the seller must meet. The forwarder determines whether the client can meet these conditions and, if it cannot, will advise the client that the letter of credit must be amended. The buyer and buyer's bank must be notified before the order can be processed further.

Booking Space on Carriers.   Space is frequently more difficult to obtain on international carriers than on domestic ones for several reasons. Vessel or aircraft departures are less frequent, and the capacities of planes or ships are strictly limited. Connections with other carriers are more difficult to arrange, and the relative bargaining strength of any one shipper vis-à-vis an international carrier is usually weaker than it is with respect to domestic carriers. Forwarders are experienced at keeping tabs on available carrier space, and because they represent more business to the carrier than an individual shipper does, they have more success when finding space is difficult.

---

[15] Ocean *liners* that carry cargo call on a regularly scheduled basis and carry less-than-shipload lots of relatively high-value general cargo. *Cross-traders* carry cargo between other nations. An example would be a ship or plane registered in country A that carries traffic between countries B and C.

Preparing an Export Declaration. An export declaration is required by the U.S. government for statistical and control purposes and must be prepared and filed for nearly every shipment.

Preparing an Air Waybill or Bill of Lading. The international air waybill is a fairly standardized document; the ocean bill of lading is not. The latter may differ between ocean lines, coastal areas through which the shipments are moving, and for a variety of other circumstances. Ocean bills of lading are frequently negotiable, which means that whoever legally holds the document may take delivery of the shipment. Because nearly every ocean vessel line has its own bill of lading, a forwarder's experience is necessary to fill it out accurately.

Obtaining Consular Documents. Consular documents involve obtaining permission from the importing country for the goods to enter. Documents are prepared that the importing country uses to determine duties to be levied on the shipment as it passes through customs.

Arranging for Insurance. Unlike domestic shipments, international shipments must be insured. Either the individual shipment must be insured or else the shipper (or forwarder) must have a blanket policy covering all shipments. International airlines offer insurance at nominal rates. Rates on vessel shipments are higher, and the entire process is complex because of certain practices that are acceptable at sea. For example, if the vessel is in peril of sinking, the captain may have some cargo jettisoned (thrown overboard) to keep the vessel afloat. The owners of the surviving cargo and the vessel owner must then share the costs of reimbursing the shippers whose cargo was thrown overboard.

Preparing and Sending Shipping Notices and Documents. The financial transaction involving the sale of goods is carefully coordinated with their physical movement, and rather elaborate customs and procedures have evolved to ensure that the seller is paid when the goods are delivered. The export forwarder handles the shipper's role in the document preparation and exchange stages. It is necessary to have certain documents available as the shipment crosses international boundaries. (The forwarder serves to coordinate the logistics, documentation, and payment channels.)

Serving as General Consultant on Export Matters. Questions continually arise when dealing with new products, terms of sale, new markets, or new regulations. The forwarder knows the answers or how to find them. A conscientious forwarder also advises a shipper as to when certain procedures, such as similar shipments to the same market, become so repetitive that the shipper can handle the procedures in its own export department at a lower cost than the fees charged by the forwarder.

Export forwarders' income comes from three sources. Similar to domestic forwarders, they buy space wholesale and sell it retail—by consolidating shipments they benefit from a lower rate per pound. Second, most carriers allow the forwarders a commission on shipping revenues they generate for the carriers. Third, forwarders charge fees for preparing documents, performing research, and the like. Figures 11-5 and 11-6 show forms used by forwarders. Figure 11-5 is used to prepare cost estimates for the client to use when quoting a price to a potential overseas buyer. Figure 11-6 is the form that a forwarder uses to bill a client for handling a shipment.

Nonvessel-Operating Common Carriers (NVOCCs)

In recent years, a modified form of the forwarder operation known as the **nonvessel-operating common carrier (NVOCC)** has developed:

> Since the Motor Carrier Act of 1980, the NVOCC sector has been an extremely easy one to enter. The only requirement at present is that a prospective NVOCC owner must file a tariff with the Federal Maritime Commission and pay a small registration fee. Consequently, the industry has become extremely attractive both for an entrepreneur who wishes only to establish an NVOCC or for other transport-oriented companies that wish to extend their current range of services into the ocean segment of the logistics chain.[16]

NVOCCs can perform most—but not all—of the functions of a freight forwarder. However, they have much greater ability to enter into rate agreements with ocean and inland carriers, and they may issue single-rate quotations between inland points in one nation and inland points in another. NVOCCs frequently affiliate with forwarders so that they can offer their customers a more complete package of services.

Customs House Brokers

An opposite, but similar, function is performed by **customs house brokers**. They oversee the efficient movement of an importer's goods (and accompanying paperwork) through customs and other inspection points and stand ready to argue for a lower rate in case one of two commodity descriptions apply.

Export Management Companies

Sometimes the manufacturer seeking to export retains the services of an **export management company**, a firm that specializes in handling overseas transactions. These companies represent U.S. manufacturers and help them find overseas firms that can be licensed to manufacture their products. They also handle sales correspondence in foreign languages, ensure that foreign labeling requirements are met, and perform other specialized functions. When handling the overseas sales for a U.S. firm, the export management firm

---

[16] David J. Pope and Evelyn A. Thomchick, "U.S. Foreign Freight Forwarders and NVOCCs," *Transportation Journal*, Spring 1985, p. 29.

EXPORT QUOTATION WORKSHEET

DATE_____ REF/PRO FORMA INVOICE NO._____
COMMODITY_____ EXPECTED SHIP DATE_____
CUSTOMER_____ PACKED DIMENSIONS_____
COUNTRY_____ PACKED WEIGHT_____
PAYMENT TERMS_____ PACKED CUBE_____

PRODUCTS TO BE SHIPPED FROM _____
                        TO _____

SELLING PRICE OF GOODS: $_____

SPECIAL EXPORT PACKING:
   $_____   quoted by_____
   $_____   quoted by_____
   $_____   quoted by_____ $_____

INLAND FREIGHT:
   $_____   quoted by_____
   $_____   quoted by_____
   $_____   quoted by_____ $_____

   Inland freight includes the following charges:
   ☐ unloading   ☐ pier delivery   ☐ terminal   ☐ _____

OCEAN FREIGHT		AIR FREIGHT	
quoted by	tariff item	quoted by	spec code
$_____ _____	#_____	$_____ _____	#_____
$_____ _____	#_____	$_____ _____	#_____
$_____ _____	#_____	$_____ _____	#_____

Ocean freight includes the following surcharges: Air freight includes the following surcharges:

☐ Port congestion   ☐ Heavy lift   ☐ Fuel adjustment
☐ Currency adjustment ☐ Bunker   ☐ Container stuffing
☐ Container rental   ☐ Wharfage   ☐ _____
☐ _____   ☐ _____
INSURANCE ☐ includes war risk   ☐ INSURANCE   ☐ includes war risk
rate:_____ per $100 or $_____   rate:_____ per $100 or $_____

TOTAL OCEAN CHARGES $_____   TOTAL AIR CHARGES $_____ $_____
notes: notes:

FORWARDING FEES: $_____
Includes: ☐ Courier Fees ☐ Certification Fees ☐ Banking Fees ☐ _____

CONSULAR LEGALIZATION FEES: $_____

INSPECTION FEES: $_____

DIRECT BANK CHARGES: $_____

OTHER CHARGES: _____ $_____
                                                                 $_____

TOTAL: ☐ FOB_____   ☐ C & F_____
        ☐ FAS_____   ☐ CIF_____ $_____

Form 10-020 Printed and Sold by *UNZ&CO* 190 Baldwin Ave., Jersey City, NJ 07306 • (800) 631-3098

Figure 11-5 A forwarder's export quotation sheet showing factors to include when determining the price to quote a potential buyer of a product. (Reprinted with permission of Unz & Co., 190 Baldwin Ave., Jersey City, NJ 07306, USA.)

⌐			**INVOICE NO.**	
			DATE	
			YOUR REF. NO.	
∟				
CONSIGNEE:				

FROM:				CARRIER:	
TO:		☐ AIR	☐ OCEAN	B/L OR AWB NO.	
INLAND FREIGHT/LOCAL CARTAGE					$
EXPORT PACKING					
AIR FREIGHT CHARGES					
OCEAN FREIGHT/TERMINAL CHARGES					
CONSULAR FEES					
INSURANCE/CERTIFICATE OF INSURANCE					
CHAMBER OF COMMERCE					
BROKERAGE FEES					
FORWARDING					
HANDLING AND EXPEDITING					
DOCUMENT PREPARATION					
MESSENGER FEES					
POSTAGE					
TELEPHONE					
CABLES					
CERTIFICATE OF ORIGIN					
BANKING: (LETTER OF CREDIT/SIGHT DRAFT)					
MISCELLANEOUS					
As amended by the United States Shipping Act of 1984.				TOTAL	$

_____ has a policy against payment, solicitation,
or receipt of any rebate, directly or indirectly, which would be unlawful under the United States Shipping
Act, 1916, as amended

Figure 11-6 Invoice form used by a freight forwarder to bill client for handling an export shipment. (Reprinted with permission of Unz & Co., 190 Baldwin Ave., Jersey City, NJ 07306, USA.)

either buys and sells on its own account or else provides credit information regarding each potential buyer to the U.S. manufacturer, which can judge whether to take the risk.

Export management companies and international freight forwarders are closely related because together they can offer a complete overseas sales and distribution service to the domestic manufacturer that wants to export but just does not know how. Sometimes international forwarders and export management firms work out of the same office, the only apparent distinction being which phone line they answer. Export management companies are also retained by large firms that have exported for many years because they can perform their very specialized service less expensively than could the client.

Export Trading Companies

Export trading companies (ETCs) attempt to combine all facets of international business: sales, finance, communications, and logistics. They are widely used by the Japanese. The Export Trading Company Act of 1982 relaxed some of the antitrust restrictions that had prevented firms that competed in domestic markets from cooperating in overseas ventures. In addition, banks were given the right to acquire up to 100 percent equity interest in export trading companies (with the Federal Reserve Board's approval).

Shippers Associations

Widely used in foreign countries, **shippers associations** are trade groups that represent shippers of similar cargo that join together to bargain as a single entity with ocean steamship conferences (groups of ocean liner operators). They were not allowed in the United States until the Shipping Act of 1984.

Export Packers

As with the other export functions discussed to this point, there is a specialized service of export packing performed by firms typically located in port cities. **Export packers** custom pack shipments when the exporter lacks the equipment or the expertise to do so itself. However, when exporters have repeat business, they usually perform their own export packing.

Export packaging involves packaging for two distinct purposes (in addition to the sales function of some packaging). The first is to allow goods to move through customs easily. For a country assessing duties on the weight of both the item and its container, this means selecting lightweight packing materials. For items moving through the mail, it might mean construction of an envelope with an additional small flap that a customs inspector could open and look inside without having to open the entire envelope. For crated machinery, this might involve using open slats rather than completely closed construction (the customs inspectors would likely satisfy their curiosity by peering and probing through the openings between the slats).

The second purpose of export packing is to protect products in what almost always is a more difficult journey than they would experience if they were destined for domestic consignees. For many firms the traditional ocean packaging method is to take the product in its domestic pack and enclose it in a wooden container. Ocean shipments are subject to more moisture damage than are domestic shipments. Variations in temperatures are also more extreme. Canned goods moving through hot areas sweat, causing the cans to rust and the labels to become unglued.

Recent transportation equipment innovations have helped overcome the climatic problems of ocean shipping. International air freight, a post–World War II development, has made it possible to reach major cities throughout the world within twenty-four to forty-eight hours, avoiding the long sea voyage. Packaging for international air freight is sometimes no different than packaging for domestic markets. Containerships are able to provide better care for cargo since shipments are in individual containers that come equipped with freezing, refrigerating, or air-circulating equipment in case the cargo demands it. Each container can be handled differently, and the ship's personnel are detailed to check temperature gauges outside the containers several times daily.

In a 1994 meeting with Chinese businesspeople, one of the authors was queried at length as to why packaging was needed. The Chinese also could not understand why a separate packing industry was needed; they apparently relied on scrap around their operation to serve as packaging materials. The answer given was the following: Packaging is also needed for wider-scale distribution of one's product; as channels and supply chains lengthen, it is more necessary that the product be protected. Consumers also want assurance that the product they intend to buy was well protected.

Goods sold in foreign markets require additional labels. The metric system is widely used outside the United States, so most measurements of products must be expressed in metric terms.

For goods moving in foreign trade, it is not safe to assume that handlers can read English. Hence, cautionary symbols must be used. (See Figure 11-7.) Cargo moving aboard ocean vessels has distinct markings that identify the

keep away from heat

this way up

keep dry

use no hooks

Figure 11-7 Some of the symbols used for packing export shipments. (Courtesy of Air France Cargo.)

shipper, consignee, destination point, and piece number (in multipiece shipments). Some cartons and crates moving internationally are marked with what looks like a cattle brand. This is a shipper's mark, and a drawing of the mark also appears on the documentation. This is for use in areas where dock workers cannot read but need a method to keep documents and shipment together. As with domestic cargo, care must be taken so that pilferable items are not identified. This may include changing the symbols every few months. Figure 11-8 shows a package with the various markings required for movement in foreign commerce. The markings should be applied with a stencil, using waterproof ink. The bill of lading, packing list, letter of credit, and other documents pertaining to a shipment must contain similar markings. Note that markings on the box are in both inches and meters. Both weight and dimensions are given, because density is a factor in determining international transportation charges.

Persons making packaging materials decisions today must be very aware of environmentalists' views as to the wastefulness of many packaging practices. Environmentalists in some areas are conducting "buy naked" campaigns that encourage shoppers to buy materials that are totally unpackaged, and to leave any packaging in the retail store for the retailer to dispose of.

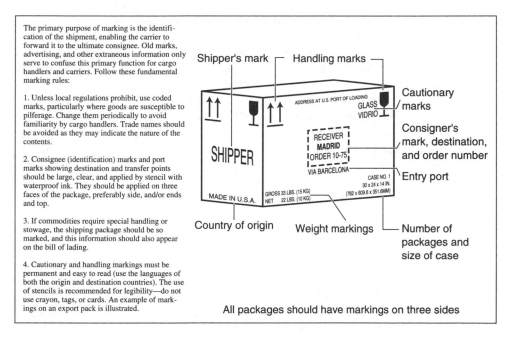

Figure 11-8 A package marked for export. (From *Ports of the World*, 15th ed., a publication of Cygna Property & Casualty.)

LOGISTICS CHANNELS IN INTERNATIONAL DISTRIBUTION

To this point in the chapter we have dealt with international negotiation, payment, and ownership channels. The remainder of the chapter addresses the logistics channel, which handles the physical movement of goods.

Most of this section deals with transportation. The first part deals with the landward move to the port or airport. The second and third sections deal with international air and ocean shipping. The last section deals with the landward leg in the foreign country. Although much of what is presented is from the viewpoint of the exporter, it is important to remember that the movement of goods requires cooperation and coordination among seller, buyer, and many intermediate parties.

Before moving to more visible forms of international transportation, we should mention pipelines that carry petroleum, petroleum products, and natural gas. In terms of tonnages and value, they are some of the most important forms of international transport. Their huge investment costs are justified only because they are used to carry major hauls.

Movement to Port or Airport

For air shipments, or for products moving by rail or truck to Canada or Mexico, the movement from the manufacturer's plant is similar to that for domestic sales. The only difference is that more paperwork accompanies each shipment. Usually the same equipment is used for the entire haul to Canada. However, for shipments to Mexico, the product is often transferred at the border into Mexican railcars or truck trailers. Delays at the Mexican border are common.

Ports that handled foreign trade were traditionally grouped for rate-making purposes. This meant that the shipper at some inland point would pay the same rail rate and the same ocean rate, no matter which port was used. Carriers and ports competed in terms of service quality. However, since the railroads were deregulated in 1980, the concept of port equalization has been destroyed and service contracts between railroads and shippers have disrupted traditional cargo routing patterns. We now see a few ports handling large shares of traffic.

Traffic destined to move through ports is first loaded aboard intermodal containers at an inland point and then sent forward without interruption. Vessel lines operating between U.S. Pacific Coast ports and Western Europe frequently find it cheaper to discharge and load their containerized cargo at East Coast ports and have it move by rail across the United States. The vessel line pays for the rail haul but saves the voyage through the Panama Canal. The shipper or consignee pays the same freight rate but benefits because time in transit is reduced by about four days. Similar service is available for East Coast firms doing business with the Orient. These services are examples of

land bridge operations. Figure 11-9 is an ad for mini-bridge service, with trains departing from the West Coast. The vessels sail from Gulf and Atlantic ports to the Middle East. The West Coast shipper gives the cargo to the ocean shipping line in either Seattle-Tacoma, San Francisco, or Los Angeles by the specified date, and the ocean carrier moves it by rail across the United States.

A UNITED ARAB

SHIPPING COMPANY   The National Flag Line of the Arabian States of Saudi Arabia, U.A.E., Bahrain, Qatar, Kuwait and Iraq

USA/Middle East Express Container Service

MINI-BRIDGE DEPARTING	DARZAN V-36	JEBEL ALI V-36	ADDIRIYAH V-35	AL WATIYAH V-35
SEATTLE / PORTLAND	JUL 13	JUL 27	AUG 13	AUG 28
SAN FRANCISCO	JUL 17	JUL 31	AUG 16	AUG 30
LOS ANGELES	JUL 20	AUG 3	AUG 20	SP 3
SAILS				
HOUSTON	JUL 26	AUG 9	AUG 26	SEP 10
SAVANNAH	JUL 30	AUG 13	AUG 30	SEP 14
NORFOLK	AUG 3	AUG 15	SEP 1	SEP 16
BALTIMORE	AUG 4	AUG 16	SEP 2	SEP 17
NEW YORK	AUG 6	AUG 18	SEP 4	SEP 18
ARRIVES				
JEDDAH	AUG 22	SEP 3	SEP 20	OCT 4
DUBAI	AUG 28	SEP 9	SEP 26	OCT 10
BAHRAIN	SEP 4	SEP 16	OCT 3	OCT 17
DAMMAN	AUG 30	SEP 11	SEP 28	OCT 12
JUBAIL / ABU DHABI / DOHA	SEP 4	SEP 16	OCT 3	OCT 17
KUWAIT	SEP 1	SEP 12	SEP 29	OCT 13
BOMBAY	SEP 4	SEP 16	OCT 3	OCT 17
MUTTRAH	SEP 4	SEP 15	OCT 2	OCT 16

FCL to Iraq all vessels.
LCL accepted from EC/GULF to all ports except Iraq.
Cut off date for LCL cargo from EC/GULF ports is three (3) working days prior to ETD.
Reefer containers available from EC/Gulf ports.
Ras Al Mishab on inducement.
FCL accepted from Jacksonville, Miami, Tampa, Charleston, Philadelphia, Boston, Montreal and Toronto.

GENERAL AGENTS

KERR STEAMSHIP COMPANY, INC.

LONG BEACH	SAN FRANCISCO	PORTLAND/VANC., WA	SEATTLE	VANCOUVER	HOUSTON
4401 ATLANTIC AVE.	ONE MARKET PLAZA	ONE S.W. COLUMBIA ST	800 FIFTH AVE.	1135 TWO BENTAL CENTRE	2727 ALLEN PARKWAY
(213) 422-1132	(415) 764-0200	SUITE 450	(206) 628-6700	(604) 682-5881	SUITE 1500
		(503) 220-2500			(713) 521-9600

Figure 11-9   Mini-bridge schedule. (Courtesy of United Arab Shipping Company.)

International Air Freight

In relative terms, air freight has probably had a more profound effect on international distribution than on domestic distribution because the airplane has reduced worldwide distances. While transit times between the two U.S.

coasts have shrunk from five days to less than one, some international transit times have shrunk from as many as thirty days down to one or two.

There are two types of international air freight operations: chartered aircraft and scheduled air carriers. Chartering an entire aircraft is, of course, expensive, but sometimes the expense can be justified. For example, chartered aircraft have been used in the international transport of livestock sold for breeding purposes. One charter airline carried 7,000 cattle from Texas to southern Chile. Nineteen flights were involved, each lasting fifteen hours. The comparable time by sea was twenty days, and past experience showed that the sea journey was hard on the cattle, causing either lung damage or long delays before the animals could be bred. The cost of the chartered aircraft was justified by the reduction in time that the breeding stock was nonproductive. The aircraft were specially equipped with lightweight flooring, gates, and kick-panels (an animal's sharp hoof can pierce the side of the plane). Prior to being loaded aboard the plane, the livestock were kept in feedlots and given a transitional diet that combined both the food to which they were accustomed and the food they would be getting at their destination.

The schedules and routes of international air carriers are established by negotiations between the nations involved. Rates are established by the **International Air Transport Association** (IATA), a large cartel consisting of nearly all the world's scheduled airlines. The principal function of international airlines is to carry passengers. Freight is a secondary product, although a few scheduled airlines use some all-freight aircraft in certain markets. Lufthansa, the German airline, was the first airline in the world to use an all-cargo Boeing 747. It was used in trans-Atlantic service and connected Germany with the northeastern United States. It replaced several smaller planes. Compared with earlier jets, the 747 has enormous capacity. Figure 11-10 shows several configurations. In addition to the planes shown in Figure 11-10, Lufthansa flies Boeing 737s in all-freight configurations, Airbus 320s and Airbus 321s in passenger freight configurations, and four other versions of the Boeing 747. Figure 11-11 shows several container sizes used by international airlines.

In the 1980s the most significant international air cargo development was the introduction into numerous foreign trade routes of Boeing 747s with main-deck cargo configurations. The three different 747 models that can carry cargo on their main deck are the 747-200F, an all-freighter, and the 747-200C and the 747-200B, both of which can have their main deck in all passenger, all cargo, or various combinations of seating and cargo-carrying configurations. Some of these 747s have a movable bulkhead that can be changed as the relative amounts of passengers and cargo vary; this model is called a *combi*. This enables the airline to adjust for seasonal changes in passenger travel. Also, the carrier has more flexibility in case there are changes in the relative strength of passenger and freight movements.

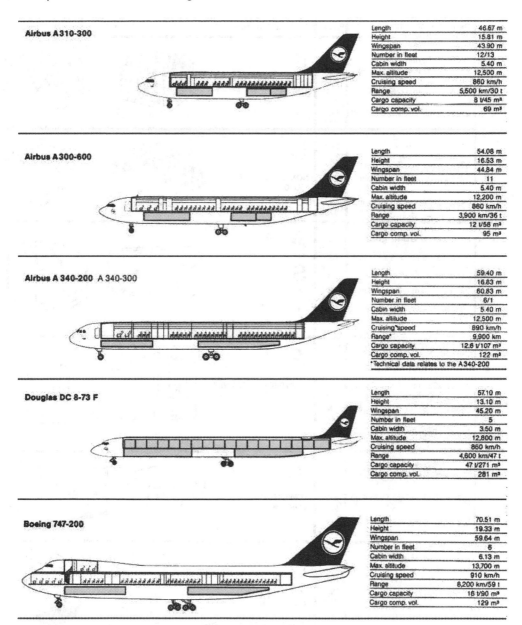

Figure 11-10 Aircraft freight capacity. (Courtesy of Lufthansa Cargo.)

For shippers of large quantities, international airlines offer a unit-load incentive in conjunction with some FAK (freight-all-kinds) rates. The airline supplies large pallets and, if necessary, igloos (a fiberglass pallet cover placed over the load to protect it and ensure that it does not exceed the allowable

Description Base Dims.	Prefix	Code and Illustration
Pallet/Net 2235 x 3175 mm (88 x 125 in) 2235 x 2743 mm (88 x 108 in) 2438 x 3175 mm (96 x 125 in) 2438 x 6058 mm (96 x 238½ in)	PA PB (PD) PM (PQ) PG (PS)	**P** AIRCRAFT PALLET AND NET 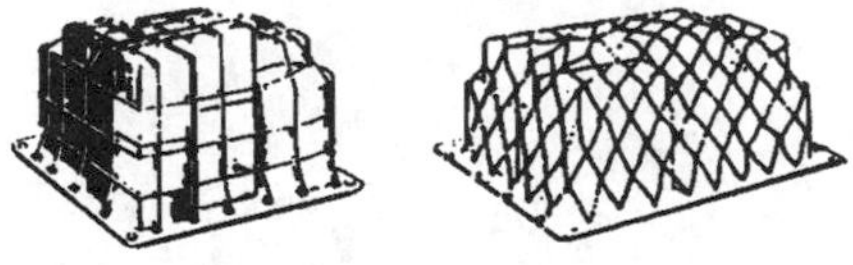
Igloo/Net 2235 x 3175 mm (88 x 125 in) 2235 x 2743 mm (88 x 108 in) 2438 x 3175 mm (96 x 125 in)	UA UB (UD) UM (UQ)	**U** NON-STRUCTUAL IGLOO 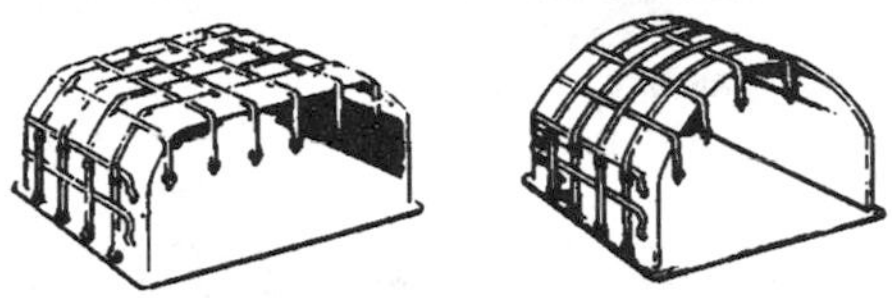
Structual Igloo 2235 x 3175 mm (88 x 125 in) 2235 x 2743 mm (88 x 108 in)	AA (SA) (TA) AB (AD)	**A** or **S** or **T** STRUCTURAL IGLOO 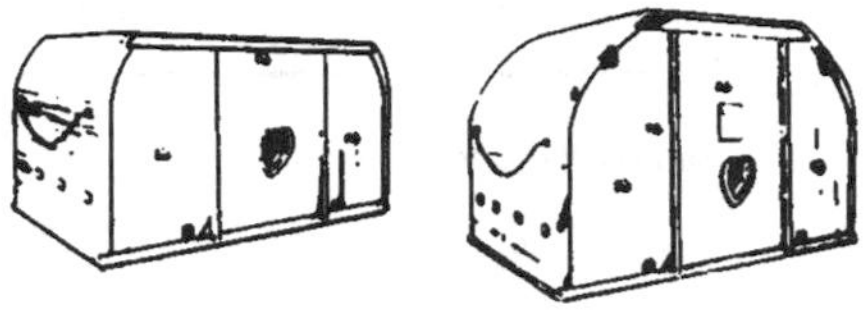
8' x 8' Maindeck Container 2438 x 2981 mm (96 x 117¾ in) 2438 x 3175 mm (96 x 125 in) 2438 x 6058 mm (96 x 238 ½ in)	AF (AR) AM (AQ) AG (S)	**A** MAIN DECK CONTAINER 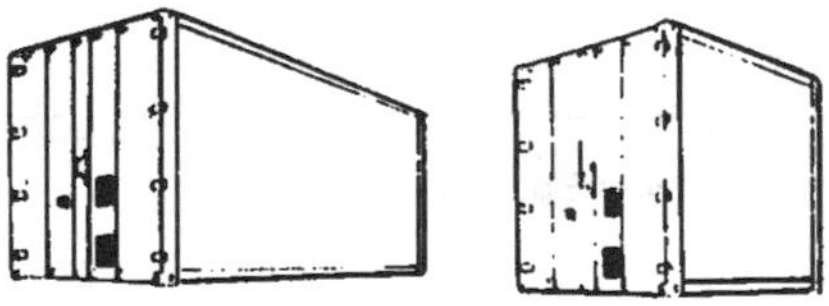
Lower Deck Certified Cont. 1534 x 1562 mm (60.4 x 61.5 in) 1534 x 3175 mm (60.4 x 125 in)	AK (AV) AL (AW)	**A** LOWER DECK CONTAINER 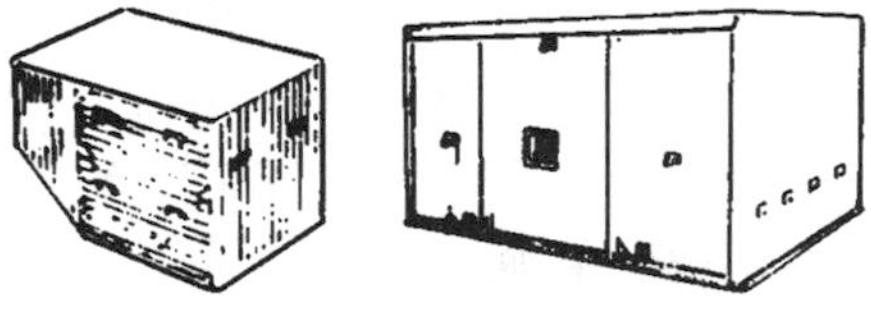
Non-Certified Aircraft Cont. 1534 x 1562 mm (60.4 x 61.5 in) 1534 x 3175 mm (60.4 x 125 in)	DK (DV) DL (DW)	**D** NON-CERTIFIED CONTAINER (May be made from material other than metal) 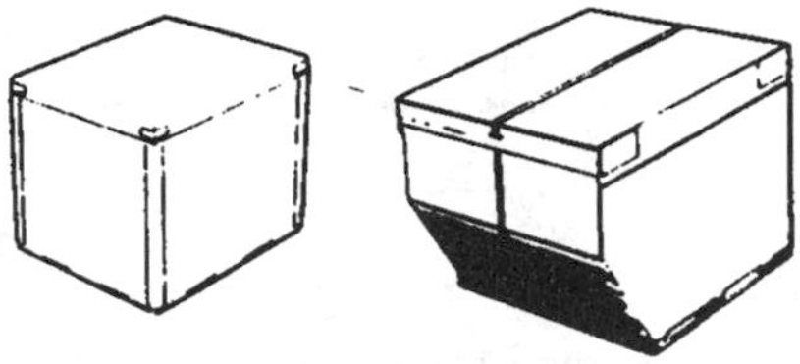

Figure 11-11 Large containers used by international airlines. (Courtesy of International Air Transport Association.)

dimensions). To obtain the lower rates from IATA carriers, the shipper must tender the pallet loaded to airline specifications; at the other end of the journey, the entire pallet must be destined to one consignee. A special charge is made if it is necessary to unload or partially unload the pallet for customs inspection. Both the shipper and consignee may have the pallet for forty-eight hours each before demurrage charges are assessed.

The result of the IATA incentives to use containers and unit loads has been to increase the average size of shipments handled by the airlines. This has reduced the number of individual packages each airline terminal must handle. Air freight forwarders have benefited since they are frequently in a better position than individual shippers to take advantage of incentives offered for larger shipments.

International air freight forwarders use a document entitled the Shipper's Letter of Instructions, which is frequently the only document the shipper must execute. Shippers not using forwarders need to have their own airway bill prepared.

International air cargo rates are published in tariffs available from the airlines. There are both general cargo rates and lower specific commodity rates. Rate breaks encourage heavier shipments. Excerpts from a tariff with freight rates from Houston to some Latin American destinations are given in Figure 11-12. Most rates today are computerized.

A new development in international air freight has been international parcel services offered by well-known carriers such as UPS, FedEx, and DHL. The couriers provide land pickup and delivery services for documents and small parcels. These courier services are of special significance to international logistics because they often provide the fastest service between many major points. They are also often employed to carry the documentation that is generated by—and is very much a part of—the international movement of materials. These services also handle documentation services for their clients.

Ocean Shipping

The past decades have seen two significant advances in shipping technology: larger vessels and improved cargo-handling techniques. Newly constructed tankers in use today have thirty to forty times the capacity of World War II–vintage T-2 tankers. Methods of handling cargo are now much more efficient, especially in the handling of break-bulk general cargo. For centuries it had been loaded or unloaded on a piece-by-piece basis after being lifted by the ship's boom and tackle.

The capacity of a merchant fleet is measured in terms of deadweight tonnage. Of the entire world's fleet in 1990, some 39 percent of the total tonnage was for oil tankers, 30 percent was for ore and dry bulk carriers, 6 percent was for combi carriers, 16 percent was for break-bulk general

BULK GENERAL & SPECIFIC COMMODITY CARGO RATES FROM THE U.S. AND CANADA

From: HOUSTON (HOU)

Airline	Item	Commodity Description	Minimum Charge($)	1	100	220	440	660	880	1100	2200	4400	Note	Flight Days
		To: COZUMEL (CZM)												
AMERICAN AIRLINES (AA)	GEN	General Commodity	37.00	68	59	57	57	53	53	50	50	50		
		To: CURACAO (CUR)												
EASTERN AIRLINES (EA)	GEN	General Commodity	40.00	144	108	108	108	102	102	83	83	83		
VIASA AIRLINES (VA)	GEN	General Commodity	50.00	146	108	108	108	102	102	88	88	88		
		To: DOMINICA (DOM)												
CARICARGO (DC)	GEN	General Commodity	50.00	121	97	97	97	97	97	79	79	79		
		To: FORT DE FRANCE (FDF)												
CARICARGO (DC)	GEN	General Commodity	50.00	115	94	94	94	94	94	79	79	79		
EASTERN AIRLINES (EA)	GEN	General Commodity	40.00	155	108	108	108	108	108	97	97	97		3
		To: FREEPORT (FPO)												
EASTERN AIRLINES (EA)	GEN	General Commodity	35.00	90	69	69	69	69	69	57	57	57		
		To: GEORGETOWN (GEO)												
CARICARGO (DC)	GEN	General Commodity	50.00	125	112	112	112	112	112	95	95	95		4
		To: GRAND CAYMAN (GCM)												
CAYMAN AIRWAYS (KX)	GEN	General Commodity	39.00	80	66	66	66	66	66	55	55	55		
CAYMAN AIRWAYS (KX)	GEN	General Commodity	39.00	80	66	66	66	66	66	55	55	55		
CAYMAN AIRWAYS (KX)	0006	Foodstuffs, Spices, Beverages								35	35	35		
		To: GRENADA (GND)												
CARICARGO (DC)	GEN	General Commodity	50.00	116	94	94	94	94	94	78	78	78		1
		To: GUADALAJARA (GDL)												
AMERICAN AIRLINES (AA)	GEN	General Commodity	37.00	44	34	34	34	34	34	31	31	31		
		To: GUATEMALA CITY (GUA)												
AVIATECA AIRLINES (GU)	GEN	General Commodity	45.00	81	59	59	59	56	56	50	50	50		1,3,5
EASTERN AIRLINES (EA)	GEN	General Commodity	45.00	137	104	104	104	92	92	78	78	78		
TACA INTERNATIONAL (TA)	GEN	General Commodity	45.00	78	78	56	56	56	56	50	50	50		1,3,5,6
AVIATECA AIRLINES (GU)	1081	Baby Poultry						44	44	44	44	44		
	2199	Textiles, Clothing or Footwear						45	45	38	38	38		
	4206	Surface Vehicle Parts						45	45	38	38	38		
TACA INTERNATIONAL (TA)	4742	Oil Drill Machines/Parts												
AVIATECA AIRLINES (GU)	6001	Chemicals,Drugs,Pharm.Medicine						50	50	42	42	42		
		To: GUAYAQUIL (GYE)												
AECA AIRLINES (2A)	GEN	General Commodity	50.00	117	89	89	89	68	68	68	68	54 ag		
AEROPERU (PL)	GEN	General Commodity	50.00	131	98	98	98	80	80	69	69	69		
AIR PANAMA (OP)	GEN	General Commodity	40.00	131	98	98	98	80	80	69	69	69		
EASTERN AIRLINES (EA)	GEN	General Commodity	50.00	228	171	171	171	145	145	120	120	120		2,3,5,6,7
ECUATORIANA (EU)	GEN	General Commodity	50.00	224	168	168	168	142	142	117	117	117		
LADECO AIRLINES (UC)	GEN	General Commodity	50.00	166	125	125	125	101	101	88	88,	88		
		To: IQUIQUE (IOQ)												
FAST AIR (UD)	GEN	General Commodity	50.00	370	279	279	279	279	279	198	198	198		
LAN-CHILE (LA)	GEN	General Commodity	50.00	375	283	283	283	283	283	211	211	211		Daily
		To: IQUITOS (IQT)												
FAUCETT AIRLINES (CF)	GEN	General Commodity	45.00	193	138	138	138	116	116	110	110	110		
LAN-CHILE (LA)	GEN	General Commodity	50.00	256	200	200	200	161	161	140	140	140		3,6,7

Figure 11-12 Excerpts from an air freight tariff showing rates from Houston to several Latin American points. (Courtesy of CRS Publishing Division, Miami.)

cargo, and 4 percent was containerships.[17] Other categories accounted for 5 percent.

Types of Ocean Cargoes.   Much of the world's shipping tonnage is used for carrying petroleum. The tankers are either owned by oil companies or leased (chartered) by them from individuals who invest in ships. The leased vessels are chartered for specific voyages or for large blocks of time. The charter market fluctuates widely, especially after events such as the closing and opening of the Suez Canal and the announcement of large U.S. wheat sales overseas. International commodity traders follow the vessel charter market closely because they know the differences in commodity prices in various world markets. When the charter rate between these two markets drops to the point that it is less than the spread in the commodity prices, a vessel is chartered to carry the commodity.

Dry bulk cargoes, such as grain, ores, sulfur, sugar, scrap iron, coal, lumber, and logs, usually move in complete vessel-load lots on chartered vessels. A bulk carrier is shown in Figure 11-13. There are also large, specialized dry cargo ships often owned by shippers. Nissan Motor Company of Japan, for example, owns eight auto-carrying ships, four of which can carry 1,200 autos apiece and the other four of which carry 1,900.[18] Most of these vessels carry autos to the United States and can then load with soybeans for the return voyages.

Independent dry cargo vessels, often referred to as *tramps*, can be chartered for carrying relatively large shipments of high-value cargo in situations where the cargo can be assembled at one time. The traffic manager of General Electric International noted that one advantage of chartering an entire ship to carry all equipment and materials needed for an overseas project is better scheduling, in that all participants do everything possible to be ready for the sailing of the ship. The procedure has worked better than the traditional approach of sending the equipment and materials on a series of liner sailings. With chartering, however, those involved must all meet one specific date because there is not "always another vessel" sailing next week.[19]

If a single shipper's needs do not fill the vessel completely, the vessel is topped off with compatible bulk cargo, such as grain, that can be loaded into an unused hold. This helps defray the total voyage costs for the party using the ship. Agents specialize in chartering fractional spaces (often individual holds) in vessels.

[17] United Nations Conference on Trade and Development, *Review of Maritime Transport, 1990* (New York: UN, 1991), p. 17.

[18] The term *neobulk* is sometimes applied to cargoes, whether manufactured or processed, that move in volume on specialized or dedicated vessels, such as autos, steel, logs, and cattle.

[19] Comments of Jack Scally, traffic manager, GE International, at Port of Oakland's International Transportation Conference, October 26, 1978.

Figure 11-13 An ocean bulk carrier being loaded with export coal carried by a mechanical device at far left. (Photo courtesy Electro-Coal Transfer Corp., Davant, Louisiana.)

Another type of vessel that combines aspects of several is the parcel tanker. These vessels have over fifty different tanks, ranging from 350 to 2,200 cubic meters. Each can carry a different liquid and is loaded and unloaded through a separate piping system. The tanks have different types of coating; some are temperature-controlled. Some of the vessels go on round-the-world voyages and carry palm oil, coconut oil, chemicals, and refined petroleum products. Stolt-Nielsen is the firm best-known for this service. The firm's planning director, Robert F. Matthes, described its operations as "a loosely defined liner service."[20] He also noted that there is a significant adjustment in business planning taking place toward a concept of through transportation services. This not only includes offering through bills of lading and overland transport but other services necessary for the transport of bulk liquids. Note that this is an example of a carrier widening the range of services it makes available to its customers.

[20] *American Shipper*, May 1986, p. 78.

Shipping Conferences.   Ocean general-cargo (or break-bulk) liner rates are set by **shipping conferences**, which are cartels of all vessel operators operating between certain trade areas. Conferences provide stability in markets where cargo offerings fluctuate. Members agree to provide relatively regular service, and a shipper that agrees to use them exclusively pays a rate that is lower than that charged to shippers that do not agree to use the conference exclusively. Many different conferences serve U.S. ports. Examples are the Gulf/UK Conference, which handles trade from U.S. Gulf Coast ports to England, Ireland, Scotland, and Wales; and the Israel/U.S. North Atlantic Westbound Conference, which handles trade from Israel's Mediterranean ports to U.S. ports from Portland, Maine, to Hampton Roads, Virginia. Some conferences are very stable and well disciplined; others are not. Recently the number has declined, with each covering a larger geographic area. Some are now being called "rate agreements."

Service contracts are permitted under the Shipping Act of 1984; they are drawn up between conferences and specific shippers or shippers' associations. A service contract consists of "a commitment by the shipper to the conference or carrier of a minimum volume of cargo, usually expressed in TEU (20-foot container equivalent units) with rate levels indicated as intermodal, point to point, or port to port. The contract is for a specific period of time. The carrier or conference must guarantee regular service, perhaps a particular port rotation and specialized equipment."[21] "Port rotation" means the pattern in which the vessel calls at ports. There are also clauses for damages in case the shipper does not live up to its commitment—a typical shipper's problem is loss of overseas sales. Most contracts cover containerized cargo and many have a most-favored shipper clause, meaning that if the conference gives another similarly situated shipper a better rate, the initial contracting shipper also gets it. Some contracts have a "Crazy Eddie clause," named after a former New York appliance dealer who vowed in television commercials never to be undersold. This clause requires the ship line to match any rate offered by a competitor.

An example of a service contract is for FAK (freight-all-kinds) rates to a number of inland U.S. points from Hong Kong and Taiwan. The contract is for one year, and the shipper commits to 1,000 FEUs. If 1,001 to 1,500 FEUs are shipped, there is a 1.5 percent discount; if over 1,500 FEUs are shipped, the discount is 2.5 percent. For a twenty-foot container from Hong Kong to Long Beach, Oakland, or Seattle, the rate is $950; for a forty-foot container, it is $1,250. For the same shipments to Portland, Oregon, charges are $1,150 and $1,450. To New Orleans, costs are $1,950 and $2,700. To Boston, Jacksonville, and Philadelphia, rates are $2,300 and $3,000.[22]

---

[21] "Are Service Accords Destined to Survive?" *Handling and Shipping Management,* February 1987, p. 27.

[22] *American Shipper,* December 1986, p. 16.

Note the higher rates to Portland, Oregon, compared with rates to other West Coast ports. Containerization, larger container vessels, and the use of double-stack container trains have reduced the number of ports handling cargo to a few *load center* ports, an idea that favors the few.

Containers.   Today operators of general cargo vessels might never handle, or even see, cargo on a piece-by-piece basis. Their ships are fully containerized, which means the only way they can load or unload cargo is to have the cargo stowed inside containers. Shippers or forwarders tender full containers, and if a shipper tenders a less-than-container lot, the vessel operator must load all the less-than-container lots into containers so that the cargo can be loaded aboard the containership.

Figure 11-14 shows the side and top views of a large containership. Note that some of the containers are carried above the level of the deck; this increases the vessel's cubic carrying capacity.

LASH (lighter aboard ship) vessels handle floating containers. They can be used most advantageously where the central port is connected to inland areas by shallow waterways. Similar conditions must exist on both ends of the voyage, so the applicability of the system is somewhat limited. LASH barges are approximately sixty feet long, thirty feet wide, and thirteen feet deep, or about 20,000 cubic feet. They carry about 400 short tons. The LASH concept is relatively new, and its success is still being evaluated. The Seabee concept is similar except that the barges are larger. A typical Seabee barge is 100 feet long, 35 feet wide, and 13 feet deep.

RO-RO (roll on–roll off) vessels are somewhat like large floating parking lots. They have large doors in their stern or on their sides. Ramps are stretched to the shore, and cargo is moved on or off the ship in trailers. RO-RO vessels are used to carry vehicles that can move using their own power. A RO-RO vessel that operates between Florida and Puerto Rico is shown in Figure 11-15.

Although the various types of vessels have been discussed separately, many vessels carry cargo loaded by various techniques. Most LASH and RO-RO vessels, for example, also carry conventional containers.

Surface Transport in Other Countries

The quality of transport facilities in foreign nations varies. Some are as well developed as those in the United States, but two important differences should be pointed out. First, few foreign nations have as wide a range of modes to choose from, because the United States makes a greater effort to encourage all modes of transportation. Second, the degree of nationalization of transportation is higher in most foreign countries than in the United States.

The widespread use of seaborne containers has brought about hopes of standardizing land vehicles for carrying containers on the landward legs of

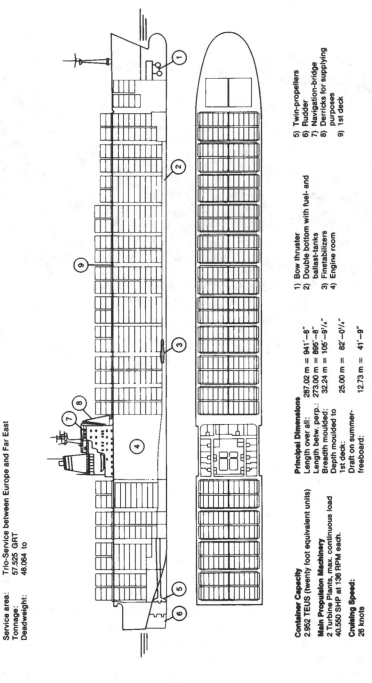

Containership "Hongkong Express"

Service area: Trio-Service between Europe and Far East
Tonnage: 57.525 GRT
Deadweight: 48.064 to

Container Capacity
2.952 TEUS (twenty foot equivalent units)

Main Propulsion Machinery
2 Turbine Plants, max. continuous load
40.550 SHP at 136 RPM each.

Cruising Speed:
26 knots

Principal Dimensions

Length over all:	287.02 m =	941'–8"
Length betw. perp.:	273.00 m =	895'–8"
Breadth moulded:	32.24 m =	105'–9¹/₄"
Depth moulded to		
1st deck:	25.00 m =	82'–0¹/₄"
Draft on summer-		
freeboard:	12.73 m =	41'–9"

1) Bow thruster
2) Double bottom with fuel- and ballast-tanks
3) Finstabilizers
4) Engine room
5) Twin-propellers
6) Rudder
7) Navigation-bridge
8) Derricks for supplying purposes
9) 1st deck

Figure 11-14 Side and top views of the layout of a containership. (Courtesy of Hapag-Lloyd AG.)

Figure 11-15 A RO-RO vessel in Jacksonville, Florida. (Courtesy of Jacksonville Port Authority.)

their journey. The European Common Market has been making progress in its attempt to standardize truck dimensions within its member countries. Truck-borne containers are now familiar sights throughout much of the world. Trucks appear to be in universal use. However, there is growing opposition to trucks in some European nations, such as Switzerland, that trucks cross while moving between other nations. They are trying to force the use of containers on rail.

Rail equipment sizes and clearances vary throughout the world, and most nations use equipment that is much smaller than that used in the United States. Containers that can be loaded two to a railcar in the United States are frequently carried on individual railcars elsewhere. A variety of rail gauges complicates the exchange of traffic between nations.

One of the difficulties in implementing international transport technological improvements is that fairly identical handling equipment must be in place at each end of the trip. In a few parts of the world, grain and sugar are still stowed or unloaded by stevedores carrying individual bags on their shoulders and walking up and down gangplanks. In handling relief cargoes to Africa, one finds that cargo handling techniques there are primitive. Aircraft may be unloaded by workers carrying bags of grain on their shoulders. In Somalia the port at Mogadishu had been inactive for some time because of silt and sunken hulls, and it could not receive loads of relief cargo on vessels of sizes in common use.

The incidence (or burden) of costs is also significant. RO-RO shipping involves the use of trailers rather than containers to be carried aboard ship as though it were a large ferry boat. Once loaded, there is considerable waste space—essentially the height of each trailer box above the deck floor. Thus, a vessel cannot carry as much cargo within a given amount of space. Yet the required port facilities are relatively inexpensive; there need only be a ramp for driving the trailers on or off the ship. The trailers can be hitched to tractors and hauled directly to or from their landward destination. So, although more is spent per ton of cargo on vessel operations, less is spent for port operations. Vessel lines can sometimes force a port to add cargo-handling equipment by placing a surcharge against the port for all shipments until such equipment is installed.

INTERNATIONAL TRADE INVENTORIES

Even under the best conditions, the movement of products in an international supply chain is never as smooth as a comparable domestic movement. Because there are always greater uncertainties, misunderstandings, and delays in international movements, safety stocks must be larger.

Firms involved in international trade must modify their inventory policies, or at least give them careful thought. Most nations represent smaller potential marketing areas than the United States; thus, the inventory necessary to serve any one of them will be smaller. An inventory held in one nation may not necessarily serve the needs of markets in neighboring nations because there may be minor, but significant, variations in the specifications of the product sold in each country.

> The thorniest conflicts between domestic and international interests [within a firm] often center around issues of market size. Plans for domestic production and inventory tend to be geared to demands of the company's primary market—usually the domestic one. So when a compromise is struck for purposes of export modification, as one executive notes: "A lot of that compromise is based on who is going to buy the most, and what market has the greater potential."[23]

Also, duties may have to be paid each time a product crosses a national boundary, although there is frequently a provision for *duty-drawbacks*, which provide the rebate of all (or nearly all) of a duty if the imported product is exported, usually within a specified time period of its initial entry.

[23] *Adapting Products for Export* (New York: Conference Board, 1983), p. 23.

Return items are virtually impossible to accommodate in an international distribution operation, especially if the return involves movements of the goods across a national boundary. This has some implications to a firm trying to achieve a high level of customer service standards on an international basis, since it may be unreasonable to tell buyers to return a defective item to the factory where it was built. One U.S. retail chain tells its stores to contact directly the domestic producers with questions regarding product defects. However, for imported products, there is no recourse. The stores are told to destroy the products or sell them at salvage prices.

Import and export quotas affect values of inventories. Inventory valuation on an international scale is difficult because the relative values of various currencies continually change. The value of wheat held in a nation's grain elevators will be the world market price, adjusted for transportation, unless the government places an embargo on wheat exports (or imports). The value of the wheat within the nation then becomes the domestic price. When a nation's (or the world's) currency is unstable, investments in inventories rise because they are believed to be less risky than holding cash or securities.

Computer programs have been developed that aid in managing international inventories. One such system, used by the Cummins Engine Company, is located at that firm's Brussels warehouse, which handles distribution to eighteen countries in Western Europe. Some of its unique features include its multilanguage capabilities and its use of current relative values of the various national currencies. The multilanguage capability allows translation into whatever languages are necessary to prepare shipping documents, invoices, and so on. The currency conversion feature enables invoices to be drawn in the buyer's home currency. In addition, a feature is used to instruct the warehouse to fill the order in a way that minimizes the amount of duty to be paid. To accomplish this, the computer needs to know the applicable tariff rates between the goods' nation (or nations) of origin and the nation of sale. It must also take into account that day's relative values of world currencies, because this will have an impact on the true amount of duties that must be paid.[24]

SUMMARY

Chapter 11 covers various aspects of international logistics. It differs from domestic logistics in many respects, such as by having a requirement for numerous documents. It is also dependent on fluctuating currency values, since they cause shifts in the flows of commerce. Governments attempt to influence foreign trade, in part because export sales help their economies, balance of payments, and currency values. They also may discourage imports

[24] The system was developed by Distribution Systems Management Systems, Inc., of Lexington, Massachusetts, and is described in the firm's brochures.

by imposing tariffs or other restrictions (sometimes known as nontariff barriers). Governments subsidize their international shipping and airlines.

International sourcing is a new term that means looking anywhere in the world for inputs to one's production process.

Because international logistics is complex, many firms rely on specialists to help with export and import transactions. These foreign trade specialists include freight forwarders, NVOCCs, customs house brokers, export packers, and others.

Finally, the chapter examines the transportation elements involved in an export shipment. These include the move to a port or airport, the move aboard a plane or ship, and delivery overseas. A brief discussion of international trade inventories is also given.

QUESTIONS FOR DISCUSSION AND REVIEW

1. In what ways does international logistics differ from domestic logistics?
2. What are some of the documents required in international trade?
3. Why are international freight forwarders needed? What functions do they perform?
4. How are transportation rates for international shipments set?
5. Why are international air carriers and vessel operators using more containers? What impact does this have on the individual shipper?
6. What is a land bridge? A mini land bridge?
7. How are international freight forwarders compensated?
8. Why do developing nations prefer that their own citizens rather than foreigners be employed in new industries?
9. Why should international shipments be insured? What is especially unique about the need for insuring cargo on vessels?
10. What services do export management firms perform?
11. What are the differences between managing an inventory of goods for domestic consumption and managing goods destined for consumption in foreign countries?
12. What functions do import brokers perform?
13. How are irrevocable letters of credit used in international transactions?
14. Why do governments exert considerable control over international trade?
15. How does export labeling differ from labeling for domestic markets?
16. How does export packing differ from packing for domestic shipments?
17. What is international sourcing? Give some examples.
18. What is the IATA? What functions does it perform?
19. What are the differences between using a tramp vessel and using a conference liner vessel?

20. Discuss briefly each of the following:

  a. RO-RO vessels

  b. TEU

  c. NVOCC

  d. Service contract

SUGGESTED READINGS

Bagchi, Prabir K., and Tage Skjott-Larsen. "Logistics Strategy in Integrated Europe." In James Masters (ed.), *Logistics at the Crossroads of Commerce* (Columbus: Ohio State University Transportation and Logistics Research Fund, 1994), pp. 97–121.

Brooks, Mary R. "The Ocean Container Carrier Market—Is It Segmentable?" *Proceedings, 35th Meeting of the TRF, 1993,* pp. 351–361.

Bruning, Edward R. "Code of Conduct for Liner Conferences: Its Significance for Developing Nations." *Transportation Practitioners Journal,* Spring 1985, pp. 340–348.

Clayton, Brian R., et al. "International Transactions: An Integrated Systems Approach." *Papers, CLM 1988 Annual Meeting,* vol. 1 (Oak Brook, Ill: Council of Logistics Management, 1988), pp. 133–160.

Dresner, Martin, and Robert J. Windle. "The Liberalization of U.S. International Air Policy: Impact on U.S. Markets and Carriers." *Journal of the Transportation Research Forum* (1992), pp. 273–285.

Ellram, Lisa M. "Patterns in International Alliances." *Journal of Business Logistics,* vol. 13, no. 1 (1992), pp. 1–25.

Fawcett, Stanley E., and David B. Vellenga. "Sea-Air: Opportunities and Challenges in Intermodal Transportation." *Journal of the Transportation Research Forum* (1988), pp. 101–110.

Foggin, James H., and Carol M. Foggin. *Bibliography on International Logistics Environments.* (Oak Brook, Ill.: Council of Logistics Management, 1988).

Mathe, Herve (ed.). *Managing Services across Borders.* (Cergy Pontoise Cedex, France: European Center for Research in Operations and Service Management, 1991).

Murphy, Paul R., Douglas R. Dalenberg, and James M. Daley. "Analyzing International Water Transportation: The Perspectives of Large U.S. Industrial Corporations." *Journal of Business Logistics,* Spring 1991, pp. 169–190.

Peng, Li, and Martin T. Farris. "Recent Chinese Port Developments and Problems." *Waterways and Transportation Review,* vol. 2, no. 1 (1994), pp. 1–12.

Pope, David J., and Evelyn A. Thomchick. "U.S. Foreign Freight Forwarders and NVOCCs." *Transportation Journal,* Spring 1985, pp. 26–36.

Prentice, Barry E., and Marvin D. Hildebrand. "Transborder Trucking, Institutional Barriers to Canada-U.S. Trade of Agricultural Goods." *Journal of the Transportation Research Forum* (1988), pp. 65–72.

Rao, Kant, Richard R. Young, and Judith A. Novick. "Third Party Services in the Logistics of Global Firms." *Logistics & Transportation Review*, vol. 29, no. 4 (December 1993), pp. 363–370.

Rhodes, Michael P. "NAFTA's Implications for the Transportation Industry." *Transportation Quarterly*, Spring 1994, pp. 135–148.

Rinehart, Lloyd M. "Global Logistics Partnership Negotiation," *International Journal of Physical Distribution & Logistics Management*, vol. 22, no. 1 (1992), pp. 27–34.

Seguin, Vernon C. "An Introduction to the Challenge of Logistics Support for Business with the People's Republic of China." *Papers, CLM 1988 Annual Meeting*, vol. 1. (Oak Brook, Ill.: CLM, 1988), pp. 161–169.

Sherwood, Charles S., and Robert Bruns, "Solving International Transportation Problems." *Review of Business*, vol. 14, no. 1 (Summer–Fall 1992), pp. 25–30.

Tangeman, Nanci A. "The International Logistics of Freight Forwarding: Performance Measurement at the Harper Group." *National Productivity Review*, vol. 13, no. 1 (Winter 1993–1994), pp. 107–114.

Tansuhaj, Patriya, and George C. Jackson. "Foreign Trade Zones: A Comparative Analysis of Users and Non-Users." *Journal of Business Logistics*, April 1989, pp. 15–30.

Wilson, Wesley W., and Kenneth L. Casavant. "Pacific Northwest Agriculture and the Shipping Act of 1984." *Journal of the Transportation Research Forum* (1988), pp. 73–79.

Wood, Donald F., Anthony Barone, Paul Murphy, and Daniel L. Wardlow. *International Logistics* (New York: Chapman & Hall, 1995).

CASE 11-1

HDT TRUCK COMPANY

This case situation takes place during the mid-1970s. HDT Truck Company is a small firm that has been located in Crown Point, Indiana, since 1910. Its only products—large trucks—are built to individual customer specifications. The firm once produced automobiles and light trucks as well, but dropped out of the auto business in 1924 and out of the light truck business in 1937. The firm nearly went out of business at that time, but by 1940 its fortunes were buoyed by receipt of several military contracts for tank retrievers—large-wheeled vehicles that can pull a disabled tank onto a low trailer and haul it to a location where it can be repaired.

Since World War II, HDT has manufactured only large off-the-road vehicles, including airport snowplows, airport crash trucks, oil-field drilling equipment, and the like. HDT purchased all components from small manufacturers that were still clustered in the Milwaukee-Detroit-Toledo-Cleveland area. Essentially, all HDT does is assemble the components into a specialized vehicle containing the combination of frame, power plant, transmission, axles, and cab that are necessary to do the job.

The assembly line was relatively slow. After wheels were attached to the frame and axles, the night shift labor force would push the chassis along to its next station on the line so it would be in place for the next day's shift. By using one shift, two trucks could be assembled each day. If large orders for identical trucks were involved, it was possible to assemble three trucks per day. Quality declined whenever the pace became quicker. HDT officials had decided they could not grow and became satisfied with their niche in the very heavy truck market. With only two exceptions, since 1960 they had always had at least a four-month backlog of orders. In the 1960s their best market had been airports, but since 1970 their best market had been for oil-field equipment, first for the North Slope in Alaska and then for the Middle East. This case discusses a situation that faced HDT in the mid-1970s.

In late 1975 HDT received an order for fifty heavy trucks to be used in the oil fields of Iraq. The terms of sale were delivery on or before July 1, 1976, at the port of Al Basrah, Iraq. Specifically, HDT would receive $52,000 per truck in U.S. funds FAS (free along side) the discharging vessel in Al Basrah, which meant that HDT was responsible for all transportation costs up until the time and point the trucks were discharged from the ship's tackle at Al Basrah. Once each truck was unloaded, HDT would be paid for it.

Chris Reynolds, production manager at HDT, estimated that production could start approximately April 1, 1976, and the order would take eighteen working days to complete. Because weekends were involved, all fifty trucks would be completed by April 20–25. Reynolds thought that May 1, 1976, was a more realistic completion date because he had always found it difficult to restrict the assembly line to constructing trucks for only one account. The reason for this was that Vic Guillou, HDT's sales manager, liked to have trucks being built for as many accounts as possible on the assembly line at any one time. Prospective buyers frequently visited the plant and were always more impressed when they could see a diverse collection of models being built for a wide range of uses.

Norman Pon, HDT's treasurer, always wanted to give priority to building trucks that were being sold on an FOB plant basis because that would improve his cash flow position. At the time the $52,000 price had been set on the truck sale to Iraq, Pon had argued (unsuccessfully) that the price was too low. Guillou, on the other hand, argued that the sale was necessary since the Arab world represented a growth market by anyone's definition and he wanted HDT trucks there. HDT's president, Gordon Robertson, had sided with Guillou. Robertson thought that Pon was a good treasurer but too much of a worrier when it came to making important decisions. Pon, in turn, thought that Robertson had yet to shed the image he had acquired in the

1960s when his late father was president of HDT. Pon had lost count of the number of times the elder Robertson had needed cash in order to buy his son's way out of some embarrassing situation. Guillou was young Robertson's fraternity roommate in college, and Pon thought the two of them shared a similar love of "life in the fast lane."

At the time the order was signed in 1975, Guillou argued that the FAS destination port represented the best terms of sale because ocean charter rates were declining as a result of an oversupply of tanker tonnage and the reopening of the Suez Canal. Guillou predicted that by mid-1976 charter rates would be so low that the cheapest method of transport would be to load all fifty trucks on one vessel. Pon countered that HDT should try to make a profit only from the manufacture of trucks since nobody in the firm knew much about ocean shipping. Robertson, who was a gambler at heart, of course, disagreed.

It was now March 1976, and Reynolds had the fifty-truck order scheduled to be on the line from April 2 to 29, which represented 2.5 trucks per working day. Other work was scheduled for the assembly line at the same time, so the production schedule was considered firm. Component parts for the oil-field trucks and for the other trucks were already arriving. Right now, orders were backlogged for over seven months, the highest figure since 1967. This was due, almost in total, to Guillou's additional sales of oil-field equipment to Arab producers. Three separate orders were involved and totaled 115 trucks.

Robertson and Guillou left Crown Point for an industry convention in San Diego. Robertson phoned from San Diego that he and Guillou had decided to vacation in Mexico for a while before returning to Crown Point. Robertson knew that HDT could function in his absence and knew that with Pon "watching the store," the company's assets would be safe. Several days later, a Mexican postcard postmarked "Tijuana" arrived saying that both were enjoying Mexico and would stay longer than initially planned.

Pon was relieved to learn that Guillou and Robertson would be gone for a longer time and immediately began wondering what types of bills they were accumulating in Mexico and for which ones they would want company reimbursement. Both had several credit cards belonging to the company. Based on experience, Pon also expected Robertson to phone for cash about once a week. As usual, Pon started wondering how paying for the Robertson and Guillou vacation venture would affect HDT's cash flow. Pon looked at his cash flow projections, which were always made up for six weeks in advance, in this case through the first of April when some of the bills for components of the oil-field trucks would come due. In fact, if Reynolds's schedule were adhered to, all the components would be on hand by April 10 and, if HDT were to receive the customary discounts, all of the components would have to be paid for in the period between April 8 and April 20 (HDT received a 1 percent discount for goods paid for within ten days of actual or requested receipt, whichever came later). For a moment, Pon thought that the worst might happen: that the component bills would be due at the same time as Robertson's and Guillou's travel bill. He called the Crown Point Bank and Trust Company, where HDT had a line of credit and found that the current rate was 10 percent per annum. He then asked Bob Vanderpool, who was HDT's traffic manager, when the oil-field trucks would arrive in Iraq.

"I don't know," was Vanderpool's reply. "I assumed that Guillou had arranged for transportation at the time you decided to charge $52,000 per truck. But I'll check further." He did and phoned back to tell Pon that Guillou's secretary could find nothing in the files to indicate that Guillou had checked out charter rates.

"That figures," muttered Pon. "Would you mind doing some checking?"

Vanderpool said yes, he would mind doing some checking. Pon then suggested to him that there were several other newer orders also destined for the Arab countries, so Vanderpool should start thinking about widening his area of expertise. Vanderpool reluctantly agreed, and Pon heard nothing from him for a few days until Vanderpool passed him in the hall and said the assignment was much more time-consuming than he had imagined.

One week later, Vanderpool said he had done as much as he could and would turn the figures over to Pon. He also said that he (Vanderpool) did not have the authority to charter a ship and suggested that Pon determine who could do so in Robertson's absence. Later that day Vanderpool came to Pon's office with a thick file. "It looks like you've been doing a lot of figuring," said Pon.

"No, not me," said Vanderpool, "but two outsiders. One is Bob Guider, an international freight forwarder in Chicago whom we use for our export parts shipments. And he put me in touch with Eddie Quan, a New York ship broker who is on top of the charter market. We have two alternatives."

"What are they?" asked Pon.

"Well," answered Vanderpool, "the St. Lawrence Seaway will open in mid-April, so we could use it. The problem is that the Seaway route is circuitous, especially to reach the Arab countries. Also, there aren't many scheduled Seaway sailings to that area, and because the Seaway will just be opening again, cargo space is hard to come by. Therefore, if we're not going to charter a ship, the best bet is to use Baltimore."

"What about chartering a ship?" asked Pon. "Why not use Baltimore for that?"

"In theory, we could," answered Vanderpool. "But Quan says the size of ship we want is rather small and not likely to be sailing into Baltimore. We could arrange to share a ship with another party, but many bulk cargoes are pretty dusty and might not be compatible with our vehicles. Quan says there is one foreign vessel entering the Great Lakes in April that is still looking for an outbound charter. Seaway vessels, you know, are somewhat smaller because of the lock restrictions. If we want to charter that vessel, we'll have to move quickly, because if somebody else charters her, she's gone."

"What kind of vessel is it?" asked Pon.

"The vessel's name is the *Nola Pino*, the same name as a French movie actress in the 1960s. You may recall that some Greek shipping magnate named the vessel after her, but his wife made him give up both Nola Pino the actress and *Nola Pino* the ship. At present it's scheduled to be in Chicago the last week in April with a load of cocoa beans and ready for outbound loading May 1. Quan thinks we could charter it for $1,200 per day for thirty days, which would be enough time for it to load, transit the Seaway, reach Al Basrah, and discharge the trucks by May 29 or 30."

"Tell me about the alternative," said Pon.

"Baltimore has fairly frequent sailings to the area we want to reach," said Vanderpool. "We could load two trucks per day on rail cars here and send them to Baltimore. There are two ships a week scheduled from Baltimore to Al Basrah. It would take the trucks an average of 4 days to reach Baltimore, where they would wait an average of 3 days to be loaded aboard ship. The figure should be 3.5 days, but the railroad will hustle if it knows we're trying to connect with an outgoing sailing. Sailing time to Al Basrah averages fifteen days—a little more, a little less, depending on the amount of cargo to be handled at ports in between."

"That averages to twenty-two days per truck," stated Pon, who had been putting the figures in his new pocket calculator. "What are the charges?"

Vanderpool answered: "It costs $60 to load and block two trucks on a flatcar, which is, of course, $30 apiece as long as they move in pairs. Sticking to pairs, the rail rate for two on a flatcar totals $896 to Baltimore. Handling at Baltimore is $100 per truck, and ocean freight rate from Baltimore to Al Basrah is $720 per truck. We also have to buy insurance, which is about $75 per truck."

"That totals $1,395," said Pon, after consulting his calculator. "What are the costs if we charter the *Nola Pino?* You said it would be $36,000 for the vessel. What else is involved?"

"There are two ways of getting the trucks to port," said Vanderpool. "There are no export rates to Chicago, but the domestic ones aren't so bad. The loading and blocking would be only $20 per truck because we'd be doing all fifty at one time. The rail rate per truck would average out to $90 each, and it would take one day for them to reach Chicago and another day to be loaded. We'd be tying up a wharf for one day, and the wharfage charge runs $1 per foot, and the *Nola Pino* is 535 feet long. We'd be responsible for loading and stowing the cargo, and this would cost $4,000 for all fifty trucks. The Seaway tolls are 90 cents per ton or, in our case, $27 per truck. At Al Basrah the unloading costs will be $2,100 for the entire vessel. Marine insurance will be $105 per truck."

"Are there any other alternatives?" asked Pon.

"The only other one that comes close is to drive the trucks from here to Chicago," answered Vanderpool. "We would need temporary licenses and a convoy permit and pay to have the fuel tank on each truck drained before it is loaded. The problem is that the convoy would cross state lines, and we would need temporary licenses and permits in Illinois as well."

"Do me one favor," said Pon. "Please call Frank Wood, our outside counsel, and ask him what steps we have to go through to charter a ship. Tell him I'm especially concerned about the liability. Give him Quan's phone number. I want to make sure there are no more costs involved. If Robertson's fooling around is on schedule, he'll be phoning me asking that I cable cash. I'd really appreciate it if you would summarize what you've told me in two columns, with the charter costs on the left and the overland Baltimore cost column on the right. Then when Robertson calls, I can ask him to decide."

"One question," asked Vanderpool.

"Shoot," responded Pon.

"Why should the charter figures be on the left?"

"Because on a map (see Exhibit 11-A), Chicago is to the left of Baltimore and that's the only way I'll keep them straight when I'm talking on the phone."

Exhibit 11-A   Map of the northeastern United States.

Questions

1. Assume you are Vanderpool. Draft the comparison Pon just asked for.

2. Which of the two routing alternatives would you recommend? Why?

3. Assume that the buyer in Iraq has made other large purchases in the United States and is considering consolidating all of its purchases and loading them onto one large ship, which the buyer will charter. The buyer contacts HDT and, although acknowledging its commitment to buy FAS Al Basrah, asks how much HDT would subtract from the $52,000 per truck price if the selling terms were changed to FOB HDT's Crown Point plant. How much of a cost reduction do you think HDT should offer the buyer? Under what terms and conditions?

4. This case was written some years ago when interest rates were lower. Assume, instead, that the year is 1980 and that HDT's line of credit with the Crown Point Bank and Trust Company would cost about 18 percent per annum. How, if at all, does this affect the cost calculations in the answer to Question 1?

5. Is there an interest rate that would make HDT change from one routing to another? If so, what is it?

6. Assume that it is 1980 and the cost to HDT of borrowing money is 18 percent per year. Because the buyer will pay for trucks as they are delivered, would it be advantageous for HDT to pay overtime to speed up production, ship the trucks as they were finished via the Port of Baltimore, and collect their payment earlier? Why or why not?

C A S E   1 1 - 2

BELLE TZELL CELL COMPANY

Headquartered in Tucson, Arizona, the Belle Tzell Cell Company manufactured one standard-size battery for use in portable power tools and in military weapons. Nell Tzell was the company's current president. Her mother, Belle, had retired from active management ten years before, although she and several of Nell's aunts still owned a controlling interest in the company. Belle and her late husband, Del, had founded the firm in 1945, and it had prospered by selling batteries and dry cells to a number of electronics firms that had sprung up in the Arizona–New Mexico area after World War II.

Toward the end of her presidency, in the late 1960s, Belle had taken one action that increased the capacity of the firm. In response to a bid by the Mexican government, she had moved part of her operations south of the border into Nogales to take advantage of low-cost Mexican labor and Belle's fears that both the U.S. and Arizona governments would increase their controls on pollution and require safer working conditions for employees. The Mexican government provided a low-cost loan and required Belle to enter into a partnership with a Mexican citizen, who would own 51 percent of the Belle Tzell Cell Company's Mexican operation. The operation that Belle moved to Nogales was the facility for making lead panels. This operation involved combining strong acids with lead, and was considered hazardous to employee health. Noxious vapors damaged the workers' lungs, and the acidic wastes left over from the curing processes were dumped into a nearby stream bed, killing aquatic life for at least ten miles downstream.

Belle retired a few months after the Nogales plant went into production and told Nell that it would take "only a few more months to get the bugs out." That was well over fifteen years ago, and, if anything, the bugs had increased. Although actual production costs remained low and the Mexican plant was still nonunion, its production was very undependable. Because it was under Mexican ownership, the Mexican who owned 51 percent of the stock insisted that most of plant's management be Mexican also. However, neither the Mexican who owned the 51 percent of the stock nor most Mexicans capable of managing the operation cared to live in Nogales. They preferred the bright lights of Mexico City. The plant's work force was continually changing. Despite the fact that wages were high by Mexican standards, new workers soon suffered either burns from acid splashes or lung irritation because of the fumes and would leave. Also, because Nogales was just south of the U.S.-Mexican border, Mexican workers would prefer to cross the border illegally and work at higher-paying jobs in the United States until they were found by U.S. immigration authorities and deported.

Although Nell would have preferred to close her Nogales lead panel plant, the cost of establishing such a facility in the United States made such a move impossible. This was because of the new worker safety requirements of the federal government, operating through OSHA, and new controls on air and water pollution and toxic waste disposal administered by the U.S. Environmental Protection Agency (EPA). Transportation costs for delivering acids to the plant would also be very high because carriers considered them to be an extremely hazardous material requiring specialized, expensive trailer tanks to avoid acid spills.

Although the Mexicans were capable of turning out high-quality products, lax supervision resulted in wide variations in the quality of the final product. Sometimes this would not be noticed until the workers in the Tucson plant attempted to install the lead plates that had been received from Nogales.

Relatively little of the Tzell Company's operations were in Tucson. Their offices were on the second floor of a building, cramped on a narrow lot with little room for expansion. Downstairs, the lead plates from Nogales were combined with printed circuits from Taiwan and placed inside plastic cases purchased from one of several suppliers in Tucson. Each day's production filled two thirty-five-foot trailers parked at the north end of the building. At night the two trailers would be delivered to various buyers. The Tucson plant was operating at capacity and rarely ever caught up with sales. Several times Nell had wanted to increase the number of production lines, but she was unable to expand the building at its present site. In addition, Nell's aunts, who still controlled the company, were unwilling to allow her to relocate to a new site or larger plant because the financial resources required for the move would cut into their current incomes.

The present Tucson plant was a long, narrow building set in a north-south direction between two parallel streets. The south side fronted on 17th Street and contained a receiving dock that was built to accommodate only one trailer. There was no street parking allowed on 17th Street, and neighbors would complain to the Tucson Police Department if a truck parked on the street for even a few minutes. The building stretched north, with the east and west sides within a foot of their respective lot lines. The north end of the building was on 16th Street. Here was a large parking lot used by employees and the loading dock that could accommodate three trailers. Prior to the opening of the Nogales plant, the employee parking lot filled every day, with all thirty-two slots occupied. Today, only about ten slots were used because employees were using car pools and local buses. Even Nell was in a carpool, sharing rides with David Kupferman, her operations manager, who lived in the same apartment complex as she did.

Kupferman had worked for the Tzell Company for only a few weeks, and as he and Nell were driving from work one day, she said, "Dave, you know I'm caught between two rocks and two hard places. My mother and aunts won't let me expand here in Tucson, and our Nogales plant produces more ulcers than anything else. Your predecessor left because the strain of coordinating the two plants was too great. Believe it or not, the majority of our operations take place in Nogales. You'd better visit there, soon, to see what it's like."

"I can hardly wait," responded Kupferman. "After my last argument with them over poor quality, I'm afraid they'll dunk my head in an acid vat if I ever set foot inside that plant. How come you became so dependent upon Mexico for your operations?"

Nell explained the reasons, already given here, and added: "For many years these savings gave us a competitive edge. In cost or money terms, two-thirds of our operation is down in Nogales."

"Two-thirds?" asked Kupferman. "That seems high. How do you figure it?"

"Look at it this way," said Nell. "We take in a little over $4 million per year, or about $16,000 per working day. We spend about $15,000 per working day. Of that, about $10,000 is spent at Nogales for labor, raw materials, and overhead. We spend just over $1,000 a day moving the lead plates from Nogales here, although $800 of that is import duties on the lead plates. Here in Tucson, our manufacturing operation takes only about $3,000 per day; about two-thirds for labor and one-third for the printed circuits and plastic battery cases. The remainder of the money goes for companywide overhead and for profit."

"I see," said Kupferman. "How, then, do you see the problem?"

Nell answered, "First of all, our problems are caused by our success in selling. Right now we have a backlog of orders, but I am unable to expand capacity either here or in Nogales. Mother and my aunts won't allow major capital improvements, and while I might be able to build a small addition to the north of the Tucson plant, the cost would be prohibitive, especially when one considers the small increase in capacity that would result."

"It's too bad your family won't let you expand more," offered Kupferman.

"Actually, I don't blame them," said Tzell. "Our business is really volatile, and I've also been unable to interest serious outside investors in helping me expand. Several bankers told me that I'd have to get my production act together before I should think about either expanding or borrowing much outside money. Right now, the banks will loan me any working capital I want at 12 percent, if it's secured by inventories or equipment. However, I'm unable to assemble enough funds for any type of expansion."

"I still don't understand your coordination problem," said Kupferman. "Your Nogales plant produces one trailerload of battery plates per day, which is exactly the input you need for a day's output at Tucson. The battery plates can be trucked at night, and if you can get your quality control act together at Nogales, you'd have a smooth, continuous operation."

"I hate to say this," said Nell, "but your predecessor said just about the same thing eight months ago. And like you, he thought that quality control at Nogales was the key to solving my problem."

"So what did he do wrong?" asked Kupferman.

"He was going to use a two-pronged approach, which I'll tell you about in the office," said Nell as she wheeled her Porsche from 16th Street into the parking lot at the north end of the Tucson plant. "Get a cup of coffee and we'll continue this conversation in my office," she said as they climbed the stairs to the second floor offices.

Kupferman got two cups of coffee, walked into her office, and sat down. Nell was looking through her messages and exclaimed, "Dammit, it happened again! We just got penalized $3,000 because of a late delivery to Jedson Electronic Tools. They then were late on delivering a government order and decided we were responsible because our delivery was late, which it was. Their purchase order to us had a penalty clause in it and now they're going to collect. This is exactly the problem we have to lick! The Nogales plant either misses making a shipment or sends a load of such poor quality that we can't use it right away. We then assign our people here to other tasks for the day, such as inserting only the printed circuits into the plastic cases. They do this until the battery plates arrive, and then they add all the battery plates. At the end of two days we're caught up, except that yesterday we made no deliveries and yesterday's promised output is one day late. That's why we lose customers. To them, we're just another tardy supplier. Right now the industry practice is to specify a delivery date, with cost penalties included for either early or late deliveries. Indeed, some of our customers are adopting JIT inventory systems and are trying to specify a sixty-minute window during which they'll accept our daily deliveries. Our major competitors are already dancing to this tune, and we will have no choice but to follow."

"How often do we have this kind of problem—when we can't make deliveries because of some foul-up in our quality?" asked Kupferman.

"For a long time, it was only once a month or so," responded Tzell, "but as we reached our plants' capacity and there was less slack, the problem has been happening almost weekly. One week, about two months ago, we hit the jackpot and had three days of bad production in a row. That threw us out of kilter for nearly two weeks, even after paying overtime both here and at Nogales. That's when your predecessor's ulcer started bleeding and he left. Too bad, too, because I think he was just about ready to solve our problem."

"What changes had he intended to make?" asked Kupferman.

"Well," responded Tzell, "your predecessor had studied probability in college and had computed the chances of foul-ups in Nogales occurring one right after the other. He calculated that we should close down our Tucson plant for five days or have the Nogales plant run five days of overtime so that it could produce a five-day supply of lead battery plates. He said that if we kept the Nogales plant scheduled so that there was always five days' worth of plates between Nogales and Tucson, we would never have to be out of usable lead battery plates here in Tucson."

"If his calculations are accurate, why haven't you implemented his plan?" asked Kupferman.

"We couldn't figure out where to store the approximately five loads of battery plates," responded Tzell. "It's more complicated than you think. Here, let me read to you your predecessor's memo, written while he was recovering from surgery, no less. It says, and I quote, 'There are three alternatives: warehousing in Nogales, warehousing here in Tucson, or leasing five truck trailers and parking them either outside the Nogales plant or in the 16th Street parking lot here in Tucson.' " Tzell looked at David directly and continued, "David, what I want you to do is to figure out the costs of these three alternatives and get back to me with a recommendation."

Kupferman took his empty coffee cup, walked back to his office, and started gathering the cost figures Tzell had asked for. He discovered that to warehouse the five loads of lead battery plates in Nogales would cost $300 per week, plus $120 per week for local drayage in Nogales (that is, trucking the plates from the plant to the warehouse). To truck the plates directly from the Nogales plant to a Tucson warehouse rather than to the Tzell Tucson plant was the second alternative. Few Tucson warehouses wanted to touch the business for fear that the plates would contaminate other merchandise they were storing. The best quote David could get was for $350 per week plus a requirement that Tzell provide a bond to protect the warehouseman from damages the plates might cause. Local drayage costs within Tucson from the warehouse to Tzell's 17th Street receiving dock would be $150 per week.

The trailer idea involved leasing five trailers, loading them with battery plates, and parking them at either the Nogales plant or at the 16th Street lot of Tzell's Tucson plant. Trailers could be leased and licensed for use in both Mexico and Arizona for $3,000 per year each. In addition, a used truck-tractor, costing approximately $5,000, would have to be purchased and used for shifting trailers around whichever of the two plants where they were stored.

The advantage of storing the trailers at Nogales was to delay the payment of import duties of about $800 per trailer load of battery plates. However, a problem with the current system was that Mexican border agents, sensing the urgency in the Tzell shipments, attempted to shake down the Tzell drivers to let the trailers exit from Mexico. Trailers were subject to delays and sometimes would be searched thoroughly to make certain that they were carrying no works of art or Mexican national treasures. One Mexican agent inspected trailers ever so slowly, complaining aloud that the reason he moved slowly was that he was depressed by the fact that Christmas was coming (no matter what month it happened to be) and that he lacked sufficient money to buy gifts for all of his family.

Kupferman had yet to visit the Nogales plant, but before presenting his findings to Tzell, he wanted to make certain that the parking lot at the Nogales plant was fenced. He phoned Juan Perez, the Mexican plant manager, who said very little until he realized that Kupferman was not calling to complain about something. Perez answered Kupferman's query by saying that the yard was not fenced but that it would be possible to park the loaded trailers with their closed rear doors against a solid masonry wall, making entry impossible. "Besides," he added, "this plant had such a bad reputation for causing illness and injury that no local thief would come within a mile of it."

Kupferman was trying to think of a witty response and the Nogales manager continued, "But you said 'up to five trailers.' Why so many?"

Kupferman then told him of his predecessor's calculations that the Nogales plant should produce five days of output in advance of that needed by the Tucson plant.

"Why so many?" repeated Perez.

"To make sure that Tucson never has to shut down or be late with orders," answered Kupferman. "The only reason we have problems here is because of delayed or poor-quality shipments from you. When Tucson falls behind, we can't make deliveries and that costs us money."

"Nonsense!" responded Perez. "You blame all your problems on us. Let me tell you two things. First, not all production delays are caused down here. It's just that we're not in the same building as the home office, and we tend to get blamed for everything. Second, because the Tucson plant makes a single standard product, it would be cheaper to have them produce a day or two's inventory in advance, ready to use in case *either* the Tucson plant or my operation fouls up. You'll have to excuse me now. We've just had another acid spill."

Kupferman heard a click and then a humming sound. He hung up. He decided to walk to Tzell's office and tell her what Perez had said.

She admitted that Perez was correct, "just a bit," about some of the delays being at the Tucson plant. In fact, she conceded that Kupferman's predecessor had overlooked the problems at the Tucson assembly line when he made his calculations that the Nogales plant produce a five-day advance supply of battery plates as a cushion. She told Kupferman to start over and assume that delays could occur by conditions in either plant or both. She felt that Kupferman would find that sales should be cut back for a few days so that either or both plants could turn out some advance production that would serve as a continual cushion of safety stock. She wanted enough inventory in reserve that the Tzell Cell Company could fill 99 percent of all orders on time. Kupferman would have six months to set up the system and another six months to test and debug it. After that, he would be expected to maintain a 99 percent performance level of filling orders on time.

During the next few days of ride sharing, Tzell and Kupferman talked about everything except work. Tzell commented that she missed seeing David at the swimming pool. Kupferman responded that he had been spending his time indoors, studying probability.

After several weeks, Kupferman had finally calculated the probabilities that would allow Tzell Cell Company to maintain Nell's required 99 percent level of on-time deliveries. First of all, his predecessor had been correct, insofar as he had calculated. One solution was to have the Nogales plant produce five days' worth of battery cell plates in advance of the Tucson plant. This was because the Tucson plant was responsible for only two of the delivery delays in a year of 250 working days. However, Kupferman also made calculations about the sizes of completed stocks for the Tucson plant to manufacture in advance and keep as a safety stock cushion. If the Tucson plant produced and maintained as safety stock one day's output of completed batteries, the Nogales plant would only have to maintain a four-day lead in production of lead battery plates ahead of their use in Tucson. If the

Tucson plant produced in advance and maintained as safety stock two days' output of completed batteries, the Nogales plant would have to produce only two days' worth of battery plates in advance of their use in the Tucson plant. And if the Tucson plant made three days' output in advance and held it as safety stock, the Nogales plant would not have to produce a surplus of plates in advance of what was required each day at Tucson. That is, each night the truck would leave with the Nogales output and drive to Tucson, where the plates would be used the next day. Even if there were problems with the Nogales shipment, there would be a three-day safety stock of finished batteries in Tucson.

Kupferman intended to determine warehousing costs for the safety stocks of completed batteries in Tucson, but Tzell told him to plan on using the trailer idea instead. The trailers would be parked in the 16th Street lot. At night they would be parked so that none of their doors were exposed. For $3,000 the lot's fence could be made more secure and a gate would be added. Tzell told Kupferman that deliveries would be made out of the trailer that had been parked the longest (usually two or three days). This would ensure orderly inventory turnover, which was important, since batteries have a limited life.

Kupferman took a clipboard with a pad of paper and made four columns, one for each of the alternatives. The column headings looked like this:

I	II	III	IV
Five days' worth of plates in Nogales	Four days' worth of plates in Nogales	Two days' worth of plates in Nogales	No extra plates in Nogales
No extra batteries in Tucson	One day's worth of batteries in Tucson	Two days' worth of batteries in Tucson	Three days' worth of batteries in Tucson

Each alternative would give the firm the ability to provide a 99 percent or better level of on-time order filling.

Questions

1. What are the total inventory carrying costs of alternative I?
2. What are the total inventory carrying costs of alternative II?
3. What are the total inventory carrying costs of alternative III?
4. What are the total inventory carrying costs of alternative IV?
5. Which alternative do you think Kupferman should recommend? Why?
6. Tzell "wanted enough inventory in reserve that the Tzell Cell Company could fill 99 percent of all orders on time." This is, as you may recall, a

customer service standard. How reasonable is a 99 percent level? Why not, say, a 95 percent level? How would Tzell and Kupferman determine the relative advantages and disadvantages of the 95 percent and the 99 percent service levels? What kind of cost calculations would they have to make?

7. Jedson Electronic Tools invoked a penalty clause on a purchase order that Tzell Cell Company had accepted, and the Tzell Cell Company had to forfeit $3,000. Draft, for Tzell's signature, a memo indicating when and under what conditions the Belle Tzell Cell Company should accept penalty clauses in purchase orders covering missed delivery times.

8. In your opinion, is it ethical for a U.S.-based firm to relocate some of its operations in Mexico so as to avoid the stricter U.S. pollution and worker-safety laws? Why or why not? Discuss.

Part Three

Analyzing, Designing, and Implementing a Logistics System

Parts 1 and 2 present an overview of logistics and focus on the individual components of the logistics portions of the supply chain. Part 3 examines methods of analyzing, implementing, and controlling logistics as used by the firm and by those firms with which it is linked.

Chapter 12 focuses on the techniques involved in logistics systems analysis, design, and reengineering. These techniques are designed to isolate inefficiencies in logistics operations so that corrective action can be taken.

Chapter 13 examines the various control systems that must be implemented to ensure that the logistics system operates efficiently. Controls are also needed to minimize losses from pilferage and theft.

Chapter 14 is based on combining the supply chain that one might have designed in Chapter 12, along with the controls that Chapter 13 indicates are necessary. The result would be a more integrated logistical approach. Chapter 14 discusses various organizational and partnership strategies and their implementation.

Finally, Chapter 15 looks at some of the anticipated changes that may confront logistics managers in the later 1990s and into the twenty-first century.

Reengineering Logistics Systems

A thinker, aided by a computer, is pictured in this consultant's brochure entitled "Managing Complexity: Logistical/Marketing Strategies." (Credit: Ernst & Whinney/Shycon Associates, Inc., Waltham, Mass.)

Texas Instruments previously had 24 warehouses around the world. By early 1997 it would like to have just one each in Europe, the United States and Japan, with another one elsewhere in Asia and possibly one in Canada.

Journal of Commerce
September 19, 1994

Goodwill streamlined operations—for example, it now tries to sell donations locally rather than ship them to central distribution centers. As a result, administrative costs fell from 12 percent of 1988's income of $555 million to 8 percent of last year's $644.1 million.

Money
December 1991

With its many benefits, simulation of materials handling systems has become a key step in the design process, especially of larger companies. One Ford Motor Company plant has created a simulation model of the entire facility. Before a change is made in any area, the automaker looks at how that change will affect other areas.

Modern Materials Handling
November 1991

Put away that monkey wrench and get out the whole toolbox. Reengineering involves much more than just tinkering with existing processes.

Modern Materials Handling
February 1995

Key Terms

- Benchmarking
- Channels audit
- Competition audit
- Customer audit
- Design implementation
- Direct product profitability (DPP) analysis
- Environmental sensitivity audit
- Existing facilities audit
- Industry standards analysis
- Logistics system design
- PERT (program evaluation and review technique)
- Product audit
- Reengineering
- Simulation
- System constraint
- System goal
- System objective
- Systems analysis
- Vendor audit

Learning Objectives

- To examine the problems and opportunities involved in systems analysis
- To relate the importance of industry standards to systems analysis
- To discuss the steps involved in reengineering a logistics system
- To explain the utilization of PERT and simulation in data analysis

REENGINEERING

Logistics concepts and practices are well in place. Sometimes they are too well in place and might even be considered as inflexible. This chapter deals with how a logistics system is analyzed with the idea in mind to redesign, or reengineer, the system if that is found to be necessary. Part of the reengineering effort also recognizes that the firm sees itself as part of a supply chain and that today's system must have closer links with both suppliers and customers than was once the case. **Reengineering** can be described as follows:

> Reengineering takes a blank-sheet-of-paper approach to rethinking how critical business systems and processes should be organized. Processes are redesigned to minimize hand-offs, cut cycle times, and reduce costs while enhancing flexibility and output quality. In general, reengineering strives to achieve processes that add the most value at the lowest cost.[1]

This chapter has two main parts. The first deals with system analysis, and the second deals with system design.

WHAT IS SYSTEMS ANALYSIS?

Because few things in the business world are static, a system that optimizes yesterday's situation may be less than optimal today and, especially, tomorrow. Logistics, of course, is no exception. For example, the deregulation of intrastate trucking on January 1, 1995, has allegedly reduced intrastate trucking rates in some states to the point that distribution centers serving that state are now placed inside that state. Previously, they had been just outside the state because the unregulated interstate trucking rates were far less than the regulated intrastate rates, so it had been cheaper to ship goods from nearby out-of-state points.

Markets shift constantly; even public utilities do not consider their demand patterns fixed. Consider, for example, the many changes that have taken place in the telephone and other communications industries in recent years. Relationships with partners in the supply chain also change.

As used here, the term **systems analysis** refers to the orderly and planned observation of one or more segments in the logistics network or supply chain in order to determine how well each segment and the entire system function. Systems analysis can be a simple operation, such as a time and motion study of individuals who handle incoming freight at a receiving dock. Or it can be nationwide or global in scope, with the idea of completely redesigning a firm's entire logistics system, including its relationships with many long-time suppliers and customers. The observations provide data that are then subjected to statistical analysis. In some situations the next step is to

---

[1] Michael H. Sargent and Keith P. Creehan, "Managing the Complexities of Product Proliferation," *Mercer Management Journal*, 1993, no. 1, p. 10.

incorporate the data into programmed models of the logistics network. A model simulates real conditions to determine how well the present system or a contemplated system would respond to various happenings. Based on the simulation and other analytical analysis, the final procedure may involve redesigning the entire logistics system.

Many firms have personnel who conduct systems analysis projects throughout the firm. Other firms prefer to use outside consultants because they can be more objective. Although consultants vary in quality, they bring outside viewpoints and broader perspectives to bear on most problems. In supply-chain situations involving related firms, a consultant may appear to be more neutral than a representative of either firm.

For any type of analysis, several general questions must be asked. One set of useful questions is offered by consultant William Copacino:

Why do we perform each task?

What value is added by it?

Why are the tasks performed in the order they are?

Can we alter the sequence of the processing steps to increase efficiency?

Why are the tasks performed by a particular group or individual?

Could others perform this task?

Is there a better way for the system to operate?[2]

PROBLEMS INVOLVED IN SYSTEMS ANALYSIS

How to focus a logistics systems analysis (or audit) is the first and often the most difficult part of the task. Should it focus on the work practices at the receiving dock, on the dock's location in the building, or on the building's location in the system? Are the products being handled properly? Are customer service standards adequate, or should the order-processing function be automated? What is the competition doing?

The types of systems analyses that might be performed are limited only by the analyst's imagination and the amount of money that the firm or client is willing to spend for the analysis. Figure 12-1 shows a checklist prepared by a consultant; it lists some of the questions that a firm should address in determining whether systems analysis is needed. Firms with high scores (more needs) are advised to "conduct a strategy study to redirect the logistics functions to more closely correlate to the business strategy of the company."

Another problem of focus deals with the time span for the implementation of new ideas. Some improvements might deal only with specific adjustments within the supply chain without altering the chain itself. Ordering

[2] Cited in James Drogan, "The Role of Information Systems in the Preparation and Management of Transportation Service Packages," in *Proceedings of Forward Motion: A Conference Sponsored by Burlington Northern* (Dallas, November 3–4, 1988), p. BNS-5.

To analyze your business, answer the following Key Logistics Strategy Questions........

Circle the appropriate number next to the question.

	Significant	Moderate	Somewhat	Not Applicable

COMPANY MARKETS

1) Has your company recently opened (or closed) new market areas generating need for additional logistics and customer service capability?	6	4	2	0
2) Has there been a shift in the shipments to the types of customers within your company? (wholesalers, distributors, retailers, etc.)	9	6	3	0

COMPANY PRODUCTS

3) Have there been additions and/or deletions to your company's product lines?	6	4	2	0
4) Has a recent ABC analysis produced a difference in major and minor volume products?	4	3	2	0

CUSTOMER SERVICE

5) Has a survey of representative customers indicated service problems?	4	3	2	0
6) Has the customer service complaint level increased recently?	4	3	2	0
7) Have there been any changes in EDP systems or order processing which have resulted in modifications to order cycle times?	6	4	2	0
8) Have other system changes altered inventory reporting, resulting in increased stock outs?	6	4	2	0

LOGISTICS OPERATIONS

9) Have internal distribution center operating factors such as labor or facility costs caused changes in location and/or operations?	6	4	2	0
10) Has purchasing, engineering, or marketing made changes to type, quality, pack, unit, or size of product packaging?	6	4	2	0

11) Has marketing or sales altered the characteristics (size, cycle, timing, etc.) of product promotions?	6	4	2	0
12) Have you reached capacity in terms of volume or inventory of existing distribution facilities?	9	6	3	0
13) Do you shuttle amounts of product between distribution locations?	6	4	2	0

TRANSPORTATION OPERATIONS

14) Has the profile of product shipments changed in terms of TL, LTL, UPS, etc.?	6	4	2	0
15) Does the company move inbound and outbound products across common shipping lanes?	6	4	2	0

PRODUCT OPERATIONS

16) Has the company changed or introduced new production source points for products?	9	6	3	0
17) Has product capacity been changed at existing production locations?	6	4	2	0
18) Do frequent changes occur in production schedules and between product source points?	4	3	2	0

OTHER

19) Have distribution and transportation costs increased as a percent of sales?	9	6	3	0
20) Have there been internal structural changes within the company resulting in integration or segregation of primary business operating units?	9	6	3	0

TOTAL POINTS

If your total points are:

* *Less than 40* - you have outlined minor issues which should be addressed as a part of your overall planning process

* *Between 40 and 70* - you should prioritize these issues and structure an analysis effort to resolve them as a part of a specific plan

* *Over 70* - you should conduct a strategy study to redirect the logistics functions to more closely correlate to the business strategy of the company.

Figure 12-1 A scoring checklist used to determine logistics planning or strategy study. (Courtesy of Robert E. Murray of REM Associates.)

procedures or packaging may be changed, or a decision might be made to link all warehouses by computer. More basic changes, such as changes in the number and location of distribution centers, take more time to implement. There might be a period of overlap when the old system is being phased out as the new one is being phased in. Maintaining levels of customer service during this period would be difficult. Long-range changes (taking from two to five years to implement) result from decisions to redesign a firm's entire logistics system and its relationships with others in the supply chain.

Friction is inherent in any attempt to analyze and redesign a logistics system. Operations managers are typically performing as well as they can. Systems analysts, whether employees of the firm or outside consultants, cannot continue in business by telling every client that all aspects of the present operation are perfect. If analysts did so, they could not justify their functions. Thus, their goals and the goals of operating personnel and operating managers differ. Labor may view with suspicion any suggestion that appears to be a "speed-up," that might reduce the hours or numbers of workers needed, or that hints that facilities might be closed.

PARTIAL SYSTEMS ANALYSES

It is often not feasible to examine all functioning aspects of a system. What follows are examples of analysis focused on a single aspect of logistics. Sometimes, for the purposes intended, partial analysis is sufficient. However, its confined focus is also a limitation, because whatever findings are developed are also narrow. They cannot be used to improve an entire system.

Figure 12-2 illustrates a large metal basket with fold-down sides mounted on a pallet. It provides the advantages of unit-load handling while allowing a wide variation in the size and shape of the individual cartons (or smaller building blocks). The use of such equipment would probably be justified after analysis of practices at both the distribution center where they are loaded and at the retail outlets where they are received and unloaded. The combined savings in both the warehouse and retail stores must be sufficient to justify the investment in the equipment. If the savings are not evenly divided between the warehouse and retail outlets, the party enjoying the greater share of savings may have to compensate the other, in order for the other party to agree to make whatever changes are needed to accommodate the new equipment. Such decisions would be the result of partial systems analysis. The only danger posed by making decisions based on partial analysis of a system is that one might inadvertently commit the entire system without having tested whether the entire system would benefit. An example is a commitment to use only railroads for outbound shipments of over-sized machines while the firm's marketing planners might be deciding that the best potential for sales growth is, for various reasons, customers who are not located on railroad sidings.

Figure 12-2 A metal basket container mounted on a pallet. (Courtesy of Interthor, Inc., Broadview, IL 60153.)

Partial analysis is one of the building blocks of total systems analysis. It is difficult to measure a system's overall performance without measuring and understanding the performance of the various components that make up the entire system. Partial analysis contributes toward an understanding of how an entire system functions. Several examples are cited on the following pages. An explanation of why partial analysis was performed in each case is also offered.

Customer Profitability Analysis

Our first example is an old one but a very useful teaching tool. It deals with a route-analysis system that a large dairy chain used to help its delivery personnel analyze the profitability of each stop on their routes. The accompanying forms are filled out by hand. Although both the forms and the procedures appear unsophisticated by today's standards, they force the individual involved to focus directly on the question of what makes a customer profitable or unprofitable. Figure 12-3 is a time tally sheet completed by the driver/sales-person's supervisor on a day he or she travels along, carrying a stopwatch.[3]

The data collected on the form shown in Figure 12-3 and from the driver/salesperson's monthly records were transferred to several other forms so that they could be analyzed more critically. Figure 12-4 is a tally sheet showing each customer's dollar volume across the top and the number of deliveries the customer receives along the vertical axis. It uses the same data and points out which customers are to be considered overserviced. A high dollar volume combined with a low number of deliveries per month is the goal. Thus, entries toward the upper right-hand corner of the chart show more desirable stops. Entries in the lower left-hand corner of the chart repre-sent less desirable stops. A step downward, a diagonal line is drawn between the upper left-hand and lower right-hand corners. The inference drawn is that entries below the diagonal should be shifted either upward or to the right or both (or eliminated).

The reason these forms are relatively unsophisticated is that the driver/salesperson is an independent or semi-independent operator. He or she sells, delivers, and decides who should and should not receive various types of service. Because the driver/salesperson is paid a salary plus commis-sion, the commission portion of his or her pay is an incentive not to waste time. However, the dairy is interested in time utilization because it pays the salary part of the wages. Rather than tell the driver/salesperson whom he or she can and cannot serve, the dairy has to use this approach to demonstrate how time can be reallocated in a more productive manner.

Warehousing Productivity Analysis

In the late 1970s the National Council of Physical Distribution Management undertook a large-scale study concerning measurements of distribution pro-ductivity. One of the several activities studied was warehousing. To give an idea of the extent of detail involved:

1. Approximately ten different warehousing activities were defined (such as storage, packing and marking, and shipping).
2. About twenty different input or output terms were defined (such as vehicles, weight, pallets, SKUs, cartons, demurrage time, and demurrage charge).
3. Approximately forty different tables containing lists of various measures were used. These were divided into measures of productivity, utilization, and performance and were compared with inputs of labor, equipment, warehouse space, and financial investment. One could make these various

---

[3] The dairy supplying these forms asked not be identified. See Donald F. Wood, "The Driver/Salesman and His Changing Role," in *Proceedings, Transportation Research Forum, 1973* (Oxford, Ind.: Cross, 1973), pp. 631–637.

```
AM Starting Time, Load a/o Unload_____    Time  4:10   Salesman _____
Starting Mileage (at plant)_____  568       Time  4:15   Route #  9
Mileage at First Stop_____  569          Time  4:18   Super. _____
Mileage at Last Stop_____  590            Time  11:45
Ending Mileage (at plant)_____  513        Time  11:54
PM Ending Time, Load a/o Unload  45 min     Time  12:41
Check In (Finish Day)_____  12 min       Time  12:56
                    Total Time:  Hours  8        Minutes  46
```

	Front Porch	Back Porch	Inside or Ask	Solicitations
Time 1st hour: 5:18	45 35 30 / 55 30 35 / 40 110 120 / 63 55 34 / 88 35 / 50 55 / 45 51 / 45 30	85 / 75 / 85 / 103 / 50	NONE	Hour 6th Time :51 / Hour 6th Time 5:03 / Hour 6th Time 1:01 / Hour___ Time___
Miles 1st hour: 574				
Dollars Sold: 30.31 ave 1.13				
Accounts Served: 20 / 5 / 10				
Time 2nd hour: 6:18	20 35 42 30 / 23 81 38 30 / 35 60 28 50 / 30 30 25 70 / 182 38 48 60 / 30 108 70 / 23 64 82 / 45 44 37	75 / 120 / 60 / 61 / 60	NONE	Collections from Customers not receiving delivery: / Hour 3rd Time 3 0 / Hour 7th Time 33
Miles 2nd hour: 577				
Dollars Sold: 75 ave 1.11				
Accounts Served: 27 / 5 / 10				
Time 3rd hour: 7:18	20 30 40 / 25 38 23 / 42 41 / 55 41 / 70 28 / 72 65 / 22 45	120		Hour___ Time___ / Hour___ Time___ / Hour___ Time___ / Total → 3 33½
Miles 3rd hour: 580				
Dollars Sold: 33 ave 1.93		NONE		
Accounts Served: 18 / 0 / 1				
Time 4th	44 / 30 / 17 / 20 / 29	53 / 56 / 120 / 55 / 50 / 60 / 95	85 195 / 128 240 / 95 / 98 / 97 / 120 / 20	Rest/Eating Stops: / Hour 3rd Time 30 0 / Hour 4th Time 11 8 / Hour 7th Time 31 4 / Hour___ Time___ / Hour___ Time___ / Total → 58 min 12 sec
Dollars Sold: 31 ave 1.00				
Accounts Served: 10 / 2 / 9				
Time 6th hour: 10:18	20 / 31 / 10 / 75 / 55 / 58 / 30	73 / 73 / 90 / 45 / 75 / 75 / 126 / 117	170 / 110 / 85 / 60 / 180 / 120 / 120 / 126	REMARKS: / MARK UP Book 1st. 7.00 / " " " 2nd 5.20 / " " " 3rd 3:00 / " " " 4th 4:00 / STRAIGHTEN' TRUCK OUT 6.00 / MARK UP Book 6th 3:50 / Total → 28 min 50 sec
Miles 6th hour: 586				
Dollars Sold: 34.01 ave 1.48				
Accounts Served: 7 / 8 / 8				
c 7th hour: 11:18	30 / 48 / 23 / 47 / 42	65 / 60 / 63 / 40	77 / 240 / 77 / 85 / 90	BROKE UP 2 TIMES BECAUSE OF DEAD END STREET TOOK = 30 SEC
Miles 7th hour: 589				
Dollars Sold: 14.49 ave 104				DELIVERIES 170 / DOLLAR SALES 191.53 / COMMISSION 32.92 / SALES PER STOP 1.13
Accounts Served: 5 / 4 / 15				

Figure 12-3   Home delivery route management growth program tally sheet.

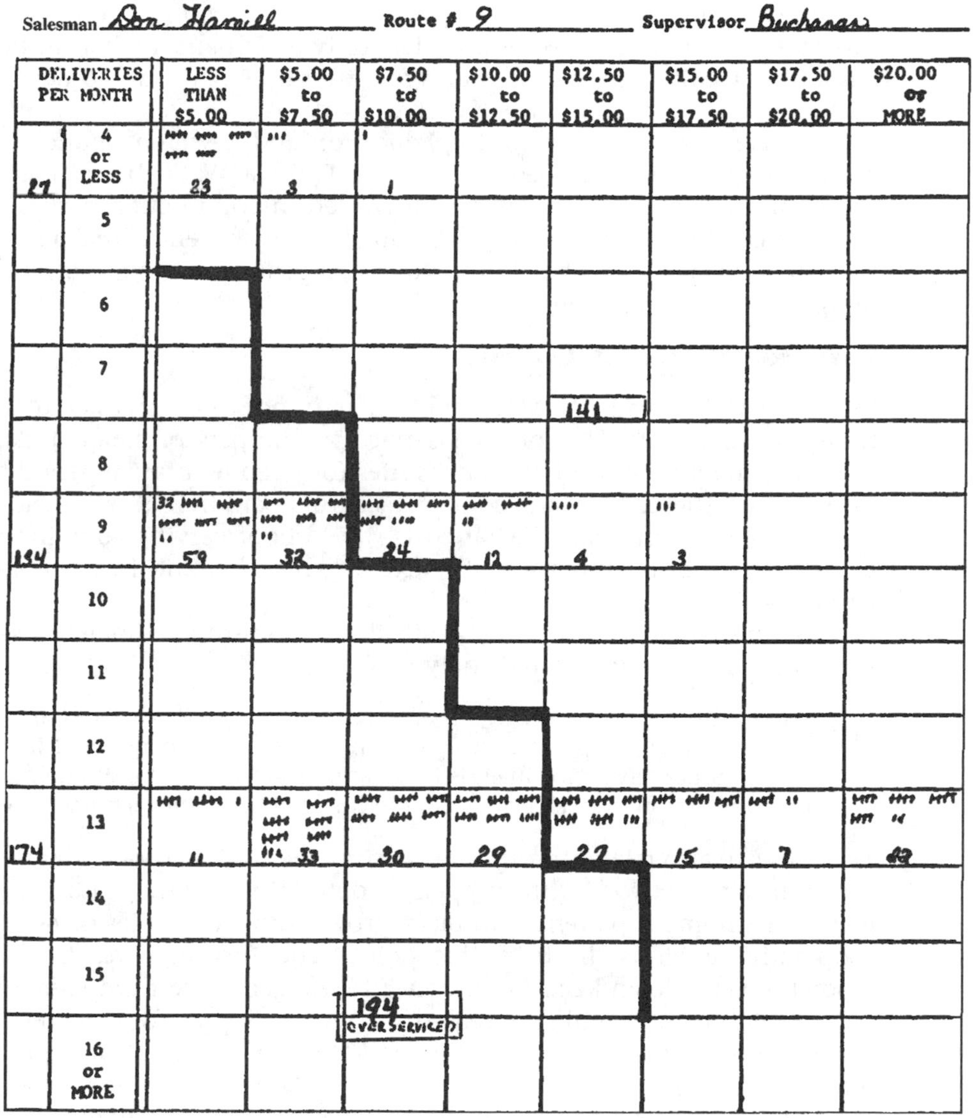

Salesman *Don Hamill*   Route # *9*   Supervisor *Buchanan*

DELIVERIES PER MONTH	LESS THAN $5.00	$5.00 to $7.50	$7.50 to $10.00	$10.00 to $12.50	$12.50 to $15.00	$15.00 to $17.50	$17.50 to $20.00	$20.00 or MORE
4 or LESS 27	23	3	1					
5								
6								
7								
8						141		
9 194	59	32	24	12	4	3		
10								
11								
12								
13 174	11	33	30	29	27	15	7	42
14								
15		194 OVERSERVICED						
16 or MORE								

Figure 12-4 Home delivery route management growth program graphic analysis.

comparisons for each warehouse activity (such as packing and marking) or for all specific activities combined (in the category of overall output or throughput).[4]

[4] A. T. Kearney, Inc., *Measuring Productivity in Physical Distribution* (Chicago: NCPDM, 1978). See also Stephen L. Frey, *Warehouse Operations: A Handbook* (Beaverton, Ore.: M/A Press, 1983), chap. 9.

The analyst then applied these suggested measures, ratios, and other indicators to the warehouse operation under study. Comparisons had to be made with other facilities or with measures for other time periods in order to determine the relative performance of each activity.

In late 1991 the Warehousing Education and Research Council released a software package developed by Professor Thomas W. Speh for determining warehousing costs. The model, which is used in conjunction with a LOTUS 1-2-3 spreadsheet, allows costs to be analyzed by several variables (such as handling expense per labor hour, storage expense per gross foot, and handling and storage costs per unit).[5]

Transportation Cost Analysis

With the widespread use of computers, it is now much easier to analyze transportation costs. UPS offers a service to shippers of small packages. It examines inbound or outbound deliveries for a representative period of time using data gathered from the company's actual paid freight bills. The service also includes an analysis of what costs would be if varying combinations of UPS's three priority systems—UPS Next Day Air, UPS 2nd Day Air, and UPS Ground—are used.

Burlington Northern makes available to its customers some PC software that allows more sophisticated analysis:

> The Logistics Cost Page is the fourth screen. The page calculates all the data entries through the previous screen. In this screen's shipment size field, the user may conduct sensitivity analysis by changing the size of the shipment and the F5 "run" option to recalculate what the costs would be for each revised weight.[6]

The software also relates transportation strategies to inventory policies.

Carriers also work with shippers to determine whether individual shipments or shipment patterns can be improved. Two examples of rail/shipper cooperative analysis illustrate this point. The first involves Conrail and Procter & Gamble and the movement of detergent base from Cincinnati to Lima, Ohio. After a number of requests from the shipper for emergency shipments, Conrail decided to give this market special study (since trucks were sometimes being substituted in emergencies). After some joint shipper/carrier analysis, Conrail decided to run a special minitrain (nicknamed the "Tide Train") weekly, and the transit time was cut to fifteen hours from an average of 6.7 days. Because rail equipment was being used more intensively, Procter & Gamble was able to reduce the number of leased cars it committed to this haul from 230 to 66. There were additional energy savings in winter because

---

[5] *A Model for Determining Total Warehousing Costs for Private, Public, and Contract Warehouses* (Oak Brook, Ill.: Warehousing Education and Research Council, 1991).

[6] *Distribution,* January 1988. The program handles more than transportation issues. See Yosef Sheffi, Babak Eskandari, and Haris N. Koutsopoulos, "Transportation Mode Choice Based on Total Logistics Costs," *Journal of Business Logistics,* September 1988, pp. 137–154.

it was less necessary to heat the arriving tank cars to warm the detergent base to the point where it was liquefied and could be pumped. The new train system saves Procter & Gamble $4 million per year.[7]

The other example involves CSX and Lipton Tea Company and the substitution of bulk for bagged sugar in Lipton's ice tea blending operations at Suffolk, Virginia. The change involved the use of covered jumbo hopper cars (rather than boxcars) and the construction of a bulk unloading system to receive the sugar (rather than unloading the bags into a warehouse). The savings are in transportation costs, because covered hopper costs are less than boxcar costs, and in warehouse labor costs. "Lipton's one-year cost savings in transportation alone are estimated to be in six figures."[8]

Consolidation Analysis

Transportation costs are lower per unit of weight for larger shipments. Because of this there is always a motivation to consolidate small shipments into larger ones. Figure 12-5 is from a worksheet once used for consolidation analysis. One would write the shipments going to each state on the sheet. Today, computer programs that handle shipping documentation generate similar analysis using ZIP codes.

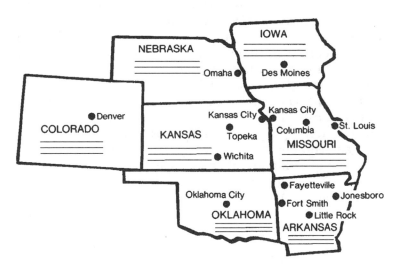

Figure 12-5   Excerpt of forty-eight-state worksheet for preliminary freight consolidation analysis. [Interstate System, Marketing Department, Physical Distribution Audit Map (Grand Rapids, Michigan, 1978). Reproduced with permission.]

[7] Conrail's entry in the *Modern Railroads* 1989 Golden Freight Car competition, unpublished.

[8] CSX Transportation's entry in the *Modern Railroads* 1989 Golden Freight Car competition, unpublished.

Direct Product Profitability (DPP) Analysis

Often used in the food industry, **direct product profitability (DPP) analysis** involves calculations of the "real costs and profitability of distributing each individual product item for the manufacturer, through all the distribution activities (transportation, handling, storage, order processing, etc.) to the final customer."[9] A LOTUS 1-2-3 spreadsheet is used, though some simplifying assumptions have to be made regarding cost allocation (for example, how does one determine and allocate the costs of shelf space in a retail store or of slots in a warehouse?). Even determining the precise costs of the goods may be difficult because some discounts and allowances are based on the dollar size of the entire order, whereas transportation costs or savings are often based on the order's total weight (or cubic volume). The DPP system is most useful to manufacturers looking to analyze alternative packaging and product densities, different routes, different handling systems, and the like.

Benchmarking

Benchmarking of logistics operations, as practiced by firms in the United States today, involves having four to six noncompeting firms get together to analyze and measure how they compare with each other when performing various tasks. For benchmarking, one tries to find other firms that are logistically similar enough that something can be learned from studying their operations. A firm would be concerned when costs of its operation seem high compared with those of other participants in the same category. For example, five firms that all warehouse pallet loads could compare warehouse operations and costs in terms of costs as percentage of sales, costs per units handled, and units per worker hour. Costs could be broken down into labor, space, and equipment.

A group of liquid bulk motor carriers engaged in a benchmarking exercise agreed to compare costs per mile of labor, fuel, operations, overhead, repairs, tires, insurance, and benefits. One of these participants advised future benchmarkers:

- Don't be caught in the NIH ("not invented here") syndrome. We all have much to learn from each other.
- Use consistent definitions, but recognize that different accounting systems will categorize some costs differently.
- Despite your best efforts, it may be impossible to obtain absolute accuracy with the numbers. Don't bother trying. Benchmarking should be focused on

[9] Donald Firth, Jim Apple, Ron Denham, Jeff Hall, Paul Inglis, and Al Saipe, *Profitable Logistics Management*, rev. ed. (Toronto: McGraw-Hill Ryerson, 1989), p. 316.

an overview—a direction to look for cost savings. When red flags appear, then you can focus in on more detail.

- An absolutely flawless "apples-to-apples" comparison will be elusive. Again, don't even try. Look for obvious areas of improvement. That is where you'll want to focus your efforts anyway![10]

Industry Standards Analysis

Industry standards analysis is performed by a trade association (rather than an individual firm) on an industrywide basis. Individual firms cooperate by supplying data about their operations to a centralized research body. The researcher then compiles data for the entire industry and reports the data in a manner that maintains each firm's anonymity. The participating firms then use the tabulations to determine how their performances compare to that of the industry as a whole.

One example of such a study involved periodic tabulations regarding operations of grocery chain distribution centers. Respondents responsible for operating fifty different distribution centers supplied the data. The researchers then compiled and analyzed the data and found five key measures: tons per worker-hour of direct labor, cases per worker-hour of direct labor, tons per hour of total labor, cases per hour of total labor, and cases selected, or picked, per worker-hour. Data were also given for rates of unloading trucks, picking orders by use of various types of equipment (tow trains, chain tows, hand trucks, and pallet jacks), and loading outgoing trucks with cargo that is unitized or in baskets or cages. Good performance by some criteria must sometimes be paid for by poorer performance by other criteria.

Industry standards are also sometimes used by industry groups to bring about industrywide changes that will result in the smoother, lower-cost flow of materials. One example is the grocery industry, which is trying to get standardized pallet and unit-load dimensions, minimum standards for load stability, maximum weight per carton, and uniform markings.[11] Or a dominant firm may try to get the industry to move in a more efficient direction. Apple Computer, for example, is trying to get the computer industry to move from the use of pallets to slipsheets.[12] One reason for this is that many of the industry's inputs originate in Japan, where the cost of wooden pallets is about five times their cost in the United States.

---

[10] Thomas R. Henkel, "Benchmarking: The Key to Your Future?" *Private Carrier,* February 1994, p. 41.

[11] See *Voluntary Industry Guidelines for Dry Grocery Shipping Containers,* a report issued jointly by the Food Marketing Institute, the Grocery Manufacturers of America, and the National-American Wholesale Grocers' Association, January 1988.

[12] Steven Foster, comments at Warehousing Education and Research Council meeting at Apple Computer Distribution Center at Santa Clara, Cal., April 6, 1989.

LOGISTICS SYSTEM DESIGN

Logistics encompasses a wide range of activities. Because the various functional areas of logistics interact, **logistics system design** is a complex undertaking that requires sophisticated analytical techniques. Two commonly used procedures—PERT and simulation—are examined briefly later in the chapter.

Unlike partial systems analysis, in which a part of the system is examined, logistics system design looks at the entire logistics system in an attempt to determine how well all of its components function together.

Establishing Objectives and Constraints

Before a logistics system can be designed or redesigned, it is imperative that the **system goals** and the **system objectives** of the analysis be delineated. Is cost-cutting the objective? Are profits and return on investment the goals? Must customer service standards be improved? How would improved control over the flow of inbound materials influence the performance of the assembly line? Are the goals long- or short-term in nature?

Here is an example of a clearly stated objective:

> Eighteen months from the start of this study, the objectives stated here will be achieved at the lowest possible cost.
>
> Objectives:

1. Order transmittal time for our customers will be less than twenty-four hours.
2. Orders will be processed within sixteen working hours of receipt.
3. Eighty percent of orders will be completely assembled within sixteen working hours. All orders will be assembled within twenty-four working hours.
4. Order delivery time from our dock will be no longer than ninety-six hours for 85 percent of all customers. All domestic orders must be delivered within six days of tendering to the carrier.
5. Stockouts will not be accepted for greater than 7 percent of units requested. Customers experiencing a stockout will be immediately advised by phone. The out-of-stock product will be replaced within ten days, and expedited transportation will be used to reach the customer.

Note that the example presents measurable objectives. This is important because when the study is completed and the new system implemented, it is possible to determine whether the objectives are being met. Objectives that can be measured also serve as a psychological stimulus to managers, who can use them to determine whether their efforts are successful.

Goals tend to be somewhat broader than objectives; examples are increased market share, cost minimization, and profit maximization. As logistics consultant Harvey N. Shycon, in reviewing studies over the last several decades, notes:

> Over the past twenty years most logistics planners have been designing distribution systems to a concept of low cost. Utilizing sophisticated mathematical models with many variables and costs, even trumping their optimizing characteristics, the "scientific method" has been applied. On the basis of such studies there has been a major movement in the past two decades toward fewer distribution centers and a larger proportion of the distribution dollar spent on transportation.
>
> The criteria for these distribution evaluations have almost universally been lowest total cost; that is, the mathematical and financial criteria have been low cost. But when the question is then posed whether the service provided by such a system is adequate, a qualitative examination is made, some minor adjustments frequently made in the results obtained (possibly destroying the optimality of the result identified), and the system is implemented.
>
> But, companies are not in business primarily to reduce cost. Companies are in business to generate profit, growth, and a reasonable return on investment. Why then do we not use these criteria when we design the distribution system?[13]

Two frequently mentioned goals today are developing and adhering to "quality" programs, and being a "leading edge" logistics partner.

Quality Programs

Quality has always been important to logistics operations, and today nearly all firms appear to be pursuing so-called quality objectives. There are several reasons for this. One is the just-in-time inventory system approach, which leaves no spare stores to fall back on in case a defect is found. A second is the replacement of mechanical devices by electronic devices, with the latter being much more accurate, a common example being watches. A third reason is that as possibilities for partnership arrangements present themselves, a company is wary of being linked to a supplier that does not share similar ideas or beliefs about quality measures or concepts.

An article about Xerox Corporation's ten-year quality program said:

> Thanks to its quality efforts, the company has reaped a bounty of heralded results: A 78 percent decrease in the number of defects per 100 machines, a 27 percent reduction in customer service response time, a 30 percent decrease in the time it takes to bring a new product to market, a 50 percent cut in unit manufacturing costs, and a 20 percent increase in revenue per employee.[14]

Today nearly any firm engaged in reengineering its logistics system would keep quality objectives in mind. Quality is important for the functioning of

---

[13] Harvey N. Shycon, "The Folly of Seeking Minimum Cost Distribution," a paper distributed by Shycon Associates, Waltham, Mass., 1983, unpublished.

[14] *World Trade*, December 1993, p. 80.

the firm itself as well as with its partners in the supply chain. At present, ISO 9000, a quality assurance program formulated by the International Standards Organization, is one method for a firm to use to demonstrate to others that it has a system for developing, sustaining, and managing quality.

Leading Edge Logistics Programs

Some firms have already achieved such outstanding competence in their practice of logistics that it sets them apart from their competitors. For some, this is slightly different than a quality program, in that its focus is on activities in the logistics chain. For a firm that already has a leading edge logistics operation, those attempting to design or reengineer the system should realize that this is an advantage that should be maintained. Efforts should be made to get other functions of the firm and its supply-chain partners to function at an equally high level.

A firm that is already at a leading edge position might not be engaged in reengineering its processes. However, it would keep reorganizational and restructuring options open. Planning—whether it involves structural change or not—is important.

> A hallmark of top level logistical competency is the fact that most operational events occur according to plan. The planning of leading edge logistics begins with direct involvement with and commitment to business unit strategic plans. The details are executed through comprehensive logistics operating plans. These plans . . . are . . . blueprints to guide the allocation of human and financial resources dedicated to the logistical process. Among leading edge firms, such logistics plans are typically projected from three to five years forward and are updated on at least an annual basis.[15]

Before system design or redesign can be initiated, there must be agreement on the goals and the measurable objectives. System constraints must also be considered.

System Constraints

System constraints, if any, must also be specified; these involve factors in the system that cannot be changed for various reasons. The following are some examples of system constraints:

1. The distribution center at Detroit will not be closed nor its employment decreased because the firm has publicly pledged to support the downtown area of this city.
2. Order transmittal will continue to be based on a telephone system because this equipment was purchased just six months ago at a cost of $2.5 million.

[15] Donald J. Bowersox, Patricia J. Daugherty, Cornelia Droge, Dale Rogers, and Daniel Wardlow, *Leading Edge Logistics—Competitive Positioning for the 1990s* (Oak Brook, Ill.: CLM, 1989), p. 296.

3. The Wardlow Trucking Company will be utilized whenever it has competitive trucking rates.

In one sense, each system constraint simplifies the situation because it tends to reduce the number of alternatives to be analyzed. However, it is usually fair for the study team to question some of the constraints, especially if their impact may run counter to the stated goals and objectives.

An example of a real constraint from a fantasy situation involves Disneyland in Anaheim. Only nighttime (11:15 P.M. to 7:15 A.M.) deliveries are allowed from a central warehouse to 110 vending locations throughout the theme park. When Disney World in Florida was built, this constraint was overcome by constructing "a network of tunnels beneath the new park, so that shops and restaurants would be serviced, invisibly, at any time."[16]

Another system constraint is shown in Figure 12-6. Here the bridge opening limits the width of what can pass through.

Organization of the Study Team

Once the measurable objectives are established and the system constraints outlined, the next step is to organize the firm's personnel for the analysis. It is preferable to have two separate groups working on the analysis. One group, the working analysis team, includes the managers of the functional areas involved and other staff and quantitative specialists. The customer service director, traffic manager, warehousing manager, director of purchasing, production scheduler, and other relevant managers are members of this team. Any outside management consultants that are used work with the working analysis team on a daily basis. The team is responsible for the actual analysis performed and for the testing, design, and implementation of the new system.

The other group, the management supervisory committee, works with the working analysis team. Its members represent a broader perspective or the overall viewpoint of the firm. Marketing, law, finance, and production personnel as well as accounting executives are represented on the committee. The group is on call to clarify and amplify system objectives. It also occasionally probes the working analysis team about why certain actions are being taken.

Data Collection

Another important stage in designing a logistics system involves data collection. Obviously, the validity of the study can be no stronger than the accuracy of the data base. Seven comprehensive audits must be performed. They are the product, existing facilities, vendor, customer, channels, competitor, and environmental sensitivity audits.

[16] *Distribution*, January 1988, p. 64.

Figure 12-6   A floating dry dock passing through a bridge in Portland, Oregon.
(Courtesy of Port of Portland.)

Product Audit.   The **product audit** is a comprehensive analysis of both the existing product line and new product trends. The specific information that must be determined for each product includes (1) annual sales volume, (2) seasonality, (3) packaging, (4) transportation and warehouse information, (5) present manufacturing or assembly facilities, (6) ease with which manufacturing of product can be scheduled, (7) warehouse stocking locations, (8) present transport modes utilized, (9) sales by regions, (10) complementary products that are often sold at the same time as the product under consideration, (11) relationship to other products in the firm's total product line, and (12) product profitability. This list is not exhaustive; it simply indicates the type of product information needed. Most of the information needed to perform a product audit is available in a firm's existing records.

Existing Facilities Audit.   The **existing facilities audit** is performed next. Since each logistics system is unique, the working analysis team must have a comprehensive audit of its facilities. This includes (1) the location and capacity of production plants, (2) the location and capacity of storage warehouses and distribution centers, (3) the location of the order-processing function, and (4) the transport modes utilized (especially when the firm is somewhat locked into use of a particular mode). When constraints are present, they typically involve aspects of existing facilities that are not to be changed. The existing facilities audit, which tells where a firm is utilizing facilities, provides essential data for determining (or limiting) changes in the system.

Recently it was reported that U.S. exports of frozen food to Japan were being stored in the United States, rather than in Japan. "With the rate of exchange for the dollar and the yen and the high price of real estate in Japan, it's about 2-1/2 times more expensive to store frozen food in Japan [than] it is on the West Coast."[17] Japanese importers buy more cautiously and store less in Japan, leaving U.S. exporters holding the inventory on the West Coast. Note that in this case the change taking place along the supply chain is caused by the relative values of currencies in different countries where supply-chain members are located.

Vendor Audit.   The **vendor audit** looks at sources of supply for raw materials and components. This includes (1) their location, (2) their dependability, (3) quality of work, and (4) the costs and performance of inbound transportation.

In all these audits of existing conditions, it is also permissible to include other options, in this case, say, potential vendors. In fact, before the audits begin, those establishing the study objectives should give some indication of the direction in which they want some studies to go. For example, "Texas Instruments is reducing its number of vendors as part of a company plan to shift its manufacturing from making goods in the hope of selling them to making products as it receives orders for them."[18] It will be helpful to those auditing the existing vendor situation to know in advance that the company is contemplating—or has as a goal—a change in its manufacturing philosophy.

Customer Audit.   The **customer audit** focuses on determining the characteristics of current customers. Potential new customers are also analyzed. The following information must be collected: (1) the location of present and potential customers, (2) the products that each customer orders, (3) the

---

[17] *Journal of Commerce,* September 30, 1993, p. 3A. The article went on to state that the costs of building cold storage plants on the U.S. West Coast "is so high that it's difficult to foresee a reasonable return on investment without looking to the explanation that cold storage in Japan would be even more expensive."

[18] *American Shipper,* November 1994, p. 58.

seasonality of customers' orders, (4) whether customers buy FOB-origin or destination, (5) the importance of customer service, (6) special services customers require, and (7) the volume and profitability of sales for each customer. The customer audit provides a key input for system analysis because, in the end, the system is designed to satisfy the needs and requirements of a firm's customers. Professors J. U. Sterling and D. M. Lambert suggest the use of accounting contribution analysis to report profitability most accurately by product, customer, and channel segment.[19]

Channels Audit.   Since current logistics thought includes the development of long-term, supply-chain relationships with other firms in one's distribution and supply channels, a logistics system design study should include some contact with these parties in the logistics channel to determine whether mutually beneficial agreements might be negotiated or, if in place, continued. This is the **channels audit.** At the very least, one wants to keep these options open and remain flexible in terms of being available for future partnerships. (See Figure 12-7.) When looking at suppliers and customers, one should also examine the possibilities of leveraging the assets of both.

They're a heck of a nice outfit to do business with!

Figure 12-7   Flexibility makes it easier to work together. (Copyright © *Seaway Review,* the Les Strang Publishing Group. Reproduced with permission.)

---

[19] Jay U. Sterling and Douglas M. Lambert, "A Summary of the Accounting Techniques Used to Measure Profitability of Marketing Segments," *Council of Logistics Management Fall 1987 Annual Conference Proceedings,* vol. 1 (Oak Brook, Ill.: CLM, 1987), pp. 205–229. In the same work, see Martin Christopher, "Assessing the Costs of Logistics Services," pp. 195–204.

Regarding logistics planning, D. J. Bowersox and R. E. Murray note that "effective strategic logistics requires the leveraging of combined assets of a company with key suppliers of material and services. The purpose of leveraging is to achieve customer loyalty."[20] While leveraging is often thought of in monetary terms, it could be in other terms also, say, customer service.

Channels audits are also used today to determine whether some channels can be shortened. With the advent of electronic data interchange (EDI) between buyers and sellers, the services of some agents are no longer needed. Wal-Mart, for example, is among "the first of what is expected to be a long line of companies to cut once-vital players [that have been] rendered into economic deadwood by technological advances." Sears's director of EDI implementation is quoted in the same article: "You no longer need the input of whatever role the middleman played."[21]

Channel or supply-chain rearrangement is always a possibility. Here is another example:

> To ensure that the tomatoes arrive at supermarkets faster and in better condition, Calgene is doing its own tomato picking, packing and distributing, eliminating several layers of industry middlemen.
>
> The company's attempt to reinvent the tomato-distribution process—including employing patented packing boxes and a state-of-the-art central distribution facility in Chicago—is just as critical as genetic engineering in its efforts to deliver a tastier tomato.[22]

The problem may be with the sales channels. Record producers are finding that most music stores and record outlets stock only the most popular current hits and are reluctant to stock slower-moving "classics" of only a few years ago.

> Although the compact-disc boom has encouraged record companies to dig into their vaults and re-issue scores of older catalog albums, many retailers, especially stores located in shopping malls, fail to carry essential titles by enduring artists such as the Beatles, Elvis Presley, the Grateful Dead, Chuck Berry and the Rolling Stones.[23]

Hence the manufacturers may have to resort to selling their older titles through retail catalogs. A common example of channel rearrangement is for a firm to start printing and distributing mail-order catalogs.

Competition Audit.   The **competition audit** outlines the competitive environment within which the firm is selling. The following informa-

[20] Donald J. Bowersox and Robert E. Murray, "Logistics Strategic Planning for the 1990s," *Council of Logistics Management Fall 1987 Annual Conference Proceedings,* vol. 1 (Oak Brook, Ill.: CLM, 1987), pp. 234–235.

[21] *Journal of Commerce,* December 16, 1991, p. 3B.

[22] *San Francisco Chronicle,* September 30, 1993, p. B1.

[23] *Rolling Stone,* September 3, 1992, p. 80.

tion should be ascertained: (1) the order-transmittal methods of competitors, (2) the accuracy and speed of competitors' order processing, (3) the speed and consistency of carrier movements used by competitors, (4) the ratio of orders given to competitors that could not be filled because of a product stockout, (5) competitors' experience with loss and damage claims, and (6) a narrative statement regarding customers' perception of the customer service strengths and weaknesses of the firm and its competitors.

Unlike the other audits, the information required for the competition audit is generally not available within a company's own records, although salespeople can often provide some of it. Outside marketing research firms are used to survey competitors to gather the required data. Outside research firms can usually design the questionnaire in such a manner as to disguise the ultimate recipient of the information.

Environmental Sensitivity Audit.   Many firms operate in markets or in political areas where there is a growing public awareness of environmental protection issues. The **environmental sensitivity audit** should look at current practices along the supply chain regarding packaging materials used and the recyclability of both packaging and product. A related study would be of the potential markets for the materials being recycled; they must be strong enough to yield prices that will support recycling.

> Avoiding stock-outs and late shipments, going the extra mile to meet your customer's emergency needs, and shortening your customer's order-to-delivery cycles may seem like sure-fire ways to win and retain customers across the [European] continent. But new environmental legislation, as well as environmentally conscious customers, are demanding more.
>
> In fact, as they rationalize their European operations and pursue supply chain logistics strategies, many companies may be wondering, "Where is that 15 to 20 percent cost savings associated with distribution in a barrier-free Single Market [resulting from Europe '92]?"
>
> They may want to look at their costs of complying with environmental laws for the answer [as to where the savings went]. Increasingly legal requirements and consumer preferences are making a supplier or manufacturer responsible for a product beyond its sale and delivery. In parts of Europe, the manufacturer is now responsible for taking back and disposing of packaging, rejects and excess, as well as curing any environmentally unfriendly aspect of the end product. As a result of these laws, Single Market opportunities are no longer the only driving force behind supply chain logistics management. Traditional approaches to logistics management are giving way to "green logistics."[24]

Analysis of the Data

Once the information from the various audits is assembled, the next step is to examine and analyze it. This can be accomplished using relatively unso-

[24] Jack Berry, Greg Girard, and Cynthia Perras, "Logistics Planning Shifts into Reverse" *Journal of European Business*, September–October, 1993, p. 35.

phisticated techniques or complex methods. The sophistication of methods has improved greatly with the widespread use of computers, which both generate data in a form that can be easily analyzed and can analyze it. The scale of problems addressed is also greater. Not long ago the pin and string method of routing trucks was frequently used. It involved a wall map with a thumbtack stuck at each place a delivery had to be made. One end of the string would be tied to the thumbtack at the distribution warehouse, and then an effort would be made to loop the string in a manner that touched all thumbtacks, and returned to the origin, using the minimum length of string. Contrast this with the following abstract of a paper entitled "Consolidating and Dispatching Truck Shipments of Heavy Petroleum Products," published in 1994:

> Mobil Oil Corporation consolidates and dispatches truck shipments of heavy petroleum products—lubricants in packages and in bulk—from ten lubricant plants nationwide. They dispatch hundreds of orders daily either individually, or as consolidated truckloads, using a very non-homogeneous fleet of Mobil-controlled and contract vehicles, and common carriers. Shipments schedules may span several days, and include stops to pick up returned drums or entire trailers. Shipping costs depend upon the vehicle used, the shipment size, the locations of all required stops, and the route distance and time. Candidate consolidations are generated automatically, or with dispatcher assistance. Then, an optimal, minimal-cost set of schedules is selected. Mobil has been using this system for three years, reducing annual transportation costs by about $1 million (US).[25]

Many computer and operations management courses taught in business schools today contain some assignments associated with logistics operations. This book will touch on only two methods: PERT and simulation. PERT is of value when the analyst is attempting to determine the relationships among all tasks that must be performed. Simulation is much broader and assumes that the relationships are known; it is used to determine how well an actual or proposed system will perform under varying stresses.

PERT.   PERT (or **program evaluation and review technique**) is a form of network analysis that places all component tasks in the sequence they are to be performed. It recognizes that some tasks can be performed only in a certain order, whereas for others no such relationship exists. There is a period when either of two tasks, neither, or both can be performed. Following is an example of how PERT can be applied to the export process, where some twenty different steps are involved.[26] They are listed here and

[25] The paper is by Dan O. Bauch, Gerald G. Brown, and David Ronen and has been accepted for publication in *Interfaces*.

[26] See James W. Tatterson and Donald F. Wood, "PERT, CPM and the Export Process," *OMEGA*, vol. 2 (1974), pp. 421–426.

assigned identifying letters. Letters early in the alphabet are assigned to tasks that must be performed first. However, there is no absolute relationship between the letter assigned to a task and when, in comparison with other tasks, it must be performed. Although the word *task* is implied, the word *event* will be used. Event means that the task has been completed.

Event A: An order from a foreign customer is received.

Event B: Applicable government controls concerning the export transaction are determined.

Event C: Transportation mode, carrier, and routing are selected.

Event D: The goods needed to fill the export order are made available.

Event E: The export declaration is prepared.

Event F: Space is reserved on the carrier.

Event G: Insurance coverage for the shipment is obtained.

Event H: Packaging requirements for the export shipment are established.

Event I: The delivery permit for the export shipment is obtained.

Event J: The commercial invoice covering the shipment is prepared.

Event K: The shipment is packed, marked, and weighed.

Event L: Inland transportation to point of exportation is arranged.

Event M: The certificate of origin covering the goods is prepared.

Event N: The bill of lading or airwaybill for the shipment is prepared.

Event O: The consular invoice is obtained from the government representative of the importing country.

Event P: Any special certificates required for importation are obtained.

Event Q: The shipment is onloaded aboard an inland carrier for transport to the point of exportation.

Event R: The shipment arrives at the point of exportation, and a receipt for the goods is issued.

Event S: The shipment is loaded aboard the international carrier; the bill of lading or airway bill is issued.

Event T: The shipment arrives at the designated point of entry. (For the purposes of our analysis, this is as far as we are concerned. Beyond this point, the buyer assumes responsibility.)

To perform the PERT analysis, it is necessary to have some real figures as input data. The example used is a 2,000-pound shipment from an exporter in the San Francisco area destined to a consignee in Manila. The shipment quotation is CIF (cost-insurance-freight) Manila; this means that the exporter is responsible for the performance of all export process events until the shipment is off-loaded in Manila. In addition to the regular documentation required, the shipper must obtain a delivery permit from the steamship company. Shipment value is $36,000. The exporter purchases the merchandise at event A and receives payment from the customer at event T. No mode, route, or time limit is specified. Because of the high value and small size of this shipment, the shipper is uncertain whether to ship by sea or air or whether to expedite the shipment.

Estimates of cost and time must be made for each of the twenty tasks or events. Sequential relationships between events must be recognized. Figure 12-8 depicts all the various relationships in network form. Tasks that must be performed in sequence follow along the same line. Tasks that can be performed simultaneously are shown on parallel lines. Cost figures in dollars are represented by the first number; the second number represents time in days. Four alternative types of shipment are involved. Each line between event A and event T is a path. The time to travel along each path is then added, giving these results:

Network path	Number of days required to traverse path
ADHKQRST	44.0
ADHKNORST	46.5 (critical path)
ADHKJMORST	45.5
AFGJMORST	41.5
AFILQRST	37.5
ABEILQRST	37.5

These figures are for the normal shipment via water. Even though all paths must be traversed, one path—ADHKNORST—has been designated as the critical path because it takes the longest time to traverse. The reason it is considered critical is that if one wishes to speed up the normal surface process, the time-saving improvement must be made on one or more events that occur on this path. It would do no good to speed up task J because even if J is accomplished in less time than originally estimated, it will not affect the total time of the tasks on the critical path.

In fact, the shipper could allot more time to task J than it presently takes without slowing down the export process. The question is, How much? This is where the path concept is useful. Note that event J appears on several other paths, although not on the critical one. Path ADHKJMORST contains task J and is closest in time value to the critical path. It takes 45.5 days to complete, while the critical path takes 46.5 days. Thus, the shipper could add one more day to the time to complete task J without affecting overall delivery time. Other tasks not on the critical path could be analyzed in a similar manner. If the shipper does not want to improve delivery time, it can reduce costs by allowing more time for the completion of tasks that are off of the critical path.

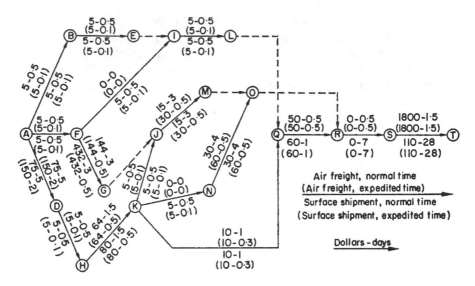

Figure 12-8 A sample network for an export shipment. (Reprinted from *OMEGA*, vol. 2, no. 3 (1974), p. 424, with kind permission from Elsevier Science Ltd., The Boulevard, Langford Lane, Kidlington OX5 1GB, U.K.)

Figure 12-8 can also show how to improve delivery time. Using the normal surface transport figures, the shipper would concentrate on tasks that are on the critical path since overall time could be reduced only be reducing their required times. Task D (or event D) appears on the critical path. Any reduction in time to complete D will reduce the time required to traverse the critical path by the same amount. At present, D takes five days. If event D could be completed in, say, 0.5 day, this would reduce the critical path from 46.5 days to 42.0 days. There is a limit to improvements that can be made on the critical path, however. Saving time on events D, H, and K, for example, is useful up to a total savings of five days. At that point, path AFGJMORST becomes the controlling, or critical, path, and D, H, and K are no longer critical.

The PERT chart suggests how the shipper should go about adjusting the time allocation for each task. Costs of altering the time spent on each task should also be known. For events off the critical path, time allowances could be extended if cost reductions will occur. For events on the critical path, any change in time allowance has a direct impact on system performance. This holds until the time saving becomes so great that the path itself is no longer critical.

Note the usefulness of the PERT chart in evaluating a complete process. It enables the user to relate tasks and focus attention on any task without losing sight of where it fits in the overall picture. The foregoing example is old, but one of the authors has always found it to be a useful introductory example to use in class. Today one would also include the time investment in inventory as part of the daily costs, even taking into account the fact that the cost of each completed task increases the investment in the transaction under way. In a course the same author teaches that deals with international logistics, students are expected to find a real export or import shipment and then prepare separate PERT charts for the financing, logistics, and documentation channels and then a single chart that combines all three channels into one.

Simulation.   The computer technique that is most widely used for logistics system planning is **simulation.** It usually involves a computer model that is a series of mathematical relationships. Simulation reliability is achieved by making the model as close to the real world as possible. Such factors as transport mode availability, transportation costs, location of vendors, warehouse locations, customer locations, customer service requirements, and plant locations must all be accurately reflected in the model. Although logistics simulation models may require many programmers working together for long periods, they enable the firm to answer questions such as these:

- If we reduce the average order cycle time for our customers from twelve days to seven days, what will be the additional cost involved? Will sales increase?
- If we presently use our trucks for outbound movements only and are debating whether to use them to pick up some of our inputs on their return trips, how will this affect our current schedules of outbound deliveries?
- If we reduce the number of distribution warehouses from thirty-two to nineteen, what will be the effect on customer service standards? What about costs?
- If our vendors improve the accuracy of their delivery times, by how much can we safely reduce our stocks of components?
- If the minimum order accepted is increased from $20 to $100, what will be the effect on total sales?
- If private carriage is substituted for motor common carriage, what will be the changes in total logistics costs, and what effect will this have on customer service standards?
- What will happen if we shift the order penetration point nearer to or farther from the customer? (The order penetration point is when and where a specific item in an inventory or production process is earmarked for a particular customer.)

Here is an example of simulation applied to a specific routing problem. It involves the routing pipe that is used in pipeline construction. A natural gas pipeline being built between Saskatchewan and Iowa required more than 800 miles of steel pipe. The pipe was delivered by rail from three domestic mills and three foreign sources. The initial allocations between domestic and foreign sources were dictated by government requirements for local content. Simulation took into account the work schedules at the mills, the time needed to load the pipe aboard railcars, the vessel-rail transfer times in ports, train speeds, allowances for overheated rail wheels (bad orders) on three of four trains (assigned at random), three possible derailments of the 170 trains being used (derailments were assigned at random, and each derailed train was assigned to be delayed three days, but following trains could be rerouted), defective pipe (involving both defects that could be remedied at the site and those that could not), defects caused by welding, and some barge logistics (for example, one route for imported pipe was by water from New Orleans to St. Louis).

> Simulation results showed that the pipe could be delivered on time. As we gathered the simulation statistics, we realized that the company could get the pipe delivered in the assigned 260 days with 20 percent fewer railcars than originally proposed (1,358 were needed and 1,703 had been planned). At a cost of $50 for leasing one railcar for one day, this translated into a savings of $4.5 million. The total cost for the study was $29,800. Thus the benefit-to-cost ratio was 150 to 1.[27]

The primary advantage of simulation is that it enables the firm to test the feasibility of a proposed change at relatively little expense. In addition it prevents firms from experiencing the public embarrassment of making a major change in their logistics system that might result in a deterioration of customer service levels or an increase in total operating expense.

Career logistics people should familiarize themselves with computer simulations because they are important to logistics planning and will become even more important in the future. Many consultants have developed expertise in simulation techniques and have devised models that can be used by various clients. Figure 12-9, from a consultant's brochure, describes three different computer systems useful to a client making decisions involving the location of distribution facilities.

Consultant Paul S. Bender writes:

> The structure of a logistics system can be represented by a network, containing two types of entities: nodes and links. Nodes represent stationary inventory locations, such as suppliers, plants, warehouses and customers. Links represent moving inventories, such as transportation moves.
>
> In any logistics system, the network defined by nodes and links is fully described by their attributes. In any situation, the attributes of nodes and links can only be of three types: costs, or their negative, revenues; numerically expressed constraints such as minimum or maximum capacities; and nonnumerical, logical conditions such as legal, technical, policy or service conditions that must be respected to arrive at a practical logistic strategy.
>
> Those concepts form the basis for the automatic generation of customized logistic models.[28]

[27] Deepak Bammi, "Northern Border Pipeline Logistics Simulation," *Interfaces*, May–June 1990, p. 10.

[28] "Developing Optimum Global Logistics Strategies Using Artificial Intelligence and Large Scale Optimization," (Arlington, Va.: Bender Management Consultants, 1990, unpublished.)

LOCATE Network Planning Software Systems

LOCATE3+

LOCATE3+ is an interactive PC-based, strategic decision-support system that helps companies solve complex multi-echelon, multi-product manufacturing and distribution network problems. The system utilizes advanced simulation and optimization techniques to help operations and logistics executives analyze alternative supply/production/distribution configurations to optimally determine the least-cost, most service sensitive physical distribution network. LOCATE3+ thus will help make decisions on: the number and location of plants and distribution facilities; customer sourcing assignments; replenishment flow paths; product stocking strategies (e.g., central-ized stocking of slow-moving items); inventory investment levels; distribution facility configurations (e.g., DC, pool point, cross dock, etc.); and certain issues surrounding transportation management. In general, the model will help answer the question "How do I construct a network of facilities and transportation links that will optimize the flow of product through the supply chain, while respecting capacity constraints, and maintaining or enhancing my service objectives?" The system provides easy data entry, creation, and editing features, as well as detailed tabular and graphical information outlining all logistics costs and product movements throughout the supply chain.

LOCATE/CP

Although LOCATE3+ can incorporate manufacturing costs and capacities as factors in supply chain and facility location decisions (including plant location), it does so at an aggregate level (i.e., at a product/plant level). LOCATE/CP adds *detailed* manufacturing capacity planning capabilities into the facilities network decision. The system maintains all of the functionality of LOCATE3+, but allows you to define production information (such as run rates, costs, and capacities) at the plant/line/product level. You can further constrain solutions by defining capacities of key raw materials and their consumption rates. Therefore, LOCATE/CP has the capability of answering the question "Which products should I manufacture on which lines at which plants and in what quantities?" and ascertaining how these manufacturing considerations impact decisions surrounding the entire physical distribution network. The "CP" model also adds profit maximization logic to the "least costing" capabilities of LOCATE3+.

LOCATE4 for Windows

LOCATE4 for Windows is a complete rewrite of the DOS-based LOCATE3+ and LOCATE/CP systems. Based on the modules utilized, the software can accomplish the same tasks as LOCATE3+ and LOCATE/CP, but takes advantage of the benefits inherent in Windows-based systems. Therefore, LOCATE4 incorporates a GUI interface with simple interfaces to other Windows applications; is more flexible and easier to use; has relational database logic; and can solve for a more detailed/complex problem. In the future, the modules comprising LOCATE4 for Windows will completely replace both LOCATE3+ and LOCATE/CP.

Figure 12-9   A summary of the system simulation services offered by a consulting firm. [Courtesy of CSC (formerly Cleveland Consulting Associates).]

An H. J. Heinz Company study conducted some time ago gave an indication of the possibilities that simulation studies offer.[29] The H.J. Heinz Company was concerned with the configuration of its warehouse network. Specific questions involved the following issues: (1) How many warehouses should be utilized? (2) Where should they be located? (3) Which customers should be served from each warehouse? Because of the size and complexity of the problem, consultants Harvey N. Shycon and Richard B. Maffei decided that a simulation model would be the best analysis technique.

When the study was initiated, Heinz had sixty-eight warehouses in the United States. Over time, Heinz officials had noticed that the "Mom and Pop" retailers were becoming less important in grocery distribution. Chain stores were the dominant factor, and they received their products in fewer locations and in much larger quantities. It was obvious that Heinz had too many warehouses.

Once the objective of the study had been determined and the working analysis and management supervisory groups established, the product, existing facility, customer, and competition audits were completed. Shycon and Maffei determined that three alternative distribution methods could be used. First, products could be shipped directly from the production plant to the customer. Second, products could be transported from the factory to other production facilities, consolidated with other products, and transported immediately to the customer. Or, third, the products could flow from the factory to a storage warehouse and then to the customer. The first two alternatives did not use warehousing facilities. Warehouses were needed for customers that do not order in large enough quantities to warrant direct shipments and for those that require relatively short order cycles.

The computer was told to try various numbers and locations of warehouses for shipments that required intermediate warehousing. For each configuration, a year's worth of sales data were simulated and the costs and customer service levels were determined. Each alternative configuration required approximately seventy-five million mathematical calculations by the computer. When each alternative was tested, the results indicated that the optimum number of warehouses was about forty. With this number of warehouses, customer service standards were achieved and total distribution costs were minimized. Note that this study was conducted prior to 1960, although the type of analytical problem faced then is no different from today.

---

[29] Harvey N. Shycon and Richard B. Maffei, "Simulation—Tool for Better Distribution," *Harvard Business Review*, November–December 1960, pp. 65–75. See also Donald J. Bowersox, "Planning Physical Distribution Operations with Dynamic Simulation," *Journal of Marketing*, January 1972, pp. 17–25; O. Keith Helferich and Lloyd B. Mitchell, "Planning for Customer Service with Computer Simulation," *Transportation and Distribution Management*, January–February 1975, pp. 17–21; and Katy Lawrence, James H. Stone, and Walter L. Weart, "Computer Assisted Modeling of an Automobile Distribution Network," in *Council of Logistics Management Fall 1987 Annual Conference Proceedings*, vol. 2 (Oak Brook, Ill.: CLM, 1987), pp. 321–337.

Arthur Geoffrion and Richard Powers, who have long been involved in logistics system design, traced the development of system design processes over the twenty–year period from 1975 to 1995. Desired outputs have always been answers to questions such as the following:

- How many stocking points should there be, and where should they be located? Should they be owned?
- Should all stocking points carry all products or specialize by product line?
- Which customers should be served by each stocking point for each product?
- Where should the plants be located?
- What should be produced at each plant, and how much?
- Which suppliers should be used at what level?
- What should the annual transportation flows be throughout the system? Should pool points be used, and if so, where should they be?[30]

The two authors then went on to describe the evolution of algorithms used in these problems, including nonoptimizing cost calculators, heuristic methods, linear programming, and specialized optimizers. Increased computer capacity has helped, and "new advances in factoring embedded network structures have yielded remarkable computational improvements that already have proven valuable for an immense logistics model (about 550,000 constraints and 7,000,000 variables)."[31]

Geoffrion and Powers have their own program, and they gave some examples of its use:

- Baxter Healthcare Corporation had acquired another company in the same business, and it used the program to integrate the two distribution systems.
- Pet, Incorporated, uses the program to evaluate shifting production among plants and introducing new products.
- Clorox Company used the program to test the distribution synergy and implications of acquiring Pine Sol and distributing it in the same channels as bleach.
- Eastman Kodak was interested in possibilities of recycling, and it "used the package to evaluate how best to collect spent film products from film processors and get them back to recycling facilities. To accomplish this recycling project, the usual model was inverted, with customers

[30] Arthur M. Geoffrion and Richard F. Powers, *20 Years of Strategic Distribution System Design: An Evolutionary Process* (Los Angeles: Western Management Science Institute at UCLA working paper No. 431, 1994), pp. 2–3.

[31] Ibid., p. 9.

becoming suppliers and the recycling facilities becoming the cus-tomers."[32]

Many other, different logistics system simulation programs exist. They differ according to their mathematical approach, the computer capacity they need, and the amounts of data inputs. Some are proprietary and are used by consultants or third-party logistics services providers. Many of the programs have as their initial focus the improvement of customer service. A second focus is to integrate inbound and outbound logistics functions.

As Figure 12-10 illustrates, there is very little business behavior that can-not be simulated.

Design Implementation

The final activity in logistics system design is **design implementation.** However, only rarely is an operating logistics system completely revised at

"It can't actually think, but when it makes a mistake, it can put the blame on some other computer."

Figure 12-10 Computers can simulate many forms of business behavior. (Reproduced by permission of the artist and the Masters Agency.)

[32] Ibid., pp. 16–17.

one time. A one-time, across-the-board revision is typically too traumatic for most firms to tolerate because it inevitably results in a breakdown of customer service functions. Orders are lost, incorrect quantities are shipped, stockouts are frequent—these are the typical problems that occur when a system is changed too radically in a short period of time. In addition, personnel may resist the changes.

Most firms prefer to use their simulation and PERT analysis to find those areas that should be changed first, because these functions are the greatest bottlenecks to efficiency. Also, the payoffs may be greater.

Design implementation may also involve the design, construction, and placing into operation of very large and specialized facilities. Figure 12-11 is a drawing of automated warehouse equipment. For a facility of this size,

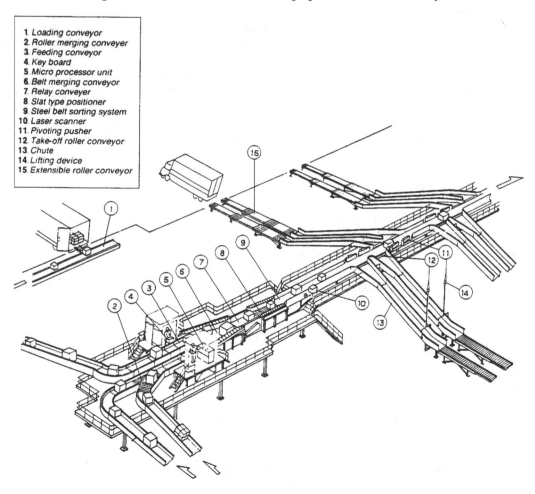

1. Loading conveyor
2. Roller merging conveyer
3. Feeding conveyor
4. Key board
5. Micro processor unit
6. Belt merging conveyor
7. Relay conveyer
8. Slat type positioner
9. Steel belt sorting system
10. Laser scanner
11. Pivoting pusher
12. Take-off roller conveyor
13. Chute
14. Lifting device
15. Extensible roller conveyor

Figure 12-11   Schematic drawing of automated warehouse equipment. (Source: Sandvik Process Systems.)

considerable analysis would be needed to determine the amounts of materials flowing into and out of the facility and to select the site. A facility such as this is but part of a total system.

SUMMARY

This chapter covers two main topics: the analysis of logistics systems and their design. Most systems analysis undertaken is considered partial in nature; that is, it looks at how well some specific activity is performed or is functioning. Total system analysis involves looking at the overall picture. It is often performed by an outside consultant with a mainframe computer because it is usually a massive undertaking. In addition, outside consultants may be more objective.

Several examples of partial analysis are given, including customer profitability, vendor quality control, warehouse productivity, and transportation costs.

One approach to total system design involves establishing objectives and constraints, organizing the study team, collecting data, analyzing the data, and so on. Two analytical techniques, PERT and simulation, are usually performed through the use of computers. Finally, assuming that changes are called for, the new system must be implemented.

QUESTIONS FOR DISCUSSION AND REVIEW

1. Describe the importance of systems analysis in logistics.
2. What are the strengths and weaknesses of systems analysis as applied in logistics?
3. "Systems analysis is the most important activity supervised by senior logistics management." Do you agree? Why or why not?
4. Why are outside consultants frequently employed to analyze a firm's logistics practices?
5. Why is partial systems analysis so commonly used?
6. What is your reaction to the customer profitability analysis utilized by the dairy driver/salesperson? Could it be improved? Discuss.
7. What are the advantages of having a trade group collect and then distribute data concerning the relative efficiency of its various members' operations?
8. What is direct product profitability (DPP) analysis?
9. Discuss the basic procedure used in system design. Does this procedure appear logical to you?
10. Why is it important to specify clearly the objectives of a study?
11. What are system constraints? Are they important? Why?
12. "Design objectives should not be measurable because, if they are, they tend to make the systems analysis inflexible and difficult to implement." Do you agree? Why or why not?

13. Assume that you want to determine the average length of time that it takes a first-class letter to be delivered in the United States. What will you measure? How will you set up your sample? Explain.

14. Discuss the information that should be contained in each of the following audits: product, existing facilities, vendor, customer, channels, and competition.

15. Which of the seven types of audit is the most important? The least important? Why?

16. What is PERT? What types of problems can be solved using this technique?

17. What is the critical path? Why is it important? Discuss.

18. What is simulation? What are its strengths and weaknesses?

19. Outline the problems and procedures used in the H. J. Heinz simulation. Did the analysis appear logical to you? Discuss.

20. "Design implementation is often accomplished in stages rather than all at once." Is this logical? What are the strengths and weaknesses of a gradual approach?

SUGGESTED READINGS

Allman, William P. "A Cost-Minimization Planning Model for the Coal Sourcing/Transport Network Problem, Emphasizing Environmental Emission Restrictions." *Energy Systems and Policy,* vol. 15 (1991), pp. 65–73.

Ballou, Ronald H. *Business Logistics Management,* 3d ed. Englewood Cliffs, N.J.: Prentice Hall, 1992.

Beierlein, James G., Jack Kirkland, and Melissa Cummins. "A Systems Approach to Minimizing the Total Cost of Moving Milk from Farmers to Consumers in Pennsylvania." *Journal of the Transportation Research Forum* (1988), pp. 80–85.

Bingham, John E., and Paul S. Pezzini. "Systems Design for International Logistics." *International Journal of Technology Management,* vol. 5, no. 4 (1990), pp. 472–479.

Blanchard, Benjamin. *Logistics Engineering and Management,* 4th ed. Englewood Cliffs, N.J.: Prentice Hall, 1992.

Bookbinder, James H., and Carolynn I. Barkhouse. "An Information System for Simultaneous Consolidation of Inbound and Outbound Shipments." *Transportation Journal,* Summer 1993, pp. 5–20.

Campbell, James F. "Designing Logistics Systems by Analyzing Transportation, Inventory, and Terminal Cost Trade-Offs." *Journal of Business Logistics,* vol. 11, no. 1 (1990), pp. 159–179.

Clark, Richard L., and Kent N. Gourdin. "Measuring the Efficiency of the Logistics Process." *Journal of Business Logistics* (Fall 1991), pp. 17–33.

Dawe, Richard L. "An Investigation of the Pace and Determinants of Information Technology Use in the Manufacturing Materials Logistics System." *Journal of Business Logistics,* vol. 15, no. 1 (1994), pp. 229–259.

Droge, Cornelia, and Richard Germain, "Evaluating Logistics Management Information Systems." *International Journal of Physical Distribution & Logistics Management,* vol. 21, no. 7 (1991), pp. 22–27.

Gattorna, John L. "Creating an Effective Logistics Systems Solution: The Role of People." *International Journal of Physical Distribution & Logistics Management,* vol. 22, no. 3 (1992), pp. 11–14.

Gomes, Roger, and John T. Mentzer. "A Systems Approach to the Investigation of Just-in-Time." *Journal of Business Logistics* (Sept. 1988), pp. 71–88.

Mentzer, John T., and Brenda Konrad. "An Efficiency/Effectiveness Approach to Logistics Performance Analysis." *Journal of Business Logistics* (Spring 1991), pp. 33–62.

O'Neil, Brian F., and Jon L. Ivenson. "An Operational Procedure for Prioritizing Customer Service Elements." *Journal of Business Logistics,* vol. 12, no. 2 (1991), pp. 157–191.

Rinehart, Lloyd M., and Robert A. Novack. "Development of an Integrated Introductory Logistics Course." In *The Transportation and Logistics Research Foundation Papers.* Columbus: Ohio State University Press, 1991, pp. 1–22.

Sheffi, Yosef, et al. "Transportation Mode Choice Based on Total Logistics Costs." *Journal of Business Logistics* (Sept. 1988), pp. 137–154.

Tarski, Ignacy. *The Time Factor in Transportation Processes* (Amsterdam: Elsevier, 1987).

Tyworth, John E., and William Grenoble. "Spreadsheet Modeling in Logistics: Advancing Today's Educational Tools." *Journal of Business Logistics* (Spring 1991), pp. 1–25.

Windle, Robert, and Martin Dresner. "Productivity Measurement in Transportation Industries: A Summary." In *Proceedings, 35th Meeting of the TRF, 1993,* pp. 141–148.

C A S E   1 2 - 1

EASING IRA'S IRE I

Ira Pollack was difficult to work for. A self-made millionaire, he paid extremely high salaries but demanded much from his subordinates, including being on call twenty-four hours per day. In his Las Vegas penthouse, he would study and restudy each detail of his conglomerate's performance, and then call some unlucky underling—at any hour—to vent his anger and demand that something or other be improved. His tantrums were legendary.

One of Pollack's underlings, Tamara Wood, was driving her new red Mercedes convertible along Rodeo Drive in Beverly Hills, looking for a parking space. Her college class (at Northern Illinois University at DeKalb) was holding its fifth reunion in Chicago, which Tamara planned to attend. She wanted to buy a new outfit for the event, to show her old classmates that she had "arrived." A chauffeur-driven Rolls pulled away from the curb, leaving an empty space right in front of Tamara's favorite couturier. Tamara expertly swung her Mercedes into the empty space, looked up, and was pleased to see that there was still nearly an hour left on the meter. "Daddy was right," she thought to herself, "clean living does pay off."

As she turned off the ignition, the telephone mounted below the dash started buzzing. Tamara hesitated. Would it be John, calling to thank her for that wonderful evening? Would it be Matt, seeing if she were free to spend next weekend on Catalina Island? Or maybe it was Jason, who was always wanting her to accompany him to Waikiki. Tamara finally picked up the phone and sweetly said "hello."

"Dammit! Don't 'hello' me!" shouted a man's voice at the other end.

Tamara's stomach churned, her muscles tightened, and she said, weakly, "Sorry, Mr. Pollack, I was expecting somebody else."

"That's obvious," he retorted. "At this hour of the day, you're on *my* time and *should* be thinking of business. How come you're not in the office?"

"I'm just making a customer-service follow-up," responded Tamara, hoping that Mr. Pollack would not ask for too many details.

"Well, you *should* be worried about customer service," said Pollack. "That's why I've called. I've been studying performance records for all my operations dealing with the amount of time that elapses between our receipt of an order and when our customer receives a shipment. The performance of your distribution center in West Hollywood *stinks! Drop* what you're doing and *get back to your office* and figure out what's wrong! Then tell me what's needed to speed up your operation. Call me at any hour."

Tamara heard the phone click. She forgot about DeKalb. She forgot about Chicago and the new outfit. She forgot about her night with John, about Catalina Island, and about Waikiki. She heard a faint beep to her left. She saw a maroon Jaguar, with a Beverly Hills matron motioning with one of her white-gloved hands as if to say, "If you're leaving, may I have your parking spot?"

"Dammit," thought Tamara as she pulled away. "If it weren't for one hundred thou a year, I'd tell Pollack what he could do with his order-processing system."

Still muttering, she pulled into her reserved slot next to the West Hollywood distribution center. "Aloha!" chirped Ellen Scott, her assistant, as she walked in. "Jason has called three times about wanting you to fly to Hawaii. Also, you have two calls from John, one from Matt, one from your mother, who asked why you never phone her, and one from some fellow who wouldn't leave his name, but said it was very personal. Tell me about the outfit you bought. I'll bet it's stunning."

"Forget about them, and hold all my calls," said Tamara, crisply. "I'm not going anywhere. Pollack called me and is mad because our order-processing and delivery times are out of whack."

Two days passed. Tamara had put her social life on hold and had not even phoned her mother. All her time was spent trying to figure out how to speed up her order-processing system. But she didn't know how to start. The accuracy of the system was not an issue, although additional costs could be. When Pollack paid his bonuses last year, he had told Tamara that if her operation had cost one cent more to run, she would not have received a bonus. Because her bonus had paid for her new Mercedes, Tamara was cost-conscious, to say the least.

Ellen helped her, too—at least through late Friday afternoon. Ellen explained that she couldn't work on Saturday and Sunday because she'd accepted an invitation to spend the weekend at Catalina Island with an unnamed friend. Before Ellen left, she and Tamara had decided that there were twelve distinct operations involved in processing and shipping orders. Some could be performed at the same time, whereas others had to be performed in sequence—that is, one could not be started until the other was completed. These tasks, the amount of time it takes to complete each, and the sequential relationships, if any, are shown in Exhibit 12-A.

EXHIBIT 12–A   ORDER-PROCESSING AND SHIPMENT TASKS IN APPROXIMATE ORDER OF COMPLETION

Task	Description	Duration (in days)	Precedence relationships (tasks on right of < cannot commence until tasks on left are completed)
A	Order received and entered into computer	0.25	A<D
B	Determine whether to fill from warehouse or ship direct from factory	0.50	B<C
C	Print picking order	0.30	C<H
D	Verify customer's credit	0.35	D<G, E
E	Check and determine buyer's eligibility for discounts	0.15	E<F
F	Prepare invoice and enter in accounts receivable file	1.00	F<K
G	Determine mode of transport and select carrier	1.65	G<J
H	Pick order at warehouse	0.75	H<I
I	Pack and label shipment	1.20	I<L
J	Notify carrier and prepare shipping documents	2.25	J<L
K	Transmit copy of invoice to shipping dock	1.20	K<L
L	Transport order to customer	3.50	

After completing the information shown in the exhibit, Ellen left. Tamara was left with the task of trying to relate all those tasks to each other. She recalled a college textbook that she had never much cared for but that she had come across a few weeks earlier as she was searching for her Northern Illinois University yearbook. Tamara looked at a PERT chart in that book and knew that she would have to construct something similar in order to analyze the distribution center's order-processing and shipping operations. She studied the text accompanying the chart, sighed, and thought to herself, "Where was I—or at least where was my mind—the day the professor explained all of this in class?"

Questions

1. Arrange the tasks shown in Exhibit 12-A in a network or PERT chart.
2. Determine the critical path. What is the least amount of time it takes between receipt of an order and its delivery to a customer?
3. Offhand, looking at your answers to questions 1 and 2, what areas of activity do you think Tamara should look at first, assuming she wants to reduce order-processing and delivery times? Why?
4. Now that she's a Californian ready for the race down the information superhighway, Tamara wants to be able to impress Pollack in terms of her knowledge of current technology. Recently a sales representative from a warehouse equipment company called, trying to interest her in installing a "Star Wars–Robotic" order picker for the warehouse. Controlled by lasers and powered by magnetic levitation, the device can pick orders (task H) in fifteen minutes, rather than six hours (0.75 day), the current time. How valuable would such a device be to Tamara? Why?
5. Another alternative is to use faster transportation. How should Tamara choose between paying more for faster transportation and paying more for other improvements? Assume that her only goal is speed.
6. To offset some of the costs of speeding up the system, does the PERT chart indicate where there might be some potential savings from assigning fewer people to some tasks, thereby increasing the amount of time needed to complete these tasks? If so, which tasks are likely candidates? Why?

C A S E   1 2 - 2

ANALYZING THE SYSTEM

This case requires the same computer disks as those used for Case 6-2. Note the introductory comments for that case.

Questions

1. Your firm is headquartered in Little Rock, Arkansas (ZIP code 72204). You send 3,000-pound shipments of packaged product each day to Dallas, Texas (75062); Atlanta, Georgia (30303); Baton Rouge, Louisiana (70803); Wheeling, West Virginia (26003); Elmira, New York (14903); New Orleans, Louisiana (70148); Savannah, Georgia (31411); Jackson, Mississippi (39210); Dayton, Ohio (45469); and Milwaukee, Wisconsin (53188). At present your product's classification is 200, but you are considering redesign of the product so that it will weigh 8 percent less when packaged. How would this change affect transportation costs? Explain.

2. (This is a continuation of the situation described in question 1.) You are considering a new packaging process that would permit a new classification of 175; however, the packaged shipments would weigh 4 percent more (1.04 times 3,000 pounds). How much would this new packaging process be worth to you?

3. Your firm is located in San Jose, California (95192). A good market for your product exists in Boston, Massachusetts. Each day you sell and ship twenty-five parcels to the Boston area, each weighing an average of twenty-five pounds. A representative sample shipment is as follows: Boston (02289), seven parcels; Boston (02101), one parcel; Boston (02299), five parcels; Boston (02201), six parcels; and Boston (02188), six parcels. In a trade magazine you note an advertisement from a local parcel delivery service in the Boston area, which delivers packages of the size you ship from its location (ZIP code 02217) to all nearby areas where you have customers. The parcel delivery service charges $5 per delivery. Your product's classification is 200. Consider whether you should consolidate your Boston business, shipping all twenty-five parcels as a single shipment to the parcel delivery service and paying it to make the local deliveries. How much, if anything, would you save?

4. Your firm is located in St. Louis (63130) and your product, classified at 350, is used for Thanksgiving decorations. Using FAX, you determine that you have three buyers in Bayonne, N. J. (07002) that will buy your product, though you are haggling over the details with each buyer. You decide that the product will be sold to one of the buyers and that you need to start trucking it east today. Since you are uncertain of the exact consignee, you decide to use the diversion and reconsignment option. To whom should you consign the shipment? How does use of this option affect your costs?

5. Assume that your firm is located in the community where you attend college. List five state capital cities in neighboring states. Then determine the costs of shipping a product in 200-pound lots once a week to each of those cities. The product's value is $3 per pound, and its freight

classification is 100. Each is a single shipment, and no discounts or accessorial charges are involved. You absorb the freight charges. What are the costs?

6. (This is a continuation of the situation described in question 5.) Since you and your customers have some storage space available, you are thinking about consolidating shipments. Production would remain at the same rate, but you would ship 1,000 pounds to a single customer every five weeks (instead of 200 pounds a week). Of course, your customers would have to hold more inventory than before; they calculate annual inventory carrying costs at 25 percent of their average investment in inventory. How much of a financial incentive, if any, should you offer your customers to accept the larger shipments made every five weeks, rather than the smaller weekly shipments? Explain.

Logistics Systems Controls

"Write a letter to Santa? It's easier just to break into his computer distribution system."

Even the most traditional supply chains are vulnerable. (Cartoon © 1992 Harley Schwadron. Distributed by Sandhill Arts.)

Thieves are now going aboard ships calling Nigeria to steal parts even before the automobiles are off-loaded.

Journal of Commerce
September 22, 1994

A jury rules that Portacock in Napa breached its contract by supplying corks coated with an emulsifier that acted as a glue, virtually cementing the stoppers.
Sonoma-Cutrer Vineyards had to recall most of its 1986 vintage and build a special corking machine to extract the corks.

Marin Independent Journal
February 23, 1995

Installing robots and getting rid of bad workers might seem costly and time-consuming. Still airline executives would do well to consider Pan Am's example. There, observers have said, the gross mishandling of cargo shipments led to the loss of many accounts and played a role in driving the former aviation giant out of business.

American Shipper
August 1993

Qualcomm Inc. has signed multimillion-dollar contracts to provide several truck lines with its OmniTRACS two-way mobile satellite communications and tracking systems.
Trucking companies are moving rapidly to develop satellite tracking systems to help them keep up with cargo and communicate with drivers.

American Shipper
May 1993

Some grocery warehouses never encourage their [forklift] operators to speed. That would be against company rules. They do however, pay by tonnage. Even though there is not a scale in sight, they judge their operators by the tonnage they move in a day. Well, if tonnage doesn't convert to speed, what does it convert to? Certainly not safety. Tonnage does convert to speed and that converts to product and equipment damage and accidents.

Material Handling Engineering
November 1994

Key Terms

- Accounting control
- Batch number
- Building security
- Computer security
- Document security
- Organized theft
- Pilferage
- Product recall
- Short-interval scheduling
- System security
- Truck security
- Warehouse work rule
- Worker productivity

Learning Objectives

- To understand the use of accounting techniques for logistics system control
- To examine the worker productivity issue
- To discuss problems and solutions involved in a product recall
- To learn how to reduce pilferage and organized theft

INTRODUCTION

If logistics management entailed only establishing a system and putting it into operation, it would be a relatively simple task. But logistics systems and supply chains do not always work the way they are expected to. The potential problems confronting the logistics manager are numerous. This chapter deals with various logistics topics ranging from the problem of out-of-control costs to that of protecting shipments from theft.

The chapter is of special importance to those training for an entry-level position in logistics management. Much of the initial performance with a new employer is evaluated on the basis of how well new employees exercise control responsibilities. The inability to carry out control functions is easily spotted at the beginning levels of management.

In the process of reengineering a logistics system, the need to control the system must not be overlooked. Indeed, the control mechanisms must be built into the system, and their effectiveness must be continually monitored. This chapter deals primarily with controlling functions that are somewhat protective in nature. They must be employed to keep a firm's position from worsening. In a competitive world with small and sometimes shrinking profit margins, application of tight controls may enable a firm to maintain its position while competitors fall behind.

The word *control* is chosen deliberately. The problems discussed here cannot be eliminated; they can only be controlled. A person involved in logistics management will confront the issues and problems presented in this chapter many times during the course of her or his career.

Indeed, logistics managers must have plans in anticipation of things going wrong. Jerry D. Smith, of Tompkins Associates in Raleigh, notes that formal contingency plans can help to protect warehouses from conceivable circumstances that occur on an unpredictable basis. He suggests that warehouse managers do the following:

1. Make a list of the conceivable bad things that can happen in an operation.
2. Rank those bad things in terms of their consequences or probability of occurrence.
3. Starting with the highest-ranked problem, carefully determine, in as much detail as possible, the proper steps and actions that should be taken to resolve, eliminate, or deal with the problems when and if they occur.[1]

ACCOUNTING CONTROLS

Budgets are a form of control called **accounting controls.** Yet they also serve other functions. In the early stages budgets are planning mechanisms and a means of fulfilling corporate goals. The logistics manager assembles a

---

[1] *Distribution Center Management,* April 1991, p. 1.

proposed budget to indicate how much money is needed to carry out the various planned logistical tasks. In drawing up the budget, all activities "must not only be expressed in terms of units or financial values, but also in volume, weight, pallets, boxes and order or invoice lines."[2] Later, after the budget for a time period has been approved, it becomes a control mechanism.

In the early 1970s a number of firms belonging to the National Council of Physical Distribution Management funded a pioneering study conducted by Professor Michael Schiff that dealt with accounting controls in physical distribution management. In his report Schiff was critical of two industry practices, both of which dealt with what he saw as improper cost allocation. Schiff noted that physical distribution costs should be considered as selling costs, insofar as they determine sales strategies and incentives. He found that goals were set for salespeople, but the goals ignored distribution and logistics costs and therefore sales personnel ignored this expense item.

Schiff also noted that decisions to increase inventory should be subjected to the same amount of management scrutiny as decisions to commit a like amount of funds to another undertaking. He suggested that this problem can be overcome by assigning an imputed interest charge on the additional investment in inventory to the unit of the firm responsible for the decision to increase inventory size.

Schiff devoted a chapter to methods of controlling physical distribution costs, in which he described four methods: use of budgets, use of standard costs, comparing shipment costs with costs of similar movements stored in a computer's memory, and establishing costs and standards for maintaining desired levels of customer service.[3]

In the 1980s the CLM commissioned studies involving the use of accounting tools as they relate to logistics. Reports resulting from these undertakings include *Transportation Accounting and Control—Guidelines for Distribution and Financial Management* (1983) and *Warehouse Accounting and Control* (1985). Controls compose an important segment of these reports; for example, topics covered in the transportation study include responsibility accounting, management by exception, performance accounting, and internal controls.

Here is how John J. Mahan, director of distribution for the Gillette Company, describes the distribution accounting function in his firm:

> Distribution accounting reports to Distribution on a dotted line basis and provides financial consulting services to distribution management. It prepares operating

[2] M. J. Ploos van Amstel, "Physical Distribution Cost Control," *International Journal of Physical Distribution and Materials Management,* 1987, p. 71.

[3] Michael Schiff, *Accounting and Cost Control in Physical Distribution Management* (Chicago: NCPDM, 1972). See also Howard M. Armitage and James F. Dickow, "Controlling Distribution with Standard Costs and Flexible Budgets," in *NCPDM 1979 Meeting Papers* (Chicago: NCPDM, 1979), pp. 99–122; and Joseph Cavinato, "How to Play the Budget Game," *Distribution,* August 1990, pp. 102–104.

and capital budgets and interim forecasts, as well as establishes performance standards. The group also prepares management reports on freight expense, private fleet results and public warehouses, and operating expense variance analysis.

In addition, it maintains and operates an internal control system for distribution and ensures its adherence to corporate guidelines for the approval and payment of invoices, contracts, leases, capital expenditures, and the protection of company assets. Finally, it ensures accurate reporting of all finished goods inventory.[4]

Note that many of the functions described by Mahan are of a controlling nature. In addition it is possible to establish statistical controls over logistics systems, setting tolerance ranges within which performance is considered to be satisfactory. Other functional areas within the firm are also concerned with the accounting controls and systems of the logistics operations. Logistics costs, for example, are part of the costs shared by or assigned to the other functions. An example is the determination of the total costs of producing or distributing a product.

Professor D. M. Lambert has written extensively about accounting controls and their impact upon logistics activities. He says costs can first be categorized by their nature or within the framework of analysis that one is working. Cost categories are:

Controllable versus noncontrollable

Direct versus indirect

Fixed versus variable

Actual versus opportunity

Relevant versus sunk[5]

Lambert advocates the use of "standard costs" and "flexible budgets." Standard costs involve two steps. First, one must establish standard or acceptable costs for each activity. Second, one must determine how acceptable deviations from these standard costs are. "The use of standard costs represents a frontal assault on the logistics costing problem because it attempts to determine what the costs should be, rather than basing future costs predictions on past cost behavior."[6] The standard costs developed should be applied to activities to determine their reasonable budget; if the standard cost of handling a pallet is

[4] John J. Mahan, "Management and Control of Distribution Costs," in *NCPDM 1983 Papers* (Chicago: NCPDM, 1983), p. 967. "Dotted line" refers to the firm's organization chart and as used here implies that distribution accounting is not under the direct, complete control of the firm's distribution function manager.

[5] Douglas M. Lambert, "Logistics Cost, Productivity, and Performance Analysis," in *The Logistics Handbook* (New York: Free Press, 1994), pp. 264–265.

[6] Ibid., p. 281.

three dollars and 10,000 pallets are handled, then $30,000 should be budgeted for handling pallets. If the standard costs per unit change as volume handled changes, this should be reflected in the budget also. The budget is flexible in the sense that it is tied to actual activity.

WORKER PRODUCTIVITY

Labor is expensive, so its efficient use is necessary for a profitable operation. The two most frequent uses of labor in physical distribution are in warehousing and in transport of goods. Both warehousing and trucking involve heavy investments in capital equipment (which frequently reduce the need for workers). The workers and the equipment must be used in a manner that achieves the lowest cost for a given volume of output. In many areas warehouse workers, drivers, and helpers are unionized, and work-rule provisions influence **worker productivity.**[7] In areas where warehouse workers' unions resist changes in work rules, a warehouse may become prematurely obsolete—not because of its structure or equipment, but because of high-cost work practices that the union insists on continuing.

Use of labor is usually made more efficient by scheduling work in advance. In a warehouse the time for performing each task (such as opening a truck door, stacking a pallet, or picking a case of outgoing goods) is calculated. Precise time breakdowns—to the number of seconds—are used. The location of the pallet load in the warehouse or its height above the floor makes a difference. Outgoing cases being picked require different amounts of time, again depending on their location, volume, and weight. Picking and assembling an outgoing order comprising of cases of different dimensions require more time than if the cases are of the same size. These data are used in two ways. First, they indicate that the goods within the warehouse should be arranged so that the more popular or faster-moving items are located in slots where they will require less time for storage and retrieval. Second, through the use of computer programs, an order picker's travel sequence can be arranged in a way that minimizes the time that he or she (and whatever equipment is being used) will require. According to Myron H. Nerzig, a warehouse management consultant:

> Almost every individual will work to a target, goal, or objective. We measure ourselves even if a company does not have a measurement system. That is our personal way of providing output to meet our own objectives or to satisfy our supervisors.

[7] See Frank Dorsey, "Preparing the Union for Work Standards," in *NCPDM 1982 Papers* (Chicago: NCPDM, 1982), pp. 581–594. See also "Fleming's Fast Rise in Wholesale Foods," *Fortune,* January 21, 1985, p. 54.

Without good standards and a reporting system, workers will not meet a level of production that is acceptable to management. . . . Most workers want to do a fair day's work but will become disgruntled and their morale lowers when they see other employees get away doing as little as possible, and in some cases, nothing.[8]

As might be expected, work scheduling systems become involved in labor-management controversies.

Short-Interval Scheduling

One useful method of analysis, **short-interval scheduling,** involves looking at each worker's activity in small time segments. An amount of time is assigned to each unit of work, and then the individual's work is scheduled in a manner that utilizes as much of each worker's time as possible and maximizes output for each worker.

The scheduling technique is useful to supervisory personnel. Each day's work for the operation is plotted out and is in essence a summation of each worker's tasks. For a warehouse the scheduling may also be tied into departure times for delivery trucks (also controlled by computerized scheduling) and arrival of trucks with incoming freight. Large buyers frequently require suppliers' trucks to arrive within rather limited time blocks (say, thirty minutes or an hour) because this reduces congestion at the receiving dock and spreads the arrival of inbound materials throughout the working day. Because an operation's entire work day can be prescheduled, the supervisor can tell as the day progresses how the actual progress compares to the schedule. If at the end of the first hour in an eight-hour shift, less than one-eighth of the work has been completed, the supervisor must take steps to catch up within the second hour (or at least to fall no further behind).

Short-interval scheduling can also be used by intermediate management to assess the effectiveness of supervision. One firm uses a "Lost Time Review" report that is filled out by the immediate supervisor on a daily basis. In case the immediate supervisor fails to note or explain the lost time, the information appears on a form entitled "Unexplained Lost Time," which intermediate management prepares to cover instances when more time was spent on a job than had been assigned *and* the immediate supervisor failed to report it.

Improving Worker Performance

Knowledge of supervisory techniques is important to students of physical distribution and logistics because fairly early in their career, they are likely to receive an assignment that includes supervision of others. Some workers are more obviously in need of supervision than others (see Figure 13-1); the skills of workers assigned to the same task also may vary (see Figure 13-2). The

[8] Comments made before the Northern California chapter meeting of the Warehouse Education and Research Council, January 28, 1988.

"That new man may bear watching."

Figure 13-1   The objective of supervision is to improve performance.
(Reproduced by permission of the artist and the Masters Agency.)

supervisor's goal should be to improve worker performance. Emery Air Freight Corporation uses a three-part approach consisting of performance audit, feedback, and positive reinforcement. After a worker's performance is measured, it is important that this information be fed back to the worker, so that he or she is aware of it. According to a spokesperson for Emery, several clues indicate that lack of feedback is a cause of poor performance:

1. When asked, workers do not accurately and immediately know their level of performance.
2. When asked, workers do not know that a performance standard exists.
3. Whenever a specific performance is consistently below standard.
4. When employees say they do not know what is expected of them.[9]

Once performance information is made available to workers, the next step is to reinforce their good performance with some form of reward—from an approving nod to a large Christmas bonus.

Although union work rules are often inflexible and difficult to change, sometimes, as part of the bargaining transaction, it is possible for management to

[9] Paul F. Hammond, "Increasing Productivity through Performance Audit, Feedback, and Positive Reinforcement," in *1974 Papers of the American Society of Traffic and Transportation* (ASTT, 1974), p. 31.

Figure 13-2 Employees have varying degrees of skills. (Reproduced by permission of the artist and the Masters Agency.)

get unions to agree to alter some work practices. Usually management must demonstrate that neither the union as a group nor its members as individuals will be adversely affected by the proposed changes. Thus, when performance standards are measured, some attention should be paid to those standards that are influenced or controlled by contractual work rules. During collective bargaining sessions, management must know the savings of eliminating or altering a work rule because these calculations establish a value for each contemplated change.

Performance standards, as such, may not be included in the contract. However, provisions have to be made for giving management the right to establish and use them. Unions want protection from unreasonable standards, and mutually agreed-upon procedures are necessary for handling new or continuing employees who consistently fall below established standards.

In order to maintain and improve productivity, it is necessary to have **warehouse work rules** and to enforce them. Work rules serve many purposes, but their most important function is to keep the work force (or its individual members) from backsliding into poor performance. Figure 13-3, from *Warehousing Review,* shows one public warehouser's set of work rules.[10]

---

[10] See also Thomas W. Speh and Jennifer E. Heil, *A Model for Developing Warehouse Work Rules* (Oak Brook, Ill.: Warehousing Education and Research Council, 1988).

Ours is a company that has been built on service to its customers. Our business has grown both in the number of customers and in the area which we serve. We are constantly striving to improve our service, because it is only through growth and progress that a company can give to its employees the good wages, increased benefits, and job security that everyone wants.

In order to meet these aims it is necessary to adhere to a set of rules. Whenever people work together they have certain rights and privileges. Along with these rights they have certain obligations and responsibilities. So that each employee will know what is expected of him we have drawn up a list of work rules which are necessary for the orderly and efficient operation of our business. By following these rules you contribute to the progress of the company and therefore to the stability of your own job. These rules therefore benefit you rather than hinder you. They are fair rules and to keep them fair to everyone they will be enforced in every required situation.

These rules are listed in two groups, by type of violation, and are as follows:

- Violations subject to discharge on the first offense.
- Violations subject to constructive discipline.

Violations Subject to Discharge on the First Offense

(1) The possession of, drinking of, or use of any alcoholic beverages or narcotic drugs on company property; or being on company premises at any time under the influence of alcohol, or drugs, or while suffering from an alcoholic hangover which materially affects work performance.

(2) The transportation of, or failure to notify the company of, unauthorized persons on company equipment or its property.

(3) Theft or misappropriation of company property or the property of any of its customers or employees.

(4) Deliberate or malicious damage to the company's equipment and warehouse facilities or to the merchandise and property of its customers.

(5) Intentional falsification of records in any form, including ringing another employee's time card, or falsifying employment application.

(6) Fighting while on duty or on company premises or provoking others to fight.

(7) Smoking in a building or van, or any restricted area, or while loading or unloading merchandise and other items.

(8) Immoral or indecent conduct which affects work performance or makes the employee unsuited for the work required.

(9) Unauthorized possession of, or carrying of, firearms or other weapons.

(10) Insubordination — refusal to perform assigned work or to obey a supervisor's order, or encouraging others to disobey such an order.

Violations Subject to Constructive Discipline

The rules printed below are subject to constructive discipline. This means that for the first offense you will be given a constructive reprimand. For a second offense you will receive a disciplinary layoff without pay, the length of which will depend upon the seriousness of the offense; subject to the terms of the collective bargaining agreement which may exist between employee and union. For a third offense you will be discharged, subject to the collective bargaining agreement.

If you have had a violation, followed by a record of no violations for a nine (9) month period, the original violation will be withdrawn from your record.

(1) Excessive tardiness regardless of cause. (Being tardy and not ready to perform work at the designated starting time may at the company's option result in the employee being sent home without pay.)

(2) Absenteeism without just cause and excessive absenteeism regardless of cause. If you must be absent for a justifiable reason notify the company in advance. Justified absence will be

Figure 13-3 Sample warehouse work rules. (Courtesy of American Warehouse Association.)

excused if the company is notified as soon as possible before the beginning of the shift; however, too many justified and excused absences may be grounds for constructive discipline as well as unjustified, unexcused absence. If you are absent from work for three consecutive work days without notification followed by failure to report for work on the fourth day you will automatically be removed from the payroll with the notification "quit without notice."

(3) Failure to work reasonable overtime.

(4) Unauthorized absence from assigned work location.

(5) Failure to observe proper break periods, lunch periods, and quitting times, unless otherwise directed by your supervisor.

(6) Disregard for common rules of safety, safe practices, good housekeeping and sanitation.

(7) Unauthorized or negligent operation or use of machines, tools, vehicles, equipment and materials.

(8) Loss or damage to the property of the company or its customers which could have been reasonably avoided.

(9) Failure to complete work assignments within a reasonable length of time or loafing on such assignments.

(10) Garnishments not satisfied prior to the hearing before the court issuing same.

(11) Gambling on company premises.

(12) Use of immoral, obscene or indecent language on company premises.

(13) Trying to persuade or organize other employees to disobey any of these rules and regulations. ■

Figure 13-3   (Continued)

Financial incentives may also be used to improve worker performance. Sometimes they are given as bonuses to warehouse supervisors. They can also be used carefully to encourage teamwork on the part of all employees. Some warehouses pay a bonus (beyond whatever provisions exist in the contract with workers) when certain performance elements, such as the percentage of accurately filled orders, are improved.

Another important concern in setting performance standards is safety. There is the risk that, as performance or production is increased, the potential for accidents that injure workers or damage merchandise or equipment also increases (see Figure 13-4). In warehousing, back injuries are a significant problem and are the basis for many disability claims.

Driver Supervision

When discussing supervision of logistics labor, a distinction has to be made between warehousing and trucking. In warehousing, the supervisor is physically present and expected to be on top of any situation. However, once on the road, truck drivers are removed from immediate supervision. In addition, they are in day-to-day contact with customers. While on the road, they and their trucks can be seen by thousands of motorists. Because of these factors, different types of supervision as well as different types of workers may be needed.

"I said not such a heavy load, Hooper!"

Figure 13-4   There are dangers associated with overachieving. (Reproduced by permission of the Masters Agency.)

When a worker in a warehouse falls behind schedule, it is usually noticed immediately and corrective action can be taken. A supervisor can choose from a range of supervisory techniques to provide an incentive for the worker to improve performance. However, the work of a truck driver is more difficult to evaluate. If a truck driver falls behind schedule, it may be because of traffic conditions or a bottleneck at the consignee's loading dock. Initially, all a supervisor can do is accept the driver's explanation. Still, it is necessary to have a control mechanism so that drivers who often encounter delays can be distinguished from those who do not. Figure 13-5 is a computer printout showing the monthly delivery performance of drivers. Shown are the number of cases and weight handled and the amount of time spent waiting and unloading. The *P* indicates that pallets are utilized and that the receiver uses a forklift to unload the trailer. *C* means specialized wheeled carts are used instead of pallets. Various comparisons are made, including the average cost per ton and the average cost per case. "Adjusted cases per hour" takes into account both waiting and unloading time.

The arrangement of data shown in Figure 13-5 can be used, for example, to support a driver's contention that his or her relatively poor performance is caused by delays at the customer's receiving dock. The contention could be verified by having a different driver make deliveries to determine whether

ASSOCIATED FOOD STORES INC.   PAGE NO. 2

DELIVERY PERFORMANCE ANALYSIS
WEEK ENDING 11/01/

REPORT NO. 2 —STORE—

	DRIVER	P	STORE	CASES	WEIGHT	WAIT	UNLD	CS/HR	ADJ CS/HR
B	,D.	P	BEL AIR MARKET #7	467	30,699	.1	.3	1,556	1,167
D	,P.	P	BEL AIR MARKET #7	1,055	6,000	.1	.5	2,110	1,758
F	,J.	P	BEL AIR MARKET #7	242		.1	.4	605	484
M	,J.	P	BEL AIR MARKET #7	120		.2	.3	400	240
			TOTAL	1,884	36,699	.5	1.5	1,256	942
F	,J.	C	BELL MARKET #1	1,038	24,525	.1	1.1	943	865
F	,J.	C	BELL MARKET #1	446	14,306	.1	.9	495	446
F	,J.	P	BELL MARKET #1	50	2,000	.1	.2	250	166
			TOTAL	1,534	40,831	.3	2.2	697	613
F	,J.	C	BELL MARKET #2	300	12,000	.1	.7	428	375
M		C	BELL MARKET #2	729		1.2	1.5	486	270
M		C	BELL MARKET #2	1,242	30,420	.1	1.8	690	653
V	,B.		BELL MARKET #2	1		.1	.1	10	5
			TOTAL	2,272	42,420	1.5	4.1	554	405
G	A.	C	BELL MARKET #3	913	23,049	.2	1.0	913	760
M		C	BELL MARKET #3	1,200	30,601	.3	1.0	1,200	923
			TOTAL	2,113	53,650	.5	2.0	1,056	845
M		C	BELL MARKET #4	408	10,392	.2	.9	453	370
M	J.	C	BELL MARKET #4	671	15,109	.2	.9	745	610
			TOTAL	1,079	25,501	.4	1.8	599	490

Figure 13-5 Delivery performance of truck drivers. (Courtesy of Associated Food Stores.)

the delays still happen. If they do, the supplier would approach the customer with these printouts and indicate that improvements are needed in the receiving procedures.

If it is determined that the cause of the problem is an inadequacy of the customer's receiving ability, care would have to be used in informing the customer. The supplier's marketing staff would have to be made aware of the problem, and calculations would be needed of how profitable the account is at the present time, given the unloading handicaps. If it is determined that the unloading delays make servicing the account unprofitable, the supplier might threaten to discontinue service or raise prices. If it is found that servicing the account is profitable in spite of the unloading delays, a more tactful approach would be employed.

The preceding example illustrates an important interface between marketing and logistics and within the supply chain. Care has to be used when establishing customer service standards to ensure that they do not become a drain on profits. In this example one does not know what one's competitors would do; they are probably handicapped by the same inefficiencies at the customer's receiving dock. The buyer might respond that the problem is not at its dock, but that it runs a friendly and relaxed operation, and if delivery drivers want to have a cup of coffee and chat for a few minutes before unloading their trucks, the buyer does not mind. What the buyer does mind, however, is having this friendly atmosphere labeled as inefficient by some supplier's computer. In this situation, the customer has indicated that he or she likes the supplier's drivers but does not like the supplier's computer. The point of this example is that supervision of the driver could be related to a firm's selling efforts.

Another device used to aid in controlling truck drivers' performance is the *tachograph,* a recording instrument that is installed inside the vehicle and produces a continuous, timed record of the truck, its speed, and its engine speed. Figure 13-6 shows a printout of the activity recorded by a tachograph. From the information on the tachograph chart, one can tell how efficiently the truck and driver are being used. If the driver works on a regular route, it may be possible to rearrange the stops so that the driver can avoid areas of traffic congestion. Bad driving habits, such as high highway speeds and excessive engine idling, can also be detected. In case of an accident, the tachograph chart is invaluable in reporting and explaining what occurred just prior to impact.

According to an article in a trucking magazine:

> The use of tachographs in its eighty-five-van fleet has improved gasoline use by 15 percent, largely through improvements in driving habits, . . . reports Auto Glass Specialists.
>
> The company sends its installers from seventeen service centers in Wisconsin, Michigan, and Iowa to the customers' site, where they replace windshields and windows in vehicles. The customers include commercial fleets and farmers, as well as auto and truck dealers and body shops.
>
> . . . The firm knows in advance how long each installation will take and the distance between jobs. By correlating the tachograph records with the installers' logs, . . . the company ensures that equipment and installation time is maximized.
>
> Good driving habits are readily identifiable from the tachograph charts, such as holding speeds on upgrades, reducing idling time, maintaining smooth acceleration and braking, and . . . driving no faster than 55 mph.[11]

The most recent development in the supervision of trucks and their drivers involves global satellites. In this system the manager of the fleet and the truck drivers are connected by way of numerous satellites that circle the

[11] *Transport Topics,* July 14, 1980, p. 24.

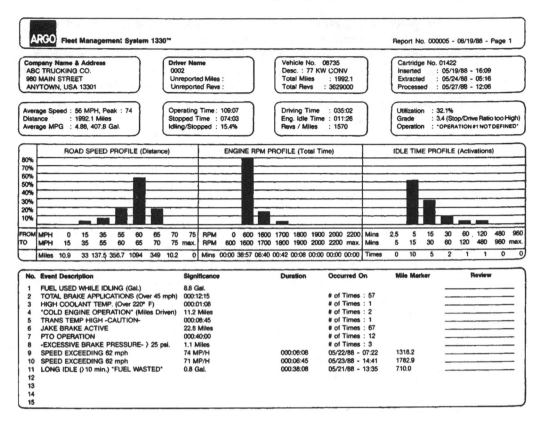

Figure 13-6   Printout from a truck tachograph. (Source: Argo Instruments, Inc., Fleet Management Systems.)

globe. During Operation Desert Storm, for example, U.S. soldiers "were able to pinpoint their positions in the trackless desert by consulting boxes the size of paperback books that took readings from the satellites."[12]

PRODUCT RECALLS

A vexing physical distribution logistics problem, and one that can cost physical distribution or product-line managers their jobs, involves the inability to cope with a product-recall crisis. A **product recall** occurs when a hazard or defect is discovered in a manufactured item that is already in the distribution channels. It necessitates a reversal in the usual outward flow of merchandise. Here is an example:

---

[12] *Business Week*, February 10, 1992, p. 120. With respect to commercial trucking, the article notes that by combining the satellite reading system with other data, "such as digitized land maps, more intriguing systems are possible. For example, intelligent vehicle-tracking systems could show drivers, on small dashboard screens, how to circumvent a traffic jam, or where the nearest automatic teller machine is [located]."

Last summer [1986] Pepsi-Cola General Bottling Company of Kansas City, Kansas, received a firsthand lesson in . . . crisis management when 2,500 cases of Mandarin Orange Slice and Apple Slice had to be pulled from store shelves in northwest Missouri and northeast Kansas. Heavier-than-normal yeast counts had been found in the product, a situation attributed to closure failures on a 2-liter bottle. Pepsi General acted quickly, notified the Food and Drug Administration, dispatched ninety route sales[people] to the affected stores to pull product, and ran newspaper and radio ads explaining the situation to consumers.[13]

One manufacturer that undertook a product recall instructed all of its retailers to ship the goods in question back to its plant. To its dismay, the manufacturer discovered that many of its retailers did not know how to write a bill of lading or to take any of the other necessary steps to accomplish the backward movement of goods.[14]

In recent years there have been well-publicized recalls involving soups, drugs, toys, produce with pesticide residue, autos, and Perrier mineral water. From the manufacturer's standpoint, the publicity is undesirable. This is an instance where the saying "There's no such thing as bad publicity" does not hold. If the manufacturer plays down the amount of publicity, it runs the risk that a user will be harmed by the defective product after the defect was known to the manufacturer. In a subsequent lawsuit, the injured consumer might allege that the manufacturer failed to devote sufficient effort and publicity to the recall campaign.

The best-known recall involved the drug Tylenol in 1982. It cost Johnson & Johnson an estimated $50 million. The firm undertook the recall action on its own after several individuals in the Chicago area died after using the product. The pain reliever had been tampered with by an individual who was believed to have removed the bottles' caps and added cyanide-laced capsules. The company already had a recall plan in place, so it could respond to the emergency effectively. The product was reintroduced with more tamper-proof packaging, and within a year the firm had regained more than 80 percent of its one-time market share.

Another Tylenol scare occurred in 1986; it resulted in the product's removal from sale. Johnson & Johnson said that "it cost almost $150 million before taxes to recall the current supplies of Extra Strength Tylenol capsules on the market and to stop further production."[15]

Once a recall campaign is completed (or under way, depending on how it is conducted), the manufacturer and its distributors must take immediate steps to refill the retailer's shelves with either defect-free batches of the same product or a substitute product. Although this step is not as important as the recall, it must be

---

[13] *Beverage World,* July 1987, p. 20.

[14] Information obtained in an interview during a research project that resulted in the following paper: Ronald S. Yaros and Donald F. Wood, "Recalling Products in the Drug and Cosmetic Industry," *Journal of Business Logistics,* vol. 1 (1979), pp. 48–59.

[15] *Business Insurance,* February 24, 1986, p. 2.

undertaken to minimize losses. Otherwise competitors will take the opportunity to suggest that the retailer use their own products to fill empty shelf space.

Sometimes products are recalled through different channels from those through which they are distributed. The National Wholesale Druggist Association favors a policy that eliminates the wholesaler in product recalls. Goods are returned to the manufacturer even though it may simply destroy them after they are received. In theory it seems easier to authorize retailers or wholesalers to destroy the recalled product. However, if the goods are hazardous, it may be desirable for the manufacturer to supervise their destruction. There are always the risks that the defective goods will not be properly disposed of and that individuals will be injured. Accounting controls are necessary to ensure that individuals returning the recalled materials are reimbursed only for the goods they return.

Product recall takes many forms, depending on the type of product. The responsible government agencies (including state and local as well as foreign governments) have their own procedures. The degree of danger posed by the defect also differs, the worst defects being those that are discovered to be directly life threatening. Less serious are the defects that are possible threats to life, such as those linked to causes of cancer if exposure is over a long period of time. An even less serious problem is posed by products that are mislabeled (such as a label that reads "contents 16 ounces" when the product contains only 12 ounces). Sometimes the problem can be overcome by merely changing the product's label or adding a warning label. A lamp manufacturer might be required to add a sticker to each lamp, saying, "Do not use light bulbs larger than 100 watts in this lamp." In this instance the manufacturer could have the stickers attached at some intermediate point between the place of manufacture and the retail outlet.

Federal Agencies Involved with Recalls

The Food and Drug Administration (FDA) is concerned with food, drugs, and cosmetics. In what it considers a *Class I Recall* (i.e., the most serious of hazards, such as botulism toxin in foods), the FDA will insist that the product be recalled at the consumer level and all intermediate levels and that 100 percent effectiveness checks be made of all distribution points. The FDA will also issue a public warning.

Another federal agency involved in product recalls is the Consumer Product Safety Commission (CPSC). Its main objective is to ban the sale of products deemed hazardous, thereby making it an offense for a retailer, wholesaler, or other distributor to sell a banned product. If the CPSC bans the sale of a specific item, the product becomes frozen in all distribution channels because it cannot be sold. Manufacturers and distributors are required to repurchase the banned items.

The CPSC is a relatively new agency that took over the product safety functions of several older federal agencies. It also administers some programs, such as those dealing with flammable fabrics. From a distribution control standpoint, note that the FDA has procedures for recall that result in a reverse flow of the defective products from the consumer back to the manufacturer. The CPSC merely bans sale of the product and halts it in its place in the distribution network.

The National Highway Traffic Safety Administration is concerned with motor vehicles and their accessory parts. It does not engage in recalls; it is responsible only for causing the manufacturer to notify purchasers that a defect has been discovered. Buyers are instructed to take their vehicles to the nearest dealer to have the defect corrected at no cost. The method of notification is registered mail to the first purchaser of record. Sometimes it is not necessary for the owner to take the vehicle back to the dealer. In one instance the manufacturer issued a corrected sticker showing different tire pressures; the owners were instructed to place the decal over the original one (or to see a dealer if they had difficulty following the instructions).

Publicity, Liability, and "Fire Drills"

Whatever form it takes, product recall is an extremely serious matter for the manufacturer and all parties in the distribution network. Adverse publicity and large lawsuits can be devastating. Top management must be involved in any recall activity. Other involved staff should include members of the firm's legal, controller, public relations, quality control, product engineering, and marketing staffs. Management, who may never have known how the firm's logistics system functioned, will be anxiously examining its effectiveness in handling a product recall. Usually a firm designates one individual to be responsible for handling recall activity. Some firms even have practice, or "fire drill," recalls to determine their speed and degree of coverage. All actions that a firm takes to prepare for a hypothetical recall are important for two reasons. First, they allow better performance when the real emergency arises. Second, in case the recall is not completely successful and lawsuits result, a portion of the firm's defense might be the precautionary measures it had undertaken.

Public relations expert Deborah Lowe, in writing about crisis management associated with product tampering, notes the following:

> Media experts believe that the company must tell its side of the story in the first 24 hours for the public to perceive that the company cares. Although the company is a victim of an attack on its products and on its customers, if it does not handle the tampering crisis effectively, it can jeopardize its positive public image and this can hurt the company economically. Some suggested media guidelines for tampering incidents that have proved successful include:
>
> 1. Respond to the tampering crisis within 24 to 48 hours to the media and show concern for the victims.
> 2. With or without media inquiries, do a swift withdrawal of the threatened products from the stores or area the threat includes.

3. Limit the number of media spokespersons but train all top managers for crisis interviews on tampering so the same facts reach the media.
4. Prioritize media call backs during the crisis.
5. Log all phone calls and actions.
6. Respond to questions, but be brief.
7. Characterize the company as a victim, not a villain.[16]

Batch Numbers

The possibility of defective products and product recalls increases the need for positively identifying each product or batch as it leaves the assembly line with a **batch number.** If a defect is detected, it is easier to identify and locate a group or batch of items produced at about the same time (which should, at least, be inspected to ensure that they are not also defective). Items such as office machines contain serial numbers, and their entire move through a distribution system is recorded by that number. In a recall they are relatively easy to trace. For items that do not have serial numbers, batch numbers are commonly used. For example, the batch number 33 C 3 B 2 5 would indicate the following information:

33: day of the year (February 2)
C: plant
3: year 1993
B: production line B
2: second shift
5: fifth hour of that shift

A computerized inventory control system can record the batch number stenciled on each carton. (This information is also used to ensure that the inventory is being turned in proper sequence.) If the batch numbers are recorded as the goods move through the distribution system, in a recall it would be possible to trace each carton to a warehouse or to a retailer. The problem, and the accompanying adverse publicity, could then be more regionalized than if the manufacturer had to undertake a nationwide search campaign.

Figure 13-7 shows one public warehouse's inventory activity report (prepared for one of its grocery customers). Every time it receives a shipment of an item, that item is given a new lot number; at any one time, the warehouse may have large quantities of the same product whose only difference is their lot numbers. The warehouse's computer is programmed to pick up the oldest lot for outgoing shipment. In the event of a product recall, the warehouse's records would indicate which customers received goods from the affected lot or lots.

[16] Deborah Lowe, "Crisis Management Marketing for Tampering: Strategies for International and Domestic Marketplace Terrorism," *San Francisco State University School of Business Journal,* vol. 1 (1990), p. 87.

```
IRP04                              LEDERER TERMINAL  WAREHOUSE CO.
    ANDERSON CLAYTON FOODS          0085
  MERCHANDISE STORED AT-                    INVENTORY ACTIVITY REPORT        AS OF   1/31/80        PAGE  1
        LEE ROAD
```

DATE	ITEM #		DESCRIPTION	SHP/RLS # B/L-OSD#	RCPTS	SHPPD	ADJ.	BAL
12/31/79	01058	CS	12/8-7 SEAS HERBS & SPICES			BEGINNING BALANCE		610
1/03/80	LOT# 5240		TRLR 847L40LT RIGGS	3923379 C 8611	160			
1/28/80	LOT# 6506		ACF TRK	3925754 C 8980	160			
1/30/80	LOT# 6717		G220958 COLDWAY	3930165 C 9028	320			
1/02/80	LOT# 3508		AMERICAN SEAWAY FDS INC	3923035 3923035		60		
1/02/80	LOT# 3508		SCOT LAD FDS INC	3923465 3923465		60		
1/03/80	LOT# 3508		A & P TEA CO INC	3922970 3922970		9		
1/03/80	LOT# 3897		A & P TEA CO INC	3922970 3922970		31		
1/08/80	LOT# 3897		SCOT LAD FOODS INC	3924771 3924771		100		
1/09/80	LOT# 3897		MCLAIN GROC	3925427 3925427		13		
1/11/80	LOT# 4167		HEINENS INC	3926031 3926031		23		
1/11/80	LOT# 3897		HEINENS INC	3926031 3926031		16		
1/14/80	LOT# 4167		SEAWAY FOODS INC	3926635 3926635		60		
1/15/80	LOT# 4167		SCOT LAD FOODS INC	3926610 3926610		77		
1/15/80	LOT# 5036		SCOT LAD FOODS INC	3926610 3926610		13		
1/18/80	LOT# 5036		THOROFARE MARKETS INC	3928014 3928014		80		
1/21/80	LOT# 5036		CAHRLEY BROTHERS	3928421 3928421		52		
1/22/80	LOT# 5036		SCOT LAD FOODS INC	3928492 3928492		15		
1/22/80	LOT# 5240		SCOT LAD FOODS INC	3928492 3928492		65		
1/23/80	LOT# 5240		MCALIN GROC	3929105 3929105		26		
			ITEM WEIGHT	7,700	640	700		
						ENDING BALANCE		550
12/31/79	01582	CS	12/8-7 SEAS GREEN GODDESS DRSG			BEGINNING BALANCE		1,185
1/28/80	LOT# 6621		RIGGS	3929538 C 9008	320			
1/02/80	LOT# 9579		SCOT LAD FDS INC	3923465 3923465		20		
1/03/80	LOT# 9579		TAMARKIN CO	3923569 3923569		39		
1/04/80	LOT# 1373		GOLDEN DAWN FDS	3924195 3924195		5		
1/04/80	LOT# 9579		GOLDEN DAWN FDS	3924195 3924195		5		
1/07/80	LOT# 1373		FRANK FORTUNE GROC CO	3924551 3924551		10		
1/08/80	LOT# 1373		SCOT LAD FOODS INC	3924771 3924771		60		
1/08/80	LOT# 1373		BETSY ROSS FOODS INC	3924972 3924972		20		
1/09/80	LOT# 1373		CARDINAL FDS INC	3925085 3925085		25		
1/09/80	LOT# 1373		MCLAIN GROC	3925427 3925427		26		
1/11/80	LOT# 1373		HEINENS INC	3926031 3926031		13		
1/14/80	LOT# 3565		TAMARKIN CO	3926630 3926630		38		
1/14/80	LOT# 1373		TAMARKIN CO	3926630 3926630		1		
1/15/80	LOT# 3565		SCOT LAD FOODS INC	3926610 3926610		20		
1/17/80	LOT# 3565		ASSOCIATED GROCERS INC	3927559 3927559		10		
1/18/80	LOT# 3565		THOROFARE MARKETS INC	3928014 3928014		80		
1/21/80	LOT# 3565		CAHRLEY BROTHERS	3928421 3928421		40		
1/21/80	LOT# 3565		CAHRLEY BROTHERS	3928421 3928421		12		
1/22/80	LOT# 3767		SCOT LAD FOODS INC	3928492 3928492		38		
1/22/80	LOT# 3580		SCOT LAD FOODS INC	3928492 3928492		22		
1/22/80	LOT# 3580		THE TAMARKIN CO	3928498 3928498		78		
1/22/80	LOT# 3580		CARDINAL FOODS INC	3928736 3928736		20		

Figure 13-7   Excerpt from a warehouser's activity report tracing lot numbers from manufacturer to retailer. (Courtesy of Lederer Terminals, Cleveland, Ohio.)

CONTROLLING RETURNED AND SALVAGE GOODS

In addition to product recalls, goods may be returned because they are damaged or unsalable (due to their poor condition or the disappearance of a market). Returned goods must be carefully counted and the various accounting records adjusted accordingly. Unsold newspapers, magazines, and paperback books are often returned for credit. Frequently it is necessary only to return the copyright page or the book's cover to receive credit. In the paperback book industry some publishers were defrauded by dealers who had fake book covers printed to collect credit.

Some unsold goods are "salvaged," meaning that they are saved until a decision is made concerning what to do with them. In 1993, 788 Subaru autos stored at a company distribution point were damaged by a flash flood. The company decided to strip the cars of recyclable parts, which would be sold as reconditioned parts, and to have the remaining parts of the vehicles crushed. A company spokesperson said, "We are taking this precaution because we want to control the process. We do not want parts to get into our parts supply or into new vehicles."[17]

As firms increasingly become involved in recycling, they must enforce controls that will prevent them from becoming victims of fraud. The system that controls outgoing movements must also control inbound movements of materials being recycled. There are likely to be many disagreements about the content and quality of materials placed into the recycling effort.

PILFERAGE AND THEFT

An ongoing problem facing nearly all businesses is theft, especially **pilferage**—employee theft. The materials stolen in pilferage are usually for the employee's own use, whereas what is considered theft is more likely to be conducted by outsiders, although one's employees may be involved. Theft is conducted on an organized basis, and it is likely that the goods are stolen for resale. An East Coast importer made the distinction this way: "Theft we consider as individual packages, or the loss of the whole package; pilferage is where packages are opened and a certain portion . . . taken."[18] Both result in inventory shrinkage (i.e., unaccounted-for losses of product).

Since pilferage involves a firm's own employees, controls must begin with the hiring process and continue with supervisory practices. This is an area where double standards exist. A warehouse employee caught carrying a can of the company's gasoline out of the warehouse and placing it in his or her private auto would be subjected to disciplinary action or might even be fired. Yet the warehouse superintendent may use the company car, with company gasoline, to run personal errands.

Pilferage is widespread and cannot be completely eliminated. Employees at lower levels who engage in pilferage tend to view it as their opportunity to obtain disguised (and nontaxable) income. Most firms find it less expensive to tolerate a small amount of pilferage than to impose a system of total control. The principal cost of total control is in employee turnover; many individuals choose not to work under such close scrutiny and supervision.

A toll bridge authority installed an elaborate toll-collection monitoring system that made it virtually impossible for toll collectors to cheat. Turnover among toll takers increased drastically for two reasons: The total income of most toll takers was apparently reduced, and without a chance to attempt to beat the supervisory system, the tedious job of toll collection became even

---

[17] *Journal of Commerce*, October 6, 1993, p. 3B.

[18] Statement made by Edwin A. Elbert before the U.S. Senate Committee on Commerce considering cargo security legislation, S. 3595 and S.J. Res. 222, September 29 and 30, 1970, p. 85.

more tedious. Costs of increased employee turnover soon exceeded the savings from the cheat-proof system. The bridge authority then decided to adopt an unannounced policy of letting each collector pilfer up to $10 per week. That is, even though it knew exactly what a toll collector should have collected, it would say nothing until the losses for which the worker was responsible exceeded $10 per week.

> The toll-collection manager has an informal system to signal to collector[s] that [they are] under suspicion. A brightly painted authority police car parks right in front of the malefactor's toll booth. The toll taker gets the message. Theft drops back to a tolerable level.[19]

Obviously, handling pilferage is a difficult job for the supervisor. Some consider that the best policy is to declare that all taking of others' property is wrong, and proceed from that principle.

Organized theft involves the efforts of outsiders to steal merchandise while it is in the firm's distribution channels. Sometimes thefts and pilferage occur while the merchandise is within the custody of a common carrier or a warehouser. In this case the common carrier or warehouser is liable. However, the incident may still be disadvantageous to the shipper for several reasons:

1. The planned flow of the goods in the channel has been interrupted and may result in a stock-out at some later stage.
2. The carrier's or warehouser's liability may not cover the entire value of the shipment.
3. Time, telephone, and paperwork costs are not covered.
4. Employees who had knowledge of the shipment's route and timing may come under suspicion.
5. The stolen products may reappear on the market at a low price to compete with goods that have moved through legitimate channels.

Among the concerns about employees who use drugs is that they are vulnerable to outsiders who attempt to coerce them into aiding in thefts. "As a warehouse manager, perhaps your greatest risk is an employee who steals to raise money to acquire the substances which are abused."[20]

Building Security

In recent years there has been increased interest in providing **building security** for warehouses and other distribution facilities. Figure 13-8 shows some of the security measures that can be built into a warehouse.

---

[19] Lawrence R. Zeitlin, "A Little Larceny Can Do a Lot for Employee Morale," *Psychology Today,* June 1971, p. 64. See also Joseph F. Hari Jr., Ronald R. Bush, and Paul Bush, "Employee Theft: Views from Both Sides," *Business Horizons,* December 1976, pp. 25–29.

[20] Kenneth B. Ackerman, "Substance Abuse in the Warehouse," in *Council of Logistics Management Fall 1987 Annual Conference Proceedings,* vol. 1 (Oak Brook, Ill.: CLM, 1987), p. 81.

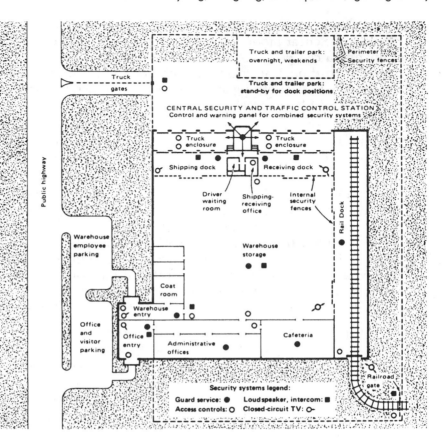

Figure 13-8   How to plan a thief-resistant warehouse. (Courtesy *Modern Materials Handling.*)

Electronic devices are available to perform three different functions. First, closed-circuit television cameras can be used to view different areas. The picture is shown on a monitor screen constantly observed by a guard. For areas where there should be no movements, it is possible to have monitoring devices store the image that contains no movement in digital memory and, "when a change in the image occurs—such as would be caused by an intruder in a freight storage area—initiate an alarm."[21] The second type of electronic device is used for access control. An example is a magnetically encoded tag that each employee must insert into a sensing device that records the event and determines whether the door or gate should be unlocked. The third and most common device is continuous wire circuits on

[21] Miklos Korodi, "Stop Thief!" *Distribution Worldwide,* December 1974, p. 47. See also "Warehouse Security," *Warehousing Review,* Summer 1979, p. 20; and "Controlling the Risk of Mysterious Disappearance," *Warehousing and Physical Distribution Productivity Report,* September 1982, pp. 1–14.

all doors, windows, and other openings that cannot be broken without triggering an alarm. There are also invisible photoelectric beams and many types of listening devices that can record unauthorized movements. Within a warehouse, heavier security may be placed around areas where higher-valued material is kept. Outside firms are sometimes retained to provide nighttime security for warehouse buildings. There is no limit to the sophistication or cost of the security devices that can be employed. It is, unfortunately, another cost of doing business.

Truck Security

Methods and equipment have been developed to discourage thefts from (or of) trucks and to improve **truck security.** Numbers can be painted on top of truck trailers to make them easier to spot from the air in case they are stolen (see Figure 13-9). An alternative is to place a transponder (a small device that responds to radio signals from an outside source) aboard trailers that are likely to be hijacked.

Figure 13-9　Suggested markings for the top of a truck, trailer, or container. (Courtesy of U.S. Department of Transportation.)

Improved locking devices are helpful. Thieves have been known to climb onto the rear of a truck waiting at a traffic signal and then force their way inside the vehicle. This is an area where continual training of employees is necessary. Figure 13-10 is from a late 1940s trucking firm's employee newsletter; despite its obvious sexist overtones, it was meant to serve as a warning against roadside hijackings.

Computer and Document Security

Computer security and **document security** can be difficult to maintain when individuals (usually employees) know how a company's various computer and paperwork systems work and then use their knowledge to defraud the company. They may be able to manipulate the system so that it ships additional products, issues unauthorized refund payments, or the like. As firms adopt computerized systems to handle their logistics functions, they

I should've known he wouldn't stop. It's one
of those safety minded B. F. Walker drivers.

Figure 13-10   A 1940s warning about roadside hijackings. (Courtesy of
B. F. Walker, Inc., Denver. This cartoon appeared in the June 1947 issue of
Boll Weevil Newspaper, a company publication.)

must take steps to ensure that the systems are safeguarded against unauthorized access and that sufficient controls are incorporated to prevent fraud.

In a situation involving the security of Revlon's new computerized distribution system in 1990, the cosmetics manufacturer had its inventory control software shut down by an unexpected phone call from the software
developer-vendor with whom it was having a dispute. Revlon was unhappy
with the performance of the partially installed system and balked at making
further payments. The software producer "responded by using a phone link

and Revlon's computer access codes to shut down its software in Revlon's computer systems. . . ."[22]

International transactions and movements are especially susceptible to documentation fraud. In these instances the owner of the goods may be thousands of miles away from the cargo and be dependent upon the honesty of many different parties in different lands who prepare and verify the cargo's documents.

Product Identification Number Security

Inventory control systems based on product serial numbers or product batch numbers have certain advantages with respect to discouraging theft and pilferage. If items are discovered missing, it is possible to identify them by number. This makes it possible to reclaim the goods if they are recovered and facilitates prosecution of those in possession of the goods. These facts are also known to pilferers, thieves, and fences and tend to make the "hot" merchandise somewhat less valuable. Altering or destroying the serial or batch numbers is time-consuming and arouses the suspicions of legitimate buyers.

Truck leasing companies, in an effort to thwart truck theft, now etch vehicle identification numbers "in forty different locations on each vehicle— glass, frame, drive-line components, various engine parts, and virtually any other part with resale value."[23] The number is cut on a special stencil and a sand blast gun is then applied. Some autos also have their serial numbers stamped on various parts.

System Security

One of the most effective methods of protecting goods is to keep them moving through the system. Goods waiting in warehouses, in terminals, or to clear customs are more vulnerable to theft than goods that are moving. No list of methods of improving **system security** (that is, security throughout the entire supply chain) is complete; determined thieves are likely to overcome almost any hindrance or barrier placed in their way. However, a few suggestions are offered here, mainly to reflect the breadth of measures that might be taken.

- Decals are required for autos in employee parking lots.
- Forklifts in warehouses are locked at night, making it difficult to reach high items or to move heavy items.
- Seals (small wirelike devices that once closed cannot be opened without breaking) are used more and more, with dispatchers, drivers, and receiving

[22] *San Francisco Chronicle,* October 25, 1990, p. 1. The matter is still in litigation. See also "Is Your Software Holding You Hostage?" *Distribution,* April 1991, pp. 48–50. This feature is nicknamed the "drop-dead device" because buyers of the systems are often unaware that it exists.

[23] "Vehicle Identification: How Leasing Companies' Experience Can Help Your Operation," *Private Carrier,* August 1984, pp. 46–48.

personnel all responsible for recording the seal number and inspecting its condition.

- Some companies have a continuous receipt system, so that an employee is considered responsible for each item until he or she can pass the item on and have the receiver sign a receipt. Although somewhat cumbersome, it has been helpful because it enhances the sense of personal responsibility of the employee, who tends to view any effort to steal or tamper with the goods as an assault on his or her own integrity.

- Electronic tags or strips are embedded in products at the time of their manufacture, and they can activate alarms at warehouse or retail store doors.

- One retail chain requires its retail stores to report any overages received from company warehouses. On occasion, it deliberately ships too much to determine whether the overage will be acknowledged.

- Sealing tape having a pattern containing the company's logo is used for sealing all outgoing packages and cartons. Although it does not prevent theft, it does make it more difficult to cover up evidence of pilferage or theft.

- A shoe manufacturer plagued with thefts from trucks decided to ship left shoes in one truck and right shoes in a different truck. The shoes were later matched and boxed at their destination.

This brief section has dealt only with domestic theft. When goods move in international commerce, they are much more vulnerable to theft. Entire shiploads of cargo have been known to disappear:

> [Some] ships have met diverse fates. Some have been scuttled after their cargo was surreptitiously unloaded at an unscheduled port. Some have vanished only to reappear under a new name and a new flag, with the old name faintly visible under the new paint. Some are diverted to a different port, where the cargo is sold to the highest bidder while the original purchaser waits in vain.
>
> Rustbucket fraud . . . involves chartering an aged ship that is loaded with goods worth more than the ship. After setting sail, it makes an unscheduled stop, sells off the cargo to the highest bidder, and exchanges its regular crew for a "scuttling crew" that takes it out to sea, where it runs into bad weather or an "accident" and sinks. The crew manages to escape and the hulk lies too deep for divers to examine it.[24]

ENERGY-SAVING CONTROLS

With the sudden and large increases in energy costs that took place in the 1970s, logistics managers had to pay increasing attention to keeping energy costs under control.

There are two areas in logistics systems where most energy costs occur and where energy-saving measures should be focused. One is in warehouses, where both design factors (such as not placing doors on the north side of

---

[24] "Modern Pirates Prey on Ships Taking Cargo to the Third World," *Minneapolis Tribune*, December 16, 1979.

a building) and operating procedures (such as having workers turn out unneeded lights) can lower energy consumption.[25] Solar energy can be employed to reduce purchase of the other forms of energy. One California walnut-processing and storage facility now uses shells from shelled walnuts as fuel to heat the structure.

The other area of logistics where considerable amounts of fuel can be saved is transportation. Almost any changes in shipping practices and patterns that reduce transportation costs probably utilize less fuel. Indeed, part of the rationale for deregulating the domestic transportation system in the United States was to do away with some of the inefficiencies (including fuel inefficiencies) of the regulated system.

HAZARDOUS MATERIALS HANDLING

Mention has been made several places in the text of hazardous materials and the fact that they must receive specialized and more careful handling. A firm or agency handling them would probably establish a special logistics channel to provide the additional protection required by government regulations, insurance requirements, and company policy. These precautionary measures would extend through the entire supply chain. Those handling hazardous materials must have in place training programs and haz-mat accident investigation procedures.

It is imperative that anybody handling or receiving hazardous materials be informed. In order to save time, some shippers have avoided labeling their shipments as hazardous and have later been subject to large fines. In one instance a plant manager labeled a shipment of ethyl mercaptan as "valves" so that it would be accepted for shipment by air. The package leaked, and forty-one people were hospitalized. The shipper faces up to thirty years in jail, and the company faces both fines and lawsuits from those who were hospitalized.[26]

MAINTAINING CHANNEL AND SUPPLY-CHAIN INTEGRITY

As channel relationships evolve into supply chains, a continual matter of concern is maintaining the integrity of the product and the product flow. While one must trust his or her partners, one cannot assume that the partners will be able to detect everything that goes wrong. One must continually monitor the quality of materials shipped and received, as well as performance in some of the other channels.

There are also outside threats. Product tampering is the most common, and although it usually occurs at the retail level, the retail store, the product, and the product's name all suffer from bad publicity. Usually several parties along the supply chain suffer.

---

[25] *Modern Materials Handling,* November 19, 1984, p. 29; and *Organizing and Managing for Energy Efficiency* (New York: Conference Board, report no. 837, 1983).

[26] *Journal of Commerce,* January 31, 1994, p. 12A.

In early 1995 a story was unfolding in California regarding the alleged sale of fake Similac, a baby formula, in Safeway Stores. Allegedly an individual purchased some powdered baby formula destined for export, packaged it in cans that were nearly identical copies of the Similac can, and sold it to a food broker that regularly supplied Safeway. The broker then sold it to Safeway, and the fake Similac ended up on Safeway's shelves. When the Food and Drug Administration moved in, over 6,000 cans of the fake Similac were recovered from wholesale and retail stocks. As might be imagined, lawsuits are now being filed. One class action suit filed alleges that Safeway "owed consumers a duty to ensure that the product it was purchasing and reselling was what it was represented to be."[27] The purpose of mentioning this incident here is that it shows how an existing channel can be broken into.

Sometimes no actual tampering takes place; a person need only announce to the media that he or she has tampered with some product, and the ensuing publicity will have a similar effect.

In an effort aimed at terrorism, the Federal Aviation Administration requires airlines to have air freight forwarders and air cargo agents certify that they have either physically inspected or X-rayed all cargo that they tender to airlines. These rules took effect in early 1994, and they matched similar requirements already existing for international shipments. Note that this shifts some responsibility for security along the logistics channel of the supply chain.

SUMMARY

Chapter 13 demonstrates the need for various types of controls. Of special importance are accounting controls and controls on worker productivity, both in warehouses and on the roads. A list of warehouse work rules is needed, including violations subject to discharge and violations subject to corrective discipline.

Supervising drivers is usually more difficult than supervising warehouse workers because drivers are on the road and out of their supervisor's immediate sight. Also, they are in contact with both customers and the public, whereas warehouse workers are not.

Product recalls are common. They involve reversing or freezing the movement of goods in the channel. Different products are subject to varying federal recall controls. Johnson & Johnson's difficulties with Tylenol is probably the best-known recall incident.

Pilferage and theft are two other important control issues. Pilferage is informal or casual thefts by employees, while thefts are committed by outsiders. Both are continuous hazards and require constant vigilance to protect against them. In recent years, computer security has become a problem.

Finally, energy-saving controls are important, especially in terms of fuel costs.

[27] *San Francisco Chronicle*, February 22, 1995, p. A15. In August 1995 a similar story was emerging regarding Head and Shoulders shampoo.

QUESTIONS FOR DISCUSSION AND REVIEW

1. What is the difference between pilferage and theft? From a management stand-point, which do you consider more significant? Why?

2. Describe how the tachograph functions. What bad driving habits can it detect?

3. What steps can be taken to discourage thefts from trucks and truck hijackings?

4. What steps can be taken against pilferage?

5. Do you think job applicants should be subjected to lie-detector tests? To drug testing? Why or why not?

6. What steps should a firm take to prepare for a product recall?

7. Why are serial numbers and batch numbers important?

8. What kind of accounting controls are used in logistics?

9. What is shrinkage? How would you measure it?

10. Give some examples of how a logistics manager might reduce a firm's use of energy.

11. What is short-interval scheduling? How is it used?

12. What questions might you ask employees to find out whether they are aware of their relative level of performance?

13. List the similarities and differences in controlling outbound shipments moving on one's own vehicles and on common carriers.

14. Read the warehouse work rules in Figure 13-3. Referring to the violations in the first list that call for immediate discharge, are there violations that you would (a) add to this list, (b) transfer to the second list, or (c) delete entirely from the first list? Why?

15. Why should a firm control access to its computer system?

16. What are product recalls? Give some examples.

17. List and discuss the various federal agencies that might be involved in product recalls.

18. Why do you think logistics systems controls are a matter of continual concern to management?

19. Of the various problems discussed in this chapter, which do you think are the most serious? Why?

20. Have you ever worked in a situation where pilferage was taking place? If so, describe the situation.

SUGGESTED READINGS

Curtis, Ellen Foster. "Quality Circles in Transportation: The Milwaukee Road Experience." *Transportation Journal,* Spring 1984, pp. 63–69.

Dorsey, Frank. "Preparing the Union for Work Standards." In *Annual Proceedings of the NCPDM.* Chicago: NCPDM, 1982, pp. 581–594.

Gallagher, Patrick (ed.). *Logistics: Contribution and Control*. Cleveland: Oberlin Printing, 1983.

Lambert, Douglas M. "Logistics Cost, Productivity, and Performance Analysis." *The Logistics Handbook*. New York: Free Press, 1994, pp. 260–302.

Lowe, Deborah. *Product Tampering: A Worldwide Problem*. Los Angeles: Foundation for American Communication, 1993.

Loyden, John J. "Nabisco Brands: Budgeting for the Distribution System." In *Annual Proceedings of the NCPDM*. Chicago: NCPDM, 1984, pp. 637–642.

Mentzer, John T., and John Firman. "Logistics Control Systems in the 21st Century." *Journal of Business Logistics,* vol. 15, no. 1 (1994), pp. 215–227.

Murphy, Paul R., and Richard F. Poist. "Management of Logistic Retromovements: An Empirical Analysis of Literature Suggestions." *Journal of the Transportation Research Forum,* 1988, pp. 177–184.

Novack, Robert A. "Transportation Standard Cost Budgeting." In *Annual Proceedings of the NCPDM*. Chicago: NCPDM, 1984, pp. 607–622.

Snitzler, James R., and James A. Caron. "Measuring Productivity in Distribution Operations of Regional Farm Supply Cooperatives." In *Annual Proceedings of the Transportation Research Forum*. Arlington, Va.: TRF, 1984, pp. 300–302.

Sterling, Jay U. "Measuring the Performance of Logistics Operations," *The Logistics Handbook*. New York: Free Press, 1994, pp. 199–240.

Voss, Bristol. "Uncovering Hidden Costs." *Journal of Business Strategy,* vol. 15, no. 3 (May–June 1994), pp. 37–47.

White, John A., Jr. "Management Guide to Productivity." *The Distribution Handbook*. New York: Free Press, 1985, pp. 319–369.

C A S E   1 3 - 1

BRANT FREEZER COMPANY

Located in Fargo, North Dakota, the Brant Freezer Company manufactured industrial freezers. They came in one size and were distributed through public warehouses in Atlanta, Boston, Chicago, Denver, Los Angeles, Portland, and St. Louis. In addition, some space was used in the company's Fargo warehouse. Young Joaquin (J.Q.) Brant, with a fresh MBA degree from the University of South Alabama, returned to the family firm, where he had once worked during summers. On his first day of work, J.Q. met with his father. His father complained that they were being "eaten alive" by warehousing costs. The firm's controller drew up a budget each year, and each warehouse's monthly activity (units shipped) and costs were tallied.

Exhibit 13-A shows actual 1996 figures for all warehouses, plus actual figures for the first five months of 1997. In addition, projected twelve-month

EXHIBIT 13-A   WAREHOUSE PERFORMANCE

| | 1996 figures | | | | 1997 figures | | | |
| | Units shipped | | Warehouse costs | | Units shipped | | Warehouse costs | |
	12 months Jan.-Dec.	5 months through May 31	12 months Jan.-Dec.	5 months through May 31	Projected 12 months Jan.-Dec.	Actual 5 months May 31	Budgeted 12 months Jan.-Dec.	Actual costs through May 31
Atlanta	17,431	4,080	156,830	35,890	18,000	4,035	178,000	40,228
Boston	6,920	3,061	63,417	27,915	7,200	3,119	73,000	29,416
Chicago	28,104	14,621	246,315	131,618	30,000	15,230	285,000	141,222
Denver	3,021	1,005*	28,019	8,690*	3,100	1,421	31,000	14,900
Fargo (company warehouse)	2,016	980	16,411	8,883	2,000	804	17,000	9,605
Los Angeles	16,491	11,431	151,975	109,690	17,000	9,444	176,000	93,280
Portland	8,333	4,028	73,015	36,021	9,000	4,600	85,000	42,616
St. Louis	5,921	2,331	51,819	23,232	8,000	2,116	56,000	19,191

*Denver warehouse closed by strike March 4–19, 1996.

1997 budgets and shipments are also included. If you are familiar with Lotus 1-2-3 or other spreadsheet software, you might try using it here.

Questions

1. When comparing performance during the first five months of 1997 with performance in 1996, which warehouse shows the most improvement?

2. When comparing performance during the first five months of 1997 with performance in 1996, which warehouse shows the poorest change in performance?

3. When comparisons are made among all eight warehouses, which one do you think does the best job for the Brant Company? What criteria did you use? Why?

4. J.Q. is aggressive and is going to recommend that his father cancel the contract with one of the warehouses and give that business to a competing warehouse in the same city. J.Q. feels that when word of this gets around, the other warehouses they use will "shape up." Which of the seven should J.Q. recommend be dropped? Why?

5. The year 1997 is nearly half over. J.Q. is told to determine how much the firm is likely to spend for warehousing at each of the eight warehouses for the last six months in 1997. Do his work for him.

6. When comparing the 1996 figures with the 1997 figures shown in the table, the amount budgeted for each warehouse in 1997 was greater than actual 1996 costs. How much of the increase is caused by increased volume of business (units shipped) and how much by inflation?

7. Prepare the firm's 1998 warehouse budget, showing for each warehouse the anticipated number of units to be shipped and the costs.

8. While attending classes at the university, J.Q. had learned of logistics partnerships. Should Brant Freezer Company attempt to enter into a partnership relationship with these warehouses? If so, what approach should it use?

C A S E   1 3 - 2

RED SPOT MARKETS COMPANY

The Red Spot Markets Company operates a chain of grocery stores in New England. It has a grocery distribution center in Providence, Rhode Island, from which deliveries are made to stores as far north as Lowell, Massachusetts, as far west as Waterbury, Connecticut, and as far northwest as

Springfield, Massachusetts. There are no stores beyond the two northernmost points in Massachusetts. There are stores to the west, but they are supplied by a grocery warehouse located in Newburgh, New York. The Providence grocery distribution center supplies forty-two Red Spot retail stores.

Robert Easter, Red Spot's distribution manager, is responsible for operations at the Newburgh and Providence distribution centers. By industry standards, both were fairly efficient. However, of the two, the Providence center lagged in two important areas of control: worker productivity and shrinkage. Warehouse equipment and work rules were the same for both the Newburgh and Providence centers, yet the throughput per worker hour was 4 percent higher for the Newburgh facility. Shrinkage, expressed as a percentage of the wholesale value of goods handled annually, was 0.36 percent for the Newburgh center and 0.59 percent for the Providence center. Jarvis Jason had been manager of the Providence distribution center for the past three years and, at great effort, managed to narrow the gap between the performance of the two Red Spot facilities. Last week he requested an immediate reassignment, and Easter arranged for him to become the marketing manager for the Boston area, which would involve supervising the operations of eleven Red Spot markets. The transfer involved no increase in pay.

Easter needed a new manager for the Providence distribution center, and he decided to pick Fred Fosdick for the task. Fosdick graduated from a lesser Ivy League college, where he majored in business with a concentration in logistics. He had been with Red Spot for two years and rearranged the entire delivery route structure so that two fewer trucks were needed. As part of this assignment, he also converted the entire system to one of unit loads, which meant everything loaded on or unloaded from a Red Spot truck was on a pallet. Fosdick was familiar with the operations of both the Providence and Newburgh centers. He has been in each facility at least fifty different times. In addition, he spent two weeks at the Providence center when the loading docks were redesigned to accommodate pallet loading. Fosdick was surprised that Jason requested his reassignment to a slot that did not involve an upward promotion. That was his first question to Easter after Easter asked whether he was interested in the Providence assignment.

"I'm sorry you started with that question," said Easter to Fosdick. "Now we'll have to talk about the troublesome aspects of the assignment first, rather than the positive ones. To be frank, Fred, one of the union employees there made so much trouble for Jason, he couldn't stand it."

"Who's the troublemaker?" asked Fosdick.

"Tom Bigelow," was Easter's answer.

Fosdick remembered Bigelow from the times he had been at the Providence center. Thomas D. Bigelow was nicknamed T. D. since his days as a local Providence high school football star. Fosdick recalled that during work breaks on the loading dock, Bigelow and some of the other workers would toss around melons as though they were footballs. Only once did they drop a melon. Fosdick recalled hearing the story that Bigelow had received several offers of athletic scholarships when he graduated from high school. His best offer was from a southern school, and he accepted it. Despite the fact that the college provided a special tutor for each class, Bigelow flunked out at the end of his first semester and came back to Providence, where he got a job in the Red Spot warehouse.

In the warehouse Bigelow was a natural leader. He would have been a supervisor except for his inability to count and his spotty attendance record on Monday mornings. On Mondays, the day that the warehouse was the busiest since it had to replenish the stores' weekend sales, Bigelow was groggy, tired, and irritable. On Mondays he would even hide by loading a forklift with three pallets, backing into any empty bay, and lowering the pallets in position (which hid the lift truck from view), and he would fall asleep. The rest of the week Bigelow was happy, enthusiastic, and hardworking. Indeed, it was he who set the pace of work in the warehouse. When he felt good, things hummed; when he was not feeling well or was absent, work dragged.

"What did Bigelow do to Jason?" Fosdick asked Easter.

"Well, as I understand it," responded Easter, "about two weeks ago Jason decided that he had had it with Bigelow and so he suspended him on a Monday morning after Bigelow showed up late, still badly hung over. It was nearly noon, and he told Bigelow to stay off the premises and to file a grievance with his union shop steward. He also told Bigelow that he had been documenting Bigelow's Monday performance—or nonperformance—for the past six months and that Red Spot had grounds enough to fire Bigelow if it cared to. He told Bigelow to go home, sober up, and come back on Tuesday when they would discuss the length of his suspension. Bigelow walked through the distribution center on his way out, and I'm sure Jason felt he had control of the matter.

"However," continued Easter, "by about one o'clock, Jason realized he had a work slowdown on his hands. Pallet loads of bottled goods were being dropped, two forklifts collided, and one lift truck pulled over the corner of a tubular steel rack. At 4:00 P.M. quitting time there were still three trucks to be loaded; usually they would have departed by 3:30. Rather than pay overtime, Jason let the work force go home, and he and the supervisor loaded the last three trucks.

"On Tuesday, Bigelow did not show up, and the slowdown got worse. In addition, retail stores were phoning with complaints about all the errors in their orders. To top it off, at the Roxbury store, when the trailer door was opened, the trailer contained nothing but empty pallets. Tuesday night somebody turned off the switches on the battery chargers for all the lift trucks, so on Wednesday, the lift-truck batteries were dying all day. I got involved because of all the complaints from the stores. On Wednesday Jason got my permission to pay overtime, and the last outgoing truck did not leave until 7:00 P.M. In addition we had to pay overtime at some of our retail stores because the workers there were waiting for the trucks to arrive. While I was talking to Jason that afternoon, he indicated that he had fired Bigelow."

Easter lit his cigar and continued, "On Wednesday I decided to go to Providence myself, mainly to talk to Jason and to determine whether we should close down the Providence center and try to serve all our stores out of Newburgh. This would have been expensive, but Providence was becoming too unreliable. In addition, we had a big weekend coming up. When I showed up in Providence, Jason and I had breakfast together in my hotel room Thursday morning, and he told me pretty much the same thing I've been telling you. He said he knew Bigelow was behind all the disruption and that today (meaning Thursday) would be crucial. I've never seen Jason looking so nervous. Then we drove to the distribution center. Even from a distance, I could tell things were moving slowly. The first echelon of outgoing trucks, which should have been on the road, were still there. Another twenty of our trucks were waiting to be loaded. On the other end of the building, you could see a long line of arriving trucks waiting to be unloaded; usually there was no line at all. I knew that our suppliers would start complaining because we had established scheduled unloading times. However, I decided not to ask Jason whether he had begun receiving phone calls from them."

"Inside the center the slowdown was in effect. Lift-truck operators who usually zipped by each other would now stop, turn off their engines, dismount, and carefully walk around each other's truck to ensure there was proper clearance. Satisfied of this, they would then mount, start their engines, and spend an inordinate amount of time motioning to each other to pass. This was only one example. When we got to Jason's office he had a message to phone Ed Meyers, our local attorney in Providence who handles much of our labor relations work there. He called Meyers and was upset by the discussion. After he hung up he told me that Meyers had been served papers by the union's attorney, charging that Wednesday's firing of Bigelow was unjustified, mainly because there existed no provable grounds that Bigelow was behind the slowdown. Meyers was angry because, in firing Bigelow on Wednesday, he (Jason) may have also blown the suspension of Bigelow on Monday. Jason and I started talking, even arguing. I talked so much that my cigar went out," said Easter, "so I asked Jason, who was sitting behind his desk, for a match. He didn't carry matches but looked inside his center desk drawer for one. He gasped and I didn't know what was the matter. He got up, looking sick, and walked away from his desk. He said that a dead rat had been left in his desk drawer, and he wanted a transfer. He was in bad shape and the distribution center was in bad shape, so I had the opening in the Boston area and I let him have it. Actually, right now he and his family are vacationing somewhere in eastern Canada. He needs the rest."

Fosdick was beginning to feel sorry that he knew all the details, but he persisted. "Then what?" he asked Easter.

"Well, I took over running the distribution center. I phoned Meyers again, and he and I had lunch. He thought that Jason had blown the case against Bigelow and that we should take him back. So on Friday, Meyers, Bigelow, the union attorney, the shop steward, Bigelow's supervisor, and I met. Jason, of course, was not there. It was a pleasant meeting. Everything got blamed on poor Jason. I did tell Bigelow that we would be documenting his performance and wanted him to know that Jason's successor, meaning you, was under my instructions to tolerate no nonsense from him (Bigelow). Bigelow was so pleasant that day that I could not imagine him in the role of a troublemaker. The amazing thing was, when he went out into the center to resume work, a loud cheer went up and all the drivers started blowing their lift-truck horns. For a moment, I was afraid all the batteries would run down again. But I was wrong. They were plain happy to see Bigelow back. You know, the slowdown was still in effect when Bigelow walked onto the floor. I'd say it was 10:00 A.M. and they were an hour behind. Well, let me tell you what happened. They went to work! By noon we were back on schedule, and by the end of the shift we were a half-hour ahead of schedule. In fact, the last half-hour was spent straightening up many of the bins that had been deliberately disarranged during the slowdown. I tell you, Tom Bigelow does set the workpace in that warehouse!"

"So what do you suggest I do at the center?" asked Fosdick.

"Well, the key is getting along with Bigelow. Talk to Meyers about the kind of records you should keep in case you decide to move against Bigelow. Be sure to consult with Meyers before you do anything irreversible. Frankly, I don't know whether Bigelow will be a problem. We never had trouble with him that I knew about before Jason was there. According to Bigelow and the union attorney, Jason had it in for Bigelow. If I were you, I'd take it easy with Bigelow and other labor problems. See what you can do instead about the inventory shrinkage."

On the next Monday morning, Fosdick showed up at the Providence distribution center. After gingerly looking in all his desk drawers, he had a brief meeting with his supervisors and then walked out to meet the entire work force on a one-to-one basis. Many remembered Fosdick from his earlier visits to the facility. Because it was a Monday morning, he had not expected to encounter Bigelow. But Bigelow was present, clear-eyed, alert, and enthusiastic. He was happy to see Fosdick and shook his hand warmly. Bigelow then excused himself, saying he had to return to work. The truck dispatcher said that the work force was ahead of schedule again: it was 11:00 A.M. and they were about fifteen minutes ahead. Fosdick returned to his office, and there was a phone message from Ed Meyers. Meyers asked to postpone their luncheon for that day until Tuesday noon. Then Robert Easter called to ask how things were going on Fosdick's first day. Easter was pleased that things were going smoothly.

It was lunchtime. Fosdick decided to walk to a small café where he had eaten at other times. It was two blocks from the distribution center and on the side away from the office. So he walked through the center, which was quiet since it was closed down for lunch. He walked by the employee's lunchroom where there were the normal sounds of fifty people eating and talking. Just outside the lunchroom was one lift truck with an empty wooden pallet on it. As Fosdick watched, one of the new stock clerks came out of the lunchroom with an opened case of sweet pickles from which three jars had been taken. Next came another new stock clerk with an opened carton of mustard from which two bottles had been removed. One of the clerks suddenly saw Fosdick and said weakly, "We take these opened cases to the damaged merchandise room." Fosdick went into the lunchroom. There, on the center table were cases of cold meat, cheese, soft drinks, catsup, and bread. All had been opened and partially emptied to provide the workers' lunch.

Bigelow was making himself a large sandwich when he saw Fosdick approach. "Don't get uptight," he said to Fosdick. "You've just come across one of the noncontract fringe benefits of working at the Red Spot Providence distribution center. May I make you a sandwich?"

Questions

1. How should Fosdick respond to the immediate situation?
2. What controls, of the types discussed in this chapter, might have been used by Red Spot Markets to reduce or eliminate the problems discussed in the case?
3. What longer-range steps should Fosdick take to control the operations of the Providence distribution center?
4. What longer-range steps should Fosdick take to improve the Providence distribution center's productivity?
5. What longer-range steps can Fosdick take to reduce the distribution center's high rate of shrinkage?
6. Assume that Fosdick decides that the practice of free lunches from the opened cases of goods must be stopped. Develop and present the arguments he should give in a meeting with the union shop steward.
7. (This is a continuation of question 6.) Assume, instead, that you are the union shop steward. Develop and present your argument that the free lunches represent a long-standing employee benefit enjoyed by the distribution center's employees, and that management's attempt to stop them is a breach of an unwritten contract and will be resisted.
8. Much of the situation described in the case seems to evolve around the personality of T. D. Bigelow. How should he be treated? Why?

14

Supply-Chain Integration and Management

Although we tend to think in terms of high speeds, quick turnovers, and large volumes, it is important to remember that many markets function at a slower pace. Shown here is an Overnite Transportation Company tractor-trailer crossing the Ohio River between Marion, Kentucky, and Cave in Rock, Illinois, via ferry. (Courtesy of Overnite Transportation Company.)

The women's long crepe jumper with tie sides advertised on the cover of today's Target sale section will not be available. . . . This style of jumper does not meet Target's high quality standards. The short twill jumpers on sale at $17.88 will be available.
Also, the kids' Greatland-R flannel pants advertised are not available due to manufacturer's shipping problems. Please fill out a rain check so that we can notify you by mail when they are in stock. We regret any inconvenience this may cause.

San Francisco Examiner
August 20, 1995

Wal-Mart told suppliers it would no longer deal with wholesalers and other [agents] and would only buy directly from manufacturers. By eliminating the intermediaries, Wal-Mart stands to reduce its costs further.

San Francisco Chronicle
April 6, 1992

Chrysler Corp. relies on the Harper Group to manage its annual volume of 65,000 vehicle exports. The EDI program known as HarperLink provides worldwide inventory control, invoicing to all parties, and basic information such as ports, carriers, and customs documentation.

World Trade
June 1993

Why would any businessman who looks at logistics as a strategic advantage want to go to a third party?

Clifford M. Sayre
American Shipper
January 1994

Supply-chain information sharing requires total trust and high levels of confidentiality. In some cases these meetings [of manufacturers, raw material suppliers, end users and transportation providers] have led to as much as a 40 percent improvement in costs.

Journal of Commerce
July 28, 1993

Key Terms

- Channel management
- Contract warehousing
- Decentralized logistics organization
- Linking-pin organization
- Matrix management
- Status quo organizational structure
- Third-party, or contract, logistics
- Unified department organization

Learning Objectives

- To examine a number of organizational alternatives
- To describe a number of techniques for achieving logistics coordination
- To distinguish between centralized and decentralized logistics organization
- To understand concepts of supply-chain integration
- To appreciate the logistics practices of not-for-profit agencies

INTRODUCTION

To some observers logistics is a mature concept, and each firm or agency has adopted whatever aspects of logistics that best suit its needs. Indeed, the term *logistics reengineering* would lead one to believe that logistics systems have been around for a long time. The authors of this book have followed and written about this topic for some time. Earlier editions of the text placed greater emphasis on the physical distribution aspects of logistics, that is, those aspects dealing with the movement of product from the end of the assembly line to the retail customer. Today we think more in terms of *total logistics,* meaning balanced concern with both inbound and outbound movements and with the development of channel or supply-chain relationships on a long-term basis with suppliers and customers.

While there continue to be many changes in how each user organizes in order to meet its logistics needs, the intellectual concepts are well in place. Much depends on the importance that a firm places on logistics. Often this translates into how much, as a percentage of sales, the firm is spending on logistics. Other factors may be what the competition is doing, how centralized or decentralized the firm's management is, and whether the same should hold for the firm's logistics management. Today there is also interest in "farming out" some logistics functions to be performed by others.

Organizations that are thought of as providers of services, rather than of goods, also have formidable logistics requirements. At the United Airlines main maintenance base near the San Francisco airport there is an inventory of over 170,000 different SKUs, all needed to keep the airline's fleet operating. This system processes over 100,000 inventory transactions each month. Firms also have their own internal logistics needs to deal with the transport within the firm of materials, supplies, and people. For example, a firm's own printing operation may produce all the forms, letterheads, brochures, and so on that the company uses. These printed materials must then be shipped within the firm's internal communications and logistics network. Figure 14-1 shows a custom-built desert vehicle used to carry portable offices and equipment sheds needed to support an oil exploration operation in the Middle East.

Some firms provide logistical services to others. Traveling music groups retain firms to handle the transportation of performers, instruments, sound systems, and stage equipment from tour site to tour site. Specializing firms also transport, assemble, and disassemble traveling displays used by their clients' marketing managers who are, say, conducting a series of sales meetings throughout the nation.

One-time functions also may have major logistical needs. One example is the 1984 Summer Olympics, held in Los Angeles. In addition to providing for the athletes and guests, there was a large quantity of specialized equipment to be handled, such as each team's yachts, rowing shells, canoes, gym equipment, or judo mats. Over three hundred horses were brought into the

Figure 14-1   A mobile office. (Courtesy of Arabian American Oil Company.)

country for use in equestrian events. At Super Bowl XIX, played in Palo Alto, the ABC television broadcasting operation required twenty-four trucks and one helicopter. To cover the 1988 Olympics, NBC used a fleet of over forty mobile units valued at over $60 million.[1] As this book is being revised, the O. J. Simpson trial is under way and views outside the courthouse show a huge collection of broadcast vans.

This chapter will deal with logistics as it is organized within the firm. Then it will look at the practice of some firms that farm out some of their logistics activities to be performed by others. Then it will look at supply-chain integration, usually evidenced by partnership relationships along the channels or chain. Last, it will look at logistics operations in nonprofit entities.

LOGISTICS WITHIN THE FIRM

Earlier editions of this book dealt with how many of the different functions listed in the chapter should be under the control of the firm's logistics director. This continues to be a matter of interest. In an annual survey of logistics executives, Professors Bernard J. LaLonde and James M. Masters of Ohio State University list a number of logistics activities and inquire whether, in the respondent's firm, they fit under the logistics umbrella. The activities and the

[1] "'Olympic Fever' Is Heating Operations for California Customshouse," *Air Cargo News,* February 1984, p. 9; *Marin Independent Journal,* January 25, 1985, p. TV; and *Port of San Francisco Wharfside,* August 1988, p. 9.

percentages of firms including them under logistics are as follows: traffic management, 95 percent; warehousing, 94 percent; facility location, 90 percent; inventory control, 80 percent; global logistics, 80 percent; general management, 79 percent; order processing, 59 percent; procurement, 47 percent; order entry, 46 percent; packaging, 41 percent; product planning, 36 percent; and sales forecasting, 28 percent.[2] The logistics staff shared responsibility with other groups in areas such as packaging, strategic planning, sales forecasting, and so on.

Professors K. C. Schneider and J. C. Johnson, in a similar survey, received responses from over 150 firms and found that the following percentages of firms assigned these listed activities to their logistics staff: transportation of finished products, 88 percent; warehousing, 74 percent; finished products inventory, 53 percent; transportation of inputs, 47 percent; materials handling, 45 percent; order processing 31 percent; protective packaging, 32 percent; purchasing, 30 percent; and customer service, 26 percent.[3]

While this chapter deals mainly with domestic corporations, brief mention should be made of several other forms of organization in which the principles mentioned here may also be applicable. International corporations with operations in many countries, for example, must organize whatever structure suits their multinational interests best. The international logistics manager must be familiar with domestic logistics operations in many nations and with the physical and legal complexities involved in transferring materials between nations.

Dispersion of Logistics Activities

The size of a firm also influences the placement of logistics functions. In small firms there are definite limitations as to how thinly managerial talent can be spread. In such situations one consideration in organization may be to even out the workloads of supervisors. The integration of inbound and outbound movements should not be surprising. Current professional thinking is that this type of coordination is needed. As Andre J. Martin pointed out:

> Most books on distribution inventories assume that allocating the inventory once it is available is the problem. They must believe that the inventory which the distribution centers need just appears out of nowhere! The real problem is planning manufacturing, be it within one's own company or with outside suppliers, to make sure that the inventory will be available when needed. Integrating the production planning for distributing inventories with the production planning for manufacturing inventories is a subject that has

[2] Bernard J. LaLonde and James M. Masters, "The 1994 Ohio State University Survey of Career Patterns in Logistics," in *Council of Logistics Management Annual Conference Proceedings* (Oak Brook, Ill.: CLM, 1994), p. 96.

[3] Kenneth C. Schneider and James C. Johnson, "Marketing Logistics, Necessary Evil or Strategic Marketing Function?" *Logistics Spectrum,* Winter 1988, p. 8.

gotten little attention in the conventional literature on distribution inventories.[4]

Achieving Coordination

Effective logistics operations cannot exist without a high level of coordination among the various functional areas. George A. Gecowets, of the CLM, once noted that the key to implementation is coordination and that it may involve only an ongoing exchange of information among the traditional functions that combine to form the logistics department.[5]

To achieve a high level of coordination within the firm, one can choose one of the three organizational strategies: making no change in the present system, experimenting with unique ways of coordination with the existing system, or reorganizing the functional areas of logistics into a logistics department. There are other alternatives, but they are only variations of these three strategies. Which strategy to choose may depend on a firm's strategic plans, including those formulated to cover its logistical activities. Considerable thought must go into organizing or reorganizing the firm—and its vendors and buyers—in order to achieve a more desirable flow of goods and services.

The Status Quo

For some companies it is feasible to obtain the required coordination among the logistics functional areas without any formal change in the organizational structure. This is accomplished by both formal and informal operating procedures that guarantee that the various areas will coordinate and discuss their various problems and proposals. This concept of coordination is generally most feasible when the overall size of the firm and the number of employees trying to coordinate across departmental lines are not large. For many firms this is a viable alternative, and it avoids the problems associated with actually transferring and reassigning functional areas.

One problem of maintaining the **status quo organizational structure** is that the influence of logistics thinking never gets an opportunity to express itself. Because logistics activities are scattered throughout the firm, they always remain subservient to the objectives of the senior department (i.e., marketing, manufacturing, finance) in which they are housed.

The Linking-Pin Concept

Another organizational structure, similar to the status quo option, is the **linking-pin organization.** Here certain individuals are assigned the responsibility of ensuring coordination among logistics activities. Known as "linking pins," they are assigned to work in two or three functional areas. An

[4] Andre J. Martin, *Distribution Resource Planning* (Englewood Cliffs, N.J.: Prentice Hall, 1983), p. 2. Martin was an associate of the late Oliver Wight, one of the principal figures in the development of MRP.

[5] George A. Gecowets, "PDM—Pro and Con," *Distribution Worldwide*, March 1973, p. 39.

individual may simultaneously be assigned to the traffic department (which is a part of production) and to the warehousing department (which is a part of marketing). The advantage of this system is that the linking-pin members of each work group are able to coordinate and express the problems and concerns of each decision as it relates to the respective department within which the linking pin operates.

However, there are some serious problems with the linking-pin concept. The most basic is that it violates the classic organizational principle of unity of command. Linking pins in effect belong to two or more departments, so who is their boss? Who evaluates job performance? Who decides about promotions? Linking pins may find themselves in the position of having no home. It is possible for linking-pin members to alienate all the departments for which they work. The departments may feel that the linking-pin members are too global in outlook and no longer members of the home department's team. Also, under the linking-pin arrangement, logistics is close to being considered a staff rather than a line function, with the accompanying inference being that staff activities are never quite as important as line activities.

A Unified Department

The **unified department organization** combines all functional areas of logistics into one department. This approach is intuitively the best because coordination among traffic, warehousing, inventory control, production, and other functional areas is facilitated when they are combined into one operating department. This alternative has worked well for many companies and appears to be the preferred solution to overcoming the coordination problems in a logistics department. Under the unified department strategy, logistics is a line activity.

Professors Jeffrey Miller and Peter Gilmour have long advocated that the materials management department of a firm be on the same level as the traditional departments of manufacturing, finance, and marketing. As an example of the type of firm needing such an organizational structure, they cited an electronics manufacturer that once had grown with little competition and is now in a mature market, confronting many new competitors. Cost control was of increasing importance, and the decision was made to have a single materials manager.

> Most important in justifying this reorganization was a plan for a new procurement program that promised to save the company millions of dollars a year by long-term contracting for groups of related materials instead of buying each material separately on a spot basis.
>
> The production planning group figured prominently in the proposed program because it controlled materials inventories and thus determined when releases needed to be placed against the new contracts. This the production controllers would be in contact with vendors on a more frequent basis than the purchasing department.

Through their expediting and ordering decisions, the production planners could also significantly affect contract prices. Some managers felt that if production planning and purchasing reported together, their boss, the materials manager, could be sensitive to both materials costs and vendor relations along with inventory and ordering costs.[6]

A 1993 consultant's survey of 300 firms sought to determine the level to which the head of the firm's logistics operations reported. In 29 percent of the instances, the president was reported to, meaning that the logistics function was on a level with the firm's other major functions. For 26 percent of the respondents, the operations vice president was the individual reported to; for 16 percent, the manufacturing vice president; for 9 percent, the finance vice president; and for 6 percent, the marketing vice president.[7]

Another consultant reported that the "new" logistics manager (titled "chief logistics officer") was in the middle of the organization and concerned with five major areas: corporate strategies, information systems and flows, procurement, manufacturing, and sales. The consultant believed that the chief logistics officer dealt more with general management than with specific logistics issues. The consultant used the categories "old logistics" and "new logistics": the old logistics included managing the logistics pipeline, managing and collaborating with logistics personnel, partnering with logistics suppliers, and integrating the elements of the physical distribution function. The new logistics, instead, includes creation of breakthroughs in customer delivery practices; partnering with other functional heads, customers, and suppliers; and selecting and developing the best system to get the job done, often changing elements inside and outside the company. "The old system emphasizes costs. The new system emphasizes profits. The old contained limits (a system could only become so efficient). The new is limitless (as it helps grow the company). The old rewarded creative rearrangement of familiar elements. The new takes its creative practitioners into unfamiliar ground."[8]

Centralization versus Decentralization

An important issue in logistics organization strategy is whether the logistics department should be centralized or decentralized. A centralized logistics organization implies that the corporation maintains a single logistics department that administers the related activities for the entire company from the home office. A **decentralized logistics organization,** in contrast, means that logistics-related decisions are made separately at the divisional or product group level and often in different geographic regions.

---

[6] Jeffrey G. Miller and Peter Gilmour, "Materials Managers: Who Needs Them?" *Harvard Business Review,* July–August 1979, p. 147.

[7] *Logistics Management and Technology* (Chicago: KPMG Peat Marwick, 1993), p. 2.

[8] Jim Stone, "The New Logistics," *Logistics Resource,* 1993, no. 2, p. 2.

The size of a firm, its product, and the geographic area over which its sales are made and its inputs are purchased are what determine whether centralized or decentralized decisions should be made. There are several arguments in favor of the centralized logistics organization, and two will be given here. One is related to the information sciences and computers, which are revolutionizing many aspects of business and changing many traditional ways of interacting both inside and outside the firm. Logistics managers control some of a firm's most important, timely, and sensitive data, since so many of their activities deal with sales and orders. Today there are more than a thousand different software programs available for use in logistics functions. The various programs are divided fairly evenly among personal and mainframe computers. The important point is this: As firms and markets restructure themselves around the functions of information handling, processing, transmittal, exchange, and control, logistics should end up doing well. In situations in which closer communication is needed with customers, the logistics function will be in an enviable position. Computers and communications are likely to lead firms in the direction of centralized management (even if only through linked computers).

The second observation has to do with relations within the firm. Here we continue to see an increasing interest in combining the outbound product flow functions with inbound product and input flows, in part because of the computer. It is now possible to link via computer the incoming orders for a firm's output to its own orders of replenishment stocks. When negotiating a contract with a carrier, one can press for a lower rate by offering a greater total tonnage or more balanced (inbound-outbound) hauls. Thus load balancing (or any form of freight consolidation) appears to work best in a centralized system.

The arguments in favor of the decentralized logistics organization stress the unmanageability of a centralized system in large, multidivisional firms. In highly decentralized firms it is often preferable for the line distribution functions to remain in each autonomous division. The decentralized organizational system appears to function best when the various product lines of each division have very little in common.

Advocates of decentralization question the ability of a centralized logistics department to provide required levels of customer service. Customers willing to wait thirty to sixty days to receive orders may be adequately served by a centralized logistics department of a multidivisional firm. However, for customers requiring twenty-four-hour service, the centralized logistics function may not be responsive enough. In order to meet these customers' needs, an in-house department (i.e., one within the division) is needed, one that is attuned to the specific requirements of the division. In this case, too, geography is a factor. Many global firms need to decentralize operations because centralized management may be impossible to achieve. Figure 14-2 shows a firm that sells medical supplies having sources spread throughout the world.

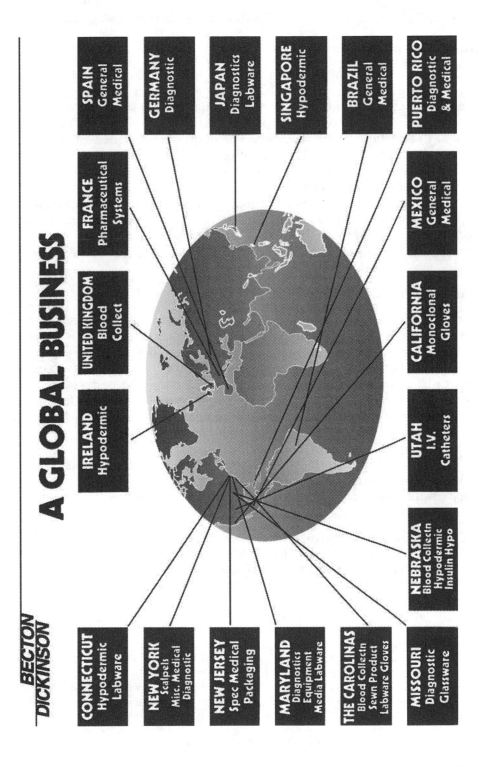

Figure 14-2 Becton Dickinson's worldwide sources. (Courtesy Becton Dickinson and Company.)

BECTON DICKINSON

A GLOBAL BUSINESS

SPAIN
General
Medical

GERMANY
Diagnostic

JAPAN
Diagnostics
Labware

SINGAPORE
Hypodermic

BRAZIL
General
Medical

PUERTO RICO
Diagnostic
& Medical

FRANCE
Pharmaceutical
Systems

UNITED KINGDOM
Blood
Collect

IRELAND
Hypodermic

MEXICO
General
Medical

CALIFORNIA
Monoclonal
Gloves

UTAH
I.V.
Catheters

NEBRASKA
Blood Collectn
Hypodermic
Insulin Hypo

CONNECTICUT
Hypodermic
Labware

NEW YORK
Scalpels
Misc. Medical
Diagnostic

NEW JERSEY
Spec Medical
Packaging

MARYLAND
Diagnostics
Equipment
Media Labware

THE CAROLINAS
Blood Collectn
Sewn Product
Labware Gloves

MISSOURI
Diagnostic
Glassware

Matrix Management

Another useful form of management organization is referred to as **matrix management.** In this approach the firm maintains a conventional management structure for handling most routine matters. However, certain employees are periodically assigned on a short-term basis to teams established to deal with specific, unique problems. The employees assigned to these short-term projects are chosen because they possess special skills. An example of a one-time assignment would be to deal with the closure of a plant and the relocation of some of its operations.

Although matrix management may seem similar to the linking-pin concept, the latter involves a much longer-term commitment toward achieving coordination among several logistical activities. Matrix management, in contrast, involves short-term projects undertaken by teams that are only temporary.

FARMING OUT LOGISTICS ACTIVITIES

Very few firms conduct absolutely all of their own logistics activities. Some are farmed out to be performed by others. A common example is using UPS to deliver one's parcels. This practice is sometimes known as **third-party,** or **contract, logistics.** Public warehouse personnel perform many assembly and distribution functions, and in some states they also perform deliveries. These channel members act as intermediaries between the manufacturer and the ultimate customer. Some intermediaries perform more logistics functions for the manufacturer than others. And of course, for doing this they expect to be additionally compensated.

Sometimes operations are given to others in order to reduce exposure to risk. Since the *Exxon Valdez* disaster, U.S. oil companies have been cutting back on their ownership of tankers, in order to reduce their exposure to law suits:

> Some companies have been so afraid of liability risks from operating their own fleet that they have begun large-scale sales of their ships, combined with farming out operations responsibilities to outside companies. . . .
>
> The farming out of ship operations represents a near-complete abandonment of the marine industry for these oil companies. Most of the major oil companies—whose collective fleets have shrunk to 180 tankers today from about 600 in 1974—already had been reducing the percentage of oil they carried in their own ships. . . .
>
> In another sign that the majors are distancing themselves from shipping, many companies have been changing the names of their ships to remove any obvious connection between a ship and its oil company owner. In the most dramatic move, Exxon Corp. even changed the name of its shipping subsidiary to SeaRiver Maritime Inc. from Exxon Shipping Corp.[9]

[9] *Journal of Commerce,* February 28, 1995, pp. 1A, 10A.

In a similar manner, chemical companies are replacing their own truck delivery fleets with fleets provided by outsiders. They are doing this "because of the high cost of maintaining their own fleet, precipitated by low market prices for commodity chemicals . . . , the difficulty in attracting drivers, and their increasing perception of the risk of transporting their own products."[10]

Logistics personnel within firms are often suspicious of the motives of potential outside logistics providers, fearing that the outsiders' ultimate goal is to replace them. At a National Industrial Transportation League meeting, a traffic executive from a major firm complained that "his firm's top brass constantly received letters from third-party providers that start out by stating that in-house logistics operations are costing the company dearly."[11]

Total Logistics Firms

There are firms that contract to perform the entire range of logistics services for others. One such firm is Martin-Brower, which handles all distribution functions for food chains such as McDonald's and Baskin Robbins. Martin-Brower operates hundreds of tractors and trailers and controls the inventory levels for its customers. The firm also handles purchasing, pricing, sales analysis, and planning functions for its clients. It delivers food, napkins, plastic containers, and so on in quantities that both make good use of the truck trailer's capacity and take into account the limited storage space in the franchise restaurants. Each restaurant receives one delivery of all it needs. Franchise Services, Inc. (FSI) is the distribution subsidiary of Pepsico that handles logistics for Pizza Hut and some Taco Bell restaurants. These large logistics firms that have assumed responsibility for supplying the restaurant chains are among the nation's largest purchasers of food and restaurant products.

Monitoring Third-Party Performance

It is necessary to monitor the performance of third-party logistics providers. Methods of monitoring are often specified within the agreement. Two examples of monitoring measures will be given here.

The first is the process used by Kimberly-Clark Corporation's Health Care Sector. Kimberly-Clark uses a report card system for the distribution centers with which it has contracts. Measures used are as follows:

- Number of orders shipped on time.
- Number of outbound orders confirmed on time. (The distribution center must confirm to Kimberly-Clark that the orders were sent and were accurate.)
- Number of orders picked and loaded accurately.
- Number of transfers of goods confirmed within twenty-four hours.

[10] *Journal of Commerce*, February 9, 1994, p. 2B.
[11] *American Shipper*, January 1994, p. 37.

The total orders shipped plus transfers made are added and become the denominator of the scoring equation. The numerator is the number of orders shipped accurately and on time plus the number of transfers made accurately, less the number of billing errors and less any damage to product reported by customers.[12]

Toyota Motor Sales, U.S.A., inspects carriers that move Toyota automobiles and light trucks. Their evaluation form lists nineteen different items with accompanying scores. The points, which are merits or demerits, total 104. Items worth up to ten points are equipment condition, tie-down procedures, truck loader training, vehicle clearances, and vehicle handling. Items worth up to five points are height measurement of truck, lighting, pavement surfaces, seat and floor protectors, skid and ramp angle settings, and supervision. Items worth up to three points are handling of keys, houskeeping, loaded vehicle condition, loaded vehicle in park/neutral, security, storage of excess tie-down chains and hooks, striped bay markings, and vehicle inspection prior to loading.[13]

SUPPLY-CHAIN INTEGRATION

Supply chains are integrated by having various parties enter into and carry out long-term, mutually beneficial agreements. These agreements are known by several names: partnerships, strategic alliances, third-party arrangements, and contract logistics.[14] These terms are used loosely. When a firm enters into a partnership arrangement with a source or with a customer, it must keep in mind how this relationship will affect the entire supply chain. Ideally all links of the supply chain will meet at one time and work out whatever agreements are necessary to ensure that the entire supply chain functions in the most desirable manner.

In order to integrate one's supply chain, one must recognize the shortcomings of the present system and examine the channel arrangements as they exist and as they might be, with the "might be" often meaning partnership arrangements. All this is done within the framework of the firm's overall strategy, as well as any logistics strategies necessary to support the goals and objectives of the firm's top management.

To begin organizing one's supply chain, it is necessary to recognize some of the problems that exist under present arrangements. How good, or how bad, is present performance? What are competitors doing? Figure 14-3 shows some of the supply-chain challenges facing a global medical supply

[12] *Outsourced Logistics,* vol. 1, 1994, p. 3.

[13] Colonel's Island Railroad Company's entry in the 1993 *Railway Age* magazine's Golden Freight Car contest, unpublished. On one of the actual forms the facility earned 10 demerits under the "vehicle handling" category because one of the workers had an exposed belt buckle which might have scratched autos.

[14] They are defined in Chapter 2.

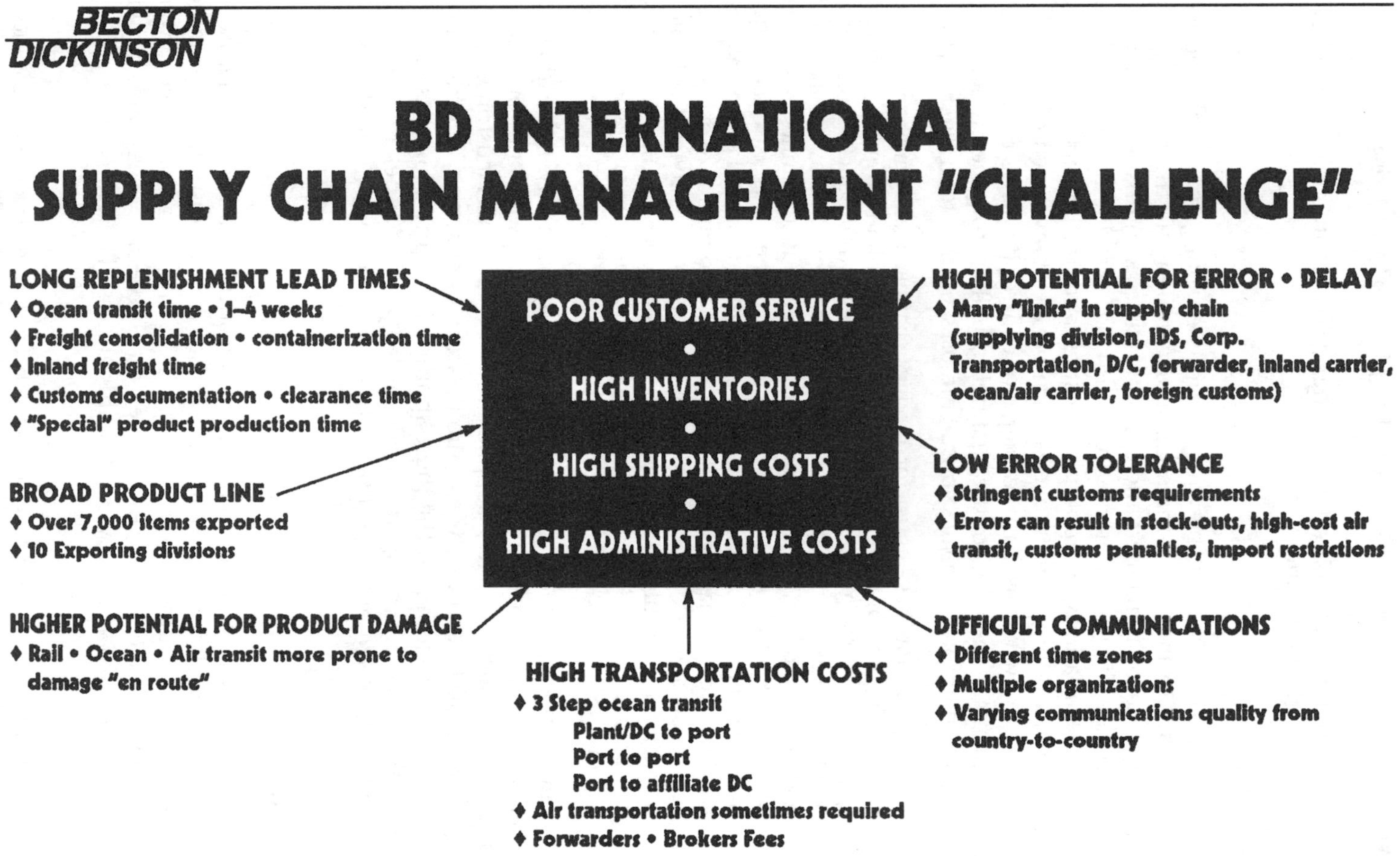

BECTON DICKINSON

BD INTERNATIONAL
SUPPLY CHAIN MANAGEMENT "CHALLENGE"

LONG REPLENISHMENT LEAD TIMES
- ◆ Ocean transit time • 1–4 weeks
- ◆ Freight consolidation • containerization time
- ◆ Inland freight time
- ◆ Customs documentation • clearance time
- ◆ "Special" product production time

BROAD PRODUCT LINE
- ◆ Over 7,000 items exported
- ◆ 10 Exporting divisions

HIGHER POTENTIAL FOR PRODUCT DAMAGE
- ◆ Rail • Ocean • Air transit more prone to damage "en route"

POOR CUSTOMER SERVICE
•
HIGH INVENTORIES
•
HIGH SHIPPING COSTS
•
HIGH ADMINISTRATIVE COSTS

HIGH POTENTIAL FOR ERROR • DELAY
- ◆ Many "links" in supply chain (supplying division, IDS, Corp. Transportation, D/C, forwarder, inland carrier, ocean/air carrier, foreign customs)

LOW ERROR TOLERANCE
- ◆ Stringent customs requirements
- ◆ Errors can result in stock-outs, high-cost air transit, customs penalties, import restrictions

DIFFICULT COMMUNICATIONS
- ◆ Different time zones
- ◆ Multiple organizations
- ◆ Varying communications quality from country-to-country

HIGH TRANSPORTATION COSTS
- ◆ 3 Step ocean transit
  - Plant/DC to port
  - Port to port
  - Port to affiliate DC
- ◆ Air transportation sometimes required
- ◆ Forwarders • Brokers Fees

Figure 14-3 Some supply-chain challenges facing a global firm. (Courtesy Becton Dickinson and Company.)

543

firm. It is also necessary to understand the various channels that are relevant to the movement of product.

Channels

Channel management can be thought of as enabling firms and people to work together to move raw materials and components through processing and manufacturing to retailers and customers. Earlier in this book there was a more elaborate discussion of channels, and six were identified: ownership, financing, negotiations, promotions, logistics, and, for international transactions, documentation. The individual firm decides how much of each channel it wishes to own as well as the degree of control it wishes to exercise over other segments of members of the channel (usually through contract).

David Anderson, a logistics consultant, uses another term, *product channel:*

> The organization best suited for product channel management would integrate production (or for retailers, merchandise distribution) and logistics functions by product group. Instead of focusing on production or logistics functions, channel management organizations would focus on maximizing end-market profitability. Specialists within the product channel management organization would focus on the three key decision areas: customer requirements, production scheduling and inventory allocation, and end-market profitability. The organization would work as a team to minimize overall product acquisition and delivery costs while meeting customer service requirements. In addition, it would coordinate with other product channel management groups to ensure optimal return on corporate production, processing, and distribution assets.[15]

The term *supply-chain management* has also been covered earlier. It is related to channel management in that it also deals with the total flow of materials from one's suppliers' suppliers to one's customers' customers.

It is crucial to consider the entire network of channels in which a firm operates before deciding on the most appropriate form of logistics organization or supply-chain arrangements. Knowledge of channel relationship is also a prerequisite to entering into partnership arrangements with suppliers and customers.

Partnerships

Partnership is a relatively new term in the logistics field. It is loosely used to describe positive, long-term relationships between a firm and its suppliers and customers. Partnership agreements are drawn up in a way that rewards all partners when cooperative ventures are successful. They also provide incentives for all parties to work toward success. There are some strategic

---

[15] David Anderson, "Product Channel Management: The Next Revolution in Logistics?" booklet distributed by Temple, Barker & Sloane, Lexington, Mass., ca. 1988.

benefits from alliances,[16] and the goals of alliances must be congruent with the goals of all partners.

Partnerships are becoming more important and more popular in the logistics field for several reasons. Deregulation of carriers has given them more flexibility to enter into long-term agreements with shippers. Shippers now typically divide their business among a smaller number of carriers than before. And the use of JIT and EDI systems has forced closer, more disciplined relationships with a smaller number of vendors.

Partnership arrangements can be loose or formal. An example of a loose arrangement would be for the two parties to exchange business cards at the end of a casual office visit. At the other extreme, consider this description of an RFP (request for proposal) received by an international freight management company from a large Midwestern shipper:

> The shipper, as is its regular practice, had sent out a request for proposals to a number of companies, asking them to bid against one another for a contract to carry the next year's freight. As is standard practice, the request had gone out in the form of a computer diskette, which the carrier fills out and returns to the shipper.
>
> What made this year different was that the amount of information requested wouldn't fit on a single diskette. For the first time, the amount of data required on a shipper's request for proposals, or RFP, was so extensive that a second diskette was necessary.
>
> "It was the mother of all RFPs," said an exasperated sales manager for the carrier company.[17]

A study conducted by the Warehousing Research Center at Miami University developed some definitions and explanations of **contract warehousing** that are useful when attempting to understand partnership arrangements. They define contract warehousing as "a long term, mutually beneficial arrangement which provides unique and specifically tailored warehousing and logistics services exclusively to one client, where the vendor and client share the risks associated with the operation."[18] Exclusivity means that the arrangement is unique in the sense that it would not be available on the same terms to everyone else. Shared risk means that both parties have an investment in the agreement and stand to lose if it does not work out. Extended time frame means that the contract should be durable and neither party will immediately begin searching for a replacement partner. Tailored services mean that each side is making some physical adjustments to make the supply chain flow better.

---

[16] Donald J. Bowersox, "The Strategic Benefits of Logistics Alliances," *Harvard Business Review,* July–August 1990, pp. 36–45.

[17] *American Shipper,* January 1995, p. 30.

[18] *Contract Warehousing: How It Works and How to Make It Work Effectively,* prepared by the Warehousing Research Center at Miami University for the Warehousing Education and Research Council, 1993, p. 7.

An example of a successful partnership is the agreement between Libby-Owens-Ford (L-O-F) and Schneider National, a large truckload motor carrier. The product carried is plate glass, used in buildings. After a period of operation, here are some of the results:

- While paying Schneider a slightly higher freight rate than previously, L-O-F has reduced costs by about $1 million a year.
- Average loads have increased from 44,000 pounds to 48,000 pounds.
- Schneider invested in a terminal located adjacent to the L-O-F plant.
- Schneider's satellite communications with its trucks allows L-O-F to perform instant tracking, sometimes important to L-O-F and with its customers at construction sites.
- EDI connections between Schneider and L-O-F have eliminated 25,000 sheets of paper.
- L-O-F, Schneider, and Wabash National Corporation, Schneider's trailer supplier, worked together to design a patented trailer to handle this business.[19]

One can also enter into partnership arrangements with others within the same firm, especially when the firm is decentralized and many activities are somewhat autonomous.

In the 1970s and 1980s many firms integrated their logistics operations on an internal basis, often meaning that a single logistics department pulled together the firm's various related logistics activities. The 1990s carries this integration outside the specific firm. Through partnership arrangements, logistics activities all along the supply chain can be integrated. "This drive toward external integration has resulted from a channel member's desire to gain competitive advantage through improving overall channel efficiency by reducing costs, reducing risk, and effectively leveraging the corporate resources of specific channel members."[20] The challenge is that one must manage across organizations.

With regard to ideal logistics organizations, D. J. Bowersox, D. J. Frayer, and J. M. Schmitz write:

> As companies head into the twenty-first century, it is becoming increasingly clear that logistical performance will remain a critical success factor. What is not clear is which logistical organizational blueprint will fully satisfy the dual requirements for internal process integration and external enterprise integration. As exacting logistics performance becomes increasingly critical, firms will seek more efficient and effective ways to organize and manage customer service.

---

[19] *Purchasing,* December 10, 1992, p. 61.

[20] James M. Masters and Terrance L. Pohlen, "Evolution of the Logistics Profession," in *The Logistics Handbook* (New York: Free Press, 1994), p. 24.

This will require creation of entirely different organization solutions that extend well beyond the internal operations of a firm. . . . It is likely that formal logistics organization structures will become increasingly seamless as all units of the overall organization become sensitive to logistics performance. It is also likely that formal command and control structures will give way to teams linked by information networks. . . . The logistics system of the future will require the capacity to surge and capture new opportunities. It is the development of a ready and waiting reserve capacity to do the extraordinary that translates logistical competency into competitive advantage. As managers apply their creativeness to determine how best to organize, the answers will be customized to individual circumstances. It is doubtful that textbooks of the future will be able to diagram what constitutes an "ideal" logistics organization.[21]

LOGISTICS IN NOT-FOR-PROFIT AGENCIES

While the book is centered on logistics as practiced by business enterprises, many logistical activities are conducted by government or by nonprofit organizations. One of the largest logistical exercises in the United States occurs daily as school buses pick up and deliver students. At all levels of government—federal, state, and local—there is considerable activity involving the purchase, storage, and distribution of materials. These agencies follow many of the practices mentioned in this book in order to increase their operating efficiencies.

Local charities have collection boxes and pickup routes for donations of old clothing and household items. All the goods are inspected and sorted. A decision is made as to which goods can be sold in second-hand shops, which should be given directly to the needy, and which should be disposed of. Soup kitchens receive daily donations of food to feed the homeless.

Collecting and disposing of municipal wastes is a large-scale logistical undertaking. Often available disposal sites are many miles away. Recycling of paper, metal, plastic, and glass is justified in part because it reduces the flow of municipal trash taken to landfill sites.

Military logistics is a specialty in itself, and we must remember that many facets of business logistics as we practice them today originated in the U.S. military establishment. In the Falkland Islands dispute, the British demonstrated their ability to manage a military operation in which the logistical challenges were likely greater than the challenges of actual battle. Civilian ships, including the *Queen Elizabeth II,* were requisitioned for military transport service, and a row of commercial tankers was positioned the length of the Atlantic Ocean for fueling ships.

During the war in the Persian Gulf, there was renewed interest in military applications of logistics. About 120 civilian vessels, flying U.S. flags and

---

[21] Donald J. Bowersox, David J. Frayer, and Judith M. Schmitz, "Organizing for Effective Logistics Management," in *The Logistics Handbook* (New York: Free Press, 1994), pp. 782–783.

flags of other nations, were chartered to carry supplies. In Operations Desert Shield and Desert Storm, from August 1990 through March 1991, the Department of Defense used over 18,000 aircraft flight and 466 voyages of ships to carry troops and supplies.[22]

Logistics of Famine Relief

Logistics in not-for-profit agencies often follows a different channel pattern than logistics as practiced by for-profit organizations. Consider, for example, the logistics of famine relief operations as have occurred in recent years in Somalia and Bosnia. They follow, by only a few years, major relief efforts in Ethiopia.[23]

Famines occur because food is not where it is needed. Effective logistics is the essence of famine relief because the task in providing aid is getting the food to the people who are starving. The logistics of famine relief are unique for three reasons. First, the political environment plays a pivotal role in the entire operation. Second, while such operations can occur anywhere in the world, they often occur in less developed regions, which usually have inadequate infrastructures and are some distance from major traffic lanes. Third, the consumer of the final product is not the customer of either the supplier or the carrier. How do these three factors influence the management of the relief logistics efforts?

As for political concerns, relief is foreign intervention in a society in an effort to help local citizens. How this is conducted can either help or hurt. The distribution of free food can disrupt existing local agriculture and transportation and distribution systems, delaying their development and postponing the area's becoming self-sufficient. In addition, one cause of a famine may be a war or political unrest, and those handling relief efforts must avoid being caught in the middle.

Many relief efforts are carried out under the bright lights of publicity, and many conflicting signals are heard from all areas of the world as to what is being done right and what is being done wrong. In many of these situations there is no agreed-upon leader. Governments may resent relief aids to groups that are out of political favor; indeed, some governments use starvation as a political instrument and may order soldiers to intercept the relief shipments. The persons managing relief efforts will receive many mixed signals.

Relief organizations can be branches of the UN or of governments of nations, or private voluntary organizations (PVOs), often associated with religious groups. Some organizations will enter a situation and remain for several years; others will be in and out with a single dose of emergency aid.

From a management viewpoint, persons at the top of relief operations have to be politically attuned, and those at middle and lower levels must deal

---

[22] *Journal of Commerce,* February 21, 1992, p. 1B.

[23] This discussion is based on Douglas C. Long and Donald F. Wood, "The Logistics of Overseas Famine Relief," *Journal of Business Logistics,* vol. 16, no. 1 (1995), pp. 213–229.

with getting food to the starving. The actual movement and distribution of the food is often carried out in a military or paramilitary fashion. Army trucks are often used because commercial trucks cannot operate on the available roads. Armed convoys are used for protection from thieves and to assist each other along the route.

Third is the question, Who is the customer? In humanitarian relief efforts the sponsor is the constituent, and the victim is a third party, with very little voice in the process. The relief workers must first answer to their sponsor before they can serve the victims, and if the needs of the victims and the sponsors do not correspond, the relief workers will have a very difficult time serving both.

Sponsors provide the money and sponsors call the shots. Many sponsors are charitable organizations and have an eye on future fund-raising efforts back home. They are conscious of the value of publicity. In the past decade they and their donors have also been very concerned about stories of inventory shrinkage, so more controls have been enacted that have resulted in a higher percentage of the food reaching its intended destination.

Other chapters have dealt with commercial logistics practices. How do they differ when one is involved with famine relief? Let us consider these functions: demand forecasting, purchasing, packaging, inventory management, warehousing, site or route selection, transportation and communications, parts and service support, and overall management.

Demand forecasting is difficult because in most famine areas, very little data are kept. The needs of disaster victims are presumed initially by people far away, based on limited information. Assumptions are made regarding the kind of supplies needed, where they are needed, and how they will be distributed. Initially supplies are pushed. Once relief personnel are in the area, they reassess the situation and correct the mistakes. Once better assessments have been made, a pull system is put into effect.

Language and terminology vary with each organization, making coordination difficult. For example, when the Ethiopian Relief and Rehabilitation Commission published their analysis of relief supplies needed during the famine of 1984, their statistical measurement was numbers of families, not individuals. This made their analysis difficult for Western relief agencies to translate.[24]

Forecasts also include allowances for shrinkage in the pipeline between the source and the recipients. For example, theft of supplies by armed forces cannot be prevented, but the food is still accounted for. Logistical planning can only estimate how much food will be lost before it gets to the recipients, and plan accordingly.[25]

[24] *Situation in Drought-Affected Areas of Ethiopia—April, 1976* (Addis Ababa: Ethiopia Relief and Rehabilitation Commission, 1976).

[25] "Death by Looting," *The Economist*, July 18, 1992, p. 41.

The *purchasing* function attempts to buy the foods from nearby nations with surpluses. This keeps down transportation costs, and the foods, usually grains, are closer to what those being fed are used to. The Red Cross is often offered food that is unsuited for relief work. They have a list of recommended food, such as whole grains, salt, and sugar. Then there are restricted foods, such as milk products, and precooked and instant food. Finally, there are foods that are not recommended, such as liquids, frozen and refrigerated food, and canned baby food.[26] The supply chain therefore needs to have at the origin some mechanism to discriminate among donations.

Packaging is needed to protect the food in a harsh environment. The most common unit of food used by relief agencies is the fifty-kilogram bag. They are as large as possible while still capable of being carried by an individual. When a ship of bulk grain arrives, the cargo must be transported at once to the bagging station, bagged, and then sent on to its final destination.

Inventory management is difficult. Shrinkage has already been mentioned; it is a serious problem. First, it deprives starving people of food that was intended for them. Second, it undermines donors' confidence in the relief efforts, and they then reduce their contributions. Usually, large inventories of food are not stored. They are purchased when needed and then moved expeditiously to the starving.

Relief operations also involve a myriad of nonfood commodities, such as tools, fuel, shelters, and water purification and sanitation equipment. Sourcing these supplies is a matter of determining what contingency stocks are available or where they can be purchased quickly. Relief supplies also include service support requirements, such as fuel and spare parts, hand tools, and medicines. Medicine poses unique logistical problems. Many medicines can tolerate only a certain range of temperature, which complicates matters immensely. Refrigerated vaccines must be kept cold with the use of portable generators.

Warehousing facilities are unavailable in most areas where famine relief efforts are underway. This is unfortunate, since both moisture and rodents cause considerable damage to the bagged or bulk foods. Thefts of food and other relief supplies is a never-ending problem.

Storage in transit is a common technique in which the ship slows down to add a few days to a long journey. This saves fuel and the cost of storage upon arrival. This method is useful only in prolonged famines for which a pipeline of supplies has developed and there is not an immediate urgency. Storage in transit may occur involuntarily, since some ports are incapable of handling more than one ship at a time.

The U.S. Office of Foreign Disaster Assistance (OFDA), which conducts the emergency operations, maintains seven contingency warehouses worldwide,

[26] "ICRC/League Policies in Emergency Situations" (Geneva: International Committee of the Red Cross, November 2, 1992), pp. 9–11.

close to air and sea port facilities. They contain basic disaster commodities such as blankets, plastic sheeting, water containers, tents, gloves, hard hats, dust masks, and body bags.

We think of *site* or *route selection* as a traffic management function. Routes are selected by conventional methods after political or security concerns have been taken into account. In handling the cargo, local labor should be used as much as possible. Local leaders will then take more personal interest in the success of the operation, and local knowledge of the area should ensure that relief is conducted effectively. This also increases local pride and the motivation to rebuild after a disaster.[27]

Cost efficiency dictates that food be distributed at centralized facilities, where the hungry come to the food. However, this method of food distribution can cause people to become refugees when they must leave their homes behind and travel long distances to get the relief food. Starving people are traveling, which can be life-threatening for the weak, or it means that only the strong will get the food. Once people are uprooted, refugee camps become necessary, creating still more logistical problems. Hence, distribution of food should be as decentralized as possible.

The port of importation must be chosen. Important pieces of information in assessing a port are location, connections to roads leading to where food is needed, water depth, cargo-handling and storage facilities, security, and availability of customs and other governmental agencies. In Mogadishu, Somalia, it was necessary to use U.S. Navy SEALS (diver commandos) as divers to lay out a navigable channel for larger ships. It was also necessary to move a sunken tug that was blocking a cargo berth. Five warehouse structures filled with "human and animal waste" had to be cleaned "with bulldozers and high pressure hoses."[28]

Air transport can move cargo quickly into remote areas that lack roads, though at much greater cost. This mode of transport is most valuable in emergencies, when time is more important than cost, or when civil strife makes overland transport unsafe, as occurred in Ethiopia. Medicines and medical supplies move by air. Sometimes air cargo drops are used. In certain planes, such as the U.S. military's C-130 or C-141, the cargo door in the tail can be opened, and palletized cargo can be pushed out. Helicopters are very expensive to operate.

Trucks are the most common mode of land transport. Since famines rarely strike in regions with well-developed roads, the trucks used must be able to handle rougher roads with higher clearance requirements and with fewer refueling facilities. Rugged terrain increases service requirements to the

---

[27] Mary B. Anderson and Peter J. Woodrow, *Rising from the Ashes: Development Strategies in Times of Disaster* (San Francisco: Westview, 1989), p. 64.

[28] Capt. Patrick Buckner, quoted in *Journal of Commerce*, March 9, 1993, p. 8B.

extent that Catholic Relief Service assumed in its planning that only 75 percent of its fleet would be available at any one time.[29]

Accurate assessment of the road infrastructure is critical. A road in Thailand may be a five-foot-wide strip of mud only inches above the water line that can accommodate only scooters and livestock. Bridges have weight limitations.

Communication is related to transport control. UN agencies have developed the UN International Emergency Network (UNIENET). This on-line system provides much of the organizational information for planning, such as contact personnel, situation reports, and electronic mail (E-mail) for disaster workers.[30]

The logistical requirements increase dramatically when a relief agency assumes responsibility for maintaining the *parts and service support* for a truck fleet. Mechanics and garages must be available near the area of operations, and an inventory of parts must be maintained. As if protecting the food were not difficult enough, auto parts are valuable and lucrative to steal. Most PVOs either contract for locally owned trucks or charter trucks from other relief agencies. In Ethiopia the supply roads soon became littered with abandoned trucks that had broken down and could not be repaired because of lack of parts. Some were surplus military trucks that had been donated by various nations.

If aircraft are used, service support includes a professional mechanic, spare parts, and aviation fuel. During the Ethiopian relief effort, Transamerica Airlines, which had the contract to fly cargo, was using up its aircraft tires at the rate of one per day.

As for *overall management,* here is one example: World Vision International, a church-based group deeply involved in Ethiopian famine relief efforts, developed a manual based on its experiences in the early and mid-1980s. The Ethiopian logistics organization in 1985 (at which point it was supplying food to 500,000 people) consisted of these eight functions:

1. Project management.
2. Flight operations (two small twin-engine aircraft were used for communications, parts supply, and the like).
3. Procurement.
4. Port clearances to make certain cargo was received and moved through port.
5. Supply management—responsible for food and all other supplies.
6. Warehousing.

---

[29] Interview with David Palasites, Logistical Operations Manager, Catholic Relief Service, Baltimore, September 12, 1991.

[30] Interview with Mila Manalansan, UN Department of Humanitarian Affairs, New York, November 23, 1992.

7. Transportation.

8. Equipment maintenance.[31]

These functions are nearly the same as the logistics elements of famine relief discussed above. So, in a sense, the supply chain would be managed by coordinating and leading these different functions.

The effort can also be viewed as one of channel management. The logistics channel is the easiest to track. The financing channel would involve obtaining donors to pay for or donate the relief supplies and the equipment needed to move them. In many situations the financing and negotiations channels would be closely linked. Negotiations would probably also include government representatives of the donor and recipient nations. In some situations military forces might be involved, whether to deliver the supplies or to provide protection. The actual ownership channel is probably less important since many of the supplies have been donated. However, parties along the supply chain are all held responsible for ensuring that the relief supplies reach the famine victims.

SUMMARY

Chapter 14 covers various approaches to organizing a firm's logistics system. An initial concern is the relative importance of logistics (usually expressed in terms of cost) to a firm's overall operations.

A study conducted by LaLonde and others concerning the number of different logistical activities assigned to a firm's logistics department indicates that firms that assign more activities are presumably more advanced in adopting the logistics concept.

The centralized versus decentralized organization issue is discussed, as are the various organizational means of achieving coordination: the linking-pin concept, unified department organization, matrix management, channel management, partnerships, and contract, or third-party logistics. Relying on outside parties to perform logistics functions is becoming more common. Also discussed are supply-chain management, supply-chain integration, and logistics of famine relief.

QUESTIONS FOR DISCUSSION AND REVIEW

1. Management consultant John F. Magee once stated that "logistical system management poses some puzzling organization problems to the typical, functionally organized firm." Discuss this statement.

---

[31] Ben Boyd, *Getting It There: A Logistics Handbook for Relief and Development* (Monrovia, Cal.: World Vision International, 1987), pp. 21–25.

2. Describe the various stages through which a company may go as it develops its logistical organization.

3. One of the sections in this chapter discusses the dispersion of logistical activities. What is scattered, and why does this make the organizational issues more difficult?

4. It has been said that effective logistics can be a great assistance to the accomplishment of a high level of customer service. Why is this true?

5. Why is the support of top management necessary to establish an effective logistics department? Discuss.

6. Effective coordination is often thought to be one of the most important aspects of logistics. This chapter suggests several methods that can be used to achieve this objective. Discuss each briefly. Which one do you feel is the best? Why?

7. Who is a linking-pin person? What problems and opportunities does this organizational alternative present?

8. Discuss briefly the pros and cons of an independent logistics department that is equal to the marketing, manufacturing, and finance departments.

9. Why, and in what ways, might one monitor the performance of outside firms performing contract logistics services?

10. What is the difference between a centralized and a decentralized logistics department? Which is more desirable? Why?

11. Carefully present an argument for the centralization of logistics departments.

12. What is matrix management? Do you believe it is a practical solution for logistics organizations? Why?

13. Discuss the advantages of a unified logistics department.

14. What is contract logistics? In what situations is it used? Why?

15. What is supply-chain integration? How is it achieved?

16. Assume that you are instructed to establish a logistics organization in a firm that presently has logistics functions scattered throughout the organization and everywhere on the map. How would you start? Why?

17. Continuation of Question 16: What steps would you take? Why?

18. In what ways might military logistics differ from logistics as practiced by conventional business firms? List and discuss.

19. What is channel management? How might it affect a firm's choice of logistical organizational structures? Why?

20. Discuss some aspects of the logistics associated with famine relief. How do they differ from logistics in the regular business sector?

SUGGESTED READINGS

Bagchi, Prabir K. "International Logistics Information Systems." *International Journal of Physical Distribution & Logistics Management,* vol. 22, no. 9 (1992), pp. 11–19.

Bowersox, Donald J. "The Strategic Benefits of Logistics Alliances." *Harvard Business Review,* July–August 1990, pp. 36–45.

Cooper, Martha C., and John T. Gardner. "Building Good Business Relationships—More Than Just Partnering or Strategic Alliances?" *International Journal of Physical Distribution & Logistics Management,* vol. 23, no. 6 (1993), pp. 14–26.

Ellram, Lisa M. "Patterns in International Alliances." *Journal of Business Logistics,* vol. 13, no. 1 (1992), pp. 1–25.

Gattorna, John L. "Building Relationships in Distribution Channels." *International Journal of Physical Distribution & Logistics Management,* vol. 21, no. 8 (1991), pp. 36–39.

Gourdin, Kent N., and Richard L. Clarke. "Winning Transportation Partnerships: Learning from the Desert Storm Experience." *Transportation Journal,* vol. 32, no. 1, pp. 30–37.

Gustin, Craig. "Integrated Logistics: The Perceptions and the Future." In *Annual Conference Proceedings of the Council of Logistics Management,* vol. 2. Oak Brook, Ill.: CLM, 1990, pp. 127–156.

Heskett, James L. "Leadership through Integration: The Special Challenge of Logistics." In *Papers, CLM 1988 Annual Meeting,* vol. 1, Oak Brook, Ill.: CLM, 1988, pp. 13–21.

LaLonde, Bernard J., and Martha C. Cooper. *Partnerships in Providing Customer Service: A Third-Party Perspective.* Oak Brook, Ill.: CLM, 1989.

McGinnis, Michael A., and Jonathan W. Kohn. "A Factor Analytic Study of Logistics Strategy." *Journal of Business Logistics,* vol. 11, no. 2 (1990), pp. 41–63.

Murphy, Paul R., James M. Daley, and Douglas R. Dalenberg. "Selecting Links and Nodes in International Transportation: An Intermediary's Perspective." *Transportation Journal,* vol. 31, no. 2, pp. 33–40.

Novack, Robert A., Steven C. Dunn, and Richard R. Young. "Logistics Optimizing and Operational Plans and Systems and Their Role in Achievement of Corporate Goals." *Transportation Journal,* Summer 1993, pp. 29–40.

Rao, Kant, Alan J. Stenger, and Richard Young. "Corporate Framework for Developing and Analyzing Logistics Strategies." In *Papers, CLM 1988 Annual Meeting,* vol. 1. Oak Brook, Ill.: CLM, 1988, pp. 243–262.

Rinehart, Lloyd M., and David Closs. "Implications of Organizational Relationships, Negotiator Personalities, and Contract Issues on Outcomes in Logistics Negotiations." *Journal of Business Logistics,* Spring 1991, pp. 123–144.

Sheffi, Yosef. "Third-Party Logistics: Present and Future Prospects." *Journal of Business Logistics,* vol. 11, no. 2 (1990), pp. 27–39.

Williamson, Kenneth C., Daniel M. Spitzer Jr., and David J. Bloomberg. "Modern Logistics Systems: Theory and Practice." *Journal of Business Logistics,* vol. 11, no. 2 (1990), pp. 65–86.

Wood, Donald F., Anthony Barone, Paul Murphy, and Daniel L. Wardlow. *International Logistics.* New York: Chapman & Hall, 1995.

COLUMBIA LUMBER PRODUCTS COMPANY

The Columbia Lumber Products Company (CLPC) was headquartered in Portland, Oregon, where it had been founded in 1899. For many years its principal product had been only lumber; in the 1940s it began producing plywood, and in 1960, particle board. The first two products, lumber and plywood, were produced at various sites in Oregon and marketed on the West Coast and as far east as Chicago.

Particle board was produced in Duluth, Minnesota, at a plant built with a U.S. Area Redevelopment Administration Loan in 1962. Initially, the input to the plant was trimmings and other scrap from CLPC's Oregon operations. Particle board sales increased so quickly that the Duluth operation consumed not only all of the former waste from CLPC's Oregon plant but also waste purchased from various lumber and wood products operations in Minnesota and northern Wisconsin.

In terms of product volume, CLPC's sales doubled between 1960 and 1990. However, nearly all the growth had been in particle board; lumber and plywood sales remained relatively constant (although varying with changes in the home construction industry). In 1996, exports accounted for 9 percent of CLPC's sales. Nearly all of this was plywood sold to Japan. Fifteen percent of CLPC's 1996 purchases were from foreign sources, 5 percent was mahogany from the Philippines used for plywood veneer, and 10 percent was wood scrap purchased from Ontario, Canada, for use in CLPC's Duluth plant. Particle board produced in Duluth was marketed in all states east of the Rocky Mountains, although sales in the southern United States were somewhat less than spectacular.

The slowdown in home production, which started in the late 1970s and, in the Midwest, really never ended, resulted in many years of little or no growth in CLPC's sales. Common stock dividends had been cut several times. In 1996, they were 37 cents per share, down considerably from their peak—in 1976—of $2.21.

Stockholders, the outside directors, and various lending institutions were becoming increasingly unhappy. After a long, tense board of directors meeting, agreement was reached only with respect to what some of the organizational problems were. A partial list follows:

1. The corporate headquarters was in Portland, although what growth there was, was in the Midwest. Possibly the headquarters, or at least

more functions, should be shifted to an office in Duluth, where the plant was, or to Chicago, where the largest sales office was. A major relocation away from Portland would be difficult. Many employees would choose to remain on the West Coast. Even for those willing to relocate, there was a split between those willing to relocate to Duluth and those willing to relocate to Chicago.

2. There were too many vice presidents. (See Exhibit 14-A.) Because four vice presidents (engineering, finance, human resources, and purchasing) would reach mandatory retirement age by 1997, the number of vice presidents should be reduced from nine to no more than six (plus one executive vice president).

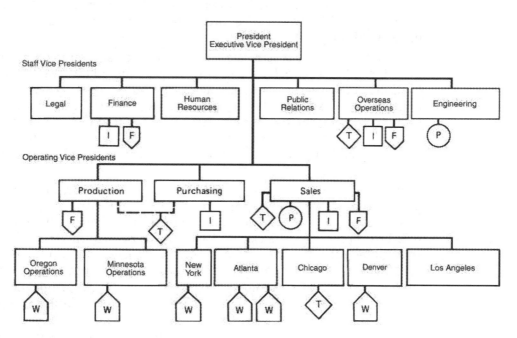

Exhibit 14-A   Columbia Lumber Products Company's organizational chart (as of January 31, 1996).

3. Logistics and distribution costs were higher than industry averages. The majority of customer complaints dealt with poor deliveries. In Exhibit 14-A a *T* shows where a traffic management function was located. Geographically, the traffic manager for overseas operations was located in Seattle, which was a foreign trade center for the Pacific Northwest. The Chicago sales office had a traffic manager who handled all fiberboard distribution, and lumber and plywood distribution east of the

Rockies. Production and purchasing shared a traffic manager who was headquartered in Portland and whose principal duty was overseeing shipments of waste products from Oregon to Minnesota. Another traffic manager (in Portland), who reported to the sales vice president, was acknowledged to be the firm's senior traffic manager and more or less coordinated the efforts of the other three. Recently Irwin Buchanan III had been promoted to that post. He was the only one authorized to initiate action before regulatory bodies, and he also handled the negotiations with carrier rate-making bodies and with carriers. (CLPC used contract truckers and rail for most of its shipping.)

4. The purchasing department handled the details of fleet management, which included about one hundred autos on long-term lease for use by management and by the sales force. Several light trucks were leased for use around the plants.

5. CLPC also owned two small aircraft, which often were the target of questions during stockholders' meetings. One plane was based at Portland, the other at Duluth. Each was used in its respective region for trips to sites without scheduled airline service. Both planes were under control of the production department. Other departments, especially sales, complained that the planes were being used for the benefit of the production department, rather than for the benefit of the entire firm.

6. *P* in the exhibit shows two packaging engineering functions. The one under engineering was located in Portland and dealt with plywood products. The one under sales was located in Chicago and handled particle board products. The two packaging engineering functions saw their roles differently. The one in Portland was concerned mainly with safe packing and packaging of products moving between CLPC plants or from CLPC plants to customers. The Chicago packaging engineers were interested in finding new markets for particle board and lumber as packaging materials to be sold to others. *W* in the exhibit shows where there are company-owned warehouses. Numerous public warehouses were also used, although not continually. *I* shows locations of individuals concerned with inventory levels. All four individuals were located in Portland. *F* indicates where sales forecasting took place. Only sales and production devoted much staff to forecasting. Each quarter, however, the financial vice president's office coordinated all forecasts to ensure comparability. Computer operations were under control of the engineering division. CLPC's executive vice president determined priorities for computer access and use.

7. The human resources department handled employee moves, although only a few had taken place since 1980. An outside director, who was

familiar with current federal legislation, suggested that CLPC negotiate a contract with a household goods carrier to handle all CLPC employee moves. This action would be especially significant if a major reorganization resulted in numerous employee transfers.

Questions

1. Draw a new organization chart for Columbia Lumber Products Company that you feel overcomes best the directors' criticisms of CLPC's present (January 31, 1996) organization. Indicate the geographic location of all operations shown on the new chart. Explain why you established the organization chart the way you did.

2. Assume that the firm should be reorganized in a manner that emphasizes sales and marketing. This would include a physical distribution system, which would support the marketing effort. Draw an organization chart that you think would accomplish this aim. Indicate the geographic location of all operations on the new chart and explain why you drew the chart as you did.

3. If the channel management approach is followed, how would CLPC be reorganized? Describe and discuss.

4. Assume that a major reorganization appears unlikely, but you are told to draw up a plan for implementing the linking-pin concept. Describe how you would accomplish this. Between which functions or geographic sites would you establish linking pins? Why?

5. Assume that the firm wants to reorganize into a highly centralized form, closely managed from a single home office. Draw a new chart that takes this into account. Indicate the geographic location of all operations on the chart and explain why you organized it as you did.

6. Assume, instead, that the firm wants to reorganize into a highly decentralized form, where many important decisions can be made out in the field. Draw up a new chart, including the geographic location of all activities. Explain why you drew it up as you did.

7. Young Irwin Buchanan III, the firm's senior traffic manager, heard rumors that the number of vice presidents was to be reduced. He felt that this would reduce his chances of ever achieving vice presidential— or presidential—status. Luckily, he had access to some money in a family trust fund. He wondered whether he should propose to form a separate, third-party firm to contract with CLPC to perform CLPC's logistical operations. What functions should it offer to perform?

8. (This is a continuation of the situation described in question 7.) Assume that young Buchanan does decide to form an outside firm to handle CLPC's logistics operations. Draft his letter to CLPC's management containing such a proposal.

EASING IRA'S IRE II

(*Note to the instructor:* This case should be assigned to students familiar with STORM software, although other general business analysis software programs with PERT applications might also be used.)

This is a continuation of Easing Ira's Ire I, Case 12-1. After manually constructing a PERT chart, Tamara began reading more about the methods and did a more thorough job of evaluating the time it took to complete each of the tasks. She discovered that there was an average time, although sometimes the actual time was a little longer or a little shorter. This, she learned, was the variance. While, in theory, it would all even out, on days when everything went right the total time used to process an order was much less than the average. Conversely, when one or more things went wrong, total time requirements escalated.

Tamara constructed a new chart (see Exhibit 14-B) that shows one additional task—loading the shipment—she had overlooked in her earlier analysis. In addition, the exhibit shows three time estimates for each task: the

EXHIBIT 14-B   ORDER PROCESSING AND SHIPMENT TASKS (IN APPROXIMATE ORDER OF COMPLETION)

Task	Description	Optimistic	Most likely	Pessimistic
			Estimated duration (days)	
A	Order received and entered into computer	0.20	0.25	0.35
B	Determine whether to fill from warehouse or ship direct from factory	0.45	0.55	0.60
C	Print picking order	0.30	0.30	0.30
D	Verify customer's credit	0.30	0.35	0.70
E	Determine buyer's eligibility for discounts	0.15	0.15	0.15
F	Prepare invoice; enter into accounts receivable file	1.00	1.10	1.30
G	Determine mode of transport; select carrier	0.50	0.65	0.80
H	Pick order at warehouse	0.65	0.75	0.80
I	Pack and label shipment	1.10	1.20	1.30
J	Notify carrier; prepare shipping documents	0.20	0.50	0.70
K	Transmit copy of invoice to shipping dock	0.90	1.10	1.40
L	Load shipment	0.15	0.20	0.30
M	Transport order to customer	1.50	3.50	4.8

optimistic, the most likely, and the pessimistic. The same precedence relationships between tasks as shown in the table for Easing Ira's Ire I exist. The new task, loading the shipment, is labeled L, and cannot be started until task I, "Pack and Label Shipment," is completed; and the new task must be done before the goods can be transported to the customer, now labeled M.

Use STORM 2.0 or some other software that enables you to perform this type of analysis and prepare PERT charts. If standard deviations are called for, they are 20 percent of the most likely duration.

Questions

1. Determine the network and the critical path.
2. Determine the shortest possible project completion time.
3. Determine the slack time for each activity. What is its significance? Show each activity with its corresponding slack time in a graphical presentation.
4. Tamara wants to guarantee a certain order-processing and delivery time, so she wants to know the 95 percent confidence level. That is, within what time span will 95 percent of all orders be processed and delivered?
5. Answer the same question as is asked in question 4, but for the 90 percent confidence level.
6. Once Tamara knows a 90 percent or 95 percent confidence level of processing-shipping times, how can she use this information in determining a guarantee? What, precisely, should she guarantee? Draft the guarantee.
7. If Tamara is to reduce the typical order processing-delivery time, on which activities should she focus first? Why?

15

Logistics: Future Directions

This car may soon be on its way to a successful logistics manager. (Courtesy of Austrian Airlines.)

In the 1980s, logistics strategies could best be thought of in terms of independent boxes (storage centers) linked together by transportation services. In the 1990s, the model [is] shift[ing] to that of a pipeline, with emphasis placed on integration. By the late 1990s, the more appropriate model will be the hose, where product velocity is increased and the system is flexible enough to respond quickly to changing customer demands.

David L. Anderson and Robert G. House
Private Carrier
April 1991

Japan's leading groups of companies plan and operate with military-style bureaucracies, both within the company and outside. These groups of companies control large sectors of industry—from procurement through provision of services and sales right up to financing. They maneuver aggressively in key sectors. This planned, systematic aggression toward the outside world results in the conquering of market shares and indeed entire markets.

Frankfurt AirCargo Letter
January 1993

True EDI communication between computers using standard formats—is supplanting faxes, "800" phone numbers and proprietary software packages.

World Trade
June 1993

Japan has identified the non-metric nature of U.S. products as a specific barrier to the importation of U.S. goods.

PC-Trans
Fall 1994

Key Terms

- Artificial intelligence (AI)
- Electronic data interchange (EDI)
- Metric conversion
- Multinational firm
- Production sharing
- Recycling
- Service economy

Learning Objectives

- To understand how increased international business will affect logistics
- To learn more about the U.S. trend toward a service economy
- To realize the possibilities of expert computer systems
- To note the snail's pace toward metrication in the United States
- To appreciate the present and future importance of recycling

INTRODUCTION

The preceding chapters of this book examine the fundamentals of logistics and supply-chain management as they are practiced today. In this final chapter we look at some future trends in logistics. The topics chosen for discussion here are likely to bring important changes to the field of supply-chain management. These changes will affect those readers who are in the process of preparing for a career in logistics.

This chapter focuses on the following future trends in logistics and supply-chain management: the continued importance of international trade, the shift to a service economy, the use of EDI in place of hard copy and printed documents, the development of artificial intelligence systems to handle inventory and customer service problems, the inevitable conversion to the metric system, and the recycling of both products and containers.

INTERNATIONAL TRADE

The field of international logistics (discussed at length in Chapter 11) is expected to take on increased importance in the future. In the early 1990s the United States was the world's leading exporter and importer of merchandise. Germany was second for both exports and imports; Japan, third; France, fourth; the United Kingdom, fifth; and Italy, sixth. The remaining leading exporters, in order, were the Netherlands, Canada, Belgium-Luxembourg, and Hong Kong. The remaining leading importers, in order, were Canada, the Netherlands, Belgium-Luxembourg, and Hong Kong.

If we instead look at **multinational firms**—those headquartered throughout the globe—we see the entire world as a market and source of inputs; such firms are willing to locate their manufacturing, assembly, and storage facilities just about anywhere in the world. United States–based multinational companies contribute significantly to offsetting the U.S. balance-of-trade deficit by repatriation of dividends, royalties, technical assistance fees, and interest on and repayments of loans by foreign subsidiaries. Most important, however, is the direct influx of funds that results when U.S. products are sold by multinational firms in foreign commerce. Astute logistics managers of the future must adapt to the cultural shock that is often inherent in dealing with foreign logistics operations. The late 1990s, for instance, will continue to be a time of developing and expanding trade with former Communist nations and China, which are in the process of changing their economic systems.

One powerful factor propelling world trade activity is the concept of **production sharing.** For example, 95 percent of the baseball gloves sold in the United States are manufactured in Japan. However, the leather used to make the gloves is typically American cowhide, shipped to Brazil for tanning before traveling to Japan for manufacturing. Many of today's products that state

"Made in Japan" are actually assembled in Singapore, Indonesia, or Nigeria, where labor rates are considerably lower than in Japan. This trend is likely to accelerate. National Semiconductor Corporation designs and fabricates computer chips in California's Silicon Valley. The chips are then transported to developing countries, such as Sri Lanka, Barbados, the Philippines, the Virgin Islands, and Panama, to be assembled and tested. Finally, the finished products are transported back to the United States and other countries for distribution to customers around the world. Another example of production sharing, or worldwide production, involves the Caterpillar Tractor Company. It recently closed a plant in Mentor, Ohio, that produced lift trucks and moved production to less costly plants in Korea and in Norway.

Yet not all such situations involve the loss of U.S. manufacturing jobs to other countries. In the 1980s Ford Motor Company announced that after years of utilizing engines made by its foreign subsidiaries and then assembled and sold in the United States, the firm would start shipping engines to its European subsidiary. Ford noted that its Dearborn, Michigan, plant was producing four-cylinder engines so efficiently that it became advantageous to run that plant at high-level output and ship the surplus production to Europe. From an international logistics viewpoint, this trend is both challenging and fraught with opportunities for disaster. International logistics is inherently complex. Henry Wagner, a well-respected logistics executive, aptly observed that "international distribution is truly an octopus."[1] An example of the perplexing issues involved in international shipments is export documentation. An export shipment can typically require between ten and twenty separate documents. Most of the paperwork is required by the receiving country.

In addition, foreign sales typically involve larger ratios of inventory to sales because of longer lead times between when orders are received and when they arrive. Professors Donald J. Bowersox and Jay U. Sterling once estimated that multinational firms require up to 50 percent more in inventory level than domestic operations to support foreign sales.[2] For this and other reasons, international logistics is an expensive undertaking. Whereas the logistics costs of domestic operations are estimated at 5 percent to 6 percent of the total cost of each order received, for international shipments the figure jumps to between 10 percent and 25 percent.

There is great potential in developing overseas markets and sources.

The headlines are full of stories of new joint ventures, partnerships, acquisitions, direct investments, and outsourcing arrangements.

[1] Quoted in James C. Johnson and Donald F. Wood, *Contemporary Physical Distribution and Logistics,* 2d ed. (New York: Macmillan, 1982), p. 437.

[2] Donald J. Bowersox and Jay U. Sterling, "Multinational Logistics," *Journal of Business Logistics,* vol. 3, no. 21 (1982).

- Coca-Cola and Pepsi are expanding into Mexico by acquiring existing companies to take advantage of their established logistics networks.
- Wal-Mart and other major retailers are establishing their own free trade zones to facilitate international trade.
- Kao Infosystems, the world's largest producer of 3-1/2 inch diskettes and the leading U.S. software duplicator, is using its global distribution network to provide services to software companies that want to outsource their logistics operations.[3]

THE SERVICE ECONOMY

One change already under way and likely to continue is the shift toward a **service economy** in the United States. This means that an increasing percentage of U.S. economic activity will be devoted to providing services rather than physical goods. The implications of this trend for logistics are significant. Much of the logistics field has developed around the need to organize and manage the orderly flow of products. The relative decline in importance of the heavy industry in the Great Lakes industrial belt is one example. Another is the fact that the U.S. gross national product (GNP) increased by 25 percent in the 1980s, while intercity ton-miles of freight increased by only 12 percent during the same period. Over the same period, intercity passenger travel increased by 26 percent. More developed nations devote a greater portion of their GNP to services. According to some dated United Nations' statistics, in 1981 nations where services accounted for a fairly high proportion of GNP included the United States, Israel, many countries in Western Europe, Canada, Singapore, and Greece. Nations where services provided a smaller part of GNP included China, Ghana, Uganda, Somalia, and India.[4]

Since so much of logistics deals with inventories, it is important to note that services are difficult or impossible to store. A service provider obviously cannot store repair calls, shoeshines, or consultants' visits. "In many services, the unit of demand is the customer. And customers can be inventoried. For example, in a restaurant customers are regularly inventoried in a holding area often known as a bar."[5]

Moreover, services are used to enhance the value or usefulness of a good that already belongs to a consumer. Recall earlier discussions of post-sales customer service. In these instances, sales of service are very much linked to

[3] *Mercer Management Consulting Logistics,* Summer 1994, p. 4.

[4] Dorothy I. Riddle, in *The Emerging Service Economy,* ed. Orio Giarini (New York: Pergamon, 1987), pp. 84–85. In Japan and South Korea services are relatively less important than in the United States. However, manufacturing is relatively more important in Japan and South Korea.

[5] James L. Heskett and Carl D. Evans, "Logistics in the Service Industries," in *The Logistics Handbook* (New York: Free Press, 1994), p. 861.

sales of product. A computer or software purchaser today is influenced by the level of product support she or he may want in the future.

Logistics also deals with transportation, so we can look at services in terms of who has to travel. In some instances the service provider must travel (e.g., plumbers who make home repairs, workers who travel to a construction site). In other instances, however, the user of a service must travel (e.g., visits to a hospital). At yet other times both the user and provider may travel (e.g., servicepeople who travel in small trucks to replace tires or windshields or to repair large trucks, off-road construction equipment, and the like). It may be less expensive for the repair truck to drive to the site where the larger truck is down than it would be for the larger truck to drive or be towed to the repair shop. Also in this category would be the case where both the user and provider are capable of traveling but the user prefers to pay an additional amount to have the provider do the traveling (e.g., a dog-grooming service that makes home visits).

Proximity between provider and user is a key issue in the logistics of service industries. Certain services can be provided by use of telephone or other means of electronic communication. Sounds from a patient's heartbeat can be transmitted via telephone and diagnosed by a physician listening many miles away. Cable television provides home shopping channels that display products and enable buyers to place orders through use of a toll-free 800 telephone number. Other shopping services are available on a subscription basis to personal computer users who can use a telephone modem. Note that telemarketing has brought changes in the ownership, negotiations, and logistics channels in that there are no retail stores stocking goods.

Communication and transportation are now considered services, as are freight forwarding and many other ancillary services associated with the transport of goods and people. Labor practices also result in the increased use of services. Frequently the user firm pays so much in fringe benefits to its regular employees that it becomes cheaper to rely on outside firms to supply some services (rather than to place additional persons on the payroll). United States railroads, for example, contract out much of their equipment maintenance because the service firms have lower labor costs. It is important to note that not all employment in the services field is high-paying, a fact to which many college students will attest.

Services exist in both domestic and international markets. There are, for instance, "Norwegian exports of seaborne transport services; British exports of financial services; U.S. exports of computer software; [and] South Korean exports of building services."[6] South Korea has recently become a major provider of worldwide construction services, a role once associated with Western European nations and the United States. Often large movements of

---

[6] Brian Hindley, in *The Emerging Service Economy,* ed. Orio Giarini (New York: Pergamon, 1987), p. 46.

foreign labor to the construction site are involved. This is as true today as it was a century ago, when railroads and canals were being built throughout the world. Along the U.S.-Mexican border many Mexicans offer their day labor services to U.S. employers.

J. B. Richardson lists a number of services that can be thought of as international in scope: travel and tourism, air transport, maritime transport, banking, insurance, construction, information services, other business services (accounting, legal, advertising, and the like), and cultural services (performing arts and television).[7] Consider how closely related to—if not part of—logistics these services are.

Several issues related to service industries should be mentioned. One is that U.S. firms are generally expected to switch toward producing more services and fewer goods. In turn, supply chains will need to switch from moving products to moving people and ideas. Another issue is whether service transactions will become subject to more foreign trade (import-export) restrictions. Recall from Chapter 11 that there are tariff and nontariff barriers that hinder the flow of products and increase the tasks of those handling logistics for the products that do move. In addition, restrictions exist on the flow of currency, banking and insurance services, and labor. Most of these restrictions were initially enacted to protect a nation's own establishments and workers. If firms providing these types of services persuade their national governments to restrict the use of foreign providers of service, the latter will have to adapt in the same manner as manufacturers and bankers have been doing since World War II.

Travel and tourism are service sectors where growth is dependent on geographic, cultural, and historical endowments.

> The main characteristics of tourism are large volume, rapid growth, and qualitative change. In 1984, international tourist receipts amounted to some $100 billion; that is, about 5 percent by value of total world exports. These figures make international tourism the second largest item in world trade preceded only by oil and petroleum products.[8]

The travel industry employs many, but often at low wages.

The aircraft, which has revolutionized the inventory, warehousing, and customer service strategies of U.S. domestic firms, is doing the same in the travel and tourism industry by reducing the time and money it takes to reach all corners of the globe. In this area there will be continued growth and more situations to which logistics principles can be applied. Teleconferencing, for example, is now a substitute for business travel.

---

[7] John B. Richardson, in *The Emerging Service Economy,* ed. Orio Giarini (New York: Pergamon, 1987), pp. 74–80.

[8] Christine Richter, in *The Emerging Service Economy,* ed. Orio Giarini (New York: Pergamon, 1987), p. 216.

In 1991 the Council of Logistics Management released a major study concerning logistics in the service sector.[9] The study examines in some detail logistics in four industries: hospitals, telephone companies, retail banks, and high-tech field service organizations. The study concludes that

> while the terminology and titles are quite different, the essence of logistics is quite similar within the goods and service industries. Often, the similarities are striking. For example, the logic used to determine the best location for a bank branch or automated teller machine is similar to that used to determine the location of a field warehouse, or just-in-time (JIT) techniques to minimize inventory can be applied to reduce turnaround time for test results in a hospital.[10]

Information handling, reporting services, and communications are among the growth areas in the service sector. Of great interest is the mushrooming use of FAX machines and E-mail, which are taking the place of high-speed document delivery services.

ELECTRONIC DATA INTERCHANGE (EDI)

"In the old days, our distribution cycle was pushed and pulled by the movement of materials. Today, the impetus is movement of information."[11] Consultants David L. Anderson and Robert G. House note that by the year 2000 more money will be spent on information systems ($215 billion) than on inventory carrying costs ($205 billion). These expenditure patterns represent a fundamental shift in logistics strategy away from asset-intensive strategies (e.g., many warehouses and high inventory levels) and toward information-intensive control systems.[12]

Clearly, improved information and information exchange will continue to bring significant changes to logistics. Of particular importance is **electronic data interchange (EDI).**

> [EDI] involves the direct, computer-to-computer transmission of intercompany transactions. Although many people think of EDI as relating to ordering transactions, EDI often involves a broader set of credit memos, shipping documents, or any other routine transactions between companies. EDI can be used to link a company to all external parties—not just customers but also suppliers, transportation carriers, public warehouses, freight forwarders, customs clearance houses, and others.[13]

[9] *Logistics in Service Industries* (Oak Brook, Ill.: CLM, 1991).

[10] Ibid., p. xxi.

[11] Robert B. Footlik, "Performance, Packaging, and Distribution," in *Proceedings of the 1988 Annual Safe Transit Conference* (Chicago: National Safe Transit Association, 1988), p. 14.

[12] David L. Anderson and Robert G. House, "Logistics in the 1990s," *Private Carrier,* April 1991, p. 14.

[13] Arthur D. Little, Inc., brochure, ca. 1988.

In the early 1990s use of EDI in the logistics field was increasing at a rapid rate. George Klima, director of accounting systems for Super Valu Stores, Inc., noted:

> By electronically transmitting the order versus calling it in, we are saving about $1.20 to $1.30 per purchase order. We are transmitting 5,000 purchase orders a week. That's beginning to add up to some money.[14]

Similarly, in a study prepared for the CLM, Ernst & Whinney points out:

> Inland Steel increased its market share over the past few years (the only domestic steelmaker to do so)—a feat many industry observers attribute, in part, to the firm's channel computer system. Customers can enter orders on their Inland Steel terminal, and check shipping dates (customer order status). Inland executives believe the firm's ability to give customers these options and to ship promptly and reliably produce inventory savings that more than pay for the computer system. In effect, the terminals help Inland counter the cost advantage of its foreign competitors.[15]

EDI is important to the development and functioning of supply chains because "it often is the glue that ties long term relationships together. EDI is a communications technology that offers a variety of benefits to channels."[16] A typical EDI buyer-seller loop proceeds as follows:

- The buyer issues an EDI purchase order to the supplier.
- The supplier issues an EDI acknowledgment, either detailed or abbreviated, to the buyer.
- The supplier automates its order-entry system using the EDI listing from the buyer.
- The supplier issues shipping information via EDI to the carrier and may send a copy to the buyer via EDI.
- The supplier issues an EDI invoice to the buyer for the goods shipped.
- The carrier issues an EDI acknowledgment to the supplier.
- The carrier generates a freight bill using the supplier's EDI data.
- The carrier issues shipment status information, upon request, via EDI.
- The carrier issues an EDI invoice for freight charges to the paying party.
- The buyer issues the EDI payment to the supplier for the goods.
- The carrier is paid via EDI.[17]

---

[14] "Insight on EDI," *McDonnell Douglas SourceLine*, 1988, p. 8.

[15] Ernst & Whinney, *Corporate Profitability and Logistics: Innovative Guidelines for Executives* (Oak Brook, Ill.: CLM, 1987), p. 65.

[16] Lisa R. Williams, "Understanding Distribution Channels: An Interorganizational Study of EDI Adoption," *Journal of Business Logistics,* vol. 15, no. 2 (1994), p. 173.

[17] Lee Winrode, "Why EDI?" *Private Carrier,* May 1988, p. 12.

Buyers and sellers involved with EDI transactions are closely integrated:

> With K-Mart, Wal-Mart, and others, it's all done strictly by bar code. The inventory is set up on bar-code scanners. Every time something is taken out of the stockroom and put on the shelf, it's scanned and considered used. That information then goes directly to the supplier. [It] then knows that the last box has been taken out of the storeroom, and that triggers the supplier to ship the lot size [it is] programmed to ship.[18]

The benefits of using EDI are many; they include reductions in document preparation and processing time, inventory, carrying costs, personnel costs, information float, shipping errors, returned goods, lead times, order cycle times, and order costs. In addition, increases in accuracy, cash flow, sales, turnover, productivity, and channel management opportunity are possible with EDI. Interestingly, EDI is also used by buyers and sellers to exchange bids and ask questions directly, sometimes bypassing the traditional agents. As a result, the channels through which goods move are affected to the extent that the negotiations and logistics channels are related.

Sea-Land allows its customers to pay freight bills through a variety of EDI programs. When the funds are sent directly to the bank, Sea-Land receives notification of payment immediately. This is especially significant in ocean commerce because carriers sometimes do not release cargo until the freight bill is paid.

EDI reduces the need for transporting printed paper copies. "Large car producers, such as General Motors and Ford, have asked all their major suppliers of components, national and international, to connect to their Computer Aided Design system in order to reduce design time and increase quality."[19] One result of the electronic linkage has been to reduce the flow of drawings between the motor car manufacturers and their suppliers. With regard to customer service, EDI makes it possible to diagnose some electronic equipment at a distance as well as to give the repairperson instructions.

Professor Margaret A. Emmelhainz, in a study of the strategic issues related to several firms' adoption of EDI, makes the following observations:

> The decision to implement EDI [is] neither cost driven nor technology driven, but rather driven by the desire to obtain competitive advantage.
>
> Top management support for implementation [is] crucial because, to be successful, EDI's potential value [is] so widespread both within the firm and with its allied suppliers and customers.
>
> Third (or outside) parties [are] often used to implement and run the EDI systems.
>
> EDI is an essential ingredient of any just-in-time production-inventory system.

[18] *WERCsheet,* October 1990, p. 2.

[19] Juan F. Rada, in *The Emerging Service Economy,* ed. Orio Giarini (New York: Pergamon, 1987), p. 164.

> The most common starting point for implementing EDI [is] the link [of] a
> high-volume vendor with a corporate division [that has] personnel interested in
> EDI.[20]

International tariffs are being standardized (or "harmonized") so as to reduce
the number of different classifications or descriptions of a good as it moves
through an international transaction. However, the potential of EDI is not
spread evenly throughout the world. Two-thirds of the world's population
lacks access to telephones.[21] As a result, EDI will be used in developed markets primarily and its use there will continue to spread. However, there are
many different EDI transmission formats, such as the WINS (Warehouse
Information Network Standard) format used in the warehousing industry.
The EDI Association, formerly the Transportation Data Coordinating Committee (TDCC), coordinates the standards of several of these group formats.

Since EDI systems link buyers and sellers, it is more difficult for a competitor to break into the arrangement. This is part of the development of
partnerships along the various marketing channels and the supply chain.

> New types of competitive systems are arising, driven by product channel logis-
> tics. The traditional competitive entity, defined in terms of a single firm, is start-
> ing to be replaced by the product channel system, where all the firms involved
> in producing and distributing a product think and act as a single competitive
> entity. Operating in this type of environment requires each firm to think about
> its impact, not just on its immediate customer but [also] on its customer's cus-
> tomer.[22]

EDI is therefore helping to restructure the framework of logistics and supply-
chain relationships.

Artificial Intelligence (AI) Systems

More than any other single factor, computers are responsible for many of the
changes and advances that have taken place in the field of logistics during
the past two decades.

> Most "experts" agree that the next wave of computer-systems development—
> after integrated systems—will be in the area of decision support. Enter decision
> support systems.
>   A new category of decision support systems—encompassing artificial
> intelligence (AI) and expert systems—is under development at some pioneering
> companies. Broadly speaking, they are computer systems that perform at the

[20] Margaret A. Emmelhainz, "Strategic Issues of EDI Implementation," *Journal of Business
Logistics*, September 1988, pp. 55–70.

[21] Juan F. Rada, in *The Emerging Service Economy*, ed. Orio Giarini (New York: Pergamon,
1987), p. 166.

[22] Anderson and House, "Logistics in 1990s," p. 16.

level of intelligent human behavior, simulating the reasoning processes humans might use to solve a problem.

These systems draw inferences based on facts inputted into them and decision rules that are programmed in special AI languages or in conventional ones such as COBOL.[23]

Artificial intelligence (AI) is a highly sophisticated use of the computer in which it is programmed to "think" as a trained, skilled human would in specific situations. One popular application of AI is the computer-played chess game. One might ask, If a computer can play chess, are there other equally difficult tasks that it might also perform? Note the following:

> Blue Cross and Blue Shield of Missouri's state-of-the-art claim settlement system receives claims; evaluates them; writes checks and letters of explanation; and inserts, seals, weighs, meters, and sorts them untouched by human hands. In a typical transaction a claim is entered via a remote terminal at a hospital, and the computer plus bar coding and automated mailroom equipment do the rest. One operator, working 15 hours a week, can process between 75,000 and 80,000 average claim transactions a week. The secret isn't in the computer but in the decision rules it has been given.[24]

Another example of AI was developed by the Port of Singapore to develop plans for loading and unloading ocean containerships:

> Examples of . . . constraints include container size, storage location (in ship/ship yard), container contents, ship configuration, location of loading/unloading cranes, intermodal connection schedules, and ocean tides, among others. The expert planner applies these constraints to develop better loading/unloading plans than the inexperienced staff.[25]

Students familiar with basic computer instruction know that computers can be programmed to respond to different questions, often by asking a more definitive question. In theory one needs to know the questions to ask, when and how to ask them, and also the various relationships among all possible answers—a difficult but not impossible task. Consultant James Drogan notes that "expert systems are nothing more than a collection of knowledge and a set of rules whereby that knowledge can be applied to make better decisions."[26]

In logistics the task involves developing artificial intelligence systems that can handle routine matters. It is not necessary to handle all situations

---

[23] Ernst & Whinney, *Corporate Profitability*, pp. 67–68.

[24] *Customer Assurance Report*, May 12, 1988, p. 4.

[25] Mary Kay Allen and Omar Keith Helferich, *Putting Expert Systems to Work in Logistics* (Oak Brook, Ill.: CLM, 1990), p. 65.

[26] James Drogan, "The Role of Information Systems in the Preparation and Management of Transportation Service Packages," *Proceedings of Forward Motion: A Conference Sponsored by the Burlington Northern,* Dallas, November 3–4, 1988, p. BNS-14.

via AI, for conceivably the computer program could refer truly unique situations and queries to its human masters.

The Council of Logistics Management supported the doctoral research of Air Force Major Mary Kathryn Allen into the development of artificial intelligence systems for managing certain Air Force parts inventories. Allen did much of her work at the Sacramento Air Logistics Center, relying on eight human experts to assist her in developing and critiquing the long list of decision rules that the computer model had to follow to find answers to questions regarding inventory stocking levels. Each day the group addressed problems, both themselves and through the use of a developing computer program that was later named Inventory Manager Assistant (IMA). Differences were analyzed closely.

> Frequently, five or six times each day, the experts would disagree about the correctness of the advice IMA had provided. The researcher would then have the expert(s) who disagreed with IMA explain why to the other experts. Usually, these discussions resolved the issue. Usually, one expert or two had noticed an important piece of information which the other experts had overlooked. Additions to the IMA were usually required.
>
> When discussion alone did not resolve the issue, a vote of the experts was taken.
>
> Working through the fifteen cases resulted in considerable additions, modifications, and deletions to the knowledge base. Approximately forty new rules were added each night by the researcher as a result of the day's validation session. Approximately another twenty of the existing rules were modified each night to clarify the rules and make the advice provided easier to understand. Less than five rules were deleted each night. Frequently, a single rule which was deleted would be replaced by three or four rules of a more detailed nature.[27]

The final IMA expert system that was devised contained 441 rules, which gives an idea as to the magnitude of the task.

More recently, Professor R. Mohan Pisharodi examined the carrier selection process, using a survey of traffic managers who were asked to list the steps they follow in selecting a carrier. They were instructed as follows:

> You have just received shipping instructions to send an LTL shipment by common carrier (motor) to a customer located about a thousand miles from your warehouse. You have never shipped to this customer in the past. Freight is paid FOB destination. The shipment is for the product that you ship most frequently and the quantity to be shipped is your average shipment size for the product.[28]

[27] Mary Kathryn Allen, *The Development of an Artificial Intelligence System for Inventory Management Using Multiple Experts,* doctoral dissertation, Ohio State University (Oak Brook, Ill.: CLM, 1986), pp. 126–127.

[28] R. Mohan Pisharodi, "Modeling the Motor Carrier Selection Decision Process," in *Proceedings of the Transportation and Logistics Research Fund* (Columbus: Ohio State University, 1991), pp. 184–185.

The form had the first step printed at the top—"received basic shipping instructions"—and the last step at the bottom—"schedule shipment," with space for listing up to fifteen activities in between. The respondents listed a total of 120 activities, but slightly over half of the activities were listed only once. A rank order was established for each activity, with the lowest rank assigned to the activity performed first and the highest rank to the one performed last. An effort was then made to condense the list to include only activities mentioned by 5 percent of the respondents; this narrowed the list to thirty-two activities. Condensing the list to activities mentioned by 10 percent of the respondents reduced the number to twenty-four. Finally, condensing the list to activities listed by 20 percent or more of the respondents reduced the list to these fifteen activities (in order of performance): confirming shipment specifications; determining destinations; identifying carriers that serve origin-destination combinations; identifying carriers that serve destinations directly; checking routing guides; determining freight rates; choosing routes; reviewing carriers' past rates, services, and claim performance; determining carriers' transit times; determining which carrier can provide the lowest rate; evaluating carriers in terms of cost and service; selecting the carrier; contacting the carrier; scheduling the shipment; and advising the shipping department about shipping and routing.[29] A procedure such as Pisharodi's can be used when establishing an expert system to determine the sequential relationship among specific steps in a routine operation.

At the CLM's 1994 annual meeting consultant Paul S. Bender described an expert system named *Phydias*, which constructs logistics networks from data inputs and then uses them to calculate optimum strategies. "Phydias solves each problem seeking to optimize the maximum number of tradeoffs of two kinds: tradeoffs among different cost and revenue elements, and tradeoffs among different cost, revenue, and performance (e.g., service) elements."[30]

METRIC CONVERSION

Metric conversion, though not a new issue, is one that will need to be confronted. The United States is the only major country in the world that does not use the metric system of weights and measures. The federal government has been studying the metric issue for more than two hundred years. In 1790 President George Washington asked Congress to decide whether the metric system should be adopted in the United States. Secretary of State Thomas Jefferson, noting the use of the metric system in Europe, argued

[29] Ibid., p. 194.

[30] Paul S. Bender, "Using Expert Systems and Optimization Techniques to Design Logistics Strategies," *CLM Annual Conference Proceeding, 1994* (Oak Brook, Ill.: CLM, 1994), p. 233.

strongly for metrication. Congress, however, was unable to decide and therefore took no position on this issue.

More recently it was generally assumed that if the United States converts to the metric system, a relatively long conversion period would be needed to make the transition as smooth as possible. During the early to mid-1970s, the metrication bills before Congress called for a ten-year conversion period. A compromise metrication bill was signed into law on December 23, 1975. The Metric Conversion Act created a seventeen-member U.S. Metric Board, whose job was to plan for the conversion and to educate the public about the benefits of the metric system. However, the board was not given enforcement power, and its work was not subjected to a time limit for complete conversion. The softening of the ten-year deadline for conversion came at the insistence of organized labor. The board could recommend to Congress that federal subsidies were required to help meet conversion costs, especially for workers required to purchase metrically dimensioned hand tools. In 1981, with federal deficits growing, Congress searched for federal programs that could be eliminated to save funding. The Metric Board was a victim of those cutbacks; it closed on September 30, 1982.

Most U.S. business executives recognize the inevitability of conversion to the metric system. The American public, however, is less enthusiastic about the metric system. Many familiar measures will have to be replaced. Two types of conversion referred to are soft and hard. Soft conversion converts measurements exactly, with a 2-inch by 4-inch stud becoming a 50.8-mm by 101.6-mm stud. "A hard conversion would result in a nominal 50 mm by 100 mm stud. . . . The 2 inch by 4 inch stud would be interchangeable with the 51 mm by 102 mm stud, but a hard conversion to a 50 mm by 100 mm stud would be preferable, because it results in round numbers that are easier to work with."[31] Metrication lacks popular support. See Figure 15-1.

The majority of multinational firms are already involved in planning for metric conversion. One reason is the European Common Market's announcement that all products exported into its member countries would have to move in metric measurements. Substantial noncompliance penalties were also mandated. Other countries have similar laws. Kenya, for example, requires all imported products to be in metric measurements. In France "laboratory glassware must be marked in milliliters. If a U.S. company selling laboratory glassware has milliliters listed on one side of a graduated cylinder and ounces on the other, the French see this as a hazard [and] won't let the product in the country."[32] Indeed, the only nations in the world not presently using the metric system are the United States, Liberia, and Burma.

The United States continues to move toward metrication only slowly. The trade bill enacted in August 1988 designates metric as the "preferred system of

---

[31] Christopher Stone, "Metric Conversion Arrives," *PC-Trans,* Fall 1994, p. 12.

[32] *Federal Express International Newsletter,* October 1991, p. 7.

"I'm sure glad your Pa ain't alive to see this."

Figure 15-1 The metric system will bring some unexpected changes. (Reproduced by permission of the artist and *The Wall Street Journal*.)

weights and measures for U.S. trade and commerce" and required all federal agencies by 1992 to utilize the metric system in purchasing activities.[33] In 1988 Defense Secretary Carlucci signed an order requiring the use of metric specifications on development work for the Strategic Defense Initiative (SDI) systems.

> The move is simple economics. Under the gun to pare costs, the Defense Department expects relatively painless savings from the switch. It would end the dual inventories that NATO now keeps and make it easier to enlist foreign companies in joint development programs.[34]

In the early 1990s all federal agencies were instructed to develop plans to convert their operations to metric measures. In mid-1991 the Interstate Commerce Commission announced a hearing to determine whether to require that all its filings and reports be based on metric measures. Tariffs, rate contracts, report filings, data collection, and evidence submitted in rate disputes that come before that agency would have been affected by that proposal. Shippers and carriers responded without enthusiasm to the proposal.

RECYCLING

Recycling is another issue that will continue to receive attention by the logistics field in the 1990s. Most major cities in the United States are simply running out of space to dispose of garbage and waste, driving up the costs of disposal. In addition there is increasing scrutiny of industry's waste-disposal

[33] *Industry Week,* October 17, 1988, p. 29.
[34] *Business Week,* April 11, 1988, p. 123.

practices. The Green movement, which is now worldwide, is forcing nations to adopt more environmentally sound laws and businesses to follow more environmentally friendly practices.

> To comply with these tough new regulations, manufacturers are not only streamlining their packaging and expanding their distribution networks—they are redesigning their products in order to minimize their waste and maximize their recyclability. This cradle-to-grave product management demands life cycle planning that emphasizes environmental issues. As a result, green logistics affects the entire supply chain.[35]

Energy costs are yet another factor. Part of the rationale for recycling aluminum cans is to save the energy consumed in smelting new aluminum. In addition, the "recyclability of [a product's] package is a growing factor in purchasing decisions. Responding to [the question,] 'How often does the recyclability of a package affect your decision to buy one product over another?' 41.3 percent of consumers answered 'often' or 'sometimes.'"[36]

Recycling lags in the United States compared to that of other countries. "Japan now recycles more than 50 percent of its trash; Western Europe around 30 percent. The United States does not fare nearly so well: only 10 percent [of its trash] is recycled."[37] Recycling rates vary by material as well: In the United States in 1991, for instance, 64 percent of aluminum cans and 57 percent of corrugated boxes were recycled.[38] However, in 1990 the U.S. recycled 32 percent of its kitchen appliances; by 1994 the percentage had climbed to 62 "due in part to increase private and public sector awareness and the continuing development of a strong infrastructure for recovery of ferrous scrap from appliances."[39]

To the logistics professional recycling means many things: understanding how a product's ability to be recycled adds to its value; recognizing how recycling establishes new channels in the supply, distribution, and return movement networks; and appreciating how recycling influences the choice of materials for packaging a product. Recycling is related to logistics in several other ways. With regard to inventory management, for example, there are tax matters to consider when goods are donated to charitable organizations. Goods damaged in transit, moreover, are sometimes candidates for recycling.

A product's ability to be recycled adds to its value because the initial buyer realizes that at some point in time the item can be resold to another user. Automobile manufacturers boast about how well certain makes retain

---

[35] *Journal of European Business,* September–October 1993, p. 35.

[36] *Packaging,* June 1987, p. 54.

[37] *Time,* January 2, 1989, pp. 45–47.

[38] *Journal of Commerce,* April 6, 1992, p. 6C.

[39] *The Recycling Magnet,* Summer 1994, p. 1.

their original value in resales. At Apple Computer a staff of ten devotes its time to recycling computers. While some of the computers are customer returns, most are models that were previously used within the firm. Once reconditioned, the recycled computers are made available for sale to employees or loaned to school districts considering the purchase of new computer equipment.

The various markets that handle recycled products differ in sophistication and coverage. The used-car market has been in existence since the beginnings of automobile manufacture. A relatively new market is that for discarded beverage cans. Major aluminum manufacturers have made a major long-term commitment to buy back the cans; local recyclers, in turn, have developed collection and recycling procedures. In part because of the support of aluminum manufacturers and recyclers in the recycling effort, the price per ton of used aluminum cans ($600–$1,000) is much more than the prices of other separated scrap (e.g., plastic containers, $100–$200; steel, $50–$80; glass, $15–$40; and paper, $0–$20).[40] Figure 15-2 shows an aluminum can collector and crusher.

Figure 15-2   The recycling of aluminum cans (Courtesy of Aluminum Company of America.)

[40] *Plastic Bottle Reporter,* Fall 1990, p. 3.

Of special interest to the logistics professional is whether recycled goods should be handled by an existing channel that is merely reversed or by a newly established channel. In the case of beer bottles, for instance, an existing but reversed channel is often used for recycling. The beverage company driver picks up cases of empty bottles when the new supply is delivered. Grocery wholesalers have to pay a small bonus to drivers for bringing back empty pallets to replace those that were under loads just delivered. Frequently materials to be recycled must be separated. The value of recyclable wastes fluctuates, so it is difficult to pursue a profitable strategy. Recovery systems also have to deal with environmental issues; automobile brake linings, for example, contain asbestos, and auto batteries contain acid and lead.

Garage sales, flea markets, auto salvage yards, and thrift shops are examples of some of the channels set up to handle the sale of recycled products. In addition these channels may handle new products, such as slow sellers that were dumped by their retailer, wholesaler, or manufacturer. A sophisticated system of recycling exists for the sale and resale of college textbooks. Some used textbooks are sold from student to student or from the student back to the bookstore. In addition there are firms that redistribute used college textbooks throughout the country. Some firms even buy from college professors the sample textbooks that publishers distribute to instructors to consider for possible course adoption. In these instances note that the new channels both help and hurt the original manufacturer: They continue to support the market for the product, but they may also compete with the manufacturer.

A manager of a firm that makes plastic cushioning for auto parts noted the following:

> His company is already setting up methods of retrieving the cushioning from the destination plant, arranging for its transport back to the source of intermediate locations for reuse (in some cases where the application permits), but mostly for recycling. "We're talking to people about setting them up in business to handle this waste cushioning. We're looking at joint ventures for such work. We're looking at the equipment that's needed. We're working to set up a system, let's call it a network of distributor, end user, waste recycler, and source for the reprocessed cushioning. This is all aimed at meeting a market condition which will affect our ability to sell our cushioning product. We can see a situation where the cost of disposal is included in the price a customer is willing to pay. We have to be able to deal with that bidding factor and we think our waste recycling network will help us do that."[41]

Here the logistics manager is proposing that new channels be established to handle the packaging materials.

Although packaging materials that can be reused are often desirable, some materials are so stable that they do not decompose. This is not a recycling

---

[41] Charles R. Garth, "Affirmative Procurement: New Factor in Package Development," in *Proceedings of the 1988 Annual Safe Transit Conference* (Chicago: National Safe Transit Association, 1988), p. 93.

issue, but it does demonstrate the difficulty in selecting packaging methods and materials. Attorney Charles Garth predicts the following:

> Affirmative procurement to promote recycling and disposability of packaging is on the way. It will have a direct and indirect impact on the development of packaging, especially in the selection of materials and the combination of materials. Initially the pressure will come from state and local governments.[42]

By "affirmative procurement" Garth means that, in purchase orders, governments will require a product's packaging to be recyclable or made of recycled materials. The requirements may even go beyond packaging to include the bidding process, in which products that are recyclable or that contain a certain percentage of recycled input may be favored over other products.

In some cases products and packaging cannot be reused and may instead be burned as fuel. The feasibility of this approach, however, depends on the energy economics of the region and the plant and on local restrictions on air pollution.

Public demands for recycling vary in intensity throughout the country, making it difficult for national firms to satisfy all consumers' needs. Steven Lyman of Michigan State University, in a study of the use of lightweight returnable plastic containers to deliver parts to automobile assembly lines, draws the following conclusions:

> Full implementation of returnables is not completed [by] any of the three [major] U.S. automakers, even after 5 years. Chrysler is probably the furthest along in its program, implementing by car platform (style) and striving for 100 percent returnable. Next comes GM, [which], although having started at the same time as Chrysler, has lagged behind. GM implements by plant but does not hold fast to 100 percent returnable or in some cases even close. Ford has followed the lead of Chrysler and GM, allowing them to set more of the framework. [Ford], like most of GM, [does] not intend to implement returnable containers 100 percent.[43]

Part of the problem here is that each automaker has a different policy on dunnage (i.e., the packing materials found inside a container). According to Lyman, Ford mandates expendable dunnage, Chrysler uses 100 percent returnable dunnage, and "GM seems to take both sides of the street."[44] Thus dunnage is yet another recycling issue complicating automakers' decision on whether to use plastic parts containers.

As shown in Figure 15-3, many professions are faced with the dilemma of determining what type of product or packaging is "environmentally correct."

---

[42] Ibid., p. 91.

[43] Steven B. Lyman, "Plastic Returnable/Reusable Containers in the Automobile Industry," in *Council of Logistics Management Fall 1988 Annual Conference Proceedings*, vol. 2 (Oak Brook, Ill.: CLM, 1988), pp. 201–202.

[44] Ibid., p. 199.

582

Figure 15-3 Knowing which packaging to choose is a problem for many enterprises. (Copyright © 1991 by the *San Francisco Chronicle*. Reprinted by permission.)

SUMMARY

In this concluding chapter several topics likely to affect the future of logistics are discussed. These trends are expected to bring important changes to the field.

Increased international trade and operations will take several forms. Domestic firms will become more dependent on exports and imports. Some firms will become multinational in scope.

The service economy is expected to grow in the United States. This means that an increasing proportion of U.S. economic activity will be based on services and a decreasing proportion on tangible goods. Logistics systems will need to be refocused in order to deliver services instead of physical products.

Electronic data interchange (EDI) will play an important role in logistics. Electronic data interchange involves computer-to-computer interchanges between buyers and sellers, unlike the traditional exchange of verbal messages and documents. In logistics, EDI is now widely used for transmitting orders and handling customer service inquiries. It not only speeds up processes but also makes them less prone to error.

Artificial intelligence (AI) systems, which have many potential applications in order processing and customer service, will grow in use in logistics operations.

Conversion to the metric system in the United States has been a slow process, but ultimately it will have to be accomplished, as U.S. firms become more involved with the global marketplace. Finally, recycling will continue to be an important concern along the entire supply chain.

QUESTIONS FOR DISCUSSION AND REVIEW

1. Why is the U.S. government concerned about exports? In your view, should the government encourage U.S. firms to export? Why or why not?
2. Why is international logistics so expensive?
3. Discuss the implications of a world economy for the United States.
4. What makes international trade more complicated than domestic trade?
5. Why is the United States moving toward a service economy? Discuss.
6. Compare and contrast the logistical activities of a firm that delivers goods and a firm that delivers services.
7. What is the American public's attitude about the use of the metric system?
8. In your opinion, should the United States move more quickly toward adopting the metric system? Why or why not?
9. What is electronic data interchange (EDI)?
10. Describe a buyer-seller transaction made via an EDI loop.
11. Discuss why a firm would have to adopt an EDI system.
12. What is artificial intelligence (AI)?

13. In which areas of logistics do you think AI is most likely to be used? Why?

14. Why are computers so commonly used in logistics today? Discuss.

15. What is recycling? Will it become more or less important? Why?

16. How might recycling affect a firm's packaging decisions? Discuss.

17. What recycling activities do you engage in?

18. If you were able to choose the area of logistics for your first job, which one would you select, and why?

19. Discuss the impact of improved communications on logistics. Explain.

20. Will logistics be more important in the twenty-first century than it has been in the twentieth century? Why or why not?

SUGGESTED READINGS

Allen, Mary Kay, and Omar Keith Helferich. *Putting Expert Systems to Work in Logistics*. Oak Brook, Ill.: CLM, 1990.

Coyle, John J. "Preparing Logistics Systems for the Twenty-first Century." In *Annual Conference Proceedings of the Council of Logistics Management*, vol. 2. Oak Brook, Ill.: CLM, 1990, pp. 1–10.

Davis, Frank, and Karl Manrodt. "Service Logistics: An Introduction." In *Annual Conference Proceedings of the Council of Logistics Management*, vol. 2. Oak Brook, Ill.: CLM, 1990, pp. 67–91.

Kling, James A., and Curtis Grimm. "Microcomputer Use in Transportation and Logistics: A Literature Review with Implications for Educators." *Journal of Business Logistics*, February 1988, pp. 1–18.

Logistics in Service Industries. Oak Brook, Ill.: CLM, 1991.

Millen, Robert A. "Utilization of EDI by Motor Carrier Firms: A Status Report," *Transportation Journal*, vol. 32, no. 2 (Winter 1992), pp. 5–13.

Perry, James. "Emerging Economics and Technological Futures: Implications for Design and Management of Logistics Systems in the 1990s." *Journal of Business Logistics*, Fall 1991, pp. 1–16.

Rogers, Dale S., Richard L. Dawe, and Patrick Guerra. "Information Technology: Logistics Innovations for the 1990s." In *Annual Proceedings of the Council of Logistics Management*, vol. 2. Oak Brook, Ill.: CLM, 1991, pp. 245–262.

Ruth, Stephen R. "Expert Systems in Logistics: Undervalued and Oversold?" In *Papers, CLM 1987 Annual Meeting*, vol. 2. Oak Brook, Ill.: CLM, 1987, pp. 71–83.

Sheombar, Haydee S. "EDI-Induced Redesign of Co-ordination in Logistics," *International Journal of Physical Distribution & Logistics Management*, vol. 22, no. 8 (1992), pp. 4–14.

Udo, Godwin J., and Trish Grant, "Making EDI Pay Off: The Averitt Express Experience," *Production & Inventory Management Journal*, vol. 34. no. 4 (Fourth Quarter 1993), pp. 6–11.

C A S E   1 5 - 1

COALTAINERS

Prior to about 1950, coal was widely used throughout the United States for heating homes, apartments, factories, and institutions. A coal-burning furnace would provide the heat that would warm air or water or create steam that would be carried by pipes or ducts. The coal furnace was often fired by a stoker. The stoker, which was placed a short distance from the furnace, consisted of a coal hopper on top into which coal would be shoveled by hand. Below the stoker hopper and leading into the furnace was an enclosed tube six inches or more in diameter. One end of the tube was below the stoker, and the other end of the tube led inside the furnace to a point just above the grate where the fire was burning. An Archimedes' screw (a continuous screw) fed through this tube and would carry coal from the bottom of the hopper to the fire burning on the grate. See Exhibit 15-A. A thermostat, elsewhere in the building, controlled the motor to the stoker. When the temperature fell, the thermostat would activate the stoker motor, which would feed more coal onto the fire. As the temperature would increase, the thermostat would switch off, stopping the flow of coal. It was necessary, however, to maintain the continual fire in the furnace. The stoker functioned only to feed more coal on a fire that was already burning. Beneath the grate on the furnace was an ash pit. Ash and clinkers remaining after the coal had burned would collect in the ash pit and would be cleaned out by hand. About 10 percent to 20 percent of the coal, by weight, would become ash.

Deliveries to users of coal were made by two means of transportation. Railroad cars carried coal directly to factories and large institutional users, often at a rail site for the sole reason of receiving coal. Trucks, such as shown in Exhibit 15-B, were used for deliveries of smaller amounts. The conventional coal truck was unloaded by gravity. A lifting frame was often provided to raise the level of the coal load, increasing the horizontal distance that the coal would move down chutes by gravity. Buildings that used coal for heating had the furnace located in the basement for several reasons. First, it allowed delivery of coal by a gravity method. Second, coal and ash are dirty and dusty, and the basement location reduced the possibility of this dirt and dust settling elsewhere in the building. Third, heating units also relied on gravity to move the hot air or water upward and cause the colder water or air to return downward for reheating.

Just before and after World War II, coal lost popularity for home and institutional heating to two other fuels: oil and natural gas, which had numerous advantages. They were cleaner burning and produced no ash. The heating units required much less space in the building. Also, it is easier to

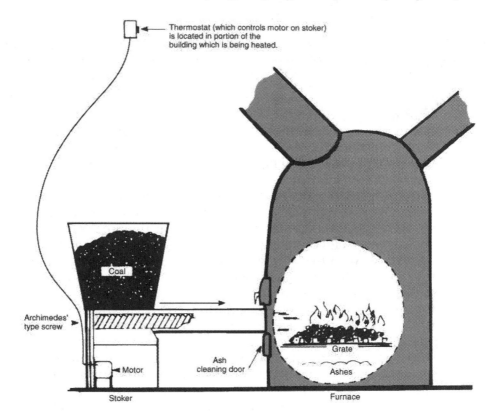

Exhibit 15-A   Conventional pre–World War II stoker and burner arrangement.

ignite an oil or gas fire, so the unit could be used intermittently in the fall and spring. (This was not as easy to do with a stoker-fed coal furnace, where the fire had to be maintained continually.) The oil and gas units had several advantages in the construction of new buildings. Less room was required, and it was less necessary to isolate the furnace unit from the rest of the building in order to reduce dirt and dust. In addition, the furnace location did not have to be near a street or driveway in order to receive coal, and pumps were developed for pumping hot water or blowing hot air, which meant that the new heating units could be on the same floor as the rooms being heated. Even in older buildings in which the owner did not wish to completely replace an existing furnace, it was possible to install the gas or oil burner inside the firebox of the one-time coal-burning furnace.

Oil and gas furnaces had one additional advantage: They required almost no labor on behalf of the building owner or custodian. It was no longer necessary to shovel coal into a stoker or to empty ashes from the bottom of the furnace. In factories and institutions this often meant that it was no longer necessary to have a fireman (one who tended fires) on the payroll.

Exhibit 15-B   Two pre–World War II methods of delivering coal to retail customers. In the top photo, a circa-1930 Diamond-T with an elevated coal body dumps the coal through a window chute, where it will fall into a coal bin and be shoveled by hand into a stoker. The bottom photo shows a 1935 Studebaker dumping coal, which falls through the grate into a bin below. (Top photo courtesy of the Heil Company; bottom photo courtesy of Fruehauf Corporation.)

Thus, coal all but disappeared as a fuel used for heating homes, apartments, stores, office buildings, factories, and other institutions.

During the fuel crises of the middle to late 1970s, prices of oil jumped and were, at times, twice that of coal in terms of BTU content. During most of the 1980s oil prices were lower, mainly because of instability within OPEC. Because of these lower oil prices, there was less interest in conversion from oil to coal. Should (or when) oil prices climb again, coal will be scrutinized as a means of heating buildings in the United States.

There are many problems involved with increasing our use of coal as an energy source. Some of these are touched on later in this discussion. One idea, which is developed here, deals with a method of transporting and delivering coal to users. The device to be employed is referred to here as a *coaltainer*. The idea is based on the open-topped metal boxes used to collect debris from large buildings and construction sites. They sometimes have small metal wheels on the bottom, and it is possible for specially equipped trucks to deposit and collect these boxes at the sites where they are used. The coaltainer is a similar box with a few modifications.

Exhibit 15-C shows one proposed coaltainer that is eight feet wide, eight feet high, and twenty feet long. The bottom is sloped on both sides down toward the center. At the bottom center, running the length of the coaltainer, is an Archimedes' screw. The coaltainer with the Archimedes' screw would be placed in position in front of the furnace, and the screw would then be used as a stoker screw to feed coal into the fire as it was needed. The power unit to move this screw could be self-contained within each coaltainer or permanently mounted near the furnace and attached to

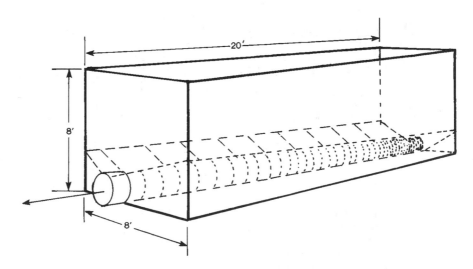

Exhibit 15-C   Coaltainer with Archimedes' screw stoker.

each coaltainer as it is placed in position. The electric motor would be controlled by the building's thermostat.

Exhibit 15-D shows the modification of the proposal for the coaltainer with a movable panel that covers an opening running along the bottom. This container does not contain the Archimedes' screw. Instead, the screw is permanently placed in front of the furnace, and individual coaltainers are placed on top of it. This has several advantages. First, the payload of the coaltainer is increased because space is not used up by the screw. Second, chances of damaging the screw while the coaltainer is in transit are eliminated. Third, the cost of the entire system is much lower because the coaltainer does not include the expensive screw installation. Last, fewer screw devices would be required.

Another modification of the coaltainers, which is not illustrated, would be to have a small, separate compartment in each coaltainer that would be used for carrying away the ash that is a by-product of the coal's combustion. The individual tending the fire would have to shovel the ashes from the ash pit below the fire grate into the ash compartment in the coaltainer. This would be a useful feature in situations where only one coaltainer was used at a time. In instances where numerous coaltainers were located at the user's

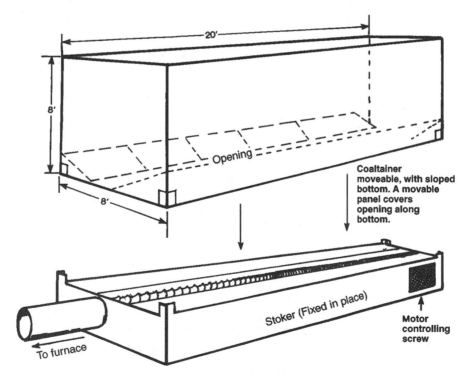

Exhibit 15-D   Coaltainer with movable panel.

site, any empty coaltainer could be used for loading ash. Exhibit 15-E shows a method of unloading a single full coaltainer and later reloading it aboard the truck when it is empty. Users of single coaltainers would probably have to maintain a small reserve of coal elsewhere to be used in instances where the coaltainer's supply was exhausted.

Exhibit 15-F shows a much larger installation. Coaltainers are delivered to the left of the picture and then moved toward the right, where they are connected with the furnace. Coaltainers farther to the right are either empty or are being used for holding ashes. The coaltainer farthest to the right is being reloaded aboard a truck, where it will be hauled back to the coal dealer for refilling.

There are many problems associated with determining whether coaltainers are a feasible alternative for delivering coal. The remainder of this case discusses some of the issues that should be of concern to an individual attempting to determine whether the coaltainer idea is feasible. In the last

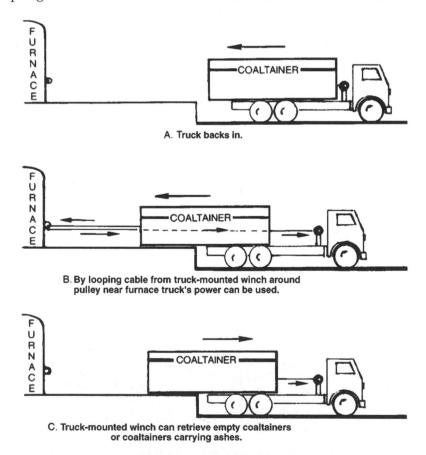

A. Truck backs in.

B. By looping cable from truck-mounted winch around pulley near furnace truck's power can be used.

C. Truck-mounted winch can retrieve empty coaltainers or coaltainers carrying ashes.

Exhibit 15-E Moving coaltainers between truck and furnace installation.

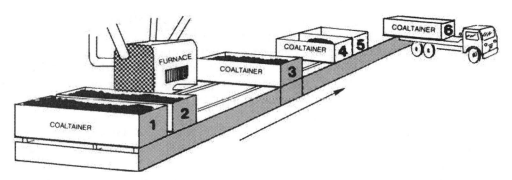

Exhibit 15-F   Large coaltainer installation.

quarter-century all levels of government have enacted stricter requirements regarding air pollution. The use of coal for heating buildings would create two sources of air pollution. The first would be the smoke from the combustion process, and the second would be dust from the coal being carried to where it is being used and from the ash being removed and taken to a disposal site. Some coals are considered to be cleaner burning than others in terms of both air pollution and ash content. One cause of acid rain is the burning of coal with a high sulfur content.

The exact dimensions of coaltainers are another issue. The eight-foot width and height are fairly universal as dimensional requirements on motor trucks. However, the length can vary. Although longer containers carry more, they require additional internal bracing to reduce the possibility of sagging in the middle. This is of particular concern because they must fit into a system that feeds the coal into the furnace. There are some advantages to handling multiple containers on one truck or truck-trailer; however, additional space is required then to maneuver the rig. (In the late 1930s many coal delivery bodies were very short; this was to enable them to maneuver into small areas in order to make deliveries.)

In some cities there are still requirements in safety codes that particular licensed individuals are needed to tend coal fires in buildings above certain sizes. Union jurisdictional disputes might also limit the amount of work the driver of a truck carrying a coaltainer could perform when removing the device from a truck and coupling with the furnace. To date, deliveries of fuel oil and natural gas have been fairly immune from labor strikes. Coal deliveries have been and could be more vulnerable. One would also have to explore whether the idea has been patented or would infringe on patents held by others.

Should the coaltainer idea be used, questions arise as to who would own the coaltainers and who should own the stoker installations. In addition, schedules of charges would have to be established that cover the cost of the coaltainer, the coal, and pickup and delivery services.

An operational problem is that the demand for coal is seasonal. Very little coal is used during the summer months for heating purposes. In the winter coal use is related to cold temperatures, and within a given area, coal use by all users would run in similar patterns. That is, if the winter were mild, there would be low use by all customers. If there was a hard winter, all users would demand more coal, and all would want additional deliveries at about the same time.

Building codes exist in many communities that govern the specifications of structures. Whether they are up to date with respect to installation of coal-burning furnaces is unknown. In addition, within each community the building codes (often influenced by local conditions and pressures of various building trades, contractors, and unions) vary so that code requirements in no two communities are the same. It would be difficult to develop a product that would meet such a wide number of building codes.

There are many operational problems in the handling of the coaltainers, especially because it is necessary that they not be damaged to the extent that they make it difficult or impossible to connect with the furnace. In addition, if one malfunctions while it is in place, connected to a furnace, it must be removed quickly because it is difficult to feed the fire with coal except by hand.

It would be difficult to convert buildings built since 1950 back to burning coal. In many instances the furnace installation would be nowhere near the street or driveway where coal deliveries could be made. Within urban areas distribution sites would have to be found where coal, received by rail or barge, could be sorted, stored, and loaded aboard coaltainers for local distribution. This particular site would also create dust, and many communities would not encourage such sites near residential areas.

As mentioned earlier, coal, when burned, creates ash. Ash disposal is a minor problem in itself. In earlier times, ash was used for surfacing driveways and roads and as an aggregate in concrete. An attempt would have to be made to find uses for ash.

Other methods are proposed for handling local deliveries of coal. One such alternative is shown on Exhibit 15-G. Rather than using the unique coaltainers, this system could rely on conventional dump trucks. Note, in this instance, that there is much less risk involved since the dump-truck bodies are relatively inexpensive and could be easily resold. Dump trucks would also carry away the ashes.

Questions

1. Assume that you work for a large coal company and have been asked to outline a feasibility study of the coaltainer. The study's budget may be as high as several million dollars. Outline such a study with all its elements.

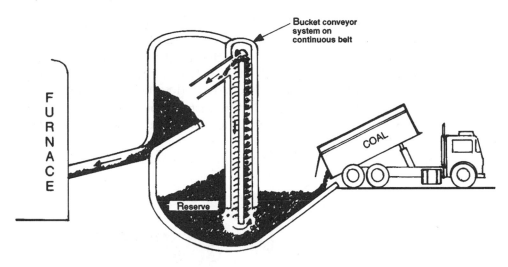

Bucket conveyor
system on
continuous belt

FURNACE

COAL

Reserve

Exhibit 15-G   An alternative to the coaltainer system.

2. Assume that you want to test market the idea in one U.S. city. What characteristics should that city have? Why?

3. The coaltainer equipment consists of the coaltainer, an Archimedes' screw, which may be part of the coaltainer or may be part of the stoker below the coaltainer and not part of the coaltainer, a truck with equipment to carry the coaltainer and load and reload it, and a furnace connection that can handle one or more coaltainers. How would you go about deciding whether the Archimedes' screw should be mounted in every coaltainer or be part of the stoker (i.e., permanently attached to the furnace)?

4. The case states that the coaltainer should be eight feet high and eight feet wide but was less definite as to its length. Assume that you are on a study team to determine the length or lengths of the coaltainers. What factors should you consider?

5. Assume that you are in the group that is attempting to determine how the firm that employs the coaltainers should go about charging for their use. In this case the users are the customers who buy the coal that is delivered in coaltainers. Items you should consider are the price of coal, which varies by BTU content; the cost of buying, delivering, and maintaining the coaltainers; the labor cost involved in handling the coaltainers; the trucking costs; whether ash removal is involved; and whether your driver or the user is responsible for connecting and disconnecting the coaltainers. In addition, you want to achieve certain levels of equipment utilization. Outline a pricing schedule for coal deliveries made to

users who receive their deliveries in coaltainers. Are there other elements of customer service to be considered? If so, what are they?

6. Exhibit 15-G shows an alternative to the coaltainer system. What are the similarities and differences between the system shown in Exhibit 15-G and the coaltainer idea? Which do you think is preferable? Why?

7. Is it feasible to have a coaltainer installation where the user has but one coaltainer on hand at any time—that is, the one in place and feeding the furnace? Discuss.

8. How sensitive are the ideas proposed here to changes in the price of oil? Discuss.

C A S E   1 5 - 2

DONELLY METAL STAMPINGS COMPANY

Donelly Metal Stampings Company is located in East St. Louis, Illinois, where it has been since its founding in 1887. In its old and relatively small plant, it operates twenty punch presses of varying sizes. Punch presses cut and shape metal pieces and parts, such as bases for scaffolding and the metal boxes used to contain electrical outlets. Donelly's principal customers are in the St. Louis area, though a number are scattered as far west as Kansas City, to the northeast as far as Chicago/Hammond, and to Kentucky in the southeast, where there are some new auto assembly plants.

The outgoing product is usually shipped by truck. If the stamped item can be nested, the shipment is very heavy. When the product cannot be nested, the loads are bulky. An ideal outgoing load is a mixture of dense, nested items below and bulky items above. Donelly operates its own fleet of eight trucks for making deliveries. Production and delivery are closely coordinated, and Donelly offers a high level of customer service (measured in terms of on-time delivery). Richard Ritter of the marketing department is in charge of scheduling the outgoing deliveries and dispatching the fleet of trucks carrying goods to customers.

The principal input is sheet steel, usually purchased from mills in the Chicago/Hammond/Gary area. Steel producers usually charge uniform amounts for their product but compete in terms of absorbing the freight costs of making the deliveries. Obtaining these concessions requires astute bargaining. Herb Wiggins is the assistant director of purchasing, specializing in transportation.

There is little coordination between those responsible for outbound and inbound shipments at Donelly. For example:

1. Ritter and Wiggins do not get along personally, and neither has been inside the other's office for as long as most employees can remember. Mail or phone calls directed to "the traffic manager" cause problems since either is offended when the other gets the letter or call.

2. Attempts to use Donelly's private fleet of trucks for carrying inbound sheet steel as a backhaul have not worked out, in part because steel is better suited for carriage by rail and in part because neither Wiggins nor Ritter has tried to make the backhaul system work. Since the *Toto* decision and the 1980 Motor Carrier Act, Ritter has developed occasional backhaul business carrying for other firms, but the depressed economy in the East St. Louis area has resulted in few inbound loads.

3. During a wildcat rail strike in the Chicago area, Donelly attempted to get some motor carriers to carry steel from Hammond to East St. Louis. It was unable to contract with any truckers because regular carriers know that Donelly usually uses rail and has its own trucks, and so the shipments of their steel represented temporary business. In addition these truckers had all the work they could handle, hauling for regular accounts during the rail strike. Harold Donelly III, the firm's president, had to personally tell Ritter to release some trucks from making deliveries to go to Hammond to pick up steel. By the time the trucks arrived in Hammond, the rail strike was over. However, the Donelly plant was without steel and had to shut down for two days. Its competitors, however, relying solely on contract truckers, were able to receive sheet steel and remain open.

The wildcat strike experience has brought matters at Donelly to a head. Withdrawing trucks from making deliveries and being shut down for two days caused the loss of several key accounts to competitors.

At this point Wiggins's boss sends a memo to Harold Donelly outlining the problem. He lays heavy blame on Ritter, recommending that a new post—director of traffic—be established and suggesting that Herb Wiggins is qualified to fill the post.

Ritter and his boss believe that Ritter has been unjustly blamed since he is not responsible for inbound movements. They counter with an even longer memo, recommending that Ritter be named director of traffic and that Wiggins serve as his assistant. They both know that Wiggins would resign rather than be Ritter's assistant, but they consider this one advantage of their plan.

Within a week, Donelly's management is split into two camps: one favoring Wiggins as the new director of traffic and the other favoring Ritter. Harold Donelly realizes that he has to make a controversial decision. If he names either Ritter or Wiggins, he will alienate the other individual as well as about half of his management team. He could bring in an outsider, but the firm cannot afford a three-person traffic department. In addition neither Ritter nor Wiggins is considered flexible or easy to work with, so it is unlikely that either one could be reassigned elsewhere within the firm.

On Thursday afternoons Harold Donelly has a long-standing golf date with some friends. He, Sid Burroughs, and Louis Milsted are sitting in the clubhouse waiting for a fourth member to arrive. Donelly tells the others about the problem.

Burroughs says, "I'd fire both Wiggins and Ritter, and start from there."

Milsted comments, "Do you need a traffic department at all? Why not buy on a delivered basis and make your vendors agree to deliver sheet steel as you need it. Sell on an FOB-dock basis, and your buyers will have to pick up their purchases. The buzz words these days are 'forming partnerships' with your vendors and customers. You'll save the cost of traffic people as well as that of your eight trucks."

Questions

1. If either Ritter or Wiggins is named director of traffic, what assignments should be given to the other?
2. Comment on Burroughs's suggestion. Should both Wiggins and Ritter be fired? Why or why not?
3. Wiggins and Ritter do not get along, and their feud has management divided. Who is responsible for the problem? Discuss.
4. Assume that both Ritter and Wiggins are no longer part of the traffic operation. You are asked to prepare a job description for a new traffic manager. Prepare the draft of such a job announcement.
5. Instead of a traffic department, should Donelly create a logistics department? Discuss.
6. Comment on Milsted's suggestion. Should Donelly follow his advice? Why or why not?
7. Are there situations, industries, or firms for which Milsted's suggestion might be more applicable? What are they?
8. In what types of situations, industries, or firms is it more important to closely control inbound shipments but not outbound ones? Give examples.
9. In what types of situations, industries, or firms is it more important to control closely outbound shipments but not inbound ones? Give examples.

ABC analysis. In inventory management, the placing of items into categories A, B, and C with respect to monitoring stock levels.

Accounting controls. The use of accounting records to determine the financial efficiency of a logistics system.

Adjustment function. Selecting a point in the exchange channel to concentrate goods, make a new selection from that concentration, and form a new selection of goods to move forward in the channel.

Backhaul. A return trip or movement in a direction of secondary importance or purpose.

Back order. Materials requested by a customer that are unavailable for shipment at the same time as the remainder of the order. They are usually shipped when available.

Bank payment plan. A service provided by banks for shippers. Carriers send freight bills to the bank to be paid. The bank pays the carrier and subtracts the payment from the shipper's account. Also called freight payment service.

Bar-code scanners. Electronic devices that read bar codes and can be used to keep track of inventory, reorder inventory, and analyze inventory patterns.

Batch numbers. Numbers put on products when they are manufactured for identifying when they were made and at what factory.

Belly freight. Cargo that is transported in the lower freight compartments of airplanes.

Benchmarking. Using measures of another's performance to judge one's own performance.

Bill of lading. A contract stating that a carrier has received certain freight and is responsible for its delivery.

Bonded storage. The most common type involves the collection of excise taxes, such as those on cigarettes. Excise taxes do not have to be paid until the product leaves the bonded warehouse.

Break-bulk cargo. In ocean shipping, cargo handled piece by piece by stevedores, rather than in bulk or in intermodal containers.

Break-bulk distribution center. A warehouse where large shipments are sent by a shipper. Shipments are broken down by customer, and each consignee receives what was ordered.

Brokers. Companies that help both shipper and carrier achieve lower freight rates and more efficient utilization of carrier equipment. They also help match carriers to loads.

Building-block concept. Combining smaller packages into larger units that can be more efficiently handled at one time.

Bulk cargo. In shipping, cargo stowed loose, without specific packing, and generally handled with a pump, scoop, or shovel.

Carload sale. An old retail advertising term, meaning that the retailer purchased an entire carload of product at a reduced cost and is presumably passing these savings on. Today the term *truckload sale* is sometimes used.

Carrier. An individual or firm in the business of carrying cargo and/or passengers.

Carrying costs. See *Inventory carrying costs.*

Cartage. Local hauling of freight.

Charter. In international transportation, the leasing or renting of a vessel or aircraft for a specific trip or time limit.

Classification. Numbers assigned to various types of freight, based mainly on the carrier's costs of handling that type of product, and, along with weight and distance, used as a basis for determining the costs of shipment.

COFC (container on flatcar). Piggyback traffic, or the shipping of containers on rail flatcars.

Commodity rate. The least expensive of the general types of freight rates. It is typically used by common carriers as a reward for shippers that ship in large quantities or frequently. The rates are specific, often naming the specific origin and destination.

Common carrier obligations. Over time, common carriers assumed four legal obligations to their customers: service, delivery, reasonable rates, and avoidance of discrimination.

Competition audit. An analysis of a firm's competition—both present and projected—that includes the products it sells, the quality it provides, plant locations, and shipping points. It is part of the data-collection phase of logistics analysis.

Concealed damage. Damage not initially apparent but discovered after a package is opened.

Conrail. A federally sponsored railroad that took over the Penn-Central and other bankrupt railroads in the East and the upper Midwest. The railroad has since been returned to the private sector.

Consignee. The receiver of a shipment.

Consignor. The shipper of goods.

Consistency of service. The dependability of a carrier's service, including the consistency of on-time pickup and delivery.

Containers. Large boxes—about eight feet high, eight feet wide, and from twenty to fifty-five feet long—that can be transported by rail, truck, air, or water carrier (though air containers are often smaller).

Contract carrier. Found in the trucking industry; recently, railroads have also offered contracts to their customers. A contract carrier provides specialized service to each customer based on a contractual arrangement.

Contract logistics. A long-term arrangement between a shipper and another party to provide logistics services.

Critical path. In network analysis, the necessary path that takes the longest to complete; it therefore is critical in the sense that attempts to speed up the total process must focus on it.

Cross-docking. Immediately moving cargo as it is being received at a warehouse to a loading dock where it is loaded aboard outbound trucks.

Cross-traders. Ships that transport cargo between two countries, neither of which is the nationality of the vessel. A U.S.-registered ship carrying products from Mexico to Spain would be engaged in cross-trading.

Cube out. Occurs when a bulky cargo takes up a vehicle's or a container's cubic capacity but not its weight capacity.

Customer audit. An analysis of a firm's customers—both present and projected—that includes their location, products typically ordered, customer service standards required, and so on. It is part of the data-collection phase of logistics analysis.

Customer service. Assisting an existing customer.

Customer service standards. A service level that a selling firm wants to achieve, such as the ability to fill 95 percent of all orders completely within forty-eight hours.

Customs collection. Tax payments collected by a government when foreign products enter its country.

Customs house brokers. Companies that help buyers bring imports into a country by preparing customs reports, arranging for transportation, and the like.

CWT. 100 pounds.

Dedicated equipment. In railroading, cars assigned for use by a specific customer.

Delivered-pricing systems. A price that includes delivery to the buyer.

Delivery window. The time span within which a scheduled delivery must be made.

Demurrage. A charge assessed by carriers to users that fail to unload and return vehicles or containers promptly.

Design implementation. The final step in logistics analysis, during which recommended changes are put into use. It can be done all at once, though usually it is implemented slowly so that the system does not break down from excessive unfamiliarity with the new system.

Detention. A payment from a shipper or consignee to a carrier for having kept the carrier's equipment too long.

Distribution center. A warehouse with an emphasis on quick throughput, such as is needed in supporting marketing efforts.

Distribution requirements planning (DRP). Inventory management of finished products that is linked to sophisticated sales forecasting.

Door-to-door. Through carriage of a container from shipper to customer.

Dovetailing. When vendors (suppliers) locate their plants in close proximity to customers. The idea is growing rapidly because of JIT inventory systems.

Draft. The depth in the water to which a vessel can be loaded.

Drayage. Local trucking, and used today to describe the truck movement of containers and trailers to and from railyards and port areas.

Drop shipments. Shipments delivered to a handful of designated sites.

Dunnage. Wood and other packing materials used to wedge and otherwise keep cargo in place.

Economic order quantity (EOQ). An order size that minimizes the combined storage and processing costs.

Electronic data interchange (EDI). Buyers and sellers are linked by computers and use computers to exchange orders and other routine information.

Embargo. A carrier's temporary refusal to accept certain shipments, usually because it is unable to deliver them (such as during a strike or a flood).

Enterprise zone. A deteriorated area designated to receive some tax relief in order to encourage new developments.

Expedited shipment.   A shipment that a carrier moves more quickly than usual.

Export declaration.   A form filled out by a U.S. exporter for governmental statistical and export-control purposes.

Export management companies.   Firms that help a domestic company become involved in foreign sales. They often locate foreign firms that can be licensed to manufacture the product in the foreign country. They also take care of the details involved in exporting.

Export packers.   Companies that prepare the protective packing for shipments transported overseas.

Export trading companies.   Companies that provide total help to exporters. They often involve a number of firms that may be domestic competitors and that are allowed to combine forces to be more effective in foreign sales.

FAK (freight-all-kinds) rate.   A rate applicable to a mixture of products.

FIFO (first in, first out).   An inventory management procedure whereby the oldest item in stock gets shipped first.

Fixed-order-interval system.   Inventory is replenished on a constant, set schedule and is always ordered at a specific time; the quantity ordered varies depending on forecasted sales before the next order date.

Fixed warehouse slot location.   Each product is assigned a specific location and is always stored there.

Flags of convenience.   Flags of nations that have lax maritime registration rules. Many ships are registered in these countries because of their lenient safety requirements.

Flying a nation's flag.   A ship that is registered in a particular country (e.g., a ship registered in France flies the French flag).

FOB (free on board) pricing.   Price at seller's place of business. Buyer must carry away.

Foreign trade zone.   An area, usually near a port or an airport, where goods can be stored or processed before entering through the importing nation's customs inspections.

Freight absorption.   A seller's absorbing part of the transportation costs in the product's delivered price.

Freight payment services.   See *Bank payment plan*.

Full-cost pricing.   The carrier prices the transportation service to each customer so that the full cost of providing the service is charged to each customer.

Goods in transit.   Goods moving between two points, often accompanied by a live bill of lading.

Grid systems.   A location technique utilizing a map or grid, with specific locations marked on the north-south and east-west axes. Its purpose is to find a location that minimizes transportation costs.

Hazardous cargo.   Goods that pose hazards to those handling them, to other cargo, or to the public and for that reason require special handling.

Hijacking.   Theft that typically involves stealing both the transport vehicle and the cargo inside it.

Hub and spoke.   A carrier's route system with many routes (spokes) radiating out from a single center (hub).

Import quotas. Absolute limits to the quantity of a product that can be imported into a country during a particular time period.

In bond. Cargo on which taxes or duties have yet to be paid. The owner must post a bond or use a bonded carrier or warehouse to guarantee that the materials will not be sold until the taxes or duties are paid.

Incentive rates. Charging less per unit of weight for heavier shipments.

Industry standards analysis. Average worker-output information available for many industries that helps a company compare itself to others in the same industry.

International Air Transport Association (IATA). A cartel, or group, that sets rates for international air transport.

Inventory carrying costs. The costs of holding an inventory, such as interest on investment, insurance, deterioration, and so on.

KD. Knocked down; when goods are packaged and shipped in a knocked-down state, so that their bulk is reduced by about 67 percent, they receive a lower classification number and a lower rate per pound is paid.

Load center. A major port where thousands of containers arrive and depart per week. These ports specialize in the efficient handling of containers.

Load factor. Percentage of capacity utilized.

Loading dock. A warehouse or factory door where trucks are loaded or unloaded.

Logistics. The flow of materials and services and the communications necessary to manage that flow.

Loss and damage. Loss or damage of shipments while in transit or in a warehouse.

Make-bulk distribution center. Frequently utilized for the shipment of production inputs. Vendors ship their relatively small shipments to a nearby warehouse. At the make-bulk distribution center a number of small shipments are combined to take advantage of the lower freight rates per pound available when large shipments are given to the carrier.

Manufacturing resource planning (MRP II). The use of computerized systems.

Maquiladora. Manufacturing plants that exist just south of the U.S.-Mexican border.

Marginal analysis. Analyzing the impacts of small changes, such as adding or subtracting one unit of input.

Market dominance. The ICC does not regulate rail rates unless the railroad in question has market dominance over the shipment involved. Market dominance is usually defined as having 60 percent or more of the freight in a specified market.

Marshaling. Accumulating products or materials needed for a project.

Materials handling. The efficient movement of products into and out of warehouses. The term also applies to bulk materials and to the handling of components on an assembly line.

Materials management. Movement of raw materials, parts, and components to the production plant.

Materials requirements planning (MRP I). Using computers to manage production inventory.

Matrix management.   A logistics alternative that utilizes task forces established to solve specific problems. Members are drawn from various functional areas that impact on the problem. Once the problem is solved, the task force is disbanded.

Measurement ton.   In ocean shipping, the use of forty cubic feet (or some similar cubic measure) as the equivalent of one ton for calculating transportation charges.

Metric conversion.   Adopting the metric system of weights and measures.

Metric ton.   2,204.6 pounds.

Nesting.   Packaging tapered articles inside each other to reduce the cubic volume of the entire shipment.

Nontariff barriers.   Governmental barriers that restrict trade but do not involve tariffs or quotas. An example is a government that requires all imports of a specific product to enter the country through one small port.

Non-vessel-operating common carrier (NVOCC).   In international trade, a firm that provides carrier services to shippers but owns no vessels itself.

Occupational Safety and Health Act (OSHA).   A 1970 federal law regulating workplaces to ensure the safety of workers.

Ocean liners.   Ships in regularly scheduled operations that specialize in less-than-shipload quantity shipments.

Opportunity costs.   The cost of giving up an alternative opportunity.

Order cycle.   Elapsed time between when a customer places an order and when the goods are received.

Order-dedicated inventory.   Inventory pledged to a customer that will soon be shipped to the customer involved.

Order picking and assembly.   In a warehouse, the selection of specific items to fill or assemble a complete order.

Order processing.   The activities from receipt of an order until the warehouse is notified to pick the order.

Order transmittal.   The time from when the customer places or sends the order to when the seller receives it.

Overnight delivery.   Goods shipped on one day and delivered the next morning.

Package testing.   Simulation of the types of problems that the package will be exposed to in warehouses and in transit.

Packaging.   Materials used to protect a shipment physically when it is in a warehouse or in transit.

Pallet.   A small platform, usually forty by forty-eight inches, on which goods are placed for handling in a warehouse.

Palletization.   See *Unitization.*

Parcel.   In transportation, a small quantity or small package.

Perishables.   Cargo that spoils quickly and requires special attention.

PERT (program evaluation and review technique).   A form of network analysis that places all component parts in the sequence in which they must be performed.

Phantom freight.   Occurs in delivered pricing when a buyer pays an excessive freight charge calculated into the price of the goods.

Physical distribution.   The flow of materials from the end of the assembly line to the customer.

Piggyback.   Truck trailers on flatcars, also referred to as TOFC.

Pilferage.   The stealing of cargo on a casual basis, usually by one's employees.

Private carrier.   Carrying one's own goods in one's own vehicles.

Private warehousing.   Owning or leasing storage space for one's exclusive use.

Product recalls.   A company asks customers to return certain products that are found to be defective.

Program evaluation and review technique.   See *PERT*.

Project cargo.   Cargo destined for one project, say, a dam being built in Africa.

Public warehouse.   A warehouse whose owner leases space and provides services to a variety of customers.

Pull inventory system.   Goods moving so slowly through an inventory system that the buyer must take action to attract the flow of goods in its direction.

Push inventory system.   To the buyer it appears that the product is being pushed toward it, and it must act to stop or slow the flow.

Rail siding.   A short rail track leading from a main line to a customer's plant or warehouse.

Rate bureau (conference).   An organization of carriers that sets rates.

Rate negotiation. Negotiation between the shipper and the carrier on the rate to be charged by the carrier.

Recycling.   Reuse of materials.

Released value.   The limits to a carrier's liability for a certain shipment, in the sense that the carrier may agree to charge a lower overall rate if the shipment's stated value is lessened.

Reorder point.   A stock is consumed, and the balance remaining drops to this point, at which time a replenishment order is placed.

Reparations.   Payment from a carrier to a shipper for having charged the shipper excessive rates in the past.

Reverse logistics.   Goods that flow from the consumer to the manufacturer (e.g., product recalls and product recycling).

Right-to-work laws.   State laws that specify that a worker at a unionized plant does not have to join the union to work permanently at the facility.

RO-RO (roll on/roll off).   Ships similar to floating parking lots that are loaded by driving tractors and trailers on ramps.

Safety stock.   A reserve inventory, in addition to that needed to meet anticipated requirements.

Scanners.   See *Bar-code scanners*.

Seamless distribution.   A logistics organization strategy that removes impediments to the flow of information and goods.

Shipment consolidation.   Freight rates are less expensive per pound shipped when large shipments are given to the carrier at one time. Therefore, shippers try to group shipments bound for the same general area.

Shippers' agents.   Firms that purchase rail TOFC/COFC service and then sell this capacity to shippers.

Shippers' associations.   Shippers that join together to negotiate more favorable ocean shipping rates.

Shippers' cooperatives.   Nonprofit groups of shippers that join to consolidate shipments.

Shipper's load and count. On a transport document, the term means that the carrier did not independently count the items said to be shipped.

Short-interval scheduling. An analysis of workers' productivity over short periods of time. Each worker is assigned specific duties that he or she should be able to complete during the time period provided.

Shrinkage. Losses in inventory that are difficult to account for.

Simulation. A technique used to model the systems under study, typically using mathematical equations to represent relationships among components of a logistics system.

Single-source leasing. A firm leases both its private truck fleet and its drivers from the same source.

Skid. See *Pallet.*

SKU (stock-keeping unit). Each separate type of item that is accounted for in an inventory.

Slipsheet. Thick sheet of cardboard placed under a unit load, instead of a conventional pallet.

Slurry pipeline system. Transports products that are ground into a powder, mixed with water, and then shipped in slurry form through a pipeline. The concept has been successfully used for transporting coal.

Stacker/retriever (S/R) system. Used in automated warehouses to store goods and remove them when needed.

Staging. Accumulating or assembling goods before sending them.

Steamship conference. An organization of liner operators that sets rates. Also called *rate agreement.*

Stockout. Being out of an item at the same time there is a willing buyer for it.

Stockout costs. Costs to seller when it is unable to supply an item to a customer ready to buy.

Strategic logistics. Using logistical competency and channelwide partnerships to gain competitive advantage by developing long-term logistical alliances with customers and suppliers of materials and services.

Stuffing. Loading a container.

Supply-chain management. Asserting positive control over one's suppliers and vendors.

System constraints. Restrictions that cannot be violated in the logistics operation being planned.

System goals. Broader than objectives and more general, such as the goal of increasing market share slowly over time.

System objectives. Measurable factors that enable management to know if it is meeting its goals, such as whether 98 percent of orders are being shipped within six hours of receipt.

Systems analysis. Analysis in which the importance of each aspect of a situation is recognized, along with the relationship of each part to all other aspects of the situation.

Tachograph. An electronic device that records the road speed and the engine RPMs (revolutions per minute) on a truck and tells a lot about the vehicle that has been driven.

Tapering rates. Transportation charges that increase as distance increases, but at a slower rate; that is, the average cost per mile drops.

Tare weight.   Weight of the empty container or vehicle.

Tariff.   A book containing a carrier's charges for transportation services or the charges assessed on items imported into a country.

Tax-free bonds.   Issued by local and state governments, the bonds carry lower interest rates than corporate bonds because the interest on corporate securities is fully taxable.

Terminal.   A carrier or public facility where freight (or passengers) is shifted between vehicles or modes.

Throughput.   A term expressing output in warehousing and in pipelines; it is expressed as the number of units moving through a specified system in a given period of time.

TOFC (trailer on flatcar).   Piggyback traffic, or loading truck trailers onto rail flatcars.

Total-cost approach.   All aspects of a logistics system must be considered as a whole, and a manager should not be too concerned about individual cost elements.

Toto authority.   A private carrier with the authority to act as a common or contract carrier in backhaul situations.

Tracing.   A carrier's attempt to find a misplaced or delayed shipment.

Uniform order bill of lading.   This form is considered negotiable, and whoever holds it may claim the goods.

Uniform straight bill of lading.   The most widely used bill of lading. The carrier may deliver the goods without requiring the original copy.

Union work rules.   See *Work rules.*

Unitization.   The placing of goods on pallets, or designing a materials handling system to accommodate pallet loads of goods.

Unit load.   A pallet load, or a similar-sized load on a slipsheet.

Unit train.   A train with cars permanently linked, used for repetitive hauls, usually of coal.

Value-of-service pricing.   Taking into account the shipper's ability to pay, irrespective of the costs of providing the service.

Variable warehouse slot location.   A warehouse where incoming products are stored wherever there is empty space available.

Vendor audit.   An analysis of a firm's vendors (suppliers) in terms of their locations, dependability, quality of work, and so on. Part of the data-collection phase of logistics analysis.

Warehouse work rules.   A set of rules that specify correct procedures at a specific warehouse. Each worker should be required to know them thoroughly.

Weight-losing product characteristics.   A product that loses weight during the production process must therefore be processed as near to its origin as possible. The finished product, which weighs less, is transported.

Wind, shipping.   Declaring that a shipment weighs more than it actually does in order to qualify for a lower per-pound rate, which results in a lower total shipping cost.

Work rules.   Often established by contracts with unions, these rules specify exactly the duties of each worker. They sometimes restrict workers from doing more than one type of function.

NAME INDEX